THERAPEUTIC
COMMUNICATION
WITH CHILDREN

The Mutual Storytelling Technique

THERAPEUTIC COMMUNICATION WITH CHILDREN

THE MUTUAL STORYTELLING TECHNIQUE

Richard A. Gardner, M.D.

Associate in Child Psychiatry
College of Physicians & Surgeons
Columbia University
New York City

Faculty
William A. White Psychoanalytic Institute
New York City

SCIENCE HOUSE, INC.

Published by Science House, Inc.
Fifty-nine Fourth Avenue
New York, New York 10003

Designed by Jennifer Mellen
Manufactured in the United States of America
Library of Congress Catalog Card Number: 71–155063
Standard Book Number: 87668–042–2

To My Parents

Amelia and Irving Gardner

By the Same Author

The Boys and Girls Book About Brain Dysfunction
The Boys and Girls Book About Divorce
On Understanding Children

Acknowledgments

My profoundest debt of gratitude is owed to the children whose stories are the heart of this book. Their stories served as the models for mine; their ingenuity and creativity have been my source of inspiration. Since they all are, or have been, patients of mine, the names used in this book are fictitious. I preserve here then their anonymity as well as their contributions.

I wish to express my deep appreciation to Mr. Gordon Lander and Professor Frances Dubner who indefatigably edited the manuscript and provided many valuable suggestions. The enthusiasm, interest, and dedication of my publishers, Dr. Jason Aronson and Miss Jennifer Mellen of Science House, have been most gratifying.

I am also grateful to Mrs. Linda Gould, my secretary, who not only typed the manuscript but also transcribed the stories verbatim from the tape recorder to typewritten form — a grueling task, if there ever was one.

I appreciate the permission granted to me by the editors to quote from the following previously published articles of mine:

"Sexual Fantasies in Childhood," *Medical Aspects of Human Sexuality*, 3, **10** (1969), pp. 121–134.

"Psychogenic Problems of Brain Injured Children and Their Parents," *Journal of the American Academy of Child Psychiatry*, 7 (1968), pp. 471–491.

"The Mutual Storytelling Technique: Use in Alleviating Childhood Oedipal Problems," *Contemporary Psychoanalysis*, 4 (1968), pp. 161–177.

"The Mutual Storytelling Technique: Use in the Treatment of a Child with Post-traumatic Neurosis," *American Journal of Psychotherapy*, 24 (1970), pp. 419–439.

"Mutual Storytelling as a Technique in Child Psychotherapy and Psychoanalysis," in J. Masserman, ed., *Science and Psychoanalysis*, New York: Grune and Stratton, 1969, Vol. 14, pp. 123–135.

Review of H. Ginott's *Between Parent and Child* (New York: The Macmillan Co., 1965), in *Psychology Today*, 1, **12**, (1968), pp. 6–10.

Lastly, my deep-felt gratitude goes to Lee, my loving wife, who patiently tolerated the absences which the writing of this book necessitated. As a respected colleague, she also provided me with meaningful and useful suggestions.

R.A.G.

Table of Contents

Foreword

Dr. Richard Gardner's Mutual Storytelling Technique is an important psychotherapeutic innovation. It is especially useful in the latency period during which products of the child's imagination are difficult to come by. Children like the idea of telling a story to an imaginary television audience and, of course, they enjoy listening to the playback. The use of a tape recorder is thus an added incentive. The author has already proven that children respond to it in most cases. The child is introduced by the therapist to the make-believe "Make-up-a-Story Television Program." During the introduction, the child is told that the story must be one he is making up right there and that after the story is told, he must tell the moral, the lesson the story teaches. The child is also told that his story will be followed by one made up by the therapist, which also has a "moral".

For this method a number of talents are required. The therapist must be a master of ceremonies who builds up his program by introducing the patient to his audience as though an active audience were present, and he must be quick to furnish help when there is a lag in the child's story. He must have a special memory for the details of the story as it was told. He must be able to improvise a new story based on immediate interpretation of the symbols that were used by the child, eliminating whatever is thought to be irrelevant while at the same time interweaving in his own story a constructive termination with a "moral" appropriate to his therapeutic purpose.

These events are the high points of sessions that include the usual methods of child psychiatry. Among other things these procedures help in learning the most useful interpretations. Judging by the demonstration I witnessed, the therapist is using an instrument in which he is keenly interested and highly skilled.

Presumably therapeutic modification is attested by modifications in the child's story and in his behavior as therapy goes on. The use of the child's own story, his familiar symbols, and his vocabulary may indeed have a reinforcing value, and where the method is applicable, it presents an original contribution with manifold possibilities.

David M. Levy, M.D.

Introduction

Eliciting stories is a time-honored practice in child psycho-therapy. From the stories children tell, the therapist is able to gain invaluable insights into the child's inner conflicts, frustrations, and defenses.

A child's stories are generally less difficult to analyze than dreams, free associations, and other productions of the adult. His fundamental difficulties are exhibited clearly to the therapist, without the obscurity, distortion, and misrepresentation that are characteristic of the adult's presentation. The essential problem for the child's therapist has been how to use his insights therapeutically.

The techniques described in the literature on child psychotherapy and psychoanalysis are, for the most part, attempts to solve this problem. Some are based on the assumption, borrowed from the adult psychoanalytic model, that making the unconscious conscious can itself be therapeutic. My own experience has been that few children are interested in gaining conscious awareness of their unconscious processes, let alone utilizing such insights therapeutically. Children do, however, enjoy both telling stories and listening to them. Since storytelling is one of the child's favorite modes of communication, I wondered whether communicating to him in the same mode might not be useful in child therapy. The efficacy of the storytelling approach for the imparting and transmission of values and insights is proved by the ancient and universal appeal of fable, myth, and legend.

It was from these observations and considerations that I developed the Mutual Storytelling Technique, a proposed solution to the question of how to utilize the child's stories therapeutically. In this method the child first tells a story; the therapist surmises its psychodynamic meaning and then tells one of his own. The therapist's story contains the same characters in a similar setting, but he introduces healthier adaptations and resolutions of the conflicts that have been exhibited in the child's story. Since the therapist speaks in the child's own language, he has a good chance of "being heard." One could almost say that here the therapist's interpretations bypass the conscious and are received directly by the unconscious. The child is not burdened with psychoanalytic interpretations which are alien to him. Direct, anxiety-provoking confrontations, so reminiscent of the child's experience with parents and teachers, are avoided. Lastly, the introduction of humor and drama enhances the child's interest and pleasure and therefore his receptivity. As a therapeutic tool, the method is useful in combination with traditional techniques. It is most useful for children who will tell stories but who have little interest in analyzing them. It is not a therapy per se, but rather one technique in the therapist's armamentarium.

In planning this book I found myself faced with a conflict: should I present a series of cases, each of which would follow the course of treatment from beginning to end, or should I describe each phase of treatment separately and provide illustrative therapist-patient story sequences characteristic of each stage? The former plan has the advantage of enabling the reader to follow the course of treatment from beginning to end. The disadvantage of this approach is that it would involve unnecessary repetition of theoretical material such as, for example, the criteria for deciding why a given story manifests a particular phase. Such theoretical redundancy would ultimately prove boring to the reader. The alternate plan, in which a group of stories typical of a given phase of treatment are presented along with theoretical information about that phase, has distinct didactic advantages. The drawback of this approach is that one loses out on case continuity.

I decided to solve the dilemma by employing both methods of presentation. In Section I, I present a general description of the characteristics of the child's story in each phase of treatment and provide illustrative examples from a number of cases.

In Section II a similar approach is used in my discussion of common clinical problems. There is, for example, a general description of oedipal problems with representative examples provided by patients. In Section III, I present four full case studies from beginning to end.

Five of the patients used as clinical examples in Sections I and II can also be read in continuity as case studies. To enable the interested reader to follow these cases in sequence, an Index of Patients has been provided. This index lists the stories of these patients in chronological order, regardless of where they may be discussed in the text.

Regarding the other children presented in Sections I and II, while a given child may appear more than once, the combined stories either do not represent a full course of therapy, or they do not lend themselves to meaningful sequential reading. However, since there may be some readers interested in following the chronological sequence of these patients as well, they are also included in the Index of Patients. A few of the stories of the four patients presented in continuity in Section III also appear in Sections I and II. The index can also be used to facilitate the reader's incorporating these additional story sequences into the Section III case studies.

This is not an easy technique to learn. Proficiency may require months and even years of practice. My hope is that this book will provide the reader with a basic foundation upon which to build his expertise.

R.A.G.

When they're offered to the world in merry guise,
Unpleasant truths are swallowed with a will —
For he who'd make his fellow, fellow, fellow creatures wise
Should always gild the philosophic pill!

William S. Gilbert
Yeoman of the Guard

Section I

The Basic Technique

1. BASIC MECHANICS OF THE METHOD

Although drawings, dolls, puppets, and other toys are the modalities around which stories are traditionally told in child therapy, these often have the effect of restricting the child's storytelling or of channeling it in highly specific directions. The tape recorder does not have these disadvantages; with it, the visual field remains free from contaminating and distracting stimuli. Eliciting a story with it is like obtaining a dream on demand.

In order to show in detail how the technique works, the tape recorder will be utilized. The same method, however, can be employed — with some modifications — with dolls, blocks, drawings, and other play material.

I introduce the child to the game by first pointing to a stack of tapes, each of which has a child's name clearly written on the end of the box. I tell the patient that each child who comes to my office has his own tape for a tape recording game which we play. I ask him if he would like to have a tape of his own. The child generally wants to follow usual practice, and having his own tape enhances his feeling of belonging. If he assents, I take out a new tape and let him write his name on the box.

I then ask the child if he would like to be guest of honor on a make-believe television program on which stories are told. If he agrees — and few decline the honor — the recorder is turned on and I begin:

Good morning, boys and girls. I'd like to welcome you once again to Dr. Gardner's "Make-Up-A-Story Television Program." As you all know, we invite children to our program to see how good they are at making up stories. Natur-ally, the more adventure or excitement a story has, the more interesting it is to the people who are watching at their television sets. Now, it's against the rules to tell stories about things you've read or have seen in the movies or on television, or about things that really happened to you or anyone you know.

Like all stories, your story should have a beginning, a middle, and an end. After you've made up a story, you'll tell us the moral of the story. We all know that every good story has a moral.

Then after you've told your story, Dr. Gardner will make up a story too. He'll try to tell one that's interesting and unusual, and then he'll tell the moral of his story.

And now, without further delay, let me introduce to you a boy [girl] who is with us today for the first time. Can you tell us your name, young man?

I then ask the child a series of brief questions that can be answered by single words or brief phrases such as his age, address, school grade, and teacher. These simple questions diminish the child's anxiety and tend to make him less tense about the more unstructured themes involved in "making up a story." Further diminution of anxiety is accomplished by letting him hear his own voice at this point by playback, something which most children enjoy. He is then told:

Now that we've heard a few things about you, we're all interested in hearing the story *you* have for us today.

At this point most children plunge right into their story, although some may feel the need for "time to think." I may offer this pause; if it is asked for by the child, it is readily granted. There are some children for whom the pause is not enough, but who nevertheless still want to try. In such instances, the child is told:

Some children, especially when it's their first time on this program, have a little trouble thinking of a story, but with some help from me they're able to do so. Most children don't realize that there are *millions* of stories in their heads they don't know about. And I know a way to help get out some of them. Would you like me to help you get out one of them?

Most children assent to this. I then continue:

Fine, here's how it works. I'll start the story and when I point my finger at you, you say exactly what comes into your mind at that time. You'll then see how easy it is to make up a story. Okay. Let's start. Once upon a time —— a long, long time ago —— in a distant land —— far, far away —— there lived a ——.

I then point my finger, and it is a rare child who does not offer some fill-in word at this point. If the word is "dog," for example, I then say, " And *that dog* ——" and once again point to the patient. I follow the statement provided by the child with "And then ——" or "The next thing that happened was ——." Every statement the child makes is followed by some introductory connective and by pointing to the child to supply the next statement. That and no more — the introduction of specific phrases or words would defeat the therapist's purpose of catalyzing the youngster's production of his *own* created material and of sustaining, as needed, its continuity.

For most children, this approach is sufficient to get them over whatever hurdles there are for them in telling a story. If this is not enough, however, it is best to drop this activity in a completely casual and non-reproachful manner, such as: "Well, today doesn't seem to be your good day for storytelling. Perhaps we'll try again some other time."

While the child is engaged in telling his story, I jot down notes, which are not only of help in analyzing the child's story, but serve also as a basis for my own. At the end of the child's story and his statement of its moral, I may ask questions about specific items in the story. The purpose here is to obtain additional details, which are often of help in understanding the story. Typical questions might be: "Was the fish in your story a man or a lady?" "Why was the fox so mad at the goat?" "Why did the bear do that?" If the child hesitates to tell the moral of his story or indicates that there is none, I usually reply: "What, a story without a moral? Every good story has *some* lesson or moral!" The moral that this comment usually does succeed in eliciting from the child is often significantly revealing of the fundamental psychodynamics of the story.

For younger children, the word "lesson" or "title" may be substituted for "moral." Or the child might be asked: "What can we learn from your story?"

Then I usually say: "That was a very good (unusual, exciting, etc.) story." Or to the child who was hesitant: "And you thought you weren't very good at telling stories!"

I then turn off the tape recorder and prepare my story. Although the child's story is generally simpler to understand than the adult's dream, the analysis of both follows similar principles. At this point, I will present only a few fundamentals of story analysis. My hope is that the reader who is inexperienced in dream and/or story analysis will, by careful reading of the numerous examples of story analysis to be presented in this book, become adept at story interpretation.

I first attempt to determine which figure or figures in the child's story represent the child himself, and which stand for significant people in his environment. It is important to appreciate that two or more figures may represent various facets of the *same* person's personality. There may, for example, be a "good dog" and a "bad cat" in the same story, which are best understood as conflicting forces within the same child. A horde of figures, all similar, may symbolize powerful elements in a single person. A hostile father, for example, may be represented by a stampede of bulls. Swarms of small creatures such as insects, worms, or mice, often symbolize unacceptable repressed complexes. Malevolent figures can represent the child's own repressed hostility projected outward, or they may be a symbolic statement about the hostility of a significant figure. Sometimes both of these mechanisms operate simultaneously. A threatening lion in one child's story stood for his hostile father, and he was made more frightening by the child's own hostility, repressed and projected onto the lion. This example illustrates one of the reasons why many children see their parents as being more malevolent than they are.

Besides clarifying the symbolic significance of each figure, it is also important to get a general overall "feel" for the atmosphere and setting of the story. Is the ambience pleasant, neutral, or horrifying? Stories that take place in the frozen tundra or on isolated space stations suggest something very different from those which occur in the child's own home. The child's emotional reactions when telling the story are also of significance in understanding its meaning. An eleven-year-old child who tells me, in an emotionless tone, about the death fall of a mountain climber reveals not only his hostility but also his repression of his feelings. The atypical must be separated from the stereotyped, age-appropriate elements in the story. The former may be very revealing, whereas the latter rarely are. Battles between cowboys and Indians rarely give meaningful data, but when the chief sacrifices his son to Indian gods in a prayer for victory over the white man, something has been learned about the child's relationship with his father.

Lastly, the story may lend itself to a number of different psychodynamic interpretations. In selecting the theme that will be most pertinent for the child *at that particular time*, I am greatly assisted by the child's own "moral" or "title."

After asking myself, "What would be a healthier resolution or a more mature adaptation than the one used by the child?" I create a story of my own. My story involves the same characters, setting, and initial situation as the child's story, but it has a more appropriate or salutary resolution of the most important conflicts. In creating my story, I attempt to provide the child with more *alternatives*. The communication that the child need not be enslaved by his neurotic behavior patterns is vital. Therapy must open new avenues not considered in the child's scheme of things. It must help the child become aware of the multiplicity of options which are available to replace the narrow self-defeating ones he has chosen. My moral or morals are an attempt to emphasize further the healthier adaptations I have included in my story. If, while I am telling my story, the child exhibits deep interest, or if he reveals marked anxiety, which may manifest itself by jitteriness or hyperactivity, then I know that my story is "hitting home." Such clear-cut indications of how relevant one's story is are not, of course, always forthcoming.

After the moral to my story, I stop the recorder and ask the child whether he would like to hear the recorded program. In my experience, the child is interested in doing so about one-third of the time. Playing the program makes possible a second exposure to the messages that the therapist wishes to impart. If the child is not interested in listening to the tape, then we engage in other therapeutic activities.

The therapist's attitude has a subtle, but nevertheless significant, influence on the child's ability to tell a story. Ideally this attitude should be one of pleasurable anticipation that a story will be forthcoming and surprised disappointment when the child will not or cannot tell one. The child wants to be accepted by those who are meaningful to him, and if a productive therapeutic relationship has been established, he will try to comply with what is expected of him.

Peer group influence is also important. When the child gets the general feeling that storytelling is what everybody does when he visits the therapist, he is more likely to play the game. Seeing a stack of tapes — with each child's first name prominently displayed — tends to foster his desire to tell stories "just like the other kids do." In my typical session, the mother and child are seen together for a few minutes. The mother then leaves, and the child and I start our time together with the storytelling game. The rest of the session is devoted to other therapeutic activities — most often initiated by the child. In this way, there is a pattern set down which both of us routinely follow. It is a *matter of course* that we proceed to the tape recorder (which is conspicuously placed in my play area) as soon as the child's mother leaves. If the child is disinclined to play the game he must break an expected pattern. Since this is hard for most children to do, he generally goes along with the game and finds it not only less anxiety-provoking than he had anticipated, but pleasurable as well.

2. THE FIRST STORY IN TREATMENT

The first dream which the adult patient presents to his therapist can be a rich source of information. Often it epitomizes the patient's fundamental problems and provides valuable information about his psychodynamics. In addition, it frequently depicts the patient's expectations from treatment and the kind of relationship he is already forming with the analyst. The nature of the incipient transference neurosis can sometimes be gleaned by careful attention to this dream. Lastly, for the patient who is a newcomer to therapy, a meaningful analysis of this dream can serve to catalyze his involvement in treatment and enhance his respect for the therapeutic process. When such a patient experiences a *feeling of amazement* that so much can be learned from his dreams — that his apparently nonsensical nocturnal imagery can reveal so many remarkable things about himself — a giant leap forward is made in his commitment to treatment. In fact, I would go so far as to say that the prognosis for the treatment of a patient who does not have this experience is poor indeed, for without the genuine conviction, born of *emotional* realization, that dreams can be helpful, he will have little motivation to utilize this valuable source of information.

The child's first dream, however, is not usually so rich a source of therapeutic data. Since his life is less complex and his experiences are limited, he has a far less sophisticated repertory of symbols and defense mechanisms. His dreams reflect, by their simplicity, his more primitive state. In addition, his dream recall is usually poorer than the adult's, his rendition is less accurate, and his tendency toward what Freud called "secondary elaboration," that is, providing the dream with a logicality and consistency which is not intrinsic, is more pronounced. All these factors lessen the likelihood that the child's first dream will furnish the therapist with as much valuable information as the adult's.

The child's first story, however, can supply the therapist with data very similar to that which the adult's first dream provides. Like the dream, the story is an invaluable projection of unconscious processes. It is told in the therapist's presence so problems of poor recall, inaccuracy, and the distortions of secondary elaborations are obviated. If short — and thereby less revealing than it might be — the story can be lengthened by the therapist's skillful but non-contaminating requests for further elaboration. All therapists have had the experience of wishing that their patient's dream had not been interrupted or that the dreamer had returned to sleep to "finish it." One can essentially accomplish this with the child's story by proper encouragement. Also, the presentation of the moral provides further information regarding the fundamental psychodynamic themes. Lastly, if the therapist can then tell the child a story which "hits home," that is, one which imparts to him a message which is so meaningful that it produces an emotional impact, he may accomplish a catalyzation into therapy similar to that effected by the well-analyzed first dream of the adult. Such an experience gives the child the feeling that there are important things to be learned from the therapist; that something significant, useful, and possibly even enjoyable is happening; and that it is a good idea for him to return for more of the same.

In analyzing both stories and dreams, the longer the therapist has known his patient and the deeper his insights are into the latter's problems, the more readily he can appreciate their psychodynamics. In adult treatment, one may have to reluctantly forego the analysis of the first dream because one's knowledge of the patient is so sparse that even with the help of free association the dream's meaning does not become apparent. Similarly, one may not know enough about a child to ascertain the psychodynamics of his first story and it may be difficult to create a meaningful story in response. In such situations, I still attempt one, in accordance with the "rules" of the television game, but I know that I will probably not provide the child with an involvement-enhancing emotional experience. My hope is that at some time in the first few sessions I will "hit home." The technique then becomes a most valuable therapeutic modality.

After presenting each first story and describing what I consider to be its psychodynamics, I will then give the story which I told in response. All stories are presented verbatim. Dashes (—) represent brief pauses or interpolations, long dashes (——) indicate longer pauses or hesitation in speaking.

Example 1

Henry, an eleven-year-old boy with a history of poor school performance, poor relationships with peers, and overdependency upon his parents told this story:

Once upon a time there was a parakeet. It could say what it wanted to. If someone said, "Go to sleep," it could repeat as well as answer the person.

One day, the man who owned the parakeet had stolen a buffalo from a neighbor and had eaten some of the meat and put the rest of it on the roof. The neighbor came and asked the man if he saw the buffalo. He said, "No," but the parakeet told the story.

The man was mad at the parakeet and put him in a big brass pot with water in it with a cloth over the top. The parakeet couldn't see what was going on. The man banged on top of the cloth on top of the pot. He made water dribble through the cloth into the pot. The parakeet thought that it was rain and thunder.

Then the man went on trial. He said that he didn't kill the buffalo and that he keeps his meat on top of the house. The parakeet called him a liar. They asked the parakeet about the weather and when he said that it was raining, they thought the parakeet was insane. The man had put the parakeet into the pot and poured the water down on him so that he would think that it was raining. Then they let the man go.

Years later the parakeet died and its son went into the jungle. He told the parakeets and all the other parrots not to speak their own thoughts because then they would get

34

into trouble. He told them only to repeat. And that's why parrots repeat and don't say things on their own.

The moral of that story is: don't believe everything you hear.

I consider the parakeet to symbolize the patient, the man in the story represents his father. The story reveals Henry's feelings that his father engages in dishonest practices, such as stealing, and that were he to reveal these transgressions to others, his father would protect himself by tricking the world into believing that the patient is insane. To protect himself, he decides to assume the form of a parakeet which can only repeat, but not spontaneously reveal, what he observes. In other words, he had better play it safe by docilely repeating what is said to him and revealing nothing. I consider the moral, "Don't believe everything you hear," to be a message to me that I should be incredulous about what I learn from both him and his parents.

Henry's father had had a meteoric rise to success in an industry which has a reputation for price-fixing and other unethical market practices. Besides this, there were other forms of subtle duplicity in the family. The parents were exhibitionistically materialistic and socially hypocritical. They had always impressed upon the patient the importance of good manners and strict adherence to the details of social propriety.

In accordance with this understanding of the story, I related the following:

Once upon a time there was a parakeet. It could say what it wanted to. It could repeat as well as answer.

One day its owner stole a buffalo from his neighbor. He ate some of the meat and put the rest of it on the roof of his house. The neighbor came around and asked if anyone had seen the buffalo. The man said, "No," but the parakeet told the neighbor the true story.

This made the man mad at the parakeet and he put him in a big brass pot with water in it and a cloth over the top. He began banging on the pot and let water drip through the top. The parakeet thought that it was raining and that he was hearing the thunder.

Then there was a trial. The man said that he always kept his meat on the roof. But the parakeet said that he had stolen it. The man tried to prove that the parakeet was insane because the parakeet said that it was raining out and that there was thunder when no one else got wet or heard the thunder. The judge then asked the parakeet where he was when he heard the thunder and felt the rain. When the parakeet described himself as being in a big brass pot, the judge and the jury became suspicious and gradually they realized what had happened. They did not consider the parakeet insane but believed that the man had indeed stolen the meat.

The man then confessed that he had lied about the meat and that he had tried to make everyone believe that the parakeet was insane so that he would not be punished for his crime. Because of his confession, the jury gave him a light sentence, but nevertheless he was punished. The man gradually realized that it was wrong to lie and steal, and in the end he was thankful to the parakeet for having served as a good example of honesty.

My story has two morals. The first is: honesty is the best policy. The second is: sometimes when you are honest, you may embarrass or otherwise cause difficulty for someone who is close to you. Most often it is still better to be honest in such cases. Even if those who are close to you may suffer embarrassment because of your honesty, they will most often be much better off if you are honest.

In my story I attempted to encourage Henry to reveal himself. I tried to assuage his fears that I would necessarily take his father's opinion over his. I tried to communicate that his ostensible disloyalty in divulging family indiscretions could be a form of loyalty in that such disclosures might ultimately be to their benefit. My story also served to lessen the likelihood that he would relate to me with distrust.

Example 2

Steve, an eight-year-old boy who was a disciplinary problem in school, told this story in his first session:

I have this friend named Andy. We get into a fight. Then we decided not to have a fight. Then Andy and I met with a big boy and we both didn't want to fight the big boy. We ignored him.

We met with this monster. It tried to burn us. Then he [the monster] got himself all smoked and burned. The fire from his nostrils went the wrong way.

Moral: never try to get into a fight unless you know what the victim is, how tough or weak.

The first part of the story reveals Steve's ambivalence over expressing his anger. The two boys get into a fight and then decide not to. When the boys meet a big boy — probably the patient's father — they decide not to fight him. Again, the notion of fighting is considered and then rejected.

In my opinion the monster symbol serves a double purpose. It represents the patient's father as well as Steve's own projected hostility. He sees his father as basically malevolent. As is so often the case, he perceives his father's rejection as hostilty, and, in addition, he probably anticipates his father's retaliation for his own unconscious resentment of him. He protects himself from his father's fury by preventing its outward expression. The fire from the monster's nostrils goes the "wrong way," becomes directed internally, and he burns himself. A more poignant representation of the internalization of anger is hard to conceive of. By the father's self-traumatization, the patient's hostile impulses toward him are also gratified. It is as if Steve could say: "He did it to himself; I had nothing to do with it." In addition, the monster, as the projection of the patient's own rage, reveals his fear of such external expression. His wrath must be disowned via projection and even then repressed and internalized. The moral epitomizes Steve's fear that overt expression of anger can be dangerous.

This story, like most, contains many themes which could reasonably be selected for elaboration in my version. I usually try to develop in my story that issue which is most dramatically emphasized — the theme, that is, which appears to be at the forefront of the child's imagination. Concentration on this element increases the probability that my story will be meaningful to the child. I attempt to reach the child at the level that is most significant. This level is not necessarily "deep," for significance and depth need not be identical. For example, in this child's story, the hostility toward the father suggests that oedipal problems are being dealt with. The most impressive element exhibited, however, was the dramatic representation of the repression of rage — the monster internally directing his own fire — and so this aspect was selected for amplification in my story:

Once upon a time there was a dragon. This dragon never noticed that he was different from other dragons in that he did not breathe out smoke and fire like the others. When the other dragons were bothered by someone, they would say to them, "Get out of here." And if those who were bothering the dragon did not go away, then the dragon would breathe out smoke and fire and that usually worked and he wouldn't be bothered again. When this dragon was bothered, however, he said nothing; did not breathe out smoke and fire and kept it all inside himself.

One day this dragon began to complain of aches and pains in his chest and stomach. He went to his doctor. His doctor examined him and then asked him what he did when he was bothered by others. He told the doctor that he said nothing and held his feelings inside himself. The doctor then said to him: "I know what's wrong with you. When other dragons get angry at someone, they tell them to stop bothering them and if that doesn't work, they breathe out smoke and fire, and that usually stops people from harming them. But you keep the smoke and fire inside you and that's hurting your lungs and stomach. I suggest that when somebody does something that bothers you, you tell them about it. If that doesn't work, then let out your anger, let out your smoke and fire, and that will usually help."

The dragon went home and thought a lot about what the doctor had said. He realized that the advice was good and he then tried to follow it. It was hard at first because he had never done such a thing before in his life. In fact, he was quite afraid to do such a thing. But the more he did it the less afraid he became. He had to return to the doctor once in a while for further instruction and advice, but he gradually learned how to do it and the pains in his stomach and chest went away.

The moral of this story is: if somebody is doing something which bothers you, tell them about it. Let out your anger. Don't keep it inside. If you do that, most often things will be better for you.

As can be seen, in my story I did not touch upon the sources of the child's anger because I could only guess them at this early point in treatment. I did know, however, that he was significantly inhibited in the expression of hostility, and I tried to help him in this regard. Anxiety-provoking communications such as these can best be digested piecemeal; too much at once only overwhelms the child and increases his anxiety and resistance.

Example 3

Martin, a seven-year-old boy, was referred because of generalized apathy, lack of involvement with peers, and disinterest in school in spite of high intelligence. He told the following story in his first session:

> Once upon a time there was a bear. He was trying to get some honey from a beehive. He got it from the beehive. He went home with it. The bear ate the honey.

The patient's father was obsessively involved in his work, was away for weeks at a time on business trips, and when home had practically no interest in his son. The mother, although physically present, was a bitter, self-indulgent woman who openly stated that she disliked her son. Biting sarcasm was her primary mode of relating to men.

I consider the beehive in the story to represent Martin's mother. She is the source of honey, that is, love, but this love is covered with stinging, poison-injecting, potentially painful contaminants. Acquiring affection from her inevitably exposes one to her venom. In the story he reveals his wish to gain her love without being traumatized by her malevolence.

The story beautifully epitomizes in a few words the mother's basic personality pattern and her relationship with the patient. It is an excellent example of how the child's first story may reveal his core problems. Since the mother's psychopathology was deep-seated and since she had absolutely no interest in entering into treatment herself, I considered her prognosis for change very poor. Accordingly, I told Martin the following story:

> Once upon a time there was a bear. This bear loved honey very much. There was a beehive nearby but he knew that the bees were not always willing to let him have some. Sometimes they were friendly and then they would give him a little bit. Other times they were not, and he knew then that it was wise to stay away from them or else he would get stung. When the bees were unfriendly, he would go to another part of the forest where there were maple trees which dripped sweet maple syrup. When the bees were friendly, he would go to them for honey.

In my story I attempted two things. First, I tried to help the patient accept his mother as she really was at that time — someone who could, on occasion, give him some affection but who, at other times, could be punitive and ego-debasing. I advised him to accept this situation and to take her affection when it was available, but not to seek it otherwise. Secondly, I attempted to provide Martin with alternative sources of gratification by suggesting that there are others in the world who can compensate him for his mother's deficiencies.

Example 4

Gavin, a six-year-old boy with poor school performance, disinterest in playing with other children, and generalized apathy, told the following story in his first session:

> Once I climbed a tree and fell down and then a bird

flew down. It was pretty big and it lifted me up back into the tree. I fell down again. And that time it didn't lift me up so I had to climb up myself.

Then I went inside my house and said, "Ma, how come — Mommy, how come I always fall down from the tree?" And my mother said because the branches break too much.

The patient's father had inherited a well-established business, and although in his thirties, he was basically a weak and inadequate person who was still quite dependent on his own mother. He had married an attractive woman because of the enhanced esteem he anticipated he would enjoy from such a beautiful wife. She was sexually inhibited, self-involved, and quite vain. Neither parent was able to involve himself deeply with the patient.

The story clearly reveals Gavin's concept of his parents and his relationship to them. The father, as represented by the tree, cannot provide him with support. Each time he climbs the branches — the father's outstretched arms — they break and he falls to the ground. The bird — the mother — also attempts to uphold him; but she, too, is unsuccessful.

Accordingly, I told Gavin the following story:

Once upon a time there was a boy and this boy loved to climb trees because when he was up at the top of a tree he could see far away and he really felt big. Well, one day he was climbing a tree and the branch broke and he fell down. He got very upset and he thought: "I'd better be careful. Next time I climb a tree I'd better test the branches and make sure that they are strong."

Well, the next day he was trying to climb a tree and it looked all right and then he tested some of the branches and they weren't too strong so he said: "Well, I'd better stay away from that tree." Then he got another idea: "I'll get a ladder" and he got a ladder and he climbed up the ladder and in this way he didn't have to step on the weak branches and he still got to the top.

Well, this boy gradually grew up and he found that he was so tall that he didn't have to stand on trees after a while because he could see what he wanted without it.

And the lesson of that story is that if a tree you want to climb has a weak branch, test it first. And if it won't hold you, then get a ladder. But know this also: everybody grows up and then they are big enough to see many things without having to climb trees.

In my story I attempted to help Gavin gain from his father that support which he was capable of providing by testing the branches. I encouraged him to use his own resources — the ladder — when his father was unable to gratify the child's needs. I also tried to offer him the hope and consolation that as he grew up he would be capable of doing more on his own and would thereby suffer less from the frustrations engendered by his parents' inadequacies.

Example 5

Bonnie, a ten-year-old girl with a school phobia, told the following first story:

Once there was this cat and it had a lot of kittens, and all the kittens were very pretty except for one. It wasn't very pretty and so the mother cat just kept it out of the litter. She wouldn't feed it. And so the man who owned the cat didn't want it either so he sold it to this family.

One day the kitten ran away and it fell into a manhole. Wait — no — the people who bought the cat were very mean to it so it ran away and fell into this manhole and it started walking and walking in the manhole. And then it came to this big door. She pushed it open with her paw and there was a catland behind the door and so there was this head cat there who said to her: "This place is for cats whose owners are mean to them and don't take care of them right." And so she stayed at the catland for a little while.

But then one day when she was in the catland this little boy came up to her and said, "Let's go peep behind that door." And she said, "No." And so he said, "Let's go peep behind the door." So she didn't want to. The head cat at catland said, "Don't go behind that door." Then the boy cat said, "Come on. There's nothing behind there that's going to be bad." And so she said, "All right." So they opened the door and what was behind that door was dogland. All these dogs came rushing in and started chasing after all the cats.

But then she woke up. It was only a dream about it and her parents liked her after that.

The story reveals Bonnie's basic feeling that she is a black sheep in her family and unloved. Other families also will find her unlovable. She might, however, find some affection with similar strays and discarded ones. The opening of the door to dogland represents the focusing upon unconscious processes which she envisions will be anxiety-provoking, possibly because the dogs represent her unconscious hostility toward her parents whom she sees as rejecting. With this understanding of Bonnie's story, I related the following:

Once upon a time there was a cat and this cat had many kittens. All of them were very pretty except one. And the one that wasn't very pretty was very sad, very sad indeed, because she saw that her mother and father were always spending time with the other kittens, but weren't spending very much time with her. This made her very sad and also very angry, but she thought, "I must not tell them I'm angry. It's very bad to be angry at one's mother and father."

Well, she spoke to another cat who was in a similar situation, and that cat said, "What do you mean it's very bad to be angry at your mother and father? Maybe if you tell them how angry you are, maybe they can do something about the situation." So she thought about that and realized that it was probably true; that it wasn't so bad to be angry after all.

So one day she went back to her mother and father and said, "You know it makes me angry to see you spend so much time with the other kittens and give me so little time." Well, she was surprised to see that her mother and father did not punish her for saying that she was angry at them or that she was mad at them, and they listened to her and said, "Well, maybe you are right. Maybe we haven't been giving you enough time." So they started to give her more time and she felt a little bit better. But she still realized that they weren't giving her as much time as she would like. About this time she said, "Well, there's no point. I've told them that I was angry. I see that it's not so bad to be angry and they've done something about it. But I still feel that I'd like to have more time with cats." So she decided that she'd better turn to friends because she couldn't get as much time with her parents as she would like and she knew that someday she would grow up, get married, have a boy cat all to her own, and then she wouldn't have to hang around waiting for her parents to give her so much time.

My story has a few lessons. The first lesson is that when somebody does something to you that bothers you it's okay to get angry. Next, it's best to talk about the problem with the person who's bothering you to try to get something done about it. Sometimes that works; the person changes, and you feel better. And the last moral is that if somebody still doesn't give you what you want, you can always get a substitute and get the same thing you want from somebody else. The end.

In my story, I attempted to help Bonnie feel less guilty about the anger she felt toward her parents for their rejection. In her story, she had relegated her anger, symbolized by the ferocious dogs, to the unconscious, to dogland, which was even more inaccessible than the underground catland where she felt herself most comfortable. In my story, the kitten learns that the anger she feels toward her parents is not only not to be feared but, by its expression, it can also be useful in helping lessen the frustrations of her rejection. She is also taught that its expression may not work to her complete satisfaction; and if that is the case, she can still derive substitute gratifications elsewhere, thereby lessening her anger even more.

With Bonnie, as in many with school phobia, the primary fear is that her unconscious hostility toward her mother will be realized in the mother's death while she is in school. By staying with the mother the child is reassured that her death wishes have not come true. Anything which can lessen the hostility and the child's guilt over this hostility can be salubrious in the treatment of this disorder.

Example 6

Tony, a ten-year-old boy with divorced parents was brought to me because of poor school performance and hostile outbursts. His father lived in another part of the country and had little genuine interest in him, whereas his mother was more involved in dating than in spending time with her children. In the first session Tony told this story:

There was two boys, and one girl and a mother and a father, and they went out in a car about five miles out of town, and they ran out of gas in the middle of the night. And they waited there for about an hour or two and then the man said, "I'm going to go back to town and get some more gas," and he walked back. He told the other people to go to sleep and after they went to sleep the sister woke up and she heard a scratching noise on the top of the roof and then she wondered what it was and she went back to sleep. And when she woke up and she heard it again. And a police was next to the car. And the police said, "Will you please get out and walk," and she got out and walked. They said: "Whatever you do, don't look back." She kept on walking and walking and walking.
Therapist: Where was the rest of the family?
Patient: They were still asleep. And when she got about one-half mile, she just had to look back and when she looked back she saw that the noise that was scratching on the roof was the biggest brother hanging on a tree with his bloody fingernails scratching on top of the roof.
Therapist: So the big brother was hanging from a tree? Was he dead?
Patient: Yes.
Therapist: Upside down? I see, and his bloody fingernails

were scratching on the roof. Is that the whole story?

Patient: Uh-huh.

Therapist: Who killed him?

Patient: That's supposed to be the mystery of the story.

Therapist: Uh-huh.

Patient: But I could make somebody up.

Therapist: Do that.

Patient: This monster and he had a big hook on his hand. There was nothing on that hand except the hook and he just takes the hook and he picked him up and he rammed it through his stomach and he took his shirt and he hanged it, and he took a rope and he hanged his feet from a tree. And then he jabbed a knife in his stomach and let him hang.

Therapist: I see. Now what about the cop? Where does he fit into all of this?

Patient: All he was doing was just telling her to get out of the car.

Therapist: Why did he tell her to walk away?

Patient: He was afraid that she would get hanged because of the man with the hook.

Therapist: So he was trying to protect her. What about the other people in the car? What happened to them?

Patient: Well, they just were sleeping, I guess. The man with the hook never saw them.

Therapist: What's the moral of that story —— the lesson?

Patient: I guess it's to get gas before you leave town. That's the first time I've ever made up the moral of that story. I just made that one up.

Therapist: Did you think of that story a lot?

Patient: Yes.

Although it was learned at the end that the story was not created *de novo* according to the rules of the television game, it is still rich in significant psychodynamic material. A repetitive fantasy is often a manifestation of powerful psychological forces, and I considered this one of equal value to the impromptu first story.

The monster represents Tony's father whom he saw as

hostile because he had abandoned the patient. Before the divorce, the father had been cruel to him. The extent of the father's hostility is dramatically represented by the sadistic murder. Tony's mother is also seen as neglectful in protecting him from his father's rage — she sleeps during the murder. His sister, however, is singled out for protection from the father's wrath. She is not only spared but also ambivalently shielded from viewing the carnage. Running out of gas symbolizes the failure of both parents to provide those elements which are vital to the sustenance of the family.

With this understanding of Tony's story, I related the following:

Once upon a time there was a family. This family consisted of a father, a mother, two brothers, and a sister. And one day while they were taking a trip, when they were about five miles out of town, they ran out of gas. And they sat around and waited awhile and then the father said, "You know, I think I'd better go back to town and get some gas. I don't think we're going to meet anybody here who is going to give us any." So the mother said, "Well, it's a dark night here and there might be a lot of scary things. I hear that there's a monster with a claw who is around here." And the father said, "Yes, I heard that, too, but you keep an eye open, Mother. You watch for him. This monster is not the kind of monster that really can hurt anyone if a big person is around to protect the children." At any rate, he went away and the children started to fall asleep and the mother started to fall asleep.

The mother fell lightly asleep and the boy was sort of sleeping too, but he knew that the monster was there too. And it was he who awakened and saw the monster outside the window. He immediately got up and said, "Mother, Mother, there's a monster out there," and the mother beat away the monster. She said, "Get out of here you filthy, ugly monster." And then the cops came and took the monster away to jail.

And the moral of that story is that if there is anything around you that is dangerous, speak up, cry out, and say something about it. Talk about it, ask for help, and that's the best way to get rid of those things.

In forming my story, I realized that it would be unrealistic to introduce any elements which would have encouraged Tony to try to change his father. The latter was geographically distant and too uninvolved emotionally to be expected to respond meaningfully to any overtures or complaints from the patient. Such encouragement would only have added to his frustration and rage. His mother, therefore, was his only hope. In Tony's story she sleeps, thereby exposing him to danger but, nevertheless, she is in the car with him. In my story he wakes her up and successfully enlists her aid. As I so often do, I attempted to get the child to actively participate in improving his own life situation.

Example 7

Joey, a seven-year-old boy, who presented complaints of enuresis, nightmares, chronic anxiety, and feelings of inadequacy, told the following story in his first session:

> Once upon a time there was a snake and he was very thin. He boasted about being so thin. Then he saw a fat snake and he said to him, "Isn't it good to be a thin snake?" The fat snake said, "Why?" The thin snake said, "Well, so I could boast that I'm thin." And the fat snake said, "Ha, is that the only thing you can do?" the thin snake said sadly, "Well, yes." He had nothing else to boast about. He couldn't dig holes. He was supposed to be a rattlesnake but he couldn't bite or be poisonous. He could never control himself; he had a bad temper. Whenever it was cold, he was always warm. Whenever he wanted to be warm, he was cold.
> The lesson of the story is: think before you boast because you will usually end up having nothing to boast about.

Joey's father was an active professional person whose deep

investment in his work often left him with little meaningful time for his children. The mother intermittently responded to life's stresses with withdrawal and depression, and thereby compromised her effective involvement with the patient. In spite of these difficulties, the parents were otherwise fairly stable people, dedicated to their childrens' welfare. I considered the two younger siblings to be within the normal range psychologically and felt that the degree of deprivation the patient suffered did not warrant or fully explain his symptomatology.

The story reveals the patient's feelings that he has nothing to boast about. He therefore attempts to raise his self-esteem by making assets out of his liabilities. Joey makes a virtue out of being thin, that is, of being small and inadequate. His inability to dig holes, an activity which he considers important for snakes to know how to do, also reveals his feelings of inadequacy. His strong desire to repress his anger is revealed by the snake's inability to bite and its absence of poison. The latter deficiency, of course, is the most striking manifestation of the patient's severe inhibition of rage. The snake's wishing to control his bad temper is another reflection of this problem. Lastly, Joey sees himself as deprived of affection when he states: "Whenever he wanted to be warm, he was cold." This suggests that the source of his rage is his feeling of deprivation of love.

With this understanding of Joey's story, I related the following:

Once upon a time there was a thin snake and he had a mother and a father and he felt pretty bad about his family. He felt that they didn't spend enough time with him. He felt that maybe they didn't like him very much or they weren't good to him. He had some feelings that they weren't right; something was wrong with them. He didn't know what. This made him feel pretty bad because if a mother or a father doesn't like you, you don't feel good about yourself.

This kind of made him mad too, but he was scared to say he was angry because he thought it would be a terrible thing if he were to tell them that he was angry at them. He thought that if he were to tell them that he was angry they would beat him or send him away or something even worse. So he kept it all in. Then one day he saw a fat snake and that fat snake was screaming at his mother. The fat snake said to his mother: "I don't like you. You don't spend enough time with me." And he said, "Gee, whiz, I never knew that kids could say such things to their parents. I guess it isn't so bad." And he went to the fat snake and he said, "I saw you screaming at your mother." The fat snake said, "Of course, when she does something wrong, I've got to tell her."

"Isn't that terrible to say terrible things to your mother?"

"Well, if they're true, they're not. That's the way I get her to fall into line. That's the way I get her to do the things I want. What is anger for if not to help you get the things you want?"

And the thin snake remembered: "What is anger for if not to help you get the things you want? Anger helps you get what you want — the things you think you may not be able to have." And he thought about that and said, "Gee, that's a good point."

So he went home and he said to his mother, "Would you be angry at me if I told you that I get angry at you?" And the mother said, "Of course not. What's anger for if it's not to help you get what you want. Anger helps you get what you want." He said, "Gee, Mommy, that's the exact same thing that the fat snake said." She said, "Yes, everybody knows that. What are you angry about? What am I doing that you don't like that makes you angry?" And he said, "You don't spend enough time with me." The mother thought about it and said, "You know, you're right. I will make an effort to spend more time with you." And so she did and then he wasn't angry any more. He also learned that it's not terrible to say you are angry when you are. It can help you get what you want.

The moral of my story is that if somebody isn't giving you something that you want, ask him for it. Express your anger because anger can help you get what you don't have.

In my story I attempted to lessen Joey's guilt over his

anger and to encourage him to utilize such anger in the service of changing the situation which brought it about. In Joey's case, I felt that the parents were intelligent and sensitive enough not to react punitively to his expression of anger. I expected them to respond with sympathetic understanding and to comply with reasonable requests on his part.

Example 8

Ronald, a ten-year-old boy with severe negativistic behavior, violent rage outbursts, and marked defiance of authority, told this story in his first session:

> Once upon a time there was a big greedy ogre who whenever somebody came near his home or tried to take anything around his home, he would gobble them up immediately. There was this prince who wanted to get the things that the ogre had and since he was only a little boy he would cry and cry until his mother and father went practically crazy, and so they said, "We'll get that ogre's stuff if it kills us." And it almost did, for when they went, the ogre himself had so many defense lines and everything that the king's guard didn't have a chance. So they just had to go home in disgrace.
>
> The next day the prince started crying louder than ever and said, "Mommy, Daddy, I want the money. I want some stuff and if I can't get that I want what the ogre has. The ogre has everything: games, money, toys —— anything I can dream of." And so the king said: "Well, young man, you are just going to have to put up with it. We are not going to have our men and ourselves killed just to get you some toys and stuff. We have enough stuff as it is."
>
> But the next day the prince got some guards and set out to kill the ogre. But when the prince took one look at the ogre he was so ugly that the prince got so scared and ran away and never came back again, and his men ran back, afraid of what might happen to them.
>
> The moral of this story is: if you can't like it, lump it. This means if you don't like it, skip it. There's another

moral: you can't get everything your own way and you can't get everything you want. And another moral is: you can fool all the people some of the time, some of the people all the time, and some of the people some of the time, but you can't fool all the people all the time.

Therapist: How does the prince fool the people?

Patient: He was trying to fool his mother and father by —— when they weren't looking —— going out to kill the ogre. But he couldn't fool the whole kingdom 'cause the soldiers knew he was going so it wasn't really a secret.

Therapist: Where did the prince run after he ran away from the ogre?

Patient: He just ran away and never came back.

Therapist: He never returned home?

Patient: No, he was practically scared stiff. He never saw a face as ugly as the ogre's.

Both parents were very angry people. The mother utilized the mechanisms of massive repression and reaction formation to handle her deep fury. She was excessively polite and exaggeratedly concerned for the welfare of others, taking particular pains to ensure that they did not endanger themselves. Her subdued anger and tense control created a subtle feeling of tension in most who were involved with her. The father was a fiercely competitive sportsman who discharged much of his hostility through sublimation and physical activity. At home, however, he was given to violent outbursts.

I understood the story to reveal Ronald's feeling that his parents could not provide him with affection as symbolized by money, games, and stuff. If he wanted love, Ronald would have to seek it elsewhere. The ogre epitomized his notion that, like his parents, the providers of the good things in life are inevitably ugly and hostile — a phenomenon Harry Stack Sullivan referred to as the "malevolent transformation." Ronald ends up alone in the world, fleeing from everyone because of his feeling that seeking love from people can be a dangerous thing. The patient's mode of acquiring affection is to steal it or forcibly extract it, rather than to earn it.

In addition, the story clearly exhibits the way in which he controls his parents through temper tantrums. His hostility toward them is also apparent: "He would cry and cry until his mother and father went practically crazy, and so they said, 'We'll get that ogre's stuff if it kills us.'"

With this analysis of Ronald's story, I related the following:

Well, once upon a time a long time ago there was this very greedy ogre who had large amounts of money and other possessions that he guarded very jealously and no one was permitted to even get near. Well, this prince used to be very envious of what the ogre had. He wished that he could have what the ogre had and he came home each day crying and crying, screaming and having temper tantrums in the hope that this would get his parents to try and get some of that money for him. But they just sat by, simply telling him that he could have as many temper tantrums as he wanted but they were not going to get that money for him. First of all, it wasn't theirs. It belonged to the ogre and that was it.

Patient: And they had enough money since they were rich. They were royalty.

Therapist: Right. They were royalty. They had their own money and they weren't that greedy that they wanted to take even more even though the ogre didn't get his money in the best possible way. Some of it was stolen and taken from people illegally. Still it was his money and they didn't feel it was justifiable for the prince to go out and try to get it. Well, he had more temper tantrums in the hope that his parents would change their minds but they didn't.

So the next thing that the prince did was to say, "Okay, I can't have the ogre's money. I want your money. I want a lot of your money." And they said to him, "Well, you're still a boy yet. We give you an allowance which is appropriate for your age and that's it." He said, "No, I want much more than that" and he started to have temper tantrums again in the hope that they would then give him more of their money because they were kind of rich. They said, "No. We're not going to give it to you and that's it."

Patient: How much money would you say the king and queen had?

Therapist: Well, I'll tell you. There's two kinds of kings and queens. There are some kings and queens who have a lot of money — millions of dollars — and own a lot and are quite rich. There are other kings and queens who look rich but really aren't and they might be very poor. And, as a matter of fact, I think the way I would like to work it in this story —— I think I'm going to change my mind and make this king and queen kind of poor. They just had enough to get by to keep up the castle, to buy the necessities required for a king and queen, and they really didn't have that much to throw around.

Patient: And yet they didn't steal any money from the ogre?

Therapist: No, they did not feel that stealing was an appropriate or right thing to do, and they just would not steal. So this prince was very angry. He had temper tantrums and he said he wanted them to get the money, and they said, "No, we don't think you should have so much money and even if we had a lot of money we wouldn't give you that much. We might give you a little bit more." He said, "What am I to do?" They said to him, "Well, like everybody else, you will grow up and you must prepare yourself to do something in life and you have to earn money on your own. Learn a trade, learn a profession, learn to do something, and then you will be able to earn money in an honest way and provide for your needs. And that is exactly what he did. He worked hard and diligently and he grew up and he earned a lot of money.

My story has a couple of morals.

Patient: Like mine?

Therapist: Yes, mine has a couple of morals. Can you guess? Can you figure out the morals?

Patient: One is, don't be greedy because you can't get everything you want.

Therapist: Right.

Patient: Business before pleasure. Well, I can't think of anything more.

Therapist: Well, one of the morals is —— you see the king and queen knew —— they were wise people —— and they knew that ——

Patient: Wisdom is better than wealth.

Therapist: That's true. They also knew that giving a kid everything he wants ——

Patient: It sort of spoils him.

Therapist: Right, it spoils him and they also knew that they weren't going to let their kid take advantage of them with temper tantrums. That would spoil him. And they knew that the best way to get something is to work for it, rather than for it to be given to you on a silver platter — as the old expression goes.

In my story the parents do not allow themselves to be coerced and manipulated by the patient's temper tantrums. Unlike the parents in Ronald's story, mine do not assist in gaining affection by overpowering and extracting it from the provider. They insist that he earn it through his own efforts. Also communicated in my story is the idea that his parents can provide him with only a limited amount of love; they insist that that is all he'll get from them and he had better accept that. But he is given the hope that he can attain more when he is older if he applies himself.

This story also demonstrates a few technical variations that have not thus far been described. In the patient's first interruption he suggests that the parents were rich. I decided to accept and incorporate this interjection because I did not, at that point, appreciate its full significance and saw "no harm" in doing so. However, his second interruption — "How much money would you say the king and queen had?" — revealed to me Ronald's desire that I provide his parents with a capacity to love which was not theirs. To have continued in the vein of enhancing their wealth would have fostered in this child unrealistic hopes for affection. Since such longings could only be frustrated, it would have been cruel to encourage them. Accordingly, with this new insight, I decided to change my story: "I think I'm going to change my mind and make this king and queen kind of poor." I have not found such midstream alterations and retractions to lessen the efficacy of my story. In fact, they usually improve it because they are introduced when I sense I have been off course and they generally serve to turn me in the right direction. Lastly, this story demonstrates how I attempt to elicit from the patient the morals of my story. When the child, on his own, is able to relate the lessons, the therapist knows that the child has fully appreciated his communications.

Example 9

Harold, a ten-and-a-half-year-old boy with minimal brain dysfunction, avoided sports because of coordination problems. Although of normal intelligence, he had difficulty in reading and arithmetic. He was referred because he had refused to attend school and had withdrawn from his peers because they constantly made a scapegoat of him. In the first session he told this story:

> Once upon a time there was a little dog. Of course, he has a master and once when his master was chopping wood the little dog got in his way. By accident he chopped the dog in half so he sewed the dog back together again. But he sewed the dog back together again wrong. He had the back feet pointing up in the air and the front feet pointing down, and that little dog was the most unusual sight in the world. Of course, the dog said to the master, "Hey, give me a bone. I'll stand on my rear feet and I'll do amazing tricks. I'll be doing somersaults for you, anything you want me to do. Please give me a bone. Anything for a bone." The dog's name was Snoopy. So his master fed him a bone and then his rear feet were turned around and then he was like a normal dog.

Harold's father was an insecure, arrogant, intermittently alcoholic, and mildly paranoid man who had little sensitivity to the emotional aspects of his son's problems. The boy's mother was subject to headaches and depressions, in part related to the suppression of the rage she felt toward the father.

The story reveals Harold's feeling that he is a freak and

that his malformations were caused by his father's ineptitude. His desire to be magically cured is revealed by his immediate transformation to normality after ingesting a bone. On another level, the bone, as a food dear to dogs, might represent the father's love — the lack of which is seen to have caused his illness and the supply of which is seen as its cure. The bone probably has phallic significance as well, in the sense that it provides masculine strength and, by implication, rectification of his abnormalities.

In response, I related the following:

Once upon a time there was a little dog and this little dog was standing near his master who was chopping wood. And by mistake or accident his master chopped him in half. Well, his master, although he was a goodhearted person, used to make a lot of errors and, by mistake, the master sewed the dog back in such a way that his feet stuck up in the air in the back and his other feet were on the ground. It really looked funny. And this dog got the idea that he could be cured of this if only his master would give him a bone. He didn't know that this was a foolish idea, that cures for such problems do not come so easily. You just don't get cured by eating a bone. So he begged his master for a bone and his master finally said, "Okay, I'll give you a bone." Then he ate the bone and was very disappointed when he found out that this did not cure him.

And then he wondered what he could do. So he decided to go to a doctor in town. The doctor examined him and said, "What you need is a special operation followed by exercises on your part and hard work. So he went in for the operation and they straightened him out. They put his feet where they should be and turned his body around, and they prescribed a long series of exercises which required a lot of work on his part and cooperation with the doctors and therapists. And after a long time he finally got back in shape, moved his legs right, and became a happy, healthy dog.

Patient: What's the moral of that story?

Therapist: Well, there are no quick cures to complicated
   diseases —— if you have a complicated disease or medi-

cal problem, you have to expect to take a long time and work very hard to help it, and your own cooperation is often required.

Since this was Harold's first story in treatment, I chose to concentrate on what seemed to be unrealistic attitudes toward therapy: the alleviation of his difficulties by the somewhat passive ingestion of a magic cure. In my story, I presented the therapeutic process as a more egalitarian experience where both doctor and patient actively work at their respective tasks. Also, placing more of the responsibility of his cure in his own hands lessens the likelihood that he will suffer the ineptitude he anticipates in others. I felt it was more important to elaborate on his misguided attitudes about therapy than to work on the elements of emotional deprivation also present in the story. This story is typical of the kind I tell during the first session because many children come with magical anticipation which is often stimulated by the parents. It is important to dispel these magical illusions as early as possible.

Example 10

Mark, a ten-and-a-half-year-old boy with chronic anxiety, feelings of insecurity, and excessive dependence on his mother, told this story in his first session:

Last night there was a hurricane, in case you might know, in Southeast Asia and not many people were hurt, but there was this one village where there was mountains all around it. And this hurricane blew down the mountains and the whole village was covered, but there were still people who were living there. The Red Cross heard about this and they sent some airplanes over there but the airplanes couldn't find the village because everything looked so much alike. So they sent for a radio plane that was going to pick up the radio signals from the people underneath the mountains —— the broken mountains. But they found the place and they couldn't, at the moment, find the way to get in. So they landed and put down men to find out if there was any entrance.

They were looking and they found a cave and some men with flashlights went in and looked around and they saw a light on the far end of the other side of the cave. And they went along and the leader of the group asked one of the other men where his friend was, but he said he didn't know and he thought he was with the other man. But the other man said he didn't know either. So they went back and looked for him and they found a deep pit. The man had falled down in there and had broken his back. So they had to put ropes down and they had to climb down and make a stretcher and tie the stretcher to the ropes. And then they pulled the stretcher up and then they had to go back to the plane and then they had to start all over again.

They went back into the cave but they couldn't find the light on the other side. So they looked around and they saw a tunnel and the tunnel mostly led to where they started but they saw it slant a little bit so they went down the tunnel and they saw a door and this door was made out of hard stone. They tried to pry it open but it wouldn't move. One of the men searched around the bottom and he touched a small stone and the door slid open. And they walked inside and they saw a tower. They climbed up into the tower and there was another door so they opened it up and stood back. Inside the door there was another tunnel but it didn't seem to end. It just kept on going and going and one of the men suggested that they go along this tunnel, so they did. They went along and they saw some more light. So they went toward it and there was these steps. So they went down the steps and they were in the middle of the village that needed supplies. They gave them the food and then everyone was all right.

The lesson of this story is: don't give up while there's still hope.

I consider the men buried beneath the mountain as well as the underground villagers to represent the patient who feels overwhelmed by his anxiety. The depth at which Mark is buried, tunnel beneath tunnel, reflects the great degree to which he feels burdened by his difficulties. The Red Cross, of course, stands for the therapist who, indefatigably searches him out in order to save him and provide him with sustenance. The story reveals Mark's strong passive-dependency and his anticipation that those around him will go to great lengths to take care of him.

With this understanding, I related this story:

Once upon a time there was a town in Southeast Asia and it was hit by a hurricane. The mountains all around it caved in on this little village so that it was completely buried. The people who were buried underneath were a very industrious group and they knew that, although they might expect Red Cross planes to come to try to get them, they themselves would have to try to do something for themselves on their own. So they figured that there were two possible things that they could do: 1) they could try to dig their way out so they sent a team to do that and 2) they also decided that they'd have to use every possible means to communicate with the outside world. So they sent another team to do things like banging on rocks with shovels in order to make noise, and there was an underground stream there so they sent notes in bottles through the underground stream in the hope that this would somehow get to the attention of people on the outside. They used their shortwave radio sets to try to communicate with the outside world, and they managed to get through communications. And people on the outside then knew that they were in distress down there and they were each able to communicate their position to the other. On the top of the surface they started a team digging down over that very spot, and the two teams dug toward one another, communicating with radio to one another. They passed pipes down into the ground in order to send air and then the two teams gradually met, and then they opened up a passageway and the people got out.

And the lesson of that story is: when you are in distress and something is bothering you, try to help yourself. Don't just depend upon the outside aid to get to you. You

60

have to work and do it yourself also if you want to get helped. The end.

Therapist: Do you have any comments about this story?

Patient: Yes, one. I think that the moral of your story was a little bit better than mine.

Therapist: Did you think yours was a bad one?

Patient: Yes, you might say that.

Therapist: Well, I'd say that your story was a good one but I've been doing this much longer than you, so I have more practice in making up stories. I wasn't unhappy or dissatisfied with your story. It was a good one.

Again, as with the patient described in Example 9, I attempted to present the therapy as an egalitarian venture in which both doctor and patient must work together toward a common goal. I included the post-story interchange because it reveals two other aspects of the Mutual Storytelling Technique. First, I often ask the patient for his comments about my story or about the "program" that day. It is important that the question be posed in a neutral manner: "Do you have any comments about this story?" If I had asked, "How do you like my story?" the child might have felt obligated to say he liked it. By careful questions, one can often learn whether the story has been meaningful to the child. Secondly, the question can also serve as a taking-off point for analytic enquiry. In this case, the child revealed his feelings of inadequacy, and I attempted to provide him with a little ego-support. Although one might expect diffident comments such as this child made to be common, in my experience they are rare. I believe that any embarrassment the child may suffer by having been told a "better" story is more than compensated for by the benefits derived from my story.

Example 11

Larry, an eight-year-old boy, was referred for treatment because of compulsive rituals. In his first session he told this story:

Once upon a time there were seven magic jelly beans and the first one said, "I'm mad." And the second one said, "There's no reason to be mad." The third one said, "How could you be mad?" The fourth one said, "Temper, temper." And the fifth one said, "Oh, my, he's about to blow his top." The sixth one said, "I guess you're right." The seventh one said, "Look at him go."

Therapist: Meaning what?

Patient: He got so mad that he launched himself all the way to the moon. The end.

And the lesson is: never try to launch yourself to the moon without a spacesuit or else you'll be floating around like anything. The end.

Larry's father was an academician who was so dedicated to his professional life that he was only minimally involved with his wife and children. The mother was devoted to the children but masochistically suffered her husband's rejections.

I cannot recall having heard a story which so dramatically reveals the various defense mechanisms which a child may utilize to justify the repression of anger. The first jelly bean is "mad." The second uses intellectualization in the service of repression: "There's no reason to be mad." The third's statement: "How could you be mad?" was said in a guilt-provoking manner, with the implication: "How loathsome can you be?" The fourth advises conscious control: "Temper, temper." The fifth predicts dire consequences for the angry one: "Oh, my, he's about to blow his top." The sixth reinforces the fifth's prediction and, lastly, the seventh sees the anger as causing one's total removal from the fellowship of mankind: "He got so mad that he launched himself all the way to the moon."

I then related this story:

Once there were seven jelly beans. Now the first one said, "I'm mad." And he was mad because somebody was doing something that was bothering him. The second one said, "There's no reason to be mad." And the first one said, "There is a reason to be mad. I'm mad because that guy over there bothers me. That boy and that girl bother me and

I'm mad at them." And the third one said, "Oh, how could you be mad? It's wrong to be mad." And the first one said, "It's not wrong to be mad. It's perfectly all right to be mad. I've a right to be mad because they bothered me." And the fourth one said, "Temper, temper." And the first one said, "What do you mean, 'Temper, temper?' I'm not going to stop my temper. If they do something that bothers me I'm going to tell them so that they'll stop doing it. That's what you get mad for — so that people will stop doing things that bother you. At least you can try to get them to stop." And the fifth one said, "Oh, he's about to blow his top." And the first one said, "I'm angry, but I'm not going to blow my top. If I go over and tell them what bothers me, then I'll feel better about myself and maybe I can get them to stop doing what they are doing." And the seventh one said, "Oh boy, you are going to get angry and you're going to fly off to the moon." And the first one said, "I'm not flying off to the moon. I'm flying right over there right now and I'm going to tell those two people over there what bothers me."

So he went over and he told them what bothered him, and to the amazement of the others most of the things that they were doing they stopped. A few things they couldn't stop, but most of the things they stopped, and they realized that the first one was right — that showing your anger helps in that you can use your anger to help you get rid of things that bother you.

The lesson of that story is: if somebody does something that bothers you and it makes you angry, use your anger to help you get rid of that thing, to help you make them stop. Go over and tell them what's bothering you. That is what anger is for. Anger is to help you to stop somebody from doing something that bothers you. And the other six magic jelly beans learned a lesson from the first one when they saw what he had done. The end.

In my story I attempted to systematically demonstrate the inappropriateness and illogicality of each of the patient's defense mechanisms against the expression of anger. I point out the use of anger "to help you get rid of things that bother you" — a use which obviates the need for the repression of anger. The boy and girl in my story represent the parents who, in my opinion, were the real objects of his anger. Clinically, his anger was being repressed, displaced, and partially discharged in his compulsive rituals. My hope was that Larry would respond to messages such as those imparted in my story by coming more directly to terms with his anger toward his parents, that he would feel less guilty about its expression, that it would provide the impetus for confronting them, and that it would enhance the efficacy of his protestations. I did not believe that he could succeed completely in getting them to be more attentive and affectionate, but partial success was certainly possible. Trying is of itself salutary. Partial success could reduce Larry's hostility, and I was prepared to deal with this issue further after some of his efforts were frustrated, as they inevitably would be.

3. THE EARLY PHASE OF THERAPY

Some children in their first stories do not provide the therapist with the kind of rich and revealing disclosures described in the last chapter. Their resistances and anxieties may be too great for them to reveal themselves — even under the protective symbolism of the story. After a few sessions, as they become more comfortable with the therapist, they may then give him their "first story."

In the early phase of therapy, the stories of many children reveal their resistances to treatment, their anxieties about the therapist, their fear of looking into their unconscious processes, their terror of revealing unacceptable thoughts and feelings, and their inability to admit faults and deficiencies. The therapist has the opportunity, through his stories, of assuaging many of these anxieties.

In this stage as well, the therapist's stories can help prime the patient for treatment. The child who expects the therapist to do all the work is helped to accept the truth that there are no magic cures for his problems and that he will have to work along with the therapist if he is to alleviate his difficulties. Also communicated is the notion that anxiety-provoking situations are not so painful as they may have seemed originally. The patient is encouraged to take his chances and expose himself to fearful thoughts, feelings, and situations.

Finally, in this phase one may see the first examples of repetitious themes and situations which may persist throughout treatment. Like the recurring dream, such repeated themes reflect powerful processes which press for expression. It is in these sequences that core problems forcefully express themselves.

In this chapter, typical story sequences from the early

phase of treatment are presented. They demonstrate not only the patterns which the child's stories usually take during this stage, but also the types of stories I tell in response to lessen initial resistances and anxieties, pave the way into treatment, and alter inappropriate attitudes and distortions about the therapeutic process.

Example 1

Steve, the eight-year-old boy with a school disciplinary problem, who told the story about the dragon swallowing his own fire, related this story two months later:

> Today my story is about how the forest fires got put out. Now once upon a time three forest fires had been caused and nobody could put them out because nobody knew anything about putting out fires. One of the trees got very unhappy and said, "We can't live well. We can't stand —— we wish we had something good to stop those forest fires."
>
> And so one of the angels flew by and they asked her what they could do and she said, "I'm sorry I cannot help you. You must find something yourself, but I will give you advice. You know the water and dirt?" "Yes," said the trees, "but what can they do?" The angel said, "Well, if you take these two things —— water is cold and fire is hot —— water will put out the fires. Just tell your friends to get enough water, and dirt will smother the fire or hold over them and mud. It will help you a lot and then you won't have your forest ruined."
>
> And so the trees obeyed and very few forest fires then happened. The end.
>
> Moral: good things may happen to everybody, even trees.

I consider the trees in the story to represent the patient and the fires, his unconscious threatening emotions — very likely hostile ones, as was the dragon's fire in Steve's previous story. The story reveals his feeling that he might be destroyed by his own anger. He seeks a magic disappearance of his rage.

66

The angel from heaven — probably the therapist — provides him with ready advice for rapidly squelching these dangerous emotions.

There is, however, another element in this story which I considered significant. The boy asks for magic help, and it is instantaneously provided. He does nothing on his own to solve his problems. I consider it vital in this phase of therapy to communicate to the child that it is he who is expected to try to find solutions for his problems and that there are no magic ready-made cures to be provided by fantasized saviors. Accordingly, in my story I decided to focus on the issues of magical solution and infantile dependency rather than on the problem of repression of rage.

Therefore, I told the following story:

Once upon a time there was a forest, and the trees in this forest were very upset because there were many forest fires and many trees were getting burned down. They wondered what they could do.

Well, one day along came an angel, flying over the forest. The trees looked up to the heavens and said, "Oh, angel, oh, angel, could you please help us. We beseech you to help us." And the angel said, "God helps those who help themselves." And they said, "We wish to protect ourselves from these forest fires." And the angel said, "The means to protect yourself are within your very sight. If you look around you carefully and think; if you look around you carefully, at your very feet are all the things that you need to fight those forest fires."

The trees wondered what the angel could mean and they looked around and said, "What do we see around us at our feet?" And the angel said, "Look, look carefully. What is at your feet?" One of the trees said, "The only thing it might be is earth." The angel said, "Think. Can that be of help to you?" Another tree said, "Yes, I remember once when I saw a fire, some earth slid down a hill and it smothered it." And the angel said, "Right. You see, you think for yourself and you will find out the answer. Another tree spoke up and said, "But there's no earth near me. I'm at the edge of a lake." The angel said, "Think, think for yourself and you will find out the answer." Now what at your feet can be of help?" Another tree said, "Well, you know that fire never goes to the lake." Another one said, "I wonder if water will put out fire?" And the angel flew away and didn't say a word.

The next time there was a fire, the first thing that they did was get earth to smother the fire, and then they got water, which put it out. The trees learned a wonderful lesson. They learned not only that fire and water could be of help to them, but if they thought about things and used their heads, they could protect themselves from that which was dangerous.

And the moral of the story is: when you are in trouble, think about that which is around you. Think about the very things that are under your very nose and you may then solve your problems. The end.

Therapist: What did you think about those stories?
Patient: Okay.
Therapist: Did you like the story I told?
Patient: Yup.
Therapist: What did you like about it?
Patient: The way that people can help themselves.
Therapist: Right.

Clearly, my main aim was to help Steve think for himself and attack his problems on his own. One could argue that my story has anti-therapeutic elements, in that I am reiterating the theme of repression of anger and thereby possibly perpetuating the child's pathology. My defense to such criticism is that I have found it best to elaborate upon a single primary theme when relating my story. Introducing more than one healthy alternative at a time lessens the likelihood that they will sink in. Emphasizing one at a time increases the chances that my message will get through. In the service of such emphasis, I may have to reiterate a pathological element on occasion, but I believe that when doing so there is time to rectify that in the future. One must consider which message deserves greatest emphasis. Here, in the early stage, I usually consider corrections of distortions which the child may have about the treatment process to have the highest priority. One must learn *how* to build a house before one can build it.

Finally, the reader should note that in my post-story inquiry, I did not accept the child's simple statement that he liked the story. I tried to get specifics. I asked him, "What did you like about it?" Steve's answer revealed that he had indeed gotten my message.

Example 2

George, a nine-and-one-half-year-old boy was referred because of disinterest in his school work, shyness, and general timidity. During the first month of treatment, George told this story:

Once upon a time there was a man who explored caves and he was famous for exploring some things he found in caves of the cavemen and that the Indians marked on the walls. Once he went in a cave and some people wanted to come with him in case he got lost. He didn't want them to. He wanted all the money for himself. He got money for the things he found. He went in there and he got lost.

The moral of the story is: don't be selfish. Let some other people share things with you. Share.
Therapist: So the moral is to share?
Patient: Yeah. Share more.
Therapist: You say he finally got lost. What happened to him?
Patient: He never could get out. He kept walking around.
Therapist: What finally happened?
Patient: He died in the cave.

I consider the underground caves to represent the child's unconscious. His exploration of these caves symbolizes his therapy, and he fears that such a dangerous journey to the unknown may have terrible consequences — death itself is not beyond possibility.

69

The people who offer to guide him represent the therapist. However, he is ambivalent about my joining him in this perilous underground excursion. At first, I am rejected — ostensibly because he would have to share with me the money he would earn from selling his findings. I believe this is a rationalization. George's real fear is that I will lead him to just those things he would rather not find. In addition, the rejection of me might reflect distrust. The boy's parents were divorced, his father was unreliable and at times excessively punitive. George's fear of therapy with me is probably related to his experiences with his father. The money issue is used to justify my not joining him in this adventure into the unknown. But without me the consequences might have been worse. Without my guidance he might become lost and even die. In the moral I do join him and protect him from the malevolent forces of the world, both internal and external.

With this interpretation of George's story, I related the following:

Once upon a time there was a man and this man was a cave explorer and he was known far and wide for the many interesting and unusual discoveries that he made in caves. He would explore the caves of ancient men and explore the caves of ancient Indians where he had discovered numerous drawings and relics from these olden days. He was known far and wide for his discoveries.

Now, once he came upon a very large and ancient cave and he said to his friends, "Although I have been hunting and trying to discover things in caves for many years, I'm quite frightened of going into this cave. I think I may get lost in there." And the friends said, "Oh, there's nothing to be afraid of in that cave." The man said, "Well, will you come with me?" And his friends said, "Okay, we'll come with you the first time and then you'll see that it isn't so dangerous and then you won't need us anymore."

So they went into the cave with him the first time. Although there were some things in there that were kind of scary, he realized that they were right; that he didn't need them to accompany him because the things were not as scary as he had thought. Then he was able to go into this cave alone and he realized that what he originally thought was quite scary wasn't that dangerous.

And the lesson of this story is: sometimes you think something is scarier than it really is. If you try to do the thing you fear, you may find out that it isn't as scary as you thought it was originally. The end.

I attempted to convey the notion that in the early phases of treatment George might need my guidance, but that gradually he would be able to do more on his own. In addition, I tried to communicate the idea that his journey into the unconscious will not be as hazardous as he anticipates, but that he can only learn this by self-exposure. Finally, in my story I incorporated the idea that I am not a dangerous person to be alone with.

One week later, George told this story:

Once upon a time there was a man with airplanes —— model airplanes and he wanted to make a model of this latest U.S. airplane. The government wouldn't let him because the other companies would find out how it was made. He took pictures when the government people weren't looking and then he made the model of the airplane. And then the other companies found out how the design was made and all that. And he got in big trouble and then the government had to make a new airplane so other companies wouldn't find out how to make it, because they didn't want them to find out how to make the plane. Then the guy who made the model got into a lot of trouble and they put him in jail.

The lesson of that story is: do not make anything that anybody doesn't want you to make anything or else you might get into trouble.

George's second story again reflects his fear that revealing himself will be followed by terrible consequences. The picture taking of the government's secret airplane is similar to the exploration of the underground cave of the previous week's story. Both reflect his fear of disclosing unconscious material. The utilization of the camera, X-ray machine, movie screen, and television set are common ways of representing self-confrontation, both in children's stories and in adults' dreams.

In order to again lessen anxieties about therapeutic disclosures, I told this story:

Once upon a time there was a man who made model airplanes and the government made a new plane. It was a commercial flight plane and he wanted to make a model of it, but he thought, "Oh, they'd never give me permission for that. It's considered to be too much of a secret."

So one day he went to where they were testing the plane and he went to the edge of the landing field and he started to take pictures. And while he was taking pictures a man from the government came over and said, "What are you doing?" He said, "I'm taking pictures." The government man said, "Well, why are you standing behind the hangar here and doing it in such a sly, secret way? Why are you hiding?" And he said, "Well, I thought that you wouldn't want me to take pictures." The man said, "Not at all. We are very proud of this plane. There's nothing secret about it. If you really want to take pictures, why don't you come right up to the hangar and take pictures both on the ground and while it's flying. We are very proud of what we did here and we'd like others to know about it, and any kind of publicity this plane gets we're happy to have." So the man did just that and he learned that many things that you think are to be kept secret are really not to be kept secret and are really better off openly discussed and exposed.

The moral of the story is that there are many things that you might think should be kept secret, but really don't have to be kept secret and you are really better off if you don't keep them secret.

As is clear, I attempted to impart to this boy the notion that things which he considers necessary to hide often need not be enshrouded in secrecy. Exposure, in fact, is often preferable to concealment. My story was another attempt to diminish George's early resistances.

A few weeks later, George told a third story which further revealed early treatment anxieties:

Once upon a time there was a man and he owned a company that made telephones. And that company made these mini-circuits for the telephones so that they would work better and so that the telephone wouldn't have to take up so much room. The men put the telephones in boxes with padding so that the mini-circuits wouldn't get broken or anything.

So once they sold a telephone to this person and it didn't work. So they complained to the company and the company found out that they didn't put padding in the box so a mini-circuit got broken. It was banging around inside. So they put in a new mini-circuit and they gave him his money back. He kept the broken telephone.

The moral of that story is that when you own a company you should make sure that things fit in a box so that they wouldn't get broken.

In this story the patient's feelings of fragility are revealed. George is essentially saying to me: "I'm too frail to withstand therapeutic confrontations. I'm too brittle to remain intact under the stress of treatment."

Accordingly, I told this story:

Once upon a time there was a man who owned a company and this company made mini-circuits for telephones. This man was a very finicky, fuddy-duddy, persnickety kind of fellow and he was constantly worried that the mini-circuits would get broken when shipped. He considered them to be very fragile and he was constantly worried about them. He insisted that the Shipping Department put a lot of padding into the boxes and as much padding that they would put in, when he would investigate it and inspect it, he would say, "Oh, no, not enough padding. Put another layer of padding."

Well, he began to notice that his company wasn't doing so well. They weren't making as much money as he would have liked and that began to upset him. So he brought an expert in — a man who looks into these things and tries to figure out why a company is losing money. And the man investigated the whole thing and he found out that the owner of the company was spending too much money on padding. He said to him, "Listen. These mini-circuits are very stable. They are not that fragile. They are not going to break that easily. You don't have to put much padding in here. In fact, they can go without any padding at all."

Well, the owner of the company was at first hesitant to accept that advice and he thought about it and he spoke to others. They said to him, "Listen, he's right. You're too concerned; you're too fearful. These things aren't that fragile. They're not gonna break that easily. I suggest that you listen to that man."

So he listened to him and at first he was scared because he was worried about those mini-circuits being sent without padding. But he did it and he sat at his phone waiting for the complaints to come in. He expected to have many complaints from people saying, "Hey, this mini-circuit is damaged." But to his surprise, there were no complaints.

And then he learned his lesson. He learned that sometimes things are not as fragile or as breakable or as easily destroyed as you might think. He realized that he was being too cautious.

Therapist: And the lesson of that story is what?

Patient: Well —— that is —— you just said it.

Therapist: I want to hear you say it so I know you understand.

Patient: That things don't get broken so easily.

My essential message, of course, was that George wasn't easily damaged, that he could withstand more than he imagined, and that he was overconcerned with protecting himself. In the story "hard knocks" of reality are not as traumatic as the man anticipates.

Example 3

Carol, a nine-and-one-half-year-old girl who entered treatment because of stuttering, generalized tension, insomnia, poor relationships with peers, and depressive moods told this story during her second month of therapy:

> Once upon a time there was a girl and there was another girl. And so the girl said, "What color is this on my new dress?" And the girl said ——
>
> *Therapist:* Wait a minute. Let's call them Girl Number One and Girl Number Two, okay? So Girl Number One said what?
>
> *Patient:* Girl Number Two said to Girl Number One, "What's this color on my dress?" and Girl Number One said, "I think it's purple." And Girl Number Two said, "No, are you dumb or something? It's orange. You must be colorblind." Now one of them was right but I'm not going to tell the one until the end of the story.
>
> Then Girl Number Two went around on her bicycle and said to everyone, "Girl One is colorblind. Girl One is colorblind. Girl One is colorblind."
>
> So a third girl came out and said, "How do you know Girl One is colorblind?" And Girl Two said, "Look at this square." So Girl Two held up a square. Girl Number Three said it was a blue square and it was a blue square. And Girl Number Two said, "No, it is yellow. You must be colorblind also." So Girl Three held up the thing to everyone and they all said it was blue and so ——.
>
> *Therapist:* Who was colorblind?
>
> *Patient:* Girl Two was colorblind.
>
> *Therapist:* What about Girl One?
>
> *Patient:* She wasn't. And the moral of the story is —— see, she was the dropout of the block because they were all laughing at her because she was colorblind and went around telling everyone that Girl One was colorblind. So the moral of the story is that when you think someone is colorblind you might be the one so go to someone grown-up and find out.

It is not uncommon for the child, when relating his story, to be unspecific about which figures are saying what. He tends to be loose with pronouns and their antecedents. He knows in his own mind which figure is speaking but often doesn't consider whether his listener clearly understands. Since a completely accurate account of the story is vital to understanding its psychodynamics, I interrupt the child when he says anything that is ambiguous.

The first few sentences of this girl's story illustrate such a potential source of confusion. Two girls are conversing and the patient is not explicit about which one is talking. When Carol assigns a name to each of the characters the likelihood of ambiguity is lessened. In general, I do not encourage the child to give a name to an unnamed figure because such designation might result in the patient's using the name of a specific person he knows. This has the effect of contaminating the story or restricting it by directing it into specific channels suggested by the real person after whom the story figure is named. To avoid this, I suggest that the figures be numbered. A person with a number is less likely to stimulate specific associations.

The story itself reveals Carol's awareness, at some level, that she tends to be colorblind, that is, that she does not see reality clearly. In it she also exhibits her tendency to deny her deficiencies and to project onto others her own blindness. If her view of a situation does not coincide with another person's, it is the latter who is distorting reality. Clinically, this was one of the patient's problems both in her relationships with her peers as well as with her parents. Carol considered her friends to be at fault in all her difficulties with them. She felt picked upon. They were always the ones "to start." The blindness to her mother served a different purpose by helping her to deny her mother's great hostility toward Carol and her frequent rejection of her.

Although her story reveals some insights into her use of these pathological patterns of denial and projection and some appreciation of how one appears to others when one uses these mechanisms, I could see no clinical evidence of conscious awareness on her part of her use of these defense mechanisms.

With this interpretation of Carol's story, I told mine:

Once upon a time there were two girls: Girl One and Girl Two. They were talking one day and Girl Two said to

Girl One, "What's this color on my dress?" Girl One said, "It's purple." And Girl Two said, "No, it's orange. You must be colorblind."

So Girl Two gave Girl One a test for colorblindness and she said that Girl One got all of them wrong. Then Girl One gave Girl Two a test for colorblindness and Girl One said to Girl Two, "You got all of them wrong." So Girl Two didn't believe what Girl One had said. And Girl Two said, "I'm not colorblind. You are colorblind."

Anyway, Girl Two went to a few other people and spoke to them and said, "Gee, there's a lot of colorblind people around here. They all seem to get this test wrong." And then Girl Two went around the neighborhood saying, "Girl One is colorblind. Girl One is colorblind."

And then they all said, "We think you are colorblind" and they tested her —— a number of people. Finally she was surrounded by a large number of people, all of whom said, "You are colorblind. We all agreed that this is blue and you see it as orange."

Well, that was quite a shock to her. First, she was quite embarrassed and then she began to realize that they were probably right — that she couldn't accept the fact that she might have some deficiency —— some defect —— some small problem. So after that she said to the girls, "You know, I'm very embarrassed and it's very hard for me to say this, but I think you are right. I am colorblind. I never realized it and I'd better go to the doctor and see if anything can be done about my colorblindness."

And the girls said, "Yes, you are colorblind, but you act like it's a terrible crime or a terrible sin, or you act like it's the worst thing in the world. We don't like you any less because you are colorblind. We would like you less or we would dislike you if you were a liar or if you were going around trying to deny it or trying to accuse others of this problem. Then we would find you the kind of person that we would have very little desire to spend time with. But just being colorblind doesn't bother us in the least, if you are nice otherwise."

So that was a real good lesson for Girl Two because she realized that it's no terrible crime or sin to have a certain number of small deficiencies or defects. And she also learned that if someone tells you something about yourself that is uncomplimentary or shows that maybe you are not perfect in some way, you should take it into consideration. There are two possibilities. It might be right and it might be wrong. Sometimes it will be right and sometimes it will be wrong. But take it into consideration. Now do you know what the two morals of this story are?

Patient: There are two?

Therapist: Yes, there are two.

Patient: Well ——

Therapist: Do you know one?

Patient: That if you think someone is colorblind you should really find out instead of going and teasing her because you might be the one.

Therapist: That's right. The moral is that if someone criticizes you, consider the possibility that it's true. It may be true or it may be false. But consider the possibility. You can learn something about yourself that may be helpful to you. And the other moral is that if you have a small deficiency or defect it doesn't mean that you are totally worthless as a human being. It doesn't mean that you have to go around hiding it and denying it. And the best thing to do is to know that you have it because then you are in the best position to do something about it. This girl, once she learned that she was colorblind, was able to go to the doctor and to do something about it. The end.

Therapist: What did you think of that story?

Patient: It was all right.

Therapist: Do you think it has anything to do with you?

Patient: I don't find anything that I would not like to know about.

Therapist: I do think it has something to do with you. What it has to do with you is this. As I pointed out to you before, I think you are the kind of person who considers it to be a very, very terrible thing if you have a deficiency or defect, and when your mother points out at times that you did something that shows one of the problems, you deny it. It can't be that your mother is always wrong about these things — not that she's always right. She makes mistakes too. She distorts also, but it can't be that she's always wrong. So that's how it applies to you. So what do you think of that?

Patient: I think it's true, but I don't always deny it.

Therapist: I think that sometimes you know it's true but you deny it. Does that happen?

Patient: Maybe.

Therapist: Well, I think that when it does it's important for you not to do that because then I can't help you with your problem unless you tell me about it — unless you admit that you have a problem. Right? (*Carol nods in affirmation.*) If you have a cut finger and you say, "No, no, my finger isn't cut. There's nothing that has to be done to it because my finger isn't cut," then you might not treat it or show it to a doctor, and then it might get worse. Right?

Patient: Right.

In my story, as in Carol's, the girl admits her deficiency. Since the patient appeared to appreciate her inappropriate behavior on the unconscious level only, I attempted in my story to lessen the resistance to conscious appreciation of her defects. Those who confront the girl with her colorblindness do not scorn her because "she was the dropout of the block because they were all laughing at her," but respond with sympathetic understanding. In addition, I imparted the message that a few deficiencies don't make one totally loathsome. Finally, I introduced the idea of going to the doctor, of doing something about one's problems — an element not present in Carol's story.

I tried to get the patient to figure out the moral of my story in order to determine whether my message had gotten through. In the post-story discussion I attempted, through direct discussion, to bring into conscious awareness the pathological tendencies revealed by her story. Although I did not get the feeling during the discussion that what I was saying was sinking in very deeply, she listened and at least superficially understood my point. This was an early confrontation and repeated exposures were necessary to break down and work through her resistances.

One week later Carol told this story:

Once upon a time there were these two clowns and the idea of the clowns was to learn the tricks wrong —— to make them funny.

And it was the day of the show. Now there was this happy clown and this sad clown —— a happy clown and a mean clown. The happy clown was yellow and the mean clown was blue. And so the mean clown went on and he did all the tricks right. He wasn't funny. No one laughed. And the people said, "This is a terrible show. Let's go." Then the other clown came out and did them all wrong and they all stayed and laughed.

Then the blue clown, the one that wasn't happy, came out again and he did them right. And they said, "This is terrible. We're leaving." And they left. Then the blue clown said, "I wonder why everybody left?" Then the yellow clown said, "I'll show you. I'm going to take you to the circus tomorrow." There, there were twin brothers —— the blue clown and the yellow clown. Same thing. Blue clown did them wrong ——

Therapist: You mean these were other clowns?

Patient: Yes. And so the second yellow clown came out. The first blue clown laughed and laughed. Then the second blue clown came out and the first blue clown said to the yellow clown, "This blue clown is terrible. Let's leave." And the yellow clown said, "That's why everyone leaves our show because you do them all right and you are supposed to do it wrong to make it look funny. But you do them right and people leave and they think just what you think of the blue clown."

And so the blue clown said, "Maybe you are right." And so he tried goofing up the whole thing. And now every single day they had visitors in their circus and they all stayed. And they got to be millionaires and they didn't have to be clowns anymore. And that's all.

And the moral is: if you are a clown you should do things wrong, but if you are a person, do them right and it will help you do whatever you are doing.

The story is essentially a rationalization for the pathological. The "right" thing to do is the "wrong" thing. Doing things wrong pays off. The two clowns did the wrong thing so well that they "got to be millionaires." It is only in the moral that a healthier alternative is mentioned: clowns do the wrong thing, but people should do the right thing. These afterthoughts tacked onto the end of the story in no way change the basic psychological meaning. Sometimes a child will end a story with, "And the boy then woke up and it was all a dream." Again, such guilt or anxiety-alleviating "undoing" in no way alters the fundamental validity of the original message.

In this story, as so often occurs in the dreams of both children and adults, each figure represents a different facet of the same personality. The blue clown symbolizes her sad, mean, and inappropriate tendencies while the yellow one stands for her happy and well-adjusted characteristics. The conflict between the clowns is, of course, Carol's inner conflict over whether to do right or wrong. The child's psyche is further fractionized by the introduction of two more alter egos — the second yellow and blue clowns. They serve the first two as reflectors, confronters, and advice-givers. The utilization of the twin in this capacity is occasionally seen in the child's story, and I have found it a helpful device in my own — even when the child's story does not introduce one. In response, I told this story:

Once upon a time there were two clowns. There was a yellow clown and a blue clown. And the yellow clown was very happy and successful in the circus. And the blue clown was not happy and successful in the circus. The reason was that in the circus it was important for the clowns to do tricks wrong and in that way they'd look funny.

And so the yellow clown said to the blue clown, "The reason why you are having so much trouble is that you are doing the tricks right." And the blue clown said, "But everywhere else in life I do things right and it pays off for me." The yellow clown said, "But in the circus you've got to do things wrong if you want to be a success."

So the blue clown learned and he did things wrong in

the circus and he was successful. However, the yellow clown was only happy in the circus, because the yellow clown would do things wrong outside the circus and he got himself into a lot of trouble because he was always irritating people; he was always rubbing them the wrong way; and he was always having a lot of difficulties because he carried out from the circus the things he was doing in the circus.

Well, one day the yellow clown came to the blue clown and said, "What's going on with me? I'm always getting into trouble." And the blue clown said, "Let's you and I visit the other yellow and blue clowns from a nearby circus at their homes — outside the circus — and see how they do things." So they visited the other yellow and blue clowns outside their circus and they found that both of them were always trying to do things *right* when outside the circus. And they said to the second yellow clown, "How is it that you are getting along so well?" The second yellow clown replied, "I try to do things right everywhere, but in the circus I try to do things wrong."

Well, the first yellow clown saw that and he learned something. So what do you think he did then?

Patient: He did things right?

Therapist: He did things right outside the circus and just did things wrong inside the circus and he lived happily ever after.

And the lesson of that story is: there's a time and a place for everything. There's even a time to do things wrong, but it's usually a very specific time and place and it only takes up a small part of your life.

Patient: Where is that? Where do I do things wrong?

Therapist: Where do *you* think you do things wrong?

Patient: At school?

Therapist: How?

Patient: By getting low marks. I guess I don't try to work as hard as I can.

Therapist: How come?

Patient: I don't know.

Therapist: Do you do things wrong anywhere else?

Patient: At home?

82

Therapist: What things do you do wrong at home?

Patient: Tease my sister.

Therapist: Anything else?

Patient: No.

Therapist: Well, all right. The important thing is that this clown found out those things in his life which he was doing wrong, which if he did right would have made him very happy. And when he changed these things he was much happier. The end.

Here I attempted to emphasize the fact that there is a limited and well-circumscribed time and place for "wrong behavior" and that when a person goes beyond the confines of those socially acceptable areas, he gets into trouble with those around him.

As the post-story discussion reveals, the story served to catalyze Carol's admission that she does indeed tend to do things wrong in certain situations. Considering the history of massive denial of *any* inappropriate behavior, this was a definite breakthrough.

Example 4

Paul, an eight-and-one-half-year-old boy with poor school performance in spite of high intelligence, presented this story early in treatment:

Once upon a time there was a TV set and he didn't like the shows he had inside him. He tried to turn the channels to shows he hadn't seen. He tried to do it from the inside but he couldn't manage it. He moved his antennas so that the picture was fuzzy.

A boy was watching it and he tried to fix it and he turned the channel to one that the TV set had seen. So the TV set waved his antennas again so the picture was fuzzy. So the boy turned it again. The boy turned it to a channel that the TV set had never seen before but it wasn't a very nice show. So the TV set turned it again and again. The boy changed it to many different shows but he never saw a TV show that was good. There were good TV shows but the boy didn't like the shows that the TV set thought were good. So the TV set ended up never seeing good shows because the boy wouldn't turn to the channels the TV liked because he didn't like the shows that the TV liked.

The lesson of this story is: never let another person do anything unless you are sure you want him to do it because you might not get what you want.

This is a resistance story typical of early treatment. The television screen symbolizes therapeutic confrontations. The boy in front of the television set, as well as the anthropomorphized television set itself, reflects the patient's ambivalence about "looking at himself." The two together somehow always manage to disagree on whether to observe each of a series of possible programs. Either the boy doesn't like the program the television set prefers to see or the television set doesn't like the program the boy wants to watch. The ultimate result is no self-observation at all.

Accordingly, I related the following:

Once upon a time there was a TV set. And this TV set was very scared to see certain shows. He was especially scared of horror stories, mystery stories, monster pictures, and stories that had a lot of fighting.

Now the boy who owned the TV set told him that there wasn't that much to be scared about. He said to him, "Try it and see." At first the TV set was frightened and he got scared when the boy turned on some of the scary shows. But the more he saw the less frightened he became, and he gradually learned that they weren't so bad after all. When the TV set really got scared, he would wave his antenna about and then the boy knew that it was too much for the TV set and then he turned to another channel. However, most often the TV set found that the stories weren't as scary as he had originally thought. As time went on he got less and less scared and he began to enjoy many different kinds of programs. From these programs he learned many interesting and useful things.

The moral of my story is: try something before you

84

say you don't like it. Most often things are less scary than you think.

In my story I informed the patient that I understood his anxieties while encouraging him to tolerate them. I suggested that Paul might find therapeutic disclosures less frightening than he anticipated and, in addition, he might learn things that would prove to be "interesting and useful."

Following this storytelling sequence, the patient drew a picture of a pond surrounded by palm trees. (Figure 1) He then told a story about a boy who chased the toads from the pond into the woods. The boy is not seen in the picture; he is said to be in the woods chasing the toads away from the pond. I considered the story to reflect even more resistance on the patient's part — resistance possibly related to further anxiety engendered by my story. The toads, who reside beneath the surface of the pond, represent unconscious anxiety-provoking complexes. One of the implications of my story was to encourage him to bring these repressed processes to the surface for direct observation. This had apparently made him quite anxious. He had to protect his unconscious material from such scrutiny. In the pond they are too readily observable since they are enclosed in one place and water is not a particularly good camouflaging agent. He therefore hides them in the woods where they are less likely to be subjected to therapeutic examination.

I decided not to follow up Paul's story with one of my own. The patient was clearly fearful and I did not consider it wise to push the confrontation issue further. Had I done so, the anxiety so produced might have inhibited him from further storytelling. Injudicious use of the technique may result in the child's fearing to involve himself further with it. The therapist may then be deprived of a sensitive source of information as well as a potent therapeutic tool.

Two weeks later, Paul told this story:

Today my story is going to be about a town and the people in the town wanted a new factory. They tore down the old school building and there was a big parking space

Figure 1

so they built the factory. A lot of people came to work in the factory and the town got larger. The streets were very crowded and they had a lot of traffic jams so one thing they did was to put one-way streets in. They tried building new streets and tore down a lot of old homes and so it was a little better.

So the people in the town —— the town started to get older and big trucks came. It was very crowded and noisy. So they had to tear down the old picnic place to build some more roads and there was no place to go have a picnic and things. Everybody had a very small backyard and a couple of new houses were very big and they took up a lot of space and so the roads couldn't go through the houses. It got very crowded again.

Then one day they decided to tear down some of the old stores and that helped and so there was less traffic running through the different roads. But there was a lot of different roads and there wasn't very many places to go. The town wasn't very exciting anymore. Nothing happened and so the people in the town started moving because they didn't want to live there. So the town got smaller and smaller. No one worked at the big factory so that it could not make things. Everyone left the town because there was hardly any money and so the town tore the factory down and put it someplace else. They fixed up the picnic area and they tried to make the town look better. And so everybody moved back and they had a nice town.

Therapist: And the lesson of that story?

Patient: Plan ahead before you do something.

Therapist: Let me ask you something. What were the main things the people objected to before they moved out?

Patient: Well, there was a lot of noise and there was a lot of traffic.

Therapist: Yes. What else?

Patient: They tore down the picnic area so the people wouldn't have very much fun.

Therapist: What else?

Patient: I don't know.

Therapist: Okay. I see. Oh, what kind of factory was it?

Patient: A steel factory.

Therapist: What did they make there?

Patient: Steel bars.

Therapist: For what?

Patient: For all kinds of things.

Therapist: For instance?

Patient: Well, like a flagpole; maybe something they'd sell to people in another factory to make it into playthings you could climb all over —— like a jungle gym.

Therapist: I see. Okay.

The peaceful town is the patient as he recalls himself prior to the onset of treatment. Suddenly in comes the factory, with its workers, its noise, and devastating traffic — a reflection of the anxiety and confusion created by the therapeutic intervention. Chaos is everywhere. All order is gone. Paul is essentially saying: "Let's get rid of all these newcomers and go back to the placid days before Dr. Gardner's arrival on the scene."

In response, I related this story:

Once upon a time there was a town and this town was doing all right but not too well. It was a calm place. It had houses, nice streets, and a picnic ground. It had troubles once in a while.

Then one day the people thought it would be a good idea to get a factory into town so they went to this place where there was an old school building. They took it down and there was a big parking lot there and they built this factory.

Well, once you build a factory you start getting more people in town. Workers would come in and they started to get a lot of traffic in the street so they had to widen some of the streets and tear down some old houses in order to accommodate the traffic — in order to let the traffic through.

Well, the town was richer because of the factory; they made more money. More people came into town and would go to the restaurants and they would go to the stores and buy a lot. The town got taxes from the owners of the factory for using the land. However, the people were very unhappy because there was more traffic, more hustle and bustle and noise in the town, and there was even some danger that they would have to rip up the picnic area.

Some people in town then began to feel sorry that they brought the factory in and other people felt that it was still a good thing and they were willing to suffer or tolerate some of the inconveniences of having a factory. So all the people in town began taking sides. Some wanted to get rid of the factory and some wanted to keep it.

Then they decided to have a big town meeting where everybody could discuss their opinions about it and they might even vote. So those people who didn't want the factory in town got up and said, "It makes a lot of noise in town. It makes a lot of traffic and we may have to lose the picnic ground." The other people said that they liked the factory even though there was more noise and traffic, the factory was a good thing to have for the town. It brought in more money, it brought in more business, and it made the town a livelier place to live in with more activity, more action. They said, "We don't need to get rid of the picnic ground. We just have to keep the factory this size. We won't let it grow any bigger. We won't destroy any more streets." So they argued back and forth and then they had a vote. And who do you think won the vote?

Patient: I don't know.

Therapist: Well, the people who wanted the factory to stay won the vote. More people realized that it was a better thing to have the factory because even though it was a little inconvenient and there was some noise and more traffic, that still they were better off because they got more money, and more life and liveliness into the town. And do you know what the lesson of that story is?

Patient: No.

Therapist: The lesson of that story is: if you want to benefit from something you often have to put up with a little bit of inconvenience. Here they would benefit from the factory but they had to put up with a little bit of inconvenience. But all these things together, they were much better off. Do you understand that lesson?

Patient: Yeah.

Therapist: Okay. That's the end. Would you like to listen to this story?

Patient: Yeah.

In my story the ambivalence over the therapist's presence is aired in a public forum. In this way Paul was encouraged to express his fears openly. He was reassured that good should ultimately come from my intervention; that with certain benefits come inevitable inconveniences, but the advantages outweigh the disadvantages.

Paul was quite interested in listening while I was relating my story and he appeared to be more relaxed when I finished it. I believe that I was effective in reassuring him about therapy through the storytelling vehicle.

Example 5

Eric, an eight-and-one-half-year-old boy, was brought into therapy because of shyness alternating with a "wise-guy" attitude, rage outbursts, a tendency to feel that he was being picked on and taken advantage of, and disruptive behavior in the classroom.

During his third session he told this story:

There was a bear and he was mixed up and he had a lot of friends that kept on getting him mixed up. He didn't know what to do. Then he tried to get them mixed up but it didn't work. So he was very angry and he wanted to plan on them not to get him mixed up anymore. He can't think that way so he went over and told them, "Don't get me mixed up." Then one guy said, "We will stop getting you mixed up," and another guy said, "We will get you mixed up." And this went on and on and on and he still couldn't do anything about it.

So one day he left and he went away and then he found some new friends and they didn't get him so mixed up. And so —— he —— and so they got him mixed up too, I mean. He went to them and talked to them, but these new friends kept on getting him mixed up. So he went away again and he still kept on getting mixed up. He didn't know what to do and he started going all over the place and he kept on getting new friends and he kept on getting mixed up.

After a long time he went to a doctor and the doctor

said —— his name was Dr. Bear. The doctor said that he should —— that it was him that was getting himself all mixed up, it wasn't his friends. He didn't know what to do to stop it so he went in his cave and just sat there. A friend came in to see him and as soon as he saw him he began to get all mixed up because the friend said something, then it looked like he said another thing, then he heard another thing, and the bear kept on getting mixed up. The doctor said it was his hearing —— that he was hearing strange things.

And so one day he went back to the doctor and the doctor gave him some pills and then they made him go to sleep and they made him feel better. And that's the end.

The moral of the story is to go to the doctor when you feel bad.

Therapist: Tell me something. Do you ever hear strange things?

Patient: Sometimes.

Therapist: What kinds of strange things do you hear?

Patient: I hear crummy noises.

Therapist: What are they due to?

Patient: They make me scared sometimes.

Therapist: You hear crummy noises that make you scared?

Patient: Yeah.

Therapist: Well, imitate a noise. What does it sound like?

Patient: (Produces a high-pitched screeching sound.)

Therapist: What do you think it's from?

Patient: Birds?

Therapist: Do you ever think it's not really there and it's just your imagination?

Patient: No.

Therapist: Do you ever hear voices that aren't really there? Did you ever have that?

Patient: Nope.

Therapist: I see. Okay.

The story reveals Eric's massive confusion and anxiety as well as persecutory trends which were also clinically present. Although he exhibits some insight into the inappropriateness of his paranoid thoughts, the story is primarily devoted to his preoccupation with them which suggests that they play a significant role in his psychic life. Also present is the magic cure expectation, so commonly seen in stories during this early phase. Lastly, the story shows pathology that had not previously been mentioned, the possibility, that is, of hallucinatory experiences: "The doctor said it was his hearing — that he was hearing strange things." In the post-story discussion this possibility was explored further.

Eric's father was an excessively suspicious man with intermittent periods of blatant paranoid thinking. It was clear that his son was now exhibiting similar tendencies.

I told this story in response:

> Once upon a time there was a bear and he was a mixed up bear, and he had many friends and he thought they were getting him mixed up. He kept blaming them for mixing him up. Really, they weren't mixing him up at all. He kept thinking they were mixing him up and he used to say to them, "Hey, you kids, stop mixing me up." And they kept saying, "We are not mixing you up. You're mixed up in your own mind." And he didn't believe them. He kept thinking that they were mixing him up.
>
> So he got a new group of friends and he found himself getting mixed up again. He said, "Hey, you kids, stop getting me mixed up." And they said, "Hey, what's the matter with you. We're not mixing you up. We're talking plain. You're mixed up yourself. We're not mixing you up."
>
> So he went to a third group of friends and the same thing happened. He said, "You're mixing me up." They said, "We're not mixing you up." Finally, he began to think about it and he realized that maybe they weren't mixing him up — that all these kids couldn't possibly be wrong and maybe it was he himself.
>
> So he went to this doctor, Dr. Bear. Dr. Bear said, "Yes, you are right. The kids are not mixing you up. You have a tendency to blame others for your own faults. You're having troubles yourself and you're getting yourself mixed up. It's not your friends." So he said to the doctor, "Well, what can I do about it? Can you give me a

pill that will stop it?" The doctor said, "No. You don't need a pill. A pill is not going to help you. You want a magic cure. You want to have this changed magically. It won't work that way. There are no pills to magically change this." This made the bear very sad, and the bear said, "Well, what can I do?" The doctor replied, "What you have to do is to come and see me and talk to me about the things that are bothering you inside." The bear said, "Ah, I don't want to talk to you about these things." The doctor said, "Now you are talking like a big shot. If you talk to me about the things that are bothering you, that's the way to stop getting mixed up."

Well, the bear thought about it and at first he didn't want to go to the doctor. So he said, "That doctor doesn't know what he's talking about. I'll go to another doctor." He went to another doctor and he said, "Give me a pill to stop me from being mixed up." The doctor said —— what do you think the doctor said —— the second doctor?

Patient: There wasn't any pill.

Therapist: He said the exact same thing as the first doctor. So what did the bear do?

Patient: He went to another doctor.

Therapist: And what did the third doctor say?

Patient: The same thing.

Therapist: So what did the bear do then?

Patient: He went to another doctor.

Therapist: And what did that fourth doctor say?

Patient: The same thing.

Therapist: So what happened then?

Patient: He went home.

Therapist: What did he do then?

Patient: He went to sleep.

Therapist: Then what happened?

Patient: Then someone came and got him mixed up again.

Therapist: So what happened then?

Patient: He went back to the doctor.

Therapist: And then what happened?

Patient: The doctor told him the same thing.

Therapist: So what happened then?

Patient: He kept on going back to each doctor and they

kept on telling him the same thing. Finally he did ——

Therapist: Did what?

Patient: Tell him all his stories.

Therapist: He told the doctor his troubles?

Patient: Yeah.

Therapist: And then what happened?

Patient: And that was the end.

Therapist: Was he better?

Patient: Yeah.

Therapist: All right. What's the lesson of that story?

Patient: Tell your doctor your stories.

Therapist: Tell your doctor your troubles and if you do that, if you work hard at it and you are very honest, it will help you with your problems — sometimes. Sometimes it won't. It will most often if you try hard to talk to him about your troubles. Most often it will help you feel better. The end.

What did you think about that story?

Patient: It was a pretty good story.

Therapist: What did you like about it?

Patient: The bear — he got so mixed up. It was so funny.

Therapist: You want to hear it?

Patient: Yeah!

Therapist: Okay.

In my story I attempted to dispel the magic cure anticipation and to advise Eric that his hopes for cure lie in communicating his thoughts and feelings to me. His "wise-guy" symptom is also touched upon in my story when the doctor confronts the bear with the fact that such an attitude is antithetical to the treatment process because it is used to cover up rather than to reveal one's inner psychic life.

As can be seen, Eric's quest for a quick cure was deep. When he joins me in telling the story he has the bear go to a series of doctors, from each of whom he seeks the magic pill. Although he finally gets the bear to reveal himself, the cure still has a magic quality in that it appears to follow quickly the patient's revealing himself. Accordingly, I introduced the notions that there is no guarantee that talking will help; that cure also depends on one's motivation, one's willingness to work, and one's genuine commitment to the therapeutic process.

At times a story strongly suggests that the patient will not be in treatment much longer. Here, the recurrent theme of going from doctor to doctor gave me the feeling that his involvement in treatment was tenuous and his motivation minimal. Unfortunately, my fears were realized; Paul left treatment a few weeks later claiming that he'd rather play. His leaving was supported by his father who was becoming increasingly suspicious of me.

Example 6

Malcolm, a nine-year-old boy who entered treatment because of multiple fears, angry outbursts, and generalized tension, presented this story during the third week of treatment:

Once upon a time there was a puppy dog that was not a German shepherd. It was a dachshund and he got lost —— they also had this big German shepherd and they went to the hall where every Tuesday the German shepherd people rented it —— a hall for a German shepherd club —— and this puppy dachshund got lost there, and he got lost right in the middle of the senior class that was running around and almost got killed by being trampled over.

Therapist: In other words, the puppy dachshund got lost in the German shepherd club. Is that right?

Patient: Yeah, in the hall and he got lost right in the middle of the senior class that was running around ——

Therapist: The senior class of what?

Patient: Of German shepherd dogs that were running around building up dog muscles and he got almost killed by being trampled over by the people. And at the end he was squeaky because he was very much hurt and the trainer blew his whistle and everybody stopped to a halt. They heard this puppy squeaking and the man said, "Why are you trampling over the puppy and why is the puppy even in here? This is a German shepherd club, not a puppy dog club. If you have a dachshund or any other form of dog besides a German shepherd, leave it in your car in a cage or not in a cage. Just leave it in your car."

So the people in the middle of the class took the dog out and put him in this little cage with some water and left him there until the end of the class. They were only beginners because they didn't notice that they were being taught how to seat their dog and the other class was running around being taught how to exercise their dogs. And the puppy was in the class that was being taught how to exercise their dogs. That was on the other side.

The moral is that if you have a German shepherd and you also have another kind of dog and you go to a German shepherd club and if the other kind of dog is a puppy, I advise you not to bring it in because you can't look after it while you're in another class with your German shepherd.

They had three dogs —— two German shepherds. The father had the German shepherd that was in the senior class and the mother had the German shepherd that was in the beginner's class and no one was taking care of the puppy.

Therapist: Okay. Very good story.

Malcolm's mother was easily enraged, and her whole family was subjected to her angry outbursts. She was also actively interested in German shepherds and spent long hours training them and attending the meetings of her local German shepherd club.

The story clearly reveals Malcolm's concept of himself as ignored by his mother whose interest in German shepherds is greater than her involvement with him. Neglected, he feels unable to cope with a world which he sees as overwhelmingly hostile. The trampling hordes are also symbolic of his mother's rage. The trainer, who represents his father and/or the therapist, is seen as one who can protect him from the devastating effects of his mother's neglect and hostility. His father attempted to play this role, but his passivity toward the mother impaired his effectiveness.

The sanctuary the child chooses for himself is a cage. There he is protected from the malevolence of the world, but he must pay a heavy price for security. But the sacrifice of his freedom is worth it — so traumatic is his environment.

With this understanding of Malcolm's story, I told the following:

Once upon a time there was a family. They had three dogs. Two of them were German shepherds — a senior class and a junior class German shepherd — and they had one little baby puppy dachshund. Now they took these dogs for dog classes and since they were classes for German shepherds only, this little dachshund felt very lonely. He was walking around there and he was smaller than any other dog. He was lonely and sad, and he felt all alone. So the first thing he did was to go over to his owners and he said, "Would you please take me to a show where they have dachshunds." And they said, "Don't bother us. We're too busy. We've got to take care of these German shepherds. They're more important than you. You're just a dachshund. You're just a small little thing and we've got to take care of these German shepherds.

Well, that made him even sadder. Then he went to the German shepherds and said, "Would you come with me to a dachshund show? I want to be with my own kind. I'm small. There are lots of people around here and big dogs and I can get trampled." And they said, "Don't bother us. We have to learn our lessons — how to sit and things like that because we're going to be in a big show."

Well, this dachshund said, "I'm not going to spend the rest of my life moping around here and waiting. So he went out the back door and he looked around and walked around and suddenly he picked up the scent of a dachshund. He tracked down the scent of the dachshund. He saw a dachshund girl and he said, "Where is the nearest dachshund center where they train dachshunds?" And she said, "Just follow me."

So off they went to the dachshund place and there, what do you know, there were hundreds of dachshunds and he began to play with them. He had a wonderful time.

Then he went back home and he said, "I found a dachshund place. Whenever you people get too involved with yourselves and you are not giving me any attention, I'm going to go to that dachshund place and there I'm going to make friends and I won't feel so sad and lonely then." Well, they realized that he was doing the right thing and he gradually spent more and more time with the dachshunds as he got older. Then when he was a teenager he met a girl and then later on he dated and he had a lot of fun on dates and things. Later on he met a dachshund whom he married and he was never lonely again and they lived happily ever after.

And the lesson of that story is that if the people you live with aren't giving you as much affection and attention as you would like, don't sit around and mope. Don't cry. Just go out and make friends elsewhere and involve yourself with others. That's the end of this story. Anything you want to say about it?

Patient: I think I do that too.

Therapist: How so?

Patient: When I am lonely I go out and look for friends.

Therapist: Right. That's the right thing to do.

Patient: Guess what? I hate those people who took care of the German shepherds. They could have made plans between each time they took the German shepherds to the club —— they should have made plans to take the dachshund to a dachshund club.

Therapist: Yes. There's no question about that.

As already mentioned, my general approach to the deprived child is to encourage him to express his resentment to those who are depriving him (most often one or both parents) in the hope that they will provide him with greater gratification of his needs for love and affection. Most parents can usually provide at least some satisfaction, and the child is helped to define the areas in which he can expect success following his assertions. Where the parents cannot or will not respond, the child is advised to seek affection elsewhere. My knowledge of the parents is helpful in deciding the degree to which I will encourage the child to approach them.

Malcolm's mother was so sick and seething with rage that her capacity for providing him with meaningful affection was seriously impaired. Therefore, the primary emphasis in my story was to direct him elsewhere for substitutive gratifications. However, he is still at first advised to express his demands. I also provide him with hope that in the future he will be less dependent on his parents and freer to pursue relationships which can be rewarding and fulfilling.

This sequence is representative of a type of early story which is not directly related to fears of treatment or inappropriate attitudes toward the therapist. In this type a fundamental problem presses for expression in the earliest phase of therapy. A child who tells such a story is getting right down to the basic work and need not work through initial anxieties and resistances.

4. THE MIDDLE PHASE OF THERAPY

It is during the middle phase of therapy, which is often the longest, that the major therapeutic work is accomplished. During this phase much of the working-through is done. Themes are reiterated and the therapist's messages gradually "sink in" and become an intrinsic part of the child's personality structure. New ideas and alternative modes of interaction are repeatedly considered and experienced and the fears associated with these unfamiliar adaptations gradually diminish as the patient becomes comfortable with them. Repetitious desensitization to the novel and the anxiety-provoking is an intrinsic part of the working-through process. If meaningful changes are to take place, however, the child must not only accustom himself to maturer adjustments in his stories, but he must translate what he has learned into action. He must have similar experiences in reality if the healthier resolutions are to become truly therapeutic. The technique is *not* one in which the child and therapist indulge themselves in fancy; it is a stepping stone to constructive action in the real world.

The hallmark of this phase is the patient's incorporation into his stories of messages which have been derived from mine. Such utilization of ideas from my stories can occur on both conscious and unconscious levels. When revealed consciously, the child's story bears an obvious resemblance to a previous tale of mine. But more often, my communications reveal themselves symbolically and I then know that I have reached the patient on a deeper level. There are, of course, stories which reflect both conscious and unconscious appreciation of what I have imparted to the child.

It is commonly held that conscious imitation is not as therapeutic as unconscious, symbolically revealed comprehension. The theory is that ideas implanted in the unconscious change something in the basic psychic structure, whereas conscious cognitive changes are considered "superficial," and by implication, less therapeutic. I do not believe this to be always the case. The five-year-old who admonishes her two-year-old sister by saying, "Be a good girl and never run into the street," is clearly imitating her mother; but such imitation is a clear manifestation of the process by which she is incorporating her mother's superego into her own. Conscious verbal and cognitive reiteration serve to entrench important communications. Soon, this five-year-old can be trusted not to run into the street. Conscious cognitive processes can be quite deep-seated and can be relied upon to affect behavior in a significant way. One should not, therefore, consider the child's stories which have obviously been "lifted" from the therapist's to be necessarily less therapeutic. The child considers such messages valid and worthy of repetition. He is attempting to become comfortable with them in order to make them part of his own way of thinking. Of course, such imitations can be used in the service of resistance and it may be difficult, at times, to differentiate resistance reiteration from healthy imitation. When a story has a rote quality it is probably being told in the service of resistance. The therapist should attempt to discourage this by such comments as: "Come on, that story's exactly like the one I told last time. I'm sure you can make up a good one of your own."

It is during this phase that the child, having become more comfortable with and trusting of the therapist, will tell stories which may be more revealing of his inner conflicts than those which he has told in earlier stages of therapy. Some will touch upon very early conflicts of the patient's life — issues which may have been too anxiety-provoking to reveal earlier. The therapist, because he knows his patient more intimately and has more information about him, is in a better position to understand the child's stories as well as to create more accurate and meaningful ones of his own.

During the middle phase the stories, like other aspects of

therapy, reflect the patient's progressions and retrogressions. A series of healthy stories may be followed by a few unhealthy ones as the child regresses in response to the anxiety engendered by the maturer adaptations.

Like the repetitious dream, the repetitious story reveals deep-seated problems which press for expression. If the therapy is going well, there is a gradual change in the stories as the therapist's messages become "heard" and then utilized.

The criticism is occasionally made that the Mutual Story-telling Technique is a kind of "brain-washing," and that I am imposing my values on the child. There is no question that I am doing this; but there is also no question, in my opinion, that every other therapist is doing this as well — although he may be using more subtle techniques. Even the most classical adult analyst, who considers silent listening with only occasional catalytic comments to be the mainstay of his therapeutic approach, is imposing his own values on his patient. The times when he chooses to speak are highly selective; there may have been hundreds of the patient's comments which he could have chosen to comment upon but which have been allowed to pass. His focusing on a specific issue is related to *his* notion that that particular element is "pathological," "needs to be changed," or "is maladaptive," according to the therapist's value system. The Mutual Storytelling Technique, like other forms of psychotherapy, can be dangerous, and much damage can be done. Hopefully, the therapist is a relatively healthy person whose values are such that their embodiment by the patient will be in his best interests. The storytelling method is not, however, a technique by which one indiscriminately attempts to impose his values on the child. It carefully considers what the child is presenting; what is at the forefront of his conscious awareness. Such imagery is derivative and representative of the child's unconscious needs at the moment. The technique directs itself quite narrowly and often, I might say, exquisitely to the issues which are of greatest concern to the child at that particular time. The child is then provided with helpful communications in response to *his* request.

Example 1

Joey, the seven-year-old boy with enuresis, nightmares, chronic anxiety, and feelings of inadequacy, related this typical middle phase story:

> Once upon a time there lived a pelican and this pelican went like that — eeee. He was embarrassed with that noise. He tried not to do it but that's all he could say. So then he tried to kill himself.
> *Therapist:* Because of this noise? Because he couldn't say anything else he tried to kill himself?
> *Patient:* Yeah. And then he tried to say something else. Then he found out that he didn't have to kill himself. That's the end.
> *Therapist:* Tell me something. What was it that made him realize that he could talk?
> *Patient:* Because he never tried to.
> *Therapist:* I see. He never tried to and when he did——
> *Patient:* He found out that he could.
> *Therapist:* And what is the moral of that story?
> *Patient:* You better try.
> *Therapist:* Very good story.

The "eeee," in my opinion, represents the concealed verbalization of thoughts and feelings which would be guilt-and anxiety-provoking if released in their undisguised form. The high-pitched sound also reflects the anxiety associated with expression of even the symbolized material. Trying to kill himself serves many purposes: it reflects his desire to put an end to the exasperation and frustration he feels in not being able to express himself; it frees him from the loathsome guilt and painful anxiety he suffers over his unacceptable ideas and affects; and, finally, it is a self-punishment for his harboring such unacceptable thoughts and feelings. My comment, "Because of this noise? Because he couldn't say anything else he tried to kill himself?" implies that this is certainly not a grave enough difficulty to warrant such drastic action. Joey picked up my message and incorporated into his story the notion that such a speech problem doesn't justify suicide. In addition, Joey carried it further and introduced the idea that the original guilt-engendering material is not so terrible to verbalize in its undisguised form. He talks and finds that what comes out is not so horrible that he has to attempt to assuage his guilt through self-destruction.

The story demonstrates that when the child has ostensibly finished his story, the therapist can introduce comments which may encourage him to continue it, add to it, or alter it in a salutary way.

In response, I told a story which stimulated a discussion that ultimately involved the patient's mother as well. My story and the ensuing discussion is presented in its entirety:

Once upon a time a long, long time ago in a distant land, far, far away, there lived a pelican and this pelican had a very strange problem. The only thing he could say was eeee. For those of you who don't know how to spell eeee, it's spelled: e e e e, four e's not three e's or five e's, but four e's. You won't find it in your dictionary. Everytime this elephant — I mean pelican wanted to talk, the only thing that would come out would be eeee. Well, he wondered why. And he went to his father and he said, "Why is it ——

Patient: You mean eeee. I thought he could only say eeee.
Therapist: You're right. He didn't say it. He wrote it down on a piece of paper, "Why is it I always say eeee?" His father said, "Sometimes that happens when somebody has some troubles that he's afraid to talk about. So every time instead of talking about his troubles, out comes the eeee – that he's all blocked up —— that there are things inside him that are bothering him that he doesn't talk about and he's so afraid to talk about them that the only thing that comes out is eeee. If he were to talk about the things that were bothering him — his troubles and his problems and possibly something he doesn't like that is going on in the house or something like that — if he would talk about these things, perhaps, perhaps, he wouldn't say eeee anymore."

Well, the pelican thought about that and there were a few things that were bothering him in the house, that he hadn't wanted to talk about. So the next day he went to his parents and he started to talk. The first thing that came out was eeee and he knew that he didn't want to say eeee. He wanted to tell them the troubles so he waved his hands, meaning wait, and the parents were very patient. Then he tried again, and he started talking and he went, "I —— I —— I —— w —— w —— w —— eeee." Then the eeee came back again. "w —— want t —— t —— to." It was getting easier. "t —— tell yooou." And it was even easier. "a —— about some things that are bothering me about what goes on in this family."

Well, the parents were amazed and they said to him, "That's right. When you speak about the things that trouble you and you don't bottle them up and you don't close them off, then the eeee doesn't come out. Then the pelican discussed with his parents what the troubles were and when he did that they were able to solve many of them and then he didn't have so many troubles anymore. And he found that whenever he held things in, whenever he didn't want to talk about his problems and the things that bothered him, then the eeee, eeee would come out. But when he talked about the problems and the troubles, then he could speak just like you and me.

And the lesson of that story is — do you know what the lesson of that story is?

Patient: Same thing as mine.
Therapist: What?
Patient: Try.
Therapist: Try. And also I would say more specifically: if you have any problems that you are not talking about, talk about them and you will see that you won't have to choke up. The end.
Patient: What does choke up mean?
Therapist: Choke up means: You can't get it out. You choke on the words. That's what this pelican was doing. He was choking on his words because he was

afraid to let them out. Tell me something. What did you think about that story?

Patient: I think it was great.

Therapist: What was the part you liked the most?

Patient: Well, I liked it when you were saying what the pelican was saying.

Therapist: Tell me. Do you have any problems, any complaints that you haven't spoken to your parents about — things that bother you?

Patient: I have to get more baseball cards.

Therapist: And any other problems that you don't talk about?

Patient: I think that's all.

Therapist: Isn't there anything?

Patient: What do you think that dream I had last night meant? The one about the scary witch who said, "Oooh." All she could say was oooh and she was really ugly. I can't figure out what that dream means.

Therapist: Do you have any guesses?

Patient: No.

Therapist: Well, that witch, that ugly witch dream could mean —— there are a number of possible meanings for that dream.

Patient: Could you tell me a few of them?

Therapist: Yeah. I'll tell you two of them. One of the possible meanings —— let's discuss each one by itself. One of the possible meanings is that your mother does certain things that bother you, that scare you, that you don't like.

Patient: You mean the witch is my mother?

Therapist: She may stand for your mother, yes. She may. See, your mother has both good and bad parts. Right? *(Joey nods affirmatively.)* Everybody has good and bad parts. Right? No one is perfect. Right? *(Joey again nods in agreement.)* And maybe the witch stands for the bad part of your mother. Your mother has very good parts. She's a very fine woman and I like her very much, but she's not perfect and she does things at times which I'm sure you don't like.

Patient: What does the oooh mean?

Therapist: She's saying oooh, just a scary oooh, like a scary ghost or something like that. That's just the part of your mother that you see as bad. You see, lots of kids think that their mothers have to be perfect. You know, they can't stand —

Patient: That's what I think.

Therapist: You think your mother has to be perfect?

Patient: Sometimes.

Therapist: Who is perfect? Do you know anybody who is perfect?

Patient: Not my brother. He's never perfect.

Therapist: Most kids say that their brothers and sisters aren't perfect. What about your mother and father? Do you think they are perfect? Do you think they should be perfect?

Patient: Sometimes.

Therapist: I think that you think that your mother should be perfect all the time. Do you think I'm perfect?

Patient: Yeah.

Therapist: You really do?

Patient: Yeah?

Therapist: I'm not.

Patient: You're not?

Therapist: I am not. I am not perfect at all.

Patient: How come you never yell at me?

Therapist: That does not mean I am perfect. Look at me. I just made two mistakes in my story. I said an elephant instead of a pelican and I had him talk when he could only say eeee. And you corrected me on that. Remember that? A perfect person doesn't make mistakes like that. Does he?

Patient: No.

Therapist: I yell at kids sometimes. If you did something— here —— if you were to go over —— let's say I was sitting over there and you went over and tried to push that typewriter off the table — that's a very expensive typewriter — I'd scream, "Hey, get away from there. Don't push that typewriter off the table." I'd scream at you. Don't you think I would?

Patient: No.

Therapist: Yes, I would. I'd be very mad at you if you

pushed my typewriter off the table. Don't you think I'd have a right to be mad at you?

Patient: Yeah.

Therapist: I would think so. That's a very expensive typewriter. That's an electric typewriter. It costs a lot of money. It costs about $250. If anybody was going to push that off the table I'd get mad. What do you think about that?

Patient: Yeah.

Therapist: What does "yeah" mean? [I did not get the feeling that Joey was agreeing with conviction.]

Patient: I don't know.

Therapist: You sound a little surprised. You look surprised that I would get mad.

Patient: I know. I know.

Therapist: (Phone rings.) This is Dr. Gardner —— Hello —— *(Hangs up phone.)* Sometimes people call and they don't speak so I just hang up.

Patient: How come?

Therapist: Well, if they're not going to speak, I'm not going to waste my time getting them to talk to me. Now, you looked surprised when I said that I would get mad if anyone tried to push my typewriter off the table.

Patient: Yeah.

Therapist: Why were you surprised?

Patient: You never yelled at me before.

Therapist: You don't think I should yell. I don't yell at you because if you don't do anything that bothers me I don't yell at you. If you do something that bothers me, I'll yell. You just haven't done anything to get me mad. Right?

Patient: Yeah.

Therapist: Yet you think that I shouldn't get mad. Huh?

Patient: I think you should, but I never dreamed you would.

Therapist: I would get mad if you did something that hurt me or bothered me. Do you think that's wrong?

Patient: No.

Therapist: I think you think that a really perfect person wouldn't get mad.

Patient: I know. A real perfect person wouldn't.

Therapist: You're wrong. You're one hundred per cent wrong. First, there's no such thing as a perfect person. Second, even the people who are the closest to perfect get mad. Getting mad is part of being human.

Patient: People have to get mad sometimes.

Therapist: Sure. If somebody does something to bother you. If you're playing a game and your little sister comes in and she kicks the board, do you get mad at her?

Patient: Sometimes. But you know why only sometimes?

Therapist: Why?

Patient: Because we have lots of games.

Therapist: Let's say your brother came in while you were playing a game and dumped the whole board.

Patient: I hate my brother. I hate him anyway.

Therapist: I understand that, but if you were playing a game of Monopoly and your brother dumped —

Patient: When I get mad I really beat the hell out of him.

Therapist: All right. So you get mad at your brother. What about getting mad at your mother or father? What do you think about that?

Patient: I get mad at them.

Therapist: Do you think it's right for your mother or father to get mad at you?

Patient: Yeah.

Therapist: Do you think it's right for me to get mad at you?

Patient: No. Sometimes.

Therapist: If you do something that bothers me I will get very mad at you. If you went and let the air out of my tires, do you think I would get mad at you?

Patient: Yeah.

Therapist: Boy, would I be angry at you. Right?

Patient: Yeah.

Therapist: Do you think I'd have a right to get angry at you?

Patient: Yeah, and I wouldn't do it.

Therapist: Well, I'm just telling you. All I'm saying to·you is that —— I'm saying that you think that people should not get mad at one another —— that it's bad to get mad or that it's wrong to get mad. Huh?

Patient: I think sometimes I think like that.

Therapist: You think that it's wrong to get mad.

Patient: Yeah.

Therapist: Well, why is it wrong to get mad? Where did you get that idea?

Patient: From you.

Therapist: I told you that it's wrong to get mad? When did I ever say that? I said that!

Patient: Just now. (*Laughs.*)

Therapist: When did I say it's wrong to get mad. Come on?

Patient: A few weeks ago (*still laughing*).

Therapist: You want to hear the tape so we can listen and see where I said that.

Patient: Okay.

Therapist: Now you know I never said that.

Patient: Oh, yeah, you said that it's not wrong to get mad.

Therapist: Right. It's not wrong to get mad. When somebody does something to bother you it's not wrong to get mad.

Patient (laughing): I got mixed up.

Therapist: You got it clear now.

Patient: Yeah.

Therapist: What did I really say?

Patient: That when somebody bothers you it's right to get mad.

Therapist: Right! And what will happen to a boy —— let's take a boy who thinks that it's wrong to get mad when somebody bothers him. Let's say this boy is playing in the street and some kid comes over — some bully — and starts pulling his bike away and the boy doesn't get mad. He thinks it's wrong to get mad. What happens then?

Patient: What does the boy say?

Therapist: What do you think he says?

Patient: Thank you.

Therapist: Then what happens?

Patient: He just rides away. I guess the boy just rides away with his bike.

Therapist: What would happen if he got mad?

Patient: The boy wouldn't.

Therapist: Why?

Patient: Because if he'd see that boy again he'd really punch him.

Therapist: Right. The boy would be able to punch him. What would he say? What kinds of things would he say?

Patient: You idiot.

Therapist: Yeah. What would you say about the bike?

Patient: That's what I would say to my brother.

Therapist: What would he say about the bike?

Patient: You better give that bike back to me or else I'll put it on your head.

Therapist: Right, something like that. If he didn't get mad he might lose his bike. If I didn't get mad at you if you were going to push that typewriter off the table, I might not stop you from breaking my typewriter. Getting mad helps you.

Patient: It does?

Therapist: Getting mad can help you.

Patient: Yay! Then I could always get mad at my mother.

Therapist: Sure you can get mad at your mother. What kinds of things would you get mad about?

Patient: My mother isn't listening in here.

Therapist: Sure she's not listening. She's outside.

Patient: I know but if I got mad at her maybe she'd do something to me.

Therapist: Like what?

Patient: Well, hit me.

Therapist: If you got mad at her she'd hit you? Did I understand you correctly? Did you say that you thought that if you got mad at her she would hit you?

Patient: Yeah.

Therapist: Where did you get that idea?

Patient: I just thought of it right now. You see, as soon as you said that it was good to get mad.

Therapist: Well, did she ever tell you that she would hit you if you got mad at her?

Patient: No. I never really show it.

Therapist: I know. Can you give me an example of a situation where you don't show it?

Patient: Like when my mother —— let's suppose it's a weekday —— and it's ten o'clock in the morning and she didn't wake up. I can't even go upstairs and tell her to wake up.

Therapist: Why?

Patient: Because she would get mad at me.

Therapist: Well, did you ever try?

Patient: Nope.

Therapist: Well, what would happen if you went up there?

Patient: I fear that she'd get mad at me.

Therapist: Do you think she would be mad that you're mad?

Patient: Yeah, at her and then I'd show it.

Therapist: Do you think it's bad to show that you are mad at your mother?

Patient: Yeah. I think it's bad to show it to my mother and father.

Therapist: You think it's bad to show that you are mad at your mother or father. Do you want to have her come in and ask her opinion?

Patient: Okay.

Therapist: Why don't you ask your mother to come in. See what she says. Okay. Have your mother come in here.

Patient: Okay. *(Gets mother.)*

Therapist: We want to get her opinion. Right?

Patient: Okay.

Therapist: Do you want to ask her the question or shall I?

Patient: I think you'd better.

Therapist: Are you scared to ask her?

Patient: Yeah.

Therapist: Okay, well, I'll ask her. Let's see what she says. Joey and I were having a conversation and he was telling me that he thinks it's wrong for a boy to get angry at his mother, no matter what the reason. He has told me at times he gets angry at you for something and he gets scared to tell you that he's angry because he thinks that it's wrong for a boy to get mad at his mother and that you would be very angry at him if he were to get mad at you no matter what the reason. I think we have to find out just what your ideas are on that subject.

Patient's Mother: I don't think that it's wrong for a boy to get angry at his mother. After all, a mother gets angry at her boy and a mother loses her temper at her boy, and even sometimes at her husband, and I think a boy has a right to do as his mother does. Also, you see Michael (*Joey's younger brother*) losing his temper constantly and nothing very much happens to him really.

Patient: But he usually yells at you.

Patient's Mother: Sure he does. Michael yells at everybody.

Therapist: Well, what do you think about what your mother just said?

Patient: Fine. Thanks.

Therapist: Thanks?

Patient: Yeah.

Therapist: You didn't know that before. Did you?

Patient: No.

Therapist: Let's go back to the example that you were giving me before. You said that if your mother were sleeping upstairs — remember that example you gave me a few minutes ago?

Patient: Yeah.

Therapist: Let's ask your mother what she would do. Okay?

Patient: Okay.

Therapist: You want to give the example?

Patient: No.

Therapist: You want me to give the example?

Patient: Yeah.

Therapist: Okay. Joey was saying that —— he was giving an example that —— let's say that you were sleeping upstairs. Is this on a Sunday morning?

Patient: No.

Therapist: You mean during the week your mother sleeps upstairs in the morning?

Patient: Yeah, she sleeps during the week.

Therapist: Who gets up to take care of the children when they get prepared for school?

Patient: Ma.

Therapist: Well, how could she sleep and do that at the same time?

Patient's Mother: Well, Joey considers seven fifteen late.

Therapist: He said ten.

Patient: No, let's just suppose —

Therapist: Okay, suppose. Give us a suppose.

Patient: Well, suppose it was ten in the morning and you were sleeping, I would be scared to tell you that it was ten.

Therapist: What would you be scared of?

Patient: That she'd hit me.

Therapist: You'd be afraid that she'd hit you?

Patient: Yeah.

Therapist: Now tell me something. You said to me before that you would be scared to let your mother know that you were angry at her.

Patient: Yeah.

Therapist: All right now. Let's see what your mother has to say about that. If you came up and told your mother that it made you very angry to see her sleeping so late.

Patient: Yeah, at ten on Monday or on Tuesday.

Therapist: Has that really happened?

Patient's Mother: It has never happened.

Patient: I know. It's just an example.

Patient's Mother: Oh, I think Joey is so anxious about getting to school in the morning that he gets up quite early. He's an early riser and it probably seems to him that we're sleeping forever up there — waiting until seven fifteen or seven thirty. We never sleep late ——

Patient: But this is only an example.

Therapist: Okay, take that example. I think the example is this: if you wanted to sleep later than he wanted you to sleep and he said to you that he was angry that you were sleeping so late, but you still felt that you were justified in sleeping as late as you wanted, would you be angry at him for being angry?

Patient's Mother: No.

Therapist: Would you hit him for being angry?

Patient's Mother: No. But I wouldn't get up as early as he wanted me to get up either. You could get angry.

Patient (practically in tears): But Mommy, this is an example!

Patient's Mother: That's just it and I'm giving you an example of what I would do to your example. I'm giving you another example. I know it's an example.

Therapist: What are you so upset about?

114

Patient's Mother: I would not get angry at you. I'm trying to tell you.

Therapist: Hold it a second. What are you so upset about?

Patient (crying): I don't think you understand my example.

Therapist: Okay. You tell the example again. You tell it again so we can try to understand it.

Patient: Well, suppose you were sleeping until ten and I was just waiting in the den.

Therapist: Yeah.

Patient: And then I got up at around, maybe around a quarter to eight. Then you were just sleeping until ten.

Therapist: All right, and if your mother wanted to sleep until ten.

Patient: No, if she was just sleeping.

Therapist: Yes, she was sleeping and she was over-sleeping by mistake, you mean?

Patient: Yeah.

Therapist: And you were angry about it?

Patient: Yeah.

Therapist: If she was over-sleeping by mistake?

Patient: Yeah.

Therapist: All right. If you were over-sleeping by mistake and he was angry, what would you say?

Patient's Mother: Well, first of all, I'd thank you for waking me up because if I over-sleep it really ruins my whole day and Daddy would be late for work and I'd be late for a new hairdo. I would thank you.

Therapist: Do you think there would be something wrong in his getting angry?

Patient's Mother: No, no. I'd be kind of angry myself — if I slept late by mistake on a day when we had things to do — because you would be late for school, I'd be late to get to the store for whatever I had to do, Joey's daddy would be late for work. It would be terrible. I'd be mad at me.

Therapist: Also, your mother would be happy that you got angry. Because you were angry at her, it helped her get up in time.

Patient's Mother: That's right. I would say, "Joey, I am awfully glad that you got angry enough to wake me because if you didn't the day would just be more ruined."

Therapist: What do you think about that?

Patient: Fine! *(Said with conviction and relief.)*

Therapist: Let me say two things before we stop.

Patient: Dr. Gardner says that anger helps you.

Therapist: Right.

Patient's Mother: Yes, it does. Could you see how it could help in the example you just gave?

Patient: Yeah.

Therapist: It helps you get what you want. Now sometimes you don't get what you want. Let's say that your mother —— it was a different kind of situation where your mother just wanted to sleep late and she didn't think that she should get up, so she would say, "I'm sorry Joey, I'm not getting up but you can be as angry as you want and I can see how you are angry. It's all right to be angry, but I'm still not getting up." Other times she would say, "I see how you are angry and I'm glad you came to wake me up." In either case she wouldn't get angry at you for being angry. Do you understand that?

Patient: I know. I really get angry. I bet I'd practically spank her if it was on a weekday and she slept until practically ten.

Therapist: I could see how you might *feel* like doing that.

Patient's Mother: I can understand that. You know, I'd want to spank myself if I slept late on a weekday.

Therapist: But would you think that there's something wrong with him for getting so angry that he would want to spank you?

Patient's Mother: I wouldn't blame him a bit. I wouldn't blame him a bit. I would be just as angry at my mother if she tried to ruin my day that way.

Therapist: And you know sometimes kids get so angry in such situations that they think even worse things. They get so angry that they even think of worse things than spankings. Some kids will even think of killing their parents they are so angry. They get so mad. They wish they were dead. They wish they didn't live in the house and things like that. Do you ever have thoughts like that?

Patient: Yup!

Therapist: Right. And that's how most kids feel when

something happens that their parents do that they don't like. You know, you have some very strange ideas about getting angry. You think that it's a terrible thing to get angry. Isn't that right?

Patient: Yeah.

Therapist: And you think that your parents are going to punish you for getting angry. Is that right?

Patient: Yeah.

Therapist: They don't.

Patient's Mother: And we haven't.

Therapist: You know what I think. We have to close right now. I would suggest that when you go home that you and your mother and father talk about this all together.

Patient: What about the other thing? You said there were two things that the dreams meant.

Therapist: Oh, about that ugly witch?

Patient: Yeah.

Therapist: Well, the other thing that I think it might mean is that it's your own anger inside that you are not letting out, that comes out in a dream. Anger can look like an ugly witch in a dream. If you let it out then you won't have the dream of ugly witches, because when it doesn't come out it stays inside you and at nighttime it comes out in your dreams.

Patient's Mother: I think it would be a good idea if Joey would make it a point of letting us know whenever he is angry. We can talk about it.

Therapist: You need practice in that. What do you think?

Patient: Okay.

Therapist: I think that's your homework — to practice when you get angry — to tell your parents and to see what happens. All right?

Patient: Yeah.

Therapist: Anything you want to say before we stop?

Patient: No.

In my story I tried to communicate that the eeee is a symbolic verbalization of repressed material which is too anxiety-provoking to be expressed in its undisguised form. The reader should note that in my story I make no particular reference to the actual nature of the problems that were being repressed and just refer to them as "troubles" and "problems" which, when openly discussed, were solved. Although I suspected from previous experiences with Joey that they related to hostility, I tried to first elicit from the child himself statements about the exact nature of the repressed material. In this way, I avoided contaminating his associations with my hypotheses, hunches, and guesses.

Following the story, I asked Joey to describe specific problems he had which he didn't talk about. His first answer was that he didn't have enough baseball cards. This was clearly a resistance response. When asked again, he immediately thought of a dream of the previous night: of a fighting witch who produced scary oooh sounds. I understood the dream to indicate a problem in his relationship with his mother, a problem involving hostility that he needed to repress. It suggested that Joey considered expression of hostility as inappropriate and a manifestation of an imperfection. This led to a discussion in which I first attempted to get him to realize that his mother, like all people, has both assets and liabilities and that no one is perfect. To emphasize my point, I used the examples of my own errors in telling my story — having said "elephant" instead of "pelican," and having the pelican talk at a time when he could only say eeee. Such actual living experiences can be emotionally corrective for the child. He has actually been witness to my fallibility and this experience, more than any statement on my part, can help him lower his standards for both himself and others.

I then attempted to demonstrate how one can use one's anger to remove provocations and irritations. Quite early in this discussion, a telephone call provided me with the opportunity to demonstrate this directly to Joey. The silent caller slightly irritated me and I expressed this by hanging up. This provided the child with another first-hand experience in which he observed me to be practicing what I preached.

In discussions of expressing hostility, I usually do not let the child dwell on anger toward siblings. Such hostility is usually fierce and normally contains a significant element of anger

118

which is displaced from the parents. I therefore try to direct the child's attention to the primary hostilities, not the displaced ones.

There are some who might take issue with my having brought the mother in. One could argue that I was depriving the child of the living experience of handling the hostility problem with his mother in a naturally occurring situation and thereby obviating a potential growth experience. Also the procedure could be dangerously anxiety-provoking and thereby might have slowed down or even shut off further therapeutic inquiry and endeavor in this area. Although such objections are based on sound therapeutic principles, there are times when there are good reasons to be more directive and this situation was, I believe, just such a case. I did not believe that the confrontations would be too anxiety-provoking for Joey at that particular time. I gave him the option regarding inviting her in, and certainly would have respected his request not to do so. I suggested that *he* bring her in to be even more certain that he was ready to handle the hostility issue. In the interview, however, he preferred that *I* pose the question and later that I present the example of his mother sleeping that he had given to me when alone. I complied with both requests. At each point, I was sensitive to his anxiety level and did not push him into areas which I felt he preferred to avoid. One cannot know beforehand how much anxiety a child can take. One must be sensitive to the guidelines the child provides.

Whatever was lost by the somewhat artificial atmosphere in which the discussion took place, more was gained, I believe, in therapeutic time-saving. I might have waited weeks and even months for this child to confront his mother. Such structured discussions, therefore, can shorten therapy. One could argue that he should have been brought to the point where he could confront his mother without my protection, and that the procedure thereby infantilized him. I felt that the child needed me to help and even "protect" him, if you will, at that point. Similar situations were arising frequently enough (especially with his father, who was less readily available for such discussions) to assure me of many future opportunities for similar confrontations on his own. This indeed turned out to be the case and I feel that the help I gave him the first time made it easier for him subsequently to confront his parents on his own. In my presence, the anticipated repercussions were not forthcoming, and he had the *living experience* that my "protection" was unnecessary.

In the discussion with the patient and his mother, I directed their attention to a *specific example* of a situation which might engender hostility in him. Otherwise the discussion might have been quite philosophical, remote from reality, and thereby untherapeutic. In this discussion, the patient preferred the theoretical example (the anger he would feel *if* his mother *were* to sleep until ten a.m. on a school day), and I let him discuss it at this level because a more realistic example might have produced far greater fear and resistance. Even in the discussion of the theoretical example, the patient's anxiety mounted and he had to emphasize the fact that his mother overslept *by mistake*, that is, she really didn't want to do it and so she is less blameworthy. He, therefore, has less justification to be angry at her; so there is less need to be guilty and anxious.

After discussing the example in which the mother angers the child *by mistake* and observing the patient's alleviation of anxiety after he has the living experience that his mother will not retaliate punitively, I carried the problem one step further and introduced the alternative situation in which the mother purposely stays in bed. The whole discussion provided an excellent opportunity to further explore the issue of anger and its utilization.

This vignette demonstrates how the story sequence can be used as a point of departure for further therapeutic work. In this case an analytically orientated psychotherapeutic inquiry evolved, as well as a therapeutic discussion involving the patient's mother.

Ten days later, Joey related this story:

A long long time ago there lived a calf and this calf

couldn't give milk. All the other calves around her could. They began to tease him. Everyday he didn't have anybody to play with and he began to cry. Then his mother said, "All you have to do is let a farmer milk you and then you'll be able to give milk." The reason why he couldn't give milk was that he was afraid of the farmer.

He went to the farmer and he said, "Could you milk me?" The farmer said, "Why, yes." Then the calf gave milk.
Therapist: Why was he afraid of the farmer at first?
Patient: Because he saw lots of chickens being killed and he got scared that he would be killed.
Therapist: What made him change his mind?
Patient: His mother said not to be afraid.
Therapist: I see. The moral of that story is ——
Patient: Don't be afraid of people until you know that they are bad.

I considered the calf to represent Joey. Although milk-giving, and therefore suggestive of the mother, it is clearly a young calf, one who assumes the child's dependent role in its relationship with his mother and the farmer. He is frightened to freely express his feelings, that is, he is so fearful of the farmer that he can't give milk. The fear relates to his notion that the farmer is his potential murderer. Although oedipal fantasies could certainly be imputed here, in view of previous discussions I considered the farmer's hostility to be more likely a projection of the patient's own.

Joey's story revealed that he was becoming less fearful of exposing himself to anxiety-engendering situations. He allows the farmer to come close after his mother reassures him that there is no danger. He has the experience, albeit only vicariously in the story, that people are not so frightening as one might anticipate. The moral epitomizes this idea.

The story clearly demonstrates the way in which messages which are transmitted both in story and through other therapeutic modalities can be incorporated into the patient's subsequent stories.

With this understanding of Joey's story, I told the following:

121

Once upon a time a long long time ago, even before your great-great-great-great-grandmother's great-great-great-grandfather's grandfather was born; in fact, so long ago that even that man could tell you it was before his great-great-great-great-grandfather's great-great-great-great-grandmother was born — it happened around that time — that there lived this calf —

Patient: What was the date?

Therapist: Something I would say about —

Patient: 1000 B.C.

Therapist: No, no, I would say about the year 1248 or thereabouts. Anyway, somewhere around that time there lived this calf and this calf was a very tense calf. He was frightened all the time. He was walking around stiff and frightened and fearful — so fearful that he couldn't give milk.

One day his mother said, "Why are you so scared?" He said to the mother, "You promise you won't tell anybody?" The mother said, "Sure I won't tell anybody. I am your mother. I will keep it a secret." He said, "Well, I've been watching that farmer and you know he kills those chickens." The mother said, "Yeah, I know that." The calf said, "I'm afraid —— you see, I get angry at him sometimes —— when he makes me go into the barn at night and locks me up in there. I know that he has to do it and he has to keep us locked in the barn, but it makes me angry at him. Sometimes I get so angry at him that I wish he was dead." The mother said, "So what?" The calf said, "You mean that's all right?" She said, "Of course, it's all right." He said, "Do other calves think that?" She replied, "Of course, other calves think that." Then he said, "Isn't it bad to think that?" She said, "Of course not." He said, "Won't he die if I think that so much?" She said, "Of course not. Your thoughts can't harm him." The calf said, "Well, wouldn't he be angry at me if he knew that I had such thoughts?" She said, "Why don't you try it out. Let's call him over."

So they called over the farmer and she said, "Now listen, this calf wants to tell you something and I want you to tell me your honest opinion, whether or not you are angry at him for what he says." So the little calf was very fearful and he finally said to the farmer; he was stuttering as he said it, "Sometimes I wish you would die." The farmer said, "Yeah, what else?" The calf said, "That's all." The farmer said, "So what? What's so terrible. I would imagine that you would sometimes wish I would die when I lock you up in that barn at night when you don't want to be locked in there. It's reasonable that you get angry." Well, when the calf heard that, what do you think he thought?

Patient: Real happy.

Therapist: He felt relieved. Right. He felt relieved because he had thought that the farmer would be very angry at him for such thoughts and then he said to the farmer, "Tell me, are you scared that you may die that I think that?" What did the farmer say?

Patient: No.

Therapist: The calf said, "Well, why? Why wouldn't you think you are going to die if I keep thinking that all the time?" What did the farmer say then?

Patient: He said, "No, thoughts can't harm."

Therapist: Right! right! Well, after that the calf really felt relieved because he wasn't the only calf in the world to have such angry thoughts and realized that it was normal to have such thoughts. Then he also found out that his thoughts can't really harm the farmer and then he really felt relieved. What do you think happened about his giving milk?

Patient: I don't know.

Therapist: Well, if he was much more relaxed and relieved, do you think he could give milk then?

Patient: Yes.

Therapist: Right. Now what do you think was the reason that he couldn't give milk?

Patient: Because it was like that story that you told me last time.

Therapist: What was that?

Patient: About someone who could only say eeee because he wouldn't say his troubles.

Therapist: Right. And when he told his troubles what happened?

Patient: He could give milk.

Therapist: Yeah, he could say eeee; he could say anything. This calf, when he let out his troubles, was then relaxed and he could give milk. So what's the moral of my story? Actually, there are two morals to my story.

Patient: Thoughts can't harm.

Therapist: Right.

Patient: And the moral that I had.

Therapist: Which was?

Patient: Don't be afraid in advance that people will be mad at you.

Therapist: Right, and I would have another moral: that all kids have the angriest and worst thoughts toward their parents at times. And a fourth moral would be that if you let things out, you'll feel much better. The end.

Therapist: Do you want to say anything about these stories?

Patient: I'd say that they were good.

Therapist: Do you want to listen to them?

Patient: No.

The reader should note that the introduction of fanciful humor in the beginning of the story serves to enhance the child's interest and lessen the anxieties which may result from the author's tale.

My story begins with the same theme of the calf becoming so fearful of the farmer that he cannot relax enough to give milk. The underlying anger which was producing the anxiety is elaborated upon and attempts are made to dispel the child's irrational ideas regarding anger — ideas which are at the very foundation of his neurosis.

Of interest is the fact that the child, on his own, realized that the story was similar to the previous ones. He saw the close relationship between the pelican who could only say eeee and the cow who couldn't give milk. He then understood that both became less inhibited when they freely expressed their feelings. This insight was genuine, I believe, self-related, and played a role in freeing Joey from his neurotic inhibitions.

Five months later, Joey told this story:

Once upon a time there lived this billy goat and he was very smart. He always went to school every single day and he liked it a lot. Then one day he had a streak of eighty straight excellent papers and he was very happy. His mother was real proud of him. Then he played with his friends because there was finally a vacation for two days. After that he practically always got excellent papers. That's the end.

The moral of the story is: get excellent papers.

The story has healthy elements which reflect the child's positive feelings about himself. There is, however, a compulsive, perfectionistic quality about the story, and so I told Joey this story:

Once upon a time there was a billy goat. He was a smart billy goat. He went to school every day and he liked it a lot. Now sometimes he would get excellent and sometimes he would get very good. Sometimes he would get good, sometimes he'd get fair, and sometimes he would even get F. Most of the time he got excellents and he figured that's the way it is. You try your hardest and sometimes you come out doing very well, but at other times you don't do that well. That's the way life is. No one's perfect and he didn't feel very bad when he didn't get a perfect, but he ended up with very good grades anyway and was pretty happy — not like some kids who are always trying to get excellents and perfect all the time and feel that they've failed terribly if they get anything less than excellent.

The moral of that story is: it's okay not to get excellents all the time. The end.

Therapist: What do you think of that story?

Patient: I think it was very good. Are you disturbed because I didn't say excellent?

Therapist: No, not at all. I can't tell excellent stories all the time. Sometimes my stories are even terrible. Sometimes I can't even tell a good story. I try hard to make good stories, but they're not always perfect.

Patient: I mostly get excellents and very good.

Therapist: Okay. Do you feel very bad when you get a very good?

Patient: No.

Therapist: Do you feel like a real crud rat fink?

Patient: No, I brag about it.

Therapist: Good. Okay. The end .

In my story I attempted to communicate the idea that one can be quite satisfied with one's life without getting straight A's, as opposed to "some kids who are always trying to get excellents."

In the post-story discussion, the patient reveals his fear that I will be angry at him because he didn't say that *my* story was excellent. I reassure him that I do not expect perfection of myself and am not angry at those who do not consider my story excellent. This is another example of one of those actual *living experiences* which, possibly even more than insight, contribute to therapeutic change.

In the next session, Joey related this story :

Once there was a baseball player and he was a pretty average ballplayer. He hit about 250. Then one day he really had a hot streak and he hit 380. That year he led both major leagues in every category except pitching because he wasn't a pitcher. He was very proud of himself. Then he just went back to normal and lived happily ever after and he was satisfied with himself.

Therapist: And he wasn't unhappy when he went back to the 250?

Patient: No. He wasn't unhappy.

Therapist: What's the lesson of that story?

Patient: Be satisfied with yourself.

The story clearly reveals that my message from the previous session had been heard and was being incorporated. Although my communication had been received on the conscious level, such reiteration is still therapeutic.

Since the patient's story was essentially healthy, I did not introduce any new themes into mine, but merely reiterated and

126

emphasized the themes of comfort with and acceptance of non-excellence in both academics and sports. Accordingly I told this story:

> Once there was this kid and he went to school. He was one of these kids who liked his schoolwork very much and he also liked sports. He was interested in both and during school he would work at his school work and after school he would try out for different teams — baseball team, football team — things like that. He was, I would say, an above-average student in the classroom and once in a while he would have a good streak in which he would do very, very well and other times he would fall down and do average, sometimes even below average. But all things together, he was above average. He had a pretty good healthy attitude towards the whole thing. When he would do very well he'd be very proud of himself and when he would do poorly, he'd be a little disappointed; but it wouldn't break him up and it wouldn't make him feel like it was the end of the world. So things went pretty well for him in school and it was the same way on the field in sports. He had a fairly good average at baseball. When he would fall down he'd feel a little bad, but when he would do very well he would feel very good. He never really got shattered when he would drop down from very good to average and he didn't have the feeling that it would be the end of the world for him if he didn't keep up perfect scores.
>
> The lesson of that story is that there are many areas of life, many places in your life, where sometimes you do well, sometimes you do average, and sometimes you do poorly. If a man is doing a good job working hard and doing fairly well, there's no reason why he has to think that he has to be perfect all the time. The end.

Three weeks later, Joey told this story:

> Once there was this baseball player and he always got discouraged when he didn't get a hit. He went to a psychiatrist and they didn't know what was happening inside him.

127

Then the psychiatrist moved away and he had to go to another one. That one still didn't help him and moved away. Then he went to a different one and this one helped him. He taught him not to get discouraged and to just keep on saying to himself whenever he got at bat, "I'm going to get a hit this time." That worked and he got more confidence and he began to be a good baseball player. That's the end.

The moral of that story is: don't get discouraged.

Here Joey has become somewhat discouraged with his progress, and he reveals his desire for another psychiatrist who might help him more quickly and less painfully. He finally is helped, but the method is one of repeating a magical resolution that he will do better without any inquiry into the causes of his problems. I therefore told the following story:

Once upon a time there was a boy and he was a baseball player. He got very discouraged when he didn't get a hit and he went to a psychiatrist and this psychiatrist worked very hard with him, but the boy didn't improve very much. He thought, "I think I'm going to go to another psychiatrist." So he went in one day and he said to the psychiatrist, "I think I'm going to go to another psychiatrist. I don't think you're helping me." The psychiatrist said, "Well, if you want to do that I can't stop you, but I think you're making a mistake. I think that you have to do three things." The boy said, "What is that?" The psychiatrist said, "The first thing is to try to find out why you are having trouble hitting. The second thing is to take the things that you learn about why you are having trouble and to think about them very seriously and to use them whenever you can. The third thing is to get some practice in hitting and some more practice in baseball so you'll be a better player."

Well, the boy thought that that sounded very reasonable and he listened to what the psychiatrist had said, tried to take his treatment more seriously, tried to think more often about what the psychiatrist had told him that they had learned about the reasons for his poor baseball and he

128

also took baseball lessons and practiced. And before long, he became a much better baseball player and he got more confidence.

The moral of that story is: confidence is not magic. It just doesn't come there by your being patted on the back or the head. You get confidence by learning what's wrong, then practicing and improving.

Therapist: What do you think of that story?

Patient: It was good, as usual.

Therapist: Okay.

In my story he is discouraged from relying on methods which magically bring about personality changes, and is encouraged to look into the sources of his difficulties and to use the information so gained toward his self-improvement.

A few weeks later, Joey told this story:

Once there lived a rabbit and this rabbit was very happy but he was an orphan. Every day at night he always used to get reminded that he was an orphan and he always used to remember his real parents when he was just one year old. He didn't like this though; he really didn't. So he tried to get a book on orphans and he went to the school library and he returned all of his books that he had been reading and he got three books about orphans. So he did and he got better by it. And they told him things. It was by Richard Gardner.

Therapist: Uh-huh. I see. What did I say in that book?

Patient: Oh, about —— I forgot it.

Therapist: Come on. Make up something. What did I say in that book about orphans?

Patient: That there was this boy named Joey, that he was an orphan and that he had a foster home, and that he had very nice parents, and that there's a number you can call to get an orphan home, and this was the number.

Therapist: Wait a minute. He had very nice parents. You mean the foster parents?

Patient: Yeah.

Therapist: And it had a number to get foster parents?

Patient: Yeah, that you could call on the telephone and it was this: 569-3125. And that's the end.

Therapist: Do you know anybody who has a number like that?

Patient: No.

Therapist: So go ahead.

Patient: And they had lots of nice foster parents there and he called it up and he got some nice foster parents. The end.

Therapist: The lesson of that story is?

Patient: There are some good foster parents. Okay?

Therapist: Okay. Hold on. I just want to ask you a couple of questions. What happened to this rabbit's real parents?

Patient: One of them was forced into the navy —— the father, and the other one was a nurse and they had to stay there for a real long time for about maybe thirty years and by the time they would come back he would be a grown up. So they just called him an orphan.

Therapist: Oh, I see. By the time the father and mother came back the rabbit would have been a grown up.

Patient: Do you have any other questions?

Therapist: Yes. You told me how the rabbit became an orphan. Now what about in the book on Joey, the orphan. How did he become an orphan?

Patient: His parents went to jail.

Therapist: Why?

Patient: Because they didn't think they were being very nice to Joey.

Therapist: Because they weren't nice to Joey. What did they do?

Patient: They just didn't think they were being very nice to him.

Therapist: In what way?

Patient: Oh he complained about being put to bed at eight o'clock .

Therapist: And what did his parents do?

Patient: And his parents spanked him for nothing.

Therapist: Hhmm. I see. Okay, now I'm going to tell a story.

Joey's story has interesting implications. The patient was born three months after his father entered the navy for a two-year stint. The family lived on a naval base in the southern part of the United States, and although the father was away from home during the day, his duties did not require further separation from his family. Throughout this period of military service the father constantly complained about his duties and was quite bitter and frustrated over his assignment. The mother was a bright and intellectually active woman who found herself in a setting where there was no one with whom she could form a meaningful relationship. The father's chronic disgruntlement added to her feelings of loneliness, isolation, and depression. In addition, the patient was her first baby and she described herself as having been "overwhelmed by the responsibility." From the time the patient was four months of age until he was eighteen months old, she said she mechanically performed her child-rearing chores, but because she was so depressed, she was unable to give the baby the degree of affection and attention she knew he deserved. Her depression lifted as the time of her husband's discharge approached.

Although Joey denies any conscious recollection of this period of his life, it is tempting to hypothesize that the story reveals his awareness, at some deep unconscious level, of the deprivations he suffered during this time. In the story, the rabbit became an orphan when he was one year old. This coincides very well with the period of his father's dissatisfaction and his mother's depression. In fact, the mother describes the period around the time when the patient was one as being "the low point of our lives." In addition, the patient describes the rabbit's real parents, that is, the loving parents, as having been "forced into the navy." In the story the father's entry into the service results in his abandoning the patient. In the second rendition of the same story, the orphan Joey's parents are put in jail because they were too punitive. Their psychological abandonment is concretized as physical punishment.

Following the father's discharge, the mother once again involved herself in her former, more interesting, and enjoyable life, and the father became absorbed in far more rewarding work. Although no longer exposed to the same deleterious milieu, I believe that the patient continued to view his parents as they were during the military period. It is as if there had been a kind of imprinting which persisted beyond the time when it accurately portrayed reality. There was no question that the parents he was living with at the time of treatment were far different. The mother was not depressed, lonely, or dissatisfied with her life, and the father was quite involved in his work and deriving deep gratifications from it. The phenomenon, I felt, was somewhat similar to one's first impression upon meeting a new person. When negative, it may lessen or even preclude appreciation of more positive and ingratiating qualities which the newly met person may reveal in the future. I considered Joey's anger, therefore, a legacy of the past, an anachronism, a residue of the days when there was indeed some justification for resentment. Joey had to be brought up-to-date; he had to get a more accurate view of his parents. In addition, the guilt and anxiety Joey felt over his anger had to be dealt with. He was accordingly told this story:

Once upon a time there was a rabbit and his father was in the navy. His mother was sad and lonely when the father was away, and because of this they didn't give him very much time and attention when he was a little baby rabbit. Now the father had to give a lot of time to the navy, and while he was away the mother was lonely because they were in a place where there weren't any friends for her. This made her sad and lonely. As a result, when this rabbit was one year old, he didn't get very much attention from his mother and father. He got very angry about this and even though later on when they got out of the navy and they started to give him more and more time and attention, he still was very angry about this. He was very, very angry about it, and not only that, he also thought that it was a terrible thing to be angry at his parents. He kept on being angry at them for many years after they got out of the navy because when he was a little rabbit they had not given him the affection and the time that he had wanted. But then later when he got older, he began to realize —— what did he realize that made him less angry?

Patient: I don't know. It's your story.

Therapist: Can you think of or try to figure out what he might have realized later on that would have made him less angry?

Patient: No.

Therapist: Well, he realized later on that his mother and father had no choice at that time, that his father being in the navy, was assigned to a job he didn't like, and he had no choice but to stay away for long periods of time, but that his father really loved him and his father really wanted to be with him but couldn't. His mother really loved him and wanted to be with him but because she was so sad and lonely she couldn't give him the affection he deserved. Then he realized that they really loved him but through no choice of their own they were sad. He also saw that they were no longer the way they had been when he was a little baby; that now they were happier and did give him more time and affection. He hadn't realized that they had changed. He was still in the habit of seeing them as they had once been when he was one year old. He then felt less angry at them and also when he did get angry at them at times, he didn't think it was so terrible because he learned that it's not so terrible to get angry at people once in a while. And the lesson of that story is: sometimes you get angry at people, but when you find out that they really love you anyway you won't be so angry.

What do you think of that story?

Patient: It was fine.

Therapist: What was the part about it that you liked?

Patient: I just liked the whole thing.

Therapist: You know that story is something like you.

Patient: Yes.

Therapist: How was it like you?

Patient: I'm the rabbit.

Therapist: Yeah, and how is your experience like the rabbit's?

Patient: I don't think my mother is giving me enough care and affection.

Therapist: Is that true?

Patient: No.

Therapist: Do you think she's giving you enough care and affection?

Patient: Yes.

Therapist: But do you sometimes question it?

Patient: No.

Therapist: I think you do. What about when you were a very little boy? What happened then when you were one year old like this rabbit?

Patient: Nothing.

Therapist: Do you think your mother and father then did not give you enough care and affection?

Patient: No. I don't even remember it.

Therapist: Of course, hardly anybody remembers when they were one. But I think a part of you remembers and I think at that time there was a little trouble when your father was in the navy. I think he couldn't give you as much time as he would have liked. What do you think of that?

Patient: Could be.

Therapist: But I happen to know right now that your parents love you very deeply. Is that so?

Patient: Yes.

Therapist: But I think you sometimes question it. Okay, do you want to listen to our stories?

Patient: Yes.

In my story I attempted to alter the "first impressions" which still seemed to be operative. From the post-story discussion, it is clear that the patient had no conscious recall of the early events alluded to in his story. Although such recall would probably have made my analysis more meaningful, my important communications related to the here and now, not to the past. My aim was to get him to see his parents as genuinely affectionate; to bring about the realization that they are no longer the people he once knew, people whom he at one time might have been justifiably angry at.

134

Subsequently in this session, Joey was encouraged to discuss with his parents the whole question of their navy experience as well as their feelings about him, both then and at present. My hope was that such discussion would help his concept of them.

Some may express incredulity that the child could have recollections dating to age one, even if unconscious. To me, there is nothing surprising about this. Understanding antedates speech, and there are many children who have amassed a considerable vocabulary by nine or ten months of age, let alone one year. Psychoanalysts have repeatedly demonstrated that there is a deep well of information about the earliest years of our lives which is not in conscious awareness. There is no question that such impressions may deeply affect our present-day behavior and may reveal themselves in our dreams and fantasies.

In his next session, two days later, Joey told this story:

Once upon a time there lived a prince and this prince didn't think his mother and father liked him very much. So he decided to ask them and he did and they liked him, and they said that they really loved him. And that's the end and I have a moral: don't try to assume what your parents are going to say. Ask them.

Therapist: Now I want to ask you a question. Do you think your story has anything to do with the things we spoke about?

Patient: Yes.

Therapist: How?

Patient: Because he thinks his parents don't love him.

Therapist: Who's that?

Patient: The prince.

Therapist: Yes, and how does this relate to you.

Patient: Maybe I don't think that my parents love me, but I do.

Therapist: What makes you think that you might not think it?

Patient: Because of the story.

Therapist: What story?

Patient: This story.

Therapist: When you told this story were you thinking about some of the things we spoke about last time?

Patient: No.

Therapist: Are you sure?

Patient: No.

Therapist: You weren't thinking at all about anything you were told last time?

Patient: Yeah.

Therapist: I told you to test your parents out and ask them if they loved you and to discuss with them their reasons for their answer. Didn't I tell you that?

Patient: Yeah.

Therapist: Well, that's what you put in your story.

Patient: Do you think the story means anything good? The prince asked his mother and father.

Therapist: Right. It means that you heard what I've said and you're trying to —

Patient: Get it into my mind?

Therapist: Put it into practice —— get it into your mind.

Patient: I still think I'm having troubles.

Therapist: What are the troubles as you see them?

Patient: This trouble.

Therapist: What's the trouble?

Patient: I think about my parents in the navy.

Therapist: Did you think about that a lot since we spoke last?

Patient: No.

Therapist: What is the navy trouble as you see it?

Patient: Oh, that I don't think that my mother and father love me.

Therapist: Do you think that's so? Do you wonder about it sometimes?

Patient: No.

Therapist: Are you sure?

Patient: Yeah.

Therapist: So why do I think that? Why do I think that maybe you think that your mother and father don't love you?

Patient: Because my stupid mind is telling fibs. It is —— my unconscious mind.

Therapist: Hhmmm. All right.

Patient: If it doesn't have any conscious then how can it tell things that are true?

Therapist: I'm not clear what you are saying.

Patient: If my unconscious mind is unconscious how come it —— how come you can believe the things that it says?

Therapist: Well, just because you don't know about it doesn't mean that it doesn't say things that are true. Things can be buried, like if you buried a book in the ground. Are the things in the book still true?

Patient: Yes.

Therapist: All right. Okay.

This story is clearly related to the main theme of the previous session. The question that arose in my mind was what his true motivation might have been in telling it. First, I had to consider the possibility that he was "putting me on," and that there was no conviction on his part of the basic validity of his story's theme and moral. Such stories are presented in the service of resistance and are obviously of no therapeutic value. The second possibility was that the parental love issue was a meaningful one to him, and that he was adjusting to it and incorporating it piecemeal through reiteration. Although conscious processes might have been operative here, as already described, such repetition is an intrinsic part of the working-through process and can be most therapeutic. The third possibility was that he had no conscious awareness of the relationship between this story and his experiences of the previous session, which suggested that my communications were being appreciated at a deep and probably most therapeutic level.

In the post-story discussion the patient denied any conscious awareness that his story reflected the previous session's discussion. This could be considered an argument in favor of deep incorporation, but his denial need not necessarily be trusted. He sensed that I preferred no conscious connection, and his denial of it might have been related to his desire to ingratiate himself to me. In the post-story discussion, Joey's responses were somewhat contradictory and his puzzlement became mine.

With these considerations in mind, I did feel, however,

that my messages of the previous session had produced a certain amount of concern and preoccupation. He was grappling with the issue of his parents' love and in this sense, at least, I had "been heard" and something therapeutic was happening. At the conclusion of the discussion I did not feel that he was consciously trying to "butter me up." I felt, on the contrary, that the story revealed meaningful incorporation of my messages with some recognition of the relationship of his story to his experiences of the previous session. In order to dissuade Joey from possible tendencies to relate stories which he thought I wanted to hear, I told this one:

> Once upon a time there was a boy and he was always trying to please those around him and he always tried to do just what they said and just what they thought and although they acted friendly toward him, he didn't feel good about himself and he didn't really express what was truly on his mind so he felt kind of depressed and bad about himself. When he started to express truly what was on his mind, even though it might not be the kind of things that his friends would like to hear, he felt much better about himself and then they liked him much more because they respected him for speaking his own mind.
>
> The moral of that story is: always try to say what is on your own mind and sometimes people will not agree with what you are saying but they will respect you more. The end.

Although my story does not relate to the primary question of his parents' love, it does direct itself to the possible resistance question raised by his story. This, I felt, was an issue of higher priority because too much of the ingratiation element makes the child's stories not only less credible but also less therapeutic.

Example 2

Steve, the eight-year-old boy with school disciplinary problems, told this story during his fourth month in treatment:

Today my story is about laughing daisies. Once there were some daisies. This was a fairyland that they lived in so almost anything could talk and walk. But these daisies were very unhappy. They always cried and sometimes they couldn't even find anything well to do because their king was always telling sad things, which made almost everything in the land cry. These daisies cried a lot and even though they had friends they still cried. They couldn't stop no matter what happened — even when it was their birthday they still cried. Now everything else in this kingdom didn't cry.

One day an angel flew over and the daisies pleaded with the angel to stop the king from telling sad things, and the angel said, "Just because you are crying doesn't mean that the king has been cruel to you. What you have to do is to stop your crying and perhaps you will find yourself not in such a bad and terrible state." Now they agreed to this and they didn't cry anymore and then they got a new king who told jokes instead and made them laugh. Almost everybody was happy in the kingdom and then the daisies were called the laughing daisies and that's the end.

Therapist: I have a question. Did these daisies start laughing before the new king came in? Did they start laughing right after they spoke to the angel?

Patient: No, they started laughing when the new king told his first joke.

Therapist: I see.

Patient: The moral is: do not be discouraged. Happy things are coming your way. That means the daisies shouldn't have cried so much when they should have known that the old king was giving his place to another king.

Therapist: I see. Okay.

The story has both healthy and pathological elements. On the one hand, Steve wants to change his situation, that is, stop the crying and sadness and, in addition, he is hopeful that such changes will occur: "Do not be discouraged. Happy things are coming your way." He achieves his end, however, by magical and external means: the old king is replaced by "a new king who told jokes." There is no working out the problem.

With this understanding of the child's story, I related the following:

Once upon a time there were in fairyland some daisies and they would cry a lot. They were always crying. Now their king was the kind of person who always spoke of sad things and they cried whenever they heard these sad things. Even though they had many friends they still cried. But most of the other people around did not cry when they did.

One day they saw some angels flying overhead and they said, "Oh, good angels, we beg you. We beg you to do something for us. We beg you to do something to us with your magic wand that will stop us from crying when the king tells sad stories." The angel said, "I'm sorry. I cannot do that for you. There's no such thing as magic." And then they said, "Perhaps then you can get the king to stop telling us sad stories." The angel said, "I cannot do that. He is the king and if he wishes to tell sad stories then I have no power over him." Then they said, "Perhaps you can get us a new king, someone who tells happy stories." The angel said, "I'm sorry. There is no prospect of that happening. There's no reason at all to believe that there will be a new king coming soon."

They said, "Well, what can we do then, angel? You are wise." The angel said, "Yes, there is something you can do. You can look into yourself and ask why you are crying." One of the daisies said, "Well, we cry because we are very sensitive. We take it very seriously." The angel said, "Well, that's your first hint. That's your first reason. You take things too seriously. You can't shake them off in a lighthearted manner. You can't say to yourself, 'Oh, who believes in that stuff,' or 'That's not true,' or 'He's only saying that to tease,' or 'That's only make believe.' If you can do that and not take things so seriously, you would cry less. I suggest you think about the various situations which make you cry and you will find that when you cry it usually means that you are taking something too seriously. You have to look into other situations and find out what the reasons are, and the more you know about the reasons, the less you'll cry."

Well, the daisies thought seriously about the angel's advice and they decided to try to put it into practice. So when they did that they found that they cried less.

And the lesson of this story is: if you cry a lot when others don't, there's no magic that will cure you of it. Just find out what your particular problems are that are causing you to cry and when you solve those you'll cry less. The end.

I attempted here to encourage Steve to utilize his own powers to effect salutary changes in his life situation. In my stories magical solutions are repeatedly presented as impossible to attain and inquiry into the sources of one's difficulties is the strongly recommended alternative.

Example 3

George, the nine-and-a-half-year-old boy with shyness and disinterest in his schoolwork, expressed his early treatment anxieties in the story in which a man died while exploring underground caves. In another story, a man was sent to jail for taking pictures of a secret government airplane. Soon afterwards, George told this story:

Once there was a man who shot up space rockets and once he shot up one to the moon. No one was in it. But he couldn't get it back because it crashed on the moon and they didn't have enough fuel to get it back. Then he tried to shoot up a spaceship with him in it and he thought it would be scary to be on the moon and all that. He shot up the spaceship and landed on the moon. He got out and explored around. He found the first spaceship. He got the information on it and it really wasn't scary. He went back to his spaceship and he went back to earth.

The moral of that story is that sometimes you think that things are scary but they really aren't.

Here George has incorporated the messages from my earlier stories and reveals that he is aware that things may turn out to be less frightening than he may have originally anticipated. The story not only demonstrates that my communications were heard, but also that he is attempting to desensitize himself to his anxieties. I felt that the story might also represent his fear of approaching his divorced father who, in the past, had been quite punitive. More recently, the father's visits had been inconsistent, and when he did appear he was unpredictable in his displays of affection and his involvement. I considered the moon to possibly represent the father: remote and cold, but potentially reachable. The child himself does not go in the first shot because father can be dangerous. When the test rocket does land, nothing devastating happens. Although it has run out of fuel, the lunar environment appears safe. The running out of fuel provides him with the excuse for going up himself to "explore" and get "information." He then returns safely, his initial anxieties having been assuaged by his experience that the anticipated dangers were not forthcoming.

With these interpretations of George's story, I told mine:

Once upon a time there was a man and he used to build space rockets to go to the moon and one time he built a rocket and he wanted to go to the moon in this rocket himself. There were two things that kind of held him back. One was fear. He was afraid that his rocket would land on the moon and might crash and even if it didn't crash the moon would be a very fearful place, a very frightening place, and that terrible things might happen to him. The second thought or consideration was that he felt that the moon, if not a fearful place, might be a useless place — that if he could get nothing out of it there would be no point in going there and that there would be nothing to be gained by even trying to get there. So there was fear on the one hand; on the other hand, that there was nothing to be gained or gotten from a moon shot.

Anyway, he decided to try it out and see what happened. Well, he did land on the moon and he was surprised to learn that there really was nothing to be frightened of or very little to be frightened of. The whole trip or voyage went very beautifully. Nothing happened to frighten him. When he got there, although the moon was certainly barren, in many ways it had many uses. He was able to build underground houses. It was a very good way station for exploration into space. He was able to set up telescopes which could see outer space much better than they could see it from earth because you didn't have the earth's atmosphere interfering. That was the main use of it. And so he learned that what he thought might be useless later on turned out to be a very useful thing because they made many astronomical discoveries there.

And the lessons of that story are: 1) Not everything you think is frightening is necessarily so. In fact, many things you think are frightening turn out not to be frightening. 2) The second lesson is that not everything you think may be useless may be necessarily useless and if you give it a chance, you may find out that it may serve many useful purposes. The end.

In my story I attempted to reinforce George's statement that dangerous things may turn out not to be as frightening as one may have originally expected. In addition, considering the moon to symbolize his father, I tried to communicate the idea that with all his liabilities, his father did indeed have certain assets. There were gratifications to be derived from his father if he would look for them and if he could overcome his anxieties and shyness.

The way in which the theme of my last story became incorporated is demonstrated by the next story George told:

Once upon a time there was this man who made ship and car models and on them he wrote the history of it, who built it, and the directions. He kept on doing this. He found out information on them.

So one time he found out this information that he didn't think was right in a book about ship models —— I mean ships. So he went to the author and he said, "I don't think this thing is right." The author checked it out and it wasn't right. A part of it was right but the rest was wrong. So the author rewrote the part in the book that was wrong and they started publishing it more and there were a lot of good copies of it. Then the other person took down notes on this from the right book and then he put the information in the model with the directions.

The moral of that story is if you think something is wrong, you should go to the person. In a book you should go to the author and explain it to him, and he'll probably check it out and see if it's wrong or not.

Here George goes to his father and presents his grievances. The father — the author of the directions — is fallible and when the patient points out a deficiency, he listens receptively and makes appropriate changes. Speaking to his father can have beneficial results. George's efforts in this regard therefore need not be in vain.

Clinically, however, George was not taking significant steps in this direction. The story reflected only his wish to do so and possibly his desire to comply with my suggestion that he assert himself. Therefore, in order to encourage the patient further in the direction of taking constructive action and to urge self-assertion when dealing with authority figures, I told this story:

Once upon a time there was a man and this man's job was to write the directions for models — for ship and car models — and he would write the history of the ship or car and give various information about these things. Now in order to do this, he had to consult books written by experts about these various models and ships and things like that.

So one day while he was reading a book by a very famous expert he came across something that he thought was wrong, but he said, "No, he's an expert. He can't be wrong. I'm probably wrong." So he went to other books and he spoke to other people and it still seemed to him that the expert was wrong; the big famous expert was wrong. But he said, "I can't possibly go to an expert and tell him he's wrong. He's so knowledgeable and I'm just an unknown." Anyway, he spoke to some friends about it, and they said, "What are you talking about. You're right, you're right. That's all. Why don't you go speak to him? Nothing is going to happen to you."

So he went to the expert and he spoke to the expert, and the expert listened to him and much to the man's surprise, the expert took him very seriously, checked on what he said — checked it out — and admitted to the man that the man was right. The expert said that he had been wrong. This made the man feel good. He felt that the expert would be very severe with him or very angry with him for telling the expert that he had made an error. Then they took these changes, put them in the original book, and when the man wrote up the information for his models, he also put in the correct information.

And the lesson of that story is no one is perfect. Everyone can make a mistake. Everyone has both good and bad parts, their strengths and their weaknesses. That's the first lesson. The second lesson is: sometimes you are afraid that if you correct an expert that he'll get angry at you or do something to hurt you, but you will find most often that this isn't so and if you have the courage to talk to the expert you will find that he is not going to be so punishing. Those are the lessons of that story.

I decided to emphasize the issue of the fallibility of authorities and their non-punitive response to being corrected by depicting a "super authority" who had these qualities. This is one of the methods I use to emphasize healthy and appropriate resolutions and adaptations that are presented in the child's story.

The following sequence, typical of the middle phase, occurred during George's fifth month of therapy:

Once upon a time there was a boy who always wanted to figure out an easier way how to do a math problem and he always spent a lot of time trying to do this. After that the easy way was quicker so he could do his homework real quick. The next day he brought his math to school and told the teacher how to do it the easy way and then he told the people in the math group how to do it the easy way and the next night they all got it done in about ten minutes. It was about a page, but it was done the easy way he had found out. Everybody got all the answers right. The teacher said that the math book that he had said there was no easy way to do the problem and he found out there was an easy way. So the next time they had a problem from the math book the boy said there was an easier way to do it.

The moral of that story is: sometimes there's an easier way of doing things and you shouldn't just wait around for others to find out. You should find out.

The meaning of the story is self-explanatory. The patient was doing poorly in school, and the story reveals one of the reasons why. Accordingly, I told this story:

Once upon a time there was a boy and his name was Sam Shortcut. That was his name — Sam Shortcut — and you know why they called him Sam Shortcut?
Patient: Because he always did problems the shortcut?
Therapist: Because he was always looking for shortcuts, so they gave him the name Sam Shortcut. You might think that everybody thought that he was great and brilliant and everybody respected him, but you are wrong. If you think that, you'd be wrong. Everybody thought that he was kind of foolish.

Sam Shortcut, in spite of all his shortcuts, was one of the poorest students in the class. In fact, he was failing a couple of subjects. Now how did this come about? For example, one day they were studying math and there in the book they saw the statement: "There are no shortcuts to figuring out this problem. This problem takes about five minutes to do for the average student." Well, Sam Shortcut said, "Not for me. I'm going to figure out a shortcut." So Sam spent about four hours trying to figure out a shortcut and he never did. When he came back to school the next day, he thought he had figured out a shortcut, but he got the wrong answer

146

with his shortcut and he didn't learn anything about how to do the problem. The teacher said to him, "There you go again, Sam. Your shortcuts always take much longer than the regular way and you usually end up not only getting it wrong, but worse than that, you don't learn the right way to do it. Shortcuts are usually a way of avoiding learning and they are usually things that lazy people use."

Well, that was the unhappy story of Sam Shortcut who didn't learn very much because he didn't realize the important thing that even if you do learn a shortcut that works, in a shortcut you usually don't learn the principles. Do you know what I mean by the principles?

Patient: How to do it.

Therapist: Right. You just learn some trick method but you don't learn the basic mechanics, the basic process by which the thing is done, and it was a very sad story for Sam Shortcut. Real fun is learning how to do the thing and figuring it out so that you can use the same principles elsewhere, and Sam would not only spend more time figuring out his shortcuts than he would if he did it the long way, but he didn't learn the basic principles so he didn't really understand what he was doing.

And do you know what the lesson of that story is?

Patient: No.

Therapist: What did Sam learn?

Patient: If you know the principle you can figure out another way.

Therapist: What is the principle? What do I mean?

Patient: How to do it.

Therapist: Right —— the basic way to do it. In shortcuts you usually don't know the basic principles and usually most shortcuts end up as long cuts. In other words, they take longer. The end.

There's little that is deep or symbolic in my story. It was an attempt, through the medium of the story, to present in a pleasurable manner a somewhat unpalatable message: hard work, although unpleasant, is predictably beneficial; short cuts are ultimately to one's disadvantage.

Example 4

Carol, the nine-and-a-half-year-old girl with stuttering, generalized tension, insomnia, and poor relationships with peers, presented this typical middle phase story:

> Once upon a time there was a girl and she lived by a seashore on a desert island. Her boat crashed once with her parents in it. They can't get off the island.
>
> One day she went down to go fishing for some supper and she came to this box. The box had big, big, big letters on it that said, "Radioactive Seeds." But she didn't see that box —— I mean she didn't see the letters on the box; she didn't read it. Well, she brought it home and they planted the seeds. After one day these beautiful plants grew — beautiful, beautiful — and her father said, "Now how could these seeds grow so fast? Only radioactive seeds could grow. Now where's the cover?" The little girl said, "I used it for the table." She made the cover that said "Radioactive Seeds" for a table. Then her father took a look at the table and he turned it over and he saw on the bottom it said, "Radioactive Seeds. Be Careful."
>
> The moral of the story is: if you know how to read use your reading.

Therapist: Now what did the father do after he looked at it? You sort of left this up in the air in that story.

Patient: He fainted.

Therapist: And what happened to the family?

Patient: Well, for instance, the father ate spinach and spinach makes you strong so he could lift up this whole house. And the mother ate carrots and she could see something from miles and miles away. And the daughter ate both so she was very strong and she could see very good.

Therapist: You mean they ate from the radioactive plants, is that it?

Patient: Yes.

Therapist: All right. Is that it? Nothing else happened to them?

Patient: Hhmmm.

148

Therapist: Well, why did the father faint?

Patient: Because he found out that they ate radioactive seeds.

Therapist: I see, but was he frightened?

Patient: Yes.

Therapist: I see, but nothing terrible happened?

Patient: No.

Therapist: In fact, from what you say, good things happened.

Patient: It wasn't very good that they ate it.

Therapist: But the father became very strong and the mother could see for miles. The daughter was strong and could see for miles. Nothing bad came of it?

Patient: No.

Therapist: Only good?

Patient: Hhmmm.

Therapist: How do you explain that?

Patient: What do you mean how do I explain that?

Therapist: Well, if it's radioactive you would expect that bad things would happen but yet in this case nothing bad happened. How come that the radioactivity didn't work in the usual fashion — which is, you know, that it is dangerous? If it wasn't dangerous, how come the "Be Careful" sign?

Patient: Well, that night they went to bed and the house exploded because they kept all the seeds in the freezer in the house.

Therapist: I see. So what happened to them?

Patient: They were killed too.

Therapist: I see. Okay.

In this story the patient revealed her basic feelings that the members of her family are outcasts and isolates. In a sense, this was true in that the mother's extreme temper earned her the reputation in the neighborhood of being someone to avoid. What is most interesting in this story is the utilization of the mechanism of denial. The radioactive seeds which are referred to as being dangerous do not have their traditional lethal, or at least severely harmful, effects when ingested, but only enhance strength and vision. I consider the radioactive seeds, which grow into foods, to represent her mother's love which she sees not only as a source of comfort and potential strength, but which could also be lethal.

In my inquiry, I attempted to get Carol to admit the strongly implied dangerous aspects of the radioactivity in an attempt to provide her with the living experience that such an expression would not be followed by a reprimand. The dangerous facets, however, were denied and repressed. As already described, Carol's mother was quite frequently enraged, and Carol was only one of the objects of her wrath. The child, however, could not allow herself conscious awareness of the hostile aspects of her mother's personality. With some sanctioning on my part, however, she did allow herself to portray the mother's rage, but in highly symbolic form: the seeds are in the freezer — the mother's love is frozen — and they blow up the house — when unleashed it turns into devastating hostility. With this understanding of the child's story, I related this one:

Once upon a time there was a family and they had been shipwrecked on this desert island because the boat that they were on sank and they got into a little rowboat and they came to this island. The family consisted of a mother, a father, and a daughter.

One day the daughter was down on the beach ready to fish to get some fish for her supper when she noticed on the beach, apparently it had floated up, there was a large box with red letters on it, and she had just learned how to read and she looked at it carefully. It said "Radioactive Seeds." So she didn't know too much about radioactive seeds so she went to her father and she said, "Dad, what are these radioactive seeds?" He looked and he said, "Radioactive seeds? Wow! Where did you get that?" She said, "It washed up on shore." She looked at them and said, "It's lucky they are all wet because some of these could be dangerous. What are they used for?" He said, after looking over the box of seeds, "There are two kinds here. Some of these are very good. They are very beneficial and if we plant them we'll get flowers and vegetables that are far more beautiful and far larger and far more healthy than anything that we have ever eaten. However, there are

150

others here that are quite dangerous and when they dry out they will explode. So, let's quickly separate —— I'll show you how to tell the difference between the two." So they looked carefully over the seeds and they separated them out. They took those that were explosive and put them in one box and those that could grow into good fruit and flowers and vegetables into another. Then they took the box of those that could explode — they were still wet — and they got into their boat and they went out far, far into the ocean. They went a few miles out into the ocean. They went about ten miles out and there they dumped them overboard. They tied up the box with string and they then put a rock on the box — a very big rock — and they dumped the thing over so it went down to the bottom of the ocean. There it was safe from any kind of explosion.

The other seeds they took and they planted and out of them they got the most beautiful flowers. They got vegetables. The carrots, for instance, were very large and strong, and when they ate these carrots their sight was really very good, and then they had these very healthy spinach plants which when they ate made them very strong.

The lesson of that story is that when you have something that is a combination of good and bad things, what you have to do is separate out the good and the bad. Remove yourself from the bad qualities, the bad things, but make use of the good things. The end.

Therapist: Do you have anything to say about that story?
Patient: No.
Therapist: Did you enjoy it?
Patient: Yes.
Therapist: Okay. The end

In my story, I encouraged Carol to differentiate between the benevolent and the malevolent facets of her mother's personality. I suggested that she remove herself from that which is dangerous and involve herself with the gratifying elements.

Example 5

Paul, the eight-and-a-half-year-old boy with poor school performance in spite of high intelligence, presented a number of stories during the first few months of treatment in which various objects exhibited impotence in their ability to perform their various functions: birds and airplanes couldn't fly, cars couldn't drive, and ships couldn't sail. During the fourth month of treatment, Paul told this story:

Today my story is going to be about this piano chair that always wanted to fly and he decided that he could take a rubber band and put it around his head, put it to a car motor and it would turn his head and he would start flying like a helicopter. So he tried that but he didn't fly. So he cut out some paper wings and pasted them all around him and then he tried it. He flew a little bit — only an inch off the ground though, so he said, "If I could put more wings on I might go higher." So he took more paper and cardboard and pasted it on him and he did fly a little bit higher. Then he decided that if he could fly that same height but only in the air, he might be able to fly very far.

So he went on top of a cliff and by the side he turned on the car motor and went off the cliff. He started to fly but then he started falling and luckily he fell into a swimming pool. He said, "Well, I don't want to get my wings all messed up, so I'll go to the other side of the mountain and this time I'll take a parachute." So he used a parachute, but he still said, "If I want to fly I'll have to make an airplane." So he made the airplane and it flew pretty good.

One day he went to fly his airplane and he met this bird. The bird said, "I'll bet you that I can fly faster than your airplane cause your airplane is just a big box with a motor in it and wings," "Oh, well, I'll have you a race," said the piano chair. So he had a race with the bird but the bird won because he was made to be able to fly and the piano stool in the cardboard box with the motor on it wasn't made to fly.

The lesson of that story is that if you want to do something that you are not made to do you might not be able to do it.

Therapist: Can you tell me what was the main reason why the piano stool wanted to fly so badly in the first place?

Patient: Well, he couldn't run away because he had no feet and he hated to be sat on and so he wanted to fly away.
Therapist: I see. Okay. One other question I want to ask you. Was the bird a male or a female bird?
Patient: It was a male.
Therapist: Thank you.

The story reflects some degree of therapeutic progress in that the patient reveals not only strong attempts to do something about his feelings of impotence, but enjoys some success in this regard as well. However, the materials — paper, cardboard, and paste — which Paul uses in the construction of the helicopter — the vehicle for enhancing his self-assertion and self-esteem — certainly do not suggest strength or competence. Also, the main reason for building wings is to flee those who impose upon him, those whom he is helpless to fight. (The piano chair has no feet and it wants to fly away from those who sit on it.) The story has possible oedipal implications as well. The bird, a male bird I learned on post-story questioning, easily outflies the piano chair, further compromising the patient's feelings of adequacy. With this understanding of Paul's story, I related the following:

Once upon a time there was an old piano chair that always wanted to fly. So at first it took a rubberband and put it on its head and connected it up to a car motor. This piano chair wanted very much to learn how to fly, especially since there was a bird who lived nearby and this bird was a very good flier. He used to look up at that bird and say, "I wish that I could fly like that bird."
Well, anyway, first he got a rubberband and connected it to his head and then connected it to a car. Then he tried to make himself into a helicopter by connecting himself to the car motor. But that didn't work very well. Then he pasted paper wings on himself and first got an inch off the ground and then he put on more paper wings and flew higher and higher, but it still wasn't enough for him.
So then he went to the top of a cliff and he connected

himself to the car motor and he went off the cliff. Unfortunately that didn't work too well, but fortunately he fell into a swimming pool so he wasn't hurt.

Then he tried it with a parachute and that protected him a bit. Then finally he made an airplane and that worked pretty well. He used to fly around in his airplane and one day he met the same bird and the bird said to him, "Oh boy, some plane you have there. You can't fly too well." And he said, "I fly pretty well." The bird said, "Let's have a race." The piano chair said, "I'm not going to race you. I know that you'll beat me. You're a bird, you're older than I am, and you've been flying for a long time, but I know that when I get more experienced and I grow up, I'll be able to fly just as well as you. But I can fly just as well as other piano chairs who have made themselves airplanes — which was true. Some of the other piano chairs who had also made airplanes and were his own age — he was just as good as they were. And as the years went on he got more and more practice and he became as good as the bird. Then when he was grown up, the bird by that time was pretty old and he could even fly faster than the bird.

The lesson of that story is: there may be times in your life when you are not as good as people who are older and more experienced, but you will grow up and you will be just as good as they are if you work hard at it. The end.

Therapist: What did you think of that story?

Patient: Well, it was a pretty nice story because if the piano chair didn't have anybody else flying with him, like the other piano chairs, he might stop because nobody else might be doing it; and it might not be so much fun cause he couldn't have races or see who could go the highest or stuff like that.

Therapist: Yes, so he'd have races with friends, his equals, kids his own age, rather than trying to beat out older, more experienced things. Okay.

In my story I decided to concentrate on the oedipal theme. I attempted to lessen the inadequacy Paul felt when he compared himself to his father. Paul is discouraged from racing the bird at this time. The competition is unfair, and he can only be humiliated. I pointed out to him that whereas now he is not competent to compete with his father, as he grows older he will be. Training and practice are also encouraged to ensure that he will reach this goal.

Two weeks later, Paul presented this story:

Today my story is going to be about an apple in a tree in the back of the house. The apple never wanted to fall on the ground because when all his old friends fell on the ground he could hear them yelling because they hurt themselves when they fell. So whenever a big wind came the apple held tight on the branch.

One day he started to fall but he fell in the trunk of the tree because there was a big hole in there. When the squirrel who lived in the hole came back, he took the apple and placed it on the ground outside his home for food. And the apple said, "Well, I'm on the ground and I didn't fall, so I guess sometimes you are lucky."

So he started rolling around to the front of the house. There was another apple tree there. The apples in the front said, "How did you get up here? When you fell off the tree you must have got hurt." The apple said, "I started to fall, but the squirrel took me down the rest of the way." So the apples in the front of the yard said, "Well, why don't you go back to that squirrel and tell him to bring us down to his house." So the apple rolled back to the squirrel and said, "Mr. Squirrel, will you take my friends inside your house?" The squirrel said, "Okay." He ran to the front of the house and took all the apples to the back and then the big tree in the front had no apples. The squirrel said, "I'll take my axe and chop down the tree because there's not going to be anymore apples."

Therapist: This is the tree in front of the house?

Patient: Yes, and so the tree in the back of the house started losing their apples and so the squirrel chopped down that tree.

Therapist: Wait a minute. He chopped down two trees then?

Patient: Yes.

Therapist: The one in the front and the one in the back.

Patient: Yes.

155

Therapist: Why did he chop down the one in the back?

Patient: Because it had no more apples on it. The apples decided that they wanted more friends and so they took some old apple seeds and dug a hole and buried the seeds and a couple of years later there was a big tree and they had more friends.

One apple that the squirrel took down off the tree decided that if he could plant lots of trees he'd have more friends. So he planted a lot of trees. But the man that lived in the house didn't like apples very much so he went and raked them up and that one apple that didn't want to hurt himself got raked up and he was the first apple to hit the bottom of the trashcan. He got very hurt and so all the other apples said to him that he didn't get hurt the first time, but that he got hurt the second time. The apple said, "It's just pure luck. You can't make yourself do anything. You couldn't make yourself not get hurt. You could try not to get hurt but you couldn't stop yourself when you get hurt."

Therapist: Is that the end?

Patient: Yes.

Therapist: What is the lesson of your story?

Patient: That most things, like I guess when you are getting hurt, are just luck —— like maybe the next time you get hurt.

Therapist: Well, what happened after the apple was in the trashcan? What happened after that?

Patient: Well, all the apples were very crowded in there and they tried to get out but they couldn't.

Therapist: Well, what happened after that?

Patient: They stayed in there and all the other apples got rotten.

Therapist: Then what happened?

Patient: Until the man took them away.

Therapist: Where did he take them away?

Patient: He took them in his backyard and burned them.

Therapist: Including the one apple?

Patient: Uh. Huh.

Therapist: Okay.

When Paul was eighteen months old, his mother gave birth

to a girl who died two hours after birth. When the mother returned from the hospital, she told the patient about the baby's death but further discussion was discouraged thereafter.

The apple in the story represents, of course, the patient. The tree stands for his mother from whom he is fearful of separating: the apple hangs tenaciously onto the tree. The hole in the tree represents the mother's womb, and when he finally does fall off, he quickly returns to the warmth and protection of his mother's uterus. Finally, he does cut the umbilical cord through the intermediary of the squirrel, who represents a healthy, growth-oriented part of himself and is carefully placed on the ground rather than falling there and possibly being traumatized. Separation from mother is still a dangerous process, considering Paul's memory of his little sister, and it must be accomplished step by step. In order to desensitize himself to the dangers and traumas of the birth process, Paul must repeat it many times over — the squirrel helps all the other apples in similar fashion.

The cutting down of the trees may represent an expression of his hostility toward his mother for allowing his sister to die, or it may indicate his healthy desire to remove the womb altogether, in order to reduce his temptations to return to it. In either case, Paul quickly grows another tree with its implied potential for possessing another womb. This tree demonstrates its fecundity, thereby reassuring him that many apples can indeed survive the birth process. However, his initial fears that extra-uterine existence is most dangerous are finally realized when the farmer not so gently drops him into a trashcan where he rots and eventually gets burned.

The interpretation that the farmer represents the patient's father and that his traumatization at the father's hands is an oedipal manifestation is, I believe, a less productive interpretation than the theme of separation from his mother. Paul was at some level aware, as proved by his sister's experience, that separation was dangerous, that one could be completely destroyed by malevolent forces in the world.

As discussed in Joey's case earlier in this chapter, a story may reveal issues which date back to the earliest phases of a child's life. Although he has no conscious recollection of these experiences, they can nonetheless play a significant role in his behavior. Stories revealing such deeply repressed material may not be told until the middle phase of treatment because they may be too anxiety-provoking to be revealed before the child has had a chance to develop a genuinely trusting respect for the therapist. It is also during the middle phase that there is a greater likelihood that the therapist will appreciate their meaning because he has had more opportunity to gather background information.

With this understanding of Paul's story, I told the following story:

Once upon a time there was a little boy and he lived in a house and he used to sit and look out of the window. Outside in his backyard were apple trees and he used to watch what was going on with those apple trees. In one of the apple trees in a hole there lived a squirrel.

One day he was watching the apples and the apples would fall down as the wind would blow, and there was one apple up there who said, "Oh, oh, I don't want to fall down. I'm going to catch on to this tree. I'm going to hold on tight because if I fall down I'm gonna get hurt." The little boy heard the apple saying that, and he came out of the house and said, "Apple, you know, it isn't so frightening as you think it is. What's so terrible about falling down? It's only a few feet." The apple said, "Oh, I wish I could fall down into that hole." The boy said, "The time has come for you, apple, to grow up. You're a big apple now and when apples get big they fall off the tree and then they go and they plant and they give seeds out and grow new apple trees. That's how it is." "But I'm afraid I may get hurt," said the apple. The boy replied, "Look you're not going to get hurt. The ground is soft. It isn't as bad as you think."

Well, anyway, a wind came along and the apple fell off, and he hit the ground and he realized that the little boy was right —— that it wasn't as painful as he had thought.

Then the apple said to the boy, "Okay, you're right. I'll plant some of my seeds and grow new trees like I'm supposed to and that makes me feel very good because I feel useful. However, what I am afraid of is that some day the man who owns the house may pick me up in a barrel."

The little boy began thinking about what that apple said and he realized that the apple was right — that he can get picked up in a barrel. The apple said, "I'm afraid I'll get burned!" The little boy said, "Well, you're not going to get burned. It's very unlikely. I know the owner of this house and he's not going to burn apples. What he might do is eat them or make you into a very good apple pie and then you'll make everybody happy as they eat you."

However, the little boy began to get upset because he began to think, "Well, if it can happen to apples, maybe it could happen to me. Maybe people can take me away." So he spoke to his parents about it and they got him straight and they told him that although apples can be taken away and burned or eaten, little kids can't be. This kid was kind of scared because he thought kids, like apples, could be taken away at any time and be burned or carted away in garbage cans or thrown away or discarded. They corrected him on that and they told him that you can't get rid of kids that easily. You just can't dump a child. You can't just put him in an ashcan and cart him away. Well, that made him feel much better. That's the end of my story.

Do you know what the lessons of my story are? See if you can figure them out.

Patient: I can't figure it out.

Therapist: Well, what was one of the things that the boy thought was wrong?

Patient: Well, he thought that maybe someone could take him away.

Therapist: Was that a right idea or a wrong idea?

Patient: It was a wrong idea.

Therapist: Why?

Patient: Well, because maybe apples could because someone could eat them, but if you took a boy away you couldn't use the boy for much and anyway if you did take someone away, like a boy, you would be thrown in jail.

Therapist: You can't take a boy away. A boy cannot be taken away from his parents. The parents cannot get rid of a boy; that's the important thing. You just don't dump kids out. That's the first thing. The second thing is that it's not so bad to grow up and separate from your parents. The tree is like the parent of the apple. He was kind of afraid of separating and thought it would be painful, but these things often are not as painful as you think. And those are the two morals of my story. What did you think of that story?

Patient: I don't know.

Therapist: Did you like it?

Patient: Yes.

Therapist: What was the part you liked the most?

Patient: I liked the part where the apple is yelling, "I don't want to get off the tree."

Therapist: Uh-huh. And what did that apple learn?

Patient: He learned that some things aren't as bad as you think they might be.

Therapist: Right. Okay.

In my story, I attempted to communicate the message that Paul is not so fragile as he thinks, and that separation from his mother will not be as traumatic as he anticipates. The apple falls to the ground without the help of any squirrels and finds that it is in no way injured. I then attempted to impart to the patient the notion that human beings — unlike apples and new-born babies — are not helpless to control their fates. In addition, I tried to impress upon him the idea that human beings are treated with great respect and care and that they are not dumped or thrown away. This story, as well as the subsequent discussion, dealt with the patient's idea that his mother has the power and right to discard her babies at her whim. This idea was one of the sources of the anxiety which contributed to his symptoms.

Paul's story and his reaction to mine gave me the acute realization that the death of his sister was playing a significant role in his symptomatology. This, in turn, suggested a specific course of action toward alleviating this aspect of his difficuties.

A number of discussions ensued, between the patient and me, and between the patient and his parents, in which the whole subject of his sister's death was openly aired. Particular emphasis was placed on the mother's role — how she did not willfully cause the death, and how she did not have power over life and death, his or anyone else's. It was repeatedly emphasized that she could not discard her children at her whim. Such discussions proved to be most salutary and played a significant role in the alleviation of Paul's symptoms.

Example 6

Malcolm, the nine-year-old boy with angry outbursts and multiple fears, told this story during his fourth month in treatment:

Once there was a pen who was named BiC and he was a blue pen. He was a very sad pen because no one bought him at the store. They left him alone there on the shelf and kept putting more better big pens with him and he was still there, an old kind of big pen.
Therapist: Oh, they put a lot of big pens with him. Is that it?
Patient: And they were bigger and better each time.
Therapist: So people bought the other ones rather than him?
Patient: Yeah. First they put him with a batch because he was —— his batch was the year's thing. Then he began to get older as the others were brought out and no one wanted to buy him and so they kept on putting more better and bigger pens. The year he was put out his kind was the best big pen but no one wanted to buy him. He looked sort of strange. Then he looked old and all these newer, bigger pens were put out. He got very sad and thought all these pens were bigger and meaner each year and would beat him up. He was this small and the other pens were this big and this big compared to this small pen.
He tried to go away except he had no legs and so he

just stood there. One day there came another big pen that the people didn't like and the new pen said, "Don't mope and grope. Just walk away." "I have no legs," said the other pen. "You do now," said the second pen. She was a pen fairy. It had legs, wings, and a magic wand and a cloak and crown.

Then the other pen that had legs now walked away and then the big pens were very shy that he had legs and they didn't.

Therapist: What do you mean by shy?

Patient: That he had legs and they didn't

Therapist: Do you mean shy or some other word?

Patient: I mean some other word, I think.

Therapist: You mean jealous?

Patient: Yeah, jealous.

Therapist: Then what happened?

Patient: Then the little pen lived happily ever after.

Therapist: And the lesson?

Patient: Don't just mope and grope if no one is buying you and bigger and better pens are being put out. Just wait for a pen fairy to come and ask it to put legs on you and then you can walk away or just not pay any attention.

The story reveals Malcolm's feelings of inadequacy and unacceptability. No one wants to buy the pen which, of course, represents the patient himself. He magically solves his problem with a good fairy, a *deus ex machina* who provides him with assets — legs — which make him the envy of all the other pens, and which, at the same time, provides him with the means to leave the scene of his humiliations.

In a sense the story is typical of the early phase of treatment with its resort to the magic cure and its flight from confronting one's difficulties. Since, however, this story was told in the middle phase, my knowledge of the patient was greater, and I was able to introduce elements into my story which I would not have been able to earlier. Accordingly, this was the story I told in response:

Once upon a time there was a little pen called BiC.

He was blue and he was very sad because no one bought him at the store. The people who owned the store had him among big pens, but on the shelf there were other pens as well. There were larger pens, there were less expensive pens, and more expensive pens. But this BiC pen felt very sad and lonely. People just didn't buy him. They would buy some of the other big pens and this made him sad and lonely.

One day he said to a friend, "I wish that a fairy pen would come along here and magically give me legs so that I could walk and then everybody else would be jealous of me and then I'd have a much better time and I'd be happy." Well, the fellow whom he was speaking to said, "That can't happen. There's no such thing as magic. You are not going to accomplish anything by that. That's going to get you nowhere. There's no such thing as fairies; there's no such thing as magic and pens don't have legs and pens don't walk." He said, "Well, how can I get somebody to buy me then?" The other pen replied, "Apparently you are doing something wrong. You're doing something yourself which is interfering with people buying you. You must be doing something wrong." "Well, I don't know what it is," said BiC. The other pen said, "Well, let's ask around." So they asked another pen there who was quite a wise pen. He said, "Yes, you're doing something wrong. First of all, you don't keep your cap on straight. Secondly, you spin around and, thirdly, you sometimes let the ink spill out of you so when people try you they don't want to buy you. Who wants a pen that leaks? Who wants a pen whose cap isn't straight and who wants a pen that spins around? If you want to get people to buy you, you've got to be on your best behavior; you can't have your cap spin around and you can't have ink coming out. I'm going to refill you with some ink so you're full. Then next time someone comes you'd better stand at attention and you've got to look good and then you will be bought." Well, the pen didn't believe that advice. He thought it was just a lot of bunk. So he kept on his old ways of letting his cap fall off and letting ink drip and no one bought him. He was still sad and depressed and he still wished for the good fairy to come along.

After a while he spoke to the big pen again and the

big pen told him the same thing. He said, "Once you take my advice you will find that you'll probably be bought." Well, he decided that maybe the big pen knew what he was talking about, after all. So he kept his hat on straight and he stopped having his ink leak. He got another refill. The big pen said, "This is the last time I'm going to refill you." Lo and behold, it came to pass that someone bought him and he went home with that family and lived happily ever after.

And the lesson of that story is: if something is going on that is bothering you don't look for good fairies. There's no such thing as magic. See what you are doing that is making the situation worse and you then may make things better and live happily ever after. The end.

Therapist: Any comments you want to make about this story?

Patient: Very good.

Therapist: Okay. What was the part you liked the most?

Patient: The part when he was spinning and he was spilling his ink all over and his cap was on sideways.

Therapist: Okay. Very good.

In my story I introduced the notion that there are no magic cures, and that one has to apply oneself to solve one's problems. Because of my knowledge of Malcolm's difficulties, I was able to introduce specific problems of his which required rectification. The patient persistently defied authority, was a disciplinary problem in class, and was extremely messy in his personal habits. The pen in my story exhibits all of these behavior patterns and is thereby neglected. He initially ignores the advice of those who point out to him that these are the reasons for his rejection, and he continues to be ignored and rejected. It is only when he changes his ways that he becomes acceptable and desirable.

The story does not go into the issue of the sources of his malfunctioning and, therefore, might be considered in the "shape-up-young-man" category. This is certainly true, but it is nonetheless therapeutic. Analysis of the psychodynamic roots and therapy directed to the underlying causes are only two aspects of psychotherapy. Conscious control of one's symptoms also plays a role, as does confrontation with the effects of one's behavior. My story at this point emphasized these facets of the therapeutic process.

One week later, Malcolm told this story:

Once upon a time there was this piece of paper that was always scribbled on with stars and different kinds of marks. The boy that used the paper when he did his homework on this paper he always got his homework wrong. The teacher marked it wrong and he scribbled out the marks of wrongness and scribbled on checks and stars. This homework paper did not like the boy at all and let the boy have his consequences and it crumbled up by itself and went into the garbage, and then it went into a garbage truck and ——

Therapist: Wait a minute, he let the boy have —

Patient: His consequences.

Therapist: I'm not clear on that. What do you mean he let the boy have his consequences?

Patient: Because the boy was scribbling on him all the junk. So he crumbled himself up and threw himself in the garbage and the garbage men threw the garbage he was in into the garbage truck and he was torn apart. Then the boy began to get mad because he didn't like the consequences.

Therapist: What were the consequences?

Patient: His paper didn't want to see him anymore and he had to buy another paper.

A man came around and the boy asked him, "Why did my paper go away just because I was scribbling on it?" And the man said, "He didn't like your scribbles on him so he decided that you got to pay your consequences and that's why he's not here anymore."

Then the boy bought another piece of paper and he did not scribble on it this time. He took the marks as they were and he corrected himself if he got any wrong. Then he lived happily ever after in school without having to buy another piece of paper.

The lesson of this story is: if you want to pay the consequences you can, but if you don't want to, don't scribble on a piece of paper or do anything like that which is not right.

This story is a good example of the patient's incorporation into his story, at a symbolic level, of messages of mine presented in a previous story. In my previous story I had communicated the notion that one will suffer the consequences of one's transgressions: the pen was not purchased as long as it engaged in its various misbehaviors. In this story, the boy finds that his defaced homework paper is alienated by the boy's maltreatment, and the paper removes himself from the boy in order to avoid further mistreatment: "So he crumpled himself up and threw himself in the garbage . . . ."

Unlike the previous story, in which the problem is solved by a magic fairy, here a man, the therapist, confronts him with what he is doing. He is receptive to the advice, changes his ways, and lives "happily ever after."

It is evident here that my messages from the previous story were heard and incorporated. The child's story reveals his attempt to implement the new ideas in a constructive way. Such stories and fantasies reflecting the wish to utilize alternative adaptations often precede clinical change. The story also reveals the patient's deepening involvement with me. In it he elicits my advice, is receptive to it, and translates it into action.

With stories such as this, in which there are so many positive and healthy elements, it may be difficult for the therapist to create one that introduces further healthy adaptations. In this story, in spite of all its appropriateness, there is an underlying psychopathic element. The boy cheats and is only deterred by the desire to avoid the external consequences of his misbehavior. Nothing is said about guilt, which would be appropriate here. Accordingly, I told this story:

Once upon a time, a long time ago, there was a boy who used to do something that wasn't very nice. He was a kind of sneaky kid and when he would get a paper back from school that had wrong answers on it he would cross out the marks that said it was wrong and put in marks that said it was right. He would do this over and over again, but he was a boy that wasn't very happy. In fact, he was kind of a sad boy. He kept on doing this in school and he kept on being sad.

One day a man was passing and saw him and said, "Why are you so sad, boy?" He said, "I don't know." The man said, "Are you doing anything that would make you feel sad or bad about yourself?" He said, "No." "What about in school? Do you do anything in school which would make you feel bad about yourself?" The boy thought for a minute and the first thing that came into his mind was the cheating that he was doing and he said, "Well, there is something I'm doing. I don't know if that's the cause of it, but I must admit to you that when I get a wrong answer, I change the mark to a star or a plus." The man said, "Well, you know, there are two things wrong with that. First of all, when you do that you are not going to feel good about yourself because anyone who lies or cheats cannot but feel bad about himself and, secondly, you're not going to learn very much. The best thing you can do is what?" And the boy said —— what did the boy say?

Patient: What did you say first?

Therapist: Were you listening to what I was saying? Hhmmm?

Patient: Yes.

Therapist: You see, the boy told the man that he was cheating in school and the man said, "There are two reasons why you shouldn't do that: one, you'll feel bad about yourself and second, you are not going to learn because if you cheat and you just change the crosses to pluses then you are not going to really learn about your mistakes." So the man said, "The best thing you can do is what?"

Patient: Not cheat and take the marks as they are.

Therapist: If you do that what two things will happen?

Patient: You'll be a much happier boy.

Therapist: Because you'll not be ——

Patient: Cheating.

Therapist: You can only feel bad about yourself when you cheat. And what is the other thing that will happen?

Patient: You learn more.

Therapist: Right. The boy took that man's advice and it was true. He felt better about himself because he wasn't cheating, and he learned much more and he got far fewer wrong answers. Do you know the two lessons of that story?

Patient: No.

Therapist: Come on. Think about it. What are the two lessons? What are the two things that the boy learned?

Patient: The first thing he learned was that he'd have a much happier life when he didn't cheat, and the second thing he learned is that you learn more when you don't cheat.

Therapist: Right. The end.

In my story, I introduced the old dictum, "virtue is its own reward." He who is honest and diligent enjoys feelings of competence and accomplishment. He who transgresses may suffer external repercussions, but more important are the internal consequences — the guilt and the lowered self-esteem. In addition, there is a further practical reason for not cheating on examinations: one doesn't learn as much.

Although much of the therapist's work involves the alleviation of *inappropriate* guilt, there are times when it is necessary to instill *appropriate* guilt. All therapy involves the inculcation of the therapist's values. Even the most passive, classical psychoanalyst is continually imposing his own values on his patients. When he chooses to interrupt his patient — even to say ueh, or uh-huh — at that point he is communicating his agreement or disagreement, his acceptance or rejection. He hopes thereby to modify the patient's behavior in accordance with *his* ideas of right and wrong, healthy and sick. It is to be hoped that what the therapist inculcates is in the patient's best interests. The Mutual Storytelling Technique is another modality for such influence, and this story is an example of how it can be used in this capacity.

Example 7

Julie, a ten-year-old girl, whose parents were divorced,

entered treatment because of outbursts of rage against her mother, a chronic attitude of surliness, obsessive self-derogation, and an antagonistic attitude towards teachers and peers. In her fourth month of treatment, Julie told this story:

This story is about two different watermelons. Each of the watermelons knew that the watermelons that the farmer chose and sold to a person were the finest so they each argued about who or which one the farmer would pick. Soon it came time for the farmer to pick his crops, and he went to the watermelons first. "Shush," said the first one, "I can hear the farmer. Of course, he's going to pick me cause I'm so ripe and fresh. I don't have many seeds in me either." So the other watermelon also wanted to be picked by the farmer and the other watermelon was really ugly but you never know how somebody is inside. He was very ugly but he was good inside.

So the farmer soon came and looked at the watermelons. He looked at the first one who smiled boastfully at him. "Pick me," he whispered. So the ugly watermelon didn't say anything — just stood still like a good watermelon should. So the farmer knew which one to pick. He took the ugly one out of the ground and went back to the farmhouse. So the boastful watermelon was very angry because he hadn't been picked because he thought that he was the finest.

The moral of my story is: don't brag before you know what's going to happen.

Therapist: Anything else in your moral?

Patient: Uh.

Therapist: What about the ugly watermelon. Can you say anything about it?

Patient: Well, I think that he was happy that he was picked and he used to think that he was very ugly, but now he knew that he wasn't. But he was clean inside and the other watermelon was mean and everything like that.

Therapist: I see. You mean the one that looked nice was really mean?

Patient: Yeah.

The ugly watermelon is, of course, the patient who considers herself homely and compensates for this deficiency by being modest. The story has positive elements in that it reveals her appreciation that boasting is an alienating personality characteristic and that modesty can be an asset. Although boasting was not one of Julie's vices, modesty was certainly not one of her virtues. She was loud-mouthed and grumbled chronically. Accordingly, I told this story:

> Once upon a time there were two watermelons and they were in a patch. Each year at harvest time the farmer would come and he would pick the best watermelon. These watermelons were twins and they both looked quite good. Inside they were both quite good also. They were both quite friendly and happy inside and good people, and outside they both were quite beautiful. But there was one difference. The second watermelon, in spite of the fact that it was very beautiful at times for reasons unknown to the farmer, would snarl up its face; it would growl and complain. It was really good inside and a very friendly and nice person inside, but outside it was constantly complaining. It would constantly say, "Ah, the sun's too hot," or "There's not enough water around here," or "It's crowded around here with all these vegetables," or "It's so cold at night," or this complaint and that complaint, or "The forest around here isn't rich enough in food and all the animals come around here and they sit on me and they bother me."
>
> Well, the other watermelon wasn't one of these growling snarling complainers. Anyway, when the farmer came to chose which of the two watermelons he wished to take, which one do you think he chose?

Patient: The first one?

Therapist: Why?

Patient: Although they looked alike the first one was better inside and had a kinder heart.

Therapist: They both had kind hearts.

Patient: Well, the first one didn't complain and was satisfied.

Therapist: And the second one was the complainer. He kind of bugged and irritated the farmer. He said, "Number Two, I know that you have as good a heart as

Number One, but you are constantly bothering me with your constant complaints. For that reason, although your heart is as good as the other watermelon and you are as pretty as Number One, you bother me — you bug me — and for that reason I am going to chose Number One. Well, that year the second watermelon learned a lesson and then it made a resolution never to do that again. When the watermelon stopped it got a lot of friends. Although it never won the prize, it still lived fairly happily since it learned from its mistakes.

And the moral of that story is that people do judge you on your appearance. You may be good inside but if you are going to walk around and snarl all the time, people are not going to take to you. The end.

What do you think about that story?

Patient: It was interesting.

Therapist: Do you think it had anything to do with you?

Patient: No!

Therapist: Not in the least?

Patient: No!

Therapist: You are not like any of the watermelons in my story?

Patient: No!

Therapist: I thought there might be a slight resemblance?

Patient: No!

Therapist: Okay. The end.

In my story I attempted to direct Julie's attention to personality qualities which are more pertinent to her own problems. You may be "good" inside, but if you are obnoxious on the outside, you are going to miss out on many of the gratifications and rewards which the world has to offer. As the post-story discussion reveals, the patient would not admit that the story had anything to do with her. Such denial, however, did not necessarily mean that my message had not reached her. She was actively interested in my story and I had the feeling that at some level it had had an impact. Insisting that the child verbalize "insight" can often be anti-therapeutic. The child may consider admission of his defects a humiliation. It is not necessary to "rub his nose in them" or insist upon testimonials. If he alters his behavior in a salutary direction, this is real proof that the therapist has been heard.

Example 8

This case is presented in somewhat greater detail because it poignantly demonstrates the primary manifestation of the middle phase of therapy: the incorporation of the therapist's messages into the patient's subsequent stories. In this case, incorporation was at a deep level, and revealed itself in highly dramatic symbols.

Peter entered treatment at the age of six and one-half years, because of an excessive preoccupation with esoteric subjects, such as Egyptian history, obscure languages, and strange lands, and a fearfulness of sports and physical contact. He cried easily, exhibited very low frustration tolerance, and engaged in frequent power struggles with his mother. He had somatic complaints, including headaches and abdominal pain. He could not tolerate criticism and frequently lied. He did poor school work, even though he was highly intelligent. At school, too, Peter was in a constant battle with authority; he teased weaker boys and was picked on by stronger ones.

The boy had been adopted. The natural mother was a college student who lived in California but who gave birth to him in Hawaii. There, at five days of age, he was turned over to the adoptive parents, who had come for him from New York City. He was familiar with this background. When he was three years old, the adoptive mother gave birth to his brother, his only sibling. The mother, a very intelligent science writer, assertive, domineering, and intellectualized, was genuinely interested in the boy and made great efforts to cooperate in his treatment. The father, a public relations man, confined himself almost exclusively to intellectual endeavors with him, and was extremely passive in his relationship with his wife. Both parents were obsessive-compulsive in their character structures.

Peter was seen three times weekly; adjunctive work was done with the parents. During the first year, the boy was uncommunicative and denied all of the difficulties reported by his parents. He was highly intellectualized and severely restricted in his ability to express feelings. He would not create stories around any modality and so other therapeutic techniques were utilized.

Since geographical subjects were one of his main interests, much was learned of his psychodynamics through games of travel and discussions about various countries. Hawaii and Alaska, as states recently acquired and remote from the others, had lower status for Peter, just as the adopted child had. The cold Alaskan environment symbolized the home atmosphere created by his rigid mother and withdrawn father. Mountains were frequently a symbol for his mother, and he often depicted himself as an explorer. The stories of his expeditions provided vital information about his relationships with his parents.

At the beginning of the second year of his treatment, the patient was still unable to talk openly about his difficulties, to relate dreams, or directly analyze, but he did begin to tell stories with the tape recorder. About the middle of the second year, when he was eight years old, he related the following story:

It was a freezing cold morning at Point Barrow, Alaska, and the L.G.U. Expedition [surname initials of the patient and two friends] had begun. They had gone five hundred miles when they reached Mt. McKinley. They wondered how it would be to drill a hole through it but they then decided not to because they found out it would take them three months. So they climbed to the top in three weeks and down the rugged side in three weeks, so it took six weeks in all.

All at once the blizzard had struck. This was very serious because this blizzard was the blizzard of Nome, which is a city right on the point of the Bering Strait. The Bering Strait has a division which changes the property of the U.S.A. and the U.S.S.R. They decided to turn back and go towards the Yukon River. They had gone the other five hundred miles back. They were going back because they had found how high Mt. McKinley was and how rough.

They had taken photographs when they got back safely

173

to Kodiak Island. Many years later, Robert E. Peary had discovered the North Pole, but this expedition was to find out all about Mt. McKinley. So ever since, people have wondered how high, how long, and how rough is Mt. McKinley. The answer is that it was not even a quarter as rough as the moon; it was 1,270 feet high, and in width it was a quarter of a mile long.

The moral of this story is: don't depend on your eyes, but depend on the measurement of man.

The main purpose of this story was "to find out all about Mt. McKinley . . . how high, how long, and how rough." Temporarily consideration was given to drilling a hole through the mountain. These factors, plus his frequent use of the mountain to symbolize a breast or the mother, justifies the assumption that the story expressed Peter's attempt to move closer to his mother. But he was hesitant and ambivalent. He must get more information about her. In order to diminish his anxiety, he must first learn "how high, how long, and how rough" she is. His initial idea of achieving intimacy directly — by drilling a hole — seems too dangerous; he takes photographs, which are safer. The hostile and sexual elements implied by the drilling are, of course, obvious.

I viewed these considerations on Peter's part as a positive step, in that they revealed his desire to approach his mother. My story was geared to helping him gratify this wish:

The following year, the L.G.U. Expedition was doing some further exploratory work on mountains. This time their goal was to find out all about another mountain, Mt. Victoria [the name of the patient's mother].

It was a very, very cold winter, but they finally reached the foot of Mt. Victoria. Then they thought: What should they do? Should they drill a hole through it or should they go up the side? One of them said, "Mt. Victoria is a very beautiful structure and it would be a pity to drill holes through it or to destroy it in any way." One of the other members of the party said, "It's quicker. Who cares what it looks like? Who cares if we destroy it?" And someone else said, "No, no, it's not right to destroy it." Then someone else said, "Yeah, but if we go up on the outside, we might freeze." And the other one said, "I know that's a risk, but we can't go around destroying nature's beauty."

And so he won out and they agreed to follow the rule of the forest which was not to molest, not to harm or hurt the natural beauties. So they began to go up and it got colder and colder, and colder and colder; and they thought for sure that this was the end of it for them and they feared that they might even die on this cold mountain.

But then, lo and behold, Mother Nature provided for her children. There they saw a cave and they went into this cave, which protected them completely from winds and the cold. They found some dry wood and cut down wood from the nearby dead trees. They started a nice warm fire and cooked some of their provisions and warmed up. They felt much better about things.

The following day they made their dash to the peak and obtained all the measurements they had sought. They planted an American flag on top of that mountain. And next to the flag was a plaque with the names of the members of the expedition. The plaque said: "On this spot, on such and such a day, stood L. [the patient], G. and U. [the friends], the first men to reach the peak of Mt. Victoria. Such expedition was possible only because these men had respected the rule of the forest and had preserved and kept intact nature's beauties. Therefore they were protected by the mountain and the forest and by nature, and were made warm and comfortable during this cold winter."

The moral of this story is: if you will follow the rules of Mother Nature, you will find that Mother Nature will provide for you with warmth, happiness, and success.

The main objective of my story was to convey the idea that one may find a warm spot in the heart of even the coldest mother; if you cooperate with such a mother, you may derive the benefits of this warmth; if you attack her — drill a hole — she will be hurt and marred. The hostile rather than the sexual connotation of this act was selected for incorporation into my story, since I considered the hostile to be the more meaningful element for him at that time. The story attempted to help the boy see his mother more realistically — a cold person but nevertheless one who could give him some warmth and tenderness if he could only meet her half-way and let up on some of his attacks.

Two days later, extremely tense and rocking in his seat, he told the following story:

The characters in this story are Nuka, an Eskimo boy, Polea, an Eskimo girl, and Kimige, their Husky dog. [The names were made up by the patient.]

"The good season is here," said Nuka. Polea followed, close on to Nuka's footsteps. Even Kimige, the Husky dog, was happy that the winter was here. "The good season is here," he barked. Nuka said, "Please let us go back to the tent.' They had to pack because they were going to the seacoast because everything gets frozen inland, but not at the seacoast where it's warmer. Everybody else in the camp had left.

Nuka stuck his head into the tent and no one was packing. Nuka asked his father why they hadn't packed yet. He said. "Because we haven't found my bone knife." When they were all ready, the little grandmother sat on top of the sled. Kimige was the lead dog of both sleds.

Two days later they reached the seashore, where it was much warmer. The igloos looked like a big gigantic plate of marshmallows. When they had pitched their igloo, the family feasted on a fine buck, which they had shot on the way to the seashore. Kimige was the one who showed the children the buck in the herd of caribou, and Nuka had shot it.

The guests were excused early because they wanted to go outside and give some of their food to the dog Kimige for showing the children how to shoot the buck. The hardy heart of the animal was saved for Kimige too. But when it came time he would not eat it for he had eaten all the other food the guests had given him. So the next day, Kimige ate the heart. And that's it.

The moral of this story is: sometimes depend on other people to watch out for danger or food for the poor and sometimes keep a watch-eye out yourself.

This story incorporates some of the themes I introduced in my story the previous session and carries them further. The patient in his own story is represented by Kimige, the dog who eats outside the igloo. He is an outsider, like the adopted child. The patient is also symbolized by Nuka, who kills the buck — an appropriate symbol for the mother because of her assertive masculine traits and domineering rule over her passive husband. The father who loses his bone knife, that is, who is castrated, is present *qua* father. The little grandmother sitting on top of the sled is also the mother; as in the family, she is very much "on top" but, as presented here in an old, diminutive form, less of a threat to the patient. This is wishful thinking, for she appears later as the buck — a more accurate representation. The moral portrays Kimige as watching out for "danger or food for the poor," the two qualities the mother symbolizes to the patient. She is killed — the danger is removed — and her "hardy heart," the love that he was told lies deep within her, is orally incorporated, after some delay, into his empty food-craving stomach. *The warm cave in the cold mountain of the therapist's previous story and the buck's heart are the same.*

Peter has incorporated my suggestion that, within this cold mother, he may still find some warmth in her heart. Then, in primitive fashion, he rips her open and hungrily eats her heart. Pursuit of warmth is also symbolized by the journey from the cold inland regions to the warm seashore.

Peter greedily wants the heart all to himself, a situation at odds with the needs of the other members of the family, who also want some of mother's love. Furthermore, his appetite is too selective: he wants the choice meats, and leaves the rest to the others; he does not take the bad with the good. These two themes were selected for healthier resolutions in my next story:

> It was almost winter again, and Nuka and Polea were in their home in the middle of the old part of the land where they lived. They said to their parents, "It looks like it's time for us to go to the seashore; winter is coming and it's going to be very cold here." The father said, "Yes, that's how it is. Part of the time we live here, where it's very cold, and other times we live where it's warmer. And that's how

we lead our lives; sometimes we are comfortable and sometimes we aren't; we must take the bad with the good." And the children readily accepted that.

So they got into their sled, pulled by their Husky dog, Kimige, and off they went to the seashore. While on the way, what should they come across but a large herd of caribou and of course, the first one to detect the caribou was Kimige because he was a dog and had a very powerful sense of smell, and he could smell them long before anyone could smell them. And he could hear them long before anyone could hear them because he had very fine sharp ears. Well, he warned Nuka that the caribou were coming and that there was a large herd of them, and then Nuka put his ear to the ground and sure enough, he too heard the distant rumblings. And so, when they finally did come, Nuka was prepared and he killed one of the bucks.

Now, since night was falling, they decided to camp where they were. So they decided to eat the buck and Kimige said, "I should get the heart, the best part, because I was the first one to detect him." But Nuka said, "You may have been the first one to have detected him but it was I who killed him. I should get the heart." And they started to argue and then the father said — what do you think the father said?

Patient: Split it.

Therapist: Right! The father said, "Just as we live here where it is beautiful in the summer, and we have excellent weather and even flowers grow, and we have wonderful fish to eat, in the wintertime it gets pretty cold and we've got to go to the seashore where it's warmer. So we have to take the bad with the good. It's the same thing with this buck, now. There is no reason why one person should eat the heart and all the others have to eat the less desirable and less tasty meat. We have to split it and share and share alike because all worked together in killing that buck and we should all enjoy it."

So that's what they did; they split it up and everybody had on his plate some good parts and some poor parts. Then they were all well nourished, felt well, had a restful night and in the morning proceeded on their journey.

The moral of this story is: you must take the bad with the good; nothing in life is perfect and often, if you want to enjoy something, you have to take the bad things as well. Another moral is that often the good things must be shared.

In the following session, Peter did not wish to tell a story; he wanted me to tell him one. He was therefore told of Kimige who, when completely alone, tracked down and killed a buck all on his own and who therefore, all agreed, was entitled to eat the heart himself. To help the patient resolve his oedipal jealousy, he was given the hope that, when he was grown up and independent, no longer sharing mother's love with father and brother, he would be free to get a love of his own.

At the next session he told a story about Japanese pilots — representing himself — who planned to bomb and destroy Diamond Head Mountain in Hawaii — the mother — but then changed their minds. He presented this moral: "Don't try to destroy things that are beautiful to other countries and they won't try to destroy things that are beautiful to you."

These stories typify the sequences in Peter's therapy. Frequently a theme I introduced could be linked with one utilized by the patient in a subsequent story, confirming the theses that such communications are deeply felt, understood, and utilized.

5. THE LATE PHASE OF THERAPY

In the late phase of therapy a greater percentage of the stories are healthier than they are in earlier phases. Fewer neurotic adaptations are present, although backsliding is certainly seen. The child's stories show that many of the therapist's messages have been incorporated. This progress is reflected in the child's clinical behavior as well. The primary criterion, in fact, for determining whether a child is indeed in the late phase of treatment is *not* the nature of his stories, but the clinical picture. It is in the latter area that one can know with certainty whether the therapeutic approaches — of which the Mutual Storytelling Technique is only one — have been effective.

Pathological stories may be easier to identify than healthier ones. Louise Bates Ames[1] did an excellent study of the fantasies of 270 nursery school children, 135 boys and 135 girls. Analysis of the spontaneous stories they told, revealed that in children from two to five years of age the predominant theme for both sexes was that of *violence*. The number of stories revealing some kind of violence ranged from a low of 63 per cent for boys of two to a high of 88 per cent for boys of three and one-half. Among the 15 two-year-old boys (mean age 2.5), 60 per cent of the stories dealt with violence, and for the girls the figure was 68 per cent. Other themes in the two-year-old group were: food and eating — girls 27 per cent, boys 14 per cent; sleep — girls 28 per cent, boys 7 per cent; good and bad — girls 21 per cent, boys none; possible sibling rivalry — girls 28 per cent, boys 21 per cent; possible castration — girls none, boys 14 per cent; and reproduction — girls 7 per cent, boys none.

In their study, "Children Tell Stories," Pitcher and Prelinger[2] also attempted to learn about children's fantasies through their storytelling. One hundred and thirty-seven children (70 girls and 67 boys) ages two to five told 360 stories. Eight main themes were found: aggression, death, hurt or misfortune, morality, nutrition, dress, sociability, and crying. One or more of these eight themes could be found in each of the 360 stories. *Aggression* appeared most often — 124 times. Hurt or misfortune was the next most frequent theme, appearing 89 times.

I am not surprised that violence and aggression were the predominant themes found in these studies, for this has been my own observation as well. The child is constantly being told: "Don't do this," "You can't have that," and "Don't say such and such." Failure to comply with these admonitions causes the child to loose the affection, to a greater or lesser degree, of the most significant figures in his environment — the figures upon whom his very life depends. The child is thus exposed to multiple frustrations. The anger which inevitably results from these frustrations is generally not permitted full release. It must be suppressed, repressed, displaced, sublimated, or symbolically released. Its unbridled expression could bring about even further alienation and punitive responses from parents and other important authorities. I am not referring only to severely restrictive parents who cannot tolerate even minimal hostility. The most permissive parents continually thwart the child's primitive and natural impulses. Such children are still prevented from ingesting poisonous substances; walking, running, and climbing in dangerous places; inflicting significant physical harm on others; and wandering off alone. All children are sensitive to the loss of parental affection that the breaking of rules threatens. Repression of resentment, then, is ubiquitous. The child's life is, in a sense, a continual struggle to handle such frustrations and resentments. He is ever sharpening his discrimination between the hostilities he can express and those he cannot. He is ever perfecting his techniques for effectively dealing with his pent-up angers. The healthy balance is hard to maintain and it is constantly being tipped too far — either in the direction of dangerous release or in that of pathological repression.

In interpreting the child's story, then, the expression of hostility may be a poor criterion for differentiating the healthy from the pathological story. When most morbid, with rotting bodies and putrid blood, for example, it is easy to designate the story pathological. Too many non-hostility stories, however, too many "sunny skies" and "sweet-smelling flowers," imply denial and repression. The normal and healthy child tells occasional stories which reveal maladaptation — especially around the issue of hostility.

With regard to determining a patient's position in treatment, the story is similar to the dream. As a patient improves, his dreams are healthier. Although in the late phase of treatment there are fewer pathological dreams, the patient still presents many with inappropriate adjustments and neurotic elements. Even the termination dream (when the therapist is lucky enough to get one), which suggests that treatment is ready to end, relates primarily to treatment and only secondarily to freedom from maladjustment. There will still be residual difficulties and unresolved problems for the continuing dream work to handle. Dream work is never done — a statement which also applies to the freely-fantasied story.

The stories in the late, or pre-termination, phase are basically free of significant neurotic conflicts and manifest many of the therapeutic communications imparted by the therapist throughout the earlier stages of treatment. In this phase, the "finishing touches" are put on; minor adjustments are made; and further "tailoring" may still be indicated. The overly submissive child, or one with too strong a superego, may go too far in the healthy direction and may have to be "loosened-up." In some, the healthy adaptations have essentially been made but the child may still be somewhat uncomfortable with them. He needs further desensitization, reassurance, and anxiety-alleviation. In this phase, more than in preceding phases, the child may have reached the point where he can directly analyze his story, as he would a dream.

The following stories demonstrate the various aspects of the late phase and show the kinds of stories I tell in response to a child's healthy story. I also give examples of inappropriate reactions on my part, as well as deteriorated therapeutic situations. It was often in this phase, after numerous attempts to salvage therapy, that my efforts finally proved futile. It is in such periods of frustration and disappointment that the therapist's countertransferential reactions are most likely to manifest themselves.

Example 1

Joey, the seven-year-old boy with enuresis, nightmares, chronic anxiety, and feelings of inadequacy, told this story during his thirteenth month of treatment:

> Once upon a time there was an ape and all the other apes used to call him: "You big human being; you big fat human being." He got tired of being teased all the time and so one day he teased them back because he really got mad that time and he just thought of it. They said, "What did you say?" Then they started to cry and went home after he teased them back.
>
> He was real happy and he told his mother. His mother was very proud of him.
>
> The next day that they teased him again —— well, early in the morning he was sort of sick and by mistake, just as he was about to tease them back, he vomited on them and it went in their mouths.
>
> From now on everybody likes the primates.
>
> *Therapist:* Now why do they like the primates?
>
> *Patient:* Well, they sort of feel sorry for the primates because when a primate makes a sad face they always say, "Ah, poor, poor monkey or poor poor chimp."
>
> *Therapist:* Well, what has this got to do with your story? I don't understand.
>
> *Patient:* Because all of them got vomit in their mouths.
>
> *Therapist:* So why should people like them if they have vomit in their mouths?
>
> *Patient:* I mean feel sorry for them.
>
> *Therapist:* Now everyone likes and feels sorry for the primates.
>
> *Patient:* Well, some people like them — not all the people

— but practically everybody feels sorry for them when they make a sad face.

Therapist: Because ——

Patient: They all have vomit in their mouths.

Therapist: And that's why people feel sorry for them?

Patient: Yeah because they make a sad face. And the moral of that story is: if people tease you, tease back and it's only a coincidence if you vomit on them.

The story was told soon after Joey had made a major clinical breakthrough. He had been quite repressed in expressing anger toward his father, and after months of therapeutic work, he had finally gotten up enough courage to express his criticisms. The father responded with sympathetic understanding and made an attempt to implement the child's requests. The patient's *experience* that his self-assertion and expression of resentment was not followed by vindictive punitive measures, but led rather to constructive utilization of his requests, was salubrious.

This story shows evidence, in his fantasy life, of similar changes. In it he asserts himself, responds in kind to his teasers, and does not let himself be taken advantage of. The recipients of his retaliatory invective go home to their mothers in disgrace. There is, however, definite ambivalence over full expression of his hostility. He vomits on his taunters because he was "sort of sick." The implication is that were he to have voluntarily vomited there would have been some kind of retribution. Since the vomiting was not his fault, he cannot be too severely punished for it. In the moral as well, he takes care to point out that "it's only a coincidence if you vomit on them." Joey is getting there, but he needs more encouragement in fully expressing his anger without fearing repercussions. With this goal in mind, I told the following story:

Once upon a time there was an ape and he lived with all the other apes. The other apes used to call him names and tease him. They would pick on him. Sometimes they would even call him names like, "You're a big fat human

184

being." Well, at first, this ape decided that the best way to handle that was just to ignore them, but then he didn't feel good inside when he ignored them. He felt ashamed of himself and he felt small. He wasn't proud of the way he was handling things.

Then he decided one day that he wasn't going to let them take advantage of him. No siree. So what he did was that the next time they came along and teased him, he teased them back and he teased them back hard. They ran away and started to cry. Then he felt good about himself because he had stood up for his rights and he had not let them take advantage of him.

Well, the next day they came back and started to pick on him. The first thing they did was to call him names. So he called them names back. But they didn't stop at that point; they decided to try something else. Suddenly one of them went over and hit him in the belly very hard. Well, when someone did that the ape suddenly vomited because when they hit him in the belly up came the vomit. He had just eaten a big meal and the vomit went all over those other guys. Well, this ape said, "You deserve what you got." They said, "Aren't you ashamed of yourself? Isn't that a terrible thing you did? You vomited on us." He said, "I'm not ashamed of myself one minute. In fact, I'm glad I vomited on you. You deserve every speck of that vomit."
Patient: "I'm glad I vomited!"
Therapist: "I'm glad I vomited on you." Right. "Every speck of that vomit." They got vomit on their eyes; they couldn't open their eyes. *Ick!* They got vomit in their nose and it stunk. They got vomit on their mouths — *ick* — and they had to taste the vomit and they got vomit in their ears and it plugged up their ears so they couldn't hear. They got vomit on their clothes. That served those apes a lesson. The first ape who vomited was glad that it happened and he said, "That will teach you guys to stay away from me." They said, "Aren't you a little bit sorry that you vomited on us?" He said, "No, not at all. Why should I be sorry? You guys punched me in the stomach and you got what you deserved."

Well, after that they respected him much more.
Patient: So would I.

Therapist: Right. Of course. They liked him much more and they then not only did not pick on him, but they also respected him more and played with him nicely. And the lesson of that story is what?

Patient: Vomit on people.

Therapist: If they deserve it. It's not so terrible. If somebody picks on you or teases you, tease him back. If somebody does something worse to you ——

Patient: Vomit on them!

Therapist: Well, if they do something that is terrible the vomiting on them is certainly one of the things you can do to get them back. The end.

In my story, the ape not only guiltlessly vomits on his provocateurs, but relishes his retaliation. The ape does not, in bully-like fashion, vomit on the innocent; he does so only in response to provocation. The attacker brings the vomiting down on himself. The barrage of vomit is a direct response to the blow to the abdomen. The attacker truly suffers the consequences of his misbehavior; he brings about his own misfortune. My elaboration of the vomiting incident, with the detailing of the effects, was designed to sweep up the patient emotionally in my story; to catalyze with humor his indentification with the ape who vents his full rage on his tormentors. Such involvement may require the therapist to use the most primitive, and often inane, kinds of humor, but it is a valuable contribution to his story and significantly enhances its therapeutic efficacy. Joey's verbalizations of his absorption in my story were recorded — "I'm glad I vomited!" and "Vomit on them!" Not recorded were his facial expressions of gleeful enthusiasm and rapture as I elaborated on the ape's behavior. I was communicating with Joey at a level that was causing every cell in his body to respond. In such states of resonance, the most meaningful kinds of therapeutic experiences occur.

Example 2

Ronald, the ten-year-old boy with severe negativistic behavior, violent rage outbursts, and marked defiance of authority, told this story during his ninth month of treatment:

Once upon a time there lived a KCH and he had a wife named FCKH. Now KCH and FCKH had a son named PPP. They also had another son, who was P's brother named HHH, like a breath. K, F, P and H were a happy family until one day they had a baby girl named SHCKHK. You can call her S. But when S was only one year old she was making so much trouble for the family and by that time she was a smart girl; you see, she knew better by then. She was a very intelligent girl, but she kept making so much trouble for her family that they wanted to kick her out, you know, when she was always misbehaving. After a while they couldn't even believe a thing she said or nothing was right. She was a fink.

So after that, I guess, they went to a child psychotherapist named Richard A. Gardner and he told them what to do.

Therapist: What did he tell them to do?

Patient: Oh, he told them what to do. Well, I can't think clear 'cause I——

Therapist: Well, what did he tell them to do?

Patient: First of all, he started out by telling her that if she didn't behave the whole family would break up and she started crying. Then she tried and after a while they just got along together and then K, F, P, H, and S were so happy that when they got a new baby —— another baby girl called TSK; I'll say T —— and when they also got a baby they were happy and even when they got a dog named RITZ —— they lived happily ever after.

The moral of the story is that if you try hard enough, you can do almost anything.

Therapist: And this is shown in the story by?

Patient: S's reforming. Right?

Therapist: Okay.

In spite of nine months of treatment, Ronald continued to have severe behavior problems. His outbursts of defiant rage against his parents were fierce and frequent. In his sessions, most of the stories that he told were of the resistance type. This story was certainly in that category. The letters representing the various characters were not meant to be initials; Ronald ostensibly chose the letters at random and denied their having any specific meaning. It is obvious, however, that some of the names are thinly disguised profanities. Regarding the mother's name, FCKH, little imagination is required to surmise what his basic feelings toward her are. Both the sexual and the hostile elements are pointedly revealed in this name. The son, PPP, who represents the patient — an only child — has obvious urinary connotations and reveals the patient's basic feelings about himself — he is an excretion, a waste product, someone worthy only of being flushed down the toilet. The siblings, HHH, SHCKHK, and TSK all represent, I believe, facets of the patient's personality. HHH is described as being "like a breath." Perhaps this refers to the anxiety which the mother's subdued anger and tense control produced in the patient. Possibly it relates to his feelings that his parents would prefer that he be invisible, that he evaporate. The SHCKHK is close enough to "schmuck" — the Yiddish equivalent of the English vulgarism, "prick" — to warrant the interpretation that it stands for his feeling that he is basically stupid. SHCKHK's behavior is identical to the patient's. She is "intelligent," "she kept making so much trouble for the family that they wanted to kick her out;" "she was always misbehaving;" "they couldn't even believe a thing she said;" and lastly, "She was a fink." The alter ego TSK suggests, "Tsk, Tsk," that is, "How unfortunate, how sad" he is. The father's name, KCH, does not suggest any obvious interpretation to me.

The patient would have ended the story at the point where Dr. Gardner tells the family what to do. No information is given as to what the specific recommendations were, and the implication is that a quick cure was effected. The story would have ended there; he would have satisfied my request that he tell a story; he would have gotten me "off his back;" but there would have been no insight, no working-through, and certainly nothing of therapeutic value. To break through this resistance, I urged him to describe exactly what Dr. Gardner suggested. The recommended cure involved evoking the child's guilt — "if she didn't behave the whole family would break up" — which fostered a resolution to stop misbehaving and to "reform." The "How-can-you-do-this-to-your-family" and "I-promise-never-to-do-it-again" approaches can only produce specious changes and clearly serve the forces of repression and resistance. They are antithetical to the treatment process; they foster additional inappropriate guilt; they encourage duplicity and, therefore, only deepen the patient's problems.

With these considerations in mind, I told this story:

Once upon a time there was a family. The father's name was KCH. I'll just give the first letters of the parents' names. The father's name was K, the mother's name was F, and there were two sons named P and H. Now they were not too happy a family. This family was not particularly happy even before they had any children. After they had a child they were even less happy. They had a little girl and her name was S and she was always in trouble. She was trouble of all kinds and they reached the point where they wanted to kick her out.

They went to this doctor, Richard Gardner, who was a child psychiatrist —— Richard A. Gardner. Anyway, the mother said, "Do you think if we tell her that if she doesn't stop doing what she's doing it's going to break up the family, that will get her to stop?" Dr. Gardner said, "No, I don't think so. Not only will this make her feel guilty but it doesn't get to the roots of the problem as to why she is being so bad. She's being bad because she's angry about things going on in the family. The thing that we have to do is to find out what she's angry about." So he told stories with her and she drew pictures and things, and through these things she learned about her problems. What do you think she learned as to why she was so angry?

Patient: I don't know. I'm not a psychiatrist. You are.

Therapist: Well, he learned that she was very angry at her mother for many things and once she learned what she was angry about, she told her mother. Then they were able to change some of those things and then she wasn't as angry and things were much better.

The moral of that story is: if you want to change

your behavior, you have to try to find out what you are angry about. You just can't change it by promising you are going to change it. The end.

This story typifies what I call the "anti-resistance story." It directs itself primarily, if not exclusively, to the resistance elements in the child's story. Whatever else of psychodynamic importance there may be in the child's story, if the resistance elements are significant, they should be worked with first. This is a well-proven psychoanalytic truth. Insights are sterile if they are gained in a setting where the patient, for whatever reason, is basically uncommitted to their explication.

In my story, I directly state that reform through guilt evocation will worsen the child's difficulties. I suggest inquiry into the problems. I was safe in introducing the anger issue as significant, not only because the names of the figures in the story suggested it, but also because the clinical situation showed that it was the central problem. My attempt to elicit from the patient specific statements regarding what the child in my story might have been angry at was met with a cement wall of resistance: "I don't know. I'm not a psychiatrist. You are." With so much resistance, there was little point to my having provided specific answers myself; Ronald's unreceptivity was such that he would not have "heard." I accordingly reiterated the basic principle that expression of anger, rather than its repression, can be useful. As I was talking, however, I had no feeling whatever that I was "getting through."

Four months later, Ronald told this story:

There was a little boy named Oaf and there was a girl named Loaf. There was a mother named Poaf and there was a father named Shoaf. Now Oaf, Loaf, Poaf, and Shoaf were all in the same family and they loved each other and everything and all that jazz and all that stuff. That's the end of my story.
Therapist: That's the most exciting story I ever heard. I'll give you one million dollars for it.
Patient: You got it. And so one day this boy named Story

190

came along and he hated stories and he didn't like his name. And one day he met a doctor named Richard A. Gardner who was taking care of them —— just in case the Oaf, Loaf, Poaf, and Shoaf family had any arguments. He took care of them. He was like a family psychiatrist but he made it that they hardly needed him. He didn't like the idea of this.

Therapist: He didn't like what idea?

Patient: Of this Richard A. Gardner guy helping all these people. He didn't like hearing stories, he hated his name and he hated everything. He was a bigot and everything and so he went around and he killed all the psychiatrists. He killed this Richard A. Gardner and he spent his life in jail for murder. And that's the end of my story. I know what that means. I just said the first thing that came into my mind.

Therapist: What does it mean?

Patient: I don't know. It means I feel like murdering you.

Therapist: Why should you feel like murdering me?

Patient: I don't know. I belong in a looney bin. Ha, ha, ha. That's the end of my story.

Therapist: Why should you want to murder me?

Patient: I belong in a looney bin. Ha, ha.

Therapist: No. It sounds to me like you may be angry at me about something. What might you be angry at me about?

Patient: Don't ask me, brother.

Therapist: Come on, tell me why you should be angry at me.

Patient: Ask your mother, brother.

Therapist: It sounds like you're angry at me about something. What might it be?

Patient: What would I be angry at you for?

Therapist: That story shows that you are kind of angry at me for something.

Patient: If you can't take that for a story, you can't take any others because that's the only one I have in mind. I just don't feel like a story today.

Therapist: Why didn't you tell me you don't feel like a story? Why do you have to kill me in your story? See, my advice to you is that if you don't want to tell a story, you don't get angry at me and kill me in a story. Just tell me you don't want to tell a story today and we'll do something else.

Patient: I don't know why. I just said the first thing that came to my mind.

Therapist: Doesn't it sound like you are angry at me because I asked you to tell a story? Huh? You see, you know what my point is?

Patient: Yeah.

Therapist: What's my point?

Patient: I shouldn't have said it in the first place.

Therapist: Yes. You should have said to me that you really don't want to tell a story, rather than getting angry and then just telling a story and killing me.

Patient: Okay. I want to say something that I said on my tape.

Therapist: What's that?

Patient: Get ready. Don't make any noise. Okay? (Makes loud noise.) And now DG has a story to say.

Both of Ronald's stories are good examples of resistance stories. In the first, he essentially states: once there was a family. They loved each other. The end. In the second, he kills me so that he doesn't have to tell any more stories.

It is clear that my general attitude toward Ronald was one of irritation and exasperation. His resistances were extreme. Meaningful communication was almost impossible. He involved himself in each therapeutic modality for the purpose of thwarting me. He was told that he was free to play with anything he wished, and could do anything, within reason, with any of the materials in the playroom. He could talk if he wished, but he didn't have to. Nevertheless, whatever he chose to involve himself with, he attempted to involve me in a way that would be irritating. If he decided to have a catch with a ball, he would throw it hard and aim for my head. He ignored me when I said I would stop playing if he continued trying to hurt me. Inquiry as to why he wanted to hurt me would have been ludicrous, so defended was he. I would therefore discontinue the game when he got too rough. When he chose to play games like checkers and cards, he would openly cheat, try to change the rules in the middle of the game, and engage in other maneuvers which would ultimately bring about a deterioration of the game. Direct expression of the irritation I felt seemed only to encourage further provocations. As can be seen from this example, Ronald used the storytelling in the same way.

Following the first story, I let the patient know that I would not permit him to dupe me. He chose to play the game, and immediately mocked its intent. I responded to his mockery with sarcasm: "That's the most exciting story I ever heard. I'll give you a million dollars for it." There are times in treatment when sarcasm on the therapist's part is indicated; judiciously utilized, it can enhance the efficacy of the therapist's communications. It can also serve as a vehicle for the release of the therapist's irritation (hopefully appropriate). My comment is also an example of one of the ways I respond when a child tells a story that is stereotyped, short, or otherwise devoid of significant psychodynamic material. I tell the child that the sponsors of the television program certainly aren't going to spend very much money for such a short story, or that I don't believe the audience is going to find the story very interesting. I encourage him to try again because I know he can do better.

The therapist should, of course, try to prevent situations deteriorating to the point where he becomes angered, but in this case I seemed to have little choice. The only way to predictably avoid being provoked by Ronald was to refuse to involve myself at all with him. This, of course, would have made his visits meaningless. What I did was to permit my involvement to the point of mild irritation and then try to use the situation in a therapeutic way. This usually involved expressing my resentment, for the purpose of extracting myself from the irritating situation as well as confronting the child with the effects of his behavior. My hope was that the child, too, would learn to handle his frustrations and resentments in a similar way, rather than let them build up to explosive force. For example, with Ronald I would say: "Well, that's the end of the ball game. I'm not going to stand here and let you throw balls at my head. What would you like to do instead?" In the context of the therapeutic interchange, the child is provided with a living example of the kind of response I am trying to get him to utilize.

In response to my displeasure over his first "story" Ronald told another. In the second, he revealed the murderous rage he felt toward me. I knew quite well that the hostility was displaced from his parents, but he was nowhere near the point where he could possibly deal with it. To a minor degree he was angry at me for "having" to tell a story. In actuality, he was not pressured into telling stories. He was told that he could do anything he wanted in the playroom. His anger toward me was also related to the frustration he felt when I would not let myself be used as a scapegoat. If Ronald had had his way, he would have used all his session time for this purpose. On the one hand, he wanted to tell a story or he would not have voluntarily gone over to the tape recorder and told one. His main purpose, however, in doing so was to utilize it as a weapon against me. On the other hand, he did not wish to reveal himself in his stories. He was not ready to deal with his core problem of rage toward his parents, and he was sorry that he had started the game because his first specious story was unsuccessful in deceiving me. His anger then, at that point, related to his frustration over this inner conflict. Had Ronald not gone to the tape recorder he would not have been so angry. When he said after some coaxing that he didn't want to tell a story in the first place, I used this as the central focus for the ensuing discussion. I tried to get him to see, in a situation in which he was presently involved, that asserting oneself can help avoid frustration. I gave him the message that he would probably not have wished to kill me if he had chosen not to go to the tape recorder in the first place. Furthermore, if I had coerced him to use it, it behoved him to assert himself and refuse. He would not then have wished to murder me or express his resentment in other ways such as insults: "Don't ask me, brother," "Ask your mother, brother," and "Now DG (Dick Gardner) has a story." The interchange also reveals the terrible feelings of self-loathing he feels over his rage. He refers to himself as a "looney," a "bigot," and as someone who " hates his name."

In discussing the telling or not-telling of a story, I hoped to impart to Ronald a message that might serve him in good stead with his parents — the knowledge that hostility directed at the source of provocation is preferable to displacement or repression. As can be seen from Ronald's reactions, I did not get very far with him. In the hope that the same communication, woven into my story, might "reach him," I related the following:

Once upon a time there was a boy and his name was Warren X. This boy Warren X was going to a doctor and this doctor's name was Richard Alan Gardner, M.D. He came in and the first ten minutes were spent with his mother. Then he went over to the tape recorder in order to tell a story. Now he really didn't want to tell a story. He didn't want to tell a story but he didn't say to Dr. Gardner, "I don't want to tell a story." What he did was first he made up a nonsense story and then he made up a story in which a boy named Story killed Dr. Gardner and he then realized that he would have been better off telling Dr. Gardner ——

Patient: I did not. I think I'm going to redo what I did.

Therapist: Let me finish my story. As I was saying, he then realized that he would have been better off telling Dr. Gardner: "I don't want to tell a story" rather than getting so angry inside that he had to make up a story in which he killed Dr. Gardner.

The moral of that story is that if you are angry about something, tell the person so maybe you won't have to do the thing that you don't want to. What do you think of that story?

Patient: (Makes noise and laughs.)

Therapist: Okay. The end.

Again, my efforts were in vain. Ronald's resistance was too great. He responded only with derisive laughter.

As is obvious, these interchanges reflect a deteriorated therapeutic situation. About two months later I told the parents, in the presence of the child, that I did not feel that I was getting anywhere in treatment and that if things did not improve after three months more, I would recommend discontinuation of work with me and consideration of transfer to another therapist. Three months later, with no significant change, therapy was terminated. The parents chose not to try again with someone else.

Some might consider my anger inappropriate, a neurotic manifestation. I believe that such responses can be used in the service of therapeutic goals. Whether my reactions were neurotic or not, the proper course was to suggest that Ronald try another therapist. My efforts had failed. We cannot be all things to all people. We cannot establish rapport with every patient who comes our way; each of us has his own personality — it cannot possibly attract everyone. Every therapist has residual neurotic patterns and inappropriate responses no matter how many years of analysis he has undergone. These inevitably appear and impede work with patients. The prudent therapist, as his experience increases, gradually comes to recognize the kinds of patients with whom he gets into difficulty, and does not treat them. To say to a patient or parent: "I'm sorry, but I cannot offer you treatment. My experience has been that I, personally, do not do well treating this type of problem. I can, however, refer you to another doctor whose experiences have been better," does not alienate most people but rather invokes their gratitude and respect. In spite of the therapist's best efforts to "screen out" those with whom experience has shown he works poorly, he sometimes finds himself in the situation described in this sequence. It then behooves him to recommend another therapist.

Example 3

Steve, the eight-year-old boy with disciplinary problems, presented this story in the latter phase of his therapy:

Today my story is about the happy cat and the sad mice. Once upon a time there lived a poor old peddler who had a cat and some mice. But the cat felt proud of himself because he could go fast and was bigger than the mice. He was apt to brag a lot and thought himself the best person in the house all because he was a cat. He was very happy.

Now the mice were sad at the thought of being so small and being caught in a mousetrap all the time. They wished something good would happen like the cat would grow as small as a marble. They weren't happy at all.

One day an angel came and they asked the angel, "Please help us. We just want to be even with the cat." So the angel said, "I'm sorry. I have no power. Animals are made the way their master made them. You shouldn't be so sad moping about in your happy life. You are better than the cats yourself. You are smaller and cannot be caught as easily as cats can. You should not be moping about all because of your size. Your size does not prove anything about you. It is about your skill and niceness. You mice are nice even though you get caught in mousetraps and there are people bigger than you. You should be happy about yourself."

So some of the mice did this and they found out that soon the cat got tired of the mouse and left them alone. So the mice were very happy and they lived happily ever after.

Moral: you should not be sad about people bigger than you are. You have something better to do too.

The mice represent the patient who feels himself small and inadequate in comparison to adults who are symbolized by the cat. To change their lot, the angel is brought in, but he replies: "I have no power." The angel, who in previous stories magically solved all problems, is now impotent. Steve has heard my message that there are no magic cures, and in this story he is accustoming himself to this painful realization. The angel does, however, give the mice some good advice about accepting themselves the way they are with both their assets and their liabilities. This, too, is a healthy thing for Steve to be reminding himself of; especially since he had in the past been filled with feelings of self-loathing.

The story is typical of the late phase. One recognizes the remains of old problems still not completely worked out. Steve needs the angel for advice; he still has some doubts about himself; but the adaptations are essentially healthy. Accordingly, I told this story:

Once upon a time there was a cat and some sad mice and the cat was much bigger than the mice and because of this the mice felt very sad. They used to mope around a lot being very sad and they said to themselves: "What can we do about this? He's so much bigger. He's so much faster." One mouse said: "Maybe there will be an angel who might come down from heaven and he could give us some advice." A second mouse said: "There are no angels. There's no such thing as an angel. Angels are something that exist in the imagination of people and animals. There's no such thing as an angel." Well, the first mouse said: "How then can we get advice?" The second mouse said: "We have to figure it out ourselves. Now what can we do? That's the problem here." Another one said: "Well, we could wish we were big as cats." The second one said: "There are no mice as big as cats. A mouse is the size of a mouse and a cat is the size of a cat. The best thing we can do for ourselves is to do mouse things and not waste our time moping around and hoping and praying that we'll become as big as cats because we never will." Another one said: "Yes, that's right. That's a good idea. It's kind of stupid just to mope around and hope that we'll become cats. We'll never become cats."

And so they decided to do more mouse things and mouse games and when they did that they felt much better about themselves and were no longer sad.

The lesson of that story is 1) there are no angels and 2) if something is bothering you, try to figure out for yourself what the solution is. The end.

In my story I emphasized that there are *no angels at all*. The patient's angel is unable to *do* anything although he still provides the mice with advice. In my story, I go one step further and stress their non-existence. Self-reliance and self-analysis are encouraged instead. The mice's situation is seen accurately, and appropriate accommodations are made.

Steve's story probably has oedipal themes as well. The cat represents the patient's father and the mice's dissatisfaction with their size is a symbolic representation of oedipal jealousy. I considered this theme, in a sense, to be less meaningful than the question of magical solutions. The oedipal issue might be deeper and more basic here, but it is also more remote. The Mutual Storytelling Technique is most effective when it directs itself to those issues which are closest to the child's conscious awareness. Had I wished to direct my attention to the oedipal theme, I would have told a story about mice who envied their father's strength and tried to vie with him for his adult prerogatives. They would come to see the futility of this and focus rather on the gratifications of childhood. In addition, they would realize that some day they would grow up to be big mice and, if they worked hard, they would enjoy all the gratifications of adulthood.

Eleven days later, Steve told this story:

Once upon a time there were some trees and some rain. The trees bragged about their colors being very beautiful and the rain was very depressed. He'd always pray every time for angels. One day a wise cloud asked him, "Well, what are you doing?" He said, "I'm hoping angels will come and help me from those trees." His friend said, "Sorry, there are no angels. I just have to tell him about that. There are no angels. Stop wasting your life feeling sad all because of the trees. You are just as great as the trees. You can make rainfall. Can the trees?" "No," said the rain. I see what you mean. I think I wasted my life just praying for angels when there are none. I just think I ought to stop this and I think I just ought to tell the trees how good I feel about it and maybe they'll know not to pray for angels themselves."

So the rain said to the trees, "You think you are great. You think you can do everything. Can you make love? Can you make rain?" Then the trees said, "No. We ought to stop this bragging ourselves and we ought to stop praying for angels to do the things we can do. There are no angels to help any of us. We got to figure out things for ourselves."

So the trees stopped bragging and the rain felt much happier and he was very happy most of the time. The end.

The lesson of that story is: don't feel guilty about what other people can do. You can do things like them.

The story demonstrates how my message imparted in the previous sequence has been embodied in the child's. Here there are no angels. The patient is becoming accustomed to that unpleasant fact and to handling life's problems more realistically.

The story also reveals further attempts to deal with his low self-esteem problem. Steve is attending more to his own assets, appreciating them more and spending less time comparing himself unfavorably to others. The wise cloud not only represents the therapist, but also an internalized derivative of him that is becoming incorporated into the patient's own psychic structure. It is during the later phase of treatment that "wise owls," "older brothers," and "wise old men" who are the bearers of the therapist's messages appear comfortably internalized in the patient's mental life.

When the patient tells a story with so many healthy elements and resolved issues, the therapist may find it difficult to create one that introduces further salutary adaptations. At such times I often weave into my story unresolved clinical issues which have not appeared in the patient's stories. One of this boy's problems that still remained with him was his tendency to blame others for causing his misbehavior. "They started," "It's all his fault. He called me stupid, so that's why I punched him," and "He brags just to make me feel bad," are examples of this trend. Although the mechanism of projection is operative here, the phenomenon is so ubiquitous among seven- to eight-year-old boys that one must even hesitate to call it a "normal paranoid phase." I consider it a manifestation of the normally weak ego of the child of this age. Accepting one's imperfections can be at times intolerable to even the healthiest child, and he may often resort to projection to protect himself from conscious awareness of his liabilities. This boy, with less than average ego strength, was even less tolerant of his deficiencies and utilized the projection mechanism to a mildly pathologic degree. In the attempt to help Steve with this problem, I told the following story:

My story is called "The Rain and the Trees."

Once upon a time there were some trees and they were always bragging about their beauty, and there was the rain who was very sad and depressed. He said, "I hate those trees. Those trees bother me. They bug me. All they do all day is brag about their colors. I have a feeling sometimes that they are plotting against me, that all they want to do is make me feel bad and that they plot behind my back and secretly make agreements to bug me and bother me and boast in front of me. I wish there was an angel that would get those trees to stop doing that. I wish there was an angel who would make things stop plotting against me."

Well, a cloud overheard him talking and the cloud said, "I'm sorry to have to tell you, my friend, there are no angels." The rain said, "Well, how am I going to get the trees to stop plotting against me?" The cloud said, "What makes you think that they are plotting against you?" He said, "I know it. I just know it because they are always bragging." The cloud said, "Just because they are bragging doesn't mean that they are plotting. There's a difference between plotting and bragging. They can brag and that doesn't mean that they are plotting against you or that they are having secret meetings." The rain said, "I don't believe you." The cloud said, "Now, look, you're rain. You can be invisible. You can put yourself into the form of little water droplets and they won't even see you. Why don't you go around and listen."

So the rain thought that that was a good idea. He went with the cloud together and listened to the trees all night and all day and after a few days the rain started getting tired hanging there in the air in little droplets. He said to the cloud, "You know, you're right. I guess they aren't plotting against me. They're just boasters. They are just like big balloons, blowing themselves up. They just like talking a lot." Then the rain realized that they weren't plotting against him and he realized that he could lead a very good life without worrying about their boasting. From then on whenever he thought that somebody was plotting against him, he said to himself, "I wonder if it's my imagination. I wonder if the alternative is possible that they aren't really plotting against me, that they are just doing things on their own and they are not really plotting." Well, he learned that lesson.

The moral of that story is: When you think somebody is plotting against you, consider the possibility that this isn't necessarily so. People have better things to do with their time than plot. The end.

In my story I purposely exaggerated the projection mechanism in the hope that it would help the patient appreciate its inappropriateness. My aim in this story was *not* to direct therapeutic communications to the mechanisms which underlay the exaggerated need to project, but rather to help the patient see and appreciate that he had this problem. Even in the treatment of adult paranoids, this approach has its place. In the child, where the tendency to project is not as deep-seated, such confrontation can be even more useful.

Some readers will probably consider my story a naive approach to the problem of projection. I must admit that when reading the transcript I myself had similar doubts. However, the true judge of the applicability of the story and the validity of my communication is the child. He was transfixed during my telling of the story. His attitude led me to feel that I was on the right track and I was thereby encouraged to go on in the same vein. When I finished, Steve smiled and asked me if he could write something on my note pad. I of course agreed, and after scrawling for a moment, he handed me this note: "I like you!" After a few similar stories, there was a definite diminution in his tendency to project. Of course, other things were going on as well, things which contributed in other ways to helping the problem, but appeals to conscious awareness and control were, I believe, contributory to the change.

A few weeks later, Steve exhibited a definite increase in his feelings of self-loathing and self-derogation. After the slightest frustration or disappointment he would berate himself with such comments as: "I'm no good," "I should be dead," and

"Why was I ever born?" This followed an incident in which a neighborhood woman chased the patient and his friend off her property. From what I could learn, their play was innocent and non-destructive. The patient returned home and angrily told his mother that he wished the neighbor were dead. The mother, who was quite inhibited herself in the full and appropriate expression of anger, told the patient that it was wrong for him to have such feelings. In the following weeks, the sessions were almost completely devoted to the anger issue. In a session with the parents I was able to help the mother become at least intellectually aware that her attitude toward hostility was causing in her child an added burden of unnecessary guilt. Specific suggestions were made about how she might respond to the patient's hostility. With the encouragement and support of her husband who was somewhat less inhibited, she was able to implement my suggestions with meaningful conviction. I met with the patient and his mother together so that she could impart to him directly her new ideas and more relaxed attitudes on anger. Within a few weeks there was a marked diminution in self-deprecatory statements. In fact, they fell to the level that I would consider to be within the normal range. It was at this point, when the hostility problem seemed to have been almost worked through, that Steve told the following story:

Once upon a time there was a prince and this prince was very happy and rich. He was very wicked and cruel. He took over all the countries and stole all the gold. He killed anybody that wanted to protest against him. The people were very poor.

There was a poor man. He was very poor. His house had been burned so he was alone wandering. One day he met another wanderer and he said, "You know this prince? I hate him with all my might. I wish the prince was dead." The other guy said, "Now you can't wish that. That's very wrong. That's a naughty thing to do." And the wanderer got very unhappy about what the other wanderer had said to him and he kept on going. He met another wanderer and the second wanderer did the same thing when he said he

wished the king were dead —— I mean the prince. He said
the poor man was wrong to wish someone dead. He walked
and walked and walked. Finally he saw a third wanderer
and he said, "You know this prince? I hate him with all
my might. I wish he was dead. I don't feel happy wishing
that he's dead. I met two other wanderers and they said it's
not good to wish people dead." So the wanderer said, "It's
perfectly normal to wish people dead, even to say it to
somebody. It's not right to say it to the person that you
wish was dead."

So that wanderer learned a lesson.

Moral: you can wish people dead or tell somebody
that you wish a friend was dead because he doesn't like you,
but you can't say to the person, "I wish you were dead!"

Therapist: That was an excellent story. You want to say
    something else? Go ahead.

Patient: Well, pretty soon the prince grew old and he died
    and his son became a wise king and ruled over the people
    happily. So everybody lived happily ever after.

Therapist: Hmm. I have a question. Do you think that the
    prince died because the old man and other people wished
    him dead?

Patient: No.

Therapist: Why not?

Patient: He didn't die because people wished him dead. He
    died of old age.

Therapist: Hhmm. Why didn't he die because people wished
    him dead? Wouldn't that make the king die?

Patient: No.

Therapist: A lot of people wished him dead. Wouldn't that
    make him die?

Patient: No.

Therapist: Why not?

Patient: He can't just go up to heaven and somebody says
    —— you just can't go to the stars or your thoughts can't
    go to the stars. They can't go to a God and he'll send
    down lightning upon the prince and kill him.

Therapist: Hhmmm. I see. Right. In other words, thoughts
    can't harm. Right?

Patient: Yeah.

Therapist: Okay. Thank you very much. That was an excellent story and now it's time for me to tell my story.

The story clearly reveals that my messages, imparted both directly and in my stories, have gotten through. The patient is badly treated. His house is burned by a cruel prince, and he is so enraged that he wishes that the prince were dead. The two wanderers — his parents — who would make him feel guilty over his anger, are ignored. The third wanderer professes the therapist's position that it is reasonable that one would be so enraged at a prince who wantonly burned down one's house that one might wish him dead. Since he was a prince, it might not be judicious to directly express one's feelings to him. It certainly would, however, be appropriate to reveal the murderous feelings to a friend. The patient has become more comfortable with his anger and is discriminating well between the ways in which it can be released and the ways in which it cannot.

In response, I told this story:

Once upon a time there was a prince. He was very rich, but he was wicked and cruel, and he took over all the country and he stole all the gold. He killed all those who wanted to protest against him.

Once there was this very poor man and his house had been burned down and he said, "I hate that prince with all my might. I hate that prince with all my heart. I wish he was dead." Now he met a man who he told this to and the man said, "It's wrong to wish anybody dead." And the man said, "It isn't wrong. The prince burned my house down. He took all my gold. I'm poor because of him and I only wish the worst things for him." Then he met a second man and he told the same thing to the second man that he wished the prince was dead. The second man said, "The prince may die if you wish he's dead." The man said, "He won't die from my wishing he was dead. He can't die from my wishing he was dead. Thoughts can't harm. Thoughts can't make him die. I still wish he were dead." Then he met a third man, and he said, "Do you think it's wrong for me to wish that the prince was dead?" And the third man said, "No, it's not wrong. However, you have to be careful who you tell these thoughts. For instance, it would be very unwise if you told the prince himself that you wish he was dead because he might punish you. However, it's all right to tell me because I'm a friend of yours. For instance, children, for example, will often have thoughts —— most children, if not all children, have thoughts of wishing people dead. They have other thoughts in which they think bad words. Now every kid knows that you can't say such things to a teacher or to a principal or to speak that way to a parent, but if another kid his own age were to call him a name or hit him, or say, "I wish you were dead," it would be all right because that person bothered him very much and if the other kid does a terrible thing then it's reasonable for the first kid to have a wish that the other was dead and even to say it. So it's important to remember that there are people you can say certain things to and others you can't, and you have to learn who you can speak that way to and who you can't. But you also have to remember that it's perfectly all right to have those thoughts and feelings if somebody bothers you very much."

Do you know what the lesson of that story is?

Patient: Thoughts can't harm.

Therapist: That's one lesson. But I have one more moral. It has to do with who you say it to.

Patient: Oh, um. You don't say it to a principal or a parent or a teacher. You might say it to a friend if he makes you really angry.

Therapist: Right, and that you have to learn, as you get older, who you can say what's on your mind to and who you have to keep it to yourself or do something else instead. The end.

Do you have any questions about that?

Patient: No.

Here I reiterated the main themes of Steve's story and added another aspect of the hostility issue which we had been focusing on during this period — the idea that thoughts can't harm.

Example 4

George, the nine-and-a-half-year-old boy with presenting complaints of shyness, disinterest in his schoolwork, and timidity, became progressively more resistive to treatment. During his seventh month of therapy, George told this story:

> Once upon a time there was a man who made calendars and they were like this. Everytime you could rip off a thing like that. Well, so, the person who bought this calendar came to the month of July and it had already been ripped out. So he complained to the company and they gave him a new calendar plus they gave him two new calendars.
> The moral of that story is to be careful when you make things. All right?

Therapist: I appreciate that story but you know it's very similar to many stories that you have been telling and I think it would be a good idea to try to make up another story.

Patient: Do I have to? Please.

Therapist: No, you don't have to. You've been telling almost the same story each time now.

Patient: Well, I can't think of different stories every week.

Therapist: Well, each time you tell me the same story. Each time you give me the exact same story. Why don't you try to think of something else?

Patient: Noooo.

Therapist: Well, come on. You can do something entirely different I know.

Patient: I know I can't though. I just know I can't.

Therapist: Okay, I'll think of a story for myself.

The calendar maker in the story is George, who pays no penalty for his slipshod work. The factory replaces the defective calendars he has produced without any attempt to rectify the problem at its source. The patient's schoolwork was similarly performed and although there were repercussions, he was oblivious to them. His attitude toward me in the treatment session was in a similar vein. His involvement was minimal, all activities bored him, and his stories were told in a perfunctory manner. He would often repeat the exact same story for weeks at a time. The repetitious stories were not manifestations of core problems which were being worked through, but rather resistance stories which were repeated to further entrench his therapeutic stagnation.

In using the Mutual Storytelling Technique it is sometimes helpful to encourage a timid child, or mildly coax a hesitant one, into telling a story. Coercion is always contraindicated; it is not only antitherapeutic in general, but the stories so gained are of little, if any, therapeutic value. In the discussion that followed this story there is a definite coercive quality which stemmed from my frustration and irritation with this boy. His lack of involvement and his passive aggression thwarted me. Reaching out to him inevitably caused me frustration. Not to reach out would result in wasting the session in silence. In a manner similar to that involving Ronald, I extended myself to the point of mild irritation and then tried to utilize my resentment therapeutically. In such situations it is often difficult to determine at what point predictable, appropriate hostility ends and neurotic anger begins. In either case, it was with some resentment that I told this story:

Once upon a time there was a man and he made calendars. One day a person came to him and said, "Say, this calendar is defective. The month of July isn't there." And he said to himself, "Uh – oh, it must be that worker that I know of, that Mr. Jones. He's always fouling up." But the boss was kind of afraid to say anything to Mr. Jones. The boss was one of these people who used to hold in his feelings and the boss would not tell people when he disagreed with them or when they did something that he didn't like. So he said, "Okay, I'll give you two new calendars." But he didn't tell Mr. Jones that he was making this error and Mr. Jones would get the calendars and make them and sort the months.

Well, a few days later another man came in and said, "Hey, look at this. This calendar is missing the month of

August." Again he gave him two new calendars and said he was sorry, but he never told Mr. Jones. Again, he was afraid to criticize anybody, afraid to say what was on his mind.

Well, this kept happening and he kept on holding in his feelings and it reached the point where business was getting worse and worse. He was losing more and more money because he wasn't saying anything. He didn't realize that this was the cause of it and finally he brought in an expert, a man who investigates businesses that are failing. And he said to him, "Why is my business losing money?" Well, this investigator found out what the problem was. He found out that this man Jones was fouling up and he went over to Jones and said, "Listen, Jones, you're losing this company a lot of business. You're doing a sloppy job on the calendars. If you don't shape up we're going to have to discharge you," Well, Jones didn't listen and he kept on producing poor calendars. The company kept losing money. Finally they fired Jones, got rid of him, got a new man who was more careful, and then the company started making money again.

The lesson of that story is: if something is bothering you, speak up and do somthing about it. Don't just hold it all in or else you'll get into trouble. The end.

In this story I attempted to impart to George the idea that one suffers the consequences of one's negligence. George's calendar maker goes on blandly, never suffering the slightest discomfort for his sloppiness. In my story, the calendar maker is concerned about inefficiency. He warns his sloppy worker, and when he doesn't shape up, the worker is fired. Perhaps my harsh treatment of the worker reflects exaggerated hostility on my part toward the patient. A less drastic course would have been to demote the worker and then, after he learned his lesson, restore him to his former position.

In the character of the boss, I transmitted another message to George, a message which touched upon his core problems. An important factor in his resistance toward me, teachers, and other authority figures was anger displaced from his divorced father. He was most fearful of expressing his pent-up hostility directly, and the boss serves as an example of someone whose business suffers because he does not express himself.

As the reader can readily see, at the time of this sequence things were going very poorly in George's therapy. It was no surprise to me when, two weeks later, the child told his mother that he didn't wish to continue. I suggested another two weeks trial at salvaging therapy, but this proved futile and treatment was then discontinued. The sequence is presented as an example of late phase stories which presage therapeutic failure. Regardless of the magnitude of George's problems, I cannot dismiss completely the possibility that inappropriate hostility on my part contributed to the deterioration of treatment. If this is the case, then this story sequence is also an example of countertransference (used in the sense of *inappropriate* emotional reactions).

Example 5

Paul, the eight-and-a-half-year-old boy with poor school performance in spite of high intelligence, told this story in his seventh month of treatment:

Today my story is going to be about a man and he wanted to know how to carve things out of wood and make things, and he knew this friend who knew how to do it real good. So he said to him, "Will you carve me something out of wood?" His friend said, "Well, okay. What would you like?" He said, "A picture of a snake." The friend said, "Well, that will be kind of hard so you'll have to wait at least a week."

When the week is over he goes back to the man's house and says, "Is the snake finished yet?" The friend said, "Yes, I just have to paint it." The man said, "Never mind painting it. I'll paint it." So he gives the man the snake and the man goes home and he tries and copies the man's work. So then when he copied it as good as he could and it still didn't look the same, but he thought that if he wrote

210

his own name on the snake that the other man did people would think that he knew how to make things real good. Then he did and showed everybody it and they said, "That's a good job. Can you make me something?" So he wrote down a list of all the things people wanted him to make. Then when he went back he started trying to make things. He thought he was real good because he had forgotten that he had took the wrong snake; he put his name on his friend's snake but not on his own; and it looked pretty much the same. So people said, when he brought back their things, "These are just as good as the other one." So the man thought that he was real good.

Therapist: You mean he made things other than snakes?

Patient: Yeah.

Therapist: And they were just as good as the friend's who was the woodcarver?

Patient: Yeah.

Therapist: So he knew how to make them real well?

Patient: Yeah, and so then he got a job in the toy store carving wooden snakes and things and got a lot of money for doing that. That's the end.

Therapist: What's the lesson of that story?

Patient: Don't try and trick some people. Try and see how your work is and it might be better.

Therapist: I'm not exactly clear —— at first he put the name of the other man on it — the original woodcarver — is that it?

Patient: No, he put his own name on it.

Therapist: He put his own name on it at first. What did the people think?

Patient: They thought he did it.

Therapist: Now how did he try to trick people?

Patient: Well, because he thought he had the other man's snake. He thought that he had taken the other man's good work and wrote his name on that, but he really didn't because they were so good and looked so much alike.

Therapist: He thought he had put his own name on the good woodcarver's snake but it was really on his own snake, and people thought it was good. Then he realized what had happened?

Patient: Yes.
Therapist: And that gave him confidence. Is that it?
Patient: Right.
Therapist: I see. Okay. Thank you.

The story reflects a feeling of self-confidence which was not present during the earlier phases of Paul's therapy. Recall, for example, the story of the fleeing piano stool who had wings made of paper, cardboard, and paste. Here Paul creates woodcarvings which are competently made and sell well. However, the patient is insecure about his abilities. He plans to put his own name on the woodcarving of the known master and sell that first. In error he labels his own. It is good enough to be confused with the expert's: it is well received, and he later learns that it is his own work after all that is enjoying so much attention. The duplicity here is not due to deep-seated psychopathy on this boy's part, but rather to insecurity — he doesn't really have faith in his newly acquired competence. In a sense his hesitancy about his new-found abilities — better school performance and improved relationships with peers — was valid. He hadn't yet had enough time with his new modes of adaptation to provide him with the depth of confidence that can only come with experience. In order to help him in these areas, and thereby strengthen the basically healthy adaptations revealed by the story, I told the following story:

Once upon a time there was a man, a young man, who admired very much a woodcarver who was an expert master woodcarver and was known far and wide for the excellent carvings that he would make. This young man went to the older woodcarver and asked him if he could train him — if he could spend a couple of years working with him as an apprentice. Do you know what an apprentice is?
Patient: Yes, somebody who helps him.
Therapist: Yes, a helper who is there to learn the trade. And the young man said, "Can I spend a few years with you as an apprentice learning the trade so that I can be a wood-

212

carver myself?" The master woodcarver said, "Yes, I'd like to have you work for me and I will teach you this art, this trade."

Well, the young man worked very hard and he spent a couple of years working for this master woodcarver and then he came to the point where it was time for him to leave and go out on his own. The master said to him, "Well, my son, you have learned your lessons well and the time has come for you to go out and start making things on your own." Well, the young man became quite frightened. He was fearful that people would not like his work. The old man said, "Now, listen. The same thing happened to me when I was a young man and I was ready to start out on my own. It's natural to be nervous and everybody gets scared, but if you're going to hide from this and not do the work you'll never be successful. My suggestion to you is to go out on your own and you've got to push through your fear. You've got to do your work in spite of the fact that you're afraid people won't buy it and then see what happens. I'm sure that you'll be successful because I'm sure that you're good."

So the young man decided to try that and he went out into business on his own. Although he was scared, he still persisted and he still carved woodcarvings. Much to his surprise people came into his store, although he thought at first that his stuff wasn't very good; people thought it was good and he gradually became very successful and then he was less scared. Then he was happy that he had done the thing which frightened him and realized that it wasn't so fearful after all; it wasn't so frightening after all.

Therapist: And do you know what the lesson of that story is?

Patient: Don't be afraid to do something or else you might not get a chance to do it at all.

Therapist: Right, if you are afraid, you've got to do it anyway even though you are scared and you'll see most often that what you're afraid of isn't so frightening after all. You've got to do it in spite of the fact that you're afraid.

And the second moral is: you have to work hard if you're to do something well.

As is clear, in my story I attempted to communicate to him that true competence only comes with hard work and practice, otherwise one's feelings of proficiency will be shaky. I also impressed upon Paul that all new experiences are anxiety-provoking, and that one inevitably has to suffer such fears if one is to enjoy the rewards of one's efforts. Placing the products of one's labors before the world and waiting for their judgments can only be frightening.

The story is a good example of a pre-termination story. The basic adaptation is healthy: his new-found feeling of competence is clearly present. What needed to be done was to help him become more secure with these changes and my story was created to serve this end.

Example 6

Donald, an eight-year-old boy with generalized immaturity, poor school performance, and overdependence on an overprotective mother, told this story two months prior to the termination of one year's treatment.

Once upon a time there was this boy and he was always fooling around in the doctor's office. Every single day he had to go to the doctor so that he could find out how he was doing. He was always fooling around and wherever he went he was careless. So the doctor said, "All these troubles are because he's careless and he doesn't care about anything." So then they solved the problem and he started being careful and he improved a little and a little every day. After the year ended he was very careful. Whenever it was a red light and not even a single car was coming, he wouldn't cross the street, not even if no cars were around on the street or else they'd get twenty years in jail; he wouldn't even cross at the red light. So he would always use a pencil so if he makes a mistake he could erase it and fix it and he was very careful. The moral of that story is: you should always be careful and if you're careful it could save your life. The end.

The story was told after a period of definite clinical improvement. He was much more attentive in school, more reliable with his homework, and generally more independent of his mother. The story reveals a basic commitment by the patient to following socially acceptable rules and regulations. There is, however, an exaggerated quality about the story. The penalty for crossing against a red light is twenty years in jail. Being careful can save your life. Donald needed some strengthening of his superego, but the story indicates that it had become somewhat hypertrophied. It was necessary, then, to help the patient reach a more moderate point of adaptation. It is during the pre-termination phase that such adjustments take place. In order to help Donald achieve such modification I told this story:

Once upon a time there was a boy and he used to fool around a lot in the doctor's office. Then finally the doctor said that he fooled around too much and the boy realized that he was and so he started to buckle down. He stopped being so careless and he stopped fooling around. Then he was much happier because he was doing much better in all things. He started to do better in school; he would do his homework every day. He started to be more careful when he crossed the street. He would not cross against the red light. He used a pencil so he could erase so his homework would be good and he concentrated much more in class. He would listen to what the teacher was saying; he wouldn't daydream in class and he studied hard and then his problems all got solved. He was happy afterwards that he had decided to buckle down.

The moral of that story is: when you buckle down, you do better. The end.

In my story there is a deliberate absence of terrible consequences for transgressions. When he adheres to the regulations

215

and expectations of society he feels better about himself. Good work is done for its own sake rather than to avoid the painful penalties of wrongdoing. In essence, I was attempting to reinforce Donald's gains, substitute a healthier reason for appropriate behavior, and tone down a somewhat rigid superego.

Example 7

Helen initially came to treatment at the age of seven because of frequent nightmares, obsessions over losing things, and hypermature behavior. The parents had been divorced two years prior to my first seeing her, and the patient was living alone with her mother. The mother suffered marked mood swings of elation and depression, which at times bordered on the psychotic. Helen was treated for one-and-a-half years with good results. She returned again at age ten with complaints of poor concentration, insomnia, and deterioration of her schoolwork. She was very bright and had always been among the highest in her class. During the six months prior to returning to treatment the mother had been hospitalized as a result of an attempted suicide. Subsequent to her discharge, she became agitated, went on buying sprees, and became sexually promiscuous. It was clear that she was suffering with a manic-depressive psychosis. Helen's second treatment experience lasted four months. This story was told during the second month:

On an Easter holiday a little girl named Julie went to her grandmother's house for the weekend and her grandmother lived in Florida. This little girl went there for a vacation just because she had never been to Florida before and her cousins were going to be there and she hadn't seen them in a long time. So while she was there — her grandmother lived right on the ocean — in the morning if she wanted to get up and go for a swim, if you had somebody watching you so nothing would happen, you could just get up and go. You wouldn't have to go to the beach or anything. It would be right in front of your house.

One morning Julie decided to go swimming and she got her cousins to go with her. She had two cousins. They were both girls, I guess. They all went swimming together and this happened practically every morning as a routine because they all liked swimming so much.

One morning one of Julie's cousins decided she should go swimming all alone because she wanted to go swimming and everybody else was asleep. They had been up late the night before trying to get something on the new television that they had gotten for Christmas. She didn't wake up anybody. She just went swimming and all of a sudden a big wave came and it knocked her over. Nothing serious happened to her and she thought it was nothing. But it was very rough and she wasn't very sure about staying out in the ocean or not. So she went on swimming and she got knocked over again. This time her head got hit against a rock on the bottom of the ocean and it began to bleed. She was conscious and she got up but she didn't want to tell anybody what had happened to her. So her sister, one of Julie's cousins, found out that she had hurt her head and so then she thought that she should tell some adult because something could have happened to her, but she didn't want to. She wasn't going to squeal on her own sister.

Finally Julie found out also and Julie felt that it would be more important to have her cousin healthy and everything than it would be not tell anybody just because she didn't want anybody to know that she had gone swimming alone. So Julie did tell her grandmother and they went to a doctor and the doctor said the cousin was okay but it could have been a lot more serious if they hadn't done anything about it. Julie's cousin was mad at her for a while because she had told, but afterwards she realized herself that it's better to be healthy than it is to be, you know, than it is to try and hide something.

The moral of this story is: tell the truth and it will help you to stay healthy.

The cousin whose head got hit against a rock and who almost drowned represents the mother and her attempted suicide. That Helen depicts her as a peer is not surprising in that the mother, in her illness, was exhibiting many childish qualities. The patient was indeed assuming adult responsibilities in her relationship with her, and I would not have been surprised if the mother had appeared as the patient's child in the girl's stories. The cousin's request that no one be told about the accident relates to the patient's awareness, at some level, of her mother's wish to deny her illness. In fact, the mother, although in treatment, had practically no insight into the depth of her difficulties. Julie's mature decision not to honor the cousin's request for secrecy was a message to me that the patient was seeking my aid in handling her mother. Living alone with a mother who is intermittently psychotic is an overwhelming burden for any child and although this patient was doing admirably, she still needed help. The story was a clear statement of this need.

Although she did not at first appreciate its significance, the girl was bright enough to analyze the story. We then directed our attention to ways in which she could more effectively handle the situation with her mother. In subsequent sessions, we spoke about what she could do about her mother's irresponsibility in caring for the home; her leaving the child alone for long periods of time; her bringing men into the house; and her excessive spending. The girl responded to these challenges with a degree of maturity and efficiency that was at times amazing.

Six weeks later, Helen told this story. Again, instead of telling a story in response, I analyzed her story with her. This time the analytic inquiry was recorded.

There was a girl named Linda and it was a rainy day and she was inside the house. It was too rainy to go outside so she decided to make something out of an old cardboard box and some paints and brushes and other things that she had. So she took the box and she cut four sides of it and she made like an old-fashioned dollhouse and it was very nice and she painted it. She decorated it and made furniture for it out of the remaining part of the box. When she was finished with that and finished admiring it, she decided to go over to her friend's house. She went over there and played for a while and when she came back she saw her cat looking guiltily and the cat had by accident pushed down the house. It wasn't completely ruined but she had to repair a couple of parts of it and so she decided that since she was going to fix it up anyway she would add some more things to it and make it nice enough to give for a present to her mother. So she got some old clothes of hers and she made some curtains and tablecloths and such things for it. She put them in and she decorated it and instead of having it all covered so that you wouldn't be able to look in if you just passed by —— you'd have to open up or look through the windows or lift up the roof or something. So she took some glass that had been broken before from a window when somebody had thrown a ball through by accident, and in just the right shape, so she made like a big glass window so you could see clear through. So now it was very dark and she had to get it out of the cat's reach so that she could save it for her mother's birthday. So she put it high on top of her closet and when her mother's birthday came she gave it to her. Her mother was very pleased with it.

The moral of the story is: if something terrible happens, don't feel badly enough so that you can't repair it again.

Therapist: That was a very good story, Helen. Now let me take a little time out to think about what it means. I have some idea what your story means, but I'd like to hear from you what you think it means. See if you can figure it out. Let's put this microphone in between us. It will pick up what both of us are saying. Now, let's just talk about it. What do you think?

Patient: I think the girl is me and the house is my mother, but I can't think what's left.

Therapist: You think the girl is you and the house is your mother. If the house is your mother, what does it mean then?

Patient: That when she gets sick I repair her.

Therapist: When she gets sick you repair her. What about that?

Patient: But I don't think that's the way I feel.

Therapist: Now I'll tell you what I think the story means. I think you divide your mother into two parts there — — the sick part of your mother and the healthy part of your mother.

Patient: What's the healthy part?

Therapist: The healthy part of your mother is your mother

as she appears and the sick part of your mother is the cat. And the house is your house. Here your house is very nice and then your mother gets sick and that kind of wrecks the house in a way. The sick part of your mother wrecks the house. Right? Disorganizes it, gets it all upset. Then you are put in the position of having to repair it again because your mother is too sick. Then you repair it and you hide the house from the sick part of your mother. You don't let the sick part of your mother destroy the house again, just like you —— in the story you put the house ——

Patient: But then I gave it to her.

Therapist: You just hide it up in the closet so that the cat can't get to it.

Patient: I know, but who is the person I gave it to?

Therapist: The healthy part of your mother. You preserved the house for the healthy part of your mother. You're watching that the sick part of your mother doesn't destroy things again. Aren't you?

Patient: Yeah.

Therapist: Aren't you on the lookout for the sick parts of your mother?

Patient: I feel it's kind of fiction-like. It's not really realistic enough. I'm not on the lookout and I'm not like saving the house from her.

Therapist: Aren't you on the lookout when you say that you'd better be careful if she's "high" [manic].

Patient: I know but ——

Therapist: Don't you kind of see your mother as having two personalities, a sick and a healthy personality?

Patient: No.

Therapist: Well, when she's high, isn't she different than when she's not high?

Patient: Yes. She's still the same person.

Therapist: Yes, but she changes. Not that she's completely different, but she changes in a way. When she's sick her personality changes. Doesn't it?

Patient: Uh-huh.

Therapist: When she's high her personality changes. She buys a lot of things. She also gets very depressed when she's sick. It's almost like two people. It's the same person but she has two different aspects to her personality.

Patient: Right.

Therapist: It's the sick part that you've constantly got to watch out for. Right?

Patient: No. Cause if you —— it's not really my job, but if I —— like if somebody finds out that she's high fast enough she won't necessarily get lost.

Therapist: Right, but you have to watch out for that.

Patient: I know, but in those aspects, you know; are you talking about high and low or are you talking about normal?

Therapist: Normal and sick.

Patient: Oh, well. That's my job.

Therapist: That's right. You keep your eye open for her if you see signs of sickness and I think the sick part of your mother is the cat, which can jump and do dangerous things and destroy the house. The healthy part of your mother is the normal mother whom you give the present to. The cat destroyed the house once — not completely — but it did a lot of damage — when it was your sick mother. Now you're more cautious. You take the house and you put it up in the closet so that the cat can't get to it, which stands for your watching out that your mother — the sick part of your mother — isn't destructive again. And then in the story you're successful in doing that and then you and the healthy part of your mother enjoy the house.

Patient: All right. That's what the dream means but what does it mean in aspect to me. I mean what's actually happening?

Therapist: In aspect to what? Well, it tells what did happen. Right? The cat destroyed the house — well almost destroyed the house. That means your mother when she was very sick almost destroyed the house.

Patient: The way I look at it.

Therapist: Right. And now what this dream — it's not a dream really — what this story is saying is that you are going to be more cautious. You're watching carefully and you're going to protect the house from the sick part of her and it expresses the hope that you will be successful in avoiding the sick part of her and that you and she can enjoy the healthy part or the good parts of the house together.

The story reveals how at times a patient's clinical improvement can be a step ahead of psychodynamic understanding. Helen was very much involved in looking for signs of her mother's decompensation and actively participated in keeping the household organized. In spite of our discussions regarding the details of these activities, she had difficulty analyzing the story when we came to the point of discussing her mother as sick. Helen wished to consciously deny this in spite of the fact that all her behavior indicated acute awareness of her mother's pathology. On further discussion she was able to appreciate the story's significance. Such analysis was helpful in further clarifying her role and, I believe, supported and mobilized her further in her tasks.

I might add here that I intermittently communicated with the mother's psychiatrist. We both felt that the situation, although a very difficult one, was not grave enough to warrant the mother's hospitalization. In spite of her difficulties, the mother was effectively working; she was meaningfully involved in her treatment; and there was no significant danger of suicide.

One week later, Helen reported this dream:

I was on a beach with my mother and father. Something bad was going on. There was a monster or a bad person there. It wasn't bad enough to get worried about. I don't know what he was supposed to do. I went swimming and nothing happened with the monster. Then we got into a beach jeep and went off.

Helen and I discussed the dream and concluded that the monster represents the sick part of her mother which the child is coming to see as less threatening as she develops the means to handle her. In addition, the presence of the monster does not interfere with her involving herself in her usual activities, which are symbolized in the dream by going swimming.

Later in the session, Helen told the following story:

There is a girl named Laurie and she went to a school in New York. She had a friend in her school that wasn't very smart and they had a test in grammar and Laurie got a very good mark, but her friend did not. Her friend got very upset about it and she made many resolutions that she would do better in the future. They were coming right up to spring vacation and she took practically all her books home and said that she was going to study a lot. Her friend's name was Stephanie.

So Laurie called Stephanie up during their vacation and asked her how much she had studied during the vacation. She hadn't done very much. Then she called her up towards the end and she still hadn't done very much, and when she came back to school she still hadn't done very much.

Laurie, instead of getting all upset about how her friend hadn't been trying, went out and had a good time anyway, but she was still a little concerned about how her friend ought to be doing better. So she let her friend know about this because she thought that if she didn't start working harder she might not pass the grade or anything. So her friend did start getting better marks until finally she was just as good and sometimes even better than Laurie.

The moral of this story is that if a friend of yours isn't doing well in something, try to help them as much as you can, but don't go overboard and get yourself all into the problem and concerned all about it. Just try to help as much as you can.

Therapist: Let's see if we can analyze this story. Do you have any ideas?

Patient: No.

Therapist: You really do not have any ideas about this story? Not at all? Are you telling the truth?

Patient: I think I understand the moral.

Therapist: What's your idea about the moral?

Patient: About the same thing that had to do with the dream.

Therapist: All right. How so?

Patient: Well, instead of getting all upset about the monster and not going swimming; to be concerned about it a little bit, but still go swimming.

Therapist: Does the story deal with the same thing?

Patient: I don't know. I really don't.

Therapist: Well, let's say that you're Laurie. Who would your friend be?

Patient: Well, wait a minute. After spring vacation —— you mean ——

Therapist: You see, you're Laurie and Stephanie is your mother and she's doing poorly in her tests means that she has some trouble with her health and you have to worry about her and you're concerned.

Patient: Oh, I understand.

Therapist: Go ahead. Finish it.

Patient: I get concerned and I start telling her that she ought to start getting better and see a doctor or something and then she does get better.

Therapist: Which is what's happening to your mother now. Isn't she kind of better?

Patient: Oh, yes.

Therapist: So you bugged her awhile and she did get back in shape. Hmm?

Patient: What about the concern of me? I mean at the end, about not being concerned about the ——

Therapist: But at the end you say: "Laurie, instead of getting all upset about how her friend hadn't been trying, went out and had a good time anyway, but she was still a little concerned about how her friend ought to be doing better." So it's just like it was in your dream: you're concerned but not too much. I think it's the same thing as the dream. What do you think?

Patient: I think the dream was better.

Therapist: In what way?

Patient: I don't know, except that it seems that I was more concerned in this one.

Therapist: You're more concerned in this story. Well, the story tells about what you're feeling today.

Patient: And the dream?

Therapist: The dream is telling you what was happening a few days ago — the day that you dreamed it.

Patient: Oh, can a dream tell what is happening on that day?

Therapist: Mainly that day and the day or two before —— about how you've been feeling about things.

Patient: So you think that's good too?

Therapist: Yes, I think it's pretty good. It still shows some concern but there's an awareness that something has been done and things have gotten better. Okay?

Patient: Okay.

The dream and story are typical of the pre-termination phase of therapy. They reveal that major problems are close to being resolved. There is a realistic concern for her sick mother, but not the exaggerated involvement which would deprive her of her own gratifications. A healthy balance is being achieved. They also demonstrate how, in this stage of treatment, the therapist may use the story like a dream and directly analyze it rather than using it as the nucleus of his own story.

6. THE TERMINATION PHASE OF THERAPY

In this chapter, stories that indicate that the major therapeutic work has been accomplished and that therapy can be terminated are presented. The decision to discontinue treatment, however, is not made on the basis of the story, but rather on clinical evidence that there has been an alleviation of the symptoms which originally brought the child to treatment. The termination story confirms the clinical impression that the child is ready to leave, but it is not vital to the decision. When it is presented, the therapist can be more secure in his decision that the child is ready to leave. It may never be told because, as I have said, such stories imply only that *pathological* problems have been worked through. *Reality* problems will continue to recur, as will minor neurotic adaptations. These will exist throughout the patient's life. Stories and dreams will always be helpful in working these problems out.

As I did in the discussion of late phase stories, termination stories of children whose treatment has been a failure are presented along with those of children whose therapy has been a success. The child's presentation of a termination story at the end of a successful treatment experience is one of the most fulfilling moments for the therapist practicing child psychotherapy. Such work can be most discouraging; the therapist must often wait for years to see the results of his labors; he can never predict with certainty that the outcome will be favorable. These considerations make the presentation of a termination story one of the therapist's most cherished experiences.

Example 1

Joey experienced significant clinical improvement by his

fourteenth month of treatment. The nightmares and enuresis had become rare occurrences and he was much more assertive with both peers and authorities. About one month prior to the termination of his treatment, Joey told this story:

Once upon a time there was a tape recorder and, well, his master was a teen-age hippie. Well, this teen-age hippie always recorded this rock stuff and his mother was seventy-six and she didn't like that stuff so much. So she was so dumb so she stopped him from doing it and she made him record things like "She'll Be Coming Around the Mountain" and "Hush Little Baby." Now he knew that this was wrong because, well, he knew that all she would have to do was not listen to it and just let him go on with it.

So he told his mother that and she agreed because she hadn't thought about that before.

The moral is: express your thoughts.

Therapist: Now I would like to ask you a question. You said that this hippie liked to record rock stuff. Could you give me the names of some of the rock songs he liked to record?

Patient: Well, all sorts of different kinds.

Therapist: Speak into the microphone.

Patient: Okay. "I'll Follow the Sun."

Therapist: "I'll Follow the Sun." Yeah.

Patient: "I Wanna Hold Your Hand."

Therapist: "I Want to Hold Your Hand." Yes.

Patient: It isn't "I Want to" — "I Wanna" — (Spells.) w-a-n-n-a.

Therapist: I wanna. Yeah.

Patient: "I'm the Walrus."

Therapist: "I'm the Walrus." Yeah.

Patient: "Julia."

Therapist: "Julia." Yeah.

Patient: Oh, yeah, "Rocky Raccoon."

Therapist: "Rocky Raccoon." Now I want to ask you something. What is there about rock music —— let's say that there was a foreign boy who came to your neighborhood and he didn't know what rock music was and he said, "I'm just learning the language. Can you tell me what rock music is?'' What would you say to him?

Patient: Well, I would say to him, oy, I can't even explain it.

Therapist: I know it's a hard thing to do.

Patient: Well, there's all different kinds of rock and roll music. I don't know how to explain it.

Therapist: Well, make believe I'm the foreign boy: "But I don't understand English too well. Could you tell me what rock and roll music is? Describe it to me in some way."

Patient: Well, it's a different style of singing, like folk songs. Folk songs are songs sung by folks. (*Starts to laugh.*)

Therapist: Folk songs are sung by folks. (*Laughs too.*) Okay.

Patient: And, oh, I just can't explain it. I can't.

Therapist: Can you try to imitate it?

Patient: No, I'm a terrible singer.

Therapist: Why didn't his mother like it?

Patient: I don't know. It's just different from other kinds of music.

Therapist: It was a different kind of music. That was the main thing about it. Well, what was there about it that she didn't like? Try to tell me that.

Patient: Okay. It isn't about it, but he played it at the highest volume that he could get.

Therapist: Were you thinking of that when you told the story?

Patient: No, I just thought of it.

Therapist: Okay. Think of something else. What was another reason why she didn't like it? You know, she could tell him, "Lower the volume a minute, but you can still play it." What else didn't she like about rock and roll music?

Patient: Can't we drop this?

Therapist: Just tell me one other thing about rock.

Patient: Sometimes it's noisy and sometimes it's quiet, but he liked the noisy music and he played all the noisy music.

Therapist: Okay. All right. I have another question. You

said that his mother instead wanted him to record songs like "She'll Be Coming Around the Mountain" and "Hush Little Baby." Why did she like those kind of songs?

Patient: I don't know.

Therapist: Hhmmm. Okay. Anything about that that she liked over rock. What was the main thing she liked about those songs over rock and roll?

Patient: Well, they weren't as noisy as the kind that he taped.

Therapist: Oh, I see. Now it's time for my story.

I consider the rock music to symbolize unbridled expression of pent-up emotions. I attempted to elicit from him comments about rock music which might either confirm or refute my hypothesis. I have often found the "foreign boy" mode of inquiry to be helpful in obtaining the child's associations and elaborations. Joey's responses, I believe, confirmed my supposition: the mother didn't like rock music because it was too noisy, especially because he preferred to play it at high volume.

His mother's suggestion that he confine himself to songs like "Hush Little Baby" reflected, I felt, his concept of his mother as one who represses him. In order to confirm this, I tried to get him to name other songs which the mother disapproved of — songs that might reveal similar repressive elements. Although unsuccessful in obtaining further confirmation, I still consider my original interpretation to be the most likely.

In the story Joey asserts himself and in response his mother agrees to tolerate the commotion. The moral, "Express your thoughts," not only epitomizes the main message of the story, but was the primary goal of his treatment as well.

The only possible inappropriate element I could find in the story was the mother's readiness to comply with his request. The story does not take into consideration her feelings; it does not consider the possibility that some mothers might be bothered by the loud playing of rock music. Even though the story might contain this possible "flaw," there are so many other healthy aspects to it that I considered it to confirm my clinical impression that Joey would soon be ready to terminate. In response, I told this story:

Once upon a time there was a tape recorder and his master was a teen-age hippie, and this teen-age hippie loved rock and roll. What he liked about rock and roll was the bounce, was the noise. When you could rock and roll you could jump around and you could scream and you could yell.

Patient: And you could have an excuse for it.

Therapist: And you would have an excuse for it, right. That's right. He could jump around and scream and run all over the place and shout and he could really go crazy a little bit or go to hell with himself or really scream a lot. While singing it he could dance and he could shout and let off steam. That was important — to let off steam.

Now his mother was an old lady of seventy-six and she didn't like rock and roll music and she used to say, "Why don't you play some nice songs like "Coming Around the Mountain," or "Hush Little Baby"? And he said, "Hush Little Baby?" That's just the kind of song that I don't want to hear, I don't wanna hear songs about hushing little babies. Not for me. I want to hear songs with noise, loud songs, racket songs."

Patient: Well, rock and roll songs are not racket songs. They don't have to be racket songs.

Therapist: But they can be!

Patient: Yeah.

Therapist: They can be. Anyway, so he said to his mother, "What's wrong with a teen-ager just letting off a little steam and singing a little loud?" She said, "All right. You can do it once in a while but I don't want the racket all the time." And he thought that that was a good compromise and she agreed to tolerate it and recognized that the boy was right — that once in a while would be okay for him to let off some steam and to play his rock and roll.

Patient: Well, I thought he liked it all the time.

Therapist: Yeah, but the thing is that he couldn't play it all the time because people had to go to sleep at night and things like that. But he was able to play it most of the time that he wanted to.

Patient: He just couldn't play it until twelve midnight.

Therapist: Right. He couldn't wake up people with it, but most of the time when he wanted to play some songs his mother realized that there was nothing wrong in his doing that.

And the lesson of that story is that if somebody is trying to impose something on you and you disagree with them and you think that they are wrong, express yourself, tell them your opinion, and, more often than you may think, you will get what you want.

As already discussed, the Mutual Storytelling Technique is a useful tool for helping inhibited patients express themselves more freely. One extremely effective way in which it can accomplish this is for the therapist, when telling his tale, to embellish it with non-verbal communications, intonations, and humorous interjections, which are emotionally arousing to the child and which tend to sweep him up in the spirit of the story. While telling this story, I gesticulated dramatically and rocked rythmically as I spoke about how when one listens to rock music. The boy responded in kind; but at one point he must have experienced some anxiety over having joined me in such an abandoned fashion. He stiffened up slightly and said: "Well, rock and roll songs are not racket songs. They don't have to be racket songs." I realized that residual fears had motivated this statement; he needed my reassurance that they need not always be so expressive. I decided to try to bring him back into the swing of things rather than get into an intellectual discussion on how much racket a rock and roll song makes. Therefore, when I responded with: "But they can be!" my associated body movements and intonations were rhythmic in the manner of a musical refrain. The boy responded with a loud "Yeah!" which clearly revealed that he was back on the bandwagon. The primary purpose of my story was to provide the child with a living experience in which emotions are freely expressed without the expected unpleasant consequences. He had gone far enough in his treatment to appreciate this, and his story reflected such appreciation. I was just providing him with more of the same message in a non-verbal and more dramatic and physical way. Of secondary importance was my message that he must take into consideration the needs of others when he wishes to "blow off steam."

One month later, on what had been previously arranged to be his last day of treatment, Joey told this story:

Patient: This is going to be my last original made-up story?

Therapist: Yes, this is going to be his last appearance on this program because Joey has finished his treatment and he is going to be discharged from treatment and this is going to be his last appearance on the program.

Patient: (*Begins to cry.*)

Therapist: I feel sad too that this is your last day.

Patient: Once upon a time there was a chair and this was a gold chair made out of pure gold and a king owned it. This king was very proud of this gold chair. He really didn't want to use it. He had his own gold throne so when guests came and when the guests slept with him in the palace, he would put the gold chair in his room, in the guest's room.

Therapist: In other words, there were two chairs, a gold throne and a gold chair?

Patient: Yes.

Therapist: And he let the guests use the gold chair.

Patient: Yeah, and he had his own gold throne. One day, well, he was the king of a place and, well, he was sort of like a governor or like a senator of a place and the president of the place told him that he had to give up his gold chair for a little while temporarily because the Secretary General of the United Nations, U Thant, who was coming there and they wanted to get a chair for him. So he did, and after they gave it back when U Thant left. After that when the king wanted to borrow the president's table for his guests, the president gave it to him.

And the moral isn't an original moral: one good turn deserves another.

Therapist: I see. Okay. Good. Is that because the king had been generous in giving up his guest chair to U Thant?

Patient: Yes, temporarily.

Therapist: In other words, the president had requested it; he hadn't ordered it?

Patient: Yes, he requested it.

Therapist: Thank you very much, Joey. That was an excellent story. Now it's time for me to tell my story.

Patient: Dr. Gardner. Did my story mean anything?

Therapist: Yes, your story meant something.

Patient: What did it mean?

Therapist: Do you want to talk about what your story meant?

Patient: Yes.

Therapist: Why don't I tell my story and then we'll talk about what it meant. Okay?

Patient: Okay, but right after that we'll talk about it.

Therapist: Yes. Right.

The child was choked with tears as he began his story. He was feeling the full pain of the forthcoming separation. There was deep appreciation that these stories, which were a central and vital part of this therapy, were soon to be told no more. His relationship with me was to be terminated and we both felt sad about that as well. There are many gratifications which the therapist enjoys in his work. The Mutual Storytelling Technique offers an additional one, not provided by other therapeutic modalities: the opportunity to derive creative satisfactions of his own through the telling of his stories. So I, too, had many reasons to be sad.

The king, as is commonly the case, represents the patient's father; the president, I felt, symbolized the patient. The king is seen as someone who has valuable possessions, some of which are shared and some are not. The king alone uses his gold throne, but guests are lent his gold chair. I consider the chairs to represent the patient's mother, who is owned by the father — some of her pleasures are shared, others are not. Acceptance of this situation is central to the resolution of the oedipus complex. The king is seen as basically benevolent, giving and sharing. The patient is finally depicting his father accurately and is free from the irrational fear of his father which had so paralyzed him in the past. Such fears must be minimal if one is to truly say that the oedipal conflict has been resolved.

The patient represents himself as someone, who although enjoying slightly lower status, is still capable of relating in an egalitarian way with the king. The president has a gold table of his own — friends, mother substitutes, valuable possessions — which he is willing to share at times with the king. He has given up his quest for complete possession of his mother, on occasion enjoys her company as one of the guests who is lent the table, and finds alternative gratifications which are symbolically represented as his own gold table.

The whole flavor of the story is one of maturity. There is genuine benevolence, egalitarianism, respect for the rights of others, sharing, healthy relationship with authority, and acceptance of realistic deprivation with appropriate involvement in alternative gratifications. The child was truly ready to terminate, and his story reflected this in highly symbolic fashion. The boy's questions after telling it clearly attests to his lack of conscious understanding of its meaning.

The therapist cannot often improve upon termination stories to any significant degree, nor should he be able to. Sometimes I do not tell a story and tell the child that his story was so good and complete that there's just nothing I can add. Sometimes I will tell one which epitomizes one or two important themes from the child's therapy — themes which have been suggested by the child's story. This is what I chose to do in Joey's case.

Once upon a time there was a king and this king had a gold throne and he also had a gold chair which he would use when guests came. Now, the president of this country, who himself was a man of a certain amount of position and status, was kind of afraid of the king.

One day when U Thant was going to visit the country, he thought it would be a nice idea to ask the king if he could borrow that gold chair for U Thant's use. He thought it would go well with the gold table that the president himself had. But he was kind of afraid because the king was older than the president and more powerful in the country and he thought just because someone is older and more powerful that they would be cruel or evil or will not treat him well. So he was kind of scared to ask the king if he could borrow the gold chair. Then he gradually said to himself, "This is foolish. I have no reason to be afraid of him. I've got to look at him more clearly and see if he's so bad."

So he was kind of scared, but he asked the king if he could borrow the gold chair and the king said, "Of course. You can borrow that gold chair. It's perfectly fine."

After that the president realized that the king wasn't as frightening a person as he had thought and they got to know one another very well and they became closer and closer and then the president felt comfortable in lending the king his gold table when he had guests. They gradually became friendlier and friendlier and the president no longer feared the king, and gradually when the king got older and retired, the president was elected king.. In this country that's how it worked. You could become king after you became president. He was a good king and he ruled wisely and he was very much concerned with people in his kingdom and was very good to them.

And the lesson of that story is that sometimes you feel frightened of a person who is in a more powerful position. Most often they really aren't people to be afraid of and you can relate to them in a way in which you don't have to be fearful. Then when you grow up, you, too, can gain the same power and goodness as the person in power. The end. You want to say something?

Patient: I didn't get the hints.

Therapist: You didn't get any of the hints? Who do you think the king was?

Patient: Me?

Therapist: Who is the man in power?

Patient: You?

Therapist: Well, why might it represent me?

Patient: My father?

Therapist: Well, why might it represent your father?

Patient: Well, before I was scared of my father and seemed depressed.

Therapist: And then what happened?

Patient: Then I gradually got to know him better and I wasn't scared of him anymore. Am I right?

Therapist: Right. That's what this story means. See, in your story you're not afraid to ask the king and you also have a kind of equal relationship with the king. He does a favor for you, you do a favor for him. It's a more equal relationship, rather than of some lowly person fearing some mighty person. The end.

In my story I go through the course of Joey's own experience with his father. The man whom he considered to be punitive and threatening, when tested out, is found to be benevolent. I then carry the oedipal resolution further and assure the patient that when he grows up he will have the powers and prerogatives of his father.

In the post-story discussion, Joey was able to analyze the story, although he did not at first consciously appreciate its significance.

Example 2

Paul, the boy with poor school performance in spite of high intelligence, experienced significant clinical improvement. His teacher described him as much more attentive in class and his grades reflected this. Babyish behavior and the tendency to associate with the most immature students in his class were no longer present. Seven-and-a-half months after therapy began, he told this story:

Today my story is going to be about a man and he always wanted to be an artist, but he could never draw good enough. So he kept on practicing and finally one day he decided that maybe if he got a job he could feel better about doing it because he would be doing it for other

236

people — kind of — and he'd have more confidence in his drawings.

Therapist: How would that give him more confidence? I am not sure.

Patient: Well, he'd be doing it a lot and he'd kind of be practicing and I guess he'd think that the practicing would make him better. So he got a job and he started drawing a couple of pictures of horses and that's what he could draw the best. So then he drew some pictures of horses and then he painted them. They didn't look so good, but he thought that he could put them out in the window of his store and maybe people would like them good enough and they'd come in and buy some.

So one man who couldn't see very well looked at the pictures and he thought that they were pretty good. So he went into the store and bought a picture of a great big horse and when he got home he hung it up. He thought it looked good, but his wife didn't like it as much as he did so she decided that she was going to put it in a different room.

So the man kept on making more horse pictures and some more people came in and they bought them. One man came in and he said, "Why all the horse pictures? Don't you draw anything but that?" The man said, "Yes, but horses are what I draw the best." So the other man said, "Well, if you are just gonna keep on drawing horses you'll never be good drawing other things." So the man tried making a picture of a house. It turned out good and he started making pictures of different things, like he made a picture of a man. He made a picture of a turtle and some other things.

So the man bought one of the pictures and he took it home, but it wasn't really as good as some of the other pictures of the horses, but he decided that if he put it up in his house and got the artist to come over to his house, he might think that his paintings were real good and he would do them more and then he would get better. So the man went and he hung up the picture in the dining room and then he invited the artist to come for dinner. So when the artist came and he saw the picture and he thought that the man liked it very much. So the next day when the artist went back he drew some more pictures and he kept on practicing. After that he got to be a real good artist.

The lesson of that story is: if you try something it might turn out that you can do it pretty good.

The story, in a way, reflects the course of Paul's therapy. Termination stories will, on occasion, epitomize the treatment progress. Here, the artist develops increasing confidence after initial periods of insecurity. His feelings of competence come only after hard work and are based on the skill which can only come from practice. There is no magic acquisition of expertise. The only possible neurotic element in the story was his selling his first picture to a man who could not see too well. Although this was certainly only a minor manifestation of the feelings of inadequacy Paul had felt early in treatment (only a person with deficient sight would buy his pictures), the duplicity involved warranted some rectification. Accordingly, I told this story:

Once upon a time there was a man and he wanted to become an artist. At first, having had no training or experience, he wasn't too good, but he realized that if he were to be good he would have to work very hard. So he went to art school to learn how to be an artist and he studied very hard and he worked very hard. Then he began to draw better and better and then he started to draw horses.

Well, he drew a picture of a horse which he didn't think was too good, but he decided to try to sell it anyway. He figured that maybe some blind man would come along or something and he won't notice it. Then he thought, "No, that's not right. I shouldn't try to trick people. I shouldn't try to sell paintings to blind men. I should work hard enough until I have pictures which are good enough that I can sell them proudly and not have to fool a blind man." So he decided not to try to fool blind people and he, therefore, worked harder and decided to wait before trying to sell any of his pictures until he got better and until he was a better artist and could perfect his style. So he worked a

238

longer and longer time until his pictures were much better. Then he put them out into the window and was able to sell them to people whose sight was good and they liked them very much. Whereas he had originally started off drawing horses, he now drew other things and he got better and better as time went on and he became a very famous artist.

The lesson of that story is that if you practice and work hard there's a good chance that you will be very good. Also, you will not gain anything by trying to fool people. You may be successful in doing that but you won't feel good about yourself and you won't have the fun of doing things well. The end.

In my story I re-emphasize the patient's message that "practice makes perfect." This is one of the ways I respond to the termination story — I merely repeat the healthy message to drive it home even further. In addition, I elaborate on any possible inappropriate element in the child's story — in Paul's case, the theme of duplicity — and present a healthier alternative. The "virtue is its own reward" message in the moral also serves to underscore more salutary adaptation.

Following the storytelling, Paul drew a picture of a man diving underwater toward a red coral and told his story about it:

A man wanted a coral for his collection. He went skin diving. He saw a beautiful red coral. He went down to get it. It was deep down, and each time that he got his hands on it, he had to come up for air. He was afraid that his lungs would run out of air. He tried again and again. Each time he almost made it but he didn't. Finally after many tries he got it.

The moral of this story is: keep trying.

On its most superficial level the story is a restatement of the one told earlier in the session in the storytelling game — hard work enables one to achieve his goal. I believe, however, that there is a deeper message as well. The coral is without question heart shaped, crimson red, and probably symbolizes his mother's love. One of the goals in Paul's therapy was to improve his relationship with his mother. There was no question that she deeply loved the boy, but her misguided approaches to his upbringing left him at times with the impression that her affection was deficient. Work with both the patient and his mother succeeded in improving the situation to such a degree that the child was much more secure in their relationship. The picture and its associated story reflected this improvement. In addition, they further confirmed my clinical impression that the patient would soon be ready to terminate his treatment.

One week later, Paul told this story:

Today my story is going to be about a man and he wanted a job. So he went to his friend's house and asked his friend if he knew where he could get a job. The man said there was a job for a teacher to teach people to drive cars. He said, "Well, I know how to drive a car and so I think I'll try over there." So he went there and asked the man about the job and he said, "Well, all right, but we'll have to test you to see if you can drive well and you won't teach people to drive bad." So they tested him and they found out that he was pretty good for the job so they tried him and he taught four people how to do that.

One of the people wrote a letter to the man that said that now that they knew how to drive a car that they are going to do a lot of good things and they thanked him for teaching them so good.

So the man thought that he was real good at that and so he went back to his friend and told his friend that he got the job and he had taught a few people and they liked his teaching. So the man said, "Do you like the job?" So the other man said, "Well, it's good enough." The friend said, "Well, why don't you get a job that you like real well?" The man said, "Well, there might not be any jobs." So the friend said, "Well, what do you like the most?" The man said, "I like drawing things." The friend said, "Well, there's no job around here for drawing things." The man said, "Oh, well, I think I'll stay in the job that I have now." That's the end.

The lesson of that story is: if you ask someone if they could help you, you could get a good job.

Therapist: Okay. This man got a good job but you said there was something else he liked more; he liked drawing more. Is that right?

Patient: Yeah.

Therapist: But he settled for teaching people how to drive. Is that it?

Patient: Yes.

Therapist: Okay.

Driving a car is one of the most common symbols of independence, self-assertion, and competence in controlling events of one's life. In this story Paul reveals the security he feels in being able to do things on his own. His capability is such that he feels competent to teach others as well — and he does so with success. Up to this point, the story is quite healthy, and it poignantly reflects his therapeutic progress. The remainder, however, reveals some anxiety on his part regarding proceeding even further. Paul was aware that therapy was scheduled to terminate in two weeks, and the second part of the story indicates, I believe, his feeling of "quitting while he's ahead." Possibly he fears that without me he will not be able to continue to mature and grow. Having learned to drive symbolizes the basic feeling of self-confidence which he has gained from therapy. Learning to draw symbolizes his future career, which he still feels somewhat anxious about. This is not a sick fear, however; it is one which I would consider normal for any nine-year-old boy. With this understanding of Paul's story, I told the following:

Once upon a time there was a man and he wanted a job. So he went to his friend and he spoke to his friend about it and his friend said, "You know there's a driving school across the street. Maybe they need someone to teach drivers." So he said, "Well, I know how to drive a car. Maybe I'll go over there."

So he went over there and they did need a person and

he started to teach others, but, of course, he had to work very hard first. Even though he knew how to drive a car he had to work very hard in order to learn how to be a good teacher. Then finally after a lot of hard work he did learn to be a good teacher and then he began teaching other people how to drive. He taught four people how to drive very well. One of them sent him a letter thanking him for having given him lessons because after the lessons he had learned how to drive so well that he was able to get a good job and he was very grateful to this man for having taught him.

So he went back to his friend and told him about the teaching in the driving school and his friend said, "Do you really like it?" "Yes," he said, "but I really would enjoy art more." So the friend said, "Well, as gratifying as teaching school must be, if you really enjoy art more, perhaps that's what you should try to do. Of course, there are very few jobs." The man said, "I think that I can do it."

So he started to work very hard training to be an artist. He studied very hard — long hours, long hours, long months — and finally he was able to become an artist and was able to get a job although they were hard to find.

The lesson of that story is that it's very gratifying and a lot of fun to do the thing you want and if you are not doing the thing you want it's important to try to do it and it may be a lot of hard work, but it's important to work hard to try to reach your goal. In this story, although this man did well as a teacher, he really wanted to be an artist and he worked very hard and he finally became one. The end.

In my story Paul is encouraged to push through the anxieties, and suffer the discomforts, which forging ahead in life necessarily entails. Following my story he drew a picture of two Martians who at first feared that they would not be able to survive in the earth's atmosphere. They built themselves special space suits, descended to earth with some trepidation, and to their surprise and relief found that they could survive quite well.

Example 3

Helen, the girl who returned to treatment for help in handling her divorced, intermittently psychotic mother, told this story in her last session, which took place two weeks after her stories about the monster at the beach and the good student, Laurie, and her friend, Stephanie.

> Once there were two girls named Leslie and Joan. One week-end they went skating together in Central Park. Leslie was a fairly good skater but Joan wasn't. When Joan got on the ice she had to be careful. Leslie helped her. Leslie had a lot of fun but Joan didn't. As the day went on Joan got much better.
> The moral of this story is: if at first you don't succeed, try, try again.

The story was analyzed with Helen in a manner similar to the ones of hers previously described. She denied conscious awareness that it pertained to her situation with her mother. However, it was not difficult for her to recognize that Joan represented her sick mother and Leslie, the patient herself. Joan, like her mother, is "skating on ice." She is in a precarious life situation and "has to be careful," and requires Leslie's help. Leslie is capable of having fun, but Joan isn't — a clear reference to the mother's depression. The story ends with Joan's improvement — an accurate reflection of the clinical situation in which both the mother and the daughter were doing much better.

In the subsequent discussion we both agreed that it was time to discontinue treatment.

Example 4

Charles, an eight-and-one-half-year-old-boy, was referred for treatment because of a severe immaturity problem. He spoke in a whining, sing-song manner, had no friends other than occasional contacts with children three years younger than he. Charles had no sense of responsibility regarding his school work and household chores. He cried easily and tried to cover his deficiencies with patent falsehoods.

At the time of referral the mother was dying of leukemia. Her death occurred about two months after treatment began. Treatment during the first few months was centered around the mother's illness and death. Practical suggestions were made, regarding funeral arrangements, for example, and he was helped to work through his reactions. During the ensuing months attempts to help him with the immaturity problem proved futile. One reason for this was the father's attitude toward this boy. The father was extroverted and had always wanted a son who would be proficient in sports, outgoing like himself, and "one of the boys." Charles was just the opposite, and was thereby a great disappointment to the father, who openly berated his son with comments like: "You're just a baby" and "Why can't you be like the other kids?" Attempts to alter the father's attitudes were fruitless, and so the patient was continually exposed to his father's scorn. Therefore, in spite of my efforts, the patient's problems remained deeply entrenched and the therapeutic atmosphere became one of hopelessness. About a month before this story was told, I informed the boy and his father that I would continue treatment one month longer. If after that there was still no evidence of progress, I would recommend that therapy be discontinued. I assured them that I would be willing to resume therapy in the future if re-evaluation warranted such resumption. This is the story Charles told one month after my confrontation:

> Once upon a time a long, long, long time ago in a distant land far, far, far away there lived a mouse. This mouse would crawl under streets, houses, under chairs, under rooms — everything you could think of.
>
> So then there was this big building and he jumped off and he thought, "I want to try to fly." So he tried and he didn't succeed and he fell down, down, down, down, down, down — the Empire State Building. Everybody thought this was sad and his father said, "Tsk, poor thing."

Then they saw the mouse do this. The mouse was moving and then it woke up. Then it yawned. It was all a dream, a horrible dream.

The lesson of that story is: birds could fly, mammals can't. Thank you, Dr. Gardner.

The story is a moving statement of the boy's despair. Charles sees himself as a mouse, with all its implications of smallness, impotency, and furtiveness. He crawls under "everything you could think of." Nothing is lower than this mouse. He wants to fly, raise himself up, and achieve competence; but instead he gets killed. He envisions that his efforts to enhance himself will only result in his destruction. The suicidal element is also present here (jumping off the Empire State Building), but there was no clinical evidence that this boy had reached such a point of desperation. The father's comment, "Tsk, poor thing," was perfunctory, reflecting the patient's appreciation of his father's basic feeling that his son would not be missed. The "It was all a dream, a horrible dream" ending in no way alters the psychodynamic validity of the story. Such anxiety-alleviating "undoing" is common and I usually ignore it as a possible element in my own story.

With this understanding of the patient's story and the deteriorated therapeutic situation in which it was told, I related this story:

Once upon a time there were two boys, boy Number One and boy Number Two. Now they were very sad; they were so sad that they felt like they were little mice. They felt like they were crawling under walls and crawling under streets and crawling under chairs and crawling under rooms. They just felt lousy about themselves. They felt like such small cruds. Why did they feel small? They felt small because first, their mother had died and second, their father was the kind of person who didn't like their personalities too much because they were kind of childish.

Now one of these boys just stayed very sad and at times he would feel like jumping off a roof or jumping off a building. He was so sad that he wanted to kill himself.

That's how sad he was. The other boy thought to himself: "Am I going to let myself stay this way, stay a baby, stay sad, feel like killing myself or am I going to go out and make friends and have good times with others and feel better about myself by being friends with others?"

So the first one stayed sad, stayed lonely and lived a very unhappy life. He remained a child even though he grew up to be an old man and he was sad and lonely. Even long after his father died he was still sad and lonely and still like a child. He would talk like a child; he would sing songs; he would whine; he would cry like a baby and he would lie.

The other one changed. The other one went out and made friends, got involved with other people, applied himself, worked hard, felt good about himself, and was no longer sad. The other one remained feeling like a mouse for the rest of his life. The end.

Therapist: Anything you want to say about that story?
Patient: No.
Therapist: I want to ask you a question. Do you think that story has anything to do with you?
Patient: No.
Therapist: Not at all?
Patient: Not at all.
Therapist: You're not either one of those boys?
Patient: No.
Therapist: Why not?
Patient: 'Cause they didn't do right. I do.
Therapist: Who didn't do right?
Patient: The boys. That mouse who stayed like he was 'cause he wasn't making friends. The boy who like wasn't making friends.
Therapist: What about him? That's not like you?
Patient: Right.
Therapist: I see. Okay. The end.

In my story I utilize the "twin-brother" or "two close friends" mechanism to contrast the healthy with the sick behavior. I have found that the simultaneous presentation of conflicting facets of the personality enhances the efficacy of my communications. I avoid using names because I might choose one that would remind the patient of a specific person.

One of my goals in treating this child was to help him form more meaningful relationships with peers in the hope that this would, in part, compensate for his parental deprivations. My story reflects this effort, and like most others with this boy, it was apparently told in vain. At the end of my story, the patient had no spontaneous comments. When asked to say something about it, he still had nothing to say. He did not think the story in any way related to himself and stated that he was unlike anyone in it. The denial of his own inadequacies was as strong as ever, and his resistances were still massive. The transcript does not begin to convey the feeling of futility I felt. The story, and the subsequent discussion (if it can be called that) served to confirm my clinical decision that therapy should be terminated.

Example 5

Nancy was first referred at age three-and-a-half because of severe temper tantrums, disruptive behavior in nursery school, disobedience at home, excessive craving for physical contact with strangers, excessive masturbation, and a tendency to withdraw into fantasy (but not to a psychotic degree). Her mother was overprotective in an effort to compensate for her own feelings of inadequacy and insecurity. The father's professional life left him little time for his children.

Nancy's first therapeutic experience lasted five months at the end of which her major symptoms had essentially cleared. Some of this improvement was no doubt related to changes in her mother brought about by the latter's therapy with me. One year after termination she returned with an exacerbation of similar symptoms. After one year of further work she was again ready to discontinue treatment. Nancy told this story in her last session:

Once upon a time there was a bird and a helicopter and they went to Hawaii and they asked them if they wanted —

Therapist: Wait a minute. Who is "they"?

Patient: The Hawaiian people.

Therapist: The Hawaiian people asked the bird and helicopter if what?

Patient: If they could take a trip to the jungle with them. So they went to the jungle and then they met Tarzan. Then they were going to eat lunch up in a tree so first Tarzan showed them how to swing up. Then he came down and then Tarzan took the bird up with him. Then he took the Hawaiian people up and then they all had lunch on the tree. That's the end of the story.

The lesson of that story is: if you want to go to the jungle with the Hawaiian people and eat lunch up in a tree, you go up with Tarzan.

During her course of treatment, the patient had frequently used a bird or a helicopter to represent herself. Tarzan, I believe, symbolizes the therapist — strong, competent, commanding, and resourceful (Considerations of modesty must not deter the therapist from his interpretations.). The jungle represents the confusion and anxiety she felt when she first entered therapy. Tarzan leads her and the Hawaiian people, which are her alter egos and possibly the dependent parts of her parents' personalities, through the confusion of the jungle to a tree. The tree probably represents the healthy aspects of her parents — their strength, independence, and ability to provide her with support. He brings together a union of the child with her parents, a union which is secure (she is supported up in the tree) and nurturing (they eat lunch there).

The story summarizes what occurred in treatment. The relationship with her parents did improve, and she felt that they were more supportive and giving. The moral: "if you want to go to the jungle with the Hawaiian people and eat lunch up in a tree, you go up with Tarzan" is a flattering statement. I do not think that the dependency elements present in this story (on Tarzan, for *taking* her up the tree and on her parents, for supporting her in the tree) are pathological — such elements are normal for a six-year-old child.

The story confirmed my clinical impression that Nancy was ready to terminate and I told this story in response:

Once upon a time there was a bird and a helicopter and they went to Hawaii. The Hawaiian people said, "Would you like to take a trip into the jungle?" They said, "Yes."

Then they went into the jungle and they met Tarzan. Tarzan said, "Would you like me to show you how we can get up into the tree there and have lunch in the tree?" The people said yes, and Tarzan said, "I'll show you how to do it and as soon as you learn how to do it then you could do it yourself." They said, "Okay." So Tarzan taught them how to do it and after that they learned how to go up to the tree themselves and get food and they didn't need Tarzan anymore. When they grew up they learned how to get food on their own and they didn't even have to get it up in the tree.

And do you know what the lesson of that story is?
Patient: What?
Therapist: That when you want to learn to do something, first you have to learn from a big person and then you can do it by yourself. That's the end of the story and those people lived happily ever after.

In my story I attempted to lay down a foundation for future independence. Although I did not consider the dependency elements in the patient's story to be pathological for her age, I felt that a message regarding future self-sufficiency could not hurt. Introducing the next step in the child's maturational process is another way in which the therapist can respond to a healthy termination story.

Example 6

Dale, an eight-year-old boy, was referred because of poor school performance, hyperactivity, silliness, immaturity, provocative behavior in the classroom, and withdrawal from peers because he could not appropriately respond to teasing. The boy was of at least average intelligence but exhibited perceptual and graphomotor impairments which contributed to his academic difficulties. He was doing very poorly in a normal third grade class. His school was not aware of the basic organic component in his learning and behavioral problems.

Diagnostically, I considered him to have minimal brain dysfunction with superimposed psychogenic problems, most of which I felt would not be present if this boy were not organically impaired. I suggested a program of tutoring by someone specially trained in the education of children with this kind of learning disability. I did not recommend treatment but rather suggested that I re-evaluate him every six months. My hope was that with the academic improvement the secondary psychogenic problems would resolve and that direct work with me would not be necessary.

By the first follow-up visit improvement in both the academic and the behavioral areas was reported. In the one year follow-up, Dale was reported to be working just about at grade level, was getting along much better with friends, was no longer disruptive in the classroom, and was generally happier and more mature. I, too, found him more alert, outgoing, and optimistic. During the one year follow-up visit, Dale told me this story:

> Once there was a bear and there was a forest fire and he tried to put it out and it didn't work. So he had to get the firemen and they got it out for him.
> The lesson of that story is: don't play with fire.

The story is a statement about the child's experiences with me. When he first came he, like the bear, felt as if he were trapped in a burning forest, helpless to protect himself. His own efforts to handle the situation proved futile and he therefore sought help from firemen — the therapist — who were successful in saving him. The moral, "Don't play with fire," does not appear to be directly related to the events in the story in that it suggests that the bear started the fire, and no mention is made in the story as to who started it. It suggests that Dale may have considered himself responsible for his difficulties. This mechanism is most often understood to be a manifestation of retroflexed rage. Hostility felt toward the environment is redirected against oneself because of guilt and fear of its outward expression. Another explanation and a more reasonable one, I think, is that it is more often a manifestation of the need to gain control over an uncontrollable situation. Personal control is strongly implied in the notion: "It's my fault." The "delusion" is anxiety-alleviating in that it suggests that the child, by his own acts, could have prevented the illness and he is thereby less subject to the vicissitudes of nature. The author and others have described this mechanism, but it has not been given the attention it deserves in the psychoanalytic literature.

Although Dale had received no formal therapy, he was given an educational program which was, without question, therapeutic. Feeling more secure and competent, he had less need to resort to neurotic defense mechanisms to hide or compensate for his deficits. Indeed, there were fewer deficits. The story reflects this course of events. It is a termination story: the fires are out, and the fireman's assistance is no longer necessary. Accordingly, I told this story:

Once upon a time there was a bear and this bear was in the forest and a forest fire started. Well, he didn't know how to put out forest fires so he called the fire department and they came along and they helped the bear. The men in the fire department and the bear worked together and they put out that fire. After that the bear had learned how to put out fires because while he was putting out the fire they taught him certain things to do which helped him put it out. After that whenever there was a forest fire he was able to put it out himself. He didn't need the firemen except once in a while when there was a very big one. Then, of course, he would need the firemen to help him.
Therapist: Do you know what the lesson of that story is?
Patient: Not to play with fires.
Therapist: Well, that's one of the lessons. The other lesson is that sometimes you don't know how to do something

yourself so you should call on others to help you. Sometimes when you don't know how to do something you will call on others to help you, but after you have learned how to do it yourself, you don't need other people to help you. This bear didn't know at the beginning but later on he knew how. That's the end of that story. Do you have anything to say about that story?

Patient: That's a good story.

Therapist: What about it did you like?

Patient: Well, he learned from the fire department.

Therapist: Good. Okay.

I did not consider Dale's dependence on the firemen to be a pathological element in the story of a nine-year-old boy. In my story, I directed him more toward the time when he will be expected to use what he has learned to do. His suggested moral, "Not to play with fires," relates back to the already described need to control and reflects the power of this mechanism. It is so common that I consider it most often normal, especially when it mobilizes the patient into directing his energies into activities of rectification and self-improvement. This was certainly the case with this boy. The part he liked most in my story was where the bear "learned from the fire department." My message was received.

In the same session, the patient drew a picture of a boat and told this story about it:

This boat has ropes and sails. It goes into the Atlantic Ocean. It comes to a storm and it passes through the storm. It anchors at a place where you can dock boats and it stays there for a night. It starts off the next morning. They stop and sit around and eat lunch on the deck. They sail into the Atlantic harbor, dock for a week, and then sail back home.

The story is self-explanatory. The ship, representing the patient, has weathered the storm and now sails on calm seas. Therapy was terminated.

Example 7

Carol, the nine-and-a-half-year-old girl with stuttering, insomnia, and poor peer relationships, was placed in a most difficult bind quite early in treatment. Her mother, a very angry woman, became increasingly hostile toward me and tried to get the patient to side with her against me. She would interrogate the patient after each session in an attempt to point out what she considered to be my defects. On one occasion, after two months of treatment, the following dialogue — related by the patient and confirmed by the mother — took place:

Mother (in a tone of biting sarcasm): So what did you and Dr. Gardner talk about today?
Patient: We talked about a nightmare I had. I dreamed monsters were chasing me.
Mother: And what did *he* think about *that*?
Patient: He thought I had a lot of anger in me that I was scared to let out.
Mother: I think he's full of shit.

Following similar reports by the patient, I arranged an interview with the parents. I told them that the likelihood of therapy succeeding was small as long as the mother continued to try to undermine Carol's relationhip with me. My invitation to the mother to air her complaints to me directly, in the hope that at least some of the difficulties might be resolved, was greeted with a barrage of invective. Attempts to help her gain insight into her reactions were futile. She did agree, however, to consult with another therapist regarding treatment for herself. It was also decided that if, after another month, there was still no appreciable difference in the mother's attitude, treatment would be discontinued.

One month later the mother, although in treatment, was as hostile as ever toward me, and it was agreed that there was no point to my working further with the child, who had been in treatment for three months. The parents also decided not to seek treatment elsewhere for the child at that time. During the session, which Carol knew was to be her last, she told this story:

Once upon a time there was this household and the lady was having a beautiful party. One day the maid spilled some coffee on the drapes and she said, "Tonight's the lady's party. What can I do?" So she tried hiding them. So she pasted a piece of colored wallpaper on them.

That night at the party somebody rubbed against the drapes and the paper fell off. "Oh, dear, you have a coffee stain on your drapes!" So they marked her off because they were having a contest as to who had the most beautiful house.

Therapist: Oh, so she lost the contest?

Patient: Yes. So the next day the lady said to the maid, "Why didn't you tell me there was a coffee stain on my drapes?" And the housekeeper said, "Well, I was afraid you would scream." The lady said, "If you told me I would have gotten a new pair of drapes and I would have won."

The moral of the story is: when you have a problem, try talking it out.

The lady, of course, is Carol's mother and the housekeeper, the patient herself. Spilling coffee on the lady's drapes, and thereby causing her to lose the beautiful house contest, is the patient's way of expressing her anger. She was much too repressed to reveal it more openly. In the moral, "When you have a problem, try talking it out," Carol pays lip-service to my communications from previous stories, but she does not implement the notion in this story. She does just the opposite. She uses silence in the service of expressing hostility. By not telling the lady of the house about the stain, the maid caused the lady to lose the contest. With this understanding of Carol's story, I told this one:

Once upon a time there was a lady and she was going to have a big party in her house to see who had the prettiest house in town. Well, as the maid was preparing for the party, she spilled coffee on the drapes, and she thought about it and realized that she must have been very angry at the madame of the house if she did such a thing because spilling coffee on the drapes could really cause the madame to lose the contest. So she went to the madame and she said to her, "You know, I spilled coffee on your drapes." The madame became very furious and started screaming at her. Then the maid said, "Yes, you know, I think that's why I spilled coffee. I didn't purposely do it but maybe it was my unconscious mind that made me do it because I'm probably very angry at you for the way you always scream at me all the time."

Well, the lady of the house then began to realize that she was really being too angry at the maid and being kind of cruel at times, and that even if the maid didn't answer back, she would tend to make mistakes and errors which might express the anger that she had. Do you understand that?

Patient: Yeah.

Therapist: And so she stopped screaming and she said to the maid, "I'm glad you told me how you feel because now there will be fewer accidents around this house. That's exactly what happened. There were fewer accidents and then they had a much better relationship.

And the moral of the story is: when somebody does something to get you angry, tell them about it. Don't do things like spilling coffee on their curtains. The end.

Therapist: What did you think of that

Patient: I thought it was quite a good story.

Therapist: Fine. Okay.

In this, my "one-for-the-road" communication to the patient, I once again tried to get her to more directly express her rage toward her mother rather than displacing, repressing, and denying it. I demonstrated how such overt expression can be helpful in solving conflicts between people.

This story is typical of a last story when therapy has been prematurely terminated by the parents. When the child knows that the session is to be his last, he may epitomize his core problems in his story in the hope that the therapist will give him a rich and meaningful message to take along with him. I would like to believe that these "one-for-the-road" tales of mine have special significance for the child and contribute to healthier adaptations afterwards. Unfortunately, in Carol's case, I have not yet been given the opportunity to find out whether such efforts have been successful.

Example 8

Bonnie, the girl with massive school phobia and multiple other fears, experienced marked clinical improvement in nine months of treatment. Because of her improvement a termination date was set. This story was told one week prior to the date of discontinuation.

Once there was this dragon a long time ago and all the other dragons had wings and they could fly around, but this one was a little baby. He was about two or three years old and he didn't have his wings all grown yet, but he still wanted to fly. All of his other friends tried with their little wings and some of them did get off the ground; but he wanted to fly but he was afraid to get off the ground. So his parents also told him, "If you fly you'll get caught up in a tree or you'll fall and break your neck." Well, he really wanted to fly because he saw by his other friends how much fun it was, but he was still scared and very nervous about it. He thought it looked like fun, but he wasn't sure because he thought he might hurt himself.

So then his grandfather came over one day and he said to him, "I'll teach you how to fly if you want. You're old enough." The dragon said, "Well, I don't know. It's kind of dangerous. I better wait until I'm older." "Nonsense," said the grandfather. "All of your other cousins fly. Some of them even go up as high at clouds." So he thought, "Boy, going up as high as clouds. That's fun." "Well," he said, "my parents won't let me." His grandfather said, "Why don't you ask them?"

256

So they went to his parents and his grandfather said, "Why don't you let me teach him how to fly?" The parents said, "Teach him how to fly, are you kidding, at his age? He'll crash; he'll hurt himself; he'll break his neck; he'll never be able to get down; he'll get caught in a tree." They named a whole lot of terrible things. This made the little dragon even more frightened.

One time in the middle of the night the grandfather was staying for a month because his cave was being built over. So he woke up the little dragon and said: "Your parents are asleep. I'll teach you how to fly." He said, "Oh, no. I'll crash." So the grandfather took the little dragon and put him on his back. Then the grandfather ran out before he had time to get off and started flying. Up in the air went the grandfather with his little grandson on his back. Then the grandfather tilted a little so that the little dragon could fall off and the little dragon was flapping his wings very hard and slowly coming to the ground. Then as he almost reached the ground he started to flap a lot harder. Even if he touched the ground he couldn't have hurt himself because he was flapping so hard that he came down softly; but he flapped so hard that finally he got up in the air. He went up and up and he never wanted to come down. He flew around and he got up high and he played and his grandfather went up in the air. They had flying races and he never had any more fun in his life.

So then he showed his parents the next morning. He said, "Mommy, Daddy, I know how to fly." They were so scared and they got furious at the grandfather and they said, "What are you trying to do — kill our little boy?" and things like that. So when the little boy got up in the air he flew and he flew and he flew and they decided that maybe it wasn't as dangerous as they thought and that maybe they should let him fly. He's old enough and it's not really dangerous. That's the end.

The moral of that story is: you shouldn't be afraid of things like that and you should try them once and then if you find that they are dangerous then not try them again. You should always try. Usually things aren't as dangerous as people say they are or believe they are.

Therapist: Do you think there's any relationship between that story and anything that has happened to you?

Patient: Well, my parents were afraid of some things with me.

Therapist: What were they afraid of?

Patient: Oh, for me to swim in the deep end of our swimming pool; for me to cross the street or ride my bicycle off the circle. I couldn't do that for a long time.

Therapist: What else?

Patient: A lot of things. They were just afraid for me to do things.

Therapist: And now?

Patient: Well, some things they are not so afraid of me doing anymore, but they still are overprotective.

Therapist: When you were telling this story were you aware that the little dragon in the story was similar to you?

Patient: Well, I didn't think about it until later.

Therapist: You mean until after the story was over?

Patient: Oh, around the middle of the story.

Therapist: Then you realized it was like you?

Patient: Yeah, that his parents were afraid for him to do certain things that were just a tiny bit dangerous.

Therapist: So what's the main things that helped this dragon stop being afraid?

Patient: When he tried it.

Therapist: He tried it, uh-huh. And what was the other thing —— anything else that helped him not to be afraid?

Patient: Well, his grandfather took him out and showed it to him.

Therapist: I would say another thing was that he began to realize that the things his parents thought were not true.

Patient: Yes.

Therapist: That's very important that he began to realize that what his parents thought were frightening things were not frightening things for him. Hhmmm?

Patient: Yes.

Therapist: I see. Okay. Well, that was an excellent story. Do you think there's any story that I can make up that could improve upon yours?

Patient: Maybe that his grandfather didn't show him. He showed himself.

Therapist: It's going to be hard to improve upon that story, isn't it? That he did it on his own; that's a good idea. I would say that my story would say that gradually as he got older —— let's say that we don't have his grandfather in the story —— he realized that the things his mother and father were saying were not so because he saw that other mothers and fathers were saying different things and his friends were doing these things and they were not in any kind of trouble so he tried it himself even though it was scary at first.

So what do you think about your troubles about being afraid to do things? Do you still think you have that trouble or not?

Patient: I'm not — no — not particularly.

Therapist: I don't think so either. Tell me, if you weren't moving to Colorado do you think you would be able to stop seeing me?

Patient: I suppose so.

Therapist: Yes, that's what I think. What about next week? Do you think you should come next week?

Patient: It doesn't matter to me.

Therapist: Do you want to come just for old times' sake — since it's your last week?

Patient: Okay.

Therapist: Okay. Very good.

As Bonnie tells us herself, during the first part of her narrative she was not consciously aware that the story pertained to her. That she did relate it to herself in the latter part does not, in my opinion, lessen the story's validity. This was not the kind of child who "buttered me up."

The patient herself provided a suggested improvement, obviating the need for me to tell a story. Discussion of the plot of a story incorporating her refinement was sufficient.

During the same session, Bonnie related a dream from the previous night:

I was with this skin diver. There was a lady and a

man with us too. We were standing on a dock, ready to dive. I was scared at first; but we dived off into the bay. It was at night. We swam across the water to another dock. We got up on the other dock. There was a houseboat there and we had dinner in it. I wasn't scared anymore.

Bonnie had had some experience with me in dream analysis and thought that the two adults represented her parents and the skin diver, the therapist. She surmised that the diving into the water stood for her treatment, where she and her parents had learned to do many things which they had previously found anxiety-provoking. Swimming across the bay symbolized the successful completion of the therapeutic course. Enjoying a good meal represented her new freedom to enjoy the pleasures of the world.

The dream and story each supported my clinical decision that Bonnie was ready to leave.

Example 9

Karen, a ten-year-old girl whose school phobia problem had improved significantly over a one-year period of therapy told this story:

Once there was this lady and she was moving from her home in town, and she moved one day and her friend came with her, you know, just to help her awhile and to stay with her a few days. As she got the house decorated and her new furniture came —— she got this new furniture —— chairs and couches —— and her friend didn't like it, like she didn't like the chair the way it was decorated, you know, the cushions or anything. So she told the lady and the lady said, "You shouldn't speak out and tell your feelings about this." The girl said, "Why not? Why shouldn't I? I don't mean it to be insulting to you. I just mean to tell you what I think. I don't mean to be insulting to you. I like it a little but I just don't care about it that much."

260

So the lady got to think about what her friend said. Then she thought that you should speak out your feelings and tell how you feel it looks. And so the next day her friend was going home and she said she was sorry what she said the day before about not speaking your feelings. It's not wrong to speak out your feelings.

Therapist: So? Is that the end of the story? And the lesson is?

Patient: If you have something to say just say it. You don't mean to be insulting or anything.

Therapist: Hhmmm. Fine. Very good story. Thank you very much. That was an excellent story.

As is true in most, if not all, patients with school phobias, Karen was massively inhibited in the expression of her feelings. Freeing her in this regard was a central goal in therapy. Attempts were made to assuage the guilt she felt over thoughts and emotions which she considered unacceptable and she was encouraged to assert herself, stand up for her rights, and to vent her pent-up emotions in appropriate ways.

The lady in the story represents Karen's mother and the friend who expresses her criticism, the patient herself. In response to the mother's comment that the patient suppress her critical thoughts, she retorts that criticisms can be benevolent and not necessarily hostile. The mother realizes the appropriateness of the patient's position and accepts it. The story epitomizes what has gone on in her therapy. Whereas at the beginning of treatment Karen was extremely inhibited in verbalizing any thoughts which might have been at variance with those of her parents, she gradually became freer to do so. Her parents, who had originally considered her expressions of antagonism and disapproval to be signs of "disrespect," gradually began to accept her expressed resentments and criticisms and give them serious consideration. The patient had learned that expressing herself could not only be useful in helping her achieve her ends, but also that her anticipated rejections need not occur. Concomitant with her translating these lessons into action and experiencing them in real-life situations, there was a clearing of her school phobia and many other fears.

In response, I told this story:

Once upon a time there was a lady and she was moving from her house to another town and she had a friend who stayed with her. This friend was a very close friend and when the lady moved in her new furniture her very close friend thought that some of the furniture was not really in good taste and that some of the combinations that the lady had chosen to use were in poor taste and would really not be very attractive. So she said to her, "You know, I'm a very close friend of yours, and I feel I can tell you this and I know you will take it in the spirit I present it and that you will understand that I am not saying this to hurt you, but to be friendly with you. I think that some of these combinations are poor and I suggest that you try some others.

The lady listened because she knew her friend meant well. Now the following day another person came and this person was not too friendly with the lady and this person did not like the color combinations either, but she didn't say anything because she didn't know the person that well and that it was impolite to make criticisms of people's furniture and just to come out with it unless they're really asking.

So the lesson of my story is that there are times when it is appropriate and reasonable to speak up and criticize, that is, when it's with a close friend or if the person asks your opinion. But there are other times when you may have criticisms when it may be appropriate and wise to keep them to yourself because it might hurt people's feelings. It's important to recognize the times when you keep your criticisms to yourself and the times when you may say them. The end.

Do you want to say anything about this story?

Patient: No.

Therapist: Okay. Fine.

There was nothing I could really add to the basic message in Karen's story. What I did was to add a further refinement, the suggestion that there are certain situations in life when one does suppress one's feelings. Such a message is best imparted in the termination phase of treatment after the child has pretty well overcome his fears of self-expression. It may otherwise be confusing.

One could say that this story is more appropriately a pretermination story in that it allowed the kind of "tailoring" which is so typical of the late phase story. However, the clinical picture was one which clearly indicated that the child was ready to terminate. On the day this story was told, Karen also related this dream:

I was in Temple Sinai where my grandmother goes. I went to the Hebrew School there and it was a lot of fun. It wasn't really a classroom because it had other things in it like gym equipment and games. I had fun doing the work and the physical exercises there. I also enjoyed reading Hebrew and studying Jewish history there.

The Hebrew School situation had been the most fearful for this girl. Her panic states there had been extreme and when urged to stay in the classroom her blood-curdling shrieks resounded throughout the school. The dream reflected her clinical improvement, and confirmed my opinion that, for this girl, the story was a termination one.

7. BASIC TECHNIQUE MODIFICATIONS

The basic storytelling technique lends itself to many modifications and elaborations. Some which I have used and found helpful are described below.

USING THE CHILD'S STORY IN DREAM ANALYSIS

Example 1

Mark, the boy with chronic anxiety and feelings of insecurity, presented this dream after two months of treatment:

> I saw this big fish. That was all. I was amazed it was so big.

Mark denied experiencing any special feelings during the dream and could not associate anything to it. I had no hunches either about the dream's meaning. I then suggested that we go on to playing the storytelling game, without commenting to the child that it might be of help to us in understanding the dream. To have introduced the idea that I was turning to the story for help might have contaminated it. This was the story Mark told:

> Once upon a time there was a fisherman. He was a fairly good fisherman. He caught a lot of fishes. He lived alone in a cottage by the sea. One day he saw a large wave. It was a tidal wave and it was far off. It looked so big that it could cover his house. He knew it would take a couple of hours to get there.
> He didn't know what to do. Should he pack up and

run away or should he stay there and try to tie things down and protect the house? He didn't want the house to get blown away. So he tied down the house and put canvases over the roof. He built up the roof.

Then he went into the cellar and stayed in the corner. The wave came hurling up and swept over the beach and came up towards the house and went "swap" right over the house and the cellar started filling up with water and everything. But the waves shrank back and there was another wave and it came up and it went "schwap" and it hit the house, but it didn't fall down. The fisherman came upstairs and the roof was broken in a little bit, but his house wasn't blown away and he was happy.

The lesson of that story is: it's not always a good idea to run away.
Therapist: Is that the end?
Patient: Yes.
Therapist: Very good. Thank you very much. Now it's time for me to tell a story myself.

Just after our discussion of the fish dream, the patient told me a story about a fisherman. It is almost as if the story was a continuation of the dream.

Mark, of course, is the fisherman. In his treatment we probe for things beneath the surface; we "fish" for things. The fisherman then is the boy in treatment delving into the unknown. The water, his unconscious, contains two elements: the fish and the tidal waves. The story reflects his fears that he may be fishing in dangerous waters; he may discover things in his treatment which may overwhelm and destroy him. In the dream the danger is only remotely implied: "I was amazed it [the fish] was so big." In the story the perilous underwater forces are unleashed. He considers the alternative of fleeing, discontinuing treatment, that is, but decides to weather the storm and expose himself to the painful revelations which may arise out of the deep. Although shaken, Mark tolerates the confrontation — a brave thing for this anxiety-ridden boy to do — and, in the end, "he was happy."

In response, I told this story:

Once upon a time there was a fisherman and he was a good fisherman and enjoyed going out into the ocean and fishing. However, there was one thing that he didn't like and that was the thought of having certain types of fishes in the house. He had just had this thing about not having certain kind of fishes in his house and even though he might fish and sell these fish to other people, he made a strict rule that he wouldn't bring certain types of fishes into his house and his wife cooperated with him on this and he just wouldn't eat those fishes or have them in the house.

So one day he looked out over the sea and he saw a large wave. It was a tidal wave. Now this was in a place where there were coral reefs and he knew that he had a couple of hours before the tidal wave would reach his house. Now he had a conflict. On the one hand, he thought, "Maybe I should run" and on the other hand, he thought, "I really love this house, but if I strap it down and put canvas and ropes and everything, the wave might come into the cellar and still might bring some of those terrible, ugly fish into the house as well. That's to me the most disgusting and terrible and ugly thought of all." Well, he thought and he thought and he said, "Well, I like this house very much. I don't want to lose it." So he got rope and he decided to tie it down. He got canvas and he covered it. He went down to the basement and sure enough first the tidal wave came along and "slap" it hit the house and water started going into the cellar and with the water, of course, guess what else came in?

Patient: The ugly fishes.

Therapist: Right! Some of the fishes he didn't mind, but some of the other ugly ones —— there they were in the basement and his initial response was to be disgusted and to be angry and upset. But then he realized that he had no choice and he realized that they really weren't as bad as he had originally thought. Then along came a second wave and "slap" hit the house again, and more of those fishes came in. He had no choice but to live with them awhile, and he knew that after the waves had passed he would be able to get them out. He realized again that they weren't as bad as he had thought.

Well, the second wave passed. He got out of the house and he saw that part of his roof had been taken off, but otherwise the house was pretty much intact. So he pumped the water out of the basement and he got the fishes out too and there was no question that he had to handle these fishes and he removed them from the basement. He threw them back into the ocean. He realized that they weren't as bad as he had thought. In fact, he saved a few and he and his wife had them for dinner, along with some of the fish he had known before to have liked.

Now the lesson of that story is —— what do you think the lesson of that story is?

Patient: Well, I know basically what the lesson is.

Therapist: What is the basic lesson?

Patient: Well, that just because you think that something is bad doesn't mean that it is bad.

Therapist: Right! And if you have an experience where you come into contact with the bad thing and give it a chance, you may find that it isn't as terrible as you had originally thought. That's the lesson of the story. Sometimes certain things are less bad than you originally think. The end.

All right, what did you think about that story?

Patient: No special comments.

Therapist: Did you find it interesting to listen to?

Patient: Yes.

Therapist: Was there any particular part that you liked the most?

Patient: Yeah, when he found out that his house wasn't blown down.

Therapist: Uh-huh. Good. Okay. Fine. So long folks. Do you want to hear that again or do you want to do something else?

Patient: I want to do something else.

Therapist: Okay.

In my story I reinforced the healthy elements in the patient's story. If he will continue to have the courage to look into his unconscious, to confront himself with the unpleasant things he may find there, he will find that his loathsome thoughts and feelings are not as abominable as he anticipates.

The first thing Mark told me in his next session was that he had had a dream the night after our previous meeting:

There was a big fish. It looked exactly like the one in the first dream, except it was a little smaller. It had shrunk and I had gotten bigger.

There is little I need add. The interchange demonstrates not only the value of the Mutual Storytelling Technique in understanding unanalyzable dreams, but the therapeutic efficacy of the method as well.

USING THE POST-STORY INQUIRY IN CLARIFYING THE MEANING OF THE CHILD'S STORY

As described in Chapter 1, and as demonstrated in some of the stories already presented, the post-story inquiry can be quite helpful — at times vital — to the understanding of the child's story. Two further examples of this aspect of the technique are presented here.

Example 2

Larry, the eight-year-old boy with compulsive rituals who told the story of the seven magic jelly beans each of which was used as another defense mechanism to handle his hostility toward his father, told this story in his sixth week of therapy:

Once upon a time there was —— oh, I would say —— this happened a long time ago —— two microphones and there was something peculiar about these microphones. Well, one day they were found and sold and put into a shop like all the other microphones.

One day somebody bought these microphones and as soon as he got home the person used the microphones but afterwards when it was dinner time for that person he turned off the microphones and he went and had dinner. Then he went and watched the news and then after that he found out that while he was watching the news he should have been doing some studying, some exams.

So, then, while he was working, the microphones began to dance and then he came in and looked around, but the microphones were just as he left them. The end.

The moral of this story is: look more carefully. No. All right. Look more carefully and then you might find out what the trouble was. The end.

Patient: Do you have any questions?

Therapist: Yes, when you said look more carefully. In what part of your story should someone have looked more carefully?

Patient: In the end.

Therapist: What would he have seen if he looked more carefully?

Patient: He would have seen that the microphones weren't really in the exact place because he was fairly far away from them.

Therapist: Well, what was the trouble about that? You say, "Look more carefully and then you might find out what the trouble is." What kind of trouble was there?

Patient: Well, the microphones were fooling around, like they were messing up an old typewriter and stuff like that and breaking pencils.

Therapist: Oh, they were breaking pencils and what else?

Patient: Messing up an old typewriter and stuff like that.

Therapist: Hhmmm. I see. Okay. Thank you very much. And now it's time for Dr. Gardner to tell his story.

This story is an example of those situations in which the child uses the recording equipment as the object upon which to project his fantasies. Generally when this happens, the object is anthropomorphized and the pressure of the fantasy is so great that it is not affected by the actual form of the equipment.

The storytelling game is played with two microphones, one for the child and one for me. In this story the two microphones represent the patient. The first thing he says is that "there was something peculiar" about them — a reflection of the child's feelings about himself. Next, he says that they were "found and sold and put into a shop." In order to be "found," you first have to be lost, which implies that Larry feels abandoned. "Somebody" then buys them — evidence of the child's desire for a new parent. The "person," after using the microphones awhile, "went and had dinner." The implication here is that the microphones were left behind — abandoned — while the "person" had dinner. In the next sentence, the "person" is referred to as "he," so it is reasonable to assume that it is his father who is being served dinner by Larry's mother. The comment that he watched the news instead of "doing some studying, some exams" confirms that the man represents the boy's father because the latter was steeped in academic life. The patient here sees his father as someone who, when not involved in his studies, watches television.

Meanwhile, back in the other room the microphones are dancing, a harmless enough activity, ostensibly. They should have little to dance about, however. They have just entered a new home and have once again been rejected. Mother and father are in the next room having dinner, that is, enjoying themselves in primitive, sensuous delights. As with the seven magic jelly beans, the dancing probably serves as a cover-up for the boy's anger over his rejection. When it came to covering up hostility, Larry was an expert. There are, nevertheless, suspicions of dirty work. The child says that the microphones were "just as he left them." Why shouldn't they be? Were they up to something? In the moral he says, "Look more carefully and then you might find out what the trouble is." What trouble? The story says nothing about trouble. This whole matter sounded suspicious; it certainly warranted further investigation.

Interestingly, Larry himself invited inquiry. "Do you have any questions?" he asked me, as soon as he finished his story. As a matter of fact I did. What I learned was that there was more than dancing going on in that back room. The microphones were breaking pencils and "messing up an old typewriter." In other words, the patient was destroying his father's work equipment as a way of venting his rage. Implied is the hope that without his work materials the father might spend more time with his son.

The post-story inquiry here was vital to the understanding of the story. In response I told this one:

Once upon a time there were two microphones and they were in a store. Now they were finally bought by someone and he brought them into his home. Now this man who brought these microphones into his home was a nice man in many ways, but there were certain things that he did which the microphones didn't like and it kind of bothered them —— some of the things he did —— and they decided that when he was going out of the room. One of them said, "I have an idea. When he goes out of the room, let's mess up the place. We'll mess up his typewriter and we'll break his pencils, and things like that and he'll never know who did it." And the second one said, "No, that would be dishonest." The first one said, "What should we do then?" The second one said, "Let's tell him what bothers us. Let's tell him the things that bother us and maybe he'll change so we won't feel so bad. We're not going to accomplish anything by messing up the place. In fact, if he finds out he'll only get angrier."

So they realized that the best thing to do would be to talk to him directly. So when the man came in they told him what bothered them and he said, "I'm glad that you told me that because I didn't know that those things were bothering you. Now that you have told me, I will change them. And he did and they felt much better.

Therapist: And you know what the lesson of that story is?

Patient: No.

Therapist: Try to figure it out.

Patient: I give up.

Therapist: When somebody is doing something to bother you tell them about it. Don't keep it to yourself and if you do so you may get things done better, and they may change. The end.

Patient: I have a question to ask.

Therapist: Yes?

Patient: Why did the first microphone want to mess up the place?

Therapist: They were angry at the man for certain things that he was doing to them and they thought that they would get back by messing up the place.

Patient: You mean the first one.

Therapist: Right, and the second one told him that that wouldn't accomplish very much, that they would be much better off if they just told exactly what bothered them.

Patient: I think the second one was right.

Therapist: Right. You try to get people to change by talking to them about things. You don't just go around messing up the place. The end.

Patient: Now let's play it back.

In my story, I recommended expressing one's resentment rather than displacing and acting it out. The presence of two microphones provided me with the opportunity for a dialogue in which both courses of action are discussed and considered. The forces of "good" win over the forces of "evil" and the argument for appropriate, civilized expression of anger wins the day. The man is receptive to the critical confrontation and tries to make amends. Punitive retaliation and further rejection are not forthcoming.

I made no mention of the microphones' specific grievances. The patient was extremely inhibited in expressing anger, the hostility toward his father was deeply repressed, and it was quite early in treatment. I felt that I should concentrate first on the general subject of expressing anger, and then get to specifics when the patient was ready to handle them. Premature exposure to anxiety-laden material could have frightened this boy away, not only from the storytelling game but from treatment as well.

Example 3

Carol, the girl with stuttering, generalized tension, and insomnia, whose treatment had to be prematurely interrupted

272

because of her mother's severe antagonism to me, told this story during her third week of therapy:

Long, long ago, in a part of the earth where no one has ever been, there lived a boy and a girl. The girl's name was Mary and the boy's name was John. And so one night Mary and John always wanted to go to Mars. So one day they were sleeping and all of a sudden this big head stuck in the window, which looked like the big head of an insect. It said, "Mary, John, come here." So they quickly got dressed and rushed outside and there was a big beautiful butterfly, bigger than you ever saw.

Therapist: Wait, was this on Mars or what?

Patient: On earth.

Therapist: You mean they saw him from the window of their house. Is that it?

Patient: Yes. They live on earth, but in a part of the earth that no one has ever been. And so they looked at the butterfly and it had all different colors — yellow, purple, green, orange, blue spots, and a green neck and scarlet eyes — and all the colors you could never name. There were so many. The butterfly said, "I heard your wish about going to Mars. Will you come with me?" They said, "All right." So they got onto the butterfly and they drove away and they were halfway into the air and John said, "Oh, we forgot to tell Mom." And so they had to go back and John and Mary rushed inside and said, "Mom." And she said, "What dear?" because she was fast asleep and she just woke up. And John said, "I'm going to Mars." The mother said, "All right." So he left.

So the mother woke up. The father woke up and said, "It's 12 o'clock. What's happening?" The mother said, "Oh, the children are just having another one of their dreams."

So John and Mary got on the butterfly and they started going to Mars. The butterfly said, "Mars is really a beautiful place." John said, "How do you know?" The butterfly said, "Because I live there." And so they kept on going on higher and higher. Finally they reached

Mars and they stepped out and they were on Mars, and they didn't come back until a year after. That's the end.

The moral of the story is: your mother and father should believe where you are going so they'll know because otherwise they'll wake up the next morning and they'll think you're gone and they won't know where you are. But if they believe you in the night time when you tell them, then if they want to find out where you are they'll know.

Therapist: Your mother and father should believe you so that what will happen?

Patient: So that the next morning when they wake up, if they believe them, they know where they were and the children were gone for a year.

Therapist: Okay. What happened to the mother and father when they woke up and they saw that the children weren't there?

Patient: They started worrying and they called the police.

Therapist: Then what happened?

Patient: Then no one ever found them until a year after when they came back.

Therapist: Then what happened?

Patient: Then the mother and father said, "Why didn't you tell us where you were going? The children said, "We told you the other night we went to Mars."

Therapist: Then what happened?

Patient: Then the parents said, "Now we'd better believe them." And that's all.

Therapist: I see. Okay. So the parents must have been very worried during this year.

Patient: Yeah.

Therapist: Uh-huh. Okay. Thank you very much. Now it's time for me to tell my story. However, there are a few things I'd like to talk to you about first. Your story is about two kids who go off to Mars. Sometimes, when kids have thoughts like going off to far-off places like Mars, it means that they're unhappy about the way things are going at home. How are things going for you at home?

Patient: My mother screams at me a lot. That makes me worry a lot. Sometimes it makes me worry so much that I wish I was dead.

Therapist: How often does that happen, that you wish you were dead?

Patient: It happens almost every day that I wish I was dead. When my father screams I don't wish I was dead. It's just when my mother screams. She screams in a terrible way.

Therapist: The kids in your story leave home. Have you ever had any thoughts about leaving home?

Patient: Yes, I often think of running away from home. I ran away from home once, last year. It was in the winter time. I stayed near a brook.

Therapist: How long were you there?

Patient: Five minutes. Then my father came and got me. But I wanted to stay there all night.

Therapist: What was happening that made you run away?

Patient: It was about Sunday School. I hate to go to Sunday School, so we have it at our house; and I hate to have it there too. My father just reads us stuff from the Bible and all that stuff. I can't tell my father I don't like it because he'll just scream at me. Sometimes we sneak out; or we stay there and while my father reads to us we're bored but we don't tell him. If I told him we didn't like it, he would just tell us we have to. My mother says, "We're doing this for you, darling."

Therapist: I'm glad we discussed this. Now it's time for me to tell my story.

As already suggested in the post-story inquiry, I considered the trip to Mars to represent the patient's desire to flee from her home. Nothing was said in the story about the particular reasons why the child wanted to escape. The discussion following her story served to supply some of these answers for me. By asking permission to go to Mars, dependence on the mother is shown, although this is not necessarily abnormal for Carol's age. To ensure that the answer is yes, however, the question is posed while the mother is still half asleep. She cannot fully appreciate the implications of the question. There is an element of duplicity on the child's part. The mother's permission also assuages any guilt she may have about leaving. Also present in the story is the child's feeling that her mother doesn't believe her. The mother is told the truth about the trip's destination but she does not take the information seriously. There is a hostile element as well: wondering about the child's whereabouts worries the parents. However, their anxieties about where she is provide the girl with a degree of attention she might not have otherwise enjoyed.

In response to Carol's story, I told this story:

> Once upon a time a long, long time ago, there lived on a part of the earth where no one has ever been, there lived a boy and a girl named Mary and John, and they lived with their mother and father. They had a lot of trouble with their parents. There was always a lot of fighting and one of the reasons for this trouble was that whenever their mother or their father would do something that they didn't like, Mary and John wouldn't say anything. They would just either try to run away from doing it, which would make their parents angry, or they would do it and then they would be very angry and resentful. Do you know what resentful means?
>
> *Patient:* No.
>
> *Therapist:* Resentful means that they were very angry but they didn't show it too well. They would just kind of mope and grunt and they were very bitter, but they never said anything about it.
>
> One day the two children were talking and one of them said, "I can't stand it anymore here — all this trouble — all this fighting. If we could only go to Mars it would be nice. We could go to Mars on some big butterfly or something. Then it would be really nice and we would really be free and we would have a good time." Well, they were thinking of doing that. In fact, one night a big butterfly from Mars actually did stick his head in their window and said, "Say, would you children like to go to Mars?" They were thinking about going and then they said, "Well, we'll think about it. You come back tomorrow night."

276

So as they were thinking about it the next day, they met a friend of theirs and they said, "You know what? We're going to Mars tonight." He said, "Why?" And they said, "So we could get away from home and we'll have no more fighting." He said, "What are your parents doing?" John said, "Oh, they're always telling us to do things we don't like. They make us read books we don't like; they make us listen to them." The kid said, "You know, kids always have to do some things they don't like. Have you told your parents about this?" They said, "No." He said, "You know, I found that when I tell my parents about the things I don't like and I sit and talk to them about it, sometimes they'll change their minds and then I don't get so angry. Besides, what are you going to do up on Mars up there? There's nothing up there. That's just a rock, Mars. There's no human life up there. You won't have a good time."

So the children thought about what this boy had said and the next day they decided that instead of going to Mars they would try out his advice. So they told their parents exactly what their complaints were. In fact, they put a complaint box into the house for everybody who had a complaint. Do you know what a complaint box is?

Patient: No.

Therapist: A complaint box is a box where if you have any complaints you write it on a slip of paper and you put it in there, and your parents open it everyday and see what the complaints were. So they discussed them and sometimes the parents changed their minds and sometimes they didn't. But after that things were much better in the house and the kids were happy that they didn't go to Mars.

Do you know what the morals of that story are?

Patient: No.

Therapist: See if you can figure them out.

Patient: It's better to tell your parents your problems.

Therapist: When you disagree with your parents and your parents are doing something you don't like, it's better to tell them about your disagreement. Tell them what you disagree about and then often they will change their minds if they see that you have a good argument and then you could avoid a lot of trouble and you don't have to run away. The end.

What do you think of that story?

Patient: Good. It was good.

Therapist: What was the thing about it that you liked?

Patient: About the complaint box. I'm going to make that in our house.

Therapist: I think you ought to. You ought to have something in your house where you can tell your parents the things that bother you.

Patient: So that you don't have to face them while you are speaking.

Therapist: I see. So that's why. Why are you afraid to speak to them?

Patient: Because they'll scream.

Therapist: They scream so much that you're afraid to tell your complaints directly. Huh?

Patient: Yes.

Therapist: Okay.

The story is self-explanatory. Unfortunately, the advice imparted might have been helpful to most children, but it was of little value to this girl. The degree of flexibility exhibited by the parents in my story was something that Carol could not reasonably hope to experience with her own parents. I did not realize it at the time (as mentioned, it was only the child's third week in treatment), but I learned it only too well later on. The patient's interest in the "complaint box" stemmed, as she says in the post-story discussion, from the fact that it would enable her to communicate complaints without having to expose herself to her parents' screaming reactions. There was much truth to this. Following my story I had the mother join us for a discussion of some of the patient's complaints. It was clear that Carol would need help in fighting some of her battles. During the discussion of Sunday School, the mother came out with the identical comment that Carol mentioned in the first post-story discussion: "We're doing this for you, darling." It was expressed with such underlying seething rage that I myself cringed.

USING THE INTER-STORY COMMERCIAL

When I first began using the storytelling technique, it took longer for me to make up my stories than it does now. To gain time, I often suggested that the child occupy himself with something of his choice while I was preparing my story. A few children, since they were already "on the air" started telling commercials. While they were often verbatim repetitions of what they had seen on television, they had some psychodynamic meaning because they were selected from the countless commercials to which most children are exposed. Those which the children made up themselves were of much greater psychological significance.

Example 4

Ronald, the very bright boy with rage outbursts, severe negativistic behavior, and marked defiance of authority was a prolific narrator of commercials. Some were his own and others repetitions of those he had seen on television. His favorite was a parody of a popular Salem cigarette commercial:

You can take Salem out of the country, but, you can't take the country out of Salem.

Ronald's version was:

You can take Salem out of the sick bay but, you can't take the cancer out of Salem.

As already described, the patient harbored deep-seated hostility toward his mother, an extremely tense woman who seethed with underlying rage. She was a heavy smoker and Ronald was preoccupied with the fear that she would get lung cancer. He repeatedly warned her about the dangers of smoking in an effort to get her to stop. Although there was a realistic basis for his fear that she would die of cancer, his obsession with it suggested that his concern was a reaction formation to an underlying wish that she would die. The commercial was only one part of Ronald's overall campaign to preserve his mother's life. If she had died, he would most likely have felt it was his fault because of his death wishes toward her. His concern was thus an attempt to avoid a severe guilt reaction were she to die of her smoking.

Here is a typical interchange we had regarding Ronald's commercials:

Listen parents if you want to keep your children's hearts healthy do this: keep weight normal. Don't have too much saturated fat. See a doctor regularly. Have a heart operation and, best of all, give to the heart fund because then if you die they'll collect insurance. Here's Markie.
Therapist: Who will collect insurance?
Patient: The heart fund.
Therapist: Who collects insurance if they die?
Patient: I can't explain that. I'll have to do the whole commercial over.
Therapist: Say it over.
Patient: Listen parents if you want to keep your children's hearts normal do this: keep weight normal. Eat food low in saturated fat. Have a heart operation. Best of all, give to heart funds because then if you die of a heart attack they'll collect insurance.
Therapist: Do you mean, if the parents die from a heart attack the children or the heart fund will collect insurance?
Patient: Ah, forget it.

The commercial is somewhat perplexing, but certain messages are there. The most important is that parents may die of a heart attack if they do not follow certain precautions. In a manner similar to the cigarette smoking preoccupation, Ronald gratifies the wish, through fantasy, that his parents die, but assuages his guilt by perceiving it consciously as a fear. In addition, insisting they take precautions against heart disease also serves to lessen the guilt he would inevitably feel if they were to die, because their deaths would be considered a realization of his wish.

The parents are also advised to contribute to heart funds. To give to heart funds so that they might collect insurance is macabre and somewhat illogical. When asked to explain who "they" are a second time, Ronald becomes impatient. My guess is that it is the children who are beneficiaries, but he cannot allow himself such undisguised expression of his hostility. The money somehow has to go back to charity.

USING HUMOR TO ENHANCE COMMUNICATIONS

As previously mentioned, humor and fanciful elaborations can aid in keeping the child's interest and intensify the impact of the therapist's messages. Jack Point, the jester in Gilbert and Sullivan's operetta, *Yeoman of the Guard* tells us:

> When they're offered to the world in a merry guise,
> Unpleasant truths are swallowed with a will —
> For he who'd make his fellow, fellow, fellow
>   creatures wise
> Should always gild the philosophic pill!

Point's point is well taken. In fact, my whole technique presupposes the validity of his pedagogical advice.

Example 5

Joey, the boy with enuresis and nightmares, had a lively sense of humor and was quite receptive to its introduction into my stories. This was demonstrated in the story of the vomiting ape. During his third month of therapy, Joey told this story:

There once lived a jaguar who couldn't run very fast.

And so this slow-running jaguar asked a cheetah to teach him how to run fast. The cheetah just couldn't because the jaguar was just so slow that the cheetah couldn't help him. The jaguar asked the lion, but the lion couldn't. And he asked a crocodile, but he couldn't; a camel, but he couldn't. And then he asked a turtle and the turtle said, "Well, let's see now. All you have to do is put your front legs like this and then put your back legs right in back of your front legs like this — like that — you know," and the jaguar saw it and he was able to run real fast. Okay?

Therapist: Is that the end of the story?

Patient: Yup.

Therapist: What's the lesson of that story?

Patient: Sometimes slow things can teach people how to run fast. You know. Can you tell me what that story means?

Therapist: Okay. Why don't I tell my story first.

The slow-running jaguar is the patient, who considers himself inadequate about his ability to compete in the contests of life. By taking lessons from the turtle, the proverbial symbol of perseverance, the jaguar learned to run "real fast." While the story is a neat parable of the therapeutic process, in Joey's case the insecurity reflected by the jaguar's indiscriminate appeals for help was a crucial point. Crocodiles and turtles, after all, are not known for fleetness. With this aspect of the story in mind, I made the following response:

Once upon a time there was a jaguar and this jaguar thought that he could not run very fast. He really could and everybody knew he could, but he just thought that he couldn't. And he went around to the different animals and he said, "Will you teach me how to run fast?" And they said, "Teach *you* how to run fast? You are a jaguar; you are one of the fastest runners in the jungle. We can't teach you anything about running." He said, "I don't know how to run fast." He kept on asking different animals. He asked a crocodile who said, "*You*, a jaguar, asking *me*, a crocodile, how to run fast? You can run ten times as fast as I can. How can I teach you anything about running?" And then he went to the camel. The camel said, "You want *me* to teach *you* how to run fast? You are a faster runner than I could ever be."

Finally he went to the turtle. The turtle started laughing and the turtle said, "Ha, ha, ha." Did you ever hear a turtle laugh?

Patient: No.

Therapist: Turtles very rarely laugh. They are not known to have a very good sense of humor. So turtles are very rarely ever heard to laugh. But when this turtle heard this jaguar ask him to teach him how to run, the turtle started to laugh very loud with a turtle laugh, which people very rarely ever hear. He said, "I, a turtle, one of the slowest animals around, teach *you*, a jaguar, one of the fastest animals around, to run? Why that's absurd!" Now the turtle laughed so hard that the jaguar began thinking, "Maybe there's something to what this guy is saying. Maybe I can run fast after all."

So the jaguar went out and he started to trot. He started to run faster and faster and faster, and before you knew it, he was as fast as the wind. All the animals said, "See, we told you." And then the jaguar felt very good.

And you know what the lesson of my story is?

Patient: What?

Therapist: Try to figure it out. What do you think is the lesson?

Patient: Try.

Therapist: Try — that sometimes you think you can't do something and you really can.

Patient: I know. I used to think that I was the slowest one in the classroom too, but now I realize that I am the fastest.

Therapist: Right. I am sure you are one of the fastest. I am not surprised. The end.

Patient: Now can you tell me what my story means?

Therapist: Yeah. I will tell you what both stories mean. I think that your story means —— I think that you are the jaguar there and you don't think that you are very good in certain things.

Patient: I don't.

Therapist: What things do you think you are not good at?

Patient: Well, in writing, spelling.

Therapist: How do you do? What kind of marks do you get?

Patient: The best I ever got was, maybe, pretty good.

Therapist: What's the highest one can get?

Patient: The highest you can get is either an "Excellent" or "Very Lovely Work."

Therapist: "Very Lovely." Have you ever gotten a "Very Lovely"?

Patient: There aren't many things I'm very good at.

Therapist: So you're not too hot on spelling. Well, all right, but I happen to know that you are a pretty smart boy. I still say that you are one of the top students in your class. Isn't that right?

Patient: Hmmm.

Therapist: So you're one of the best students in your class and you pick out the spelling and say, "I'm not so good." You're much better than you think you are. You're like that jaguar. You think you're far worse than you really are. You're far better than you realize. You think like the jaguar thinks he's a slow runner. You think you are a kind of poor student and you would ask others to give you advice when you would know how to do those things yourself. You would ask people to give you advice who are less capable than you. You think that certain people who are less capable than you are more capable than you. Is that right?

Patient: Yeah. One time I asked the dumbest guy in the class —

Therapist: You asked the *dumbest guy in the class*? What did you ask him?

Patient: Well, in spelling I asked him how you spell Wednesday?

Therapist: Do you know how to spell Wednesday?

Patient: Now I do.

Therapist: And did he tell you how?

Patient: He told me the wrong answer.

Therapist: Well, you asked the dumbest guy in the class, so don't be surprised. Why should *you*, one of the smartest kids in the class, be asking one of the *dumbest* kids in the class a question? Hmmm?

Patient: I don't know.

Therapist: It tells me that you don't think you're very smart, huh?

Patient: Yeah.

Therapist: I happen to know from your mother that your teacher has told her that you're one of the smartest kids in the class. Huh? You don't seem to think so. Why is that?

Patient: I don't know. I just —

Therapist: Even though you are one of the smartest, you don't think so. Do you see how the jaguar in your story, being a very fast runner, will ask animals like a crocodile, a camel, and a turtle to teach him how to run fast. Isn't that kind of silly?

Patient: Well.

Therapist: It's like you. Hmmm? One of the smartest kids in the class asking one of the dumbest kids in the class how to spell a word.

Patient: But how come the turtle told the jaguar the right answer?

Therapist: Well, do you think that you can get the right answer from the stupidest kids? You don't think much of yourself. You don't think you have the right answers, so you go around to every kid, no matter how dumb he is, and try to get an answer because you don't really feel that the answers that you can come up with are very smart. Well, what happens in my story? What happens in my story to you? You are the jaguar in my story.

Patient: I forget your story.

Therapist: Try to remember now — anything about it.

Patient: Well, there was a jaguar. Oh, yeah, now I remember. It was a story exactly like mine.

Therapist: Except how was it different?

Patient: I don't know.

Therapist: Remember the laughing turtle in my story?

Patient: Oh, yeah.

Therapist: What was the turtle laughing about?

Patient: About asking such a slow animal.

Therapist: And then what happened at the end of my story?
Patient: Well, I was able to run real fast.
Therapist: Did they teach you?
Patient: Yeah.
Therapist: In my story did the other animals teach the jaguar?
Patient: No, no.
Therapist: What did they do?
Patient: They just laughed at him?
Therapist: Why did they laugh at him?
Patient: Because they were slow animals.
Therapist: Yeah. So what did the jaguar finally do?
Patient: He asked the turtle.
Therapist: And what did the turtle do?
Patient: Laughed.
Therapist: And then what happened?
Patient: He taught him how to run.
Therapist: No! He did it himself. The turtle didn't —
Patient: Oh, yeah, now I remember.
Therapist: You forgot that. You still couldn't believe that the jaguar could do it by himself. You still can't believe that you can do it by yourself, but you can. Hmmm? What do you think about that?
Patient: I think that's pretty bright.
Therapist: You think what's pretty bright?
Patient: The story.
Therapist: Which one?
Patient: Yours.
Therapist: In what way?
Patient: It showed me how silly some of my ideas are.
Therapist: What did you learn from this story?
Patient: That if I try I can get what I want.
Therapist: Right. That's right. That's the lesson in my story.

Unfortunately, the transcript cannot convey my incredulous intonations as each animal expressed his amazement at the jaguar's request. As successive animals were approached for lessons, the boy's facial expression revealed ever-deepening absorption in my story. And he laughed heartily with the turtle and me. These humorous elaborations helped Joey recognize

286

the absurdity of his professions of inadequacy. He was healthy enough to be able to laugh at himself. I would not have used this approach with a child with a weak ego. He would not have appreciated the humor; he could not have tolerated the powerful criticism inherent in it. The ability to laugh at oneself is one criteria for distinguishing the psychotic from the non-psychotic.

My story stimulated a lively discussion about the child's proficiencies. There, too, I had the opportunity through intonations and gestures to increase the efficacy of my communications. Again, the transcript cannot convey the tone of gross inconceivability in my statement: "You asked the *dumbest guy in the class?*", nor does it mention the shrug of my shoulders, the throwing up of my hands in despair, and my facial expression of "what else can you expect?" as I said to him: "Well, you asked the dumbest guy in the class, so don't be surprised."

Of course, feelings of inadequacy involve more than mere cognitive distortions, but the patient's awareness of the inaccuracies in his thinking is a necessary step in the alleviation of this symptom. The confrontations in my story helped Joey reach this first step.

In his eleventh month of treatment (during the middle phase) Joey told this story:

Patient: Could you start me off?
Therapist: Once upon a time — a long, long time ago in a distant land far, far away there lived a ——
Patient: Garbage can. And this garbage can had a lot of work to do. Everybody threw lots of their garbage into him, and other people wrote bad words on him like fuck and shit.
Therapist: Yeah. So then what?
Patient: He didn't like having so much responsibility because everybody had to clean him off — clean off the bad words — and he had to be carried around and he had to be all filled up with garbage and it really hurt him.
Therapist: How did it hurt him?
Patient: Because he had to use all his force to try to stand

himself but he couldn't because they put too much garbage into him.

Therapist: You mean it pushed against his sides?

Patient: Yeah. And so one day he just walked away because he was so mad. And the moral of the story is: walk away when somebody is doing things that you don't like. The end.

The garbage can is, of course, the patient who considers himself helpless to prevent others from subjecting him to various humiliations. He removes himself from those who would take advantage of him rather than assert himself, confront, fight, or otherwise more effectively handle those who expose him to indignities. In telling the story, Joey does not seem to appreciate that his self-loathing is related to his passivity and that were he to be more active in standing up for his rights, he would not consider himself so worthless. In response, I told this story:

Once upon a time a long time ago there was this garbage can and it had a lot of work to do because it used to carry a lot of garbage. Now, there were two things that used to happen to this garbage can that made it very angry: One, people would stuff far too much garbage in him —— really to the point where it would practically split his sides. And another thing that would happen was that boys used to come around and would write words on him like fuck and shit and things like that.

Well, he was standing there one day next to another garbage can and really complaining. He said, "Oh, these people. They just push so much garbage into me that I feel I'm going to burst and those boys come around and they write dirty words on me." So the second garbage can said, "Well, what do you do about it?" He said, "I don't know. I just don't do anything about it. I just feel so miserable, wretched, and depressed. I feel like I'm going to burst."

"Well," said the other garbage can, "The trouble with you is that you are not doing something about it. You should speak up. Let them know what's going on."

Patient: But garbage cans can't speak.

Therapist: In this story this garbage can can talk and even if he couldn't speak, he could communicate in one way or another. Well, anyway, the next day these boys came along and started to write fuck on him and so he said to the boys, "If you don't stop writing those words on me, you're going to get it." And the boys said, "Ha, ha, ha, what do you think you can do?" And at this he took some garbage and he threw it right in the boy's face.

Patient: What was in the garbage?

Therapist: Oh, the garbage had coffee grains and it had soup, and orange peels and mushy cereal. It had all kinds of gunk. And they went right into the boy's face. Oh, well, when the boy got that in his kisser, or a taste of that, he stayed clear of that garbage can, that's for sure.

Anyway, his next door neighbor said, "You see, you didn't even have to talk. Those boys started writing words like fuck and shit on you, just throw a lot of garbage at them. They'll stay clear of you. Stand up for your rights. Don't hold it all in. Don't just stand there and suffer."

So he did that. And then the next thing that happened was — he was just about filled — when all of a sudden someone came with another bag of garbage and they put it on top and they started stomping on it and pressing this garbage in. And the garbage can said, "Help, stop that, stop it." They didn't even listen. He said, "If you don't cut that out I'm going to squeeze my body together and I'm just going to get all this garbage together and it's going to go right in your face." And the man said, "Ha, ha. Who cares? You can't do that." Well, at this point, the garbage can squeezed his sides together and the garbage went flying into the air right into the kisser of the guy that was pushing the garbage in. And the two garbage cans started to laugh.

Patient: This time what went into their faces?

Therapist: And this time in the garbage they had —— what do you think they had in the garbage this time? You make up some things.

Patient: Rotten mush, some half-chewed cereal with some milk and chopped corn on it, and a few ants, an old apple core.

Therapist: Ugh! You know what I am going to add —— a dead mouse and there was some vomit in there that somebody had vomited in. And let's see what else was in there? And some baby's duty from a diaper. How's that?

Patient: Yeah!

Therapist: Well, with all those things in there —

Patient: Did he taste it? He had to lick it off.

Therapist: He really got it and from then on what do you think happened to that man who used to push too much garbage in the garbage can?

Patient: He never pushed any in the garbage can.

Therapist: Right. And what about those boys who wrote words like fuck and shit on the garbage can?

Patient: They never did it.

Therapist: Right. Now what's the moral of that story?

Patient: Get revenge.

Therapist: Well, if somebody bothers you and they don't take your warning to stop, then stop them with action. Right?

Patient: Yeah.

Therapist: You see, your garbage can walked away from the difficulty. Right?

Patient: Yeah.

Therapist: He let the boys write shit and fuck on him and he allowed people to shove garbage in him. All he did was run away from the problem. Right?

Patient: Yeah.

Therapist: My garbage can fought the problem. He won and when they wouldn't stop, he took action. He warned the boys to stop writing the words and when they wouldn't stop, he took action. He warned the man not to put the garbage in and when he didn't stop, he took action.

Patient: Yeah, he threw some baby shit in his face.

Therapist: Right. So don't let people take advantage of you and if they don't heed your warning, then take action. The end. What do you think of that story I just told?

Patient: Great, especially when we named all the things that he threw at him.

Therapist: Good. Okay. That's the end of the stories today.

Near the beginning of my story the patient sensed that the garbage can was going to assert himself and "speak up." This was anxiety-provoking to him and he interrupted me: "But garbage cans can't speak." I did not let this deter me. I felt he could tolerate the anxiety of my garbage can fighting for his rights and so I replied: "In this story this garbage can can talk and even if he couldn't speak, he could communicate in one way or another."

My garbage can then responds with garbage thrown directly into the face of one of his tormentors. The patient's question: "What was in the garbage?" was stated with gleeful curiosity and suggested to me that elaboration of detail here could help the boy vicariously gratify his hostile wishes and at the same time assist him in learning some valuable lessons. Later, when I described the garbage can's throwing refuse into the faces of the men who ignored his pleas to stop stuffing excessive garbage into him, he reiterates his request for a detailed description of the garbage's contents. This time I brought him in more directly to foster greater emotional involvement in the cathartic release that the story offered. Joey rose to the occasion and there followed a rollicking orgy of profanity. The patient's ecstasy heightened with each new addition of nauseating refuse. My utilization of hostile expressions encouraged Joey to release his own. Reveling in our scatological spree provided him with an emotional experience that was far more therapeutic than any purely intellectual expression could have been. If the therapist can provide the child with emotional experiences during the storytelling, his messages will carry far greater weight. To tell the child, in the context of one's story, that expression of hostility can be advantageous may be helpful. But to sweep the child up in the same story in which this message is being communicated; to make him an active participant; to get him to *feel the angry feelings,* either directly or symbolically is far more therapeutic. Humor is one way of accomplishing this.

The session ended with a more sober discussion of the meaning of our stories. I reiterated the main messages to further entrench them in the child's psyche.

Example 6

Julie, the girl who had outbursts of rage and a chronic surly attitude which were related to the divorce of her parents, told this story early in her treatment:

This story is about two orphan boys who were always wishing to be brothers and two orphan girls who were always wishing to be sisters. So one day a rich lady and her rich husband came over to adopt some children, but the boy couple and the girl couple did not like each other very much at all. Finally the rich lady and her husband made up their minds. They decided to adopt the two boys and the two girls so they became brothers and sisters.

Now they didn't like each other at all so they spent their time fighting.

Therapist: You mean the two brothers didn't like the two sisters? Is that it?

Patient: Yes, and the two sisters didn't like the two brothers. So they yelped and screamed, kicked and everything. So finally something had to be done. The rich woman said whoever could make her children stop fighting would get fifty dollars worth of gold coins.

Men and women from all around the world came. But one day a little bird came and the lady said, "What are you doing here little bird?" "I can make your children stop fighting," the bird said. So he went in where the children were fighting and he waved his wing around them. Suddenly they were all friendly together. So the bird received instead of fifty dollars worth of gold coins a gold nest.

So the people were very angry at this bird but they couldn't do anything about it. Birds from miles around came to see this nest. So the children stopped fighting and they all lived happily ever after.

Patient: I don't have a moral for my story.

Therapist: You don't have a moral? Sure you have a moral — some lesson in that story.

Patient: Don't be jealous when you can't do anything about it.

Therapist: Now how does that fit in with this story?

292

Patient: Well, the people were very jealous of the bird, but see they couldn't do anything about it —— that the bird had made the two boys and the two girls friends. They wanted all the gold coins and everything, but they didn't get it so they couldn't do anything about it.
Therapist: You mean people were jealous of the bird and the gold nest and everything else?
Patient: Yeah.
Therapist: I see. Okay.

Julie's divorced father rarely visited her, and much of the anger she felt toward him was displaced to her mother. Without a father present, and with a mother at whom she was chronically enraged, this girl was left with a feeling of total abandonment.

The angry children represent Julie. However, I was not sure why she represented herself as two brothers and two sisters. She did have one sister with whom she constantly bickered. Perhaps the two sisters stand for the patient and her sister, while the two brothers represent boys she would like to have in her household for further companionship. The children are adopted by "a rich lady and her rich husband." With this device she goes from the emotionally impovished home she sees herself to be living in to one where there is an abundance of affection which is symbolized by wealth.

The anger, by which Julie is plagued and sometimes paralyzed, is a disruptive element, even in her new home. This is magically removed by a special bird who waves his wing over the children. Although the children are now happy, the bird becomes the object of everyone's jealousy and anger because of the gold nest he receives for curing the children. The wealthy bird, I believe, is an alter ego of the patient. Its plight suggests that the patient feels that even if she got wealth, acquired affection, that is, there would still be those around her who would be critical of her. The bird's plight also implies that her pool of rage is so vast that she cannot see herself free from situations in which it is not present, either in herself or projected onto others.

With this understanding of Julie's story, I told this one:

Once upon a time there was an orphanage and in this orphanage there lived two orphan boys who liked one another very much and they wanted to be brothers. In addition, there were two orphan girls who liked one another very much and they wanted to be sisters.

Well, one day a very rich lady came to the orphanage and she said that she was interested in getting four children — two boys and two girls — and what do you know, she chose the two friends that wanted to be brothers and the two friends that wanted to be sisters. So then they became brothers and sisters.

Well, as soon as they got home to the big mansion of the rich lady they started to fight. And they fought and they fought. This little rich old lady was kind of beside herself. She didn't know what to do. So finally she decided that she would give a reward of fifty dollars in gold coins to anybody who could figure out a way to stop these kids.

Well, people came from all over the land, making all kinds of suggestions, and they just didn't work. Nothing worked. Then a little bird came along and he said, "I think that I can make them stop fighting." So the little bird went in there and he waved his wings and you know what happened?

Patient: They stopped fighting?

Therapist: No. They didn't stop fighting because the kids said to the bird, "What do you think that's suppose to do, bird?" The bird said, "These are magic wings and they are going to make you stop fighting." The kids all laughed. They said, "That's a riot, ha, ha. What are you, a nut, bird? Waving your wings is going to make us stop fighting? You must be cuckoo. That's how the cuckoo bird got his name because he thought that he could stop fighting by magic."

Well, then, in came the wise old owl. He looked the situation over and he said to these kids and the rich old lady, "I can't promise that I can help with this problem, but I will try." And the rich old lady said, "Wonderful, wonderful, anything." The owl said, "Now you come around here, you kids, and tell me what it is exactly you are fighting about?" And then they started to talk about what they were fighting about. The boys said what they felt about the girls —— the things they didn't like about the girls —— and the girls told what things they didn't like about the boys. What things did the boys not like about the girls? What did they say?

Patient: That they were sissies?

Therapist: And what did the girls say they didn't like about the boys?

Patient: That they were too rough.

Therapist: Well whatever it was, the boys and the girls each aired their grievances. Do you know what "aired their grievances" mean? (*Julie nods negatively.*) Each told what they felt was wrong with the other and some of the things they were able to change and some they weren't. So after they did that they were all less angry at one another because they had changed certain things that were bothering them. And it was after that that they were far less angry at one another and they fought less frequently. And so the owl was given the fifty dollars in gold coin. And the people all appreciated and realized that he indeed deserved it because he had come forth with the wisest solution to the problem. And do you know what the morals of that story are? There are two morals that I can think of.

Patient: Don't be jealous when you know someone deserves it.

Therapist: All right. That's one moral. I've got a couple more.

Patient: You can't stop fighting by magic.

Therapist: Right, right. Magic doesn't solve problems. That's one moral. The other moral is that problems are solved by ——

Patient: Intelligence.

Therapist: Intelligence, by discussion, by communication, by talking to one another and trying to figure out what really are the things that bother you. That's how problems are solved and that's how people get less angry. The end. Anything you want to say about this story?

Patient: It was very meaningful.

Therapist: In what way?

Patient: I don't know.

Therapist: Why do you say it was meaningful?
Patient: It should be meaningful to me.
Therapist: Is it meaningful to you?
Patient: Yes.
Therapist: What part was meaningful to you?
Patient: About the owl and stuff, boys and girls — by talking.
Therapist: Right. That's the best way. Okay?

Julie joined with me in ridiculing the bird who professed he could perform magic. I believe that my communication that there are no magical solutions to life's problems made more of an impact when presented in this manner than it would have if I had stated it categorically. The wise old owl — one of my more sneaky disguises — urges the children to look to the sources of their anger and to air them in a civilized fashion. Having utilized their anger in the service of removing sources of irritation, they feel less angry. In my story, no one is angry at or jealous of the owl. He justly deserves his reward.

The post-story discussion shows that the girl understood my messages. Julie's statement that the story was very meaningful to her was made with conviction. I believe that the humorous way in which a portion of my message was imparted contributed to her receptivity.

USING STORIES AS A POINT OF DEPARTURE FOR PSYCHOANALYTIC INQUIRY

Although most children are not interested in an analytic inquiry, there are some who are receptive to it and can profit greatly from it. For such children the stories often serve to stimulate psychoanalytic discussions. As mentioned, eliciting a story is like being able to obtain a dream on demand. The story has certain advantages over the dream. The skillful therapist can draw it out and get the child to add to and elaborate on it while the dream is presented as a *fait accompli*.

Although some of the stories already presented demonstrate the use of the storytelling technique as a taking-off point

296

for analytic inquiry, it is a sufficiently important application to warrant a few more examples.

Joey was highly interested in direct analysis of his stories and profited greatly from it. His enthusiasm in this regard was reflected in his frequent request, following his presentation of his story, that we discuss its meaning. The sequence presented in Chaper 4 demonstrates Joey's analytical facility.

Example 7

Carol, the girl with stuttering, generalized tension, and insomnia, told this story in her third month of therapy, about two weeks before treatment was prematurely terminated:

> Once upon a time there were two pencils. One was yellow and one was blue. Now the one that was blue was always blue and the one that was yellow was always happy.
> *Therapist:* Oh, the blue one was sad and the yellow one was happy.
> *Patient:* Yes. The yellow pencil was always used. Now in these days if you needed a pencil the pencil would have to sharpen itself. Now the blue one was lazy and the yellow one wasn't. Aren't you writing all that down?
> *Therapist:* Yeah, the blue one was lazy.
> *Patient:* And the yellow one wasn't.
> *Therapist:* And the yellow one would sharpen itself and the other one wouldn't. Go ahead.
> *Patient:* In these days the pencils had to sharpen theirselves and the yellow one always sharpened himself, but the blue one was lazy. He just sharpened himself only once in a while. Then he would get into a fuss, stamp around, and break the point again. So everyone was the yellow pencil's friend, but no one used the blue pencil because he was very lazy and when they wanted him to write, he'd go very slowly and make the letters sloppy because he wanted to sleep. And so they all took the yellow pencil.
> So the blue pencil said to the yellow one one day, "How come everyone's your friend and not mine?" And the yellow pencil said, "Maybe if you would cheer up and if you go sharpen yourself and write fast and not sleep

so much, they'd like you. So the blue one did that and from that day on everyone used the blue one also.

The moral of the story is: like people. If you are a mean, sad person be nice and then people will play with you, and you'll have a lot of friends.

Therapist: Good.

The story reflects some incorporation of previous messages of mine regarding the importance of work if one is to respect oneself and gain the respect of others. However, the change is brought about quite easily and dramatically. Merely upon resolution the blue pencil changes. There is no real introspection and inquiry into the nature of the problems which brought about the pencil's lackadaisical attitude. Accordingly, I told this story:

Once upon a time there were two pencils, a yellow pencil and a blue pencil. The yellow pencil was a happy-go-lucky fellow and he was very active, whereas the blue pencil was a sad schlump, kind of lazy, and naturally people took a liking to the yellow pencil because he was always optimistic and pleasant, whereas the blue pencil people didn't like too much. When they had to use him, he'd be sluggish and slow and when it was time to sharpen — those were the days when pencils sharpened themselves — the blue pencil would not sharpen himself. He was always dull and would break his point easily and wouldn't keep himself in good shape so people found themselves tending to use the yellow pencil and not the blue pencil.

Well, one day the blue pencil said, "Why is it I have no friends and why is that you have all those friends?" The yellow pencil said, "It's because you're so lazy and you're so sad and miserable all the time." The blue pencil said, "I'm going to try not to be." Well, the blue pencil tried not to be and he was able to stop being sad a little bit, but he came back one day and he said to the yellow pencil, "You know, you were right that I don't have friends because I'm so sad and lazy and mopey. I'm trying to change but I can't." The yellow pencil said, "Well, what are you sad about?" Then the blue pencil started to talk about the things that were really bothering him and he spoke to the yellow pencil a lot about different things that he had deep down inside of him that were really bothering him that he had never spoken about before. Once he started talking about these things he felt even better and then once he started to *do* something about these things — and that was the most important part — he started to do something about the things that bothered him and was able to change some of those things, he was no longer sad.

And do you know what the lesson of the story is?

Patient: What?

Therapist: The lesson of that story is ——

Patient: If you talk over your problems you'll figure it out.

Therapist: Yeah! That sometimes you just can't solve your problems by deciding that all you are going to do is just stop doing it. That's just the first step. Sometimes you have to try to understand what's going on. That's the second step. The third step is to *do* something about the thing that you are sad about if you can. Usually if you do that you will not feel so sad. The end.

Therapist: What do you think of that story?

Patient: I thought it was good but if I talk over my problems, well, sometimes it helps and sometimes it doesn't.

Therapist: Right. As I said, it's not only talking about it, but doing something about what you learn. That step is important too. Just talking about it isn't going to help. I mean, let's say a man is in jail, and he says, "Oh, I'm so sad I'm in jail. I'm so sad I'm in jail, and keeps talking about it all the time, but he's still in jail. But if he acts good in jail and is on his best behavior, he'll get out of jail faster. So he does something about what he's doing. He uses what he has learned to get rid of the thing that bothers him. Then he feels better. You see, it's not just talking. It's doing also. You understand?

Patient: Like, well, if you were in jail and you said, "Oh, I'm so sad. Oh, I'm so sad. Oh, I'm so sad," and you were good but you were really moping around, but you were good and you answered the people's questions. You'd eat and things like that but you were still very sad.

Therapist: Right. Well, there's so much you can do but you do whatever you can. In this situation you do what you can. You get out of the jail as fast as you can by being on your good behavior or making the best of a bad situation. In each situation, it's best to understand as much as possible about what the things are that are making you sad, to do what you can about those things that you can change, and to accept those things that you can't change.

Patient: Like what problems do I have that I can change?

Therapist: Well, what do you think?

Patient: Getting along with my mother.

Therapist: All right. What about that now?

Patient: Well, I could start being good, and obeying her and listening to her and helping her around the house, and we'll stop screaming at each other. That will be a help.

Therapist: Hhmmm. For sure. That's for sure. Then there will be other things, too, in terms of saying what you really think at the right time, expressing yourself, and trying to understand what is really going on. What are really the things that are making you sad?

Patient: What other problems can I do to help me?

Therapist: What other problems do you have that you can talk about and understand better, which might be of help to you?

Patient: Other problems? Get along in school better.

Therapist: What can you do about that?

Patient: Work hard.

Therapist: But you see what I said in my story was something of an understanding, something about knowing that goes beyond. It's just not that "I decided today that I'm going to work hard," but try to understand the reasons why a person doesn't work hard. What's going on with them that they can't work harder if they won't work hard? Do you know what I mean?

Patient: Hhmmm.

Therapist: Like they might be afraid of something or they can't concentrate on certain things. You know there are different things that can be going on with a person that interferes with his functioning. Now what do you think about you?

Patient: What do you mean what do I think about me?

Therapist: You know, anything bothering you that might be interfering with your working in school.

Patient: Like what kind of thing?

Therapist: I don't know. Anything. Often kids have troubles at home which prevent them from concentrating in school.

Patient: I really don't know. That's a question I don't think I have an answer to.

Therapist: Well, you see what I said in my story was that the boy or the girl who, you know in this case of course was a pencil, tried to talk about the things that really troubled him and were making him blue and sad and when he did that he felt better, and then when he did something about what he had learned, he even felt even better. Now how could you apply this to yourself?

Patient: How could I apply it to me? Well, I don't think I'm sad at home and I don't think I mope around and maybe — it can't be my mother or can it? Can or cannot it be my mother?

Therapist: Well, what do you think?

Patient: She doesn't do anything at home that should upset me at school.

Therapist: Well, does she do anything at home that should upset you at home?

Patient: Screams.

Therapist: All right. Is there anything you're doing at home? What's your reaction to her screaming?

Patient: What do you mean by that — your reaction?

Therapist: How do you respond? How do you feel? What goes on with you when your mother screams?

Patient: I'm nervous.

Therapist: When your mother screams, what thoughts come to your mind?

Patient: That she hates me.

Therapist: Okay, you feel that she hates you at that time.

Patient: Yeah.

Therapist: How do you feel towards her when you see her looking like she hates you?

Patient: Crazy names sometimes in my mind.

Therapist: What do you call her?

Patient: Stupid. Shut up.

Therapist: What do you think of a girl who has such thoughts toward her mother?

Patient: Well, she calls me names sometimes. She calls me

a bitch and she says I'm a stupid idiot sometimes.

Therapist: And what do you do?

Patient: I get angry when she says those things. I get very angry.

Therapist: You get very angry. What do you think about a kid who thinks bad things about her mother? Do you think it's right or wrong to think bad things about your mother?

Patient: I think all kids do.

Therapist: You're right. All kids do. Some kids think it's terrible to think bad thoughts about their mother. They think it's a horrible crime to be very angry at a mother. How do you feel?

Patient: I hate to get angry at my mother. Everytime I say things like "I'm not going to speak to her again" and I swear about five minutes later, "All right, good-bye Mommy."

Therapist: Well, that's another question. The real question is whether you think it's wrong to get angry at a mother.

Patient: No.

Therapist: That's right. Was there ever a time in your life when you thought it was a terrible thing?

Patient: I think I always knew children always get angry at their mothers.

Therapist: You never thought that it was terrible?

Patient: No.

Therapist: You're sure.

Patient: Yes, I'm sure now.

Therapist: Did you ever think that getting angry at your mother might hurt her terribly? Some kids think that the angry thoughts can harm.

Patient: No because she hurts me a lot of times so I don't think my thoughts will bother her.

In my story the blue pencil's resolution to change himself does not work. Understanding of the exact nature of the underlying problems is necessary before he can translate what he has learned into action and alleviate his difficulties. In my story, I did not mention the exact nature of the problems. My hope was that the patient would provide her own examples for herself, either in a subsequent discussion, a story, or a dream.

My hopes were realized in the post-story discussion when Carol brought up the problem with her mother, which was central to her difficulties. As the reader may recall, the mother was an extremely angry woman, whose underlying rage and biting sarcasm were practically incessant. It would have been foolhearty and even cruel of me to set as a goal for this girl significant diminution of her mother's rage. She was more realistically advised to attempt to change those things in herself which might be aggravating the situation and to resign herself to certain elements in her mother's behavior which she could not change. In addition, we discussed whether she felt guilt over her angry thoughts and whether she thought angry thoughts could harm. Carol denied feeling guilty. She also denied that she ever thought angry thoughts could hurt another person.

This discussion took place after only three months of treatment, so it is not surprising that much of what I said might not have been too meaningful to her. Had therapy been continued, I think there was a good chance that Carol would have profited more from such discussion, as she was bright and introspective.

Example 8

Ronald, the boy with severe outbursts of rage and generalized antagonism toward authority, told this story during his sixth month of treatment:

(*Makes "fff-fff" sound.*) Do you know what that is fans? That's a snake and that's what my story is today. My story is —— the title is —— "Snakey."

Now there was this little snake called Snakey and he had a mother called Snookey and his father was called Bookey. And Snakey, every time his mother and father went up to him, bit her — bit one of them. And, of course, not liking to be bit when they're older, they bit him back. After a while Snakey was full of holes and sores and after a while Snakey died. That's the end of my story.

Therapist: The moral of that story?

Patient: When somebody does something bad you should punish them, but nobody has the right to kill because as we said in Hebrew before, just because the Lord creates people and people kill, that doesn't mean any human really has the right to kill unless they're brain-sick or something, unless they have a good reason.

Therapist: No one has a good reason to kill.

Patient: I mean —— you know what I mean.

Therapist: I see. So that's your story?

Patient: Yes.

Therapist: Okay, then. Thank you very much Mr. X for your excellent story. It is always a pleasure having you on this program. And now it's time for me to tell my story.

The story is a sad one. It depicts a struggle to the death with his parents. It reflects the patient's awareness that violent acting out of his antagonism to his parents will only result in even more punitive retaliation on their part and that the vicious cycle could ultimately result in his death. His moral contains a weak plea for mercy, but says nothing about his restraining himself or otherwise improving the situation from his side. Accordingly, I told this story:

My story is entitled "Snakey."

Patient: (*Laughs.*)

Therapist: Once upon a time there was a snake called Snakey and he had a mother whose name was Snookey and he had a father whose name was Bookey.

Patient: (*Imitates snake sounds while laughing.*)

Therapist: Now, Snakey was having a lot of trouble with his mother and father. He was biting them and they were biting him back and the more he'd bite them, the more they'd bite him back, until the point was reached where he had holes and sores all over himself.

One day Snakey was crawling along in the grass and who should he meet but his old friend, Smarty. Smarty said, "Hey, Snakey. What's happened to you?" Snakey said, "I've been fighting with my mother and father. I'm all bitten up with holes." And Smarty said —— see Smarty got the name because —— why do you think they gave him the name Smarty?

Patient: He's smart!

Therapist: Right! You're a smart kid figuring that one out (*Laughs*).

Patient: (*Laughs.*)

Therapist: Anyway, Smarty said to him, "You know, Snakey. I think they should change your name." And Snakey said, "Yeah, what should they call me?" Smarty said, "I think they should call you Stupy." Why do you think Smarty said that Snakey should change his name to Stupy?

Patient: Because he was stupid!

Therapist: And why did Smarty think —

Patient: And it was stupid to say stupid (*laughs*).

Therapist: Well, it was smart to say stupid. Why do you think Smarty suggested that Snakey should change his name to Stupy?

Patient: Because he was a stupe?

Therapist: Why was he a stupe? What was Snakey doing that was stupy?

Patient (laughing): Well, Snakey was a stupy because he wasn't trying to cooperate with his parents and, you know, he didn't try to get along with them, so he didn't try to solve it, so he wouldn't get bitten, so none of them would be bitten up anymore and he didn't do that, so he was stupid.

Therapist: That's exactly right. So then let's make the story go as you have suggested. So Snakey says, "Why are you calling me Stupy?" And Smarty tells him just what you said, that he wasn't trying to work out the problems with his parents, instead of having to resort to biting, that they would try to work it out and figure out what was going on. So what do you think Snakey then did?

Patient: He tried to and everything went all right.

Therapist: Now I want to ask you a question. What was one of the problems that was going on between Snakey and his parents, Snookey and Bookey, that they tried to work out. What was one of the problems?

Patient: How they could stop biting each other and get along.

Therapist: Yes. What was the thing? Why were they biting each other in the first place? What kinds of specific things were they disagreeing over?

Patient: I don't know. That wasn't in my story.

Therapist: I would like you to try to —

Patient: Guess?

Therapist: Yes, guess.

Patient: Well, maybe Stupy snake — or whatever you want to call it — thought that he wanted to (*makes sounds while thinking*) he, he, he, he ——

Therapist: I'm waiting.

Patient: He wanted to —— he wanted to (*sings*). Oh! He wanted to have his own way.

Therapist: I see. Are you saying that Smarty thought that Snakey or Stupy, as we will now call him, was kind of stupid because he wanted everything his own way?

Patient: Yeah!

Therapist: So what happened then?

Patient: So they started getting in fights and biting each other.

Therapist: How did they resolve that problem? How did they work it out?

Patient: By talking together and trying to solve it by Stupy trying to stop thinking he could get everything he wanted.

Therapist: So how did it work out? What then happened?

Patient: Well, then everything went all right. What's the moral? What's your moral?

Therapist: Hold it. I want to ask you a question. I haven't come to the moral yet because I want to understand how the story goes. What did Stupy then start doing? How did he change himself? What did he do specifically?

Patient: He just behaved and never again thought that he could get everything he wanted.

Therapist: Did he get angry?

Patient: And he realized that he couldn't get everything he wanted.

Therapist: Did he get some of the things he wanted?

Patient: Well, yes, when he was good.

Therapist: He got some of the things.

Patient: Because he was good and, you know, his parents didn't mind getting them for him because he was a good little snake.

Therapist (laughing): He was a good little snake. All right. So what's the moral of the story?

Patient: I told mine. Now you tell yours.

Therapist: Okay. The moral of the story is that when you compromise —— do you know what compromise means?

Patient: Yes.

Therapist: What does compromise mean?

Patient: That means take two ideas and put them together to merge one idea into one that will settle both problems at once.

Therapist: Right. When you compromise you can avoid fights to the death and that if you compromise you give in a little. You give up some of the things you want; the other person gives up some of the things they want; in order to find some kind of a middle ground, a middle road, where each person gets something, but not everything. Then you could avoid fighting, biting, and death-dealing blows.

Patient: That reminds me. You know that thing on "Laugh-In" where they do "da, da, dat, da, da, da."

Therapist: Yeah.

Patient: That reminds me. You took this story of mine and made it something like this: "Da, da, dat, da, da, da." (*Blows.*)

Therapist: I see. I want to ask you a question. Do you notice any similarity between the story we're talking about, Snakey and Stupy, and anything that goes on in your life?

Patient: Yeah.

Therapist: What's the similarity?

Patient: Well, lots of times I ask for things that are too much for my parents to let me have sometimes and I want everything and I can't get it and I get mad a lot of times.

Therapist: Do you think you can change that?

Patient: I hope so.

Therapist: What do you think that you can do specifically?

Patient: Anything — just change it.

Therapist: Now tell me something. Were you aware that while we were telling this story about Snakey that this was like your situation? Did you realize that? Yes or no?

Patient: Yeah.

Therapist: I see. Hhmmm.

Patient: Well, uh, hold it. It's time for a commercial.

Therapist: I want to ask you another question. Were you aware at the beginning, as you started to tell the story, that this was like your situation? When you first started to tell the story, did you realize that you were talking about yourself?

Patient: A little.

Therapist: A little bit.

Patient: Okay. Hold it. We can continue this later. And now it's time for a station break and a commercial from the Anti-Lung Cancer Organization, sponsored by me, me, me! This is D.G., Dr. Gardner's television network super-high frequency.

"Da, da, da, da, da, da, da, da, da, da, da. Bing! Da, da, dat, da, da, da, da —— You can take Salem out of the sick bay but — bing! You can't take the cancer out of Salem. You can take Salem out of the sick bay but — bing! You can't take the cancer out of Salem." (*Repeats a few more times and ends with a whisper*) "You can't take the cancer out of Salem."

And now friends, back to "Dr. Gardner's Television Program." And now here he is again, Dr. Gardner!

Therapist: All right. Just one second now. Just hold on. I want to write something down and then we'll be back.

Patient: And now another song by me and my Anti-Lung Cancer Organization. "La, pa, pa, pa, pa, pa, pa, da. (*sings a Winston Cigarette Commercial ending with*) "You can't spoil lung cancer yet." So remember, don't buy Winston. Let me repeat that, Winston.

And now back to "Dr. Gardner's Television Program." Here he is.

Therapist: Now what is this —— a sidewalk interview program.

Patient: No, it's the end of the program. Remember you were writing something down? Let's finish this program. What were you doing on or about May —— you say. Are there similarities between your story and my story?

Therapist: Yeah. I was just asking if you noticed the similarities between the story you told and what actually goes on in your life?

Patient: Yeah. Okay. Thanks for inviting me again. Boys and girls, I'll see you again next week on Wednesday morning again, on this "Dr. Gardner's Television Program," channel one million, gavillion, kazillion, etc., etc., pa vooboo, super-high frequency channel, WXXXYZ and a bit of UVW in there. This program has been sponsored by the Anti-Lung —— by the Lung Cancer Prevention Association — excuse me, I had that name wrong. (*Laughs.*) And so, until next time, good-bye for Dr. Gardner and me. Dr. Gardner's "Make-up a Story Television Program" has now ended.

Therapist: Bye.

Patient (singing): D —— R —— G. D–r period, that is.

Therapist: Okay. Off the air.

Patient: And, remember. Don't smoke Salem or Winston. They (*shouts*) stink! (*Makes strange sound.*)

The post-story interchange demonstrates not only how I try to draw the child into participating in the telling of my story, but also how in the ensuing discussion I try to help him gain insight into the meaning of both of our stories. As is obvious, Ronald was extremely difficult to engage and I cannot say that I was particularly successful in getting through to him during the interchange.

The Salem commercial took on meanings beyond those interpretations previously suggested when Ronald presented it right after our discussion of his compromising with his parents. Since his mother was a heavy smoker, perhaps the cigarette represents his mother whose deadly qualities are intrinsic and unalterable. You can't get the cancer out of Salem, and you can't get the lethal elements out of mother. Perhaps he is again telling me his original story — that his battle with mother will ultimately result in his being murdered; that she is intrinsically homocidal.

Four months later Ronald related this story:

Once upon a time there were four boys: Fat, Brat, Gat, and Gnat. They were all bad. They were all walking down the street.

Gat said, "I've got to use a real gun." He thought if he dressed up in a superman suit then bullets wouldn't go through him. So he shot himself and he died.

Fat was unhealthy. Fat was so fat that he had a heart attack and he died. His teeth also fell out because he ate too many sweets.

Gnat bugged everybody. He was a wise guy. He was so fresh that someone shot him.

Brat was such a brat that no one ever wanted him. Everybody was mean to him so he drowned himself.

The moral of that story is that people can be so bad that they will get killed or kill themselves.

Therapist: Do you know what the story means?

Patient: They're all parts of me. If I don't change I'll be so bad to myself that I'd like to kill myself.

Therapist: What do you think you can do about these troubles?

Patient: Shape up or ship out.

Therapist: How?

Patient: By behaving, boy. By behaving.

Therapist: What will happen if you don't?

Patient: I'll get in a great jam. I'll get so bad that even my parents won't want me. So then I might as well be dead.

In this case I did not think that a story on my part was indicated. The post-story discussion revealed that the patient was well aware that the figures in the story represented various facets of his personality. The patient's situation was indeed a grave one. His anger at his parents had reached violent proportions. The uncontrollable outbursts of rage only discharged a fraction of the fury he felt. To let out more would have brought about dire consequences. To turn it inward might result in his own destruction.

310

The analysis, however, was only on the most superficial level. It directed itself exclusively to the issue of conscious control of his rage and did not at all touch upon the fundamental issues which were continuing to generate it: the anger of his parents and the unhappiness of their lives. Ronald was not yet ready to deal with these issues and my experience had been that attempts to do so during this phase of his therapy only enhanced Ronald's resistances and defenses.

Two months later Ronald told this story:

Hello friends. Today my story is "The Goggler" by Ronald X. (*Hums tune.*)

There was once this thing called the goggler and it was a poor little thing. It didn't have a home; it didn't have any food, hardly. It had to go around asking other rich gogglers for food.

One day he met a beautiful princess and he fell in love with her. (*Laughs.*) They visited each other secretly and they did stuff like Aladdin and the princess did.

Therapist: What was that?

Patient: You know, they met secretly and they went out together and everything. Just this part is a little like the Aladdin story. Okay?

Therapist: Okay. Go ahead.

Patient: Just that little part. Okay? Then one day they got married and they were happy together and everything and they got a lot of children and generation after generation there was a happy family. And that's the end of my story.

Therapist: The moral of that story?

Patient: I don't have a moral. I just told a story.

Therapist: Come on. There must be a lesson. Every story has a lesson or a moral.

Patient: Well, let's think of one.

Therapist: Okay.

Patient: Well, the moral of that story is that a good family is a happy family and a happy family is a good family. Do you want to know what the story means?

Therapist: Okay.

Patient: Okay. Bye, bye.

Therapist: Wait a minute. Ronald says that he is going to interpret this story before I tell mine. Go ahead.
Patient: Well, I don't want to tell it on the tape.
Therapist: Come on now.
Patient: The goggler is me.
Therapist: Yes.
Patient: The princess is somebody that I like and the princess is a girl that I like or something like that.
Therapist: Yes.
Patient: And the happiness means that we'll live happily together.
Therapist: Okay. Now I'll tell my story and see if you can interpret this story before I tell mine. Go ahead. differences between our two stories. All right?

Ronald's interpretation was, of course, valid as far as it went. He did not comment on the "goggler's" initial feelings of deprivation — it was poor, it didn't have a home, and it hardly had any food. Also, the solution to the goggler's loneliness and privation problems is quick and magical. Suddenly, from nowhere, there appears a princess who instantaneously solves all his problems for him. Love conquers all. There is no effort on his part; no acquisition of qualities which might attract her to him.

In response then, I told this story:

Once upon a time there was a goggler and the goggler was this thing. He was a poor goggler. He had no home; he had no food; and he would just go around begging food from the rich gogglers. He used to dream of someday being rich himself and marrying a beautiful girl, but he would live in a fantasy world. He would think, "Oh, I'll marry a beautiful princess."

But then a friend of his whom he spoke to about these fantasies said, "You know, you're living in a dream world, fellow. No beautiful princess is just going to come along and marry you. You've got to work to earn her love. You've got to make something of yourself so that you'll be attractive so that you will, ummm —"

Patient: Deserve her.

Therapist: "Deserve her. Thank you. You just don't get people falling in love with you if you are nothing. They've got to love something in you." Please stop fooling around with the microphone. Anyway, he thought that was good advice and he went to school first and he studied hard and he learned, and then when he grew up, he met a very beautiful girl who was just like the kind of princess he fantasied he would some day meet and then he lived happily ever after.

And the moral of that story is what?

Patient: No. It's your story.

Therapist: The moral of that story is that if you are unhappy about something now and you want to make your situation better, it's not going to come by magic. You have to work towards it. If you are unhappy with what you are getting from people now, there's always hope for the future, but you are not going to get it by just sitting on your backside. You have to study hard, go to school, grow up, and learn to do something well, so that a desirable and pretty and wonderful person will be attracted to you.

Patient: Very interesting, but —

Therapist: Okay, what's the but?

Patient: But, uh, oh —

Therapist: Bring the microphone up towards your mouth. But what?

Patient: But happy. (*Laughs.*)

Therapist: Now what do you think is the difference between my story and yours? How do you interpret my story if the goggler is you?

Patient: Well, that means that if I want to love that girl, I've got to work for it.

Therapist: And what do you have to do?

Patient: I've got to act right and I've got to do things to earn it.

Therapist: Right. It doesn't come by magic.

Patient: That's too bad.

Therapist: That's too bad. I know it. It is too bad, but that's the way the world is.

Patient: Well, anyway I can't marry this girl.

Therapist: Why?

Patient: Because she's a little too old for me. (*Laughs.*)
Therapist: I see. Well, when you grow up you'll have some-
one your own age or around your age.
Patient: She's plenty older than I am. (*Laughs.*)
Therapist: Okay, my friend.

My communication is self-explanatory. The attempt to engage Ronald in a meaningful post-story discussion was of limited success. His occasional snatches of insight and meaning-ful dialogue gave me the hope that he might be reached on the conscious level. But he was generally so distracting, so prone to resist with extraneous interjections, that I felt that my efforts were futile.

Example 9

David, a twelve-year-old boy, was referred for treatment because of significantly poor involvement in many areas of his life. His grades were poor, he had no meaningful friendships, and his relationships with members of his family appeared superficial. His chronic attitude seemed to be one of "not giving a damn."

In his third month of treatment, David told this story:

Patient: Can you start me to think?
Therapist: Yes, sure. David has asked me to help him get his story started.
   Once upon a time a long, long, long time ago, in a distant land, far, far, far away there lived a ——
Patient: Person.
Therapist: And this person ——
Patient: He was going to do his Christmas shopping. He was a teen-ager, about sixteen, and he just got his license. He was going down the highway and he was going pretty fast. He was going to one of the department stores. You know, like Paramus. The car had a blowout and it goes spinning off the road and crashes into another car that's parked in a parking lot. He gets hurt real bad and he's in the hospital. He broke his leg and he has to go to the hospital. He's in there for a couple of days, you know,

314

and when he gets out he asks his parents to take him down so he could do his Christmas shopping.

They take him down and he only has to get one more thing and it costs about three or four dollars. It's going to be a box of stationery for his father. Then when he gets out his money he finds out he doesn't have enough. So he has to wait a couple of days until he gets the money, but he doesn't know how he can get any. So he asks his mother if he could borrow it. So he borrows it and, you know, and she says when he gets better he could go out and work so he could pay her back. So he got his dad a present and he went home. They had a pretty good Christmas.

Therapist: So he borrowed money from his mother. Is that it?

Patient: Yeah.

Therapist: Hhmmm. And the moral is?

Patient: Well, I'm not sure if there is a moral. Um —— I guess it's if you try to do something, everything will turn out all right, you know.

Therapist: Okay. Thank you very much. Now it's time for me to tell my story.

The story depicts two events in which David is threatened with unfortunate consequences and each of which turns out all right, without any effort on his part. The hospital cures his broken leg and his mother is there to lend him money when he runs out. Misfortunes have a way of working themselves out. In response, then, I told this story:

Once there was a person and he was going to do his Christmas shopping. He was a teen-ager. He was sixteen. He had just gotten his license and he was going down the highway and he was kind of a careless driver. He wasn't watching what he was doing and he crashed his car and got a broken leg.

Well, then, when he got out of the hospital —— he was in the hospital a few days and was walking around in a cast —— he wanted to buy some Christmas presents for his parents so he said. "Hey, I don't have enough money." His mother said, "Didn't you save up from your allowance?" He said, "No, I didn't think too much about that. Lend me some money, Ma." His mother said, "No. I'm not going to lend you money. You did not consider the whole question of Christmas presents. You didn't concern yourself with it. You didn't worry about it. You didn't save up money and now you are going to be in a position where you are not going to be able to give anybody Christmas presents and it will be your own fault." He said, "What can I do?" She said, "You figure that out. That's your problem, not mine."

So he thought about it and decided that maybe he could get a job. So he went and he got a job and he quickly earned some money. He worked very hard for three days, carrying packages, doing deliveries, shoveling snow, and he then was able to get the money and bought the Christmas presents.

And the lesson of that story is: when you do something wrong you have to pay for your errors. This boy was kind of lax and lazy when driving and he, as a result, got a broken leg. When he was lazy in regard to his Christmas presents, he almost ended up without having money to buy Christmas presents. The lesson of that story is that you will suffer for the consequences of your own acts and you have to think in advance if you are to avoid difficulties. No one is going to take care of these things for you like in your story. No matter what happened to this boy somehow there were people around to take care of him and do it for him, whereas in my story he learns that you suffer the consequences of your own behavior.

Patient: Can I say something?

Therapist: Yes.

Patient: How could he shovel the walk and deliver packages and everything if he had a broken leg?

Therapist: Well, that's a good question. Let's say that he had a very minor fracture which involved immobilization in a cast, but which permitted him to do exercise.

Patient: He could have had a snowplow in front of his wheelchair.

Therapist (laughing): Wise guy. That's right — one of

those electrified wheelchairs with a snowplow hitched up to it with a very powerful motor.

Patient: (*Laughs.*)

Therapist: Anyway, other than that what else do you think of my story?

Patient: It was a pretty good one.

Therapist: Hhmmm.

Patient: My stories always come out happy.

Therapist: They come out happy?

Patient: Yeah.

Therapist: And mine?

Patient: Well, sometimes they don't. Yours do too, but they sort of seem like they are going to have a sad ending, but then they come out pretty good.

Therapist: Hhmmm. What do you think, now that you have heard my story, about your story?

Patient: I don't think I told a very good one because, well, my moral was nothing about the story.

Therapist: What about the boy in your story? How would you compare the boy in your story with the boy in my story in terms of their ways of handling life situations?

Patient: They were both careless, but one, you know, he got away with it, but in yours he had to work at it.

Therapist: Yeah. Your story tells that no matter what happens to this boy things take care of themselves. He has an accident and somehow that's all right. He doesn't have enough money, his mother lends it to him. He's being taken care of, whereas in my story this doesn't happen to him. Now, do you think this says anything about you?

Patient: Yeah, I guess so.

Therapist: What does it say about you?

Patient: 'Cause I don't really go out and get friends.

Therapist: What does that have to do with this?

Patient: Well, it's sort of being careless. It's sort of —— I don't know.

Therapist: We were talking before about your lack of motivation in things and I think you lack motivation in part because you somehow have the attitude that no matter what happens to you things will be taken care of.

I think your father does that. No matter what happens, no matter how he spends his money, somehow things will be taken care of. Huh? Right?

Patient: I guess so.

Therapist: I think you have that. How do you see your father having that?

Patient: Well, lots of times he just goes out and spends money he doesn't have like make a check out for it or charges it with a charge account or credit card thing. Even if he doesn't have any money in the bank, he might cash a check.

Therapist: Right. Somehow things will be taken care of and, you know, that boy in your story has that same attitude and thinks in some magic way everything is going to be all right. Hhmmm?

Patient: Yeah.

Therapist: Well, what do you think you can do about that?

Patient: Do about what?

Therapist: This attitude on your part.

Patient: I guess try to correct it.

Therapist: How would you correct it? What would you do?

Patient: You mean about motivating?

Therapist: Hhmmm.

Patient: I'll try and do it by myself.

Therapist: You see, your mother has always taken over. Whenever your father spends too much your mother tolerates it, accepts it. Right?

Patient: Yeah.

Therapist: In your story the mother lends the boy money.

Patient: Yeah.

Therapist: Like your mother when your father spends too much money; your mother will somehow cover it for him. You know?

Patient: How?

Therapist: Well, she'll —— did your mother go to work at one point?

Patient: She did a long time ago. She was a waitress at a diner.

Therapist: Yes. In order to cover his debts.

Patient: I don't know. I don't think we had too many debts then. This was maybe when my dad began doing that sort of stuff.

Therapist: Your mother accepts it both in him and in you. Okay. Let's stop here. Our time is up.

David's question: "How could he shovel the walk and deliver packages and everything if he had a broken leg?" is another reflection of his pattern of removing himself from obligations and involvements. He was an expert at devising excuses to avoid doing chores. He certainly would have maximized the incapacitation caused by any injury to avoid assuming his responsibilities. The idea of hitching up a snowplow to the wheelchair, although clever and humorous, was again motivated out of the need to minimize effort on his part.

David was able to see the relationship between his own motivational problem and his attitude that all will somehow turn out all right. His father was psychopathic, and when I suggested a relationship between the patient's attitude and that of his father, he saw it immediately. David was then able to provide examples of his father's psychopathy — his overdrafts and his loose attitude toward his charge accounts and credit cards. The post-story discussion also served to increase David's awareness of his mother's sanctioning of his father's irresponsible behavior.

The modifications and refinements presented in this chapter are the main ones which I have found useful. Others, however, are also possible.

When the therapist is not sure how to proceed with his story, he can ask the child for suggestions and clues: "And what do *you think* happened then?" Or, he might suggest two possible endings, asking the child which he prefers and why. Often the child himself is encouraged to help the therapist complete his story. If the child's story still reveals a pathologic resolution, I usually say: "Well, that's certainly one way of finishing it; I, myself, thought of this way . . ." In this way, the patient becomes more of a participant in resolving his own conflicts. Often the youngster is asked if he can figure out the moral of my story. This, of course, tells me if my message has gotten through.

On occasion, the child's story will suggest that important things have been going on which I have not heard about previously. At such times I may say: "I'd like to speak to your mother for a few minutes. Then I'll tell my story." The mother is consulted, usually in the child's presence, but alone if need be. I may then be in a better position to create a meaningful story.

Sometimes an important insight into the meaning of the child's story occurs to me after the session and I realize that the one I had told, although pertinent, could have been improved upon. In the next session I may ask the child if he remembers the story he told me last time and, if necessary, I refresh his memory. I then tell the child that I have thought of another good story about the people (animals or whatever) in his story, and I offer to relate my new one. Most often, the child is interested in hearing it.

Since the stories are taped and the total time for the telling of them is about ten to fifteen minutes, there is often time to replay the tape and thereby repeat the communications. The old stories can be played back for additional therapeutic exposure.

At times children bring their own tape recorders to the session and the stories are taped simultaneously on the two tape recorders. The child then has the opportunity for replay at home — again providing further therapeutic exposure. I have found this approach to be especially useful in the psychotherapy of brain injured children whose short attention spans and poor memories almost necessitate replay at home if my messages are to "sink in." Such home replay also serves to intensify my relationship with the child and this, of course, is most salutary.

Lastly, as I have said, the storytelling technique lends itself to almost infinite variation and the reader is encouraged to devise modifications of his own.

Section II

Utilizing the Mutual Storytelling Technique to Treat Common Clinical Problems

8. OEDIPAL PROBLEMS

According to Freud children enter the phallic phase of psychosexual development at about the age of three. At this time both normal and pathological children universally develop what Freud called the oedipus complex.[1] Briefly, the child manifests a genital-sexual attraction to the parent of the opposite sex and an associated feeling of envy and hostility toward the parent of the same sex. The urges are considered to be genital-sexual, although not necessarily specifically associated with heterosexual intercourse as the primary source of genital gratification. The fantasies, according to the classical school, may include a variety of misconceptions regarding the exact nature of the sexual life of the parents: the child might fantasize that the parents get pleasure by looking at one another's genitals; by engaging in oral-genital contact; by rubbing themselves against each other; or by going to the toilet together.[2] In each case, the child fantasizes himself or herself in the role of the rival parent. Included also are fantasies of marriage and the desire to give the mother babies or to bear the father's children. The boy may fear that his hostility toward his father may result in the latter's retaliation, especially by castration, which produces what Freud called castration anxiety.

Freud considered the oedipus complex to be part of normal human psychosexual development and regarded the failure to resolve or come to terms with it to be the central element in the etiology of all neuroses.

His explanation for the development of the male oedipus complex was far simpler than that of the female. The boy's possessive love of his mother and murderous rage toward the father is a natural extension of the loving relationship the mother has always provided him. For the girl, things are more complicated.[3] When she first observes that the little boy has a penis, she considers herself to have been deprived of a most valuable organ. Her mother, who bore her this way, is blamed and she turns to her father for love. Also, since the mother also lacks this invaluable part the girl's respect for her markedly diminishes. The father as the possessor of a penis is looked upon as a more likely source of gratifying the little girl's desire to have one herself. Through fantasied sexual intercourse with the father the female child hopes to incorporate a penis. The adult female, by bearing a male child, can satisfy her desire to produce a penis of her own.[4] Even if the baby is a female, it can still symbolically represent the longed-for penis. Other factors which contribute to the transfer relate to the girl's anger toward her mother. The mother becomes an object of hostility because she inhibits the little girl's masturbation, and the mother refuses to give up her affection for the father and devote herself totally to the child.

For the male child, the resolution of the oedipus complex[5] involves resigning himself to the fact that he cannot totally possess his mother. This resignation is made easier by his fear of castration by the father. Observing the female's absence of a penis confirms for him that his own penis can be removed. In addition, with the formation of the superego, the boy incorporates his father's dictates against incest and patricide. By utilizing the defense mechanism, "identification with the aggressor" (Anna Freud's term), he is further assisted in repressing the oedipal impulses. He develops a contempt for all who could have slept with his mother, be it himself, his father, or anyone else. The "mother-fucker" is considered most loathsome. Lastly, Freud considered biological maturation to be operative as well: "the time has come for its [the oedipus complex's] dissolution, just as the milk-teeth fall out when the permanent ones begin to press forward."[5]

Freud says less about the factors operative in the female's oedipal resolution. She too resigns herself to the fact that her mother's love for the father is such that she can never have him

324

completely to herself. Rebuffed by her father, she renounces and represses her oedipal wishes. Since her father will not provide her with the penis she so desperately wants, getting one symbolically through child-bearing is the best she can hope for and she must turn eventually to other men for this purpose.

Freud's emphasis on the oedipus complex was deep and extensive and its ramifications pervade his writings. His supporters and detractors have commented on it at length.

Carl Jung also considered the oedipus complex to have innate elements.[6] However, he regarded contributions from the child's inherited collective unconscious to be significant. Primordial images (psychic legacies of the past history of mankind) are operative in the formation of the complex. "The Mother Archetype" — the inherited psychic image of the proto-typical mother — serves as the basis for the child's deep attraction to his mother. The actual mother who is warming, protecting, and nourishing activates the archetypal mother — the "composite image of all pre-existing mothers, a model or pattern of all the protecting, warming, nourishing influences which man has experienced or which man will experience."[4] The child would want to remain at the breast of the "Eternal Mother" but reality requires him to separate from her. He is "driven by the eternal thrust to find her again, and to drink renewal from her."[7] To Jung, however, the attraction toward the mother has little to do with sex but rather revolves around the desire for protection and food. The attraction is also an ambivalent one, for she represents both the archetypal "Good Mother" and the "Terrible Mother" — the latter being the one who denies and frustrates the child.

To Jung, the child in a healthy household does not have significant difficulty resolving his oedipal ties and becoming independent of his family. It is only in a home where the child is exposed to deleterious psychological influences that he develops neurotic oedipal fears and guilts. In spite of Jung's emphasis on past factors contributing to the formation of the oedipus complex (factors not only from the child's own early life, but also from the past history of mankind), his therapeutic approach to its resolution focuses mainly on the present and the future. He attempts to work through the present problems which perpetuate the oedipal ties and considers behavioral manifestations and dream symbols to have future implications as well.

To Alfred Adler, the infant, by virtue of his size and realistic inadequacies, cannot but feel inferior in comparison to the adults around him.[8] One way in which he can compensate for these feelings of inadequacy is to predominate over his parents. Normally the child has no particular preference as to which parent he would like to dominate. However, if the mother is overprotective, the child's excessive demands become gratified and an oedipus complex develops. The overprotective mother stimulates the child by her excessive presence and she is usually seductive as well. Both of these factors elicit the child's sexual attraction to the mother. Receiving so many intense satisfactions from her, the boy tends to turn away from the father. The child may feign helplessness or use physical illness to gain extra attention and control. As he grows older the pampered child becomes increasingly ill-equipped to cope with the real world and withdraws even more into the mother's outstretched arms which further strengthens the oedipal tie.

For the girl the oedipal complex develops similarly when the father is overprotective and seductive. According to Adler, in both sexes the sexual and dependent gratifications are subordinate to the life goal of domination, possession, and exclusive control in the service of compensating for feelings of inferiority.

For Rank the most painful experience of life is birth which removes one from the most blissful state of all — intrauterine existence.[9] Throughout life one tries to recapture this lost paradise. Birth anxiety is the "primal anxiety" which is the basis for all other anxieties of life. All childhood fears and anxieties are derivatives of primal anxiety and their expression allows a gradual catharsis of the primal anxiety. Weaning is the second great trauma in the child's life. It, too, involves a painful separation from the mother, but it derives a significant part of its traumatic effect from the birth trauma.

The "primal wish" is to return to the womb. Sexual intercourse appears to be the most likely way of accomplishing this reunion with the mother. The mother's genitals, however, as the site of the original birth trauma, are extremely anxiety-provoking. The healthy boy turns, therefore, to other women whose genitalia evoke less fear. The boy with an unresolved oedipus complex obsessively tries to re-enter his mother and desensitize himself to her genitalia by repeatedly exposing himself to them. The repudiation by the mother is seen as another enforced separation similar to the birth trauma. The healthy boy accepts the rejection and seeks substitutes; the neurotic persists in his attempts to achieve the goal of re-entry. The girl may attempt to gratify the primal wish in two ways. By identifying with her own clitoris she may hope to gain partial entrance into her own vagina which symbolizes her mother's. Or she may identify herself with her own intrauterine child and consider herself to be her own mother.

The healthy person is satisfied with partial, substitutive, and symbolic gratifications of the primal wish. The neurotic will settle for nothing less than a real return to the intrauterine state, and since this is impossible he is doomed to disappointment and frustration.

Rank's concept of "will" also enters into his explanation of the oedipus complex. He uses the word "will" to refer to one's innate drive toward self-realization, individuality, and creative expression.[10] In the oedipal conflict between the father and the son, each is trying to impose his will on the other. The father tends to rob the son of individuality by trying to mold the boy in his own image. The son, to protect his individuality, may withdraw from the father out of the fear of being overwhelmed by him, and turn to the mother.[11] A similar conflict exists between the girl and her mother. The conflict is primarily one of "wills" rather than sexual prerogatives. Rank points out that in the Sophoclean play, Laius fears that a son would vie with him for power. Therefore, hesitant to father a child, he has to be seduced into the sexual act by Jocasta, and when Oedipus is born the boy is abandoned, only to return as a young man to engage Laius in the power struggle which he most feared. Forrest, in an excellent analysis of the *Sophocles Trilogy,* points out Laius' contributions to Oedipus' obsession.[12]

Karen Horney did not consider biological elements to play a role in the formation of the oedipus complex.[13] She regarded it as the result of two specific family conditions. The first is parental seduction. The child has the biological potential for sexual interest in the parent of the opposite sex but the urge is inconsequential unless there has been actual seduction — overt or covert, physical or psychological. The second and most common factor is parental deprivation of affection. This engenders in the child a conflict between his desire to approach his parents for gratification of his dependency and other needs and a wish to express the hostility he feels toward them for the rejection. The latter arouses anxiety because the expression of anger could bring about even further alienation from the already depriving parents. An attempt is therefore made to assuage this anxiety by drawing even closer — thus the obsessive "love" of the oedipus complex. The attraction has little to do with sex, but rather is toward the parent who appears most likely to offer protection and security.

For Horney, oedipal reactions can intensify problems which relate to more fundamental processes. The child normally feels somewhat alone and helpless in the world which, no matter how benevolent, must frustrate him at times and thereby appear hostile. The fears and anxieties he experiences in such a world are referred to as his "basic anxiety" and the hostility he perceives as "basic hostility." The guilt and fear he may feel over his basic hostility may result in his projecting it in order to deny its existence within himself. This projected hostility adds to the basic hostility, which in turn makes his world even more anxiety provoking.[14] These basic anxieties and hostilities and their intensifications can be experienced by normal children. When there is real parental rejection, the basic anxieties and hostilities increase. In this way rejections which engender the oedipus complex also produce other difficulties which in turn add to the child's oedipal problems.

Harry Stack Sullivan makes little direct reference to the oedipus complex in his writings. He did not consider there to be a significant sexual element in the normal parent-child relationship. The predilection of the child for the opposite-sexed parent is engendered by the parents, and is in no way related to biological determinants. Each parent feels familiar with the same-sexed child and somewhat strange with the opposite-sexed. In addition, each tends to use the same-sexed child for vicarious gratification more frequently than the opposite-sexed. Fathers pressure their sons to achieve goals which may have eluded them and mothers similarly encourage their daughters. These factors result in the tendency by the parents to be more authoritarian with the same-sexed child and more permissive and indulgent with the opposite-sexed. The child then responds to the more affectionate parent and becomes alienated from the more coercive one. The behavioral manifestations which result are those which Freud referred to as the oedipal complex. Sullivan agreed that one could observe these intrafamilial attractions but did not consider them to have much importance in the basic etiology of psychogenic disturbance.[15]

Erich Fromm regards the oedipus myth as best understood as the rebellion of the son against the father's authority in a patriarchal family.[16] Feeling coerced and overpowered, the son develops hostility toward his father, the expression of which helps him gain his independence. The domineering father is an intrafamilial reflection of an authoritarian society, and the son's rebellion is symbolic of his antagonism against a coercive social structure. Fromm claims that in societies where patriarchal authority is weak, the oedipus complex does not develop. Childhood sexual interests are normally present but he considers them to be generally satisfied auto-erotically. When the mother is overprotective or otherwise fosters excessive dependency, then the fixation on her which is seen in the oedipus complex develops.

In a more recent article[17] Fromm points out that Freud assumed that Little Hans' parents were normal and that his oedipal problems arose *sui generis*.[18] In the case presentation, however, Freud describes the mother's seductive behavior as well as her castration threats toward the child. Hans' fear of horses is not, as Freud described, related to the father (whom Fromm sees as benevolent and supportive) but rather symbolic of his fears of his mother.

Common to both Fromm's earlier concept of the father's role in the etiology of oedipal problems and his more recent analysis of Little Hans is the use of force by a parent. Such coercion in turn is seen as a derivative of a society which excessively utilizes force and threaten the attainment of its goals. To understand the oedipus complex then, "we must go beyond the framework of the family life, and enter into a critical examination of the structure of society."[17]

All of the preceding theorists were adult analysts, and their concepts of the oedipus complex were derived from data gathered from the analyses of adults, many of whom were neurotic and some probably even psychotic — some of Freud's cases would certainly be diagnosed psychotic by today's criteria. Such data must be suspect considering the distortions that are caused by fallible memory and the passage of time as well as those that are inevitably engendered by pathological processes. Even Little Hans, whose analysis Freud considered to confirm his oedipal theories, was not treated directly by him but through an intermediary, the child's father.[18] Although Anna Freud,[19] Melanie Klein,[20] and many other classical child analysts have had extensive experience with children, most of their writings indicate that they have not questioned the basic tenets of Freud's formulation of the oedipus complex. They have been, I believe, selectively inattentive to clinical material which suggests that alterations and modifications might be appropriate.

A concept of the oedipus complex which seems most reasonable to me is based on careful and receptive consideration of the theories already discussed as well as my own observations of children in both normal and clinical situations. My concept borrows much from my predecessors but also relies heavily on my own clinical data — especially children's fantasies elicited by the Mutual Storytelling Technique.

First, I believe that there is a biological sexual instinct which attracts every human being to members of the opposite sex. From birth to puberty this drive is not particularly strong because during this period the child is not capable of fulfilling the drive's primary purpose of procreation. Although weak and poorly formulated during the pre-pubertal period, it nevertheless exhibits itself through behavior which I consider manifestations of *oedipal interest*. The normal child may speak on occasion of marrying the parent of the opposite sex and getting rid of his rival. These comments may even have a mildly sexual component such as: "and then we'll sleep in bed together." Instinctive impulses for territorial prerogatives may also be operative here. But I do not believe that psychologically healthy children have the desire in this period for genital-sexual experiences with the parent, nor do I believe that their sexually-tinged comments are associated with strong sexual-genital urges. Rather, what the healthy child may on occasion want is a little more affection and attention, undiluted by the rival.

In a setting where the child is not receiving the affection, nurture, support, interest, guidance, protection, and generalized physical gratifications such as stroking, warmth, and rocking which are his due, he may in his frustration became obsessed with obtaining such satisfactions and develop the kinds of sexual urges, preoccupations, and fantasies which Freud referred to as oedipal. The instinctive sexual urges, which are normally mild and relatively dormant, have the *potential* for intensive expression even as early as birth. Getting little gratification from his parents, the child may develop a host of fantasies in which the frustrated love is requited and the rival is removed. Such fantasies follow the principle that the more one is deprived, the more one craves and the more jealous one becomes of those who have what one desires. Such manifestations can appropriately be called *oedipal problems* in the classical sense. Thus, the foundation for the development of neurosis is formed not, as Freud would say, through the failure to resolve successfully one's sexual frustrations regarding the parent of the opposite sex, but through the failure to come to terms with the more basic deprivations the child is suffering.

Whereas Freud considered the sexual preoccupation to arise in the child *sui generis,* I believe that this mode of adaptation to parental deprivation is only one of many possible adjustments, and that family and cultural factors play an important role in determining which one is chosen. Parental seduction is only one factor which tends to foster the oedipal adaptation. The seduction need not be overtly physical; it can arise through verbal provocations and titillating exposures. Without parental seduction the child is less likely to involve himself in a sexual adaptation to parental deprivation and is more likely to utilize non-oedipal mechanisms. However, I have seen oedipal problems arise without parental seduction. Such seduction then enhances the likelihood of, but is not essential to the development of, oedipal difficulties. I also believe that family and cultural factors which tend to foster the child's rivalry with the same-sexed parent can also be instrumental in bringing about the complex. I am in agreement with Fromm that the authoritarian father in a patriarchal household may be a contributing factor in the formation of the oedipus complex in the boy and with Sullivan who postulates that the parent's stricter attitude toward the same-sexed child fosters oedipal rivalry. Once again, however, I have seen children utilize the oedipal mechanism in the absence of significant rivalry-engendering behavior by the parents.

In my experience, the classical paradigm of sexual attraction to the same-sexed parent and hostility toward the opposite-sexed is an oversimplification of what one observes clinically. Most often there is great ambivalence toward both parents. The boy with a depriving yet seductive mother has good reason to be angry. He is deprived of basic affection and provided with seduction as a substitute. Clinically the anger may be revealed directly, but more commonly it is handled by a variety of defense mechanisms including repression, denial, reaction-formation, and projection. When the latter is utilized the child may become fearful of his mother's retaliation. To protect himself, his avowals of love may increase. Or his hostile impulses may take the form of his fearing that his mother will die, and this too may be handled by obsessive concern for her welfare. A variety of other possible mechanisms as well may come into play to assist the child in handling his basic ambivalence. Such a boy, in addition to his rivalrous hostility toward his father, may still harbor deep-seated loving feelings and dependent longings toward him. The hostility may engender anxiety that he may lose the father which often results in obsessive protestations of affection. Anyone who has observed what is sometimes referred to as a childhood "oedipal panic" will readily confirm that intense feelings of love, hate, and fear regarding *both* parents dominate the clinical picture. Some of the stories in this chapter will, I believe, demonstrate this aspect of the oedipal problem.

Neuroses, most would agree, are the result of many factors acting in various combinations: cultural, social, familial, psychological, and biological. For Freud, the psychobiological (especially the psychosexual) factors were crucial and he considered the unresolved oedipus complex to be at the root of all neuroses. In my opinion, whatever cultural, social, and biological factors may be operative in the etiology of neurotic symptoms, parental — and especially maternal — deprivation is essential to their formation. All neurotic symptoms are in part an attempt to cope with this basic deprivation, and the way in which the child chooses to adapt is determined by biological, cultural, social, and familial influences. One deprived child becomes overdependent, an adaptation which is elicited and perpetuated by his overprotective mother. Another reacts with schizoid withdrawal, an adjustment with which his neglectful parents are comfortable. Another discharges in sports the hostility he feels toward his rejectors — sports being, in addition, an activity which has premium value in his milieu. Another takes drugs or becomes a juvenile delinquent because that's how kids on *his* block adapt. Another uses the secondary gain of his symptoms to enjoy compensatory attention. And so it goes. One could cover the gamut of psychogenic symptoms and find the common element of deprivation in each of them. I am fully aware that symptoms are most complex and many factors contribute to their formation, but the adaptation to emotional abandonment is central and omnipresent. The well-loved child is generally relatively free from psychopathology.

Oedipal problems are one among many classes of available adjustments to parental deprivation. I use the term oedipal then to refer to those mechanisms by which the child, in the attempt to compensate for early emotional deprivation, obsessively craves for and tries to gain the affection of the opposite-sexed parent and exhibits concomitant jealous rivalry toward the same-sexed parent. Oedipal problems are likely to arise in a situation of parental seduction and/or paternal authoritarianism, but they can appear in other family milieus as well. It is possible that they were more likely to arise in Freud's culture than in mid-late twentieth century America.

The range of psychological reactions to parental rejection is broad, and many, if not most, contain elements of more than one stage of psychosexual development. Rarely does one see purely oral, anal, or phallic phase symptomatology. When the predominant theme appears to involve obsessive attempts to gain the love of the opposite-sexed parent and/or excessive rivalry with the same-sexed parent, then one can conveniently apply the term oedipal. The homosexual whose obsessive "love" of males is a thinly disguised reaction-formation to an underlying hatred of men and who fears women because they too closely resemble his forbidden seductive mother, could be considered to have oedipal problems because his difficulties fundamentally reflect the oedipal paradigm. When a patient's adjustment to the privation involves, for example, compulsive eating, the term oedipal is not usually used even though the food may be a symbolic representation of the mother's love. The more remote the overt symptom is from the themes of mother-love and father-hate, the less likely it will be labeled oedipal. However, if the compulsive eater (who is considered to be suffering with "oral" difficulties) has a dependent, thinly disguised sexual relationship with his mother, his problems would more likely be considered oedipal.

The term oedipal is a poor one, therefore, because it purports to describe a symptom complex which rarely, if ever, exists in pure form. Most often, if not always, there are elements of other stages of psychosexual development. In addition, to use the term oedipal is equivalent to naming pneumonia, "cough," or encephalitis, "headache." Just as cough and headache are the superficial manifestations of the more general underlying diseases, pneumonia and encephalitis, the oedipus complex is only one possible symptomatic manifestation of a whole class of symptom complexes resulting from the basic disorder of parental deprivation. Also, the term is both restrictive and misleading. It is restrictive because it tends to focus undue attention on the sexual elements in the adaptation while disregarding the more important non-sexual aspects. It is misleading because it suggests that the primary problem is sexual, which it isn't.

Freud's misconceptions about childhood sexuality are responsible for what I believe to be central errors in his oedipal theory.

First, concerning the child's attitudes toward his genitalia, there can be little doubt that unnatural social attitudes produce in the child a curiosity that might not otherwise have occurred. One unfortunate outgrowth of Freudian teachings was the warning that parents, by undressing in front of their child, even at ages as low as six months to one year, could produce sexual fantasies and frustrations that might contribute to the formation of oedipal problems. In my opinion, the healthy atmosphere is one in which the child (up to the late prepubertal period — ages ten to eleven) is permitted to occasionally observe his parents in the nude, in casual and natural situations. In my opinion, it is psychologically deleterious to strictly hide one's body from the child, for such an attitude fosters the development of unnatural curiosities and excessive cravings which then contribute to neurotic attitudes toward the opposite sex. On the other hand, nudity in the home should not be taken too far. It is just as inappropriate to artificially expose the child when the situation usually does not call for nudity. If the child is excessively exposed to parental nudity, then the kind of seductiveness Freud spoke about may very well be occurring. In our culture, which strictly prohibits parent-child sexuality, such seductive behavior can lead to frustrations, guilts, and other neurotic manifestations. What is to be avoided is seductiveness, not nudity. The two do not necessarily go together. Sexually stimulating verbalizations or titillating physical contact when clothed may be equally seductive.

Even with artificial stimulation, the healthy child is relatively unpreoccupied with sexuality and genitalia. A child's interest in genitalia usually is confined to occasional teasing and joking about seeing the genitals of another child, but even then the concern is usually voyeuristic and excretory without feelings of genital-sexual excitation. The child with psychogenic or emotional disturbances, however, may exhibit an exaggerated interest in the genitals of the opposite sex and may concern himself with the sexual component.

Freud says that the female child, when she first realizes that boys have penises and that she does not, considers herself to have had a penis but lost it, possibly because she was "bad." She may then develop what he called "penis envy." The male child is also said to view with horror the lack of a phallus in the female, in that its absence implies his own member can easily be removed, especially if he is "bad:" This phenomenon is said to contribute to "castration anxiety."

I do not believe that castration anxiety is present as a significant concern in the normal boy, nor is penis envy a preoccupation in the well-adjusted girl. The healthy girl may, on occasion, express the desire to have a penis, but this, I believe, is related to the general feeling of jealousy which any child has when someone has what he hasn't. The healthy child accepts his sex and has pride both in the sexual and nonsexual aspects of himself. If, however, the child is raised in a home where he has been actively threatened because he touches himself or engages in other activities unacceptable to the parents, then, of course, he may readily develop castration anxieties. Or if the female is conditioned to believe that being a male is infinitely more desirable, then the groundwork for penis envy is certainly being laid.

336

In general, I believe that psychopathological symptoms centering around the genitalia more often than not pertain to nonsexual difficulties for which the genitals are being used as a symbol. The penis usually symbolizes masculinity in general with both sexual and nonsexual connotations — the nonsexual including such attributes as self-assertion and productivity in the world. The vagina and breasts may symbolize not only simple sexuality but also the broader context of femininity — including physical attractiveness, childbearing and rearing capacity, and homemaking ability.

In moving from the symbolic aspects of the genitalia to actual genital self-stimulation in children, some clarification of terms is necessary. When the term childhood masturbation is used, differentiation is usually not made between the occasional touching of the genitalia, which almost all children engage in for the mild pleasure it affords them, and the more intensive masturbatory practices which are obsessively engaged in and which may often culminate in orgasm. Frequent genital self-stimulation by the child, whether or not it is associated with orgasm, is pathological and reflects psychogenic difficulties whereas occasional mild stimulation is normal.

According to Freud, in the phallic stage the child masturbates primarily in response to overt or symbolic fantasies of sexual involvement with the parent of the opposite sex. Masturbatory guilt is primarily the result of oedipal guilt — the child is said to feel guilty about his sexual desires for the forbidden object, his or her parent. In my opinion, the masturbating child is essentially communicating to the parent the message: "I must turn to myself for pleasure because you are deficient in providing me with love I need." By proscribing the act, the parent is protected from this painful confrontation. This is not to say that other factors do not contribute to masturbatory guilt, but what I have just described is, I believe, central. Parental deficiency in providing the child with adequate affection is a most significant element in bringing about obsessive masturbation. The child whose environment is essentially a giving and rewarding one does not obsessively resort to this compensatory concentrated pleasure.

Generally, the normal child does not have specific fantasies associated with his occasional genital stimulation. He just touches himself because "it feels good." With regard to those children who do obsessively masturbate, generally I have found that below the ages of seven to eight, children do not have specific fantasies, whereas beyond that age, from eight to twelve, children describe a variety of fantasies, both sexual and non-sexual. In such children, when the sexual fantasy is associated with a member of the opposite sex, it does not usually, in my experience, involve sexual intercourse but rather looking, rubbing, and caressing. More pathological, but nevertheless seen in this older group of children, are occasional sadomasochistic masturbatory fantasies which might include whipping and being tortured, as well as homosexual fantasies, although the latter are most often confined to the caressing type. Occasionally the child's masturbatory fantasies will include animals (most often dogs), and sometimes this is associated with actual experiences in which there has been sex play with animals.

A study by Ames,[21] as well as one by Pitcher and Prelinger,[22] confirm what I have said regarding the sexual fantasies of children in the oedipal period. Ames found that only 1.8 per cent of all stories of children from two to five related to reproduction. Among the children studied, no fantasies regarding sensual-sexual experiences with parents were described. The primary theme for the three-to five-year-old child was violence. Pitcher and Prelinger found that the main themes in the three-to five-year-old group were aggression, hurt, and misfortune. In the stories where the child describes his relationship with the parents, sensual-sexual involvements are rare. One sees instead the whole gamut of other possible modes of interaction, both friendly and hostile.

These studies have been criticized on the ground that the investigators were naive in expecting that the subjects ("normal" school children) would freely tell stories including sexual themes to a stranger. With such selective censoring, the critics argue, the data are artificially weighted with non-sexual fantasies. Parents, they claim, are much more likely to hear such productions because the child is more comfortable revealing them in his home. Generally those who are familiar enough with these studies to criticize them are in the fields of psychology and psychiatry, and have the tendency, I believe, to selectively attend to the sexual productions of children (both their own as well as their patients). This results in an exaggerated impression of the frequency of childhood sexual fantasies. My own clinical experience is consistent with the findings of these studies — the conscious fantasy life of the normal child at the three- to five-year-old level contains little overt sexual material. But one could argue that my patients, as well, are inhibited in expressing such fantasies to me. I would prefer to believe that they are not. One might interpret some of the fantasies to have a latent sexual content. In my experience, however, most of the dreams of children, both normal and neurotic, are more meaningfully interpreted non-sexually, despite the fact that a small percentage of children with psychogenic disturbance are preoccupied with sexual activities, urges, and fantasies, either overt or symbolic.

The normal child, according to Freud, resolves his oedipus complex by the age of six. He then enters a six-year period of sexual quiescence — the latency period — which terminates at puberty.

There is, indeed, little sexual interest in this period, but not because of repression of oedipal drives and resolution of the oedipus complex, but rather because, as I have described, there is relatively little genital-sexual urge to be repressed in the first place. It is not until puberty, with physiological genital maturation, that sexual urges of adult intensity are normally present. The child has the potential to exhibit such interest and achieve such gratification, but to do so would be, in my opinion, pathological.

In spite of this low level of sexual activity during this period, there is probably more sexual interest and fantasy than in the preceding phases of life, not less as Freud indicates. It is in this period that children, excited and stimulated by the proscriptions of our culture, may satisfy their curiosity about the genitals of others and engage in exhibitionistic and voyeuristic games. But here, too, the more common interest seems to be the satisfaction of curiosity rather than pleasurable genital stimulation. In the neurotic child, for whom other gratifications are not forthcoming, there may be excessive sexual urge, fantasy, and involvement with this kind of play. And, as already described, from about age eight onward, the sexual fantasies may take any form known to the adult.

In summary, then, it is my opinion that prior to the age of puberty strong sexual urges and fantasies do not play a significant role in the mental life of the healthy child. There is, however, a latent sexual potential which may manifest itself in psychogenic disturbances. The classical school of psychoanalysis considers many of the normal child's nonsexual fantasies to be symbolic of unconscious sexual drives. My own opinion is that although fantasies, like dreams, may be derived from the unconscious, what is being symbolized in the normal child has little to do with the kinds of sexual activity described by the Freudian psychoanalytic school.

Sexually exciting dreams, moreover, are extremely rare in childhood. If there were such strong sexuality in childhood, and it was not being directly revealed in fantasies (as shown by Ames, Pitcher, and Prelinger), it could be expected to manifest itself occasionally in the dream. For the dream, although it may disguise, is closer to the primary drives and can be expected, as in the adult, to provide occasional gratifications of repressed instinctive impulses. In the disturbed child, the kinds of fantasies described by the Freudians may indeed be present, but such fantasies are best understood in a broader context. Sexual material represents both sexual and nonsexual elements in the child's mental life.[23]

The concept of deprivation is by no means all-inclusive. It is not intended to explain successfully all oedipal phenomena. There are other factors which I have not discussed in detail which are contributory. There are, for example, the genetically determined differences in the individual child's need for various forms of physical gratification. Tactile, kinesthetic, visual, auditory, and other forms are all involved in describing the affection the child receives from the parent. Cognitive elements are also most important. The child must successfully pass through many stages of ego development to form oedipal involvements. He must recognize a whole series of differentiations: himself from others, his parents from strangers, and his mother from his father. As Schecter points out,[24] the child must be able to accomplish the cognitive-affective step of going from the symbiotic dyadic relationship he has with his mother to the oedipal triangle relationship which includes the father. He must be able to break the symbiotic tie and include this third person, not only in his cognitive scheme of things, but in his affective behavior as well.

I have not gone in depth into the issue of the incest taboo. Is this a legacy of the past, that is genetically embedded in our psychic structure as Freud would have us believe,[25] or are cultural determinants more influential? I have spoken of parental jealousy but little of its psychodynamics. Parents may be jealous of their children's freedom to indulge themselves in primitive gratifications. The father may be jealous of the symbiotic tie which his child enjoys with the mother. I have spoken of parental affection and its deprivation, but not of its various qualities and intensities. I have not discussed the role of parental hostility toward the child as part of the ambivalence which exists in every relationship (The child inevitably produces resentments and frustrations in his parents no matter how loving the relationship.). I have spoken elsewhere of parental seduction,[26] but not of parental "induction,"[27] the role, that is, of the parent in inducing in the child a sexual role pattern, not so much by passively being there and allowing the child to identify with him, but by more actively fostering specific, sexually associated role behavior. For example, the father who is actively concerned with his daughter's grooming and dress, who exaggeratedly encourages her to act and look "grown-up" and "like mommy," is inducing oedipal adaptations without necessarily being seductive.

So there is much to the oedipal complex that still requires re-examination and clarification. My comments, while certainly not final, do, I hope, correct certain distortions and possibly help to put Freud's basic concept more correctly in the larger scheme of things.

Therapeutic approaches to oedipal difficulties must also reflect this larger view. The problems to be resolved do not arise from parental sexual rejection but rather from more generalized emotional privation. Therefore, I consider the improvement in the parent-child relationship crucial to the alleviation of oedipal problems in the child. The boy who has obtained little gratification from his mother may become fixated in the effort to secure it. His entire life may be spent futilely in this pursuit. It is as though he reasoned that there is no point in moving on to seek satisfaction from others. If his own mother does not provide it, how can he expect strangers to offer it? A therapeutic attempt is therefore made to improve his relationship with his mother so that he will obtain some of the gratifications that are his due in childhood. Getting them at this time will make him more confident about his ability to obtain similar satisfactions with others in the future. The same rationale holds for my attempts to improve the girl's relationship with her father. The father plays a significant role in the girl's development of a healthy sense of femininity and the girl who lacks a salutary paternal experience is likely to develop pathological oedipal adjustments. An excellent article by Forrest describes this aspect of female character development.[28]

To accomplish an improvement in the parent-child relationship, the child must come to terms with the fact that there are problems in his involvement with his parents which have to be worked on. I attempt to help the child change those elements in his behavior which might be contributing to the difficulties. I try to help him gain a more accurate picture of his parents, their assets and their liabilities, the areas in which they can provide him with meaningful gratifications, and those in which they cannot. He is helped to resign himself to the fact that he cannot completely possess either of his parents and that the affection and attention of each of them must be shared with other members of the family. He is encouraged to seek satisfactions from them when and where they can be provided and to pursue elsewhere those gratifications which his parents are incapable of giving him. I try to impress upon him the fact that just because there are deficiencies in his parent's love does not mean that he is unlovable and that no one else, either in the present or future, will love him. Deeper involvement with peers is encouraged to help him compensate and he is consoled with the hope that as he grows older he will be increasingly able and free to enjoy meaningful relationships with others. For boys, identifications with assertive men are fostered so that their future chances of obtaining a desirable mate are enhanced. Identification with the therapist, a male teacher, a camp counselor, or a scout master can be helpful in this regard.

Identifications and behavioral attitudes which will increase the likelihood of the girl's attracting a mate in the future are also fostered. Whereas for Freud the resolution of oedipal conflicts comes out of fear of castration, resignation, and natural biological processes, in this approach the child is given something in compensation for his loss and is, therefore, more likely to give up the obsession. The child with oedipal problems has not pursued these alternatives on his own and must be helped to do so. I cannot imagine true resolution without such substitutes.

Attempts are also made to diminish the guilt the child may feel over his sexual and/or hostile thoughts and feelings and to correct misconceptions which contribute to such guilt. He is repeatedly told, for example, that his impulses in these areas are shared by most, if not all, children. He is reassured that hostile thoughts, as such, cannot harm. He is encouraged to use his anger constructively to bring about a reduction in his frustrations and resentments. I try to encourage his entry into situations where he may have the living experience that the expression of anger does not generally result in the dire consequences he anticipates. Little direct attention is given to penis envy, masturbation, castration anxiety, childbearing, and sexuality in general. Even when the child's symptoms are overtly sexual, emphasis on the relatively nonsexual approaches I have described is more therapeutically effective. As I have said, the sexual is most often a symbolic representation of the more basic nonsexual problems which are more directly dealt with in my approach.

In addition, I work closely with the parents and attempt to correct any misguided approaches to the child which might be contributing to the schism in their relationship with him. If the parents are motivated for, or receptive to, intensive psychiatric treatment for themselves, I help them arrange it. In such situations, I have found it preferable to work with the mother myself (she is the one who is usually more intimately involved in the child's difficulties) and to refer the father to another therapist. Individual analytic work with each parent separately presents many technical difficulties; there are nevertheless occasional couples with whom such an approach can work out. Family interviews and family therapy, however, are extremely helpful, and I use them extensively.

The Mutual Storytelling Technique can play a significant role in helping the child alleviate oedipal problems. However important its role, it is still only one part of my therapeutic approach which, as described, is multi-faceted. The children's stories presented below are oedipal (by the broader definition I have proposed), and the stories that I respond with serve to help the child resolve his oedipal problems (in accordance with the concept of oedipal resolution which I have described).

Example 1

Seymour, a ten-and-a-half-year-old boy, had a history of headache, throat-clearing tics, and generalized tension of three year's duration. In addition, he was perfectionistic at school and a "model child." His behavior was invariably exemplary. His manners were impeccable. There was an abnormal degree of hugging and kissing his mother who seductively undressed in front of him. He said of her: "She pleasures me." Her basic

344

views on sex, however, were puritanical and she imposed these values on the patient's teen-age sister. His father was an inordinately ambitious man who was extremely successful in his business. Both parents were markedly inhibited in the expression of hostility.

During the initial evaluation, Seymour told this story:

My story is about a very famous athlete. As a matter of fact, his last name was Athlete. His first name was Bob — Bob Athlete. He was a very famous shot-put thrower. His longest throw was 527 yards. That's a pretty long way. Bob was on the U.S. Olympic team, but he was from England. He was brought up in a very poor family and he had some brothers and sisters. As a matter of fact, he had 32 brothers and 53 sisters. With all his brothers and sisters and himself and his parents, they lived in a very small shack and it was hard to get around. But finally they decided to move to the United States.

When they got here they still had to live in a very small house because they were very poor. There was one thing about Bob. Even though he was an athlete, he had a very big appetite. One day, when his mother was making his fifteen dozen flapjacks, she noticed Bob had left home. Later on when she was cleaning the dishes, she saw that Bob had not eaten all of his breakfast and when she saw the amount of flapjacks left over she was surprised. There were fifteen dozen flapjacks left over. Bob hadn't eaten a single one. When she saw this, she screamed, "Aaahhhh!" She figured that Bob was gone. Either Bob was gone or he was sick to the stomach. When they searched the house, all 53 sisters and all 32 brothers, were checked, they couldn't find Bob.

When Bob had left home, he had gone to the Olympics stadium to try out for the shot-put. When he got there and he threw his shot-put with one arm 57 ft., they said, "You'll be our star shot-putter." That year — it was 1936 — they were going to go to Berlin for the Olympics and Bob was scared. He had never been away; he had never been to Europe by himself without his parents. When he got there he was very nervous. He didn't know how the Germans were going to treat him. To himself he said, "Mommy." When they came out and they announced his name for the shot-put, he didn't hear a thing. With all the other athletes he heard a cheer, but for him not a thing. When he took the shot-put in his hand, he only threw it seven feet! What happened to him? He was sick again — that stupid knucklehead! He was sick at the wrong time again. The coach of the Olympic team was there and Bob's good friend was very worried about him. If he didn't throw well, they would lose the Olympics. Finally, three hours later, it was Bob's turn to throw again. Finally, he seemed to recover a little. This time he didn't throw that far — only about 100 yards — but it still set a world's record, and then fifteen minutes later he was in the finals. He threw and he was all recovered and he threw and what a throw. It took them five days to find the shot-put that he threw. Finally they found it down in a lake some place in Italy. Some man said he had seen a flying saucer land there, not knowing that it was the shot-put Bob had thrown.

So you see, the moral of my story is: if you are going to do something, do it well. Thank you.

Therapist: Okay. I have a question about your story. Why didn't he eat the flapjacks?

Patient: He wasn't there. He had run away before his mother put them down.

Therapist: Why did he run away?

Patient: Because he wanted to be a star athlete.

Therapist: Well, why did he have to run away from home? Why didn't he just tell people?

Patient: Because his parents didn't want him to become an athlete.

Therapist: What did they want him to become?

Patient: They wanted him to follow in his father's footsteps, and his father was a candlestick maker.

Therapist: I see. Right now it's time for me to tell my story.

The story is a rich one and reveals many things about Seymour's relationships with his mother, father, and siblings. Although, in reality, the patient had one sister, in the story he has 32 brothers and 53 sisters. He is lost in the crowd with so many siblings and his mother does not, at first, realize he is gone. I regard this aspect of the story to reflect the child's basic feeling that his mother is rejecting. His one sibling seems like dozens in the competition for the limited affection she can offer. In response he repudiates her by refusing her fifteen dozen flapjacks which symbolize her profuse demonstrations of love. When he leaves her he is frozen with fear — at his age the boy could hardly be expected to react otherwise. He does not hear himself announced for the shot-put nor can he throw it with his usual facility when he finally does compete. He can only think of "Mommy." The competition, of course, is against his father. The latter is a candlestick maker, that is, a creator of inumerable phalluses. Rather than stay at home and compete with his father in what he considers to be a losing battle, he goes off to a foreign land and achieves distinction in an unrelated endeavor which nevertheless demonstrates his masculine prowess. His father's success both in the business world as well as with the patient's mother were overwhelming Seymour. His initial freezing at the Olympic competition might also be related to his fear that if he excelled over his father the latter would react punitively.

The story has many healthy elements. He leaves the rejecting mother rather than obsessively seek or pine away for her affection. He pushes himself through the anxiety associated with such separation. He does not compete with the father on the latter's own battleground but chooses a distant arena and a different skill.

With this understanding of Seymour's story, I told the following:

Well, once upon a time there was this athlete and he was a great athlete. His name was Bob Athlete and he was a terrific shot-put thrower. Now he was brought up in a poor family in England and they had 32 brothers and 53 sisters there. They were very poor and they moved to the U.S. where they also lived in a small house.

He had a very big appetite. One day his mother made him fifteen dozen pancakes, but he left the house in order to go to the Olympics. The parents wanted him to become a candlestick maker, but he didn't want to do that. He wanted to shot-put. But as soon as he left home he was very lonely and he really missed his mother's pancakes. He missed being at home with the family — his brothers and sisters — but he spoke to himself and he said, "Well, you can't live at home forever. You have to make the break sometime. I really miss the family but maybe if I find a girlfriend that will make me feel better."

Well, on the ship that crossed the Atlantic to Berlin —— you see, they were going to Germany for the 1936 Olympics —— he met a young lady there who was also going for the Olympics and she was very beautiful and she was about a year younger than he and they fell in love and when that happened he didn't miss his family so much anymore. In fact, at times he almost forgot about them completely.

Well, he went to the Olympics and on the very first shot he did very well. In fact, he broke the world's record. The reason he was able to do it was that he wanted to impress this girl so she would love him more and he thought that had she not been there he might have fouled up because of his sadness and despondency about being away from home.

The moral of my story is —— do you know the moral of my story?

Patient: No.

Therapist: The moral of my story is that if you miss your family when you grow up, you will find that it will be easier for you if you meet someone who can help you forget the loss, and who can be friendly and loving to you. The end.

Do you have any comments on my story?

Patient: No.

Therapist: Did you like it?

Patient: Yes.

Therapist: What was your favorite part?

Patient: When he threw the world's record shot-put.

Therapist: Very good. Okay.

In my story I supported the patient's fantasies of ultimate separation from his mother and avoidance of direct competition with his father. I made the separation easier for him, however, by providing him with someone (the girlfriend) who can give him the gratifications his mother cannot supply. In addition, I introduced the notion that if a man works hard in his life's endeavors he is more likely to attract, win, and keep a woman. With these communications I attempted to help him further resolve his already partially resolved oedipus complex.

Example 2

Frank, a twelve-and-a-half-year-old boy, was referred for therapy because of tics, headaches, massive tension, fear of being alone, excessive guilt over minor transgressions, and ultrasensitivity to criticism. The family was rigidly Catholic and the patient considered his symptoms to be punishments for his sins. When his tics would get partially bad he would reiterate: "I am sorry, Oh Lord, for disobeying my parents."

The mother was an extremely cold and angry woman who used her children's mildest religious indiscretions as an excuse to visit her own rage upon them. Violent outbursts were common. Her main goal for the patient was for him to become a priest, and her pressure in this regard was formidable.

The father was dogmatically moralistic, obsessed with the various principles by which one should live. The ideals which he inculcated in Frank left no room for even occasional profanity, indiscretion, disrespect, or weakness.

In his initial evaluation he told this story:

This story is about a man who killed his wife for her money 'cause she inherited a lot of money and he killed his wife. This man was greedy and he got so greedy with his money that he thought that he was the best guy going. He knew that he had a lot of money so he went and bet on a lot of different things. One night he bet and he lost all his money because he was conceited and he was selfish and he lost all his money and now he's on a street corner begging for money.

The moral of the story is: don't be greedy; don't brag about yourself because only something bad is going to happen.

Therapist: Okay. Thank you very much. Now it's time for me to tell my story.

The story is a pathetic one and reveals the extreme degree of Frank's deprivation. The wife, of course, represents the patient's mother and the man, I believe, stands for the patient himself. The mother's money symbolizes her love, which she will not voluntarily give to others. So tenacious is her refusal to provide her son with affection that he is brought to the point of killing her, thereby rendering her helpless to continue withholding her love ("he killed his wife for her money"). The murder also serves as an outlet for the rage the boy feels toward his mother, but he has his father perform the act for he is too guilt-ridden to risk fantasizing a younger person as a murderer.

But he does not deserve the love and all of it is squandered. He ends up on the street begging for more. It is of interest that the man does not lose the money as punishment for murder, but rather because he "was conceited and selfish." As the moral tells us, the man's main sin is greed. Frank's pleas for affection must have evoked tremendous fear in his mother. By communicating to him that he was worthless in craving it, she could protect herself from the anxieties which his appeals for love engendered in her.

The story clearly exhibits Frank's unresolved oedipus complex. He has certainly not given up the futile quest for love from his mother. His frustration and rage is so great that he wishes to kill her, but even then he realizes that he will be unsatisfied because he basically feels unworthy of receiving love. If he had it, he wouldn't know what to do with it. It would make him anxious just as it makes his mother anxious, and he would have to get rid of it.

Accordingly, I told this story:

Once upon a time there was a guy. He was a young fellow and his mother was a very selfish person. She had a lot of money, but she wouldn't part with a penny. She was one of these people who always counted every cent and wouldn't give this poor kid — not only wouldn't give him a nickel, wouldn't give him a penny. This poor guy felt starved for money and he felt very bad. He wanted to buy things. Other kids got allowances, other kids had a little extra bit of spending money to buy themselves things, and he was really sad. At times he would get so sad and mad he would feel like killing her, but he realized that this would accomplish nothing.

So what he did was that he decided to get a job. The first thing he did was to get a newspaper route and he was able to earn some money with that. As he got older he was able to get bigger jobs. He went to school and he got trained in something so that he could earn a nice living. And then when he earned it on his own he met a wonderful girl whom he married. She had some earnings and he earned and they pooled their money together. They had a very good relationship and he spent his life pleasurably.

The moral of that story is: if somebody is not giving you something that you want from them, don't kill them for it. Don't knock yourself out. Don't try to bug them when they can't give it. Try to find it elsewhere. Another way of saying the moral of that story is the old saying of W. C. Fields, "If at first you don't succeed, try, try again. After that if you still don't succeed forget about it. Don't make a damn fool of yourself." The end.

In my story I attempted to get Frank to recognize the fact that his mother was essentially incapable of providing him with the affection he craved. I encouraged him to seek love from someone who can provide it ("she had some earnings"), but I made it clear that he too must work and contribute. Whereas I usually try to get the patient to approach the depriving parent in those areas where the latter is capable of giving affection and to go elsewhere when love is not forthcoming, in this case there was little point in trying to help the patient make such discriminations. The mother had so little to give and so much hostility to vent that to encourage him to approach her would have been almost sadistic on my part and would have fostered further masochistic adaptations on his part. The W. C. Fields quotation is a bit of wisdom that I impart to many of my patients, regardless of their age. It is valuable advice for just about everyone.

Example 3

Daniel, a twelve-year-old boy, was referred for treatment with a four months history of marked agitation, anxiety, and hostile outbursts toward his parents, especially his father. There was a long history of poor school performance despite high intelligence, and of difficulty in keeping friends because of his "bossiness" and bullying. The father, a successful businessman, was unusually rigid, while the mother was very passive. She did not side with the boy in his conflicts with his father, even when she knew her son to be in the right. She had a compulsion to laugh in serious situations. The boy was the youngest of three children; he had two teen-age sisters, both of whom behaved seductively with him.

He also demonstrated an oedipal panic precipitated by the heightened sexual urges of puberty and intensified by the seductiveness of his sisters and his father's punitive attitude, from which he was not protected by the mother.

In the third month of therapy, Daniel related the following story:

The title of this story is "The Mysterious Cabin." Some boys from Camp Monterey were on a hike. One of the boys said he knew a short cut. He said it, but he really didn't. They started to walk through the woods. They came to a clearing, and there was a big mansion there. It was gigantic! They thought maybe there was money in it. They thought they'd get rich and use the money to buy guns for the kids at camp. Suddenly they heard a terrible noise —— oooooh —— it was like a ghost. One boy went upstairs. He didn't come down. Three hours later two more boys went up. Three hours later they still heard nothing. Then the remaining seven went upstairs. The three boys who went before were dead. The rest jumped out of the window and ran back to camp. There really were riches in the house and robbers were hiding loot there. They wired the place with records to sound like ghosts to scare people away. They killed the three boys.

The moral of this story is: don't trespass!

This story reveals the patient's unresolved oedipal conflict. The house of riches represents the mother, the robbers the father, and the boys who were killed, the patient himself. Had the plans been successful, he would have acquired riches (his mother, a treasured possession) and guns (to enhance his masculine potency). The project was a "short cut" — stealing father's woman rather than going to the trouble of getting his own.

In response I told this story:

The title of this story is "Cabins in the Woods." Some boys from Camp Monterey were on a hike. They came to a clearing and found a big mansion. It was huge. One of the boys said: "Hey, there must be a lot of money and jewels and treasures in that mansion. Let's go in there and rob some of that stuff and then we can take it back to camp and buy guns and things for all the guys." Some of the other fellows on the hike thought that was a good idea but a few of the boys were hesitant. One said: "It's not right what you want to do. I know the old man who owns that house; he's real rich now but he was very poor when he was a boy and he worked very hard to earn the money to buy that beautiful house." Then the counselor, who overheard the conversation, said, "He's right. Not only is it not fair to the old man to take what's his, but the real fun is working hard yourself and doing it on your own. That's why I'm going to college. I hope that in a few years I'll be able to earn enough to get myself a house like that also."

So the boys returned to camp, saddened that they couldn't take all that money so quickly, but gladdened by the hope that someday they too could have a house just as, if not more, beautiful. And that's just what happened to some of them.

My story has two morals: the first is that there are many cabins in the woods and you can get one if you're willing to wait and work for it. The second is that it's more fun getting something yourself than stealing it and besides, when you get it yourself, you don't hurt someone else's feelings.

During this narrative, Daniel listened with an expression of awe and transfixed interest. The story introduced themes and courses of action that served to help him resolve certain elements of his oedipal conflict. It suggested that he resign himself to the fact that he cannot have his mother but that someday, if he is patient and diligent, he can have someone just as beautiful. Just as there are many fish in the sea, there are many "cabins in the woods." Furthermore, he is encouraged to identify with someone who is pursuing this course, the counselor. And lastly, the point is emphasized that what belongs to the father was obtained by him through hard work. He will not easily relinquish it.

During the subsequent weeks, Daniel offered similar stories about stealing pirate treasures and getting caught by the police. In addition, there were many stories about building rockets — "radio-controlled rockets that go up hundreds of miles with combustion chambers and controls to operate it manually" and others "with three generators and circuit breakers."

Five weeks after the story of the "mysterious cabin," Daniel related the following story:

This story is called "The Old House." A group of explorer scouts were on a hike. They passed a big old house. The doors were beaten down and no one was around. Nobody owned it. They thought they might be able to salvage things. They explored it. They decided to rebuild the house and sell it. They got hammers and paints and put electricity into it. They built it into a beautiful split-level home. They were able to claim land by buying it from the government. They built a driveway and put up a "For Sale" sign. But people were afraid to buy it because of the many ghost stories they told about the house. A man heard a meow sound and ran away thinking it was a ghost when it was only a cat. They had great trouble selling the house. Someone else spent three weeks in it, found it safe, and bought it for $50,000.00.

In this story, the father abandons the house (which symbolizes the mother) to the patient, who then reconstructs and disguises it so as not to look like the old one. However, the father's continuing presence and objection are still manifested in the form of a ghost, who is finally removed through his transformation into a cat. Psychologically, the exposure of an object's true nature implies a transformation — the ghost is no longer what people thought it to be. Evidently the patient is beginning to build his own house and to get a woman of his own. He nevertheless constructs it along the lines of the old model because he still basically wants what is father's.

In line with this interpretation, I related the following story:

This story is called "The New House." A group of explorer scouts went on a hike and came to an old house. The doors were beaten down, the windows broken, and no one was around. They thought, therefore, that nobody owned it and decided to rebuild it. So they got hammers and paints, etc. and started to work, and then they put in electricity.

After a while a man from the bank, who happened to be passing by, heard the noise and came to see what was going on. He told the boys the old house was now owned by the bank because the man who had it could not pay off his mortgage. He also told them that even if they earned enough money to buy it, they were foolish trying to make this very old house look like new and no matter how good a job they did, it would still have the foundation and structure of an old house. He also told them that the bank had just acquired some very desirable property on the other side of the forest, which was an ideal site to build a house. The boys visited the spot, built a beautiful house there, and were glad they had taken the banker's advice.

In my story Daniel's scheme of taking his father's house and reconstructing it is foiled. The complete impossibility of acquiring possession of the mother had to be reiterated. The patient has to accept this basic fact if he is to successfully resolve his oedipus complex. Daniel is not, however, left frustrated and in despair. He is provided with attractive compensations if he is willing to expend the effort. In this case, the ideal site on the other side of the forest beyond his father's territory is available to him, but he must work for it. Nothing is free.

Two sessions later, Daniel told this story:

> Once there were two boys, Bill and Bob, who were brought up in the poorer section of town. They were brothers and both wanted bikes but their parents were too poor. They went to the bike store and found out that in two months there would be a bike sale. So they shoveled snow in order to earn money. One time Bill did most of the work and the next time Bob did. There was good cooperation. Soon they had $100.00 but the bikes were very expensive, $75.00 a bike, so they needed $50.00 more. But the weatherman said there would be no more snow and time was running out. So they got jobs cutting grass and then had $149.99. Then they found a penny and got the two bikes.
>
> The moral of this story is: if you work hard enough, you will get what you want.

The story shows that my messages were sinking in. Daniel is accommodating himself to the fact that he must work to achieve goals in life, whether the aim is to acquire a woman or other possessions. However, there is still present a remnant of the need to get something for nothing: the boys earn $149.99 of the $150.00 needed for the bikes. The remaining penny is found.

In response I told a similar story about two boys who worked to buy themselves bikes. The story emphasized the pleasures of the endeavor and the gratifications of accomplishment. Cruel taskmaster that I am, in my story all the money was completely earned by them. They had hoped to find some money to supplement their earnings but they were unsuccessful.

Four sessions later, Daniel related this story:

The title of this story is "Bill and Bob and the Summer Resort." Bill and Bob were brothers. Bill was twenty-five and Bob was twelve. Each summer they had nothing to do. The family owned a resort at a big lake a hundred miles away, but they didn't like going there. So they decided to build a summer camp of their own twenty-five miles away. So they cleared the woods and built a camp. Many parents decided it was a good summer camp and they had a good season the very first year. They had a ham radio station there. They charged $600 a child. They made a lot of money and had a good time.

The moral of this story is: doing something yourself can be fun and profitable.

In this story Daniel strikes out on his own. He builds a summer camp twenty-five miles away from his parents. He clears the woods and builds the camp; nothing is freely given to him. There is gratification in the accomplishment: "doing something for yourself can be fun and profitable."

The story reflected a healthy oedipal resolution and there was nothing I could improve upon. Accordingly, as I often do in final phase and termination stories, I told one with a similar theme and moral without introducing anything new. The clinical picture, as well, reflected the boy's improvement. His anxiety was markedly reduced and the hostile outbursts far less frequent.

Example 4

Peter, the boy whose oedipal fantasies were dramatically represented by his oral incorporation of his mother's heart in his story of the Eskimo children and their dog, told this story in a later phase of therapy:

Well, there was this man named John Cutler and he was in a very old house that was very close to a Boy Scout camp. One day the Boy Scouts were coming around with firecrackers and John Cutler was out chopping wood and he came down and his house was burned down from some firecrackers. He blamed it on the Boy Scouts. So he went to get his axe and he started to kill all the Boy Scouts that were in that troop. And he went around from country to country, from state to state, from continent to continent and then all the Boy Scouts of the world were killed. He did the same thing with the Cub Scouts and by this time all the Scout Masters had heard of it. They gave John Cutler a note and he went into this cave and he found a note that said all of his friends were killed by his act. Then the police were coming and he was right by the river so he jumped into the river and swam away into the ocean and drowned. And whenever you go by that river you always hear, "I am the ghost of John Cutler. I have come to cutler you up."

Therapist: What is the moral of that story?

Patient: Well, I think the moral would be: those who are bloodthirsty will always taste salt.

Therapist: I have a question to ask you, Peter. Why did the Boy Scouts want to pick on Cutler in the first place? Why did they go to his cabin and pick on him?

Patient: Well, I guess it was because John Cutler was always scaring the Boy Scouts because he was an expert knivesman and when one of the Boy Scouts was hiding in a tree he'd throw a knife and it would land right between his fingers.

Therapist: I see. Okay. Thank you very much for an excellent story in your usual tradition.

The story is one of violent rivalry between father and son, symbolized respectively by John Cutler and the Scouts. Because the father threw knives at the patient (barely missing his fingers), the latter burns down his father's house. In retaliation, the father kills the patient — "all the Boy Scouts of the world were killed" — and then the police pursue the father to his death by drowning. Castration symbolism abounds. The father's name is

Cutler, one who can "cutler you up." He throws knives between the boy's fingers — a most thinly disguised castration threat. This occurs when the boy is in a tree, when, that is, he has acquired a large penis for himself. However, as previously described, I believe the castration fear to be most often symbolic of a more generalized threat to one's masculinity. The father is seen as a most fearsome and powerful figure. He is not only capable of killing all the Boy Scouts in the world, but even in his death he can threaten the patient through his ghost. He cannot really be escaped.

Although Peter's mother is not mentioned in the story even by implication, I believe that the rivalry is for her love. As previously described, her capacity for love was somewhat deficient which increased Peter's deprivation. The father was himself getting little genuine affection from her. He was an extremely passive and reserved man, and repressed much of the hostility he must have felt toward his wife for *his* deprivation. He was certainly not overtly punitive to Peter, and I felt that Peter's awesome and fearful view of the father was related in part to his own hostility projected onto the father. Peter's anger stemmed not only from the frustration he felt over not receiving the love he craved from his mother, but also related to his father's failure to protect him from the mother's hostility. Because the father was in fact less threatening, he was a safer figure upon whom to vent his hostility, and in this story much anger, which is displaced from the mother, is directed toward him.

With this understanding of Peter's story, I related the following:

Once there was a man whose name was John Cutler and he lived in a very old house with his wife who was a very fine woman. Now they lived close to a Boy Scout camp and the boys at the Boy Scout camp used to come around to John Cutler's house and want to spend a lot of time with his wife because she was such a nice person to speak to. She was very warm and friendly and she use to give the boys cookies and cake which was very refreshing after long hikes. Well, Cutler at first didn't mind this too much, but after a while these boys were getting on his nerves and once in a while he'd come in and chase them out and then they'd come back.

One day he went over to these kids and he said, "You know, you boys are getting me angry. You really spend a lot of time around here." The boys said, "Yeah, but she's a nice woman, your wife." So Cutler said, "Well, why don't you go out and get someone your own age, someone more appropriate. There's a Girl Scout camp. It's not too far from here. It's right down the road. Why don't you go over to those girls." Well, the boys at first said, "We're kind of young." He replied, "Maybe so, but I'm sure in a few years you'll be old enough to want to go out with them. Besides, my wife is my age and you kids will have more fun with the Girl Scouts and more fun playing games with your friends and things like that."

So the boys felt kind of bad that Cutler was kicking them out, but then they did go out and they tried to play ball more. They enjoyed that. Then they went over to the Girl Scout camp and met some of the Girl Scouts and enjoyed their company very much. Then when they got older they found themselves really interested in these girls — dating and taking them out and having a very good time and having a lot of fun. They were really glad that they had listened to John Cutler's advice and they lost interest in his wife almost completely. They'd visit her once in a while for old times' sake, but they had good times with the girls they had met at the Girl Scout camp.

The moral of that story is: if you are lonely, the best thing to do is to get friendships with people your own age, both boys and girls. They are the ones you can have the most fun with.

In my story I bring the mother directly in. She was conspicuous by her complete absence in the patient's story. The theme of sharing the mother's love is again presented and the compromise alternative of seeking it from others is elaborated upon. My hope was that if Peter could accomplish the goals suggested in my story, he would be far less angry, thereby obviating the need for releasing his hostility by means of the various mechanisms utilized in his story.

Three weeks later, Peter told the following story. He needed some assistance getting started and was helped in accordance with the already-described technique I use in such situations:

Therapist: A long, long time ago, long before your grandfather's great-grandmother's great-aunt was born, in a distant land, beyond the desert, beyond the ocean, beyond the mountain, there lived a —

Patient: Wolf.

Therapist: And this wolf —

Patient: Was very old.

Therapist: The wolf was very old. Yes?

Patient: And his brother was very young for some reason.

Therapist: His brother was very young —

Patient: For some reason which nobody knew, and the old wolf was sort of the weakest of the pack.

Therapist: The old was the weakest —

Patient: And the young wolf, his brother, was very strong. There was a middle-aged wolf in the pack who was the chief and he was getting very, very ill and the old wolf and the young wolf who were brothers were very well known. So they had to compete for who would be chief. So they both went to a test ground which included running, jumping, diving, swimming, and jumping over fire and fighting. Now the first one, which was running, the young wolf won. The second, which was jumping over fire, the old wolf rr —

Therapist: Won, you mean?

Patient: Won. Diving the old wolf won. Swimming the young wolf won and there was one left which was fighting — fighting I guess — 'cause I guess there were two fighting matches. One of the wolves won one and one won the other and it came out that the scores were even. So the wolves had to decide in their own way. So they took a box and they put five black stones and five white stones in it and they put four on each side. So there was four white stones and four black stones and the old wolf put one white stone in the white stone pile and the young wolf put one black stone in the black stone pile and the tie was scored. So the young wolf saw that he could not beat the old wolf because the old wolf was wiser. So the old wolf put a white one out and the young wolf put a white one out. So the winner of the contest and the new chief was the old wolf. The middle-aged wolf died at that time and the old wolf became chief.

And the moral of that story is: if you are young and brave, you cannot beat the old and wise.

Therapist: Okay. Thank you very much. Now it's time for me to tell my story.

In the tradition of the primal horde as described by Freud in *Totem and Taboo*,[24] the sons vie for the father's position. Applying this scheme to Peter's story, the young wolf is the patient's younger brother; the old wolf is the patient himself, who, while older than his brother, is yet in better condition than the sick middle-aged wolf who symbolizes the father. Peter was an extremely bright young man who excelled in the classroom but who did poorly in sports. In the competition with his sibling he uses his brains to finally win out, although the white and black stone scorekeeping system is somewhat confusing. However, rather than kill the chief as in the previously-reported story, here he conveniently dies. Accordingly, I told this story:

Once upon a time a long time ago there was a wolf and he was old and he had a brother who was young. They lived in this tribe or this pack where the chief was a middle-aged chief and both of those wolves had their eyes on the chiefship. They both wanted to be chief and the two brothers would often fight to try to be chief. They would have competitions. They would set up events to compete, such as swimming, running, and fighting and even games of wit — puzzles. The older one thought that he would be more successful because he was smarter. The younger one thought that he would be more successful because he was better at sports and games and things like that.

At any rate one day the middle-aged chief said, "Gentlemen. You are wasting your time. Whether you are the winner or the loser of these particular events that you are fighting for, no one is getting my chiefship so quickly. You're going to have to wait until I die and that may be many many years. My suggestion to you fellows is if you want to be chief that you go out and find yourself wives and make new settlements yourself. Have your own children. Have your own tribe because I'm not giving up my chiefship and my doctors have examined me and told me that I am extremely healthy and that I will probably be living a long time. You may be very old men before I die. Also even if I do die your mother will be ruler as queen and you can't marry her because you're her sons and she's much older than you."

Well, they thought that was good advice and they went out and what do you think happened to them?

Patient: I don't know.

Therapist: Were they successful do you think in setting up new tribes elsewhere?

Patient: Yes.

Therapist: Hhmm. Do you think that they were very happy about it?

Patient: Well, there would be some odd parts, but I guess so, yes.

Therapist: What would be the odd parts?

Patient: Well, I don't know. There just might be. I was only guessing.

Therapist: Well, I would say in my story they each found themselves very beautiful and attractive and very nice wives and had a very good time and were very happy in their marriages. They brought up some very nice children and were happy that they had left the old tribe and gone off on their own. The end.

In my story the father does not relinquish his position so quickly. He not only informs the boys that whatever the outcome of their competition he will be around for a long time, but advises them also that even were he to die they cannot take over his position with their mother. In the primal horde, the son can take over the father's position, but he is still not permitted to marry the mother. The patient is again encouraged to accept this painful fact and to seek females elsewhere.

Following the storytelling sequence, Peter and I analyzed the stories more directly and discussed their significance to the reality of his life. He expressed awareness of his mother's impairment in providing him with deep affection and stated: "She's colder than the mothers of other kids." However painful this realization was, it did represent a step forward in the resolution of his oedipus complex.

Three months later, Peter told this story:

Once upon a time there was a cow. He liked to go on one part of the field because there was good grass there. The other cows found that there was good grass there too so they tried to move in. The original cow didn't want them to move in.

Then the sun came out. It was very hot. The whole herd started moving in to the part of the field where the original cow was. The original cow saw them coming. Then the sun dried up all the water and the good grass in that part of the field. The first cow hid in a shady spot. When the big herd of cows got there they found that there was poor grass there. The sun had dried it all up. Then they said, "Let's go back to our own grazing ground." Then the first cow came out of the shady spot and he went to another field with good grass and shady trees and had it all to himself.

The moral of the story is: you may want something badly, but each time you may be too late to get it.

The cow here symbolizes the patient. This is a good example of how no symbol universally represents the same thing. Although the cow lends itself admirably to symbolizing a female (especially a mothering one), in this story it clearly stands for the patient. The field of nurturing grass is the mother and the competing herd of cattle, the father (and possibly the brother).

In this story Peter presents an unusual and yet most interesting adaptation to his oedipal problems. He essentially decides: if I can't have my mother all to myself, then no one shall. He allows the treasured plot to be scorched to the ground by the sun rather than to give it up to, or share it with, the others.

The story is an excellent example of one of the many other possible modes of adaptation to the mother's rejection and/or the father's possessiveness. Killing the father and compulsively trying to win the mother's affection (as described in the classical oedipal paradigm) is only one of the many courses of action which the patient may consider. In addition, destroying the verdurous plot allows an expression of the hostility he harbors toward his mother for her rejection. Again it can be seen that the classical formulation is too neat and simple: there is much hostility toward the mother in the oedipus complex.

In response, I told this story:

Once upon a time there was a cow. This cow went to a patch of grass which was very shady, had a nice brook, and had very good grass. He thought it would be a wonderful place to have all to himself. As he was about to enter that part of the farm, a herd of cows came over and said that he could not stay there. They told him that they had worked for many years cultivating this piece of land and that it was theirs. They told him to go elsewhere and get his own piece of land and cultivate it just as they had cultivated theirs. The first cow was very angry and he had a wish that he could burn down the whole place or that possibly the sun might scorch the earth. He thought, "If I can't have it, no one should be able to have it." But then he realized that the herd of cows was right, that they had worked very hard to cultivate their land and that there was no reason why he should have it instead of them. Besides, if he destroyed it then no one would have anything.

So he went off and found another spot which looked like it would be a good place to cultivate. He grew some trees there which grew up to be nice and shady and he grew a lot of thick, green, good grass. There was a nice brook on the spot and he enjoyed the new place very much.

The moral of this story is that there is enough grass for all the cows and you don't have to take what's someone else's. However, if you want a good piece of land for yourself you'll have to work for it. The end.

In my story the father does not permit the patient's total possession of the mother. The boy considers the reaction of destroying her and rejects it as unreasonable. He recognizes that this would be unfair to deprive his father of what he had so diligently worked for; that he himself had no right to total possession of her; and that if he did destroy her he would accomplish nothing for himself. He would still be without her nurture. He is then provided with the more plausible alternative of resigning himself to the painful realization that he cannot have what is his father's, but is encouraged to seek compensatory gratifications elsewhere.

Example 5

Gavin, the boy with the weak and inadequate parents who related the story of the boy in the tree whose branches were too weak to support him, told this story:

Patient: I thought you were going to help me out.
Therapist: Okay. Gavin is having a little trouble, so I'll help him out.
　　Once upon a time, a long long time ago, in a distant land, far, far away there lived a ——
Patient: Boy.
Therapist: And this boy ——
Patient: Lived on an island.
Therapist: Lived on an island ——
Patient: By himself.
Therapist: And one day this boy who lived on this island ——
Patient: He didn't have any money.
Therapist: Now without money he ——

Patient: Couldn't have any food.

Therapist: And so without food he ——

Patient: Was hungry.

Therapist: And so he decided to ——

Patient: Work.

Therapist: And so he ——

Patient: Worked.

Therapist: What kind of job did he have?

Patient: Office.

Therapist: An office job? What kind of an office job?

Patient: You know, the kind my father goes to.

Therapist: He worked in an office. I thought you said he lived on an island by himself.

Patient: I know.

Therapist: Were other people on the island or not?

Patient: I said there only were a few.

Therapist: Oh, and they were in an office. They worked in an office like your father's.

Patient: Yes.

Therapist: And as a result —— and as a result of this he ——

Patient: Got one hundred dollars.

Therapist: He got one hundred dollars and after that ——

Patient: Each day he got one hundred dollars.

Therapist: Each day he got one hundred dollars and so he could then ——

Patient: Buy food.

Therapist: And after that ——

Patient: He wasn't hungry anymore. (*Laughs.*)

Therapist: Is that the end of the story?

Patient: Yeah.

Therapist: And the moral of that story?

Patient: Whenever you're broke, work — just work for money.

Therapist: Okay. Very good.

The transcript of this story cannot fully communicate Gavin's ennui. Boredom and disinterest were his characteristic attitudes toward most things in life, and his minimal involvement in the storytelling was just another example of this. Both of his parents were inadequate in their ability to cope with reality in a mature and independent fashion. They were too egocentric to be able to provide this boy with meaningful affection. One could describe the child as having "lost interest in life." Although his withdrawal had schizoid qualities, it could not be considered schizophrenic. His future was essentially planned for him : he would enter the same business his father had inherited from his family. There was little to work toward and little to be anxious about. As Thoreau put it so well, this boy was living a life of "quiet desperation."

In the story he reveals his sense of isolation —— he lives by himself on an island. He has no food and no money, he is unloved, that is, and lacks the wherewithal to obtain affection. So deprived, he somehow floats into a situation which seems to provide him with these necessities. He gets a job in an office — "the kind my father goes to." Although originally described as living "by himself" on the island, the office job is suddenly provided for him (just as it was for his father). With no particular training or effort, a windfall of one hundred dollars a day is dropped in his lap. He is then able to acquire the love, which he was previously lacking. The boy's basic feeling tone when telling the story did not leave me with the impression that he considered the food so obtained to be a particularly worthwhile commodity. In addition, his moral advising work was perfunctorily stated without any commitment on his part to such an endeavor.

Speaking of an unresolved oedipus complex implies that there is something to be resolved, some frustrations in human relationships to be alleviated, someone's love to be attained. There is anxiety, frustration, dissatisfaction, and struggle. And there is some motivation to improve the situation. Gavin lacked such incentive. He had given up the fight and resigned himself to a somewhat constricted life with little expectation that human relationships would be in any way rewarding. He would ultimately go into his father's business and thereby satisfy his basic material needs. One could say that, in a sense, this boy had already resolved his oedipus complex. Having given up, there was nothing unresolved to come to terms with.

What can the therapist do with such a child? He must try to provide the patient with living involvements with human beings other than the parents who are attractive enough to engender in him the incentive to reach out and work toward further relationships of this kind. The therapist, hopefully, will be one of the persons who will elicit such reaching out. He must also recommend other experiences and exposures such as camps, recreational groups, clubs, and sports which will enhance the likelihood of similar salutary involvements. In addition, he should *judiciously* create certain anxieties and tension. The completely complacent individual is not well motivated to improve or change his situation. Such anxieties must be most prudently engendered, because too much tension may result in even further withdrawal. The complete answer to the question of what to do with such patients involves the whole field of schizoid character disorders. In my story I focused upon two therapeutic communications which can be helpful in the treatment of the schizoid child:

Once upon a time, a long time ago, there was a boy who lived on an island. He was very lonely there because there was no one else there. He used to wish that other boys and girls would come to the island so that he could have fun with them. Finally, one day some boys and girls did move to the island, but since he had so little experience with other children he didn't know what to do with them. He didn't know how to play the games they played, or how to tell jokes and do many of the other things that boys and girls do. This made him even more sad and lonely. He used to watch them play; they were laughing and singing and having a wonderful time. And he'd just sit around doing nothing, wishing he could join in the fun.

Finally he decided he could take the lonely life no longer. He decided he was going to play with those children and join in the fun. He was scared at first, because he hadn't done it before. Also he had to pay attention to the games they played so that he could learn them. He made mistakes at first and sometimes did silly things. But gradually he got less scared and then had more and more fun. He was then glad that he had not let his fear stop him from joining them.

Now this boy's father owned a big office on the island. He knew that when he grew up that he would own his father's office. So he thought: "I don't have to work hard in school. I'll always have enough money for anything I want. My father is rich and I'll be rich someday too." So the years went by and he never studied. When he grew up he did take over his father's business. However, since he had never learned how to read and write too well, and since he had never gotten used to working very hard, the business got worse and worse. He didn't know how to run it, no one bought any of his stuff and it finally went bankrupt, that is, it went broke and he had no money.

After that he was very poor. He had no money. There was a lady on the island he wanted to marry. She loved him and he loved her. But she told him that she wouldn't marry him because he didn't have any money to take care of her and the children she hoped someday to have. This made the man very sad. He then realized what a big mistake he had made by not learning how to earn a living when he was younger. So he went back to school and learned how to do something with which he could get a job and earn money. It took a lot of hard work, but he finally earned enough money to marry the lady. And they lived happily ever after.

The morals of my story are: playing with other children can be a lot of fun, but if you've never done it before it can be scary when you first start to do it. After you get over your fright, and learn just how to do it, it's loads of fun. The next moral is: you have to work hard if you are to be a success in life. Even if your father gives you a business, you have to work hard to keep it going, you have to know how to run it or else it will fail.

In my story I tried to stimulate in Gavin an active interest in involving himself in meaningful relationships because of the pleasures they can afford him. In addition, I attempted to create some anxiety about his future and thereby engender some motivation to apply himself more diligently. I linked up these two issues by informing him that such efforts are necessary if he is to be attractive to others — the lady does not marry him until he can support her.

Unfortunately, Gavin's interest in my story was minimal. Other efforts to engage this boy proved equally futile. I ultimately discontinued treatment because I did not feel that I was accomplishing anything. A short trial of treatment for the mother was also unsuccessful. She was of low average intelligence, had little psychological aptitude, and showed no interest in introspective inquiry. Referral of the boy to another therapist was suggested, but the family refused to consider it.

Example 6

Many of the stories of Steve, the boy with school disciplinary problems, contained oedipal themes. For example, the story about the monster whose fire went the wrong way and burned him internally is a most dramatic way of handling the punitive retaliation he anticipates from his father. It is another example of the numerous variations on the oedipal theme which were not alluded to by Freud.

Early in his treatment Steve told this story:

> The name of this story is "The Witch and the Little Girl."
> Once upon a time there was a lady and a man and they had a daughter. She went out to be a servant. The parents sent her out to be a servant. No one wanted her. There was an old witch who hired girls as servants. The witch took her into her house. The witch said, "Don't look up the chimney." The girl looked up the chimney and a bag of gold fell in her lap. Each time she looked up the chimney another bag of gold fell into her lap.
> Then she ran away from the witch. She was scared that the witch would catch her and bury her. Then she came to an apple tree. She shook it and got many apples.

Then she went to a cow and the cow gave her milk.

The witch came looking for the girl and met the cow. The cow said to the witch, "No, mama. I don't know where the little girl is." The witch then hid in an oven while waiting for the little girl. The little girl then baked the witch in the oven and that was the end of her. She then grew up and married a rich gentleman.

The story, in essence, is Steve's attempt to adjust to the fact that his parents are both "good" and "bad." He tries to take what is good and rejects and flees from that which is bad. The man and the lady send the daughter (the patient) out to be a servant — a clear rejection and assignment to inferior status. Depicting himself as a female was not, for Steve, related to feminine tendencies, but was rather another way of symbolizing his relegation to inferior role. The witch (the bad parts of his mother) also has her assets — gold comes out of her chimney (vagina?) which she warns the child not to look into. I interpreted this interesting symbolism to refer to the fact that the child sees his mother as fearful of revealing the warmth which lies deep within her. The mother was a somewhat formal and intellectualized person who was inhibited in expressing her feelings. In the story, the witch reacts punitively to his elicitation of her affection — against her warning, he acquired the gold from her chimney and he fears that she will bury him in retaliation.

Steve enjoys the nurture of a tree and a cow that freely provide him with food. These represent, in my opinion, the good and giving facets of the parents' personalities as well as the benevolent treatment he hopes to receive from others in compensation for the malevolence he sees in his parents. Parental malevolence has at least three elements for all children: the realistic restrictions which healthy parents impose on their children, the neurotic rejections which the parents in reality are exposing the child to, and the fantasied deprivations which are not present in reality but which the child believes exist. The latter are, in part, projections of the child's own hostilities. The killing of the witch serves to destroy all the bad elements he sees in his mother, leaving him only with the good. Murdering her also allows expression of the anger he feels toward her.

With all the confusion regarding the parents' assets and liabilities, benevolence and malevolence, the story does reveal a healthy trend regarding the issue of the resolution of the oedipus complex. Steve does not obsessively try to obtain love when it is not forthcoming, but turns to others who will provide it: the cow, the tree, and ultimately, the "rich gentleman."

With this understanding of Steve's story, I told mine:

Once upon a time there was a man and a lady and they had a little girl. This lady, like all mothers, had both good and bad parts. When she was bad the little girl would think that her mother was a witch. When she was good the little girl liked her mother very much. Sometimes the mother would get very angry at the little girl and then she would want to send her out of the house for a short period of time — not forever, however. Other times the mother was very good and loving and the little girl then loved her very much. When the mother was angry the little girl would sometimes think how nice it would be to go out into the world and get good things like gold and apples from trees and milk from cows because her mother was not giving her good things at that time. At other times when her mother was loving and affectionate, she did not wish to get these things from others.

She gradually learned that her mother had both good and bad parts. She learned that when her mother was in a friendly mood she could have good and happy times with her. She also learned that when her mother was in a bad mood it would be best to stay away from her at those times. She also realized that her mother was the only mother that she had and that she had better make the best of it. She realized that no one was perfect and that her mother, like all mothers, had both good and bad parts.

In my story I attempted to help Steve become more comfortable with the notion that each person has both his good and bad parts, and that these two facets of one's personality coexist.

He would do best to learn when pleasurable experiences will be forthcoming and when they will not. He can thereby derive the benefits to be offered by his mother when she provides them and can go elsewhere when she is not inclined to give of herself.

The flight to the all-giving mother and the total destruction of the bad mother, which he portrayed in his story is an unrealistic fantasy. Firstly, no such people exist, and secondly, even if more benevolent mothers than his do exist, they are not available to him. He must accept the one and only mother he has and my story clearly states this. This acceptance is vital to the resolution of the oedipus complex in children (with the rare exception of the child whose mother is so destructive toward him that he is indeed taken from her).

Three days later, Steve related this story:

Patient: I'd like to say a few words to you. These stories may seem frightening. Don't worry about them. These are made up and also if you really think they are alive get it out of your head.

Therapist: Okay. I have no set idea. I know they are made-up stories and I know they are not alive.

Patient: Okay. Here I am with my first story. This will sound like "The Lion and the Mouse" from the Aesop's fables only it's different.

Therapist: Okay.

Patient: Once there was a lion who was taking a nap. All of a sudden a mouse said, "Let me get on you." The lion then kept on snoring. So the mouse said, "Watch this" and he jumped right on the lion's nose, but then his brother jumped onto him. Then the lion pounced up as though he was going to eat both.

Therapist: Excuse me. The mouse's brother jumped on the mouse. Is that it?

Patient: Yep. But then the first mouse jumped on the lion's nose and then the two mouses said that they might help him.

One day five hunters with rifles and six hunting dogs came into the woods. They caught the lion and just as they were about to kill him the two mice came and cut the ropes through and they jumped on the lion's back and he ran and ran.

The next day the hunters were after him again and their dogs. They set up a trap with a zebra behind it. This time when the lion got caught he had no chance. But he got away again with the help of the mice and the third time the lion had a narrow escape. Then the hunters caught him again and just as they shot, a mouse held up an iron rod and the bullet bounced off him and then afterwards the lion killed all the men and the dogs and the mouses were rewarded as great heroes. And that is the end of my story.

Now we present one of our most famous story-tellers, Dr. Gardner.

Therapist: Thank you very much for the very nice intro-duction, but you forgot to do one thing in your story. You forgot to tell the moral or the lesson of your story.

Patient: Oh, okay. Moral: never forsake a friend indeed when he is a friend indeed. Never forsake a friend.

The introductory comment, "These [stories] are made up and if you really think they are alive get it out of your head," is one of my favorite quotations. It clearly confirms what most child therapists know so well: that the child generally is not aware that the stories he tells refer to his own life situation even though to the adult such disassociation may seem impossible. In order to further strengthen the child's defences against such realization at this time. I agreed with him: "I know they are made-up stories and I know they are not alive."

The lion, of course, is the patient's father and the mice, the boy himself. The story demonstrates another way in which the child may handle the oedipal hostility he anticipates from his father. He becomes a friend of his foe, offers him services, protects him from his enemies, and becomes so indispensable that it would be self-destructive on the father's part to give up such a valuable ally. All this is epitomized in the moral: "Never forsake a friend."

In addition, the story provides an outlet for unconscious hostility he harbors toward his father. The lion is unrelentingly pursued by his tormentors and each time, at the last moment, narrowly escapes death. Through the mechanism of doing and undoing, the patient can vicariously gratify his hostile impulses. The last minute rescue assuages the guilt he might otherwise feel were he to let the fantasy run completely free.

In response, I told this story:

Once upon a time there was a mouse and this mouse had a little brother and they lived in the forest. One day the big brother mouse said to the little brother mouse, "Listen, I want to give you a word of advice, my friend and brother. Stay away from that lion because he is a dangerous fellow and he is known to eat up mice." Well, when the little bother heard this he said, "Now wait a minute. Are you sure of what you are talking about? Are you positive that that lion is as bad as you think he is 'cause I've heard that that particular lion is a nice fellow and that he doesn't eat up mice?"

Well, they decided to ask around some other mice and every mouse they asked told them the same thing that that particular lion was known to be a friendly fellow and that he was a friend of the little animals, including the mice.

So the big brother who had this idea felt that maybe he had the wrong idea and the next time they saw the lion he very slowly and very carefully and very gingerly walked toward the lion just to see what the lion would do. To his surprise, the lion said, "Hi there, young man. How are you?" The mouse said, "Uh-oh, maybe he's just trying to trap me or something. Maybe he's just putting on that nice sweet smile. Maybe he's not as friendly as one would think." The mouse decided to watch and wait.

Well, the lion got closer and the mouse heard him say, "Now, listen. You know I hear that you think I'm a dangerous guy, that I'm going to eat you up." And the big brother answered, "That's what I think. I think you are going to eat me up." Then the lion said, "Have you asked any of the other animals in the forest?" The big brother mouse said, "Yes, and they seem to feel you are a pretty friendly fellow and that you are a friend of the little animals." So then the lion said, "Well, what do you think about that?" The mouse said, "I don't know what to think about it. It certainly makes me confused. Perhaps they're right. Perhaps I have the wrong idea about you." The lion said, "Well, the only way you'll find out is to take your chances and spend some time with me. Do you want to risk it?" The little brother mouse said, "I'm willing to risk it. I'm not afraid of you. I believe what the other animals say."

Well, the big brother decided to take his chances. He got close to the lion and found out that the other animals of the forest were right, that the lion was not as bad as he had thought. In fact, he was a very friendly and nice person.

They then became very good friends and helped each other in many ways. Sometimes the lion would carry the mice on his back and in this way they could travel much faster and further than they would have been able to had they been traveling alone. On a few occasions some hunters trapped the lion and tied him up with rope. The mice were able to bite through the ropes and save the lion's life, and so they remained good friends for many years and lived happily ever after.

The lesson of my story is that sometimes you think someone is dangerous and you may find out that he isn't so.

As already described, one element in the child's viewing the opposite-sexed parent as dangerous is the projection of his own hostility onto the parent. Certainly one tries to lessen the patient's basic hostility so that there is less anger to project, but such attempts do not preclude the desirability of simultaneously working with the projection mechanism as well. One step toward accomplishing this reduction in the tendency to project is to help the patient see how exaggerated and unrealistic his concept of the opposite-sexed parent is. This is what I attempted to do in my story.

In addition, I confirmed and supported the patient's attempt to establish a mutually beneficial relationship with his father because such shared experiences can only be salutary. They serve to lessen the basic deprivations which are at the very roots of the oedipal disorder.

During the same session we played the storytelling game again. There is no reason to limit oneself to only one round if the child is enjoying the game and wants to play some more. This was the second story Steve told:

The name of this story is "The Tortoise and the Hare." This story may also sound like an Aesop's fable but it is really different.

Once upon a time there was a tortoise and a hare. They both bragged that they could beat everybody in a race. So they had a race and no one won. Then they had another race and it lasted three days and three nights and still they were even. Then they had a third race and this race lasted seven days and seven nights and still they were even.

Then they decided to have the longest race of all. They decided that they would run up the hill, over the river, and through the cherry tree and then if no one won the race they'd be friends. Well, no one won and so they became friends. They made up; they were friends and they didn't brag.

The moral of that story is: don't brag too much and the second moral is friends are helpful.

I consider the hare, the naturally faster runner, to represent the patient's father and the tortoise, the slower runner, the boy himself. In all tests of physical prowess they are equal. (It is not explained whether the tortoise ran uncannily fast or the hare pathologically slow.) They finally decide to stop draining their energies in competition and to "become friends" and be helpful to one another.

The story demonstrates another way in which the child may deal with oedipal hostility — in this case both his own and his father's. The two agree to repress the anger released through competition in racing, be friends, and squelch all animosity. There is nothing really to fight over, after all. That settles that problem. However, repression and its related mechanism, denial, are most unsatisfactory adaptations. To pretend the problem doesn't exist is hardly a solution.

In addition, the story serves to deny for the child the painful inequities that exist between himself and his father. In the first story of the session, the egalitarianism which he tries to achieve with his father is more realistic. The lion and the mouse are clearly unequal, but they each have skills which the other does not possess and so they can be of assistance to one another. In this second story, greater distortions of reality are brought into play in order to achieve the sense of equality.

Accordingly, I told this story:

The name of my story is "The Tortoise and the Hare."

Once upon a time there was a tortoise and a hare. The tortoise knew that the hare was a faster runner. Sometimes he would think about racing the hare, but he knew that he could not win. He realized that hares were naturally much faster than tortoises. This made him very sad.

One day as he was sitting alone and unhappy another tortoise came along. The tortoise said, "Why are you so sad my friend?" The first tortoise answered, "I wish I could run as fast as that hare." The second tortoise said, "Now that's a silly thing. You know that tortoises can never run as fast as hares. However, this does not mean that you are no good. The facts are that you can swim underwater for long periods of time and a hare cannot do that. You have a hard shell which protects you from many dangers, whereas a hare has soft skin and can be hurt from many things that will not in any way harm you." He also told the tortoise that as he grows older he will be able to do more and more things and become much more accomplished.

Well, this made the tortoise feel much better. He realized that it was a silly waste of time to keep comparing himself to another person who was naturally better in certain things. But he realized that he himself was good in certain things that the hare was not good in and, in addition, he knew that when he grew older he would get better and better in doing the things that tortoises can do.

And that's exactly what happened. As he grew older, he grew stronger and more accomplished and could do many things quite well.

There are two lessons to this story. The first is that it's silly to compare yourself to another person who has talents and skills which you do not have. It will only make you feel bad about yourself. However, you'll feel better if you realize your own abilities. The second lesson is that young people grow older and then become stronger and better at all the things that they can do.

In my story I tried to correct unrealistic fantasies which Steve entertains regarding himself in comparison to his father. I emphasized the point, which he himself made in his first story of this session, that each animal, regardless of size, possesses admirable and useful qualities. Obsessive comparison can only be ego-deflating. Taking pride in one's talents is far more rewarding. Furthermore, Steve is reassured that as he grows older he should be able to become as competent as his father and other adults.

The elicitation of fantasy is a rich source of information for the therapist. However, he must be aware that most, if not all, neurotic adaptations involve distortions of reality which are accepted as valid. Therefore, the therapist should appreciate that, in using the Mutual Storytelling Technique, there is the danger of fostering unrealistic adaptations unless he takes care to correct distortions as they arise in the context of the game. This is an old and pervasive conflict: parents read their children the most fantastic fairy tales at the same stage that they are teaching them basic reality testing. The explanation and resolution of this seeming paradox may lie in the romantic poet's request of his reader and listener for a "willing suspension of disbelief." By doing so one can enjoy the gratifications of unreality while at the same time keeping one's bearings on reality. The child is therefore told that these stories are make-believe. The stage is set for his "willing suspension of disbelief." It behooves the therapist to strike the balance and to use what he learns of the child's unreal world to help him improve his real one.

Two weeks later, while still in the first month of treatment, Steve told this story:

Once there was a king who had seven princesses and one day he wanted to know how fond they were of him. So he asked the first one, "How much do you like me?" "As much as swans," she said, "That is good." Then he asked the second one. She said, "As much as I love my golden hair." Then he asked the third one and she said, "As much as my life." The fourth one said, "As much as the world." He asked the fifth one and she said, "As much as the light." The sixth one said, "As all the beautiful colors," but the seventh one said, "As much as fresh meat lux salt."

Therapist: Fresh meat what?

Patient: Lux salt.

Therapist: Lux salt? What's lux salt?

Patient: Without any salt.

Therapist: What does lux mean? I don't understand. Without salt?

Patient: Yeah.

Therapist: Fresh meat without salt. Okay.

Patient: And the king said, "You don't like me at all. In my palace you'll stay no more," and he turned her out.

Now as she was traveling she met a prince. The prince fell so much in love with her that she fled. She did not want to be wed. And then all of a sudden a huge giant dragon swooped down and carried her off. The prince, hiding in the bushes, saw this in the meantime and went to slay the dragon.

He went to the cave of a wise woman. The wise woman told him to shoot meat without salt out of his rifle at the dragon. He did this and when it hit the dragon he gobbled it up and in one week grew so fat that the prince cut off his head. The princess was almost burned and gave her hand in marriage.

They married and the king came to the wedding feast and the princess said, "You must not put any salt on the meat." And then the cook said, "Why?" But she said, "Don't." And then as soon as the king tasted and tasted, he began to cry and he said, "Oh." His son asked what was the matter and the prince asked him what was the matter. The king said, "Oh, I had a little daughter. She was a beautiful daughter and she said she liked me as much as fresh meat lux salt. I thought she didn't like

381

me at all." Then the princess came and said, "No, meat lux salt is good. It saved my life." So they had their wedding and lived happily ever after.

Oh, yeah. Moral: do not think people don't love you when they do.

Therapist: Good.

The story, in part, reveals reception, at some level, of the message I imparted to Steve two weeks previously: one should consider the fact that distortions may contribute to one's dislike of another. Whereas in that interchange I spoke of his false perceptions regarding his father, here it is the father (the king) who, because of erroneous ideas, inappropriately rejects the patient (the princess, again without any connotations of homosexuality).

The story has a number of symbols which are unclear, the most prominent of which is the "meat lux salt." One thing is certain, however, and that is that the major theme of the story is one of irrational parental rejection. There is ancillary information involving the same theme: speaking of the princess Steve says, "The prince fell so much in love with her that she fled." This reaction to affection is clearly, as already described, that of the patient's mother. It shares in common with the major theme of the story the notion that misconceptions can bring about schisms in a relationship. The king rejects the daughter because he falsely thinks that "meat lux salt" is distasteful. The princess, at first, flees the prince because she believes that there is something about his love that is threatening. I decided, therefore, to focus on such alienating misconceptions in the creation of my story:

Once upon a time there was a king and he had seven daughters — there were seven princesses — and he wanted to know how much they liked him. So one day he said to the first one, "How much do you like me?" and she answered, "As much as a swan." Then he said to the second one, "How much do you like me?" She said, "As much as my golden hair."

Patient: I'd like to have the characters say different things like if the six were to say something different like that, like get the words mixed up. Okay?

Therapist: All right. And then he went to the third and she said, "I like you as much as all the colours." Then he said to the fourth, "How much do you like me?" She said, "As much as life." Then he said to the fifth, "How much do you like me?" She said, "As much as light." Then he said to the sixth, "How much do you like me?"

Patient: As much as the world.

Therapist: As much as the world. Then he said to the seventh, "How much do you like me?" and she said, "As much as fresh meat without salt." He said, "Well, if you can say that, you can't love me very much and I'm going to send you out of the castle. Be gone."

Patient: What he said sounded a little bit different.

Therapist: Well, out she went into the world and she was very sad that her father was so cruel to her and that he would send her off for such a flimsy reason. It made her very sad and very angry at him.

Well, she then came upon a prince and this prince liked her very much. He loved her. Now she said to herself, "I'm very happy that he loves me and I'm very receptive to his love and I'm very pleased that he loves me because my father certainly doesn't love me very much if he could have done such a thing to me and I am glad that there is someone else around who can love me to make up for the fact that my father doesn't love me." So she was very happy that this prince had expressed his interest in her because she was beginning to doubt how good a person she was if her own father couldn't love her very much. She was beginning to think that maybe no one else could love her. But once she met the prince it made her very happy to know that other people could love her.

Then a huge giant came down and tried to —

Patient: Mine was a dragon.

Therapist: Yes, excuse me, a giant dragon, I'm sorry. The prince, loving the princess very much, fought the dragon and he did this by first shooting meat without salt out of a rifle at the dragon and then he was able to slay the dragon. This made the princess even more loving of the prince because he was protective of her and that is one way of proving if someone loves you. It's how much they are willing to sacrifice for you, how much they are willing to give up for you, and how much they are willing to go out of their way.

Anyway, there was a very big wedding and she wondered whether she would invite her family. She certainly wanted to invite her six sisters because they were all very loving of her and she decided to invite her father too even though she knew him not to be very loving. She had a big feast and her father said —

Patient: Moo. Squeak!

Therapist: Come on. Let me finish this story. She had a very big feast and the father felt bad that he had sent her out of the house. He said, "You know, I really love you very much." And she said, "I don't believe that. I think you're just talking. You can't love me very much if you sent me out of the palace that way and I feel sorry for you that you have a problem that you can't love your own daughter so that I will never be as close to you as you would like because you threw me out of the house into the cold winter. So you can't convince me that you love me, however, there are certain things about you that I like and I'm glad that you came to my wedding. I enjoy spending some time with you, but I know that your love is not as great as I would like, but there's nothing I can do to change that. Besides, I've met myself a wonderful prince who loves me very much and I'm quite satisfied with my life."

And do you know what the moral of that story is? There are a number of morals to that story. Can you figure them out?

Patient: No.

Therapist: Can you figure out any of the morals?

Patient: Like people, don't hate them.

Therapist: No. That's not the moral of my story.

Patient (impatiently): Well, then, just tell your morals!

Therapist: One moral is: if somebody doesn't like you it

doesn't mean that nobody will ever like you. If somebody doesn't like you, you can always find someone else who will like you. If somebody doesn't like you it doesn't mean that you are no good. Other morals are that no parent is perfect; they have good parts and bad parts and that there are parents that don't love their children very much or who love their children some of the time and not other times, and the best thing that a child can do is to see the way the parent really is and know that some-day he will meet someone else who will give him more love. Those are the morals of my story. Do you have any comments you want to make about that story?

Patient: No, but I'd like to play over my story. And this is the end of Dr. Gardner's Make Up a Story Program.

Therapist: Would you like to hear my story too?

Patient: You just told it.

Therapist: Yes, but do you want to play over both stories or just yours?

Patient: Both.

In my story the princess is irrationally rejected by the king, but she is a model of rationality. She accepts the prince's love fully and is not fearful of him in compliance with distorted notions about his love being threatening. She uses his love to help her assuage the pain she feels over her father's repudiation. She openly states that just because there are impairments in her father's affection for her does not mean that no one else can ever love her. She realizes that there must be deficiencies in her father's character if he cannot love his own daughter, and she takes a "You're more to be pitied than scorned" attitude toward him. She accepts this defect in him as only one element in his personality and does not blind herself to his assets. The story was perhaps too long. I tried to compress too many messages into it and the patient reacted with impatience by the end. I believe that this error, in part, related to my insecurity as to the exact meaning of Steve's story. Much of the symbolism truly puzzled me. In my story I probably attempted to com-pensate for my ignorance by giving him the whole medicine cabinet in the hope that there would be something there that would be effective. Although, I believe, that some of the "pills" administered to Steve in this story were appropriate, there is also no question that I was practicing a poor type of medicine. The therapist does far better for himself and for the child to pick out one, or at most two, themes of which he is sure and to concentrate on those in his story. A multiplicity of messages can only be overwhelming and anti-therapeutic.

Seven months later, Steve told this story:

Once upon a time there was a man and this man wanted a wife and he wouldn't work for a wife. He just wanted to have a wife to come to him and say to him, "I want you to marry me." He just expected to be asked to be married without doing anything at all. Years had gone by and he was sixty-six and no one had picked him out a wife. He still kept on wondering why no girl would pick him out for a wife.

Therapist: For a husband, you mean.

Patient: Husband. My mistake. Well, anyway, he never quite understood until he was about seventy-seven. He learned that he had to work for a wife. So he worked for a wife and he lived happily ever after.

Moral: if you want a wife you've got to work for one.

Therapist: How did he work for one?

Patient: He became a doctor. He had a lot of money and then they were not fed up with him because he wouldn't work.

Therapist: I see. Okay. Excellent story. Thank you very much. Now it's time for me to tell my story.

The meaning of the story is obvious. It reveals that Steve has appreciated my communication in previous stories that one is not loved simply because he exists. One has to apply himself in order to acquire admirable traits. The resolution of the oedipus complex involves not only an awareness of this fact but also the willingness to act in accordance with its implications.

Of course, there are other important messages along this line which must also be imparted. The child, as he grows older, must find a healthy balance between his own needs and the activities he engages in and the compromises he makes. He must not prostitute himself nor should he be oblivious to the requirements of reality. Gaining competence has its own inner gratifications which are even more important than the external rewards such as money and the attraction of a desirable mate. Career and earnings are only two among many qualities which one must work to acquire if one is to respect oneself and also gain the affection of a desirable female. Loving feelings should be felt by both the man and the woman if the relationship is to be a good one, but again, these are not healthy if they totally disregard the realities of one's behavior. The younger the child, the less capable he is of appreciating many of these qualities and distinctions, many of which are quite subtle. The therapist often has no choice but to present them in the most concrete fashion to the younger child. He must recognize that he is oversimplifying and omitting important communications. Hopefully, the child, as he grows older, will come to appreciate these more sophisticated distinctions either through his experiences with the therapist or with others.

This is the story I told in response:

> Once upon a time there were two brothers and they had strange ideas. They thought that all they had to do was sit back and women would come to them and want to marry them. Well —
>
> *Patient:* This is about the same story as mine.
>
> *Therapist:* No, no, it's different. One of them, when he was about twenty years old, finally realized that that wasn't a very good plan and that he probably would be a very lonely man if he kept to that idea. Whereas the other one said, "No. You don't have to work in life. People will come to you. People will want you even if you don't work." So the one who got wise married in his twenties and he met a very nice lady. They got married and had a very good life together. The other man remained lonely

until he was very, very old, when he finally realized that you do have to work to get a wife. You can't just sit there and do nothing.

And the lesson of that story is: if you wake up young and you get the idea when you are young that it is important to work in order to get what you want, you'll lead a happier life. The end.

Patient: That moral is quite long. Okay. That's a great story.

In my story I reiterated and attempted to "drive home" the principle that one has to apply oneself if one is to accrue the benefits of benevolent human relationships. I decided that it was more important for me to strengthen this notion than to add further and more subtle modifications at this time. This story demonstrates one of the techniques I use to reinforce a communication. I call it the "twin brother approach." One does the healthy thing and enjoys the resulting benefits; the other indulges himself in his pathological ways and suffers accordingly.

A few weeks later, Steve told this story:

Well, in the old imaginary days, way long ago, when the giants stomped and the dragons blew fire all over, there lived in those old days, something called the Geloger — one of the biggest beasts in the whole imaginary world. He had two dragon heads with a lion's mane on them and snake's teeth. His body then turned down into a lizard and his tail first started out like a dragon's, and then it kind of turned into a giraffe's. At the end were lots of poisonous snakes' heads.

Lots of men tried to kill this Geloger. What was its name? I don't know, but I'll call it Geloger. They all failed. Now in the old days, you young folks, there was a boy named Barrigudi. This is an Indian story. Barrigudi lived in the Indian deserts of Accadoni. And Barrigudi made an oath that he would kill that dragon because the dragon ate his great-great-grandfather a long time ago. I'll tell you the story about the battle.

When Geloger came from one-hundred miles away, but he still —— Barrigudi still wanted to kill Geloger. So off he went. He walked and he walked through an imaginary forest. However, on his way he had lots of adventures too, such as with the haunted owl. This owl was an owl with a dragon's head. It had claws that had snakes' heads on them. It was a big fight but he survived it because he found a mouse and gave it to the owl. He found some rats for the snakes. He walked and he walked. He had already walked twenty miles. He was tired so he sat down and rested under a tree. Suddenly the tree turned into a giant. Then more giants sprang up and suddenly Barrigudi sprang up too. The battle lasted for two months. Then Barrigudi went on his way.

Soon he came to Geloger's cave. "Out with Geloger!" The battle began. Swords and everything were falling around. And he fought bravely and he killed Geloger. Taking off Geloger's skin, he put him over himself. He put Geloger's head on his head and he put the snakes on his feet, and kept the tail. As for the man and the lizard body, he put it on himself. So he took them all to his old treasure chest and walked out.

Finally he came back to his home and he was very tired, but when he got home he said to his mother, "It was worth walking all that way." The town gave him a rich reward of $100,000 and he and his mother lived happily and they gave some of their money to the poor. The end.

Moral: if you are brave and have faith you may do a good deed someday.

Therapist: All right. Thank you very much. That was an excellent story. Now it's time for me to tell my story.

The story is classically oedipal. Barrigudi is the patient and Geloger, his father. He kills Geloger and puts his skin over himself, acquiring all the accouterments of strength and power: the two dragons' heads with a lion's mane, and a snake's teeth, a lizard's body, and a tail with the heads of poisonous snakes at the end. A dramatic statement indeed, of the oedipal wish to slay the father and acquire his strength. En route to the slaughter the boy encounters another menacing father symbol who is handled with another tactic. The owl, who also represents the father by virtue of his similarity to Geloger (the owl has a dragon's head and claws with snakes' heads), is appeased by being fed a mouse and some rats. Perhaps the rodents symbolize the patient's siblings. If so, the maneuver demonstrates another way of handling the oedipal problem: having the father direct his rage against one's siblings, rather than oneself. But this doesn't work too well. Father is not too long pacified by such morsels and reappears as the giants who have been transformed from trees. Although details of the two-month battle are not provided, I assume that the giants were successfully subdued because the patient went on his way unscathed.

Following the final and complete destruction of Geloger and the acquisition of his power, the boy goes to his "old treasure chest," a common symbol for the mother. However, he soon returns home where his mother appears in undisguised form to welcome him after his conquests. It is no surprise that there is no father present in the house; he has been killed many times over on Steve's journey. The town provides him with the wherewithal to live with her in style, and "he and his mother lived happily." And, *noblesse oblige,* there is even money left over to give to the poor.

Considering Steve's clinical progress, both in the behavioral area as well as in making oedipal adjustments, the story is regressive. It reflects a retreat to some of the more primitive and futile oedipal adaptations that I was trying to help him avoid. He kills his father, magically acquires his strength, and marries his mother with funds freely provided by the community — all totally impossible. My messages about resigning oneself to these impossibilities and working to win a younger and more appropriate young lady all seem to have been ignored. Why had Steve regressed? His parents had just gone off together on a trip to the Caribbean, and I was practically certain that this was the cause of Steve's retreat into oedipal fantasies. Accordingly, I told the following story:

Once upon a time — this was in olden days — there was a boy and he lived with his mother and father. Now he

390

was kind of jealous of the affection between his mother and his father, and he felt very much that he would like to get rid of his father. Although his father was a very nice man, he used to look upon his father as if he was a terrible monster. In fact, he gave his father a name. He called his father Geloger and, although his father was a nice guy, he used to sometimes think that his father was really a terribly horrible monster. Sometimes he'd think of him as having a tail and he had snakes around him and that there were lizards coming out of him and —

Patient: A dragon's head with baby dragons sticking out on top.

Therapist: Uh-huh. All those things and he would sometimes wish that he could kill Geloger, kill his father, get rid of that guy and then have his mother all to himself. Sometimes he was even afraid when he would have such thoughts. He would think that it was a terrible thing. He didn't know that it's normal for a boy to have thoughts like that at times, that his father and mother sleep in the same room together, and often his father can be with his mother when he can't.

Patient: That's what happened when my mother and father went on vacation. I wanted to go along too.

Therapist: I see. Were you pretty upset about that?

Patient: Yeah.

Therapist: I see. It got you upset. Uh-huh. What were the main thoughts you had about that vacation?

Patient: That I should go along too.

Therapist: Uh-huh.

Patient: My thoughts were that they were having a good time and I was staying home and doing all this dreary stuff.

Therapist: Were you particularly jealous that your father was going with your mother?

Patient: Yeah.

Therapist: Would you have wanted to go along with your father? In other words, if you had a choice to go with your father alone or your mother alone, or the three of you together, which would you prefer?

Patient: The three of us together.

Therapist: And if you had to go with one of them which one would you have liked to go with?

Patient: That's hard to say. I'd like to go with both.

Therapist: Do you have any preference to go with either one? If you had to choose one to go with which one would you go with? Speak into the microphone.

Patient: My dad.

Therapist: You'd go along with him. Uh-huh. I see. Why do you say that?

Patient: Because he's a boy too. My mother is not a boy.

Therapist: Okay.

Patient: I was afraid to say that because you might be jealous that I didn't like any girls at all, that I didn't like my mother.

Therapist: Well, who were you jealous of when your parents went?

Patient: Dad. 'Cause they were taking a plane and I felt like shooting him.

Therapist: Why not shoot your mother? Why pick him?

Patient: Because he was the one —— it was his idea.

Therapist: Oh, he was the one who decided to take her. I see.

Therapist: Now let's go on. This boy used to look upon his father as a Geloger. Then he got very angry and sometimes he used to be very frightened of the anger that he felt. Then he began speaking to his older brother about it and his older brother said, "Yes, I used to be that angry too." He said, "What did you do about it?" The older brother said, "There's nothing you can do about it. Dad and Mom are married and if they want to go off together at times and be alone there's nothing we can do about it." The younger brother asked, "What can make you feel better?" He replied, "Well, it can make you feel better to know that you can have them sometimes. You can share their company sometimes. You can be with your father alone sometimes and your mother alone sometimes. But then as you grow older you'll have more and more friends and you'll have more and more fun with other people and then it will bother you less if they have all that time together. Someday when you are a teen-ager you'll meet a girl and go out with her on dates and things and then when you are older you can even get married, and then you can have a wife all to yourself. She'll be as pretty, if not prettier, than your mother." Well how do you think the boy felt when his brother told him that?

Patient: He felt pretty good.

Therapist: Uh-huh. Why is that?

Patient: Because now he knew that it was all right to wish his father dead and pretty soon when he got married he and his wife could go on vacations and all that.

Therapist: Right. Did you ever have any thoughts like that?

Patient: Like what?

Therapist: Wishing your father dead?

Patient: Yeah. Of course. Everybody has such thoughts.

Therapist: Did you ever feel it was bad or wrong? Speak into the microphone.

Patient: Yes I did before you told me.

Therapist: When did I tell you that it was all right?

Patient: After my mother and I wished Mrs. A was dead. [*Mrs. A., a neighbor, was inappropriately critical of Steve, and both he and his mother suppressed their anger.*]

Therapist: Hhmmm. Now have you been upset since your parents went on vacation?

Patient: No.

Therapist: Hhmmm?

Patient: No.

Therapist: You're sure?

Patient: No I'm not sure.

Therapist: You think that may be one of the things that is making you upset now?

Patient: Yeah, because I'd like to go down to the places where they're going to go and I'd like to go back to my home country where I was born.

Therapist: Where is that?

Patient: Denver, Colorado.

Therapist: I see. Is that where you were born?

Patient: Yeah.

Therapist: I see.

Patient: I'd like to go back to my home country.
Therapist: Okay. Anything else you want to say?
Patient: No.
Therapist: Hhmmm. Did you like this story?
Patient: Yep.
Therapist: What was the part about it that you liked?
Patient: I really didn't like a part of it. It's hard to say which part I liked most. All the parts were good.
Therapist: Any particular part you liked the most?
Patient: Yeah.
Therapist: What?
Patient: When the boy thought his father was Geloger.
Therapist: And then?
Patient: That's all.
Therapist: Okay.
Patient: I said enough.
Therapist: Okay. So long everyone.
Patient: So long.

In my story, I once again go back to the familiar theme regarding oedipal resolution. I use here the "older brother approach" wherein my messages are communicated by a respected peer. Children often listen with greater receptivity to someone their own age.

My hunch that the patient's regression related to his parents' trip was borne out in our direct discussion. Although the patient describes conscious awareness of anger at his parents (especially his father who initiated the idea), the story reveals that there was still significant repressed rage. The discussion demonstrates that in spite of such repression he was still freer to express anger than he had been prior to treatment. First, Steve could freely talk about his anger, something he was far less capable of doing when he started. In addition, he makes reference to an incident in which he, with his mother's support, had suppressed an angry reaction to a neighbor's inappropriate criticism. Our discussion of the incident in a family interview had served to loosen up both the patient and his mother regarding the acceptance of hostile feelings. Again, the Mutual Storytelling Technique is not used in isolation from other therapeutic approaches. Here, a relaxation in the mother's inhibitions over the expression of anger was very helpful in facilitating similar changes in Steve. Without her cooperation and flexibility, accomplishing this would have been much more difficult.

At the end of the discussion, Steve expresses another regressive wish, namely to return to the city of his birth, the place, that is, where all his infantile demands were satisfied, and where he had much more complete possession of his mother.

Therapy has its ups and downs, and the therapist need not be disheartened by regressive phases. The healthier periods are never completely lost. In them the child shows that he has the capability for maturer adjustment and that he has been able to overcome the anxieties over and resistances to healthier adaptation.

Example 7

Ronald, the boy with outbursts of rage and marked defiance of authority who presented many difficult therapeutic problems and whose treatment was unsuccessfully terminated, told this oedipal story in the middle of his therapeutic experience:

> Well, I am very happy that this is my sixth time on this program and today my story consists of a character named —— named —— named —— well, he was named Named. Okay? Now Named was a man who had two brothers, Shamed and Famed, and his uncle, who was very old — he was so old that he was lamed. (*Laughs.*)
> *Therapist:* He was called ——
> *Patient:* Lamed because he was lame. So one day Named, Shamed, Famed, and Lamed went together to the store —— went together to the hospital and said, "Doctor, can you cure my brother [*sic*], Lamed. He has arthritis in his leg." So he says, "Well, we might."
> You see, this is in the future. This is in the year 2157 and medical science has grown to the extent where the

395

flu, the terrible —— we think of the flu as the most terrible disease other than arthritis. Heart disease and cancer and tuberculosis and all respiratory diseases have been cured and they made microscopes fifteen million times as powerful as the electron microscopes and they finally found the cold virus which our modern electron microscopes can't.

So they took him and put his legs under the X, under the super X-X-X-Ray — fifteen million times the strength and power of our modern X-Ray and they found the arthritis. So they opened up —— so they put his legs under a local anesthesia and you see they put a blindfold on him so he couldn't see it, and they opened up his leg and they took out the pus and everything and they took out all the arthritis. Actually what is it? It's sort of a growth. Isn't arthritis sort of a growth that stiffens the legs?

Therapist: Well, in a way. Go ahead.

Patient: I forgot. Isn't it sort of a growth. It's like cancer. It's a growth.

Therapist: You tell it in the story whatever you think it is.

Patient: Okay. Let's see. They took it out and he didn't have arthritis. So Lamed, Shamed, Named, and Famed went home. The next day Famed said he had a headache and all of a sudden he fainted. When he was shipped to the hospital, the doctor said that he was was starting to get an acute case of emphysema because he fainted and had a headache because of lack of air. But in these future days modern scientists could repair and transplant the lungs too. So they put him under full anesthetics and they opened up his chest and they plugged up the space —— they didn't plug it up —— they took the spaces in the —— they took the holes in the lungs and they pulled the size of the holes together to close them up and he was normal again. So Famed, Lamed, Shamed, and Named went home.

The next day Shamed felt a pain in his groin; I mean in his right side and he started getting a high fever. So they took him to the hospital and he had an acute case of appendicitis. But in the future days they didn't have to take out the appendix. All they did was squeeze out the germ into a little sterilized cup and seal it up before the germs could escape and go through the air. So that's what they did and then they pulled —— they took the appendix and mended it up —— and then Lamed, Famed, Shamed, and Named went home.

And then it happened! The next day Named, all of a sudden, in his groin he felt a —— he felt a —— he felt a pain in his groin. So he went to the hospital and he had a hernia rupture. So even during that time the hernia rupture was the most complicated operation because during that time since men did or had to do some heavier jobs to help make the big rocket ships and everything and to keep the house going since the taxes had to be raised and everything, a lot of people worked harder and there's more strain on their bodies. So the hernias they get are much worse. So they had to open up his stomach and they had to pull the whole hernia back together, and when they saw the hernia rip they saw that there was some intestinal damage. So they mended up that and then Named, Famed, Shamed, and Lamed all went home and nothing ever happened to them again, 'cause they finally realized what to do and they all were vaccinated against every disease there ever was and ever will be. The end.

Therapist: Thank you very much and now I will tell my story. Just let me turn this off for one minute while I think of one.

Patient: Okay.

Therapist: You want to tell a commercial?

Patient: Okay. Friends, if you would like aluminium siding call me and get it. Thank you.

Therapist: Is that the end of the commercial?

Patient: Well —— this is the NBC television network. Now are you ready for NBC week? (*Makes Tarzan sounds*) Ah, ah, uh, ah —— Friday night at seven-thirty see Tarzan. Then (*humming tune*) Star Trek at eight-thirty — seven-thirty central time on the full color network — NBC. (*Hums more.*) And then at nine-thirty for a Tick-Toc-Toe and Peter Marshall with the Hollywood

Squares. (*Hums.*) Okay. (*Hums more.*) So remember seven-thirty — six-thirty central time — Tarzan. Then Star Trek at eight-thirty — seven-thirty central time. Then (*humming*) the Hollywood Squares with Peter Marshall at nine-thirty — eight-thirty central time — on the full color network NBC. And now back to our regular scheduled program, Dr. Gardner. Well, folks, we'll be going on with the game in just a moment but first this message of interest.

You got a big dirty oven going dirtier (*laughing*) and dirtier and dirtier all the time? Yet it's so rough and tough that you have to get it out with a hammer and chisel. Well, you've got to get Dial — all new Dial — the oven cleaner in the bright red can. You put it in your oven and it packs such power and punch (*laughing*) it will get your oven so sparkingly clean that you'll never have to wash that oven again. So get Dial. Pow! Pow! Now (*singing*) your coffee break. Top it off with Juicy Fruit Gum. (*Sings*):
"When you've lots of work to do,
Reach for something good to chew.
Chewing helps you stand the pace
Any time and any place. So —
Hi ho, hey, hey,
Chew your little troubles away.
Hi ho, hey, hey,
Chew Wrigley's Spearmint Gum.
Work goes faster, smoother too.
House seems brighter when you chew.
Hi ho, hey hey,
Chew Wrigley's Spearmint Gum.
Diddle dee dum!
Wrigley's Spearmint Gum makes you feel so good that you want to chew forever. So chew Wrigley's Spearmint Gum.
Hi, ho, hey, hey,
Chew your little troubles away.
Hi, ho, hey, hey,
Chew Wrigley's Spearmint Gum.
Diddle dee dum!
Get some soon!

All right! Now back to Dr. Gardner's television program!

Due to difficulties beyond our control, we shall have to wait for him. We shall have to do another commercial while waiting for our cameramen to get this fixed. Our video has been slightly disturbed; the audio is perfect. So until we get perfect video and audio a little television commercial. (*Begins to sing.*)

Therapist: Okay. Let's go now. I have to tell my story.

Patient: (*Continues singing.*)

Therapist: Our time is running out.

Patient: Okay.

The four men in the story symbolize facets of Ronald's personality. "Lamed" has leg arthritis which, as the patient understands it, is a growth. I regard the removal of the growth as a castration manifestation. "Famed" fainted because of lack of air and was diagnosed as having emphysema. This, I believe, relates to the suffocating anxiety Ronald was experiencing with his parents (especially his mother) and to the desire to have this alleviated. "Shamed" has groin pain, which turns out to be a symptom of appendicitis. That the appendix need not be taken out does not make this less of a castration fantasy. The consideration of its operative removal by the patient is enough to justify this interpretation. The futuristic cure which obviates the necessity for excision only serves to allay the patient's castration anxiety by changing the fantasy to a less traumatic form. Finally, "Named" experiences similar groin pain, but his is due to a "hernia rupture," which is much worse and, by implication, much larger than they are today. Extensive operative repair is necessary. Again, the patient suffers another operative procedure designed to remove a swelling in the pelvic area.

In summary, then, I consider the story to reflect primarily Ronald's notion, at some deep level, that he has been castrated. In addition, it reveals his feelings of being suffocated by anxiety. However, as I suggested at the beginning of this chapter, castration anxiety reflects generalized anxiety about body integrity. The penis lends itself well to such symbolization because it is not only a symbol of strength and masculinity but, in addition, its absence in the female implies vulnerability.

Ronald, as already discussed in Chapter 7, was particularly facile in providing commercials for the storytelling programs. Since they were so revealing, I would often take longer to make up my story in order to allow him relatively free rein in this area. The oven-cleaning commercial was particularly revealing. The oven, as is so often the case, represents a female; and here, I believe, symbolizes his mother. She is symbolically described as: "a big dirty oven, growing dirtier and dirtier and dirtier all the time. Yet it's so rough and tough you have to get it out with a chisel." His mother's alienating qualities are, in other words, thick and tenaciously adherent. He seeks the magic soap that will spontaneously make her so "sparkingly clean that you will never have to wash that oven again."

The Juicy Fruit Gum song, although "lifted," is still of psychological significance in that it has been selected from a multiplicity of possible commercials. The germane elements are: "Chewing helps you stand the pace," and "House seems brighter when you chew." Ronald, as the transcript of his recording conveys, was hyperactive and hypertalkative from anxiety even with sub-lethargic doses of tranquillizer. There was no evidence of a causitive organic subtrate. Chewing, that is, talking and moving, helps release some of the tension Ronald experiences in his home — it "helps you stand the pace," and then the "house seems brighter." Finally, with Wrigley's, Ronald tells us, you can "Chew your little troubles away." With Dial in his oven and Wrigley's in his mouth, his problems disappear.

This is the story I told in response:

Once upon a time there were four men and their names were Lamed, Famed, Shamed, and Named.
Patient: What?
Therapist: Their names were Famed, Shamed, Lamed, and Named.
Patient: Right!
Therapist: Now one day Lamed found that his leg was hurting and he went to the doctor and the doctor said,

"My friend, you have arthritis." He said, "Well, doctor. You're a doctor. Cure me. Cure it." He said, "This is not the kind of disease that a doctor can cure alone. This is the kind of disease that you have to cure yourself." Lamed asked, "How can I cure it myself?" The doctor said, "This is what is called a post-traumatic arthritis."

Patient: Traumatic is a type of shock. Right?

Therapist: Right. Traumatic means that he was being hurt. It means that something is hitting his leg. The doctor asked, "Has somebody been hitting you in that leg or hurting that leg in some way. This kind of arthritis comes from being hit in the leg." Then Lamed said, "Of course. I have a brother who is constantly hitting me in that leg." The doctor said, "Well, you'd better do something."

Patient: Lamed was the uncle of all the three brothers.

Therapist: Lamed was the uncle? Okay, in that case, Lamed said, "Well, I have big fights with my wife and when we fight my wife kicks me in the leg."

Patient: Right in the shin?

Therapist: Right near that bone, near the shin — in the shin near the knee. The doctor said, "Well, that might be it. You'd better straighten this out with your wife. I can't do anything for you as long as you and your wife —

Patient: Are kicking each other in the leg.

Therapist: Yeah. You are going to have arthritis." So anyway Lamed went home and he began to look into what problems he had with his wife and then he managed to work those out. So she no longer hit him in the leg. He then —

Patient: Was cured.

Therapist: Was cured of his own arthritis. But the doctor didn't do it. He really did it himself with a little bit of guidance from the doctor.

Now Famed the next day —

Patient: He was his nephew, you know.

Therapist: Famed, his nephew, was walking along when suddenly he fainted. He went to the doctor and the doctor said, "You have emphysema with lack of air." Then Famed said, "Well, cure me doctor. Cure me. You're a doctor. Cure me." The doctor said, "My friend, I have bad news for you. I can't cure you. This is a kind of condition which is caused by breathing in suffocating air. Something is going on where you live where the air is very thick, where there's —

Patient: Smog and gas.

Therapist: Something like that. The doctor said, "Gas and smog and something like that. Anyway, what's going on in your house?" Famed said, "Well, my mother cooks all kinds of things — cabbages and eggs and stuff — and it really gives a tremendous odor to the house." The doctor said, "Well, you'd better go home and try to get your mother to stop doing that or else leave the house when she is or else you'll never be cured of the emphysema."

So he went home and he spoke to his mother and he got her to stop cooking so often all those terribly smelly things which he was breathing in the house and which was causing his emphysema. She wouldn't stop altogether. So when she did cook those foods he walked around the block for a while. Then Famed got all better.

Then Shamed the next day had this pain in the groin near the right side and he had a fever, so he went to the doctor. The doctor said, "You have appendicitis."

Now remember that this was 2157 and a different kind of medicine was practiced at that time. He said, "You have appendicitis and it's due to some infection that got into your appendix. How did you get that?" Shamed said, "Well ——." How do you think he got it?

Patient: I think he got it because somebody kept coughing in his face — somebody who had just recently had appendicitis or something, and it got into his mouth and when he swallowed, you know, it went down into his intestines and the appendix is right under where the small intestine and the large intestine connect.

Therapist: Right. So then what did Shamed then do?

Patient: He said, "Stay away from anybody who has recently had appendicitis or any other type of infection."

Therapist: Right! Especially do not let them cough in your face. He did that and he was much better. Then we come to our friend Named who also had a pain in his groin.

Patient: In the middle.

Therapist: Yes. Now he went to the doctor and what did the doctor say?

Patient: He had a hernia.

Therapist: He had a hernia and what did the doctor say was the cause of that?

Patient: He was straining too much.

Therapist: Well, he had been straining too much. The doctor said, "Well, why have you been straining too much?"

Patient: To keep up with my wife.

Therapist: Straining too much to keep up with his wife. Why? What's going on?

Patient: Because his wife always wants everything, and if he doesn't get it his wife takes out a horsewhip and starts whipping him.

Therapist: What?

Patient: His wife takes out a horsewhip and (*laughing*) starts whipping him.

Therapist: So what do you suggest that Named do?

Patient: Well, I don't know what you said, but I think he suggested that Named throw out the horsewhip and make sure that he doesn't lie anymore and don't strain anymore.

Therapist: Hhmmm. It seems that there were problems in that marriage that had to be understood and worked out. [*My understatement of the week.*]

Patient: So they went to a marriage counselor.

Therapist: Named's wife was a very angry woman. What did he do about that then?

Patient: He was divorced.

Therapist: No, well, I'll tell you. His religion was one in which you can't get a divorce and he was a very religious Catholic, a very, very religious Catholic.

Patient: Are you a Catholic?

Therapist: I'm not a Catholic.

Patient: Oh yeah. You're Jewish.

Therapist: I'm Jewish.

Patient: Baruch atoh adonoy —

Therapist: Now let's talk about Named. Now Named was a very religious Catholic. What happened then?

Patient: So Named said, "Since I can't get divorced I'm just not going to be anything for my wife."

Therapist: The doctor said that the only solution was divorce. But Named said, "I can't get divorced because I'm a Catholic. It's against my religion." So then what did the doctor say?

Patient: The doctor said, "If you don't get divorced, well then you'll probably get whipped until your body is just a mess of scars."

Therapist: Then Named said, "Isn't there anything I can do? Do I just have to get beaten?"

Patient: "Well, I may not be as religious as you," said the doctor, "but I'm a Catholic and I believe that it is God's will that people should be allowed to get a divorce."

Therapist: Then Named said, "I know that. I've heard about that. I know there are some Catholics who don't believe in this, but I do. What am I going to do now? She's an angry woman, my wife, and she's always beating me."

Patient: "Well, you're going to have to either get a divorce or you are going to have to settle this one way or another."

Therapist: How did he settle this?

Patient: "As the man you're supposed to be like the king of the house and you have to prove that."

Therapist: How did he settle it?

Patient: "So if you can't divorce just hit her back. If she hits you, just hit her back."

Therapist: I'll tell you what he said.

Patient: What?

Therapist: The doctor said to him, "Look your wife is a very, very, angry woman and you're not going to change that. What you've been doing is that you've been provoking her; by doing things that she doesn't like, you make her even angrier. My suggestion to you is to stop doing many of the —— you purposely do certain things that she doesn't like because you want to get back at her, which just makes the situation worse. What you ought to do is recognize that she is a very angry woman and that she really can't love you very much because she's so angry. But you are just making it worse by provoking her in revenge." Do you know what I mean by provoking in revenge?

Patient: No.

Therapist: Provoking means doing something to hurt in revenge, to retaliate. Do you know what that means?

Patient: Retaliate? No.

Therapist: Do you know what revenge means?

Patient: Oh, yeah. Revenge! Revenge! (*Bangs fist on table.*)

Therapist: "Like when your wife says, 'I have supper ready for you,' and you say, 'Oh, I'm not hungry right now.' That is a way of provoking her. You get her angry. So you are making the situation worse. What I would suggest you do is to recognize that she is an angry woman.

Patient: (*Whistles and makes other sounds.*)

Therapist: Are you listening to the story?

Patient: Hhmmm.

Therapist: She can't really love you very much, but there are other people who you can have very friendly and happy relationships with. If you don't have them now then you'll find that you can go out and meet these other people and have good, friendly relationships with them, even though you can't have them with your wife. Then you'll be a much happier person."

So that's exactly what Named did. He took the doctor's advice and he said, "Well, my wife is this way. I've got to live with her. What can I do?" He kind of ignored as much of her anger as he possibly could. He decided that there was nothing to be gained by continuing to try to fight her or not do the things that she wanted. He did some of the things that she wanted as long as they were reasonable.

Patient: Sensible.

Therapist: Sensible requests; things that he wanted to do anyway. Sometimes, for instance, you know Named was very hungry one day and his wife had spent a long time preparing a meal and she said, "How about dinner, dear?" He said, "I'm not hungry." He was starved. That was the kind of way that he would hurt his wife and get back and even make her angrier. So now he stopped doing that. When he was hungry and she gave him food, he ate. He didn't just cut his nose to spite his face. Do you know what that means?

Patient: No.

Therapist: That you do something to hurt someone else, but you hurt yourself at the same time. You know?

Patient: You mean he was hurting himself because, you know, he was very hungry and it was bad for his body.

Therapist: Right, but it was so important for him to hurt her that he —

Patient: Didn't care.

Therapist: He didn't care about himself.

Patient: He got back at his wife.

Therapist: Then he realized that that was a kind of stupid way to spend one's life because it hurt him as much as it hurt her. So he stopped doing that and she became less angry. You know that?

Patient: No.

Therapist: Yes, it's true. That's what happened in that story.

Patient: Okay.

Therapist: Wait. Now the morals of my story.

Patient: What are they?

Therapist: The morals of my story are that in most diseases the doctor can give you a little advice and guidance, but more often than not, you've got to do some of the treatments yourself. That's the first moral. The second moral of my story is that if there is someone around you who is very angry and who is not going to change, don't keep fighting him, don't keep trying to change him. Just go elsewhere, even if you have to live with them you don't have to spend all your time with them. Get your kicks elsewhere. Get your fun from others. The third moral is that if you cut your nose to spite your face; that is, if you want to hurt the other person and in the process you hurt yourself at the same time, that's a very foolish and inefficient way of doing things, because you end up worse than you were before. Do you have anything you want to say about this story?

Patient: Well, since we're at the end of the tape we may

as well finish it with words.

Therapist: Well, why don't we discuss this story we just told, especially about Named. What about him?

Patient: Well, I think he was a pretty nice guy. It was his wife who was so bad.

Therapist: What else?

Patient: We will be returned to the end of our show after this presentation. Please stand by. (*Sings soft drink commercial.*)

Goodbye friends. This is the end of our program. (*Hums more.*) Dr. Gardner's television program has been brought to you by Dial, Juicy Fruit, and many other foods and drinks that we all love. Thank you. And now goodbye. (*Hums.*) This has been an NBC presentation. (*Hums.*) N-B-C. See Tarzan at its regularly scheduled time next week on most of these NBC stations. And now stay tuned for —

Therapist: Do you remember the morals of my story? No. Okay. That's the end of the tape.

In my story I encouraged Ronald to alleviate some of the frictions at home which were contributing to his being traumatized and suffocated.

In the "Lamed" sequence the patient is encouraged to discuss rationally with his mother problems which they have in the hope that they may be lessened somewhat. Although, as already described, the mother's basic level of repressed rage and the father's punitive outbursts were deep-seated and perhaps unalterable, they were intensified by the patient's rage reactions which, in turn, provoked the parents into retaliations that were excessively punitive and often physical. Reducing the purely physical traumas Ronald suffered at the parents' hands was certainly possible.

"Famed," who suffers with emphysema, who, that is, is suffocating from the anxiety produced by his mother's rage, is advised to avoid her at those times when her anger is particularly pungent. In the story the episodes are represented by her cooking particularly malodorous foods. "Shamed," with the patient's assistance, is advised to avoid exposing himself unnecessarily to people who can cause him distress — those who are carriers of "infectious appendicitis." This, of course, is similar to Famed's adaptation of avoiding his mother's cooking when it is nauseating.

In discussing a therapeutic course for "Named's" hernia, Ronald suggests that it was due to his being horsewhipped by his wife, the patient's mother that is. The boy's original suggestion that Named divorce his wife is not accepted for incorporation into my story. Ronald cannot so readily leave his mother. He must find some adjustment in his relationship with her within the confines of his home. In the interchange involving divorce and Catholicism, I try to so structure the views of Named and the marriage counselor that they might elicit from the patient a compromise plan which would enable him to co-exist with, rather than "divorce," his mother. He is unable to provide one and so I propose a plan that involves his taking her love when it is offered and separating himself from her when she does not provide it. Passive-aggressive maneuvers are also discouraged and their self-destructive elements are pointed out.

There were times during the telling of my story when Ronald was with me but, unfortunately, I often lost him, as his extraneous interjections show.

Four days later Ronald told this story:

Well, what do you know, I'm back. Hello.

Today my story is —— trouble is I don't know anything about a story today.

Therapist: You've told excellent stories. Should I start you off?

Patient: Hold it. I've got one. Because of my medical knowledge that's what I'm going to do it on.

One day — hold it — may I tell something about from a medical book I read.

Therapist: It has to be a made-up story.

Patient: You mean then I can't tell something about, you know, when what's his name, Banting, found the control of diabetes through —

Therapist: No, no, no. That's not a made-up story.

Patient: Okay, uh. Then I can't make one up then.

Therapist: Should I start you? You know there are millions of stories in every kid's head?

Patient: No.

Therapist: There are — millions and millions.

Patient: Yeah, but I can't make up.

Therapist: I'll show you how to get them out. I know a trick that helps you get out the stories that are inside your head.

Patient (laughing): What?

Therapist: There are millions of stories in everybody's head. Let me show you how it comes out. I start the story and as soon as I point to you —

Patient: I start getting ideas?

Therapist: You say the first word that comes to your mind and you'll see how that will help throughout the story. Okay?

Patient: Okay.

Therapist: Now listen carefully. As soon as I point, the very first word that comes to your mind will be the beginning of a story and then it will be pulled out.

Patient: I don't know whether it's going to be a regular word or a curse or whatever it is.

Therapist: See, there are millions of stories in your unconscious mind.

Patient: Yeah, but there are millions of words in my mind too.

Therapist: Right. But in your unconscious mind there are millions of stories. What we do is I start in a way that opens up a little hole into the unconscious mind and out comes a word, and then you pull out a story.

Patient: Doooooooouuuuuphh!

Therapist: Okay. Are you ready?

Patient (laughing): No.

Therapist: Ready?

Patient: Yes. That will help me when I talk like that?

Therapist: No more nonsense. Just listen. I'll start. Once upon a time a long, long time ago, in a distant land ——

Patient: That's too soft.

Therapist: far —— far away —— way beyond the ocean

———— way beyond the mountain ———— way beyond the desert ———— a long ———— long time ago, there lived a ————

Patient: A YCH! (*Laughs hysterically.*)

Therapist: A YCH. That's the first word. And this Ych ————

Patient (*still laughing*): Always said, "Ych."

Therapist: Now this Ych who was always saying Ych, one day

Patient (*still laughing*): Ych.

Therapist: And then after that —

Patient: He went over to his girlfriend and yched her all day (*continues laughing*).

Therapist: He went over to his girlfriend and yched her all day. Now what does yching mean?

Patient: Kissing.

Therapist: Kissing, I see. Ych means kiss.

Patient: It means a lot of things in this thing.

Therapist: Okay, but in this story what does ych mean?

Patient: A couple of things, but when he goes over to his girlfriend and ychs that means he's kissing ———— you know kissing.

Therapist: Okay. And he kissed her all day — did you say?

Patient: All day.

Therapist: All right. Now this Ych was kissing his girlfriend all day and then ————

Patient: While he was yching, he said, "Baavvvvuuuhhhvaaa" — the translation of that is "Darling, come closer."

Therapist: Darling, come closer.

Patient: First he said, "Baavvvuuhhhvaa."

Therapist: Okay. At which point what happened? And then? Go ahead.

Patient: And then at the end of the day when he went home to retire at night, he started ———— well, first of all he said, (*hums a long tune*).

Therapist: Which means?

Patient: Translation — no — (*continues humming*).

Therapist: Translate that for me please.

Patient: Shama Yisrael, adonai elohaynoo adonai echord. (*Laughs while singing hymn.*)

Therapist: What happened after that?

Patient: He went into his bed. I can't continue.

Therapist: Go ahead. And then in his bed ——

Patient: He had a heart attack.

Therapist: He had a heart attack. Why did he have a heart attack?

Patient: How good can Shama Yisrael get?

Therapist: All right, he had a heart attack. How come?

Patient: He was eating too many eggs so Ych had an over-supply of cholesterol in his blood which brought up his blood pressure so high that the cholesterol finally clogged his coronary artery.

Therapist: Okay, then what happened?

Patient: Well, they had to take him to the hospital for an operation and so —— and you know what the Ych's real name in our time in America —— you know what the Ych's name would be?

Therapist: What?

Patient: Moshe Rashansky. (*Laughs.*)

Therapist: Okay, and then what happens?

Patient: And then he lived for a couple of days and then he had a heart failure again and it ruptured his heart and he died. Well, you know, nobody's really a Dr. Kildare yet. (*Laughs.*)

Therapist: Okay, so what's the moral? Is that the end of the story.

Patient: No!

Therapist: Okay, well finish it.

Patient: Then Ych Number Two went to the same girl-friend's house.

Therapist: Ych Number Two went where?

Patient: To his girlfriend — to the same girlfriend, you know, the girlfriend of Number One, and said (*more gibberish*). The translation for that would be, "Come on baby. Now that Number One has died you can have me all day." So they yched all day. Translation: they kissed all day.

Then when he went to retire at night, all of a sudden he started choking and he couldn't breathe, and he went to the, uh, and then he uh, he uh, fell unconscious, and when he was in the hospital they said he should have had a DPT. He had diphtheria and a couple of days later he died of that because they —— during that time in the whole world there was only five gallons of DPT. You know diphtheria, typhoid, and whooping cough. I don't know some other medicine and tetanus, yeah.

So the next day Ych Number Three said (*more gibberish*). Translation: "Now that Number One and Number Two are dead, honey, why don't you love me all day?" See, that was the same girlfriend that Number One and Number Two had. It's always the same girlfriend. So they kissed all day and when he retired —— they yched all day. Translation: they kissed all day.

And so at night when he went home to bed, all of a sudden he felt himself, he felt himself choking. His breath was stuck and everything and you know he (*gasping*) uhuhuhuhuhuh. He didn't have diphtheria or anything. He thought it was in his lungs, way down in the bronchial tubes or something and when he got to the hospital the doctors said he was dying of rheumatic fever. So a couple of days later he died.

So the next day the girlfriend of all three said (*gibberish*). Translation: "There goes three guys I'll never forget." The end. (*Laughs.*)

Therapist: The moral?

Patient: The moral is: an ounce of prevention is worth a pound of cure because they all should have gotten DPT and things like that — they should have gotten vaccinated while there was still time. Right? And also that —— take precautions and look before you leap, you know. Take precautions. Okay.

Therapist: Wait a minute. You want to tell a commercial while I'm thinking up my story?

Patient: Uh-huh! This is the NBC television network. Are you ready for NBC week? See Tarzan at seven-thirty, six-thirty central time. Millions of adventures waiting for you in the African jungle. See Tarzan. Then at eight-thirty, seven-thirty central time (*humming tune*) "Star Trek," starring William Shatner and with his friend doctor who he calls Bones, who is Dr. McCoy or B. Forest

Kelley and with Leonard Nimoy, playing as Mr. Spock, half human, half vulcan, a creature nothing — who can withstand almost anything — who is over twice as strong as a human being — who is scientifically over one hundred times as intelligent and who can do almost anything.

Therapist: I'm ready after this commercial.

Patient: Just let me do this last one — the Beatles. (*Sings and hums tune.*) And then at nine-thirty, eight-thirty central time, up and down, up and down, here we go, Tic-Tock-Toe, three in a row, Peter Marshall and the Hollywood Squares. So are you ready for NBC week? We'll be ready for you. So remember at seven-thirty, six thirty central time, Tarzan, eight-thirty —

Therapist: That's enough — enough.

Patient: Ah.

Therapist: I want to tell my story. All right? Okay? All right. Now it's time for Dr. Gardner to tell his story.

In spite of all Ronald's horseplay and resistance, he ultimately told a most meaningful story. When he began the story, I thought that Ych Number One represented his father and Ych Number Two the patient because Number One died and was replaced by Number Two in the relationship with the girlfriend (the mother). With the introduction of Ych Number Three, I decided that all three represent the patient. They reveal his basic feeling that intimate involvement with his mother can be lethal. More specifically, it is when he involves himself affectionately that he is most prone to being destroyed by her. Sullivan[15] referred to this phenomenon as the "malevolent transformation." It is brought about in a situation where a mother professes love and yet each time the child approaches her for tenderness, he experiences some kind of rejection, humiliation, or other form of psychic pain. He thereby becomes "conditioned" to recoil from anyone who offers affection. Ronald's story poignantly demonstrates that the mechanism is operating within him. His alienating behavior becomes more explicable then: its purpose is to bring about his rejection thereby protecting him from the traumatization he thinks he would experience were he to involve himself intimately in an affectionate relationship.

The specific ways in which each of the Ychs die is also of psychological significance. Ych Number One ate too many eggs, "had an oversupply of cholesterol" which "clogged his coronary artery" and "then had a heart failure again and it ruptured his heart and he died." The eggs (mother's food) are lethal — another statement of the malevolent transformation. Also, his dying from a ruptured heart is close enough to the proverbial "dying of a broken heart" to warrant the supposition that he yearns so much for his mother that it will bring about his death. Ych Number Two "started choking and couldn't breathe," and finally succumbed to diphtheria. This relates, I believe, to the suffocating anxiety the patient experiences in his mother's presence. Ych Number Three, although his diagnosis is rheumatic fever, dies of an asphyxiating disease of the lungs — another reference to the dyspneic element in the patient's anxious reaction to his mother.

The moral, "Take precautions," has a healthy element. It suggests that he still wishes to involve himself with his mother but would like to be able to protect himself from the "heart breaking" rejections and strangulating tension he experiences when he approaches her.

With this understanding of Ronald's story, I told the following:

Once upon a time —
Patient: Yeah.
Therapist: A long, long time ago —
Patient: Uh-huh.
Therapist: In a distant land —
Patient: Yeah.
Therapist: Far, far away —
Patient: Hhmmm.
Therapist: Come on now — there lived a Ych. He was
    called Ych Number One and there was a girl in this town
    who he went to and yched all day with.
Patient: Ych! ! !

Therapist: Yched meant kissing. That night Ych got a heart attack and died.
Patient: Ych, ych.
Therapist: The next day Ych Number Two went —
Patient: Ych.
Therapist: Over to her —
Patient: Ych.
Therapist: And started yching —
Patient: Ych!!! (*Laughs out loud.*)
Therapist: And that night —
Patient: Ych!
Therapist: Choked to death.
Patient: Yyyy-ch!
Therapist: The next day Ych Number Three —
Patient: Ych!
Therapist: Came along and he started to kiss her —
Patient: Ych!
Therapist: And that night he choked to death too —
Patient: Ych!
Therapist: With pain in his heart.
Patient: Ych!
Therapist: Well, Ych Number Four —
Patient: Ych.
Therapist: Wondered about all this. His first inclination was to now go over to this girl and say, "I love you very much" and try to ych and kiss with her all day, but he said, "Three guys died." So he decided to look into this further and find out the causes of death. Now although it said on their death certificates that they were choking — you know the first one it said that he had a heart attack, and the second one that it was diphtheria, and third was rheumatic fever. He was a very clever, sharp guy. He looked into this more carefully, got a lot of data on this.
Patient: Excuse me a minute, Dr. Gardner, but I think I know what happened.
Therapist: What happened?
Patient: You see, there are a lot of people who have a disease, but it doesn't affect them. They are like carriers and that girl carried those diseases.

Therapist: You're right! There was something about this girl that was giving these guys the diseases.

Patient: But how can a girl be a carrier of heart disease? She'd have it too.

Therapist: I'll tell you what happened with this girl.

Patient: Oh.

Therapist: You see, what happened was

Patient: Leukemia?

Therapist: No. This girl —

Patient: Yeah.

Therapist: Although she kissed men, she really didn't love them very much. She only acted like she did and these — what's the matter, are you going to sneeze?

Patient: I think I'm starting to get it.

Therapist: You're starting to choke up?

Patient: Yeah.

Therapist: I see.

Patient: First signs of tuberculosis. (*Laughs.*)

Therapist: Well, anyway, this girl looked like she loved these men, but she really didn't. These men, when they were kissing her, became very upset because they were trying to get her to love them and she really didn't love them. They became so upset that it's as if they died of broken hearts.

Patient: But they died of real diseases.

Therapist: But I'm telling you what happened here really. Number Four did autopsies and things and he found out that they really didn't die of what was said on the death certificates.

Patient: But then how come, uh, there were all the symptoms of it?

Therapist: Well, sometimes —— what happened was there were two things going on.

Patient: Emotional shock?

Therapist: Emotional shock.

Patient: Can cause disease?

Therapist: Can cause heart attacks, can cause shortness of breath, or choking and heart pain and even heart failure and lung failure. These men were —

Patient: Emotional and brain failure, too.

Therapist: Yeah. Well, after the heart failed them, the brain doesn't get any blood.

Patient: Well, sometimes after you stop breathing the heart still goes on for a couple of minutes. That's how some people with heart — with breath failure — live through artificial respiration.

Therapist: Right. Now let me finish my story. Now these men really died of emotional shock with heart failure and lung failure —

Patient: And rheumatism.

Therapist: Then the fourth man said, "This girl can be dangerous. However, we live close by. There are certain things that she's very friendly about. I can have a kind of superficial relationship with her." Do you know what a superficial relationship means?

Patient: Friendly?

Therapist: Friendly. "But I'm not going to get involved with her too deeply because I'm only going to be in for a lot of trouble, disappointment, and emotional shock. I don't want to —"

Patient: And maybe death.

Therapist: Right. "I don't want to involve myself too deeply. I have to learn the lessons of my predecessors."

Patient: That means his great-grandfather, his grandfather, and his father.

Therapist: Ych Number One, Number Two, and Number Three. And so he did that. He spent some time with her, was friendly with her, but he did not allow himself to fall in love with her. Instead what he did was that he found another girl in the village who was much warmer, friendlier, and then he could ych with her a lot —

Patient: Ych!

Therapist: And he didn't have to worry about getting emotional shock, heart attacks, or lung failure.

And do you know what the moral of that story is?

Patient: Ych.

Therapist: What?

Patient: Ych! (*Laughs.*)

Therapist: What do you think the moral is?

Patient: (*Gibberish*) Translation: be careful (*laughing*).

Therapist: Be careful whom you fall in love with. Be a little more discriminating and if the person that you're in love with is not going to love you too much, don't get a heart attack over it —
Patient: And don't ych with them.
Therapist: Right and find someone else. The end.

A certain amount of jocularity always enhances the child's interest in the game. At the beginning of my story, Ronald's "ych" refrain clearly related to his emotional involvement. He was, indeed, swept up in my story and gleefully awaited each comment. In fact, throughout the story he was deeply involved.

Whereas in the patient's story he compulsively seeks the love of a rejecting woman and continues to suffer the dire consequences of such pursuit, in my story he is encouraged to recognize the futility of this fixation. Ych Number Four wisely perceives that his predecessors died from untoward emotional reactions to the woman, rather than purely physical diseases which were unrelated to her. He accepts the fact that her hostility and anxiety-engendering behavior is deep-seated and will not significantly change. He then decides to follow the course of the healthy oedipal resolution, to involve himself, that is, with his mother in those areas in which she is capable of benevolence and to seek compensatory gratifications from others. Following through with such a suggestion can help the child correct the central distortion of the malevolent transformation: "Because my mother's professions of love brought pain, everyone else's will as well." Having the *living experience* with the therapist, as well as with others, that deep trauma need not be associated with affection is vital to the rectification of this delusion.

At the point in my story where I said: "Although she kissed men, she really didn't love them very much. She only acted like she did, Ronald became overtly anxious. I had touched upon the mother's deeply-engrained but disguised hostility, and Ronald exhibited the same respiratory symptoms that he experienced at home with his mother. I could have embarked at that point on a more direct analytic inquiry, but I felt it would be less anxiety-provoking *for this boy, at this particular time in his treatment* to send my messages through the symbolic medium of the storytelling game. This is one of the most significant advantages of the technique: it enables meaningful communications in situations where they might not otherwise be tolerable.

Example 8

All the oedipal stories thus far presented have been told by children who are in what Freud referred to as the latency period (as I have said before, I do not believe it to be so "latent" regarding sexuality). Chris, about five-and-a-half at the time he told the following stories, was in the phallic phase, the period when oedipal strivings are considered by the classical school to be at their peak.

One problem encountered in story analysis of children in this age group is that their stories are often disorganized. The child is not usually too concerned whether the listener is fully appreciative of his story. They are not particularly conscientious about which antecedents their pronouns refer to and people often appear in the story as if out of nowhere. Reference is made to previous activities of theirs which the child assumes the therapist knows about, although he has never been told. Unless the therapist frequently interrupts the child for clarification, he may become totally confused. Even with such interruptions he may only be able to ascertain the general theme of the story, but this is usually enough for him to form one of his own. In addition, the child of this age cannot usually present a meaningful moral and so the therapist is deprived of that important epitomization of the theme that is most significant to the child. He can often give a title, but this usually reveals less of the story's psychodynamics than a moral.

Chris suffered from severe post-traumatic neurosis from multiple operative procedures required for the surgical repair of a harelip, cleft palate, and other abnormalities. A few months after he began treatment he told this story:

Well, there was this castle and there was a king in it and the castle had a princess in it, and the bad guys stoled the —— and then she was —

Therapist: Wait a minute. The bad guys stole the princess?

Patient: And then the king charged his men.

Therapist: Wait. The king did what?

Patient: The king charged his men to the bad guys and then the bad guys had a dragon, but all the men had spears and they, uh, threw them at the, um, dragon. Then they —

Therapist: Wait a minute. The king's men threw spears at the bad guy.

Patient: No, at the dragon. Then they threw their spears at the bad guys and they got the princess and then all of them were trapped.

Therapist: Then who was trapped?

Patient: All of them were trapped because the king, and his men and the princess and it was that that bad guy was just a robot and he had a real big rope.

Therapist: Wait. The bad guy was a robot?

Patient: Yeah, and had a real big rope. So the king's men threw a bomb that explodes. Then they killed the other one.

Therapist: They killed who?

Patient: The bad guy.

Therapist: Now tell me something. How did the King and his men and the princess get trapped? Who trapped them?

Patient: The bad guy did. Then the king got even with the bad guy. Then the princess got out of the trap.

Therapist: Why did they kill him?

Patient: Because the bad guy stoled the princess.

Therapist: I see. What's the lesson of that story?

Patient: Uh, someone taught me.

Therapist: What's the lesson?

Patient: Someone taught me.

Therapist: No, no. What's the title of that story?

Patient: What do you mean?

420

Therapist: Or the name of the story?
Patient: "The King and the Princess."
Therapist: "The King and the Princess." Okay. That was a very good story, and now it's time for my story. Now, as you know, my story will just start off like your story, but very soon it will be an entirely different story.

After all the fire and smoke of battle had cleared away I reconstructed the events as follows: the "bad guy" (with his men, dragon, robot, rope, and spears) stole the princess from the king and held her captive in a "trap." In response, the king (with his men, spears, and bomb) charged after the bad guy, killed him for his heinous crime, and rescued the princess.

With the identity of the "bad guy" in mind, I told this story:

Once upon a time there was a castle and in this castle there lived a king and a princess. Now there was this guy who liked that princess very much and he wanted to take that princess away from the king. He wanted to sneak into the castle at night and steal her away. Well, he started to sneak in and as he was walking into the castle, who should he see, but the king. The king himself was standing right there at the door of the castle and he said, "What do you want, fellow?" He said, "Well, I'd like the princess." The king said, "You can't have the princess. She's mine. She's my princess. You can't have her, and you can't take her with you." Well, that guy felt very bad; he felt very badly about it. The king said, "That's a bad thing to want to take my princess away from me. She's mine. However, my young friend. I have some good advice for you. I suggest that you go out into the town and find a girl of your own, someone who doesn't belong to anybody. There are many nice girls in that town that you can find."

Well, that's what he did. He went down to the town and there he saw many nice girls and he found one who was very pretty. In fact, she was even nicer than the princess or at least just as nice. She was just his age. You see, the princess was older than he and it was better that he have someone his own age. So they became friends and they grew up together. Then when they grew up they got married and they lived happily ever after.

And the lesson of my story is that you can't have a girl or a lady that belongs to someone else. You have to go out and get your own, and when you do that you may even get somebody who is better than the first one that you wanted. The end.

Patient: How about your other story?

Therapist: My other what?

Patient: Story.

Therapist: You want me to tell another story?

Patient: Yeah. You said it was not the same story as mine.

Therapist: Well, my story isn't the same as yours. It was a different story. It just started in the same castle. That was all. It's a story about a castle and a king and princess.

Patient: No. This time do another one.

Therapist: Another story?

Patient: Another one, not like a castle or a princess.

Therapist: Okay. Another story. Here we go.

Once upon a time there was a boy and he lived in a house with his mother and his father. He was a very good boy, except he wanted to marry his mother and he wanted his father to leave the house. Well, when he said that to his mother and he told that to his father, his mother and father said, "It's very nice that you love Mother so much that you want to marry her, but you're only a boy and she's a grown woman. Daddy and I love each other and we want to stay married." The boy said, "Well, what can I do then?" The mother said, "Well, when you grow up you'll meet a nice girl yourself and you'll marry her and she may even be prettier than Mommy."

Well, the boy thought that was a good idea and although he was sad that he couldn't have his mother to marry, it made him happy to know that someday he would marry someone himself. So he grew up and he worked and he earned money and he met a nice lady whom he married. He lived happily with her. The end.

Do you have anything you want to say about that story I just told?

Patient: Uh-uh.
Therapist: Did you like it? You liked it. You want to hear it?
Patient: Yes.

Little need be said about the meaning of my story. It is of interest that when I finished it, Chris requested that I tell him another — a clear indication that my communication was a meaningful one. In my second story, I reiterated the same theme but brought it "closer to home," by shifting the setting from a castle to a typical family scene. His request to listen again to the whole sequence confirms that something in what I said appealed to him.

One week later Chris related this tale:

There was this piece of rock and someone picked it up and then some of his big friends came and they cracked it up and it was a man's piece of gold.
Therapist: Wait a minute. It was a piece of rock or was it gold?
Patient: And they cracked it up and there was gold inside the rock.
Therapist: I see. Okay.
Patient: So the man called the police.
Therapist: Yes.
Patient: Then the police came and hurried into the, to the, hurried to the boy and they put him in jail.
Therapist: They put the boy in jail?
Patient: Hhmmm.
Therapist: Why?
Patient: Because he stealed the piece of gold.
Therapist: Yes, he stoled a piece of gold. Go ahead. Then what happened?
Patient: He put him in jail and then the man got a whole collection of gold. Then some bad guys came to steal.
Therapist: Bad guys stole the gold?
Patient: Uh-huh. Then he called the police again and so that man —— that boy that stealed the gold —— it was the man's boy. He just wanted to have it.

Therapist: Oh, it was the man's son?

Patient: And then —

Therapist: Wait a minute. Was it the man's son who stole the gold?

Patient: Yes, and then he wanted to just see, but then he called the police and they brang him back.

Therapist: The police did what?

Patient: He and all the police were in jail.

Therapist: Why were the police in jail? I don't understand. You say the man's son had stolen the gold; that he wanted to just see it.

Patient: Uh-huh.

Therapist: Did he really want to steal it or not?

Patient: No, he just wanted to see it.

Therapist: So they put him in jail for that?

Patient: Yes.

Therapist: Then what happened after they put his son in jail?

Patient: Then they brang him home and then all the police got in jail.

Therapist: Why did the police get in jail?

Patient: All the polices were trying to open up to him and then suddenly they got the bad guys to jail, but then some more policemen they got them and killed them, and then they knocked down all the other buildings.

Therapist: So what finally happened to the police?

Patient: They saved them.

Therapist: They were saved.

Patient: By killing the bad guys.

Therapist: Is that the whole story?

Patient: Hhmmm.

Therapist: And what's the lesson of that story?

Patient: About um, see, if you see a rock you don't have to steal it. It might be a little boy who wants to see it. You shouldn't call the police.

Therapist: It might be a little boy who wants to see it.

Patient: Hhmmm.

Therapist: You shouldn't call the police.

Patient: Uh-hum.

Therapist: I see. Okay. Very good. That was a very good

story and now it's time for me to tell my story.

Patient: First I want to hear my voice.

Therapist: You want to hear your voice first? Okay.

Of course, there are sections of this story which are totally inexplicable. For example, I did not have the faintest idea exactly what was going on between the boy and the police in the police station. However, certain things are clear. A boy (the patient) was punished for the crime of stealing (or possibly only looking at) his father's gold (who else could that be but the mother?). In the "lesson" Chris requests the listener not to call the police if he sees a little boy looking at a piece of gold. This may be translated: "Please don't punish me for eyeing my mother."

I told this story in response:

Once upon a time there was a father and this father thought that he would like very much to have a nice rock. So he hunted and he hunted and he looked and he looked and he saw many rocks. He finally found one rock that he thought was the nicest looking of them all and he picked up that rock and he said, "This is a very fine rock." He opened it up and what do you think he found inside that rock? What do you think was inside it?

Patient: Gold!

Therapist: Right! He found gold inside that rock. The father was very happy. Well, the son saw what kind of rock the father had and he got the idea that he would like to have that rock too. So he thought to himself, "Maybe I should steal that rock. I think I'd like to steal that rock." He said to his father, "You know, what would you think if I told you that I wanted to steal that rock?" The father said, "I wouldn't be surprised. I would not be surprised at all because this is a nice rock and I'm not surprised that you should think of stealing it. However, I wouldn't like that very much if you stole my rock."

Then the son felt very bad. He said, "I want a rock like that." Then the father said, "Well, you can have a

425

rock like that." The son said, "How?" The father replied, "Well, all you have to do is wait until you grow up, until you're big enough, and then you can start hunting for rocks by yourself." The boy said, "That's a long time. I want that rock now." The father said, "Well, I'll share a little bit of my rock with you now. I'll share a little bit of it, however, you can't have it all because it's all mine. I'll give you a little piece of this gold right now." So the father gave him a little piece of gold right then and the son gradually grew bigger and bigger, and then when he grew up and he was a big man he then went hunting for rocks. Do you know what he found? What do you think he found one day?

Patient: A rock.

Therapist: Was it as big as the father's?

Patient: Yes.

Therapist: It was. It was just as big as the father's, and he was then very happy and he lived happily ever after. And do you know what the lesson of my story is? See if you can figure it out.

Patient: I know.

Therapist: Speak into the microphone.

Patient: You should find the rock and the boy shouldn't steal and he should hunt for a rock when he was a big man and then he'll have his own gold.

Therapist: Right. The lesson of my story is that if you don't have a rock of gold of your own now, when you grow up you can get one and also that it's not so bad to want your father's rock of gold now. It's not so bad to want that at all, but usually a father will not hurt a boy or be very angry at him for wanting to have a rock of gold, even if it's the father's rock of gold. Lots of boys would like to have what their fathers have, but they usually can have just a small part of it, and when they grow up they can usually get things on their own. The end. Want to hear my story? Okay. We'll turn it back on? (*Both stories are replayed.*) Okay. Good. I'm glad you wanted to hear this story. Did you like it? What part of the story did you like the most?

Patient: Your part.

Therapist: Which part of my story?
Patient: About the rock.
Therapist: Which part about the rock?
Patient: The gold.
Therapist: The gold part. Hhmmm. Anything about the gold part. Okay.
Patient: Okay.

One of the ways in which a child can assuage his oedipal jealousies is to realize that he can have *part* of his mother's attention and affection. Sharing her with father and siblings may not be as good as having her all to himself, but it is *something,* and the child should be able to appreciate that. One cannot expect the child to be satisfied with the hope that someday, in the distant and remote future, he will be able to have a wife himself. He needs something in the here and now, and sharing mother can provide him with some gratifications in this regard.

Three days later, Chris told this story:

Therapist: It is my pleasure to tell you that Chris is here again to day and he's going to tell us another story.
Patient: You are!
Therapist: No, no. First you. The rules of the program are that the child tells the story first and then I'll tell my story. That's the rules.
Patient: Um, well, there was this house and it was real tiny and it was through where gigantic buildings were. It was in the middle.
Therapist: Wait, I don't understand the last thing you said. The house was so tiny that what?
Patient: The house was so tiny and there were some big gigantic buildings next to it and it was so little and in the middle.
Therapist: I see. It was in the middle. It was in the middle of some big buildings. I see. Then what happened?
Patient: Someone came and they wanted to live in the house.
Therapist: The little house? Yeah.

Patient: So the little house, it was very dirty. The windows were cracked and the walls were dirty and the floor was done with dust all over it, but then the boy —— they cleaned it all up. And then a mother came in and she had a whole bunch of —— and then a big ——

Therapist: The mother had what?

Patient: And then a big man came ——

Therapist: Wait a minute. The mother had what? Wait, wait. The mother had what?

Patient: Had some cookies. Then a man came in and said, "Hey, what's going on around here?" He was mad. And they said he lived in the little house.

Therapist: The man lived in the little house?

Patient: Yes. But then he tasted one of the cookies and they were delicious to him and he said, "Yum, yum, yum," and he wanted to eat all of them and the grandmother said, "No, you can't!" But then it — um — he made some more and then he ate all of them.

Therapist: Wait. Who made more?

Patient: The grandma. She made all of them.

Therapist: She made more and she did what?

Patient: She gave it to the big man.

Therapist: All right. Then what happened?

Patient: That's the end.

Therapist: What's the lesson of that story?

Patient: There's no lessons that belong.

Therapist: What's the title of this story?

Patient: What do you mean?

Therapist: The name of the story, like every story has a title.

Patient: Uh, "The Man."

Therapist: The title of the story is "The Man." Now why was that man mad when he came into the room? Why was he mad?

Patient: Because he didn't want anybody to live in it.

Therapist: He didn't want anybody to live in the house? Nobody at all? Who was living in the house?

Patient: The big man.

Therapist: Who else was living in the house? Did he live in the house alone?

Patient: Yes.

Therapist: And who else came to live in the house?
Patient: No one.
Therapist: Who came into the house? Who were the people that came into the house in your story? Tell me.
Patient: A man.
Therapist: Yes. He lived there. Who else came in?
Patient: The company that was there.
Therapist: Who was the company?
Patient: There was a boy and the mother the grandma.
Therapist: And he didn't want them there. Did he want both to leave?
Patient: Yeah. All of them; all three of them.
Therapist: I see. Hhmmm. But that grandma made good cookies, huh? So what happened after she made the cookies? Did he still want them to leave? Yeah? So how did the story end?
Patient: I don't know.
Therapist: Well, come on. Finish up the story.
Patient: I did.
Therapist: It ends that she made more cookies and she gave it to the big man. Then what happened after that?
Patient: I think that's the end.
Therapist: Okay, an excellent story. Now it's time for me to tell my story.

In this story, Chris tries to assume occupancy of his father's house and live there with his mother and grandmother (also a mother figure). When the father returns he not only wants to throw out the patient, but his mother and grandmother as well. If he has to leave, he may as well bring along his mother and grandmother as well, and he gets his father to suggest this — a clever way of winning the oedipal struggle. The father, however, does not ask them all to leave before he has had the opportunity to taste one of the mother's delectable cookies — "they were delicious to him and he said, 'Yum, yum, yum,' and he wanted to eat all of them." Chris deprives his father of mother's delicacies by having the grandmother, at first, refuse him further cookies. The grandmother, then, is part of the mother he would like to be his ally against the father. But she, too, finally complies with the father's demands and gives him more cookies.

The story ends with the patient finding himself on the horns of a dilemma. If he leaves with his mother and grandmother, he has gained complete possession of them, but is ill-equipped to take on such awesome responsibilities. If he stays, he must suffer the humiliations and jealousies associated with his father's prerogatives regarding his mother. The central issues of the oedipal struggle are being grappled with. Chris cannot make a decision; he cannot and does not end the story.

In response, I told this one:

> Once upon a time there was this little house and this house was right in the midst or the middle of many big houses. In the house there lived a mother, a father, and a little boy. This boy loved his mother very much and he thought, "This house isn't big enough for three people. It's only big enough for me and my mother. I wish my father didn't live here." And one day he said this to the father and the father said, "I know that you would like to have this house all alone for you and your mother, but that can't be. When you grow older you will have a lady just like her all to yourself. Then you can live in your own house with her, but now you are going to have to share your mother with me." Well, the boy was kind of sad about this, but it was good to know that someday he could have a lady all to himself.
>
> Anyway, this mother baked very good cookies and when she baked cookies he wanted to eat all the cookies himself and didn't want to give his father any. He said to his mother, "Give me all the cookies." What did his mother say?
>
> *Patient:* No.
> *Therapist:* Why did she say no?
> *Patient:* 'Cause she didn't want to have [garbled].
> *Therapist:* What's that?
> *Patient:* Get cavities.
> *Therapist:* She didn't want him to get cavities. Well, that was one reason, but she also said something else. "We have to save some for your father." Did she say that?
> *Patient:* Yes.
> *Therapist:* Hhmmm. Right. How did the boy feel when his

mother told him that he would have to save some cookies for his father? What did he think?

Patient: I don't know.

Therapist: Was he happy or sad?

Patient: Sad.

Therapist: Why was he sad?

Patient: Because he didn't love his father.

Therapist: He didn't want his father to have any? Right. But what happened?

Patient: I don't know.

Therapist: He had to give them anyway, even though he didn't like it, but his mother said, "Someday when you grow up you'll marry and then you'll have a wife who could bake you cookies and you won't have to give any to anybody." What do you think about that? And do you know what the lesson of that story is? What's the lesson?

Patient: (*Doesn't respond.*)

Therapist: Well, the lesson is that when you are young you have to share certain things with your father. You can't have everything to yourself — your mother's cookies or your mother herself — but when you grow older you can marry a lady and have her all to yourself.

Chris was not particularly happy with my emphasis on sharing. His very resentment, however, was evidence that he was affected by my message. Five-year-old children are not particularly famous for their generosity, and anyone who suggests that he share as valuable a thing as his mother's love — symbolized by the cookies — is going to meet formidable resistance.

Example 9

Joey, the boy with nightmares and enuresis, presented a number of stories with oedipal themes.

During his third month of therapy, he told this story:

Patient: Can you start me off?

Therapist: Okay. Joey X. is with us today and, as you just heard, he wants me to start him off, which I will be very happy to do. Once upon a time, a long time ago —— far, far away —— beyond the deserts —— beyond the ocean —— beyond the plains —— a long —— long —— time ago —— far —— far away —— there was a ——

Patient: Pigeon.

Therapist: And this pigeon ——

Patient: Boasted all the time.

Therapist: So this boasting pigeon ——

Patient: Well, I think he was boasting about his feet.

Therapist: He boasted about his feet because ——

Patient: He thought that they were so beautiful. Then the alligator who was talking to him said, "Well, why are your feet so beautiful?" The pigeon said, "I don't know. I just like to boast." I can't think of any other thing. Could that be the ending?

Therapist: I am not impressed by this story. Come on. You can do something more with it. Say you have just told me the beginning. This is a good beginning of a story about a boasting pigeon who just likes to boast about his feet. One day this boasting pigeon who just liked to boast about his feet ——

Patient: Then all of a sudden the alligator just bit his feet off. The alligator bit off the pigeon's feet. Then the alligator said, "Now you don't have anything to boast about."

Therapist: So?

Patient: The pigeon just flew off and he never boasted again.

Therapist: Now why did the alligator do this? Why did the alligator bite off the pigeon's feet?

Patient: He knew that the pigeon always boasted so he just decided to bite off his feet so he wouldn't have anything to boast about.

Therapist: Okay and the moral of that story is?

Patient: You shouldn't boast because most likely people will do something to make you stop.

Therapist: Okay. Just a couple of questions. Was this alligator a man or a lady, boy or a girl? Was it a male or a female alligator?

Patient: A male.

Therapist: And was the pigeon a male or a female pigeon?
Patient: A boy.
Therapist: I see. Okay. Now it's time for my story.

I consider the pigeon in the story to symbolize the patient and the alligator, his father. The pigeon's feet, as appendages which descend down from the trunk, probably stand for his genitalia. The story reveals Joey's fear of castration by his father were he to compete with the latter regarding masculine prowess. His exhibitionistic display of his genitalia — the boasting about his feet — would serve to attract his mother away from his father and thereby invoke the latter's wrath.

With this interpretation of the patient's story, I told this one:

Once upon a time, a long, long time ago, in a distant land, far, far, far away, there lived a pigeon and this pigeon had a habit of boasting all the time, boasting about his big feet which he was quite proud of. He would go around boasting to everybody about what big feet he had.

Well, nearby there lived an alligator and his wife and this pigeon fell in love with the alligator's wife, and he wanted to live with that alligator's wife and he wanted to get rid of the alligator. So he went over there and he said to the alligator's wife, "How do you like me? I've got the biggest feet of any pigeon. How would you like to be my wife and get rid of that old alligator?" The alligator's wife said, "I'm sorry. You ought to get someone your own size. You ought to get a pigeon. I'm an alligator. I'm too big for you. I'm too old for you." Then the alligator's husband heard this and, of course, the pigeon was kind of scared at first. He thought that the alligator would be very angry at him. The alligator wasn't very angry. He said, "I'm very flattered that you like my wife so much that you want to marry her, however, she's my wife and I think that you should go out and get yourself your own wife."

So what do you think the pigeon thought at that point?
Patient: I think maybe he agreed with it.

Therapist: But he said, "I'm only a little pigeon." So what did the alligator say to him?

Patient: I don't understand.

Therapist: The pigeon said, "I'm just a little kid. I'm not old enough to get married." So the alligator said, "Well, you get yourself friends now. You play with boys and maybe play with girls once in a while and as you get older, you'll see, you'll be able to get many beautiful young pigeon girls who would like to marry you, especially since you have such nice big feet. You'll be even more attractive. That's exactly what happened. This pigeon grew older and some pigeon girl fell in love with him and he married her and they lived happily ever after.

Do you know what the lesson of that story is?

Patient: If you can't find someone when you're young, wait until you are older.

Therapist: And then you'll get somebody.

In my story Joey is encouraged to get a more appropriate mate, someone his own size, another pigeon, rather than a big alligator. In addition, I tried to lessen any guilty fear Joey was harboring over his incestuous designs. My alligator, in contrast to Joey's is non-punitive and flattered by the pigeon's affection for his wife, but nevertheless advises him to seek his own female elsewhere. Peer relationships are also encouraged for present-day compensation.

Three weeks later, Joey told this story:

Therapist: Once upon a time, a long, long long time ago, in a distant land, far, far away, there lived a ——

Patient: A kangaroo.

Therapist: And this kangaroo ——

Patient: Didn't have any pouch.

Therapist: She didn't have a pouch and so ——

Patient: She couldn't have babies and the babies had to crawl on her head.

Therapist: So she couldn't have babies so the babies had to crawl on her head. And then ——

Patient: Then when they were old enough to have babies they were blind.

Therapist: Why?

Patient: Because the pouch has medicine in it to make them see.

Therapist: I see. Because the pouch has medicine to make them see. Okay. Then what?

Patient: They couldn't have any babies. They didn't have any pouch; they couldn't eat; they didn't have any nose and they didn't have any mouth, and they didn't have any ears.

Therapist: Yeah, go ahead.

Patient: So finally the mother died. Whew!

Therapist: Yeah.

Patient: And then the babies died.

Therapist: Yeah.

Patient: And one of the babies who was named Ricky had one living cell in him that was still living, and that cell grew up to be a little lamb.

Therapist: Hhmmm. Yeah.

Patient: And the lamb lived happily ever after.

Therapist: And the lesson of that story?

Patient: I don't think there is any lesson.

Therapist: Ah, every story has a lesson.

Patient: Well, after everything is going bad something could go right.

Therapist: Hhmmm. Good. Good story. Okay.

Patient: Do you know what the story means?

Therapist: Yes. I think so. Let me tell mine first.

This story is a most dramatic statement of Joey's notion that his mother has rejected him. She doesn't have a pouch — a warm womb-like compartment for protection and nurture. Deprived of this protection, the babies grow up with severe sensory deficiencies. They are blind and lack noses and ears. Presumably they cannot see, smell, or hear. In addition, "they couldn't eat" — the listener is not told whether or not they lack mouths; but in either case they cannot partake of any nutriment the mother may offer. Joey appears to be aware, at some level, of the fact that organs develop only in response to certain stimulation. When the mother does not provide it, organs fail to develop or atrophy if already formed. More generally, the story reflects Joey's awareness that without proper maternal stimulation, the baby will become apathetic, marasmic, and ultimately die.

Joey was certainly not exposed to deprivation that would warrant such a gruesome story. He would have been far sicker had he been. The explanation, I believe, lies in the fact that children's fantasies, like dreams (of both children and adults), tend to represent things in primitive, highly spectacular, and often exaggerated form.

The story ends on a note of hope, however. One surviving cell grows up to be a lamb who lives happily ever after. Perhaps the story epitomizes his earlier life situation, when his mother was depressed, and he did experience a mild to moderate degree of emotional rejection. He survived the ordeal, however, and now he is more hopeful that things will be all right. Possibly, his entrance into treatment may also have contributed to his optimism.

With this understanding of Joey's story, I related mine:

Once upon a time there was a kangaroo and this kangaroo didn't have a pouch. This made her children very angry because they wanted a mother who had a pouch. This made them very sad and one of them said, "You know, that makes me sad and angry that you don't have a pouch. I think we may have trouble. We may go blind or we may have trouble with our noses and our mouths growing and everything else." And the mother said, "I'm glad you told me that. I didn't realize that you wanted it so much. Let me see what we can do. Suppose I hold you in my arms and hold you very close to me and cuddle you all around and protect you and rub you. How does that feel?" Well, the little babies realized that that was very helpful and that they were getting a lot of the warmth that they thought they wouldn't get because she didn't have a pouch. In addition, what they did was, they met other kangaroos that had

436

pouches. They got in there once in a while and they got friends and cuddled with them so they got the warmth from them. Then when they grew up they got the warmth from their wives. So they did not suffer. They weren't blind and nothing happened to them and they lived happily ever after.

And do you know what the moral of that story is? See if you can figure it out.

Patient: If you are angry at your mother or father, say that you are angry.

Therapist: Because if you do ——

Patient: You won't get into trouble.

Therapist: And you may get what you want.

Patient: Yeah.

Therapist: And if you can't get what you want even if you express your anger what can you do?

Patient: I don't know.

Therapist: Get it elsewhere. You know they got some of it by showing their anger and then their mother could only give so much because she still didn't have a pouch, so they went and got it elsewhere. Right?

Patient: Yeah.

Therapist: From other places. Now do you know what your story means?

Patient: What?

Therapist: Can you figure it out?

Patient: No.

Therapist: Who does the kangaroo stand for?

Patient: Me?

Therapist: Your mother. You see your mother as not being able to give you as much protection and affection and warmth as you would like. Is that right?

Patient: I don't know.

Therapist: Uh-huh. And that makes you angry. Is that right?

Patient: Sometimes my mother won't let me buy more baseball cards.

Therapist: I'm talking about affection and warmth.

Patient: I never thought that.

Therapist: Maybe there's something to it?

Patient: No.

Therapist: Okay. We have to stop now but that's what I think the story meant.

Here, Joey is presented with a number of courses of action he can take if he feels that he is not getting enough attention and affection from his mother. He can verbalize his frustration to her; he can get substitutive satisfactions from others, both peer and adult; and he can be reassured by the hope that as he grows older he will be even more capable of seeking alternative gratifications.

Joey's inability to understand my explanation of the meaning of his story suggests that its messages were quite anxiety-provoking to him. He did not wish to accept that, at some level, he saw his mother as rejecting, and the anger he felt toward her in response could not be consciously tolerated. Such anxieties and resistances are the main reasons why children, in general, do not associate their stories with the reality of their lives.

A few weeks later, Joey described a dream which I present here because it not only bears on the question of anxieties in treatment, but on the oedipus complex as well.

Patient: I had a dream last night.

Therapist: Let's hear it.

Patient: I ate my belt. Only the buckle was left. I was scared my pants would fall down. I kept trying to keep them up. My mother was mad at me and I knew I was going to die. I fell out of bed screaming.

Therapist: Do you know what that dream means?

Patient: No.

Therapist: Well, let's try to figure it out. Suppose a foreign boy moved to your block and he didn't know English too well and he asked you what the word "belt" meant, what would you say?

Patient: It's a thing that holds up your pants.

Therapist: So if you ate your belt what would happen?

Patient (shamefully): My pants would fall down.

Therapist: Then what would happen?

Patient (cringing): My penis would show.

Therapist: What would your mother do?

Patient: She might get a little upset or mad at me.

Therapist: Would she get so mad at you that you'd think you were going to die?

Patient: No.

Therapist: So what do you think this dream means? What's it all about?

Patient: I don't know.

One might say that the dream reveals Joey's oedipal wishes. The exposure of his genitalia is a sexual advance toward his mother. By having her respond with angry recoil he protects himself from the anxieties he would suffer if she were receptive to him. These anxieties are associated with the assumption of the male adult role both in the sexual and non-sexual areas. There is also fear of retaliatory castration by his father.

Although this interpretation may very well be applicable, I believe that there is another which was more pertinent to Joey at the time. Joey's main feelings in the dream were shame and fear, and the primary emotion he exhibited when telling it was shame. I believe that this is much more a shame dream than a sex dream. In our culture there is an inordinate obsession with the covering of one's genitalia. The child is inculcated with the notion that part of his body has a very special significance, that it should be covered at all times, and only exposed under very special circumstances. Failure to comply strictly with the rules of genital coverage can result in the child's being ridiculed, teased, punished, and humiliated. The nine-year-old boy, whose "fly" is open and who is teased by some little girls because they have gotten a quick glimpse of his penis, suffers a mortification that he may recall for years. Such a boy is far more concerned with covering his penis than using it for sexual activities with his mother or anyone else. For a child growing up in this milieu, the genitalia lend themselves well to symbolizing that which is personal and private; that which one should not reveal to others; that which, if revealed, will expose one to the ridicule of the observers.

In the dream Joey is performing an act in which he reveals something most personal and private. I believe this represents therapy where he is expected to participate in discussions involving his most closely guarded secrets. In the dream it is he who exposes himself — eats the belt that allows his pants to drop. In therapy he is also expected to reveal himself. The belt, which provides concealment by preventing the pants from dropping, symbolizes the forces of resistance, the defense mechanisms which keep unacceptable thoughts and feelings safely unconscious. By taking off the belt he satisfies his desire to expose himself in accordance with the request of the therapist and in the interests of his treatment. By eating the belt, he keeps his defense mechanisms within himself — the implication being that they would be readily available to him were he to need them in the future. The same ambivalence over exposure is reflected in his attempts to keep his pants up after the belt has been removed. His mother's angry response, I believe, relates to his notion that were she to know about his abominable secrets, she would react so punitively — so reject and mortify him — that he would feel like dying. One of these loathsome secrets, I believe, is anger. He projects it onto his mother and this contributes to the hostile reaction he anticipates from her.

My explanation does not preclude the coexistance of the classical interpretation. Dreams are rich and can satisfy many needs simultaneously. My interpretation is, however, closer to the things which were bothering Joey at the time; closer to issues in conscious awareness and, therefore, of higher priority for therapeutic focus. It is better for the therapist to concentrate on those topics which seem to have the greatest emotional charge for the patient at the particular time, rather than to explore those which he considers "deeper" or more basic. To focus on highly repressed and often extremely remote themes, no matter how valid, is at best a waste of time and at worst antitherapeutic.

With this understanding of the dream, I responded to Joey's "I don't know" with the following:

Therapist: I think the dream means that there are many

things you're ashamed to discuss with me here. Things you'd like to cover up. Things you think your mother or I would get angry at you for if you talked about them.

Patient (*anxiously*): I do get scared here sometimes, like when we talk about anger.

Therapist: Would you like to talk about some of these things now?

Patient (*quite tense*): Not too much.

Therapist: Okay, we don't have to. But I hope the time will come soon that you'll be more comfortable talking to me about some of these thoughts and feelings. I think you'll see then that the terrible things you think will happen are not going to happen. But you can't know that for sure until you've tried me out. How about a game of checkers?

Four months later, Joey told this story:

Therapist: A long, long, long time ago, in a distant land, far, far, far away, there lived a —

Patient: Bird.

Therapist: And this bird —

Patient: Was a very happy bird. Now one day this very happy bird had babies.

Therapist: And after that —

Patient: They lived happily ever after.

Therapist: And the moral of that story?

Patient: Have babies.

Therapist: The moral is have babies? Well, that's a nice story but I wonder if you could do a little bit better than that in terms of length. Our sponsors are not too happy when the program has such a short story. See if you can think of another story that is little bit more juicier, a little bit longer. That was a good story though. It was very short.

Patient: Do you know what it means?

Therapist: You can't really tell much about a story like that. It's too short. Let's hear another story. Come on.

Patient: There lived an alligator.

Therapist: All right. And this alligator —

Patient: Was a very happy alligator.

Therapist: He was a happy alligator and ——

Patient: He had babies and the babies liked the alligator very much, and the alligator liked the babies very much.

Therapist: Yeah.

Patient: And they were very happy.

Therapist: Hhmmm.

Patient: They were happy until they grew up and they had to go find a girl to marry. So they kissed their mother good-bye and they went to find a girl.

Therapist: You said they were happy until they had ——

Patient: They were still happy.

Therapist: They were still happy when they kissed their mother goodbye in order to get married. Then what happened?

Patient: They went and got married.

Therapist: Then what happened?

Patient: They had babies and they lived happily ever after.

Therapist: And the moral of that story?

Patient: When you have to leave home be happy and get a wife.

Therapist: Be happy and get a wife. I see. Okay. Do you understand what that story means?

Patient: Huh-uh.

Therapist: You don't understand it at all?

Patient: No.

Therapist: Do you think the story has anything to do with you?

Patient: Yes.

Therapist: What does it have to do with you?

Patient: I don't know but I think it does.

Therapist: How would it relate to you?

Patient: Well, the sexy business.

Therapist: The sexy business?

Patient: Yeah.

Therapist: You have to clarify that for me please.

Patient: About ladies and girls.

Therapist: Could you be a little more specific?

Patient: Oh, about the girls' nakedness.

Therapist: Well, what's that got to do with your story — about girls' nakedness?

Patient: I mean about getting my own girl.
Therapist: Yeah, go ahead.
Patient: It's a problem I'm always hearing.
Therapist: What is the problem that you have about that?
Patient: I wanted to stay with my mother.
Therapist: Hhmmm. So what is the story saying?
Patient: That I'm getting a new girl?
Therapist: Hhmmm. So what do you think about that story?
Patient: Does it mean something good?
Therapist: What do you think?
Patient: Yes.
Therapist: Why?
Patient: Because I'm getting my own girl.
Therapist: Hhmmm. That's right. I think it was a good story. In fact, the only thing I would do would be to change it only slightly. Here's mine.

The story has little that is symbolic. It is the kind of story one sees in the working-through period of treatment. The child is accustoming himself to the new adaptation — in this case leaving his mother and going on to someone else. He is desensitizing himself to the painful separation by reliving it repetitiously in fantasy. Although the story is not "rich," or "deep," it is still therapeutic. Its value should not be underestimated. In addition, there are suggestions present that Joey is telling me the kind of story he knows I like to hear in order to ingratiate himself to me. This is a general therapeutic occurrence; children are just less sophisticated about it than adults. The therapist's hope should be that, although the patient may in part be doing the healthy thing from the need to gain the affection of the therapist, he will ultimately do it because he himself finds it to be a preferable way of doing things. Most, if not all, cures have within them an element of the "transference cure."

Joey's anxieties in thinking of the ultimate separation from his mother are revealed at the point where he changes what he says about the alligator's state of happiness on separation from the mother. At one point in the story, Joey says: "They were

happy *until* they grew up and they had to find a girl to marry."
In the next statement he retracts the "until" and states: "They
were still happy." His natural anxiety over anticipating the ultimate separation is revealed by the word "until." The implication
is that he was happy until he had to leave his mother, and that
following the separation he will no longer be happy. By retract-
ing the "until" he can deny his anxiety. By this "doing and undoing" he does not really eliminate the basic fear, he just deludes
himself into believing that it doesn't exist.

In response, I told this story:

Once upon a time there was a mother alligator and a
father alligator and they had some baby alligators. These
baby alligators all loved their mother and father. They
gradually grew up, and as they grew up they realized that
although they would have liked to have stayed with their
parents, they knew that they had to grow up and live with
others someday. But they knew that as time went on they
would meet others who would be younger and more to
their liking and that's what happened. The girl alligators
met boys and the boy alligators met girls who were younger and their own age and whom they enjoyed very much
and then they got married and they lived happily ever
after and had their own children. That's what happened
to their children. Their children when they were young
were scared about the thought of leaving their own parents,
but as they grew older, they got more stronger and independent, and it was easy for them to do it and they got
married. And so on and so on down the generations.

And the moral of that story is that when you are
young, you are usually scared about the thought of leaving
your mother and father, but as you get older it becomes
easier because you can take care of yourself more and you
can usually find friends who will be your own age and who
will keep you company and be with you.

I tried to impart the idea that although the prospect of
independence may be frightening for Joey *now*, as he gets older,

444

he will be bigger, stronger, more independent, more mobile, and more capable of handling life on his own. *Then*, there will be little if any reason to be scared. My story was also a reinforcement of the healthy themes presented in his.

About eight months later, by which time he had enjoyed significant clinical improvement, Joey told this story:

Once upon a time there was a bolt and this bolt was from a tape recorder, but it fell out. So the bolt wanted to get back into the tape recorder again and get the nut, but it couldn't. So it tried to go into another tape recorder and this time a bolt had come out from that and this tape recorder wasn't as slimy as the other one and so, in fact, it had a little like scales on it so he could climb up and go with the nut.

Therapist: Wait a minute. I'm not clear.

Patient: Well, the first bolt came out from the first tape recorder. That tape recorder was pretty slimy so it couldn't get up. Then he saw another tape recorder and this one had scales on it and it wasn't as slimy and a bolt had fallen out of that so the bolt from the first tape recorder came up and got with the nut of the second tape recorder and the bolt from the second tape recorder was now looking for a tape recorder. Do you get it now?

Therapist: Wait a minute. The bolt from the first tape recorder went to the second tape recorder. Was there a nut in the second tape recorder?

Patient: There already was a nut in it.

Therapist: Oh, so it got that nut.

Patient: Yeah.

Therapist: Oh, I see.

Patient: So the one that had fallen out first couldn't find any place, and so they took him and they ended up putting him into a new Apollo 11.

Therapist: Who, the bolt from the second tape recorder?

Patient: Yes. They put him in Apollo 11 because they needed one more bolt and they found him and so they put him in Apollo 11.

Therapist: Is that it?

Patient: Yes.

Therapist: And what's the lesson of that story?

Patient: Well, it's better to be in Apollo 10 than be in a tape recorder.

Therapist: It's better to be in Apollo 10.

Patient: I mean 11, 11, 11.

Therapist: Than in a tape recorder. Now let me get it straight. This bolt in the first tape recorder fell out and wanted to get back into the first tape recorder to join up with the nut, but he couldn't. Then he saw that a bolt from the second tape recorder had fallen out and he went into the second tape recorder and he went into a nut there.

Patient: Yes.

Therapist: And then the bolt from the second tape recorder had no place at first to go, but then it finally got hooked up with Apollo 11.

Patient: Yeah.

Therapist: Okay.

The story is an excellent example of oedipal resolution. It covers oedipal conflicts over three generations. The first tape recorder is Joey's paternal grandmother and the bolt from the second tape recorder, the patient's father. He fell out of a hole from *his* mother and his attempts to re-enter are unsuccessful. His father did not obsessively try to achieve the impossible, but rather turned to the second tape recorder — the patient's mother — who was more accommodating to his entry. The hole in her, which the first bolt enters, is the same one from which the second bolt (the patient) had fallen. Since her hole is occupied by the patient's father (the first bolt) it precludes the second bolt's re-entry. The second bolt, like his father before him, does not waste time in seeking re-entry into a hole which is not available to him, but finds a slot for himself in Apollo 11, a far more prestigious niche.

The story demonstrates an interesting aspect of the Mutual Storytelling Technique. As already described, the tape recorder has certain advantages over toys such as dolls and puppets as a catalyst for story elicitation. It provides the child with far fewer

446

specific stimuli that might serve to channelize the stories and restrict fantasy. On rare occasions, the child will incorporate the recorder itself into his story. However, this invariably involves an anthropomorphization of it in accordance with his specific psychological needs at that time. The forces pressuring for release in fantasy are powerful, and they are not readily restricted by considerations of reality. The recorder, therefore, lends itself to an infinite variety of distortions to conform with the needs of fantasy formation. This story is a good example of this phenomenon.

In response, I told this story:

Once upon a time there was a bolt which fell out of a tape recorder and couldn't get back into its own tape recorder. So it went on to another tape recorder and there it saw a nut that was also available because the bolt from the second tape recorder had slipped out. Well, this bolt from the first tape recorder — we'll call it bolt one — and the nut from the second tape recorder — we'll call it nut two — liked each other very much and bolt one went into nut two. Now bolt two was very angry about this. He was furious. He wanted to get back and be with nut two and he kept saying, "I want to be back with you, nut two." Nut two said, "No, I'm sorry. I want to be with bolt one."

Well, he was really angry about this and he was spending a lot of time trying to talk nut two into letting him back, but nut two said no. Then a friend of his said, "Listen. You're wasting your time. Why bang your brains up against a stone wall? Why not direct your attention towards other things and get somebody who wants to be with you because that nut two is with bolt one?"

So he thought about that and he said, "There must be another place for me." So he went down to the space center in Houston and asked them if they needed a bolt and they said, "You know, you are just the right size that we need for Apollo 11. Let's try you out for size." So they tried him out and sure enough he was just the right size and he fit right into a nut there called nut three that was a perfect size. It was a very snug fit and they were just perfect for one another and then he was quite happy and he kind of laughed at himself that he had spent so much time trying to be with that nut two when he had so much better time with nut three.

And the lesson of that story is: when you can't have what you want often you will find that if you'll turn your attention elsewhere you might get much better in another place. The end.

Although there was little I could add I filled in the details of the conflict that must have been inevitably present before bolt two left nut two for nut three, the love of his life. This served to strengthen the resolves which contributed to the oedipal resolution revealed in Joey's story.

Joey's story supported and confirmed my clinical decision that this boy was ready to leave treatment.

Two weeks later, during the session prior to his last, Joey told this story:

Once upon a time there was a doorknob and everybody used to make him all dirty with their fingerprints and people used to throw cherries at it and used to use it as a target for cherries and things like that. You know, I wouldn't throw cherries at a doorknob. I would eat them. Wouldn't you?

Therapist: Yes, of course. Go ahead.

Patient: One day he told them not to, and he said, "Stop throwing cherries at me and things like that. Why don't you use something else besides me? Why don't you hang up a target or something like that outside?" And they did and he was glad that he didn't keep his thoughts to himself.

Therapist: What was the lesson of that story?

Patient: Don't keep things to yourself.

Therapist: Okay, because ——

Patient: If you don't speak out people won't know that they are doing anything wrong and that they are bothering you or they won't stop at all if you don't tell them to stop it. The end.

Therapist: Okay.

448

The story deals with two important issues which were focused upon in Joey's treatment: the utilization of anger and the oedipal theme.

His story demonstrates that he has learned his lessons regarding the expression of his anger and the use of it in improving his relationships with others. The cherry throwers, who soil him, are told to desist and they accept his alternative recommendation to play their dirty games outside.

On another level, the story is oedipal. The doorknob, I believe, symbolizes his penis — it juts out anteriorly and has a rounded top. The cherries represent his mother — luscious and edible, round fruits are a common breast-mother symbol. Joey structures the story so that he is the innocent victim of those who throw cherries at him, rather than one who is pursuing cherries. The guilt-alleviating switch in no way changes the results — cherries and doorknob make contact. His disgust helps repress the pleasure he basically feels about the idea. The more appropriate target outdoors is his father. There, Joey is uninvolved in the sexual encounter, and he does not have to suffer the frustrations associated with observing it. The story, then, epitomizes the course of alleviation of his oedipal conflict. Although the story does not have him go on to forming a relationship with a more suitable mate, it does put mother and father back together where they belong and he removes himself from painful confrontation with their intimate liaison.

In response, I told this story:

Once upon a time there was a doorknob and this doorknob was sometimes used as a target by people.
Patient: Would they mess him up with their fingerprints?
Therapist: Yes. Sometimes they would mess him up with their fingerprints and other times they would use him as a target for cherries. Now as a result he got very sick and tired of cherries. He would find them disgusting and hateful. So one time he spoke up and said, "Listen, you can use a target on the wall. Stop using me as a target."
Patient: Or outside.

Therapist: Or outside or something like that. They did that and they said, "We're glad you spoke up. We didn't know that this bothered you so." The doorknob said, "Yeah, it bothers me so that I don't like cherries at all." So they said, "Listen, we'll use another target outside and we're not going to throw cherries at you, but you know, we have a bag of cherries with a string and we'd like to hang it on you. You know that cherries are very good once in a while, and you have an idea that they are always bad all the time.

Well, the doorknob began to think about that and he realized that they were right — that just because he got cherries thrown at him too much doesn't mean that he can't ever have a cherry at all or ever see a cherry at all or be close to a cherry at all. So after that, once in a while, he would let them hang a bag of cherries on him and he found out that cherries weren't bad. In fact, this was a kind of eating doorknob and once in a while he would even eat a cherry and found out that it was very good.

There are two lessons to that story. One, if somebody does something that bothers you, tell them about it and speak up, express yourself, so that they will stop. The second moral is that sometimes you think that something like a cherry is bad for you all the time when really it might not be that bad but you've got to try it out to see. The end.

Joey's story ended with the implication that he was going to let his unfortunate experience with cherries "sour" him on them for the rest of his life. To help him avoid a celibate existence, which some flee to in response to oedipal anxieties, I introduce other, less threatening cherry companions to him (while the heavy cherry action is going on outside). My story ends with his eating a few and realizing that cherries aren't so bad after all.

One thought of celibacy doesn't make a misogamist. One fantasy does not make a disease. I had no real fear that Joey had any significant inclination toward a misogynistic adaptation to the oedipal conflict. Everyone is entitled to a little regression as therapy approaches termination and this, I believe, is the significance of Joey's removing himself from the field of battle.

Regarding the resolution of oedipal conflicts, one final point should be made. The term "resolution" implies a final working through, a complete solution, a coming to peace with one's oedipus complex. I think that the more one has been deprived, the less the likelihood that one can fully resolve his reactions to early deprivations. All patients, I believe, regardless of their pathology and the length and success of their treatment, still never give up completely the attempt to get one more drop of milk out of an empty breast. Often, the breast has been far more freely flowing than the patient realizes. The child is ill-appreciative of the efforts of his parents and of the time and energy involved in his upbringing. He recalls more often the frustrations and the deprivations. The child's hypercritical attitude toward his parents is further intensified by his projection of his own hostilities onto them. Because of this projection he perceives them as far more malevolent than they really are. Even when he becomes a parent himself, after he has had the opportunity to view the parent-child relationship from another vantage point, he tends to maintain and preserve his own childhood distortions.

What about the so-called "normal" people (whoever they are and whatever that means); those out there whom therapists never see; those whose life adjustments are good? My guess is that they too never completely cease trying to please their mother and father and gain their approbation. In their minds' eye, even when they are old and *their* parents have long since died, thoughts like "My mother would have been proud of me for this," or "I'm glad my father wasn't alive when that happened; he would have never forgiven me," still persist. For the first five years of life, children endlessly seek their parents' approval, and for the next ten to fifteen they are still significantly dependent on it. I do not believe that such "programming" can ever be completely erased.

9. ANGER INHIBITION PROBLEMS

The words anger, hostility, and aggression are often used interchangeably in psychiatric literature. Although there is some overlap in their meanings, there are also differences which must be made clear.

Anger often connotes an internal state, whereas hostility implies externally directed action. We speak of hostility between nations, but not of anger. The word anger can often convey a greater intensity of expression than the term hostility. One would more likely say, "He was so angry that he felt his head would split," than "He was so hostile that he felt that his head would split."

Aggression can, on the one hand, be used in a complimentary sense when it means assertive: "This organization is looking for aggressive young men." On the other hand, when such aggression results in insensitivity to the feelings of others or when people are hurt, the word is definitely perjorative: "He's so aggressive, he doesn't care about who he pushes aside to get what he wants." At other times aggression is used as if it were synonymous with anger or hostility. Because of the confusion that this word sometimes creates, I try to avoid it and instead use assertive, or self-assertive, for desirable aggression, and otherwise use anger or hostility.

Anger has two components: the psychic, which includes both angry thoughts — what the brain is thinking — and the affect, anger — what the brain is feeling; and the physiologic, which includes concomitant body reactions such as changes in blood pressure, respiratory rate, and pulse rate. The physical constituent is certainly inherent, and identical responses can be seen and measured in many animals. Many higher animals also appear to be experiencing the psychic factor as well, and the tendency toward anthropomorphization often leads to the questionable assumption that they are feeling angry affect and even thinking angry thoughts.

Anger has survival value, and it is possible that it is innate. Anger builds up when there is frustration and helplessness, and it is reduced when the irritants are removed. This same anger can help to remove noxious stimuli. As long as the painful stimulus is there, anger will be provoked and increased — resulting in even more intense emotional reactions.

In seeking to dissipate his anger, man often employs maladaptive mechanisms. This is especially true of the anger-fight reaction. He may, for example, drop to his knees and pray to unseen forces for help when confronted by an enemy. Or he may direct his anger at friends who could be of assistance. Sometimes he displaces his anger upon inanimate objects (such as a nearby tree or wall), or he may totally deny the existence of anger within himself by repressing it and pretending nothing is threatening or wrong. He may direct it toward symbols of the enemy (voodooism); or he may sublimate his anger and discharge it through sports and artistic endeavours if the danger is not immediately life-threatening. He may in some cases direct his anger toward himself and commit suicide.

One of the purposes of therapy is to help the patient avoid utilizing such maladaptive reactions to anger. He is encouraged to use his anger efficaciously to deal with threatening situations and noxious stimuli. This can best be described with an example and associated paradigms:

A man gets a splinter in his finger and removes it quickly. He feels better.

Noxious stimulus + Removal →
Pleasurable relief of pain

If the splinter is too deep for him to remove it with his own fingernails, the man feels frustrated.

> Noxious stimulus + Inability to
> remove it → Frustration

The frustration serves to stimulate increased efforts to remove the noxious stimulus. He gets a pair of tweezers, takes out the splinter, and then feels all right.

> Frustration + Early removal of noxious stimulus →
> Pleasurable relief of pain + Cessation of frustration

If he cannot find a pair of tweezers his frustration increases and he gets angry: "This God-damn splinter is painful. Where the hell's a pair of tweezers?"

> Frustration + Continual inability to
> remove noxious stimulus → Anger

So angered, he is mobilized to act further. He goes next door, borrows a pair of tweezers from his neighbor, and takes out the splinter.

> Anger + Removal of noxious stimulus → Pleasurable
> relief of pain + Cessation of anger

Suppose his neighbor has a pair of tweezers, but refuses to lend them. The pain and anger continue and now there are additional feelings of helplessness. His anger changes to rage — the feeling that comes with profound impotence over removal of a chronic noxious stimulus.

> Anger + Prolonged impotence in removing
> a noxious stimulus → Rage

The rage reaction has a purpose. It's a last ditch stand. With it, irrational things are done which are in the service of removing the noxious stimulus, but which are often misguided. He rants and becomes abusive. Even if the neighbor then gives him a pair of tweezers, he suffers consequences such as embarrassment and the need to make apologies. The anger reaction is co-ordinated and directed toward a specific goal. The rage reaction is more chaotic and is less likely to be effective. Even when it is, the slate is usually not then wiped clean. There are usually untoward side effects after its utilization.

Rage + Removal of noxious stimulus → Pleasurable relief of pain + Untoward Side Effects

Fury is sometimes used to describe a degree of rage in which the inappropriate reaction reaches psychotic proportions, whereas rage is more typically neurotic. The enraged man with the splinter, who then rampages through his neighbor's house, attacking and possibly even killing his neighbor, would be considered to be in a fury. The rage has been so deranging that he has become psychotic.

Rage + Prolonged exposure to noxious stimulus → Fury

Therapeutic efforts should be directed toward helping patients remove noxious stimuli at the earliest possoble time. The sicker the patient, the greater the likelihood that he is not effectively dealing with noxious stimuli early enough and that he is harboring unexpressed anger, rage, and even fury.

Since life inevitably exposes us to noxious stimuli, anger is ubiquitous. However, the survival of society depends on a significant degree of anger inhibition. Over the millennia man has evolved various systems for protecting himself from those whose unbridled expression of anger would endanger him. The most widely efficacious system is guilt. It is very efficient because the individual deters himself from performing the hostile act and others need be less guarded. I have described elsewhere[1] the stages the child goes through in developing a sense of guilt.

Since murder is such an irreversible destructive act, society has had to utilize the most powerful mechanisms to prevent its unbridled expression. Religions have long been of service in providing ways to help man inhibit emotions which are potentially dangerous to himself and others. Religious methods have relied heavily on the guilt mechanism. However helpful the guilt deterrent has been, I believe that it has been misapplied, misdirected, and used in excess. Since anger can lead to rage, then fury, and then murder, many religions have interdicted all the low milder forms of anger as a safety measure against the expression of the violent forms. This is somewhat like banning the use of fire because it can get out of hand; or prohibiting the production of electrical power because occasionally someone gets electrocuted. Fire and electricity are certainly useful and so is anger. It need not be lethal.

Anger must be harnessed and used to help deal with life's frustrations. Children must not be taught that there are good folk somewhere who are never angry. They must not be filled with guilt over the inevitable angry feelings that they have.

The children I see in my practice are products of this heritage and it is no surprise that problems around the expression of anger are common, if not the most common. More stories elicited with the Mutual Storytelling Technique deal with the expression of anger than any other theme. Ames and Pitcher and Prelinger (previously discussed in Chapter 5) found anger to be the predominate theme in the stories they elicited from children.[2]

Such findings are not surprising. The child is continually exposed to frustrations. He is bombarded with: "Don't do this." and "Don't do that." No surprise then that he suffers many frustrations and resentments. He cannot overtly express them for fear of invoking even further criticism from his parents, especially if they believe that he should not be having any angry reactions to their restrictions. He can neither flee nor fight, and so he develops one or more maladaptations: he denies and represses his anger (with the help of his minister and Sunday School teacher); he sublimates it (plays "war"); he displaces it (hits his brother); he releases it vicariously (watches horror stories on television); and he projects it ("It's his fault." "Kids always pick on me."). His dreams and fantasies symbolically allow release of his anger and are a powerful and effective form of substitutive gratification because no one can stop him from them. They are things which he truly has all to himself.

456

The analysis of a nightmare can serve as a useful model for understanding many of the child's hostilty fantasies and stories. In the typical nightmare the child is fearful that a malevolent figure (a robber, a monster, etc.) will enter his room. Usually the intruder comes in from a window, or closet, or from under the bed. I believe that the interloper is the incarnation of the child's unacceptable angry impulses which have been relegated to the unconscious. At night, when other distracting stimuli are removed, the pent-up hostilities of the day, which continually press for expression, are attended to. Daytime activities such as sports, sibling fights, and television, which have provided some release of hostility, are no longer available. At night, residual hostility from unresolved daytime frustrations pressure for release. In the nightmare, the symbolic derivatives of the child's anger (the robber, etc.) press for expression in the child's conscious awareness (by trying to get into the child's room). The greater the child's guilt over his anger, the more it will be repressed. The urgency for release becomes correspondingly greater, as does his fear of the anger symbols when they threaten to erupt into conscious awareness. Up to a point, the more guilt-ridden the child, the more frightening the nightmare. When the guilt is extremely great, however, even the symbolic incarnations will be repressed, and the child will be "protected" from his nightmares.

The Mutual Storytelling Technique can be extremely useful in helping children with anger inhibition problems. Many of the children's stories thus far presented deal with anger problems. Those presented in this chapter demonstrate specifically the ways in which I help alleviate their difficulties with my stories. The approach presupposes the validity of the notions and theories about anger just presented. Work with parents is especially vital here. They are the ones who have transmitted social and cultural inhibitions to the child. The greater their flexibility in changing their ideas about anger, the greater the likelihood that the child will change his. They must be helped to tolerate the child's appropriate angry expression and hopefully change their own ways regarding its use.

Example 1

Joey, the boy with enuresis and nightmares, told many stories in which the theme of anger inhibition was central. During his fifteenth month of treatment, two months prior to termination, he told this story:

Patient: Could you just start me off?
Therapist: Can I just help you?
Patient: Yeah.
Therapist: Okay. You know, Joey tells excellent stories. He just feels a little lack of confidence about telling them. Usually once I get it started with him he does very well. It was a long, long time ago, longer than even your great-grandfather's great-grandfather could remember; in fact, even his great-grandfather couldn't remember that and it was extremely far away. It was so far away that it would take about three years if you wanted to walk there and if you wanted to run, it would take at least two. You would have to swim a lot to get there also because it was so far away beyond the oceans and you'd have to climb a lot of mountains because it's way above and beyond the mountains. So in this distant place, very far away, a long time ago, there lived a ——
Patient: A pelican.
Therapist: And this pelican ——
Patient: Wasn't very nice.
Therapist: He was not very nice. Well, here we have this not very nice pelican who ——
Patient: Ate every fish he saw.
Therapist: And so?
Patient: The fishes hated him.
Therapist: The fishes hated him and so?
Patient: I don't know what to say.
Therapist: Well, what did they do? Here we have this situation where you have this pelican going around eating every single fish and here you have these fishes who hate him because he's eating them up. So what happens next?
Patient: I guess they would plan to kill him.

Therapist: They are going to kill him. They plan to kill him. Okay. Now, what's going to happen then? This is getting to be more interesting.

Patient: I don't know. If it was so far back I don't know what would have happened.

Therapist: This is only a made-up story. Your mind can go back that far. Let's try to figure it out now. Here we have this pelican who is not a very nice guy and he's eating up all these fish. The fish, of course, are very angry that he's doing this and so in response they plan to kill him. Now what happens?

Patient: He tries to get out of the land.

Therapist: He tries to get out of the land. Okay, because they are going to kill him. Well, what happened next?

Patient: After a few miles he just remembered that they couldn't kill him.

Therapist: Then after a few — good, you are doing very well — miles he realizes that they can't kill him because ——

Patient: Because they can't really fight very well and they can't hurt him.

Therapist: Wait a minute. They can't kill him because — you mean that the fishes can't kill this pelican because ——

Patient: He would really just fly away from them.

Therapist: Because he can just fly away. Oh, I see, because he can just fly away. Okay. So?

Patient: He comes back.

Therapist: He returns. Yeah?

Patient: And they find out they can't kill him.

Therapist: Yeah. They find out they can't. Yeah?

Patient: So he keeps on eating them.

Therapist: He keeps on eating them. Uh-huh. Then what happens?

Patient: That's the end.

Therapist: And the lesson of that story is?

Patient: Don't be a scaredy cat.

Therapist: Don't be a scaredy cat. Thank you very much, Joey. That was another one of your excellent stories. For a kid who really thinks he has trouble telling stories, you certainly do very well. And now it's time for me to tell my story.

The fish in the water represent repressed unconscious complexes. They can come out of the dark depths and kill him. The extrusion of his unacceptable thoughts and feelings into conscious awareness is dangerous. In my experience, swarms of little animals, vermin, etc., which cause anxiety in dreams, are often representations of repressed unconscious complexes which threaten to erupt into conscious awareness. Since the pelican's primary danger is that the fish can kill him, I knew that the repressed material was Joey's anger. The boy's first reaction is to run — a response consistent with the timidity and generalized anxiety he showed at the beginning of treatment. But Joey is aware that he cannot be harmed by his thoughts. So he returns and eats the fish. By incorporating them into himself, Joey demonstrates a most intimate kind of involvement and acceptance of what was previously considered dangerous.

The story epitomizes Joey's changed attitude toward his repressed anger. At first, he tried to repress and deny it, but as treatment progressed he became more comfortable with the hostility which resided within himself. In response, I told this story:

A long, long time ago in that same distant place where your pelican lived, there was a boy and he used to have coming into his mind, angry thoughts. It was as if his mind were like the fishes in your story. Instead of the fishes coming from the sea to eat up the pelican and hurt him, in this boy's mind his angry thoughts would jump up and scare him. He was scared of his angry thoughts because he thought that they would really come true.

In other words, if he had a thought that he wished that his father were dead — every kid thas a thought like this once in a while — he was frightened because he thought that that meant that his father would die. He thought that thoughts themselves could do harm. That's what he thought, and when these angry thoughts would jump into his mind, like fishes jumping out of the sea at the pelican, he would become very frightened and he would say, "How terrible. Maybe my father is going to die or maybe my mother is going to die. I have such angry thoughts toward them." He thought that thoughts could harm a person. He started to run but you can't run from your own mind. And then he began to wonder. What do you think he wondered?

Patient: I don't have any idea.

Therapist: Well, he said, "Is it really true that thoughts can harm?" That was the question. What do you think? Can thoughts harm?

Patient: No.

Therapist: How do you know that?

Patient: We spoke about it here.

Therapist: Are you sure thoughts can't harm?

Patient: What?

Therapist: Are you sure about that? Are you sure that thoughts cannot harm?

Patient: Yeah.

Therapist: When you first came to see me did you think that thoughts could harm?

Patient: Yes.

Therapist: You did think that thoughts could harm?

Patient: And I heard yesterday that they didn't.

Therapist: Uh-huh. When did I tell you that?

Patient: I don't remember but I think you did.

Therapist: Do you remember what kind of thoughts you had that you thought would harm?

Patient: No.

Therapist: But you did think thoughts could harm. Thoughts can't harm. And then this boy gradually realized that thoughts can't harm and he saw, like your pelican saw that the fish in the sea couldn't really hurt him. He could even eat them and they wouldn't bother him. So he realized that he could keep the thoughts inside himself and he realized that thoughts themselves cannot harm and they would do him no harm either. He spoke to other kids and he found out that they, too, had angry thoughts like this once in a while. Then he decided to do something about the thing that he was angry about so he wouldn't be angry anymore. So he did that and lived happily ever after. Once in a while he would have an angry thought but he realized that that's normal but when he learned that they didn't do any harm he felt better. Do you know what the moral of my story is? You try to figure out the moral.

Patient: I don't know.

Therapist: Well, what's the main message, the main lesson of my story?

Patient: Thoughts can't harm.

Therapist: Right. That's the moral. Thoughts can't harm. I'll write that down. The second moral is: if you have angry thoughts, try to find out what they're all about and try to do something about them. The end. Do you want to say something about this story?

Patient: No.

Therapist: I want to ask you a question. What did you think of this story?

Patient: Fine. It was very good.

Therapist: You liked it. Good.

In Joey's story, the new freedom with anger is expressed in symbolic form. In the context of my story, I presented him with an analysis of his. This sequence is a good example of how the Mutual Storytelling Technique can be used to bridge the gap between the child's story and its analysis. Joey's story was told in the late phase of his treatment and he had already shown himself to be quite comfortable with his hostility. I would not have told a story like this in the early phase of therapy with a child who was still quite anxious over his hostility.

Example 2

Steve, the boy with school disciplinary difficulties, had many problems regarding anger inhibition. Both psychogenic and organic factors contributed to his difficulties in this area. The poor impulse control associated with his organic deficit made it quite difficult for him to control his angry outbursts,

462

yet he was basically inhibited over expressing hostility and would loathe himself after his displays. The story he told about the monster whose fire was internalized is a good example of his anger inhibition problem.

During his second month of treatment, Steve told this story:

All right. I'll just give the title. Okay? I'll tell you a story about Jack Annori — Jack Annori — and now my story's begun. I'll tell you another about his brother. Now my story's done. That's the title. It's a silly title.

Therapist: Okay.

Patient: Now once there was a — now this is really made up. Nobody has told this to me and I haven't read it.

Once upon a time there was a boy named Jack Annori and he lived happily (*mumbles*).

Therapist: You know, you are mumbling. He lived happily what, among what?

Patient: In a castle. There were turrets and lots of houses to rule. There was only one thing wrong. The castle had a dragon named Sarah. This dragon named Sarah burned up a lot of things and nobody could see her because she was invisible, except Jack Annori.

One day Jack Annori cut down a tree. Jack Annori really didn't. The dragon did. And he burned up the grass, but the dragon did that too. The dragon had cut down the tree and burned up the grass for the campfire.

Therapist: The dragon cut down the tree and burned up the grass.

Patient: Yeah. Jack Annori then tried to find a way to make the dragon visible. So he went to a wise woman who was up on the top of the mountain — on top of the highest mountain. And he had to use a chunk of magic rock to get up there.

Then the wise woman told him to pour some poison on the dragon's face. He did this gladly and then everybody saw it (the dragon) and then they saw the dragon burn up the grass and the fields.

Therapist: Wait a minute. The boy threw poison in the

dragon's face and it became visible from the poison. Is that it?

Patient: Yeah. Then everybody saw him burn up the grass and burn down the trees. Finally the brave, brave knight, Sir Gordon, came and killed the dragon. Then nothing happened to Jack Annori again and he lived happily ever after. And if there is another dragon there, why? The grass is still burning.

Therapist: What's that last part?

Patient: If there still is another dragon there why the grass is still burning.

Therapist: Wait. If there's another dragon there, the grass is still burning?

Patient: Yeah! Red hot! That means all the grass is red.

Therapist: Well, I don't understand that last part, what that means exactly.

Patient: It means, like, for instance, if another dragon came back and started burning the grass, the grass would turn red.

Therapist: I see. What's the lesson of that story?

Patient: The lesson of the story: invisibly doesn't help. You know why Jack Annori threw the poison into his face?

Therapist: No.

Patient: He was the only one who could see the dragon.

Therapist: I see. And this really doesn't help because —

Patient: Because somebody else can see you —— if somebody else can see you.

And now I'd like to say a few words to you. First of all, can we change schedules again.

Therapist: Why? What do you want to do? I'm not clear.

Patient: Are we going to change the schedule to Wednesday?

Therapist: No, I'm going to be seeing you again on Thursday.

Patient: Well, I'll be seeing you on Thursday folks. That's all and here and now we'd like to have Dr. Gardner speak. But first can we play over my story?

Therapist: Okay.

I believe that the female dragon symbolizes Steve's mother as well as his own projected hostility. Although the patient's mother was a somewhat intellectualized woman with a repressed anger problem herself, she was not the massively destructive creature depicted in the story. I was not exactly sure of the meaning of the tree and grass symbols. Possibly the mother's cutting down the tree reflects his view of her as castrating (in the broad sense of depriving men of their manliness). The grass, then, possibly represents the father's pubic hair. The exact meaning of the tree and grass symbols, however, is not as important as the more general fact that he sees his mother as dangerous to his life and property.

His mother is invisible to all but him. Perhaps this relates to his feeling that others do not see his mother as being as hostile as she appears to him, or that her hostility is camouflaged and not easily recognized. There was some truth to this; the mother even hid her hostility from herself. If his mother were made visible, then she would be less of a threat. It's hard to fight an enemy you can't see. If her hostility were more overt; if she were less repressed, then Steve would have a better chance to defend himself against her. However, the potion, which he uses to make her visible, is also a poison. This enables him to express his hostility toward her by poisoning her while at the same time performing a public service by making her visible for all to see. The poison, interestingly, does not exert its lethal effects. Steve is too guilty over his anger to let it work. This dirty work is left to "the brave, brave, knight, Sir Gordon." Gordon is close enough to Gardner to warrant the interpretation that Steve is referring to his therapist who does what he fears to do. However, the mother arises phoenix-like from death as another threatening dragon. Many factors, I believe, are operative in her reincarnation: he assuages his guilt over her murder by bringing her back to life. He is ambivalent about her death; he still loves and is dependent on her. And lastly, what he sees as mother's anger (symbolized by the dragon) cannot be totally obliterated since a part of it is his own projected hostility. The dragon's reappearance then reflects his appreciation, at some level, that it cannot be expunged externally because part of it exists within himself.

With this understanding of Steve's story, I related mine:

Once upon a time there was a boy and his name was Jack Annori.

Patient: The same name might get them nervous.

Therapist: No. Same boy but different things happen. He lived in the olden times and he lived in a castle with turrets and there were houses around. Now he lived with his mother and his —

Patient (loudly): M-e-o-w.

Therapist: Come on now. You want to play this game?

Patient: I wasn't meowing into the speaker. I wasn't. I really wasn't meowing.

Therapist: Do you want to play this game or not?

Patient: Okay.

Therapist: He lived with his mother and his father and at times his mother and his father —

Patient: It's boring when I have to listen to it when I am dying of hunger.

Therapist: All right. You want to interrupt first and get a doughnut or something and then we'll come back?

Patient: After the story is okay.

Therapist: Okay this boy was —

Patient: I don't like to interrupt.

Therapist: Okay, no more interruptions now. After my story we'll go to the kitchen and see if we can find a doughnut or something. Now do you want to listen or not?

Patient: I was just sliding down.

Therapist: You're blowing into your microphone. Give me the microphone.

Now this boy lived with his mother and his father and at times they would do things which got him very angry and he would get very angry and think of things like cutting down trees or sometimes he wished that he was a dragon and had fire that he could burn down the fields and everything like that. He used to walk around furious all the time.

Then one day a friend of his came over. His name was Sir Gordon. Sir Gordon said, "What are you looking so angry about?" He said, "Oh, the things my parents do that bother me." Sir Gordon said, "Well, why don't you tell them?" He replied, "Oh, no, I can't tell them." Then Sir Gordon said, "Let me tell you something. If you don't tell them, you're just going to walk around angry all the time. I bet you feel like a dragon." The boy said, "How did you know?" Sir Gordon said, "I know how it is with anger. When something bothers you and you don't let it out it just stays inside of you and builds up. You feel like a dragon. You're so angry." The boy said, "That's true. I feel like burning down fields with fire and I feel like cutting down trees." Sir Gordon said, "Yes, I know the feeling. That's the feeling I get when I'm angry at someone for something and I don't tell them what I am angry about. Then I begin to feel like a dragon inside me. I feel like doing cruel things. But if you tell the person what bothers you, then they may be able to change things to a certain amount and then you'll feel less angry."

Well, the boy decided to try to do that. He went to his parents and he spoke to them about the things that made him angry and what do you think happened?

Patient: I cannot guess, but somehow they solved his problems I suppose.

Therapist: Right. And then was he angry?

Patient: 'Tain't likely.

Therapist: What do you think the lesson of that story is?

Patient: Was it this? Don't be angry.

Therapist: No. That is not the lesson of that story.

Patient (angrily): Well, you could tell the lesson yourself! (*shouting*) You're the moraler aren't you? Aren't you the author started it (*quite upset*)?

Therapist: I am, but I want to see how smart you are in figuring out the lesson of my story. Now what do you think this boy learned — this boy, Jack Annori? What do you think he learned in my story?

Patient: He felt like a dragon on account of he was angry.

Therapist: Right! That's the lesson. You can figure it out.

When you're angry about something, tell the person who you are angry at and then if they can fix the thing and change it you won't be so angry and you won't feel like a dragon.

Steve's comment: "The same name might get them [the television audience] nervous" reveals his own anxiety about my forthcoming story. Seconds later, as soon as I mentioned his mother, he had to interrupt me out of his anxiety. My response: "You want to play this game?" gave him the opportunity to stop if his level of tension was too high. He chose to continue, but he then interrupted because it was "boring." Expressions of boredom are a common manifestation of anxiety. In this instance, Steve also wanted to assuage his tension with a little oral gratification. This was offered but refused by him.

Steve finally settled down enough to listen to my story. In it, I tried to touch upon the two central elements in his depicting his mother as a destructive dragon: 1) Her repressed hostility and 2) his projected hostility. His hostility was projected rather than expressed in the service of his getting greater gratifications from his mother. In my story I discussed the dragon within him as well as the dragon within her. Also in my story, I did not kill the dragon, but rather advised a course of action which might obviate its formation: if he were to express his resentments to his mother, she might change somewhat and she would thereby be less dragonlike. Also, he would then be less angry; there would be less anger to project, and the dragon qualities within his mother might be further reduced.

I did not feel, while telling my story, that Steve was fully appreciating its significance. My doubts were confirmed when he said that the lesson of my story was "Don't be angry." He was clearly suggesting repression of anger (his old *modus operandi*), rather than effective expression of it. When I tried to bring him to reconsider my story and try again to surmise its moral, he became instantaneously furious. This was a common occurrence with Steve. In spite of his rage I persisted. I might not have if Steve's outburst had been purely psychogenic. Steve's bark was worse than his bite. He was much less fearful and anxious than might be surmised from his overt behavior. His organic disinhibition made things look much worse than they really were. My efforts finally proved successful, and he accurately related the moral: "He felt like a dragon on account of he was angry."

Example 3

Nancy, the girl with disruptive behavior in the classroom, temper tantrums, and excessive masturbation, was about six when she told this story near the end of her second course of therapy:

Once upon a time there was a little girl and she was two years old. The girl was two years old and she went out and she saw a statute and she got scared because she thought it was real. She thought it was real, when they were going to the park.
Therapist: Okay. Then what happened?
Patient: Then they saw a gorilla. There's a few zoos there. It was summer and there were a few pools.
Therapist: It was summer and there were a few pools. Yes?
Patient: And they were, um, and the gorilla was very wild so they kept him in a cage. They played in the —— they played and they played, they played when they were at the pool and there was a little brother and he was, and they were twins. They were both two. She took her little brother and her mother pushed the little girl and her brother. And then they were —— they uh, you know where? There was a hotel and there was a lot of rooms there.
Therapist: Yeah.
Patient: And there was so much people and so they all went to sleep. They were so quiet.
The gorilla was so strong. He punched the cage of the bars and they broke and he sneaked over very quietly and he peeked into a window. Everybody was asleep. So he went and picked the house up and put them in fire.

And they smelled it and they ran out. They didn't know the gorilla did it. So they called the firemen and then they were going to call the firemen and then the firemen put out the fire. And the gorilla tried to —— then the gorilla picked one of the children up. He was —— he only killed. He was a bad gorilla because he didn't know if they were bad —— if they were bad people or not because he didn't want to be in a cage. So he carried —— they looked and he didn't hurt her. So he be nice and gentle to everybody and then they were going to, you know, they were going to do something and the gorilla had to stay in the cage because if the gorilla stayed out so long he would do something bad. Also because there was a fair there and it was so pretty and they went and it was not over. It lasted until the morning and then everybody slept in the morning because this is only a story, you know.

Therapist: All right. Then what happened?

Patient: They were going to —— then it was nighttime again. Then they woke up and every night there was a fair there. So they kept going to it and then the gorillas tried to run and whoever gets —— whoever jumps through the middle wins. Then they came and jumped through the middle and every time they were going to ——then they shot arrows and whoever got it in the middle winned. And then they were asked for pies and cakes and everybody was happy and then there was more. Then they went to sleep and then it was nighttime.

Therapist: Okay. Now is that the end of the story? Finish up the story.

Patient: Okay, and then, and then ——

Therapist: How did it end?

Patient: Then they lived happily ever after and when the girl ever saw a statute she wouldn't be scared. That's the end of this story.

Therapist: And then when she saw a statue she wasn't scared. You forgot the lesson of that story.

Patient: Ooohh yeah! And the lesson is whenever she is in fire she runs out and whenever they hear the noise of the house bump and the gorilla they would look out the window and see the fire and then.

Therapist: What's the lesson learned from that story?

Patient: Oh! The lesson is: when she ever sees a statute she will not be scared and she will touch it and look at it.

Therapist: And? And what? When she sees a statue she won't be scared?

Patient: Yeah. That's the lesson.

Therapist: The lesson is: don't be scared of a statue.

Patient: Yeah. If you see one.

Therapist: I see. Okay. That was a very good story. Now it's time for me to tell my story.

The gorilla represents Nancy's repressed hostility. By breaking out of its cage and wreaking havoc, the gorilla represents what Nancy fears will happen if she releases her repressed anger. All good times and pleasant experiences (fun at fairs) would come to an end and instead fires would be set, houses would be picked up, and children would be killed. The statue is similar to the caged gorilla. She says that "she saw a statute and she got scared because she thought it was real." As long as it remains a statue it is safe, but if it becomes live, it can be dangerous. Emotions are safest when they are caged, immobilized, and static.

In response, I told this story:

Once upon a time there was a little girl and she lived at home with her mother and her father and sometimes her mother and father would do things that would get her mad. When she got mad it was like she had gorillas inside her or it was like she had dangerous statues inside of her — things that would rumble up inside of her and make her very angry. She thought that it was a terrible thing to be angry. She didn't know that when you are angry at someone, you should tell them what you are angry about, that you shouldn't act like a gorilla or an angry statue, but you should tell them directly what you are angry about and then you won't be so angry. So each time her mother did something that she didn't like, she didn't let angry gorillas build up inside her and then she told her mother in the beginning exactly what was bothering her and when she did that she didn't have big angry gorillas building up inside of her to make her frightened.

Do you know what the lesson of that story is? What?

Patient: When you are angry and the best way to help you stop acting like a gorilla or a statute is inside you, or you should tell your mother.

Therapist: Tell your mother what?

Patient: That you are angry and that you would feel better.

Therapist: Yes. Also you would tell her what it is you are angry about so that she can change it. You understand? For instance, this little girl once wanted to go to her friend's house and her mother said no because her mother thought that the friend was sick. Well, she got very angry and she started acting like a gorilla and she would scream and yell because her mother didn't know that this girl really wasn't sick. When she told her mother that she wasn't sick, her mother called up the other girl's mother and sure enough she was all better, so then she could go and then she wasn't angry anymore. So, if something bothers you, tell your mother. Don't let it build up inside you because then it gets to be like a gorilla. Okay?

Patient: I asked my Mommy.

Therapist: What did you ask your Mommy?

Patient: If I could go to my friend's house.

Therapist: Good.

The meaning of my story is obvious. I equated the gorilla with repressed anger and encouraged her to effectively express it.

I would like to mention here an important consideration regarding the expression of anger and what I mean by "*effectively* expressing it." Freud at first considered abreaction and catharsis, the expression of pent-up feelings, to be therapeutic in itself. Although he later realized that things were not so simple, a large body of subsequent therapists (Woltmann,[3] Hartley,[4] and Arlow,[5] to mention a few) hold the view that mere expression of feelings in itself can be therapeutic. Children are encouraged to throw sand, hit punching bags, smear paint, scream, and batter the walls. Although I believe that these modalities have a place in child therapy it goes far beyond their mere use as cathartic catalysts. Others, such as Baruch,[6] Rogers,[7] and Axline,[8] concentrate on the therapist's helping the child express his feelings verbally. "That must have made you very sad when the children didn't show up to your birthday party," and "You must feel terrible, having to repeat the third grade," for example, are comments which make good starting points. The child must be encouraged, however, to use his feelings to remove his pains or else he will only consider such comments patronizing and irritating.

If a girl's parents are divorced and her father does not show up for appointed visits, what good will it do her to clobber a hunk of clay or to be told it must make her feel very sad that her father hasn't shown up. She needs to express her resentment to her father, in the hope that he will then be more punctual. If she is successful, then she will no longer be angry over this problem. If she is not, then she will continue to be angry until she resigns herself to this particular defect in her father (whatever assets he may have). She must, *in addition*, obtain substitutive gratifications from others such as friends, counselors, and scout leaders. Then she will no longer be angry over this problem. Therefore, when I use the term "effective expression of anger," I refer to this more comprehensive use, not mere shouting to the winds.

Example 4

Tom, an eight-and-a-half-year-old boy, was referred for treatment because of poor motivation in school, difficulty in forming friendships, and obstructionism at home. His father was away on business trips for weeks at a time and his mother was a somewhat simple woman, who was quite dependent on her maid and housekeeper. She exhibited passive-aggressive and passive-dependent personality disturbances.

During his second month of treatment, Tom told this story:

Therapist: Once upon a time a long, long, long time ago, in a distant land, far, far far away, beyond the oceans, beyond the deserts, beyond the mountains, there lived a ——

Patient: A fish. And this fish was a little fish and he had no friends and he used to ——

Therapist: He used to what?

Patient: He was the littlest fish in the ocean, and he had no mommy and daddy and he was mean.

Therapist: He had no mommy and daddy?

Patient: Yeah, and he was mean and he didn't know anything. He didn't go to school and he was very, very sad. One day he was looking at the school — they had a little pretend school there — and he was looking into the window and saw that all the fishes were there. He felt sorry because he couldn't come and he was very mean when the children would come out. He used to throw rocks at them and beat the people up. He used to be mean and he used to scare them.

So one day this man who fished up this fish said, "Why do you always go around schools bothering them, scaring them, beating everybody up?" And he says, "I don't know." And he said, "Well, I don't know anything and I want to go to school and I haven't any mommy and daddy." And the big fish said, "Well, why don't you go to the principal's office and then maybe he could let you come in because this is a public school and anybody can come in?"

So one day he went when school started and he asked the principal and he said, "Sure you can come in." And he went and he learned and he wasn't bad anymore. And he learned not to do anything bad anymore. The end.

Therapist: And the lesson?

Patient: You should always ask, you know, if you want to do something.

Therapist: Now what were the bad things this fish was doing?

Patient: He was fighting and he was scaring the children and he was beating them up and he was ——

474

Therapist: Why was he doing all those things?

Patient: Because he didn't know anybody and I think he was mean because he didn't have any mommy and everybody was calling him names.

Therapist: Because he didn't have a mommy?

Patient: Yeah, or a daddy.

Therapist: Okay. Now it's time for me to tell my story.

The story reflects Tom's awareness, at some level, that his angry feelings are reactive to his own parental deprivation. So rejected, he feels small and worthless — "He was the littlest fish in the ocean." He displaces his rage onto other fish — "He used to throw rocks at them and beat the people up." He then makes what superficially could be considered a healthy adjustment to his parents' abandonment, he goes to school. If he had found substitutive relationships with friends at school, and thereby reduced his anger, I would have considered the adjustment healthy. However, the improvement in his social behavior comes about by learning in school "not to do anything bad anymore." This is a repressive adaptation; there is no working through; and there is no course of action which gets to the roots of the problem. Accordingly, I told this story:

Once upon a time there was a fish and this fish was sad and lonely. The reason this fish was sad and lonely was because he didn't have a mother or a father. He was very angry about that and so he used to go around bullying kids and beating them up and fighting and really being bad.

Then he decided that maybe if he goes to school that will make him better. So he went to school, but to his surprise that still didn't make him better. He was still very angry and he was still trying to go around beating up kids.

Then one day he was speaking to an older fish. The older fish said to him, "Why are you beating up all those kids all the time? What does that accomplish?" He said, "I'm mad because I don't have a mother and a father." The big fish said, "Gee, that's too bad that you don't have a mother and father, but what do you accomplish by beating up little kids?" He said, "Well, it makes me less mad.

I feel good when I beat 'em up." The fish said, "Do you feel perfectly good? Are you perfectly fine after that? Is everything okay after you beat up little kids?" He said, "No, I still feel kind of mad 'cause I still don't have a mother or father." He said, "Do you feel better now that you are going to school?" He answered, "Not particularly. Education has not helped me that much. They keep teaching me not to be bad, but I still am." The older fish said, "Well, what can you do?" The little fish said, "I don't know what to do." The other fish said, "If you're mad at your mother and father because you don't have one —— where are they?" "Ah," he said, "they're off in some other part of the lake." He said, "Well, why don't you go over and speak to them? Find them and tell them that you are mad that you don't see them."

So the fish went over and he spoke to his mother and father and they weren't too interested in spending time with him, but they did say that they would spend a little bit didn't satisfy him because they didn't spend enough time with him and then he felt a little bit less mad. But that still more time with him. So they spent a little more time with him to make him really feel good. So he went back to the big fish and he said, "Well, you were right. Your advice that I speak to them helped a little bit because they were able to give me a little bit of time, and I'm glad I spoke up, but I still feel kind of angry so I think I'd better go back and beat up some more kids." The big fish said, "Well, that's not going to solve anything." The little fish said, "Well, what else can I do?" The big fish said, "Well, you think about it. You're going to school now, right?" The little fish said, "Yes." "Well, who do you find there in school?" He replied, "Well, there are other kids." "Do you play with them?" He said, "Not too much." So the big fish said, "Well, do you think they could be of any help to you? Do you think you could do anything with them that might help you?" The little fish thought about it and what do you think he said?

Patient: I don't know.

Therapist: Well, he thought of something. He thought:
"Maybe if I play with them I'll feel less bad about the

fact that I don't have my mother and father too much and if I stop fighting with them and enjoy them and have a good time with them, then maybe I won't feel so bad."

So he tried that out, and he played with them, had a good time with them, and then felt less lonely about his mother and his father. Then he was less angry and he didn't go around beating up kids anymore.

Do you know the lessons of that story? There are two lessons.

Patient: You should talk to somebody when you have a problem and ——

Therapist: The other one is that if people you want to love you can't give you that much love or time or affection or friendliness, then go to others and get it from others.

All right. What do you think of that story?

Patient: It was good.

Therapist: What did you like about it?

Patient: When he went to talk to his mother.

Therapist: Yes. What else did you like about it?

Patient: When he was talking to the fish.

Therapist: Yes. Anything else?

Patient: No.

Therapist: Okay. Let's stop here.

My story's meaning is obvious. Suppression will not effectively squelch anger, but effective expression of resentment and substitutive gratifications can make it less dangerous and even productive.

Example 5

Russell, a twelve-and-a-half-year-old boy, although of superior intelligence, had repeated the fourth grade and, at the time of referral, was told that he had to repeat the fifth grade. There was no evidence of a specific learning disability or brain dysfunction. His father worked eighteen hours a day, and his mother, a simple and inhibited woman, denied resenting the father's absences. During his second week of treatment, Russell told this story:

Well, I was in Florida and I was down on the keys, Key West, in that area. We were out in a ship, a one hundred-foot yacht. We were out there and we were scuba diving and we have deep sea gear, you know, which goes to the bottom, but we're just using light gear. You know, we don't have a mixture of helium and oxygen. We just have oxygen and we're just scuba diving around — me and a friend I know that's from my school — and we went down together and we see this gigantic crab. It was really —— just from the size of it I really wouldn't know how to measure it. It was so huge. So we went down there and as we saw it, we looked at it and were kind of startled, so we went back up to the ship to tell the rest of the crew what was down there. As we were going up this thing kind of reached up at us with its claw and we couldn't get away. My friend, Sam, well, he wasn't really chopped up, but it got a hold of him. It wasn't eating him up or anything. It was just holding on to him lightly.

So I went on up to the top and I told the crew. So we got the heavy gear on and we went down and I told them to hold me with a rope. The captain came down also and we went down with spear guns and everything, trying to do it, but we couldn't, you know, get him out of there. So we finally figured it out that if we took the harpoon gun from the ship's nose, 'cause, you know, you usually have a harpoon gun around. It was a high-powered harpoon gun, and we put it in a small cage and we lowered it beneath the water and we fired it and it hit right into his claw and it opened and Sam got away.

We went up to the top surface and we moved the ship out of there and we tried to get away —— we're still trying to get away. We're all on the ship. Well, we have our gear off and we're trying to move, but we find that we still have the anchor down and the crab is pretty intelligent or we're not sure really whether he is intelligent or not, but he was sitting on our anchor and we couldn't pull it up. So we tried to pull this thing up and as far as pulling up that crab that big — it was huge — and we just couldn't do it. As we try, you know, just keep trying, it just moves off enough so that we can lift it up. We lift up the anchor and we pulled out just about twenty miles away from there. We got out about minutes or so and we got, you know, we got back down again to see if it was following us from the nose. There was a thick plated window in the nose and we had turned around and looked. We went down into the nose to look. It hadn't been following us so we returned to the harbor and nobody seemed to believe us. They didn't believe us what happened. They thought it was —

Therapist: Let me ask you something. You did get rid of the crab?

Patient: Yeah, we pulled up on the thing and he moved off just enough so that we could pull up the anchor and so we returned to the harbor and nobody would believe us at all. So as we were going into port, you know, none of the people believed us. So one guy said to Sam and me, you know, us the couple that went diving down there, to take him out there and show this thing to him.

So we got out there. We weren't even in a one hundred-foot yacht anymore or in a boat or anything. We were in a motor boat and we were going out there pretty far. So we're out just in about low tide and as the tide was going down this boat was closer to the crab. We knew this but we thought that this would be an advantage to us so we wouldn't have to dive so deep, but you see, it didn't. It gave an advantage to the crab 'cause we were down there and all he had to do was reach up there and crunch our boat, but he didn't. So we see this thing and the diver that didn't believe us went down. Now he got caught down there. So we didn't have anything. We couldn't get him out. So he had enough air for two hours, so we figured it would take us about a half an hour to get out there to the harbor and about another half an hour to get back.

So we brought out the big boat, you know, with everything on it and we figured that, you know, that we didn't have any more pressure 'cause we have to sail around to build up pressure for the harpoon gun. We didn't have any pressure so we couldn't shoot it off. So we take the anchor this time and we nose this thing. You know the big window in the front that I told you about before?

Therapist: Uh-huh.

Patient: Well, that big window there, it's real big and it can stand pressure, so it's under the water at the front of the ship and the anchor is right next to it, you know? So here's this guy and he got down there. He had a walkie-talkie. Now he's telling people up on deck where this crab is, through the window, 'cause he can see and we drop the anchor straight down on him and we kill the crab, and the diver got away.

Therapist: I see. And the lesson?

Patient: Well, as far as not believing somebody, unless, you know, unless somebody says to you something that if it sounds like they're lying or telling something and everybody else goes along with them, chances are, you know, that you are out because when somebody says something and everybody else is saying the same thing, this means, most of the time, that it is true, but not to go away from the crowd. Most of the time the crowd is right because majority rules.

Therapist: Okay. All right. Good story. Now it's time for me to tell my story.

Once again, the dangerous animal that comes from the deep to threaten the life of the story's protagonist is the child's unconscious anger threatening eruption into conscious awareness. The story also relates to Russell's therapy in which one of our important goals was to help him look beneath the surface and see what lurks below. It is a resistance story, as it relates to treatment, because of its implication that one should heed the warnings of others and stay away when one is told that there are dangerous things in the unconscious depths. The story, then, is similar to other first and early treatment stories described in Chapters 2 and 3.

The crab, of course, may also represent Russell's father whose absence is seen as hostility. But, I think this is not an important contributing element to the fantasy.

In response, I told this story:

Well, once upon a time there was a boy and he went out scuba diving and this kid was quite fearful of scuba diving because he was quite afraid of the crabs that were in the water there. He would have various fears about these crabs. He felt that they might catch on to him and prevent him from coming up. He feared that they might grab on to the anchor of his boat and then his boat wouldn't be able to come into shore. He went around thinking that no one believed how dangerous the crabs were out there. Well, when he would tell people about it, people would say, "Listen, we know the crabs out there and we don't see them as you do. We don't consider them to be as dangerous as you do and we think that you think that they are much more dangerous than they really are." The boy said, "Well, my mother and father have always been warning me about how dangerous these crabs are." The people said, "Well, we believe your mother and father are wrong. The majority of the people in the town here do not consider these crabs to be so frightening."

At any rate, one night this boy had a dream in which he was going out there and a crab held him down under the water and then the next night he had a dream in which a crab grabbed on to his anchor. He had dreams in which other people would go out there and have these things happen to them too. But it did him no good. Others just wouldn't believe the crabs were so dangerous.

Well, one day he said to one of the unbelievers, "Why don't you come out there and see what's doing with these crabs? I saw a very big one." He said, "Okay." So they went down and they saw way down under the water one of the biggest. The kid said to the man who didn't believe it was so dangerous, "Let's see you go down there." The man said, "Sure." He went down and he picked up the crab. The crab tried to grab him, but he was able to open up the crab's claw and he wasn't afraid. He said to the kid, "Why don't you come down here, sonny, and you try it too." The kid was first afraid but after a while he went into the water and tried it too. He realized that even the biggest crab there wasn't as dangerous as he had thought. Then he began to realize that his mother and father had been feeding him a line all this time about how dangerous and how terrible these crabs were and his experiences had been to reveal that they really didn't have an accurate view of the situation. They had their own hang-ups where they saw these crabs as worse than they were. Well, after this, this boy was able to more freely swim in that water, scuba dive, and, of course, this is not to say that there are no dangers from crabs, but he was far less afraid of them than he originally had been.

The lesson of that story is: sometimes you'll find that things are less frightening than you imagine them to be. The end.

Is there any comment you want to make about this story?

Patient: I'd just like to ask one question.

Therapist: Yes.

Patient: How big was the crab?

Therapist: It was a pretty big one. It was about three, four feet. It was a big crab. Any other comments you'd like to make about this story?

Patient: No.

Therapist: Okay.

Russell's parents would have been quite punitive had he expressed hostility over his rejection. In my story, I attempted to help him appreciate that his parents' dictates against angry expressions are misguided. The townspeople look upon his parents as being inappropriately fearful of the crab. He learns, in my story, that his parents are in error and that certain things aren't as dangerous as they would have him believe.

The child's inhibitions are transmitted to him by his parents. Their delusions become his. One of the things the patient must accomplish in his treatment is to learn what his parents' distortions are so that he can correct his own. In the first five years of life, the child has no way to compare what his parents teach with what others believe. There is a natural tendency to indiscriminately accept all that they say as valid. Even later, when the child is exposed to alternative views, he is reluctant to go against earlier, more deeply entrenched notions. Many of these are totally irrational and maladaptive, but since they were taught to the child as never-to-be-doubted, basic premises, he does not question them. It is one of the purposes of treatment to help our patients question these assumptions and change them, when appropriate. One of Russell's commandments was: "Thou shalt not express anger toward thy loved ones." It was one of his parents' most stringently enforced dictates, and one of the functions of my story was to help him question it for the first time in his life.

One way to help a patient lessen his anger at another is to help him find cognitive fallacies regarding his attitude. If they are present, and he can come to appreciate them, then one factor in the angry reaction can be reduced, if not eliminated. One of the purposes in rectifying the patient's maladaptive dictates is that with correct basic notions there will be fewer inappropriate emotional reactions. In Russell's case, the fear reaction to his unconscious anger was based on the notion that such hostility can be dangerous, and so he had to repress it. My hope was that by changing his basic ideas about anger, he would be less fearful of it.

Example 6

Bonnie, the girl with a school phobia, told this story during the last month of her treatment:

Once upon a time in fairyland there were these fairies and it was the time to give out the wings. When you come about twenty years old they give out golden wings to the nicest fairies. So there was a group of fairies and they were all arguing on who was going to get the wings and one was saying, "I'm the nicest," and the other was saying, "I'm the nicest," and another was saying, "I'm the nicest." They all thought of something bad to say about someone else.

So finally it was the day to give out the wings, and hundreds and hundreds of fairies were there. The queen fairy interviews all of them and sees who gets the golden wings. So she interviews the first fairy and she asked the first fairy, "Do you think you deserve these wings." The first fairy said, "Oh, I'm sure I do." The queen fairy said,

"Well, what other reasons do you have for your other friends not to have wings?" She said, "Oh, they're mean; they steal and they don't share." And all these fairies had something to say about one another.

Then she came to about almost the last fairy and she said, "Do you think you deserve these wings?" She said, "I don't know. I might deserve them." The queen fairy said, "What do you think about the other fairies? Do you think that they should get the wings?" She said, "I don't know. I think the one who is the nicest should deserve the wings." The queen fairy asked, "Don't you have anything to criticize the other ones?" She said, "No, I don't think I have anything to criticize about them. I think they are all right." So, after all these other fairies were mean and told bad things about the other fairies, she was the only one who was nice about them. So the queen fairy said, "If you can be nice about your friends, you should have the wings."

All the other ones thought, "Oh, she wasn't nice about us. She just told the most horriblest thing." Then they were so mean to her and they thought they'd get her real upset and angry. But when they didn't get her real upset and angry they thought that maybe she was nice after all and maybe she didn't say bad things about us. Then they all liked her. And the next year the rest were all going to try out for their gold wings and they were going to copy her to see how nice they could be.

Therapist: And the moral?

Patient: Is that : you're often nicer when you don't say bad things about everybody else. Just be nice to other people. Do not be mean to them or say bad things about them when you really don't know them that well.

Therapist: Okay. Thank you very much. Now it's time for me to tell my story.

Although Bonnie made up the story, it is similar to the kind of pap often fed to children in fairy tales. Little Miss Goody Goody doesn't have a critical thought about anyone in her whole pretty little head. Stories such as these, which children are exposed to at the most impressionable period of their lives, perpetuate in a most effective way this culture's repressive codes

484

regarding the expression of anger. Such stories inculcate into the child's mind the notion that there are good, kind folks somewhere, Christ-like people, whose only thoughts are good-natured and tender. As long as the child considers this an ideal to be obtained, that long will he suffer feelings of guilt and inadequacy.

Bonnie was doing well in her therapy and had improved significantly regarding angry expression. I felt that the story reflected some pretermination regression, and that it was probably modeled, in part, on some tale she had recently read or heard; it is, therefore, of less analytic significance than if it were totally hers. But even the "lifted" story has some significance because it has been specifically selected from a multitude of stories to which the child has been exposed.

In response, I told this story:

Once upon a time in fairyland it was time to give out wings. See, when the fairies are about twenty years old, they give them golden wings and they give it out to the nicest fairy. Well, the fairies started talking about one another and many of them started to gossip and be critical and then the day came for the queen of the fairies to decide which fairy to give the wings to.

So she came to the first fairy and she said, "Should I give you the wings?" The first one said yes. The queen said, "What about the other fairies?" She replied, "No, not to the other fairies because this one is this way and that one is that way," and she started criticizing them. Then the queen fairy came to the next to the last fairy and she said, "Should I give you the wings?" She said, "Yes." The queen said, "Well, what about the others?" This other fairy said, "Well, they're nice too, and you could choose the nicest." The queen said, "Don't you have any criticisms of the other fairies?" She said, "No."

Then the queen came to the last fairy. Who do you think is going to get the wings?
Patient: The last one.
Therapist (laughingly): Why?
Patient: I just think that's the way you're going to end it.

Therapist (still laughing): I've got something up my sleeve, huh?

Patient: Yeah.

Therapist: Well, the queen said to this last fairy, "Tell me. Do you think you should get the wings?" The last fairy said, "Yes." The queen asked, "Well, what about the other fairies?" She said, "Well, some of them I think are fine people and are probably deserving of it also, probably equally as much as I am, and others I would be critical of. The queen said, "In other words, you like some of them, and some you don't." She said, "Yeah. That's how it is. Some people I like and some I don't." The queen said, "Well, what do you do about those that you are critical of?" She said, "Well, if they are close friends of mine or the situation is such that I think I should tell them that I am critical of them or that they do something that bothers me, I tell them, whereas other times I just ignore it." Well, the queen liked that and she said, "You know. You're the one that I am going to give the golden wings." Why did the queen say that? Why did she give it to that one?

Patient: Because she was honest about her friends that she didn't like them and instead of just saying nice things about them and just letting them be mean to tell them that they are mean, that there are bad things about them that they should straighten up — not just say nice things.

Therapist: What about the next to the last fairy?

Patient: Well, she was kind of not telling the truth about her not liking some of the fairies.

Therapist: Yes. It can't be that she liked every one of them. You know? The lesson of that story is that the best thing to do in your relationship with people is to know which ones you like, which ones you don't like, to freely express your resentment or anger and criticisms at such times when it is appropriate. Sometimes you say nothing; other times you say something, especially when the person is doing something that bothers you. The end. What did you think of that story?

Patient: Fine.

Therapist: Okay.

Perhaps my heroine is equally obnoxious. Although she is too good to be true and too healthy to be real, she's at least a more realistic model for emulation. At times, the heroes of my stories do have halos; sometimes they are somewhat simplistic. But such oversimplification is unavoidable because the therapist cannot possibly present all the subtle nuances and varied manifestations of behavior in one story. In any particular story it is best to emphasize one or two important points. Hopefully, the characters the therapist creates will be more balanced and lifelike than the patient's.

Example 7

Malcolm, the boy with multiple fears and angry outbursts, told this story after one month of treatment:

Once upon a time —— this is the same story as last time except a different chapter.
Therapist: Okay.
Patient: And each chapter that I make up starts with "Once upon a time."
Therapist: Okay.
Patient: And if I can't find any more chapters, I'll make up a new story.
Therapist: That's fine with me.
Patient: Once upon a time in this little village, the stone age had ended one hundred years ago, the bronze age had ended fifty years ago, and iron age ended a few years ago, like one or two. They just began building better cars and one of these —— no, this is a different story.
Therapist: Okay. Go ahead.
Patient: One of these cars was called —— these are just make-up cars.
Therapist: Of course.
Patient: And I'm going to tell you the car makes. One is called the Cookoo Crown and the other is the Twenty-four Typewriter and another is the Pen Pen Pencil Co. Cars, and the last one is the Lighthouse Cars. No, the last, last is the, um, is the Boat Boat Boathouse Cars

which have a little motor in the back and they could go in water too.

And a few — there were some — like one or two of these car makes, like the, um, Cookoo Crown or the Twenty-four Typewriter car makes didn't have enough money to make cars good enough so that they couldn't make real fancy and attractive cars. So they ran out of business and there were these other people still in business and there were these new groups that came in because these groups were independent or something, I don't know.

And so first came GM and GM made its own car and they called it Picture Frame GM Cars. Then they took the Lighthouse Cars and the Boathouse Cars and another new car make called the Silly Piano Play Car. Then came out another one called Ford and they picked three kinds of cars.

Therapist: Listen, you're just naming a lot of cars. I'd like you to get to the story. You're just telling me different kinds of cars. Are you coming to the story?

Patient: As soon as I finish with the cars.

Therapist: Okay.

Patient: But these are in the story to tell everyone what kind of cars what the Big Three chose or how a big company makes up cars. This is not real but the Big Three is real, and the cars makes, like the GM or the American Motors, are real, but the cars that they choose are just fiction.

Therapist: Okay. Go ahead.

Patient: And Ford came in and picked these four kinds of cars. He picked Glade Telephone Wiper. He picked Pillow Shaped Head — the Pillow Shaped Front Car, and another new car called Typewriter Telephone Microphone Car. He also picked the Laughing Pen and Pen Pen Pencil Car. Then there came Chrysler and that picked these three new cars: The Watch Car, The Lunchbox Car, and The Fan Car. Then there came this little one called American Motors and they picked just one car — not Ramblers like the real ones picked. They picked this car similar to their Rambler called The Rambling Car which is mostly used or seen in foreign places and it's made big enough, not just to drive, but enough room so that they could crawl and walk slowly around the inside of the car over the seat. That's why it's called The Rambling Car.

Therapist: Go ahead. Are you going to tell your story?

Patient: And so these people —— lots of these people wanted to buy all these kinds of cars. And they bought all these kinds of cars and this is the story.

Therapist: That's the whole story?

Patient: No. I'm almost finished with it.

Therapist: Listen, I haven't heard the beginning of it yet.

Patient: You did! You did!

Therapist: All you did was list a lot of different kinds of made up cars. But that's not a story.

Patient: That's the kind of cars I was pretending in my story.

Therapist: Listen. No, but that isn't very interesting, you know — something unusual. Just to list the names of different kinds of cars that people bought is not very unusual. It's not a very interesting kind of story. You know that. There's nothing very interesting about that plot. So make up something interesting that happens with these cars or one of these cars.

Patient: Then all of a sudden the littlest one, American Motors, one day these old broken down cars became new and not one of them ever got old. They didn't even get dirty and everybody fainted at the Rambling Cars because they never got dirty. They stayed shiny, clean, and new, and not even the seats got torn up. Even if a dog tried to rip it, it would not rip. American Motors made it so that it would not get old very soon and they could keep on making lots of cars. But soon they did not have money because these American Motors cars called Rambling Cars were not getting broken and because they were not getting broken or bashed up there is a bit less metal that was burnt at the junkyard with the smashed up cars and they have less metal coming in. There was less metal to build cars for American Motors. Soon there were no more American Motors Cars and then it began that same problem on the biggest make. So the biggest make had enough until most of their metal was out and then they had to begin sharing their metal between all these different car makes. So they had very little metal and they could only build two cars with the metal they had when they divided it. Soon there was no metal left except for the Ford.

Therapist: Then what happened?

Patient: Then everybody began to bust in at Ford and Ford was so crowded that they made thousands of dollars.

Therapist: Because Ford had a car that did break down?

Patient: Yeah.

Therapist: All right. How did the story end?

Patient: The story ended that Ford kept on having enough metal forever after. I'm not telling about Chrysler or it will take up too much time. Chrysler happened the same way.

Therapist: All right. Is that the end of the story?

Patient: Yes.

Therapist: And what's the lesson of that story?

Patient: The lesson? I don't think I know the lesson.

Therapist: Well, what does the story teach us? What can we learn from that story?

Patient: If it teaches us anything, I don't know what it teaches us.

Therapist: Well, try to think of it. What would be the title of that story?

Patient: "Car Makes that Make you Faint."

Therapist: "Car Makes that Make you Faint?"

Patient: That means that at the end it begins to make you feel like you're there and all this stuff happens.

Therapist: What's the thing that makes the people faint most?

Patient: When the cars began to stay new and there was not enough metal.

Therapist: Okay. Now one question. Was it they fainted because they couldn't believe that a car would never wear out or break down or did they faint because there was no more scrap metal?

Patient: They fainted because it stayed nice and shiny and polished and it didn't break down. It didn't crash and it

didn't have to be fixed in the motor.
Therapist: Okay.

The first part of Malcolm's "story," in which he describes at length the various names and makes of automobiles, is pure resistance. I handled this by telling him directly that he was not telling a story and, therefore, not following the rules of the game. I will sometimes, in such situations, say to the child: "If you want to play the storytelling game, you have to follow the rules, which are that you make up a story with a beginning, a middle, and an end. Something unusual, something made up, something of interest to the listener. You haven't done that. Would you rather try again or would you prefer to do something else?" By providing alternatives, the anxious child can turn to less anxiety-provoking activities, whereas others can still continue. Malcolm was clearly in the latter category, in that he finally did present something of productive psychological significance.

In the latter part of his story, he tells of the Rambler Company whose cars were manufactured to last. As a result, the company cuts off its supply of metal from scrapped Ramblers — metal which is necessary to make more cars — and so it goes out of business. The manufacturer, I believe, symbolizes his parents and the car represents the patient. By making himself permanent, Malcolm protects himself from their hostility toward him. As he sees it they feed on the waste products of their destruction of him. Were he to be indestructible, they would be deprived of vital nutriment. The fantasy was not totally unrelated to reality. The mother especially thrived on hatred and was merciless in her ridicule of the boy. Interestingly, Malcolm describes only one specific way in which cars get destroyed other than by natural aging: dogs rip up the seats. As described in Chapter 3, the mother was a German Shepherd enthusiast who, without question, vicariously gratified her hostile impulses through her dogs. In Malcolm's story, the destructive dogs are, without question, symbols of his mother.

In response, I told this story:

Once upon a time there were a group of car companies who were producing different kinds of cars. There was Cadillac and Chrysler and Chevrolet and General Motors and everything like that.

Patient: I didn't say Cadillac.

Therapist: Okay. That's my story. I can make up any story I want. There was this one car that was —

Patient: American Motors?

Therapist: Yes — we can make it an American Motors car — yes, an American Motors car which had not been made very well. In the factory where they manufactured it they were kind of slipshod. They weren't very careful in the way they handled the car and they didn't really do a very good job in handling the car and in producing it. So it came out kind of poor. And this American Motors car was sitting there one day with big teardrops falling out of the headlights. That's where the car's eyes are, you know? And the mouth, which is like the front bumper, was really sagging down on both sides, just like a mouth, you know, 'cause it was sad. The grill was sniffing, just like the nose. And this car —

Patient: Just like the nose of the — the grill is shaped more like a nose on a Grand Prix because the Grand Prix is shaped out like this and then back in like that.

Therapist: Right. And so anyway this car —

Patient: This car was just straight.

Therapist: Anyway, this car was sniffing. It was crying and somebody said, "What's the matter?" This was a man walking along. The car said, "Oh, the people who make me aren't doing a very good job and when I go out I can easily get taken advantage of in accidents and things like that. I get bumped around a lot. I'm not very strongly built because they didn't take very great care in building me and I keep wishing that a magic fairy would come along and turn me into an indestructible car — a car that never gets old and a car that never gets dirty and the dogs would jump on it and they wouldn't get it dirty. I keep wishing for that and then I would be fine." The man said, "Well, if there were magic wishes to be wished then I guess that would be fine, but I think that's all a waste

492

of your time, because there is no magic and no one is going to change you into a permanent car." At this point the car started to cry even more and he said, "I'm doomed! My life is ruined! I have nothing to live for. It's going to be terrible for me always being a terrible old car, always dirty and always getting hurt." The man said, "No. What makes you say that?" "Well, what can I do?" said the car. The man answered, "Have you spoken to the owners of the car, the owners of your plant or factory? Have you told them how sad you are and what bothers you?" "No, I haven't." "Well, my suggestion to you is try that. Perhaps they don't know how slipshod they are. Perhaps they don't know that they are being neglectful of you and perhaps they'll repair you and build better cars."

So the car went back to the American Motors people and he had to complain a lot. They didn't change the first time. They didn't even change the second time. But he spoke more and more to them and told them more about the things that bothered him and gradually they began to do things like improve the kind of metal they used and make stronger cars. Gradually the cars felt better and better about themselves and could compete better in the open market. More and more people bought cars and the cars themselves felt much better.

Now after that the cars felt very good. They were glad that they had spoken up and that the company was now making them better. However, these cars were still exposed to many of the things that can happen to cars. Even though they were made stronger they still had to be kept up. Those cars which took the trouble to keep themselves up, those cars which reminded their owners about changing oil and gasoline and getting them lubricated, those cars who made minor repairs and who got part replacements on time continued to do well and continued to be strong. However, other cars who didn't do these things did end up on the scrap heap because they gradually wore out and got old. However, as time went on more and more of the cars prevented themselves from ending up on the scrap heap by keeping themselves up and keeping themselves in good repair.

Another thing that bothered the cars were the dogs. Many dogs have a way of ripping up the seats of cars. Those cars who let the dogs rip up their seats got worn down. Those cars which did things to prevent the dogs from ripping up the seats did much better. When they would see a dog that was angry they would drive away from him, so that he wouldn't jump inside and rip up their seats or if a dog inside started to get angry they would open up their doors and shake him out or ask the owner to push him out so that their seats wouldn't get ripped. So as time went on more and more cars learned how to handle the dogs and so there were fewer ripped seats and fewer destroyed cars.

As more and more cars learned how to take care of themselves and learned how to prevent dogs from destroying them, there became less and less metal for the scrap heap. As a result, the company couldn't get enough metal to build more cars. But the cars didn't care. They said to the company people, "That's your problem, not ours. Our job is to keep ourselves healthy and to keep ourselves lasting as long as possible. If you need us to be destroyed in order for you to stay in business that's your problem." And so the cars lived happily ever after.

You know what the lessons of that story are?

Patient: No.

Therapist: Come on. What's one lesson? You can figure one out.

Patient: I don't know.

Therapist: What did the car learn from the man who was passing by?

Patient: That if you have a complaint just don't sit there and mope, just complain about what's bothering you.

Therapist: And what might happen?

Patient: And then you may feel better.

Therapist: You might get some results.

Patient: Yeah.

Therapist: And crying accomplishes nothing. What about wishing away the problem? Do you think that could help?

Patient: No.

Therapist: How come?

Patient: Because there's no magic.

Therapist: Right. So you —

Patient: There's no real magic, but there's fake magic which looks like real magic.

Therapist: Hhmmm. But there's no such thing as real magic. Right. So two morals of that story are: number one, if something is bothering you, don't just sit there and cry. Go to the people who are responsible and try to change them. Often you can. The second moral is that if something is bothering you and if you sit wishing for magic things to change you, that won't happen either because there's no such thing as magic.

I have two more morals also. One is you have to work to keep yourself up if you want to protect yourself from those who would harm you. The cars had to protect themselves from the dogs and to work to keep themselves in good shape. And the last moral is: if somebody needs your destruction for his own survival, that's his problem. The company needed the cars destroyed if they were to stay in business, but the cars wouldn't let themselves be destroyed in order to keep the company going. The end.

My story is more complicated than my usual story and I'm sure Malcolm did not absorb it all. However, the temptation to tell it was great. The story about the car company's needing the car's destruction to survive itself was most rich in meaning and was at the heart of the child's difficulties. I knew also that I could touch on each of these themes again (hopefully, separately) in future sessions.

The meaning of my story is clear. Malcolm is encouraged to express his resentment, to assert himself, to protect himself from those who would harm him, and to not concern himself with the fact that those who would feed on his destruction might suffer were he to deprive them of their sadistic gratifications.

Example 8

George, the boy with disinterest in his school work and

shyness, presented this story during his second month of treatment:

> *Therapist:* Once upon a time, a long long time ago in a distant land, far far far away, way beyond the mountain, way beyond the desert, way beyond the ocean, there lived a ——
>
> *Patient:* Person.
>
> *Therapist:* And this person ——
>
> *Patient:* Was a —— a dragon tamer.
>
> *Therapist:* And this person was a dragon tamer. Good. Now one day this dragon tamer ——
>
> *Patient:* Found a mean dragon.
>
> *Therapist:* And when that happened he ——
>
> *Patient:* Could not tame it.
>
> *Therapist:* He couldn't tame it and so ——
>
> *Patient:* He left that one in a cage and he trained a little one. Then the big one got out and he wrecked all the cages and all the other dragons got away.
>
> *Therapist:* All right. And after that?
>
> *Patient:* I think that's the end.
>
> *Therapist:* Oh, that's the end. And what's the lesson or the moral of that story? What do we learn from that story?
>
> *Patient:* Not to just leave something; not to leave it where it is and do another thing.
>
> *Therapist:* Leave something where it is?
>
> *Patient:* Yeah, and do something else.
>
> *Therapist:* How is that shown in your story?
>
> *Patient:* When he left the dragon to do another thing and something went wrong. You know, something went wrong. The moral of the thing is don't leave something.
>
> *Therapist:* Don't what something?
>
> *Patient:* Don't just leave something where it is and then do something else or else it might get out and do something ——
>
> *Therapist:* Speak into the microphone.
>
> *Patient:* It might do something or break something or things like that.
>
> *Therapist:* You mean you should keep your eye on things?
>
> *Patient:* Yeah.

496

Therapist: You should watch what you're doing? Is that what you're saying?

Patient: Yeah.

Therapist: I see. Don't be distracted by other things?

Patient: Yeah.

Therapist: I see. Okay. I get it. Let me understand something. This big one that he had left in the cage — how did he get out of the cage?

Patient: He broke out. Because he was so strong.

Therapist: He broke out. Did it have anything to do with the man's negligence, with the dragon tamer's negligence?

Patient: I don't know what you mean?

Therapist: Negligence means: had the dragon tamer made any kinds of mistakes or anything that enabled the other dragon to get out?

Patient: No.

Therapist: But you see your lesson is watch what you're doing. Now if he had watched that big dragon, could he have prevented him from breaking out?

Patient: Yes.

Therapist: How?

Patient: He could have got him back in before he got all the way out.

Therapist: I see. Okay. Thank you very much. Now it's time for me to tell my story.

The dragon is George's unconscious anger and the dragon tamer symbolizes facets of the child's ego and superego which instill in him feelings of guilt and fear regarding the expression of hostility. The dragon must be kept caged, his anger must be repressed. Its release can be dangerous. If just a little anger is freed, the rest will follow — "he wrecked all the cages and all the other dragons got away." Although not directly stated, the story implies that the untamed dragons cause devastation when let loose. The tamer was not cautious enough; had he not relaxed his guard, he could have prevented the dragon's escape: "He could have got him back in before he got all the way out." George must not relax his vigil lest his unconscious anger erupt. If he lets down his guard the results may be catastrophic.

The story is typical of the type of early treatment stories described in Chapter 3. It relates not only to George's general inhibitions over expressing hostility, but his fears of the treatment situation which fosters such expression. There is, however, one element in the story which suggests that the patient is willing to start coming to terms with his anger. The dragon tamer "trained a little one," he was willing, that is, to handle small amounts of hostility without separating himself from it and protecting himself from it by placing it behind bars.

In response, I told this story:

Once upon a time a long, long, time ago in a distant land, far, far away, there lived a famous dragon tamer. One day this dragon tamer went to the place where all the dragons were and they were all locked up in cages. Everybody said, "Be careful of all the dragons. They are very dangerous, especially that very big one in that big cage." Well, the tamer heard so much of this talk that he actually believed also that those dragons were very dangerous especially the big one. So when he came there and he started to tame some of the dragons, he picked the smallest ones first.

Well, while he was taming the smallest one, the biggest dragon of them all, the one that everybody feared most, suddenly broke out of his cage and he started walking around the place where all the other cages were. Much to the surprise of not only the tamer, but all the other people, he didn't go around smashing up the place or breaking up the other cages. Surely he snorted and snarled a lot, but he really didn't do all the dangerous things everybody said he was going to do. Then the dragon tamer finally overcame his fear. He overcame it when he realized that the dragon was not as dangerous as he had first thought. He went over to him and said, "Hey, you, get back in your cage there." The big dragon said, "You know, I really don't have to get back in my cage because I'm not as dangerous as you think. There's a rumor around that I'm really a dangerous guy, that I kill and I murder and I destroy and I break things up. This is really not so. That's a false rumor. I have a reputation that isn't right."

498

Well, the lion tamer realized that this dragon might be talking sense. So he said, "All right. I'll give you a chance. Let me see how you are. I'll watch you awhile and if I can learn to trust you and learn that you are really telling the truth, then I'll give you greater freedom." So the dragon agreed to that and sure enough it happened just the way the dragon said it would happen. Yes, he did snarl once in a while, but his bark was worse than his bite, as the old saying goes, and he really wasn't as dangerous as everybody had thought he would be. So they gradually let out some of the other dragons from their cages and everybody found out that these dragons were not as dangerous as they had originally thought.

You know what the moral or the lesson of that story is?

Patient: No.

Therapist: Well, try to figure it out. (*No response.*) Well, the lesson of my story is that often things are not as dangerous as you might originally think. Many things that you might fear are not as fearful as you might originally have thought — that often dangerous things, as the saying goes, have barks that are worse than their bites. Those are the morals of my story. Do you understand that?

Patient: Yes.

Therapist: And you see how in my story everybody thought that the dragons were more dangerous than they really were. But if you take a chance and you let them out you'll see that they aren't so bad. Okay. What did you think of that story?

Patient: Good.

Therapist: You want to listen to that story?

Patient: Okay.

Two factors are operative in the dragon tamer's changing attitude. First, he changes his opinion because his own observations contradict what he has been told. He comes to see that those who warned him about the dragons' dangers are misguided. Second, he places himself in the fearful situation, in spite of his initial anxieties, and has the *living experience* that his fears were unfounded.

My story was told in the hope that it would not only help George be less fearful of expressing his inner angers, but that he would be freer to reveal himself in the therapeutic situation as well.

Seven weeks later, George told this story:

Once upon a time there was a man who made chairs and cushions for them. There was another man who made chairs and cushions too. The other man made the chair part, the wooden part better, and the first one made the cushions better. And they were both arguing ——

Therapist: What were they arguing about?

Patient: Whose chair was better. This man came up and said they both were good as but they didn't think that —

Therapist: Wait a minute. The third man said what?

Patient: They were both as good as each other. They were as good as each other but they kept on arguing and arguing.

Once in the town where they lived there was this contest who made the best chairs and cushions for them. They were tied at the end and they both agreed that they both had good chairs.

The moral of the story is: sometimes you think that yours is better, but it really isn't and they were even.

Therapist: I see. That was an excellent story. Now it's time for me to tell my story.

The story depicts a sibling rivalry situation: the two men continue to argue about a senseless thing. The anger, as in sibling rivalry, is displaced from the parents. Although there are certainly other elements contributing to the anger exhibited in sibling rivalry, hostility displaced from the parents is central. The parents are too big to be taken on, and expression of resentment to them may bring about the alienation of those upon whom the child is most dependent. A sibling is a safe scapegoat; the repercussions are far less devastating, and the possibility of losing his affection is far less frightening. George's parents were divorced; his mother had to work; and his father

500

was somewhat irresponsible regarding visits. There was much the boy was angry about. Accordingly. I told this story:

Once upon a time there lived in this town two men. They were young men. Now both of them made chairs and they were always fighting with one another. They were always bickering and competing and arguing as to who made the chairs better. And they were fighting and fighting. Everybody in town knew that these two men were always picking on one another.

Then one day the first man was talking to a friend of his and the friend said, "Why are you always picking on that other chair and cushion maker?" He said, "Oh, I don't like the way he makes chairs." The friend said, "You know, you got much more to be angry about at home than to be angry at that guy." He said, "What do you mean?" The friend said, "I know quite well that the person you are really angry at is not that other chair maker but your mother." The first man said, "What do you mean?" He replied, "For a number of years now your mother has worked and she doesn't give you as much time. She isn't at home as much time as you would like and that must make you pretty furious at her." He said, "Well, there's nothing that I can do about that." The friend said, "Well, maybe you can, maybe you can't. My suggestion to you is to talk to her and see what can be worked out there. Instead of taking out all your anger on the other cushion maker and chair maker, why don't you talk to your mother. I think you'll be less angry then if you get something settled there."

So the first cushion and chair maker thought that might be a good idea. So he spoke to his mother and he said, "You know, I've been pretty angry at you." The mother said, "Why is that?" He said, "Because you work all the time." His mother said, "Well, I can't help it. I need the money and I have to work. However, I'm glad you told me that you're angry at me because maybe I can try to spend more time with you when I do get home." So that was a good idea. In addition, the mother said to him, "You know what you also might do? If you spend more time with friends, you'll be less angry at me."

So the first chair and cushion maker got more friends, spent more time with his mother on weekends and evenings, and do you think he was less angry?

Patient: Hhmmm.

Therapist: Do you think he fought less with the other chair maker?

Patient: Yes.

Therapist: That's exactly what happened. Now the second chair maker was speaking to a friend of his and the friend said, "Why are you always fighting with that first chair maker?" He said, "I don't know. I just hate that guy's guts." The friend said, "You know, I think that you're not angry at him so much. You're angry at your father." He said, "Why should I be angry at my father?" He replied, "Look, your father is divorced from your mother, right?" He said, "Yes." He continued, "And your father doesn't come to the house very much. Is that right?" He said, "Yes." "He only rarely comes. Is that right?" He said, "Yeah." The friend said, "That's the person you're really angry at. You're angry at your father." So the chair maker said, "Well, what can I do?" His friend said, "Well, speak to your father. Direct the anger at the right place where it belongs. Tell him that you're angry at him. Maybe something can be done."

So the second chair maker went to his father and said, "You know, I'm angry at you." The father said, "Why?" He said, "Because you don't visit as much as I'd like you to." The father said, "Gee, I didn't know you were angry. Well, I'm going to try to do something about that." So the father did something about that. He was able to visit more often and then the chair maker was less angry. Do you think he fought as much with the first chair maker? Hhmmm?

Patient: No.

Therapist: Now what are the lessons of that story?

Patient: I don't think they fought at all.

Therapist: Why did they not fight?

Patient: Because the first chair maker's friend told him that he made up with his mother and there's no more anger.

Therapist: Why is there no more anger?

Patient: Because they both have what they wanted.

Therapist: What was it that the first chair maker wanted?

Patient: He wanted his mother to spend more time with him, and the second chair maker wanted his father to spend more time with him.

Therapist: All right, so then why was he not then angry?

Patient: Because the mother was spending more time with the first one and the father was spending more time with the second one.

Therapist: Well, also, even though the mother couldn't spend as much time as he would have liked, he also got more friends and so enjoyed himself more and was less angry. Yes, the lesson of that story is: if you're angry about something tell the person who you're angry at. Don't take it out on someone else. When you do that you'll find that you'll accomplish something. When you take it out on someone else you usually don't accomplish anything. The anger still stays there because the original problem is not solved. But when you use the anger to help you solve your original problem, then you're not angry anymore. The end.

What do you think about this story?

Patient: I think it was a good one.

Therapist: Would you like to hear it again?

Patient: No.

Therapist: All right. Let's turn it off.

The meaning of my story is obvious. I encouraged George to direct his anger where it will do the most good. Sibling rivalry is a fruitless outlet because it does not deal with the real problem. It's similar to hitting a punching bag: you may let off a little steam but it doesn't change the basic sources of the anger and it continues to build up. The sequence is presented as an example of the kind of story I use to deal with children who tend to use displacement as a defense mechanism.

Two weeks later, George told this story:

Once there was a cave explorer and he always wanted to go in caves in order to —— he always wanted to go in caves. He asked this one person once and they said no because they didn't think he had the experience. So he kept on asking people and asking and asking and they all said no because they didn't have the experience.

So once he went in a cave and he always got these treasures and all that. And when he showed it to all these people they didn't believe that he really was experienced.

Then they let him go in caves. They explored things with him in the caves. Wherever he went to, he made discoveries. People that came with him — the person who came with him, he found things —

Therapist: I don't understand this. The person who went with him what?

Patient: The person who went with him, he found things and he found things. The person that went with him found things and he found things too. They both made great discoveries.

The moral of that story is: if somebody asks you something you should find out their experience before you turn them down.

Therapist: I see. Very good.

When this story is compared to the one George told nine weeks previously about the escaping dragon, there appears to be some improvement and an incorporation of my message from that sequence. Here, he explores the cave, even when others refuse to join him. His request for a companion is probably related to his desire for protection; and their refusal a manifestation of their anxiety that he is willing to expose himself to the dangers of the unknown. In the dragon story he cages the danger in order to protect himself from it. In this story, however, there is no apparent danger. All the listener is told is that he made "great discoveries" in the caves. Either he is denying the danger — the so-called "sweet-lemon" maneuver which is the opposite of sour grapes — or he has truly come to feel that what is to be found in the unconscious is not so terrible, and may even be of interest. Considering the depth of the boy's repression and his persistent timidity, as well as the relatively short time in therapy (three-and-a-half months), I regarded the danger-denial explanation to be the more likely. Accordingly, I told this story:

Once upon a time there was this cave explorer and he was very frightened of going into certain caves and although people told him that those caves were really not so bad, he just didn't believe it. He kept being frightened of those caves and finally someone said, "Come on. Let me go in with you. You'll see that it's not so bad."

So the first thing they did was they went in the cave and he was kind of scared. Then they saw this lizard. He said, "Ooh, there's a lizard. There's a f–f–frightening, t–t–terrible lizard!" The other man said, "That lizard? There's nothing to be scared about that lizard. That lizard has no teeth. It's harmless." Sure enough the lizard opened his mouth and he saw that it didn't have any teeth and he realized that that lizard wasn't as harmful as he had thought.

Then they heard some animals howling and yelping and barking. He said, "Oh, those scary animals." His friend said, "Oh, those animals aren't so scary. Their bark is worse than their bite. They make a lot of noise but they really can't do you much harm." He said, "But I've heard about poisonous fish. Look at that pond over there. Those fish must be poisonous." At that point his friend took the water and drank it. He said, "If I thought these fish were poisonous I wouldn't drink this water. Would I?" He realized, of course, that he wouldn't.

Well, after a while this cave explorer realized that the cave was not as dangerous as he had thought and he began then to go into the cave alone without any trouble.

And the lesson of that story is: sometimes you find out that things are far less scary than you had originally thought.

In my story, the dangers, which I still considered to be lurking in the cave, reveal themselves. The lizard, however, has no teeth; the bark of the yelping animals is worse than their bite; and the secretions of the poisonous fish are potable. Whereas George's story suggested denial of danger, mine encouraged confrontation, understanding, and desensitization as ways of dealing with that which seems threatening.

Example 9

Carol, the girl with stuttering, insomnia, and poor peer relationships, had many problems clustered around the anger she felt toward her extremely hostile mother. The example presented in Chapter 6, demonstrates some of these. During her third month of treatment, Carol told this story:

Once upon a time there was a girl who didn't believe in Christmas and Santa Claus. So she said to her mother and father, "I don't believe in Santa Claus and someone else brings me the presents every night." So her mother and father said, "Well, go to bed. Santa Claus is coming so you better get in bed early."

So that night the mother took a big pile of presents and so did the father. They were going down the stairs and the mother took more than she could carry. She took more presents down the stairs than she could carry and the husband was saying, "Watch out, dear. That's too much presents." She said, "No, it isn't." Then all of a sudden she tripped over a bone and the presents all fell down. Bang! The daughter rushed over and caught the mother and father lying in the middle of the presents all over, and she saw the father carrying some presents. So she knew Santa Claus wasn't true. She said, "I knew it all the time. You're Santa Claus." The parents said, "Go to bed now." She said, "Well, I still don't believe in Santa Claus." The parents said, "Go to bed." So she went to bed.

So that night she heard someone calling her name and she woke up and she really saw Santa Claus, but it was only a dream. And Santa Claus said, "I am true." The little girl said, "How come I caught my mother and father bringing the presents?" Santa Claus said, "Because I didn't have enough time to come through the chimney because it was closed and so I had to come through the attic and so

I put the presents in the attic, and your father heard something fall and he went and found all the presents in the
attic. So they brought them downstairs." The little girl
believed Santa Claus, and Santa Claus said, "If you don't
get to bed, tomorrow morning you won't have any
presents."

The moral of the story is: parents should always
check to see that their child is asleep before they bring the
presents downstairs.

Therapist: Okay. Why did the girl have this dream? What
did the dream get her to do?

Patient: Not get angry at her parents and believe in Santa
Claus.

Therapist: Hhmmm. I see. Okay. Now let me tell my story.

The meaning of the story is stated in her response to my
question about the dream in which Santa Claus advises her not
to "get angry at her parents and believe in Santa Claus." Her
moral: "Parents should always check to see that their child is
asleep before they bring the presents downstairs" if stated in its
complete form would be: "If parents don't want their duplicity
exposed to their child, thereby invoking the latter's anger and
disrespect, they should always check to see that the child is
asleep before they bring the presents downstairs." Or to take
it further: "You are not helping your child rationalize or deny
her anger toward you if you blatantly expose your lies." In the
story, the parents are evasive when she confronts them with
their duplicity. Carol has no overt resentment over this, but
rather a dream which provides a rationalization for the parents'
behavior.

In short, the story is a series of attempts by Carol to repress
the anger she feels toward her parents. However, their behavior
is so blatantly provocative that she has a difficult time denying
their hostility. In desperation then, she asks them to please be
a little more subtle about it, to wait, that is, until she is asleep
before bringing down the Christmas presents so she will not
have to be confronted with their dishonesty regarding Santa
Claus.

With this understanding of Carol's story, I told mine:

Once upon a time there was a girl and she did not believe in Santa Claus and she told her parents, "I don't believe in Santa Claus." Well, her mother was taking the presents down the stairs and she took a lot of them, more than she could really carry, and she tripped over a bone and fell down the stairs, and the presents were strewed all over the floor. When the girl came down she said, "There that proves it. That proves there is no Santa Claus. I saw you with the presents." Then the mother and father said, "Well, the presents were really in the attic. Santa Claus brought them to the attic because he couldn't fit through the chimney, and that's why I was carrying them down." The girl said, "That's a lot of baloney. I don't believe that. It gets me very angry when you try to palm off that kind of story on me."

Well, the parents began to realize that they weren't doing this girl any favors by lying. Then they said, "You're really right. Maybe it was wrong of us to try to tell you this story. We thought you'd be happy to think that there was a Santa Claus." The girl said, "I'm glad that you told me that you were lying." They said, "Well, we're glad that you spoke up. You're right. Daddy and Mommy really did buy the presents." She was just as happy to have the presents from them and was happy that they weren't giving her this baloney story.

And the lesson of that story is what?

Patient: You should speak up to your parents?

Therapist: Speak up and it's not so terrible to be angry at them and when they do something that is wrong you *should* be angry at them. The thing to do with your anger is to tell them what bothers you, rather than to hold it in. Let out your anger and use it to get the thing that you want — to stop the thing that is making you angry. What do you think about that?

Patient: Good.

Therapist: Okay then.

The meaning of my story is clear. I advised her not to let herself be duped, to express her hostility, and she may find that the repercussions she anticipates for such honest expression will not be forthcoming. However, the parents' lies were not as simple as the Santa Claus tale implies. They were far more subtle. The mother's use of sarcasm was extensive and the child was ill-equipped to understand the full meaning of many of her mother's communications. They left her confused, with some awareness of the disparity between the ostensible innocuousness of her mother's statements and the discomfort their underlying hostility evoked in her. The father's duplicity lay, in part, in his tacit support of the mother's abuse which he showed by denying her hostility. The Santa Claus issue was just a starting-point for us in getting into this problem. Unfortunately, as already mentioned, treatment was prematurely terminated, and so Carol and I never had the opportunity to pursue this problem further.

Example 10

Mark, the boy with chronic anxiety, feelings of inadequacy, and excessive dependence on his mother, told this story during his third week of treatment:

This story is about a little boy named Perry Periwinkle. Perry lived in a house in a country by a mountain and up the side of the mountain a little bit there was a school where Perry went. He liked the summer a lot because there it snowed so much in winter that you couldn't get out of your house and you didn't go out to play at all. So he liked summer a lot and he had fun in the summer, but he was going to be going to school for the first time and he got disturbed about it. So he told his mother that he was disturbed, and that he didn't know what he should do on the first day of school.

His mother told him that he was going to like his teacher a lot and that she was the same teacher that she had when she was a little girl and that she was a nice old lady. She told him what to do on the first day and to be polite and everything.

The first day of school finally came and Perry was excited. For a while he didn't want to leave. Finally he did go and when he got to school it was a large building. It had green moss all over the sides and there were vines running up the trees. Perry thought it looked pretty spooky. He went inside and there was a long corridor and he went along the corridor, way up some steps, and found the room where he was supposed to go. Sitting at the desk in the front of the room was the teacher and he came in. The teacher asked him what his name was and she told him to go sit down in one of the corners.

Therapist: In the corner?

Patient: Hhmmm. And he waited a while and lots more children came and they all got a place where they would sit permanently picked out. Perry was having fun for a while, and the teacher asked him his name and he told her his name. He told her Perry Periwinkle. She said, "Where do you live?" and he told her where he lived. Then she started asking the class questions. Perry was getting mad at the teacher because he didn't like asking questions.

Therapist: Do you mean he didn't like answering questions?

Patient: He didn't like answering questions. His mother hadn't told him about this. So he asked the teacher why she asked so many questions. She told him, "To learn more about you." Perry was not too smart so he didn't know exactly what that meant. He thought that maybe the teacher was trying to make fun of him. So he got real mad. Then she started asking him questions about words, like do you know what this word is, and Perry got so mad that he ran up to the teacher and he threw her out of the window. The teacher landed in a pond. There was a pond outside of the building and she got real wet. Perry jumped up, got his coat, and ran out of the room, and ran all the way home and ran up into his room and went to sleep. That's the end.

Therapist: And what's the lesson of that story?

Patient: The lesson of that story is: you should hold your temper. You can get mad at people, but don't get too

mad at them and don't throw people out of windows.
Therapist: Okay. Thank you very much. Now it's time for me to tell my story.

There were two issues which I considered to be of importance in Mark's story. First, the story reveals Mark's feelings that were he to be even slightly irritated, his anger would get out of hand and there would be catastrophic results. A slight misunderstanding ends with his teacher being thrown out of the window. His moral confirms my interpretation: "hold your temper" and "don't get too mad." The second issue pertains to his statement that "He thought that maybe the teacher was trying to make fun of him. So he got real mad." Mark's solution to a perceived threat is anger. While it follows that if his perception were truly changed, the anger would cease, I am fully aware that most often things are not that simple. Displacement and projection, for example, may hinder the therapist significantly in quickly correcting misperceptions.

Although the anger-explosion theme was the more dramatic in the story and was the one he considered worthy of repetition in his moral, I decided to focus on the misperception issue in my story because it was the more basic. If Mark were able to get his thoughts rectified, there would be less anger to worry about getting out of control. Accordingly, I told this story:

Once upon a time there was a boy named Perry Periwinkle and he lived in a house in the country by a mountain. Nearby was a school. He liked the summertime a lot because he liked to play there. He had a lot of fun in the summer.

Now when the winter came he was going to school for the first time and he was very disturbed about it and he didn't know what to do. He spoke to his mother and she said, "Oh, you'll like the teacher. She's the very same teacher that I had when I was a girl." She told him to be polite.

Anyway, he went to school and he thought that it was a scary place. There were all vines all around and he finally did go inside down a long corridor. He found a room and there was a teacher. He was told to sit down in one of the corners. Then the teacher started asking the children a lot of questions and this got him very angry. The first thought that he had was to run out of the classroom. Then another part of him said, "No, that wouldn't help very much and nothing would be accomplished." Another part of him said, "I know what I'll do. I'll throw her out of the window. That will solve the problem." Then another part of him said, "No, that won't solve anything. You'll just get into trouble. You're not allowed to throw a teacher out of the window."

Well, he did nothing. I'm sorry. I take that back. He went up to teacher and he said, "Why do you ask all those questions?" The teacher said, "That's how it works in school. In school I ask a lot of questions to see what you know and to see what you don't know. Then I know what to teach you. I want you to try to think for yourself, figure things out for yourself. That's another reason why I ask questions." Well, when Perry heard the reasons why she was asking questions and they seemed like good reasons then he was no longer angry at her for asking such questions, didn't feel like he wanted to run out of the school, nor did he feel that he wanted to throw her out of the window.

The lesson of that story is — what do you think the lesson is?

Patient: You should know more before you make an accusation.

Therapist: Right! I would say that sometimes if you learn more about the thing that you are angry about you'll change your mind about it. You'll change your ideas and then you'll realize that you were wrong in being upset by it and then you are no longer angry. That's what happened. When he learned that there was a purpose for questions and that the teacher could find out what he knew and that he could get practice in thinking things out for himself, he then realized that his being angry was really not a reasonable thing and he was no longer angry.

Early in my story, the use of intellectual processes for conscious control is demonstrated. The boy considers various alternatives for dealing with his irritation: whether he should run out of the classroom or whether he should throw the teacher out of the window. Each time prudence and logic win out. Following the introductory arguments for the use of force rather than nonviolent action, he questions his teacher as to the reasons for her inquiry. With clarification of her motives his anger disappears, obviating the need for the previously considered maladaptive courses of action.

Two weeks later, Mark told this story:

There was once this house and it was a very tall house and also very old. Lots of people liked the house so they wouldn't let the town tear it down.

Once this man — he was very angry at everyone. He was very very mad. So he goes down and he bumps into the house and the house starts to shake. The man gets really scared. So he runs into a nearby woods and goes and gets some water. This man is really angry and he doesn't know what he is doing. So he goes and he throws the water at the house. Just then the chimney fell over and knocked him out because of the bricks falling on his head. But the policemen were walking by and they saw the house falling apart and they got some more workers to tear down the house 'cause it was dangerous to the public.

The moral of that story is: don't ever throw water at broken houses.

Therapist: Okay. Let me ask you a question about that story. How could water do all that damage — just throwing water at the house, how could that happen?

Patient: Well, when things get really old they get — well, concrete, if they have concrete in them, starts to crumble.

Therapist: I see. Okay. Thank you very much. Now it's time for me to tell my story.

This story also presents two important themes, only one of which I chose to concentrate on when I told my story. The house — a common symbol for the person — represents the patient who sees himself as so fragile that he could be totally demolished by even the slightest display of hostility directed toward him. The madman's rage is not expressed in violent form for example, with fire or explosives, but in a most "watered-down" form (I do not know whether the pun is also Mark's). In addition, the story alludes to another, most important issue. The berserk man is described as "very very mad," but the listener is told nothing of what he is mad about or at whom: "This man is really angry and he doesn't know what he is doing." Although frenzied, he is doing one thing that is certain: he is directing his anger from its primary source(s) to any object which may lie in his path — in this story an old house. However, the man's rage is subdued out of Mark's fear that he could not tolerate it in its full force.

Although the first theme is epitomized in the moral, "Don't ever throw water at broken houses," I chose to focus on the second issue in my story because correction of the displacement problem would enhance Mark's feelings of competence and thereby lessen his feelings of fragility. I could indirectly deal with the first problem by concentrating on the second. Accordingly, I told this story:

> Once upon a time there was an old house and people liked the house. Now in the town there was a man and he got very angry at someone and he in his rage would go around kind of wild and do all kinds of strange things, but he didn't do them at the person that he was angry at. He would take water and throw it at houses, kick trees, or stamp on the ground, or throw rocks into the water. But all that didn't do him any good even though sometimes his displacement of his anger — do you know what displacement means? What does displacement mean?
>
> *Patient:* It means that you're not putting your anger where it is or where it ought to go.
>
> *Therapist:* Right. His displacement would destroy other things, but it didn't solve any problems with the person he was angry at. So one day someone said, "What are you doing when you throw water at houses, kicking trees,

you're trying to knock down trees? What is this accomplishing?" He said, "Oh, it lets me get out some of my anger." The person said, "Anger at whom?" Then he told the man whom he was angry at. The man said, "Well, why don't you go over and tell that person what bothers you and maybe then you can solve the problem. You won't be so angry."

So he thought about it and he realized that that was good advice. So he went over to the person he was angry at to discuss the problem and then that person and he found some solution. Then after that the man was much less angry and didn't have to go around hitting trees, and things like that — throwing water at houses — and he was much happier and so was the person whom he was angry at.

Do you know what the lesson of that story is?

Patient: Yeah.

Therapist: What's the lesson?

Patient: You should work out your problems with other people.

Therapist: Instead of?

Patient: I know what it means, but I can't put it into words.

Therapist: Try it. I want to be sure that you got the message in that story.

Patient: That you should talk to people about your problems instead of getting mad at yourself or, naw that isn't it!

Therapist: No, instead of getting mad at what? Not yourself.

Patient: Humph! I can't — I know it — instead of getting mad at nothing.

Therapist: Or things. If you're angry at someone to throw water at a house doesn't really accomplish much. That's it. Okay. Thank you very much.

Although I did not feel that I had been fully successful in getting my message through in this particular story, Mark subsequently became much more direct and assertive, suggesting that this and similar stories ultimately had their effect on him.

10. SELF-ESTEEM PROBLEMS

Although many factors contribute to the formation of psychogenic symptoms, they all contain attempts to compensate for low self-esteem. Although symptomatic adaptations are designed to enhance feelings of adequacy, they usually result in an even further lowering of self-esteem. For example, the unpopular boy who lies to his peers and describes interesting and unusual exploits may enjoy more ego-enhancing attention at first, but as soon as his peers learn of his duplicity (and they inevitably do), he suffers more rejection than when he had been unpopular but truthful. In addition, even before his confabulations are detected, his own dignity is compromised by lying. He is inwardly embarrassed about what he is doing, and this in itself reduces the ego-enhancement he had hoped to achieve. The class clown is laughed at but not liked by most of his schoolmates. He deludes himself into thinking that their enjoyment of his antics reflects respect; and if he is rejected in other areas he may respond with even more harebrained escapades which further alienate his peers. The child who buys friends with candy and money may experience transient respite from his loneliness and its associated feelings of worthlessness; but he inwardly knows that his friendships are specious, that they are dependent upon continual bribery, and that he is being exploited. Accordingly, he feels even more inadequate than before. In short, such symptoms are, in part, misguided attempts to bolster a lagging self-esteem. What begins as a maneuver to enhance one's feelings of self-worth, ends up lowering it. This, in turn, may stimulate further utilization of the maneuver, resulting in an even greater loss of self-respect. Parental deprivation is the primary cause of psychogenic pathology, and low self-esteem is one of the earliest effects of this deprivation. The young child, having no guidelines of his own, develops his self-image by what Sullivan calls "reflected appraisals."[1] The child's concept of himself is derived essentially from his parents' opinion of him. It is only later, when he makes friends, enters other homes, and goes to school that new criteria for his self-worth are introduced. Modifications can then be made to alter distortions which may have been derived from the parents. In healthy development, two main processes take place: 1) increased experience and further modifications result in greater accuracy and reality to the self-image; and 2) the reliance on the environment decreases and that on the deeply-formed inner convictions increases, so that one's self-esteem is determined less by the vicissitudes and capriciousness of the milieu and more by the tried and tested inner repertoire of criteria for ascertaining self-worth.

So deep and lasting, however, is this earlier "reflected appraisal," that the child whose parents despise him may never be able to gain a full feeling of self-worth. As a result, he may spend his life futilely utilizing a variety of neurotic and even psychotic mechanisms whose purpose is to bolster his low self-esteem.

The young child lives by the dictum: I am what significant figures say I am. The three-year-old child runs to his mother crying, "Johnny called me stupid." The mother replies, "You're not stupid. He's silly," and the child stops crying. Hopefully, as he grows older, his adherence to this precept will lessen, and he will consider as well his own inner repertoire of criteria for self-worth. Failure to do so leaves him at the mercy of all those who might criticize him. Since he can never be completely acceptable to everyone, he must invariably be exposed to disapproval. Indiscriminately accepting all disapprobation as valid can only result in his chronically detesting himself. It is the job of the therapist to help the child appreciate that he is not exactly what his parents or other important figures in his milieu consider him to be. The therapist must help the child enrich his set of criteria for judging his self-worth. He must help the child look *to his own opinions* as well as to those of *others outside his home*. The child must learn to consider with receptivity, but not with gullibility, the opinions of his parents and to accept what is reasonable and reject that which is not. He must be helped to see his parents' distortions and their fallibility: "Your father doesn't think too much of you because you aren't very good in sports. To your father, sports are the most important thing in the world. There are many others who don't think that any single thing, like sports, is all that important, and they don't put down someone just because he isn't good at sports."

The Mutual Storytelling Technique can be useful in dealing with this aspect of low self-esteem. With it one can communicate alternative criteria for self-worth, apprise the child of his parents' fallibility, impart the notion that he is not necessarily what others say he is, and encourage self-evaluation and respect for his own opinions and feelings.

Feelings of competence must ultimately be based on some realistic attribute or skill. The one-year-old child who builds his first tower of blocks beams over his accomplishment. His sense of mastery is ego-enhancing. The mother who says, "What a beautiful tower you've built!" directs her compliment to the product of his labors and thereby further raises his feelings of self-worth and increases the likelihood that he will build again. In contrast, the mother who responds, "You're going to be a great engineer someday and we'll all be proud of you; the family will be famous," uses the child's accomplishments for her own self-aggrandizement, lessens his pleasure and feelings of competence, and makes it less likely that he will derive ego-enhancing gratifications from building.

A common way in which parents contribute to a child's feeling of low self-esteem is through the disparagement of those who are successful. When the child does not compete successfully, he is told that others' rewards are undeserved, that they are owing to good luck, or that they are the result of special favors and influences. The child's own inadequacies which may have contributed to his poor standing are not even considered. Sullivan describes this quite well:

If you have to maintain self-esteem by pulling down the standing of others, you are extraordinarily unfortunate

518

in a variety of ways. Since you have to protect your feeling of personal worth by noting how unworthy everybody around you is, you are not provided with any data that are convincing evidence of your having personal worth; so it evolves into "I am not as bad as the other swine." To be the best of swine, when it would be nice to be a person, is not a particularly good way of furthering anything except security operations.[4]

Compliments not ultimately associated with concrete accomplishments can be ego-debasing: "What a fine boy," or "Aren't you a nice girl," makes many children squirm. They sense that they are being "buttered up," and they are insulted as well because the comment implies that the speaker thinks they are stupid enough to be so taken in. But, "What a good cake you baked," or "Great, a home run," makes a child stand a few inches taller. The adolescent who takes drugs does so, in part, to desensitize himself to the massive feelings of self-loathing he suffers because he has no area of competence or skill. The euphoria he may experience in the early stages of his addiction provides a compensatory sense of self-worth. To try to wean him from the drug without providing him with some rehabilitative program in which he can gain a sense of proficiency and mastery is futile. Many are addicted to alcohol for similar reasons. Alcoholics Anonymous helps, in part, because it provides the alcoholic with a sense of competence in helping other alcoholics abstain. In small towns, when the members run out of alcoholics to help, they often revert to drinking again because they no longer have the opportunity to engage in an activity which has provided them with their greatest source of ego-enhancement. Since analysis and psychotherapy can only go so far, it behooves the therapist, when treating children with self-esteem problems, to encourage them to develop their interests and talents. Without proficiency in genuine skills, feelings of competence can at best be unstable. The child must, however, be discouraged from pursuits in which he has demonstrated particular ineptitude. The child with minimal brain dysfunction, with an associated coordination defect, would suffer deep humiliations in a sports-oriented summer camp. The asthenic child can be reassured that many of the boys on the football team wouldn't stand a chance against him at chess. In the story-telling game one can impart messages which encourage the acquisition of real proficiency, expose as spurious the ego-gratifications which are based on fantasy, and help the child clearly differentiate between patronizing flattery and genuine compliments. In addition, playing the game itself provides the child with genuine creative gratifications. In making up a story he demonstrates his ingenuity, originality, and quite often his sense of humor.

Feeling genuinely needed is a related element contributing to one's sense of self-respect. One of the criteria I use to deter-mine if a seriously depressed person is suicidal is whether he has the deep conviction that no one in the whole world would miss him were he dead. Although children are, for the most part, dependent and need their parents far more than their parents need them, the child must still feel that his loss would be painful to his parents if he is to have a healthy feeling of self-esteem. (The healthy child in a loving home doesn't think about his parents' reactions to his loss; this is often a source of concern to the deprived child.) The younger child feels elated over the fact that he can make others laugh. The girl who, as "mother's helper," sets the table, and the boy who helps father change an automobile tire glow with the feeling that they are important and contributing members of the family team.

When playing games with a child (and this holds for therapeutic games played in session) the adult does better for both himself and the child if he selects one that is enjoyable to both. When an adult finds a game tedious, but continues to play through obligation, the child is aware, at some level, that he is not really needed as a challenging adversary. He senses the adult's boredom and lack of interest through the latter's im-patience and easy irritability, and so the game becomes a trying and oppressive ordeal to him. The sham can be ego-debasing. I have elaborated on this aspect of child therapy in an article on the use of checkers as a therapeutic technique.[2] The actual playing of the storytelling game can provide the child with just such a feeling of being needed. The therapist, too, usually finds the game challenging; trying to surmise the psychodynamic meaning of the child's story is intellectually stimulating. The child senses the therapist's involvement and pleasure and this gives him a feeling of being useful and desirable. In the context of the stories the therapist can also help the child involve himself in situations which are likely to provide him with the ego-gratifications associated with being needed and avoid those areas where he is frustrated in this regard.

A source of impaired self-respect for many children in treatment is the notion that they are the only ones who have the abominable thoughts and feelings which they harbor within them. Parents often confirm such suspicions and deepen the child's detestation of himself. The therapist's reassurance that not only has he seen many children with similar thoughts and feelings, but that he also has had, or still has, the same kinds of ideas and emotional reactions can help lessen the child's low self-respect. Such messages can be conveniently woven into the recorded stories.

The child's feeling that he is crazy because he has to see a therapist is closely related to questions of self-esteem. Many children harbor this idea and yet do not communicate it. It is important for the therapist to be aware that the child may be silent about this ego-debasing concern and to bring up the subject himself if he suspects that it is contributing to the child's low self-esteem. I sometimes approach it this way: "You know, many kids think that just because they come here it means they're crazy. Have you had any such thoughts?" If the child states that he has, I reply: "I know you well enough to know that you aren't crazy. Yes, you do have some problems, but no one would consider them so bad that they would call you crazy. In fact, most of the children I see do not look any different from other kids in their class or neighborhood. They're kids, like you, with some problems in a few parts of themselves, not all over, not in everything." For the rare child who is psychotic, I might say: "Yes, you do have a lot of problems, and some people would call you crazy. I think that's a cruel word, and I don't use it here. There's something wrong with somebody who calls someone else that."

Inhibition in asserting oneself is another source of low self-esteem. The child, who is smoldering with pent-up hostilities over not having stood up for his rights, has little respect for himself. He derogates himself because of his passivity, and his pent-up anger, in itself precludes a feeling of self-satisfaction. Progress in the realm of asserting himself, not letting himself be taken advantage of, and appropriately expressing his resentment can be most helpful in alleviating these feelings of inadequacy. Neurotic factors notwithstanding, revenge *is* sweet. Winning a well-fought battle also enhances one's feelings of competence.

Although depression, in the adult sense, is not too common in childhood, one aspect of the depressive syndrome which is seen is the turning inward of hostility with associated self-deprecatory preoccupations. Such children, like their adult counterparts, are inhibited in overtly expressing their resentments .They turn their anger inward against themselves (a safer target), and their self-flagellation and self-disparagement result in a significant lowering of self-esteem. The therapeutic goal is, as I discussed in Chapter 9, to help the child direct his hostility toward the appropriate source so that the irritations which are engendering the anger can be more effectively dealt with.

When a patient tells me, "I feel lousy about myself," I generally ask: "Are you doing anything that would make anyone feel lousy about himself were he doing the same thing?" Often, after some thought, I get an affirmative answer. The child may be cheating on tests, stealing, or lying excessively. If he has anything approaching a normal superego, he will feel guilty about these acts. Intrinsic to guilt is self-loathing: "What a terrible person I am for doing all these horrible things." The child in such a situation might be told: "As long as you do those things you're going to find that you'll feel lousy about yourself. I think you'll see that if and when you can stop, you'll feel better about yourself." Although the proverbial advice, "Virtue is its own reward," may seem trite, it is most valid.

Erikson[3] in fact, has made the concept central to his "Eighth Age of Man" — the phase of "Ego Integrity vs. Despair." The inherent rewards of virtue can be imparted quite effectively in the storytelling game.

The perfectionistic child is unable to live up to the unrealistically high standards he sets for himself. He is therefore never satisfied with his performance, and suffers from chronic feelings of inadequacy. Most often the child's standards reflect those of his parents and he must be helped to see the inappropriateness of their precepts. Comments such as these may also be helpful: "As long as you think that any grade below A is unacceptable, you'll feel lousy about yourself," or "As long as you feel you have to be the best basketball player in every game in order to be acceptable, you'll feel terrible about yourself."

The parent who, under the guise of helping his child with his homework, actually does it for him or points out his mistakes so that the child can be assured of handing in perfect papers, is seriously undermining the child's self-confidence. The child cannot possibly enjoy a feeling of mastery if he has not indeed "mastered" his subject. A few poor grades do far more for such a child than all his A's in homework. The low marks may mobilize him to learn on his own, whereas high marks, essentially obtained by his parents, may cripple him educationally. The father who makes the models for his child so that they "look better" is similarly sabotaging the child's attempt to gain a feeling of self-confidence. These are but two examples of the overprotective parent-overdependent child syndrome. Such children become psychologically paralyzed; they are incapable of performing up to their age level in many areas; they cannot help but compare themselves unfavorably with their peers; and they inevitably suffer massive feelings of inadequacy.

The foregoing are what I consider to be the more important factors contributing to low self-esteem in children. The Mutual Storytelling Technique can be helpful in implementing therapeutic approaches and suggestions designed to alleviate this problem.

Example 1

Martin, the seven-year-old boy with generalized apathy, disinterest in his schoolwork, and lack of involvement with peers, told this story one week after the tale of the bear and the beehive:

Once there was a bear in the woods ——
Therapist: A bear in the woods ——
Patient: Who was going to get honey, so he went to a bee-hive and he wrecked it and took out all the honey.
Therapist: To a beehive and he wrecked it?
Patient: Yeah. And then he ——
Therapist: And then he what?
Patient: Brought it home and then he ate it. I think that's all.
Therapist: That's all? That's the whole story? What's the lesson of that story? What do we learn from that story?
Patient: That bears get honey from beehives.
Therapist: Okay, come on now you can give us a better story. Let's hear a better story.
Therapist: Once there was a pig and he got some straw. [Martin, at times, mumbles to the point of being inaudible.]
Therapist: The pig got what?
Patient: Straw. And he took the straw and be built a nest in the yard.
Therapist: He built a nest?
Patient: Yeah. And then he went into the mud.
Therapist: He went into the what?
Patient: The mud.
Therapist: The mud. Okay.
Patient: And then he went to the other pigs and told them to get some straw. And then they all had a nest and then the baby pigs came and hided under them.
Therapist: And then the baby pigs came and what?
Patient: Hided under them.
Therapist: Hid under the ——
Patient: Yeah, pigs. Under the big pigs.
Therapist: Hid under the big pigs. Yeah, then what happened?

524

Patient: And then the men, they gave them some corn. And then they got washed and washed them off. That's the end.

Therapist: The men washed them off. What's the lesson of that story?

Patient: That pigs get corn.

Therapist: Pigs get corn. Okay. All right. Thank you very much.

The first story is, of course, related to the story sequence of the previous week. The honey in the beehive symbolizes his mother's love which, although sweet, is carefully guarded. The acquisition of it exposes Martin to her poisonous sting. The bear is the patient, himself. I had advised Martin to seek the honey when the bees (his mother) were receptive to his requests, but when they were not, to go to the maple trees in another part of the forest, to others, that is, who are more likely to provide affection. His response here was to tell a story in which he ignores my advice and even more adamantly tries to extract love from his mother: he wrecks the beehive and takes out all the honey.

When urged to tell a second story, Martin related one which reflects his extreme dependency cravings as well as his very low opinion of himself. The nest of straw where he is fed corn reveals his return-to-the-womb fantasies, but he depicts himself as a pig wallowing in mud — a clear statement of his feelings of self-loathing. Elements in the story suggest sources for these feelings of worthlessness: his mother's lack of affection makes him feel unlovable; trying to extract love from her, against her will, only makes him feel worse about himself; regressive fantasies, however gratifying, rob him of the ego-enhancing satisfactions of growth and mastery.

Interestingly, the mother is also depicted as a pig — the baby pigs are nested under the big pigs — whereas the father, as represented by the men, not only provides affection — corn — but also washes him off as well. The father is seen, in other words, as someone who can cleanse Martin of his feelings of low self-worth.

With this understanding of Martin's stories, I told mine:

Once there was this bear and this pig. And this bear's main desire in life was to go and get honey and sit and do nothing. And this pig's main desire was to build a nest in the mud and sit there and have people feed him corn. And everybody felt that these two animals were kind of lazy. And the kids used to call them babies 'cause they never wanted to do anything for themselves, they just wanted to hang around and be taken care of. And then when the other pigs and the bears grew up and were able to do something for themselves, this pig and this bear weren't able to because they were kind of lazy and never got used to doing things for themselves. And so they ended up quite unhappy and sad, whereas the other pigs and bears who would think for themselves and learned how to do things for themselves were much happier.

And the lesson of that story is: it may be nice to be taken care of, but there has to come a time when you have to do things on your own.

The end. What did you think of that story?

Patient: Fine.

Therapist: Did you like any special part of it?

Patient: Yes.

Therapist: Which part?

Patient: When they were feeding him the corn.

Therapist: I see. Okay.

In my story, I combined elements of both of Martin's stories and attempted to help this boy enhance his self-esteem. I say help him enhance his self-esteem because the job is primarily his. He has to do the things which will make him feel better about himself; he has to ⌐orrect his distortions; I can only guide and advise. He is told that peers will respect him less if he acts like a "baby:" The implication is that their values may very well become his and that behaving in an infantile manner cannot but cause him to lose respect for himself. In addition, the ego-enhancing value of mastery and growth are emphasized: "the pigs and bears who would think for themselves and learned how to do things for themselves were much happier." I did not reiterate the theme of substitute gratifications in my story. His reaction against it had been so strong — wrecking the beehive to prove me wrong — that I decided to hold off with that advice until he was more receptive to it. Unfortunately, Martin increasingly resisted treatment, and I finally recommended a trial with another therapist. As far as I know the parents did not seek further help.

Martin's comment that the part of my story which he liked the best was "When they were feeding him the corn," was a clear manifestation of his need to deny the growth-encouragement aspects of my story and to gratify his deep-seated dependency fantasies. This pressure to withdraw into fantasy which at times approached a psychotic level, and the associated denial of reality stimuli were significant elements in the failure of Martin's therapy.

Example 2

Charles, the boy with severe immaturity problems who came into treatment when his mother was dying of leukemia, told this story about six months after his mother's death:

Patient: Can you help me?

Therapist: Well, all right I'll help you start the story and then when I point my finger at you you say exactly what comes to your mind.

Once upon a time a long, long, long time ago in a distant land far, far, far away there lived a ——

Patient: Car.

Therapist: And this car ——

Patient: Helped all the people cross the street. It was like a mechanic. Then one day the car went into a crash. Its name was Auto. So all the lights were broken and the children didn't know how to cross the street. So they all got sad. So a man fixed Auto's car and they were back to normal.

And the lesson of that story is: you should always

know how to cross the street because when you go to school you're going to have to cross the street and if nobody's helping you, oh, you're in a lot of trouble.

The car named Auto represents the patient's mother who had died a few months previously. She had been his "guiding light," and, as the story demonstrates, when she dies in an automobile accident in which the car's lights are broken, the children are left without guidance — "they don't know how to cross the street." Although there is a magic restoration of the car — a reflection of the boy's wish that his mother be alive again — the moral reveals his understanding from messages imparted in previous stories, that one cannot fully depend upon others. One must develop the wherewithal to handle many of life's situations oneself or else, "you're in a lot of trouble."

With this understanding of the patient's story, I told mine:

Once upon a time there were these kids and these kids used to depend a lot on a certain car. That car did a lot of things for them. It used to take them to different places, even to short distances where they could really walk or ride their bike, and it would often light their way across the street, even when it wasn't that dark. And this car thought it was doing these kids a favor by doing all these things for these kids, but then the kids gradually realized that this car wasn't doing them very much of a favor because they weren't learning to do things on their own. If it was going to light the streets for them all the time and help them walking, they might not be able to walk as well on their own. And if it was going to drive them everywhere, it wouldn't help them in that they would not know the ways to get different places and wouldn't have the practice of doing it on their own. So gradually they decided only to use the car in emergency situations and they felt much better about themselves after that, because they had learned to do these things on their own.

And the lesson of that story is when you learn to do something on your own you feel very good about yourself.

But, on the other hand, if you depend on somebody else to do things for you, it may be more comfortable, but you really don't feel good about yourself.

Therapist: Did you understand what that story was about? What did you understand the lesson of that story to be?

Patient: Well, it was like when somebody who always crossed you and they die then you have to learn to do it all by yourself. You feel good if you learn to do things by yourself.

In my story I referred to the mother's overprotectiveness: the car would carry children distances which were short enough for them to walk; it would light their way across the street even when it wasn't dark. The children become aware of the paralyzing dependency that the car's favors threaten. They decide to do much more on their own, and they feel "much better about themselves." I stressed the important relationship between competence and self-esteem. My moral reiterates the same message.

It is of interest that, although in my story there is no mention of the mother's death and her symbolization as the car, Charles introduced these elements in his comments following my story. Although they reveal his appreciation of my communications, his general involvement in therapy after the immediate problems related to his mother's death were worked through was minimal, and therapy was prematurely terminated.

Example 3

Mike, a seven-year-old boy with minimal brain dysfunction and borderline intelligence, was referred because of somatic complaints, obsessive smelling of his hands and objects, and ritualistic movements — all of a few months duration. During his eighth month of therapy, he told this story:

Once upon a time there was a big ocean and there were clams and sharks and scallops and lobsters and bass and whales and seals and you know what. There were boys that came for a swim in the shallow water for vacation to swim.

And they swam and suddenly came a big giant whale and ate the little boy up and all the boys 'cause the whale was so hungry and she found somebody to eat up. And she ate the little boy and the boy said, "Help! Help! They're eating me up," and she took one gulp and swallowed them alive with no bites. "Help! I'm alive in his tummy, get me out of here." That's what the boy said. So then somebody killed the whale with his sharp knife, a diver, and he came and stuck and pricked him with the knife and cut her open. A slit, a big slit, and then took the little boys out and then the whale was dead and they lived happily ever after.

Therapist: And what's the lesson of that story?

Patient: And the whale sunk and drownded.

Therapist: What's the lesson of that story?

Patient: That the whale should not eat up the boys. That the whale ate up the boys and that the whale wasn't supposed to eat up the boys. And that the whale drownded and sunk and was dead and that they slit him open. And that the first part was good and that the last part was bad. And that the middle and all the rest was all bad. And, I mean, that the middle was bad and then the last part was good.

Therapist: Okay, thank you very much. That was an excellent story.

I was especially pleased that your story didn't jump around a lot. It had a beginning, a middle, and an end. And it didn't have all kinds of things changing so often. It was very easy to follow. Do you understand what I mean?

Patient: Yes.

Therapist: It was a story I could follow.

Patient: No, I don't.

Therapist: Sometimes you tell stories where lots of things jumble up and there're all kinds of things happening at the same time and it's hard to follow and understand the story. But this story, it was very easy to follow, and I like that very much and I think it's very good that you can tell a story like this.

The story suggests a number of possible psychodynamic

interpretations, none of which need be exclusive. Mike's feelings of being engulfed by overwhelming forces in the world and his desire to be rescued from such entrapment are reflected. Mike was ill-equipped to cope with the usual frustrations and discomforts of reality, and he consequently saw his environment as far more threatening than it was. The story also refers to his relationship with his mother, who is obviously represented by the whale. She was somewhat overprotective and the patient was dependent on her beyond the requirements of his organic deficits. In the story it is she who engulfs him and brings him back into the womb; but in reality Mike was far more desirous than she to perpetuate his clinging-dependent relationship. He lessens his guilt and embarrassment over his marked dependency longings by making his mother the one who pursues the pathological relationship. Having himself removed from the whale's stomach is a manifestation of his ambivalence over re-establishing the umbilical tie. Lastly, there is a definite hostile element in the story as well. Mike sees his mother as being oral-aggressive in a most primitive fashion: she eats him up. This mother was a most warm and understanding person and although she, like all mothers, had ambivalent feelings toward her son, the hostile elements were far less than average. Seeing her as hostile was the result of his own projected hostility which was related to the frustrations he felt because of his organic deficits as well as those which were engendered by his dependency on her. Exaggerated dependency invariably produces hostility The dependent person is often at the mercy of the provider. He has not developed the means to function on his own. With the awareness that at any time he can be abandoned, the dependent person cannot help but resent his situation.

Of the various elements I could have focused upon, I felt that Mike's craving to re-establish an infantile dependency tie with his mother was the most pertinent one. Accordingly, I told this story:

Once upon a time there was an ocean and in this ocean there lived a whale. It was a big mother whale and she had a little boy whale. Now this little boy whale was always hanging around his mother and he thought how nice it would be if he could be a little baby inside her belly and be taken care of by her all the time. But when he used to wish that that would happen and he would hang around and say, "Mommy, I want you to do this for me," and "Mommy, I want you to do that for me," and "Mommy, I want you to treat me like a baby," two things happened which made him sad. Number one, other children used to laugh at him and they'd say, "You're just a baby, you're a baby," and they would tease him and call him baby. And they were right in doing that, not that they should tease him so much, but at least they were right in thinking that he was a baby because he did hang around with his mother a lot. That's the first thing that made him sad when he would hang around his mother very much. The other thing that made him sad was that he didn't learn to do all the things that boys his age were learning to do. They were out playing and learning big boy games and things, and so it made him sad that he wasn't doing all these things. And one day a friend of his came over and said to him, "You know, you must be a very sad boy. You look very sad. Why are you so sad?"

And he said, "I'm sad 'cause all the kids tease me and call me baby, and I don't know how to do all the other things that other boys do."

And the friend said, "Well, of course, they call you baby because you act like a baby. You're always hanging around your mother and you never work hard to learn to play the games that other kids play."

Well, this little boy thought about this and he realized that his friend was right, so he tried very hard, it wasn't easy, and he couldn't do it very quickly, but slowly he worked hard to learn the other games that the other children played. And he played with the other boy and girl whales who were his own age and he decided that although it was a little frightening at times to be away from his mother, he found out that he was much happier because the kids didn't call him baby anymore and he learned to play a lot of fun games. And it was hard for him to do this because he was scared at times when he would go away from his mother for long periods of time. But he gradually stopped wishing that he would be back inside his mother's belly and he gradually enjoyed playing the games more and more and the children stopped calling him baby.

Know what the lesson of this story is?

Patient: That if you hang on too much with your mother then they'll call you baby, 'cause they might tease you, but if you don't and you play games, boy games and girls' games, and you play with children, then they don't tease you anymore, they don't call you baby anymore and you're much happier.

Therapist: Right. Very, very good. And there's just one other lesson in it. And that is to do this is often very hard and kids get very scared of doing this, but if they try hard and they're brave enough — remember we talked about bravery and courage — to do it even though it may make them scared, then they will find that they'll be much happier.

What did you think about that story?

Patient: Um, kind of good.

Therapist: What's the part about it you liked the most?

Patient: The good part.

Therapist: What was the good part?

Patient: That you don't hang on to your mother anymore they don't tease you anymore; they don't call you baby anymore 'cause you play with the boys little games.

Therapist: But it's hard to do that if you haven't much practice and you have to think hard about how to do it; you have to remember not to be silly; you have to remember to do things the way the other children do it, so they won't laugh at you and you won't be different from them.

A detailed description of the use of the Mutual Storytelling Technique in the treatment of children with minimal brain dysfunction will be presented in Chapter 13. This story demonstrates the importance of two elements in the approach to such children: repetition and concretism. The therapist's messages must be repeated over and over if they are to "stick," and he must express himself in the most concrete fashion. Conceptualizations and abstractions are especially difficult for such children to understand and they are best avoided. Even the simple use of the symbol may be confusing.

Actually, the meaning of my story is quite clear. I tried to show Mike that in pursuing his infantile cravings, he will suffer peer rejection, and, by extension, self-rejection as well. Such dependency will deprive him of the ego-enhancement which comes with growth and competence. When encouraging the organically impaired child to enter into learning situations (be it social or educational), it is important to appreciate that he suffers more anxiety than most normal children. His rejections have been more frequent and predictable and his humiliations, therefore more profound. He must be helped to bear anxiety, but he must not be pressured into entering situations in which he will be predictably mortified. He must become aware of those traits in himself which may result in his alienation and to alter them when possible in order to gain acceptance. In this case, infantile behavior was without question one of the reasons for Mike's difficulties with peers, and he did have the ability to correct it.

Mike's statement of the lesson of my story revealed his appreciation of at least two of its important elements: you'll be more acceptable to peers if you're less infantile, and your self-esteem will thereby be enhanced — "you're much happier."

Example 4

Malcolm, the boy with multiple fears, rage outbursts, and generalized tension, told this story:

> Once upon a time there was this man who when he was a baby they called him Picture because in the front of his face he looked like a picture with a frame around it. So, the people when he began to grow up thought that he looked like a picture frame because there was a big gigantic picture frame bone and they called him Bone Picture Frame.
> *Therapist:* Wait a minute. He looked like a bone? I'm not

clear what you're saying.

Patient: It looked like a bone — the picture frame. It looked like a bone was busting out in the shape of a picture frame. That's what it looked like.

Therapist: So it was a bone?

Patient: Yeah, they thought it was. It was just the way he was growing.

And everybody teased him and teased him and teased him and so he went away on vacation with his mother and father and on the train were all the children that teased him because it was summertime and everybody went on vacation. And so he went back the next day with his mother and father and there was no one and nobody teased him.

Therapist: Everybody teased him, and then what happened?

Patient: Next day he went back with his mother and father to the regular town and there was no one, not a single soul there that he had to play with, because everybody was on vacation. And so someone bought him this chemistry set for him during the summer and he saw something in it that made the picture frame bone go away and he rubbed it all over his face and the picture frame went away. And then they called him Mr. Green.

Therapist: Why did they call him Mr. Green?

Patient: Uh, because then he liked flowers and he had a greenhouse and there was thousands of flowers in the greenhouse, and they called him Mr. Green. And he had a dog too.

And the moral to this story is that no one is to tease just because the other person has an odd face.

The story reveals Malcolm's basic feeling that he is a freak with a disfiguring bone growing out of his head. This deformity encircles his head like a picture frame — further accentuating his malformation. He is the object of ridicule among his peers and only escapes their scorn by returning to town when they are all away on vacation. His disfigurement is magically removed with his chemistry set, and he then withdraws from the world into the isolation of his greenhouse — a place where fragile forms of life are protected from harsh reality.

With this understanding of Malcolm's story, I related the following:

Once upon a time there was a man and when he was a baby he had a strange idea about himself. He thought that a big bone was growing out of him and that this bone looked like a picture frame. This was his thought; it really wasn't the case. He didn't have a bone growing out of his head and it didn't look like a picture frame, but he had the thought not only that he had it, but that everybody was looking at him and laughing at him and making fun of him and teasing him. Now how could he get such a strange thought?

This strange thought came about because he thought he was no good. And he thought that he was like a cripple or a freak or something like that. And why did he think he was a freak? Why do you think he thought he was a freak?
Patient: I don't know.
Therapist: I think, well, it's my story so I'll tell you why he thought he was a freak.

He thought he was a freak because his mother was a person who was a very cold person, and she was a woman who couldn't give him much time and affection and attention. And his father was a man who also wasn't giving him as much attention and affection as he might have. His father was always involved with his business and things like that. So because his mother and father were so wrapped up in themselves and so involved in what they were doing that they couldn't give him much time, it made him feel very sad, it made him feel lonely, and he thought that there was something wrong with him if they were not spending time with him. That was his wrong thought. He thought that there was something wrong with him and he must be a freak or something if they don't spend time with him.

One day he was sitting around very sad about this when a boy came over to him and sat. And he said to the boy, "How can you want to stay with me? I have a bone that looks like a picture frame so everybody looks at and laughs."

536

And the boy said, "I don't know, something must be wrong with your thinking. I don't see any bone. I don't see any picture frame. But you must feel very bad about yourself."

He said "Yeah, I do. My mother and father are too wrapped up in themselves to give me much thought."

He said "That's sad. That must make you very lonely. But that doesn't mean that you're no good, that doesn't mean that no one else will ever want to love you. Lots of people have that problem and some people that have that problem want to crawl away and hide from the world and they want to stay away from everybody because they think everybody is scorning them. They'd like to hide in a greenhouse and take care of their plants or something like that, because they think that the whole world is laughing at them and teasing them. And really the world isn't. And they think that no one can love them, and that's not so. Just because their mother and father can't love them very much, doesn't mean that no one else will."

Well, when the boy heard that it gave him some hope and he knew that when he grew up and as time went on and he grew up, he would have more and more chance to make friends. And if he couldn't get very much love from his parents he could at least from other people. In addition, he realized that just because they don't love him doesn't mean that no one else does either.

Therapist: And do you know what the lesson of that story is?

Patient: No.

Therapist: You think about it. What were the main things the boy learned?

Patient: That just because his mother and father didn't spend much time with him doesn't mean that he's a freak with a bone that looked like a picture frame.

Therapist: Right, and —— what else? (*Does not respond.*) The second thing he learned was that just because your parents don't love you very much doesn't mean that no one else can ever. And that when you grow up other people can and you can even get friends now who'll like you more and make you feel better. Now I wanted to ask you something. Do you have any comments about that story?

Patient: No.

Therapist: Did you like it?

Patient: Yes.

Therapist: What was the part of it you liked the most?

Patient: I liked all the parts. When you said that sometimes you might make up your own stories and sometimes you make up stories that are similar to mine and with just about the same characters. I haven't seen you yet make up your own story 'cause you made up ones always similar to mine.

Therapist: They're always similar to yours. I just use the same characters, but different things happen to them. 'Cause that's how it works, that's how the game works. I start off with the same characters, but different things happen to them.

Patient: Oh! I wish we could hear a story of your own too.

Therapist: Did you want to hear this story that I just told? Did you want to hear that one?

Patient: Yes.

Therapist: Okay.

In my story I touched upon one of the elements which contributes to Malcolm's feeling that he is a freak: parental deprivation of affection. The patient is clearly an adherent of the dictum, "If they don't love me, I am unlovable." I attempted to show him the illogicality of this notion. I also advised him to seek others who might provide him with compensations for the deprivations he suffers in his home. Both of these messages were presented in the service of helping Malcolm with his severe low self-esteem problem.

Although the large bone might also symbolize a phallus (displaced to the head to insure its disguise), it still represents an attempt to enhance his masculinity in compensation for his feelings of low self-worth. Accordingly, by focusing on the issue of self-esteem rather than on the sexual aspect, a more meaningful response was gained. This was confirmed by Malcolm's deep interest in my story and his wish to hear it again.

538

Example 5

Donald, the boy with generalized immaturity, poor school performance, and overdependence on an overprotective mother, told this story during his second month of therapy:

Well today I have a boy. Well this story I made up myself but there's a special catch to it. I put in somethings like when I see a library I make a story of a library. Is that all right?

Therapist: That's okay. What did you see that you want to make a story of?

Patient: Well this isn't true — only about the library. I see, it's just still made up. I just got an idea from the library.

Well once there was this boy and he had a lot of books and he called itself the Storytelling Book Library.

Therapist: I don't understand. He had a library of story telling books. Is that it?

Patient: No, he had a library and he had so many books of stories, all made up by minds from people, he called it the library of storytellings.

Therapist: Wait a minute. Were these books he had?

Patient: Yeah.

Therapist: And he had them in his library?

Patient: Yeah.

Therapist: All right, then he called them the library of story books, is that it?

Patient: Yeah!

Therapist: Okay good. So now ——

Patient: So one day he earned seventy-five cents when he polished somebody's shoes 'cause he had two businesses, publishing books — giving them out for a library, and polish shoes. And once he got three dollars on shining shoes, no he got seven dollars on shining shoes, no he earned eight dollars cause he had four customers and he got fifty cents on a customer.

Therapist: Four customers, fifty cents on a customer, would be two dollars.

Patient: No!

Therapist: If he got two dollars from a customer he'd have eight dollars. Right?

Patient: Now wait a minute. He got eight dollars because he got four men and they all paid fifty cents; oh yeah, they all paid two dollars.

Therapist: All right, go ahead. Four customers at two dollars. Go ahead. Then what?

Patient: So then he was happy and he spent around two dollars on something — on very silly books, and everybody bought all the books except those books, those five books that he bought — five small books. And everybody laughed at him for those five books. The names of them were "Silly Dr. Seuss Came to the House" —

Therapist: Was that a book he was selling?

Patient: Yeah.

Therapist: And everybody laughed at him for that book?

Patient: Yeah. And another book, "The Light is Bright, Mainly on the Moon." Well he really bought three books and the last one was "Hello Dolly, Won't You Call Me Dolly." So, oh yeah, he bought five books and the next one he called "The Clock Struck Twelve and Broke his Nose."

So many people laughed at him that he wasn't really skilled in the library business, he was only skilled in the shoe shine business. This I got, well, there's a special thing. Well you see I got this moral from a book, and something like it, and he was only skilled in shoe shine so he gave up the library business 'cause he didn't gain anything and he didn't care about it anymore 'cause of laughing people on him.

Therapist: And the moral of the story?

Patient: The moral of the story is you should never try to be anything else but your own self, because you're only skilled in something that you're trained for.

Therapist: That's a very good story. Thank you very much for telling me that very interesting story. And now it's time for me to tell my story.

Patient: I have a question.

Therapist: Yes. What's the question?

Patient: Last time, well a few weeks ago, you said that you copy a story from somebody else, something like it. Right?

Therapist: Right.

Patient: Well, once you didn't copy a story anything like mine.

Therapist: I don't think so. I always use the same people that you have in your story.

Patient: No, once you didn't do it.

Therapist: I don't recall that time. I don't recall that at all.

Patient: Well, I don't recall the time that you never played a card game with me.

Therapist: I see. All right, anyway.

Patient: 'Cause you never did.

Therapist: Shall I get on with my story?

Patient: I think you'd better.

The story reveals Donald's feeling that the stories he tells in the Storytelling game are laughable and unworthy of being seriously appreciated — no one buys them. Although storytelling may not be his métier, he is quite successful as a shoe shine boy, a far more menial occupation. In the moral he advises that one withdraw from the more sophisticated endeavor in such situations: "you should never try to be anything else but your own self, because you're only skilled in something that you're trained for." In short, the story reflects Donald's general feelings of inadequacy regarding academic and other intellectual accomplishments, his flight from such pursuits, and his notion that he can only hope to achieve competence in the simplest tasks. In response, then, I told this story:

Once upon a time there was a boy and he had many books of stories. And he used to have a library of these stories, of these books, and he used to lend them to people in order to earn some money.

Patient: He doesn't. Nobody earns money in the library.

Therapist: No. There's a lending library. There's a certain kind of library where you can earn money.

Now remember, my story is going to be something like your story, except that parts of it are different.

Patient: I know!

Therapist: Anyway, this boy was earning some money with his books, but not too much because people used to laugh at the books — sometimes because they had very funny titles. Some people laughed, and some didn't.

He also had another business; he earned money selling shoe shines. He would shine people's shoes, and he would earn money that way. But, he didn't like the shoe shine business as much as he liked writing and lending books because books are interesting and fun to read, whereas shining shoes is not very much fun. But he began to get discouraged because people were laughing at some of the books, but other people didn't. And he began to wonder: "Should I get rid of this business? Should I make all my money shining shoes?" So he decided to speak to a good friend of his about this problem. His friend told him that some of his books were good, but that others showed that he really wasn't very well trained in bookwriting. The friend asked him whether he had worked hard at learning to write, and whether he had listened in class when they taught how to write. The boy was ashamed to answer but he had to be honest and admit that he didn't listen too much in class and hadn't learned very much. So the friend said, "Well, it's no surprise then that you aren't very good at bookwriting. How can you expect to be good at something if you haven't taken the trouble to learn how to do it well? As long as you don't listen in class and don't make the effort to learn, you'll feel bad about your ability." The boy realized that his friend was right. So he tried harder, listened in class, and after a long time he slowly and gradually got better and better in writing. Then people no longer laughed at his books and he felt much better about himself, and he didn't have to shine shoes anymore.

The moral of that story is that if you don't work hard at something, you won't do well at the thing. Then people may laugh at what you do, and you won't feel good about yourself. But if you work hard at something, then people will admire your work and you'll feel good about yourself.

Patient: Well people laugh at me and there's something wrong with me all right.

Therapist: What's wrong with you?

Patient: Well I'm not so smart.

Therapist: Who said so?

Patient: Well, when somebody asks me a Hebrew question, I don't always answer it.

Therapist: That's not because you're not smart.

Patient: And all the other kids in my class answer the question.

Therapist: I think it's because you're not listening in class, so you don't learn it.

Patient: I listen!

Therapist: You're not stupid. You don't listen in class. That's why you get poor grades. What do you think of that?

Patient: Well, uh, why do I always get laughed at sometimes?

Therapist: What kinds of things do you do. that people laugh at you for?

Patient: Well, uh, when somebody asks me a question I don't answer it correctly. I answer it so off the title of it that they laugh.

Therapist: For instance, give me an example.

Patient: Suppose we were talking about Abraham, like I'm talking about, I say things about, things that didn't really happen, there's nothing in the —

Therapist: Say that again. I'm not clear.

Patient: Well suppose we were on Bible stories, and we're studying Abraham and Jacob. So I answer a question so off what we're saying.

Therapist: But when you're in class you're not listening are you?

Patient: Yeah, I'm listening.

Therapist: I think you're thinking about other things when you're in class.

Patient: Yeah, so?

Therapist: Well that's why you can't answer the question right.

Patient: When I do listen I can't answer it right.

Therapist: Yeah, but when you don't listen, you don't answer the question right, then kids laugh at you. Right?

Patient: Yeah, but when I do listen it still doesn't do anything.

Therapist: When you listen more I think you'll find that you'll be getting more of the answers right. We have to stop here.

As can be seen from the post-story discussion, Donald didn't really hear the message in my story. It was early in treatment, however, and such resistance is common during this phase.

One month later, Donald told this story:

Hello. Today I have a story about an interesting man. And this man was walking on the street. And he had a very big problem. And he was almost goin' ta give up hope until he met this man, another man on the street, Mr. Psychiatrist, and he solved this problem for him.

And the moral of that story is that you should never give up hope because there's always a chance that you'll get better.

Therapist: Now I have a question. What was this man's problem?

Patient: He couldn't do things right.

Therapist: For instance?

Patient: Like say I type something, he forgot to do it. And he didn't —

Therapist: Now what was this man's problem again? He couldn't do things right and you said he would forget?

Patient: He would forget about his typing, if he needed to do something.

Therapist: Wait a minute. Don't turn the recorder off so quickly. Hold it. Keep your hand away from there. I wanna hear this, I'm not clear.

He would forget about his typing? What kind of job did he do? What kind of work did he do?

Patient: Well, he was a reporter.

Therapist: And what would he forget exactly?

Patient: What to type when he would type. And this man fixed him all up, so that's all.

Therapist: Thank you very much. Now it's time for me to tell my story.

Donald's feelings of incompetence are revealed by the man who "couldn't do things right." Although a reporter, he forgets "what to type and when to type." However, he is quickly cured by "Mr. Psychiatrist," who requires no effort or participation on Donald's part in the curative process. The patient was anxious to turn off the recorder — probably to avoid any questions from me which might weaken his neat and secure little fantasy about a magic alleviation of his difficulties. Lastly, the choice of reporter as the man's profession might relate to therapeutic resistance to telling about himself to me. By being unable to recall and type, he can conceal from me that which is unpleasant. The quick cure then could be considered a plea for help in revealing himself to me.

With this understanding of Donald's story, I related mine:

Once upon a time there was a man and he had some very big problems. He could not do things right. He was a reporter, and when he would type he would type wrong or he'd forget what to type. And he was very sad and he was ready to give up hope, when he met another man in the street who was a psychiatrist. And he said to the psychiatrist, "I want you to please solve my problem."

And the psychiatrist said, "No, I won't do it."

He said, "What do you mean you won't do it! You're a psychiatrist. Aren't you supposed to solve people's problems?"

The psychiatrist said, "No."

He said, "Well, I thought psychiatrists solve people's problems."

The psychiatrist said, "No, you've got it wrong."

He said, "Well, what do psychiatrists do then?"

The psychiatrist said, "Psychiatrists HELP people solve their problems themselves."

He said, "What do you mean by that?"

The psychiatrist said, "All I do is help you understand what your problems are, and then it's up to you to do what you want with the information you get. You have to do it yourself. The psychiatrist only gives you some information. He can tell you why you're doing certain things. He can make certain suggestions about how you can feel better. But you have to be the one to do it on your own. And that's the hard part of being a patient of a psychiatrist."

The man said, "Well, I'm willing to try."

So the psychiatrist said, "Remember, it's hard work. I'm not going to do it to you or for you. It has to be done by you. I can just be a little help."

So the man went into treatment with the psychiatrist and he learned some things about why he had trouble, but he had to work the problems out himself. He had to practice his typing, he had to try to remember, he had to try hard, and with the help of the psychiatrist he succeeded and he solved his problems. And he then lived happily ever after.

And the moral of that story is what? Can you figure out the moral of that story?

Patient: Never give up hope because there's always a chance.

Therapist: And what is the chance? How does it work? How does the chance with the psychiatrist work?

Patient: That he'll help you in most things and it's very hard for you and you can't do it. It's not possible that you can do it.

Therapist: No, that isn't what I said. The moral of this story is that a psychiatrist can't help you, you have to do it yourself. He can just be a little bit of help.

In my story I tried to impress upon Donald the unpleasant fact that any changes brought about in himself in treatment will only occur with his active effort and participation. However, my attempt to impart this knowledge was in vain. His surmised moral, "Never give up hope because there's always a chance," suggests that he hopes to be cured without activity on his part, in spite of my warnings to the contrary. His subsequent comment, "It's not possible that you [the patient] can do it," is another statement of resignation to his ineptitude.

Five weeks later, Donald told this story:

> Well, today I have a story about a president. There was once this president and he went downstairs to the UN General Assembly and he heard all the lies and he was very disappointed in all the lies that Kosygin made. Well, when he heard this he was objecting and when he objected they all turned around and they saw Johnson. So then —
>
> *Therapist:* I don't want a story that's from real life. This sounds like it's just from real life. I want a made-up, make-believe story.
>
> *Patient:* No, but this is like a made-up story. I mean —
>
> *Therapist:* Okay, well go ahead.
>
> *Patient:* Well, Johnson objected to Kosygin's lies. When they heard this, they all turned around and they were surprised to see Johnson. And when they saw him they were very surprised. And that's the end of the story.
>
> And the moral of that story is that you shouldn't lie because if somebody bluffs you it's very embarrassing. Good riddence!
>
> *Therapist:* Thank you. Now it's time for me to tell my story.

The story makes reference to another element of Donald's low self-esteem: his tendency to lie to cover up inadequacies. Kosygin, the liar, represents the patient, and Johnson, the president, probably symbolizes me or other authority figures. When they find out that Donald has lied, he is embarrassed.

This is the story I told in response:

> Once upon a time there was a president. He went to the UN General Assembly and there there were men from two countries, Communist China and Nationalist China, each representing one part of China. And the person from Communist China told a lot of lies and the person from Nationalist China didn't. And the president thought, "That man from Communist China, he doesn't know how he's fooling himself. First of all, when you lie most people know you're lying anyway, and it's a very poor way to handle

547

things, because usually since you're lying you're not the most effective and it's a poor way to handle things. The other reason for not lying is that you feel bad inside yourself," he thought. And then he spoke to the man from Communist China and said to him, "Don't you feel bad in yourself that you're such a liar? Don't you feel like a kind of fool or a hypocrite lying that way? Also your lies make the situation worse because we can't handle it."

And he said, "Yes you're right," and he decided to change his ways.

And the moral of that story — there are two morals. Lying is a bad way to handle something, and the second is —

Patient: I know.

Therapist: What's the second?

Patient: We shouldn't lie because if somebody finds out you're lying you could really make a fool of yourself.

Therapist: That's *your* moral. But the moral of *my* story is that you feel bad about yourself even if no one ever finds out. Also, if you lie it's a bad way to handle a situation. Usually by lying you make the situation worse.

In my story, I expounded the theme of "Virtue is its own reward." The ways in which lying contributes to feelings of worthlessness are that one feels bad about oneself when one lies, and one is deprived of the gratifications that go with being direct and truthful. My emphasis on the internal reasons for being truthful proves futile. Donald's interjected moral simply reiterates the external deterrent philosophy professed in his story. The sequence again reflects the tenacity with which this boy held on to those adaptations which were guaranteed to make him feel loathsome.

Three months later, Donald told this story:

Well today I'm goin' ta tell you about a guy and he made so many jokes that after he made so many jokes he wasn't very funny anymore and everybody started to hate him. So as he continued this, they started to hate him more and more, and after that they started making jokes about him and making fun about him —

Therapist: Wait a minute now. Why did people start making jokes and fun about him now? After what?

Patient: Because they started not to like him.

Therapist: Why?

Patient: Because he keep on saying the same jokes like about ten times.

Therapist: Oh, they hated him because he said the same jokes over and over again.

Patient: He thought he was so sure of himself that he laughed before anybody else did.

Therapist: All right. Then what happened?

Patient: He went to his mother and told her all about the kids making fun. And his mother said everytime they said something he should hit 'em in the arm. And everytime he did hit 'em in the arm, and even though they punched him back, he punched 'em back and they started to like him again.

The moral of that story is that if someone starts to hate you you have to have courage in yourself to bring yourself back as a student in the class.

Therapist: Now how did this boy bring himself back in your story?

Patient: He started beating up everybody, when they said something about him.

Therapist: And then what did they do?

Patient: Then they stopped.

Therapist: They stopped saying things because he beat them up.

Thank you very much.

The story has a positive element in that it reveals some awareness that being class clown does not get one the genuine affection that most people seek. Donald tended toward rambunctious behavior in the classroom as an attention-getting device and was beginning genuinely to appreciate that such antics, although they provided him with some attention, were not really gaining for him the affection from peers he so desperately craved. What Donald does with this insight, however, is another thing entirely. Instead of seeking healthier and more gratifying alternative modes of relating with his peers, he merely attempts to coerce them into suppressing their condemnations of him — a most maladaptive adjustment to the problem.

Accordingly, I told this story:

> Once there was this guy and he told a lot of jokes. And he told the same jokes over and over again until they reached the point where they weren't funny anymore. And everybody started to hate him. They hated him more and more because he would tell the same jokes over and over. And the kids would make fun of him because of this. And he spoke to his mother and he said, "I think I should hit them back, then they'll stop making fun of me."
>
> And the mother said, "No. That won't work. The best way to get them to stop making fun of you is to stop telling those stupid jokes. You stop telling those stupid jokes and they'll stop making fun of you."
>
> The boy said, "Yeah, really, that'll work?"
>
> And the mother said, "Of course it'll work."
>
> He said, "I don't believe it."
>
> And his mother said, "Well try it and see."
>
> So the boy, although he didn't believe it, decided to try it. And he stopped making jokes and what do you know — what do you think happened?
>
> *Patient:* They stopped making fun of him.
>
> *Therapist:* Did he have to hit them to stop them?
>
> *Patient:* No.
>
> *Therapist:* Right. And the moral of that story is that if you want somebody to stop laughing at you, just stop telling jokes. Hitting won't work. Then they'll just hate you even more.

As seen in previous stories, Donald's receptivity to my messages was limited. It was not a question of low intelligence, but high psychological resistance. I therefore attempted to impart only the simplest messages in the most uncomplicated fashion. Here, I suggested only that he try seeing whether refraining from horseplay in the classroom might not bring about better relationships with his peers. Substitutive, more attractive modes of interaction were not suggested, not because they weren't indicated in Donald's story, but because the boy had proved himself to be unreceptive to more than one, or at most two, messages in a single story.

Three weeks later, Donald told this story:

Hello. Today I have a story about a dinosaur and this dinosaur could talk. Everytime he'd go to another house next door like and he'd ask for a bowl of sugar. Then this guy wondered why he needed so much sugar. And then he went and he had this factory and he kept on making sugar cane [candy]. So the dinosaur said he could have most of the sugar cane —

Therapist: You mean the neighbor?

Patient: Yeah. He said he [the neighbor] could have a lot of — he could share this sugar cane with him since he [the neighbor] gave him all the sugar to make the sugar cane. So they had a very good time. So the neighbor went home and he was very quiet and he went to sleep and he had a very funny dream about a dinosaur throwing bricks of sugar at him and he was dying like because it was so much sugar and it was drowning him like. So when he woke up he said, "I'll never have a piece of sugar cane again."

The moral of that story is: if you find out that somebody comes over to you and asks so many times each day for the same thing, tell him, "What do you need this for?" If he needs it for something important you should lend it to him. The end.

Therapist: And if he doesn't?

Patient: What do you mean, "And if he doesn't?" If he doesn't what?

Therapist: And if he doesn't need it for something important?

Patient: Just tell him that he should borrow from somebody else because if you're like going to eat sugar all day it's not good for you and besides it's like stealing because I bought this out of my own money. The end.

Therapist: Now how does that relate to your story?

Patient: Oh, about the sugar. He was giving him all of the sugar and —

Therapist: It was just too much and he was drowning him in too much sugar, huh?

Patient: Yeah.

Therapist: I see. Okay.

The dinosaur represents Donald's mother and the neighbor stands for the patient. The story reveals his recognition, at some level, that his mother's overindulgence, as comfortable as it may make him feel, is not ultimately in his best interest. Donald, like the neighbor in the story, is drowning in his mother's sugar. The story reflected the clinical situation where he was becoming much more independent and self-assertive.

I told this story in response:

Once upon a time there was a talking dinosaur and this talking dinosaur went to a house and he asked for a bowl of sugar. The guy asked the dinosaur why he needed so much sugar and the dinosaur said it was to make sugar cane candy. The dinosaur said to the neighbor, "Would you like to have some sugar cane?" He said, "All right. I'll have a little." Then the dinosaur started giving his neighbor sugar cane and he gave him so much that the guy decided that he didn't have to work or do anything because the dinosaur was always feeding him sugar cane and this was all he needed to eat.

So he was ready to quit his job when he went to sleep and he had a dream and in this dream he dreamed that he was going to be completely submerged with bricks of sugar that were being thrown at him. He realized that this dream meant that it's no good to live a life where you are just taking things from everybody else and it's better to live a life where you are doing certain things on your own. So the next day he decided not to quit his job and he continued working and he only took very little of the sugar cane from the dinosaur.

The moral of that story is —

Patient: You shouldn't get fat.

Therapist: Right. You shouldn't get fat on other people's

work. You should do work yourself or else you'll turn into a kind of blooming idiot where you just sit around and everyone does something for you. You get no work done and no pleasure from doing things on your own. The end.

In my story I reinforced the healthy elements manifested in Donald's story by emphasizing the disadvantages of being all-taking and dependent. As mentioned, this boy's overdependence contributed significantly to his low self-esteem.

Donald told this story three months later:

Once upon a time there were these three boys and they wanted to go to college. They were old enough for it and they wanted to go to college. They weren't thinking about the war that was going to last about seven years and that's how much you go in the army ahout. You go for about two years. They weren't thinking about it. So they went to college and they got picked to join the army and they were very afraid. So when they got drafted they always say, "It turns a playboy into a man." And it did and they weren't afraid anymore from now on.

The moral of that story is: you should never be afraid because if you want to do something anybody can do it. You can even jump from one building to another if you think.

Therapist: Now I want to ask you something. What is a playboy?

Patient: A playboy is a person who goes out with dates all the time.

Therapist: And what else?

Patient: And that's all.

Therapist: Is that good or bad or what?

Patient: It's bad.

Therapist: Why?

Patient: Because a playboy gets, you know, like a softie and he gets to be like a softie and, you know, he gets to be a softie. He gets to be a softie and, you know, he ah, gets to be afraid of everybody and he doesn't care and if, ah, like you're eight years old and everybody calls you a sissy and that's not nice.

Therapist: Hhmmm. But how would he harden up? How did he —

Patient: Well, the moral — as I said they went to the army — the three boys went to the army and they turn into men.

Therapist: What did the army do to turn them into men?

Patient: Well, they had physical training and they went into the war and they had to, ah, do a lot of activities, very bad activities.

Therapist: Ah, I see. Now how is that you don't do that?

Patient: Because I'm not grown up enough to be in the army.

Therapist: Like Charlie's All Stars, for instance. [Donald's activity group]. You're quitting now because you fell a few times when they were teaching you how to ice skate.

Patient: No, no. I'm not doing that because it's so much money for them and I don't want them to —

Therapist: Come on. That's not the reason.

Patient: Yes! It costs about twenty-two dollars in two weeks —

Therapist: The reason is that you —

Patient: And I don't like it there too much.

Therapist: No. The reason is that you are not —

Patient: And everybody was making fun of me because I couldn't ice skate well at all.

Therapist: No, I think the reason is that you're afraid to fall and hurt yourself. You're a kind of a softie.

Patient: I'm a softie, but not because I'm a playboy, that's for sure.

Therapist: No, you're not a playboy, but you're a softie. You'd feel less like a softie if you stuck it out at Charlie's All Stars. Now it's time for my story.

The playboys, of course, are Donald. However distorted his concept of the playboy is, he does appreciate the basic weakness of those who pursue the playboy way of life: they are "softies" and "sissies." In addition, the playboy is also obsessed with women: "he goes out with dates all the time." So there is something positive and healthy in Donald's eschewing that role; it implies a wish to rid himself of his childish, immature, and mother-dependent characteristics. However, the transformation is not accomplished in the present but in the future and by army discipline. He doesn't have to change now; it will be done to him by the army which makes men out of playboys. All Donald has to do is wait passively until he is eighteen and then he'll be transformed into a man.

In the post-story inquiry Donald describes some of the masculinity enhancing activities and exposures which the army provides, and this leads into a discussion of his quitting his activity group because of the minor traumas which all boys must be willing to tolerate if they are to enjoy sports and other ego-enhancing activities. His denial of flight from such experiences is vehement. I attempted to communicate to him the fact that he is depriving himself of experiences which might help him feel better about himself, but his fears are too great and my message went unheeded.

I told this story in response:

Once upon a time there were three boys and they were playboy types, kind of softies, and they were about eight years old and one of them said, "Well, I have time enough to harden up when I'm eighteen and when I go into the army or when I go into college." The other one said, "Yeah, me too." So those two remained softies and kids would pick on them and kids would laugh at them and they were kind of blubbery and a little fat. They didn't have too many friends and they were afraid to do things like play ball and skate and things like that.

The third one said, "I can't stand being a softie anymore. I don't like it and I'm not going to wait until I'm older." So this guy decided right then and there to institute a hardening-up program. He began to join in on sports and it was hard and difficult, but he managed to do it and then he was much happier, because from the ages of eight to eighteen, during that ten-year-period, he really enjoyed himself much more and had a better time. He felt much better about himself.

Do you know what the moral of that story is?

Patient: That you shouldn't wait until you get into the army to harden up because then when you have to fight the enemy you might get killed or die or something or get a wound because you're not strong enough. You're a softie.

Therapist: Uh-huh!

Patient: You don't have time to harden up.

Therapist: Right. The end.

The meaning of my story is obvious. Although Donald understood my message, his ability to translate it into action was still impaired. About one month later, after one year of treatment, I made an unusual and somewhat risky recommendation which fortunately turned out well. He was about to be promoted into the fourth grade, but his teacher described him to be borderline for such advancement and to be still quite immature compared to his classmates even though there had been significant improvement over the year. I suggested to his parents and school officials that he repeat the third grade. I reasoned that if he were with a younger group his immaturity problem would be less obvious to his classmates and he would thereby be spared much of the taunting and ridicule he was suffering. Of course, I was aware that "being left back" might expose him to ridicule of another kind, but this I felt would be the lesser of the two unpleasant alternatives. In addition, I suggested that treatment be temporarily discontinued. While there had been definite improvement, I had the feeling that I had reached the point of diminishing returns. My suggestion was followed and the patient improved markedly. He felt much better about himself and became one of the higher students in the class. His behavior was in no way conspicuous.

11. SUPEREGO DEFICIENCIES

Two psychic functions are subsumed under the rubric, superego: the conscience and the ego-ideal. I will discuss each of these separately.

Conscience refers to those mental mechanisms which guide and assist the individual in inhibiting himself from performing acts which are considered unacceptable by significant figures in his milieu. The affect which an individual experiences when he performs, or is tempted to perform, such unacceptable acts is guilt.

There are three stages in the child's development of the capacity to experience guilt. The first, which I refer to as the Pain Stage, is the earliest. During this phase, the parent prevents the child from participating in unacceptable behavior by the direct infliction of pain. A two-year-old child who runs into the street will not be deterred from doing so again by lectures on the dangers of automobiles. A slap on the backside, not-so-gentle removal from the street, or strong castigation is much more effective. The child learns to restrain himself because he says to himself in essence: "If I run into the street, my mother or father will hurt me or yell at me — I'd better not." Living for the moment, as he does, he cannot at that age be expected to say: "I'd better not run into the street because someday I might get hit by a car."

In the next stage, the Shame Stage, the child's primary deterrent is the fear that should he perform the prohibited act, he will be discovered by significant environmental figures who will reject him. Of importance here is the child's fear of being *seen* by parents or surrogates, and thereby rejected. This stage coincides with Erikson's second stage in which the primary life conflict to be resolved is that of "Autonomy versus Shame."[1]

Erikson makes reference to the ashamed person's words to his observers: "God damn your eyes." At this stage, the deterring forces are still externalized; one blushes in front of someone, not alone.

In the final stage, the Self-Blame Stage, or Guilt Stage, the child has incorporated the parental values. Here, the inner rather than the outer voice deters.[2] This corresponds to Erikson's third stage, "Guilt versus Initiative." Alone and unobserved, the child suffers the admonition of the internalized voices of authorities. Once this phase has been reached, the parents can relax their vigil. The child can be trusted to behave because the mechanism is powerful — so powerful that it is apt to function with exaggerated severity, even lending itself to the formation of neurotic and even psychotic mechanisms.

Each stage contains two essential elements: 1) ideas and feelings of wrongdoing and 2) parental punishment. The latter, be it in the form of rejection, withdrawal of love, castigation, chastisement, or any of the commonly used disciplinary measures is the original punitive element in guilt. As the child develops, he encounters an ever-growing horde of figures, each empowered to punish him for his transgressions. Although punitive fear may be repressed or unrealized, it is never completely lost in the guilt reaction.

In adult guilt, then, there are two major components: 1) ideas and feelings of wrongdoing and 2) an associated anticipation of punishment.

If the act or thought is considered "wrong" in the opinion of the majority of significant individuals in the guilty person's environment, then the guilt is considered appropriate and its absence abnormal in the psychological and statistical sense. If the consensus, however, of such significant persons is that the act is not blameworthy, then the guilt is inappropriate. Another form of inappropriate guilt is fantasied self-blame: the individual fancies himself to be responsible for an event for which he is in no way responsible, although if he were, then he would indeed be justified in feeling guilt. Associated with the ideas of wrongdoing are feelings of worthlessness — "How terrible a person I am for what I have done."

The anticipation of punishment may not be clearly realized but it is vital to the development of the guilt reaction. Anxiety may become a concomitant of this aspect of the guilt reaction when the punishment is vague or if it is not known whether it will be administered. The individual then finds himself under a sword of Damocles, never knowing when or if it will fall.

The relationship between actual punishment and the assuaging of the feeling of wrongdoing is complex. For the child, punishment, even in the form of a period of parental displeasure, can be effective in alleviating guilt. The crime has been committed, punishment suffered, and the slate is clean. There are children who will ask for the punishment to alleviate the guilt feeling and become distraught if it is not forthcoming.

The relationship between punishment and guilt is more complex in the adult. If one feels appropriately guilty, the remorse and self-denigration usually provide sufficient punishment. For the psychopath, punishment is used as a deterrent from anti-social behavior, but not as an assuager of guilt for there is little or none. The masochist may need punishment[3] and the depressive invites it. But in both the alleviation is short-lived and the guilt, arising from neurotic elements having little or nothing to do with an actual transgression, recurs.

In general, one can say that for the adult, punishment — even if it be self-denigration — assuages appropriate guilt but not inappropriate guilt. With the latter, the individual's feelings of wrongdoing have little or nothing to do with a real transgression but stem from other sources.

Most of the children described in this book suffer with consciences which are too rigid; with superegos which are too strong. They feel excessively guilty over their hostile and sexual thoughts and feelings; they fear that their hostile thoughts may harm; and they anticipate violent repercussions to their unacceptable impulses. In this chapter I describe the use of the Mutual Storytelling Technique in the treatment of children with *deficiencies* in their consciences. All children have such deficiencies, and growing up involves, in part, the acquisition of an autonomous but not overzealous conscience. Pathology then, in this area, may be hard to differentiate from normality. Consideration of age appropriate behavior is essential. The normal seven-year-old child is expected to be restless in the classroom; to occasionally lose things; and to be somewhat sloppy. However, when he exhibits these characteristics with a frequency that interferes with his learning and possibly that of his classmates as well, a defect in the self-regulating inhibitory mechanisms may be present. I say *may* be present because identical behavior may be exhibited by a child with a normal or even rigid superego who is so overwhelmed with anxiety that he cannot control himself although he feels quite guilty about his transgressions. And the child suffering with minimal brain dysfunction may be similarly guilty about the misbehavior which results from his organic impairment in impulse control.

The problem of identifying superego defects in children is further complicated by the fact that there is no such thing as uniform and simultaneous development of superego functions. A child, for example, may be quite aware of social proprieties when visiting the homes of others, but in his own house he exhibits almost total disregard for the rights, feelings, and property of others. He may mercilessly taunt a sibling close to his age, but show a tenderness and sensitivity to a much younger child that brings tears to his parents' eyes.

When deficiencies in the superego are present in adult life, the individual is referred to as a psychopath; in adolescence, he is called a juvenile delinquent; and in childhood, the terms adjustment reaction or behavior disorder are applied. This nomenclatural abundance is misleading because it implies different disorders when, in fact, there is a constant and primary diagnostic element: a failure in the development of internalized mechanisms which can inhibit the individual from performing those acts which are considered unacceptable by significant figures in his milieu.

The ego-ideal — the other part of the superego — refers to the constellation of standards and ideals by which the child lives. They are the guidelines by which he judges his behavior. They include the models which he wishes to emulate. Like the

560

conscience, the ego-ideal is formed by the process of the child's identification with important individuals in his environment. The qualities exhibited by parents, teachers, ministers, scoutmasters, admired relatives, and famous people whom the child has come to admire are incorporated. The child wishes to grow up and be like a particular individual because he has learned that the acquisition of the selected person's characteristics enables one to enjoy significant social benefits. The internalized mental image of what the ideal person should be like is not always in the category of presidents, baseball heroes, film-stars, policemen, and firemen. It may include Mafia chiefs, business moguls, juvenile delinquents, Don Juan types, and so on.

In successful treatment, the therapist becomes another model upon which the child tailors his behavior. No matter how passive and non-intrusive the therapist is (or thinks he is) the child, if he has a good therapeutic relationship with his therapist, will tend to model himself after him. Hopefully, the therapist will be the kind of person whom it will benefit the child to emulate. If not, the child may acquire a new set of problems in addition to those he had when he first came for treatment. In Chapter 8, I described how the child's identification with a therapist of the same sex can play a role in resolving oedipal problems, and how the storytelling method was of assistance in this regard. In this chapter I describe other ways in which the Mutual Storytelling Technique can facilitate therapeutic identifications which thereby contribute to the formation of a healthier ego-ideal.

Example 1

Henry, the eleven-year-old boy whose first story in treatment revealed that he considered his father to engage in dishonest practices such as stealing, told this story three weeks later:

Once upon a time there were three boys. They went to an amusement park about fifteen miles away from their home. They went on a lot of rides. During the afternoon they lost the money they were going to use to go home with. They looked all around and they couldn't find their money.

So then they went to the Western Union office and they sent a telegram to their mother. They said that she should go to the Western Union office and there she should send them money by wire. Their mother got the telegram and she did this. She went to the Western Union office and sent them money.

When they returned they were afraid to face her. They expected to get bawled out, but their mother told them that they should be more careful in the future and they were.

The moral of this story is: be careful with your belongings; don't just leave them around someplace.

The story clearly reveals one of the ways in which the overprotective parent can deprive the child of experiences which might contribute to healthy superego formation. The child who can do no wrong, who is protected from any untoward consequences resulting from his self-indulgent behavior has little incentive to develop internal mechanisms to deter himself from such behavior. In this story Henry's slipshod attitude toward money does not cause him any real inconvenience. Western Union provides him with free telegram service and mother freely wires the required funds. His fear of facing his mother on his return home reflects some development of a conscience in this area, but his mother's failure to reprimand or otherwise inconvenience him for his transgression accurately portrays the way she would have probably handled the situation in reality. (The parents were quite wealthy and they prided themselves on being able to indulge Henry financially and materially.) The moral, too, also exhibits some appreciation, on his part, of healthier standards of behavior. I knew Henry well enough, however, to know that this was more lip-service than actual conviction.

In response, I told this story:

Once upon a time there were three boys. They weren't brothers. They went to an amusement park and had a lot of fun. The park was about fifteen miles from the city where they lived. They went on a lot of rides. During the afternoon they all lost the money they had to get them home. They looked all around and they couldn't find their money.

So they decided to go to a Western Union office. They told the Western Union man that they wanted to send a telegram to their mothers. The Western Union man said that it would cost them money to send a telegram. The boys didn't have any money. The Western Union man told the boys that he was sorry that he couldn't do anything for them and that he would not send a telegram without advance payment. One of the boys finally said, "is there anything we can do to earn some money so that I might call my mother. It costs twenty cents to call her from here." So the man said, "Well, I do have one errand that I need to be done. If one of you boys will do it I'll give you twenty cents." So one of the boys did the errand and they got twenty cents.

Then one of the boys called his mother and asked her to wire money. The mother was quite angry and although the boy said to her that he wished that she was not so angry, she still said that she was angry about it, that she would wire the money, but that she would expect the boys to pay her back.

So they got home and then they had to do errands and chores in order to earn the money to pay back the mother who had laid it out.

My story has two morals. The first is that you have to be more careful and you have to learn to do things on your own. You can't go around having people do things for you all the time. If you are not responsible, you will suffer the consequences. If you don't take care of your money you may find yourself having to go to great inconveniences as a result. The second moral is that when you take things from people, when you take advantage of them, they get angry at you even if they don't show it.

My story confronts Henry with the unpleasant facts that the world, in general, will not be as indulgent as his mother and that if he doesn't develop more personal sense of responsibility, he will suffer definite inconveniences. My Western Union man doesn't provide him with free telegraph service but requires him to earn some money to pay for communicating with his mother. The mother in my story is not only angry (the normal reaction to irresponsibility although it is one to which Henry was oblivious), but, in addition, she requires the boys to do errands and chores in order to pay back the money she wired them.

Generally, I am a hard taskmaster in my stories to children with superego defects. My experience has been that this is not only the kind of approach they need in compensation for parental laxity in this area, but that they also welcome the structure and guidance which my suggested standards can provide for them in their everyday living.

Example 2

Nick, an eleven-year-old boy was referred because of marked disinterest in his schoolwork, recalcitrant behavior at home, lying, petty stealing, and insomnia. He was a "wise guy" and his relationships with peers was poor. His mother had decided to divorce his father a few weeks prior to his first visit. His father, a salesman, was of limited intelligence. His compensatory braggadocio engendered in his wife an attitude of chronic irritation and scorn.

During his second month of treatment, Nick told this story:

Today I'm going to tell a story about me, myself, and I.

Therapist: Okay.

Patient: There was one boy named me — that was Robert Smith. There was another boy in Italy named Roberto Smitho and another person in Germany, I mean in France, named Roberto de Smith. Now, funny thing about it was that we were all born at the same time and we all look alike.

One day Roberto de Smith from France came to

564

America. By some accident I was waiting for my grandmother, and he came off the ship and we saw each other and we looked exactly alike. Now, I walked up to him and said, "What's your name?" He said, "Roberto de Smith." And he said, "What is your name?" So I said, "Well, my name is Robert Smith." I said, "I think we're look-alikes." So I was talking to him and my grandmother came off the ship, and I told her about my experience with this boy and since he was there alone, I invited him to come to my house.

A couple of days later my father was coming off an airplane from Italy and I met another boy that looked like me. And you know who that is. That's Roberto Smitho. But the same thing happened. Now he's living in my house. So he's wearing my clothes also and we have to work in the street and we're working in the street together one day —— so one of my friends saw us three and he didn't know what to do. He said, "Which of you are Smith?" We all raised our hands because all of our names were Smith. Roberto Smitho thought he said Smitho. Smith, you know, American. I thought he said my name and Roberto de Smith, from France thought he said his name. And this guy, my friend, didn't know what to do! "Which of you three live on 135 E. 134th St., Apt. 10C?" We all raised our hands 'cause all of them were living at my house. So my friend didn't know what to do. So I stood up and explained to him that I had these foreign friends over and he started to laugh like anything.

Now, then they all flew back together and I felt lonely because I didn't have any more double.

So the moral to the story is: to have doubles are much better than to have none.

Therapist: Why is that?

Patient: Well, you have more friends because, you know, each person likes somebody else and you see him and say, "Oh, yeah, I remember you," and you have a whole list of different friends. Each will like to do different things and everybody will like you. Thank you.

Therapist: Wait a moment. I'm a little bit confused. What

were some of the advantages of having these two friends there?

Patient: Well, Roberto Smitho liked to play baseball and I liked to go swimming and water skiing and all that water stuff, and Roberto de Smith liked to play football. Each of us did something else at the same time.

Therapist: What was so good about that?

Patient: Everybody liked me because I did —— like one person would say, "Oh, you swim beautifully," or say to me, "Oh, you're a beautiful football player ——

Therapist: Oh, I see. In other words, people didn't know that there were three of you.

Patient: Right!

Therapist: Oh, I see. So that ——

Patient: Only that one friend of mine.

Therapist: So then you could fool people into thinking you were a great all-round person. I see. Now I get it. Okay.

Patient: And also let's say if Roberto Smitho was better in history and there was a history test that day, I'd let him go to school instead of me.

Therapist: I see.

Patient: Thank you ladies and gentlemen. And now Dr. Gardner will tell his. So hold on until Dr. Gardner gets ready to think of his. Please tell us the name of your story?

Therapist: This is a story called "The Three Boys."

Patient: Now don't forget at the end you must tell us the moral of your story and I'll be asking you questions.

Therapist: Okay, you can. Now remember that my story can have many things that are similar to your story, but invariably at some point it gets different.

The story reveals Nick's tendency to utilize deceitful maneuvers to bolster his lagging self-esteem. He does not feel well-liked by peers. His refusal to share, to respect the rights of others, and his excessive clowning alienated other children. In the story Nick compensates for this deficiency by taking for himself the admiration and respect earned by his alter egos. They do the work and he gets the praise. Roberto de Smith plays football and Nick is told: "Oh, you're a beautiful football player." Roberto Smitho takes the history test and Nick gets the good grade. He manifests no guilt or embarrassment over his duplicity but rather prides himself on his cleverness.

I told this story in response:

Once upon a boy there was a time.
Patient: (*Laughs.*)
Therapist: Once upon a boy there was a time!
Patient: Now let's begin with the story.
Therapist: This boy's name was John Smith and John Smith felt very bad about himself. He wasn't a very good sport. He wasn't very good in athletics and he wasn't very good in school. He had a couple of subjects that he was okay in, but for the most part he wasn't real good. Are you listening to my story? What are you mumbling there? All right. Anyway, he sometimes thought about the fact that there might be in a country like Germany another kid named Johann Schmidt and he thought maybe he'd have the same name as him. And he thought that there might be in France a boy whose name was Jean Smithe.
Patient: (*Laughs and mumbles something.*)
Therapist: Well, anyway, one day while he was waiting for someone at the dock there showed up —
Patient: Where?
Therapist: At the dock and there he sees this kid who looks just like him and they go over and they start talking to each other and sure enough it's Johann Schmidt, and he takes him home to his house.
Patient: Rats!
Therapist: And then his father is traveling in France and his father meets this boy named Jean Smithe and he brought this boy home. So these three boys stay at John's house.
Patient: (*Keeps mumbling in background.*)
Therapist: And John thought of a good idea. "I think it will be a good idea — I know that these kids have certain talents and abilities that I don't have — I think I'm going to pass them off as me and everybody will like me." Stop the mumbling. If you want to continue playing this game you'll have to stop mumbling. Anyway, the boys

567

thought that was a great idea too. So what happened was sometimes when the kids would call up and say, "Hey, John, you want to go out and play football?" he'd say, "Sure." And he sent out Johann Schmidt who was a very good football player, but there was poor John sitting home alone, very lonely, and not getting any of the fun of playing football because Johann was out playing. Johann would come home and say, "Boy, that was really great! What a game —

Patient: Did the kids know there were three?

Therapist: No. He didn't let anybody know that there were —

Patient: Well, doesn't he know how to swim or anything —

Therapist: Yeah. But the thing is that he wanted everybody to think that he was a good all-around sport.

Patient: Yeah, but that's what he was doing by having them —

Therapist: Yeah, but then he was home alone. He wasn't having the fun of playing football because Johann was out playing football. Now, of course, John was a good swimmer so when they called to go swimming, John would go himself, but when they called for someone to play basketball, he would send out Jean.

Patient: (*Still mumbling things.*)

Therapist: So he was quite lonely. In fact, when he was out swimming, Jean and Johann would have to stay home and they were quite lonely and would have to play in the house because they didn't want anybody to find out their secret. So, although the boys thought at first that this would be a good idea, after a while they realized it wasn't so hot because the other guys had to walk around keeping a secret all the time fearful of discovery. You know, they didn't have much fun doing these things.

Patient: Wouldn't they all have accents?

Therapist: These boys in their countries learned pretty good English. In your story what happened to them? Did they have accents in your story?

Patient: I believe they did.

Therapist: Well, one day one boy who was playing with Johann said, "You know, you speak a little funny today.

You speak with a slight German accent." And Johann said, "No, I don't!" He said, "John doesn't speak that way. You sound a little German." He replied, "I'm not German." He said, "You don't even say German like an American. You sound like a German." Anyway, the boy began to suspect and after that when they were playing with Jean, they realized that Jean spoke with a little French accent.

Patient: Oh.

Therapist: And then they began to get wiser and they said, "We think there's something fishy." The next evening they went up to the house when the boys didn't expect them, and there they saw the three of them. Well, following that, poor John, everybody said, "Well, what kind of liar are you? Gee whiz. What kind of liar are you? You tried to put something over on us."

Patient: (*Mumbles some words.*) Yeah, yeah, yeah.

Therapist: And, of course, the two boys felt bad too, and they went back to their native lands.

Patient: Yeah, yeah, yeah.

Therapist: And poor John was very embarrassed and then he realized that it really wasn't a good thing to try to fool everybody. So what finally happened was he decided that although he might not be a star football player, it was possible for him to be a passable football player, get the pleasure of playing football, and be honest with your friends.

Patient: Right, right, right.

Therapist: And my story has two morals. Do you know what the morals of my story are? See if you can figure them out.

Patient: I don't know.

Therapist: Come on. Figure out the morals.

Patient: I don't know.

Therapist: One of the morals of my story is that the main fun from doing something comes from doing it yourself.

Patient (*with accent*)*:* You're joking.

Therapist: And the second —

Patient: (*Blows into microphone.*)

Therapist: If people find out you're a liar, they will not like you.

Patient: That's true, true, true, true, true, true, true. Thank you very much Dr. Gardner. Dr. Gardner, I'd like to ask you a question.

Therapist: Yes, please.

Patient: Well, why didn't the two children at home want to go out somewhere else; you know, like some kids would be playing baseball, some kids —

Therapist: They were afraid to be seen in the streets, two at a time. If one kid would come and say, "Hi there John." Let's say the real John was out playing football and Johann was walking in the street and some kid says, "Hey, I'm confused. I thought I just left you at the park. What are you doing out here? How could that be?" So he'd suspect not realizing that he would be seeing Johann. So once you start something like that you've got to cover yourself up if you want it to go through. They had to lie a lot, sneak, and it made them very uncomfortable.

Patient: I see. Thank you Dr. Gardner.

My story emphasized the virtue-is-its-own-reward theme in an attempt to encourage Nick to consider non-psychopathic methods of bolstering his self-esteem. Johann has fun while playing football; and Jean while playing basketball. The stay-at-homers lose out on these gratifications. Another drawback of the scheme is that they all suffer fears of discovery which are ego-debasing. When the devious plan is finally revealed, they all endure the humiliations one must inevitably experience on being so exposed.

As was often true while playing the storytelling game, Nick would present a facade of mere superficial interest; a devil-may-care attitude with which he attempted to conceal his genuine involvement. He would mumble, tap, hum, and engage in other distractions although he was, for the most part, very much with me as his post-story questions show. When told to stop his distracting noises, he would usually do so (at least temporarily). When I was able to keep these irritations at a tolerable level, he'd gradually stop the horseplay as his absorption in the storytelling deepened. This is what happened here: by the end of my story the clowning had stopped and he was definitely immersed in the game.

His comments at the end reveal his resistance to my communications. He tries to present a plan by which the two boys hiding at home could still enjoy the gratifications of sports by sneaking out and playing elsewhere. In order to discourage this subterfuge — its purpose is to fill loopholes in the scheme rather than to abandon it — I pointed out its impracticality and, more important, its drawback of producing further feelings of self-loathing — "They had to lie a lot, sneak, and it made them feel very uncomfortable."

One week later, Nick related this story:

Patient: Today is April 5, 1967. Here we are back in Dr. Gardner's office. As you remember, I told a story, and then I did the moral, and then Dr. Gardner will make up the same story, I mean another story with the same characters and make his own moral. Now until we get ready, until I think of a good story to tell them.

Today's story is about a nice young girl. Her name is Susie. Susie had a lot of imagination and she had to write a composition in school and she wrote that she could ride a horse so great.

Therapist: She wrote what?

Patient: That she rides horses.

Therapist: Oh, I see. She wrote that she rides horses well.

Patient: And a lot of compositions and they asked, "What do you do on weekends?" She wrote in her composition about what happened on her horse riding trips.

So one day one of her friends read in a comic book that there was a contest for people who could ride horses. Now this best friend sent in for Susie 'cause everyone knew by then that Susie was such a great horseback rider and she was set up in the line. She had to ride a horse and she didn't know how to ride a horse. And she kept on falling off. She couldn't ride the horse. She sat down wrong. She couldn't clean the horse or anything. Everybody disliked her because they all had hopes in her and she had to tell everyone that it was all imagination.

And the moral of this story is: if you have too much imagination you get in trouble. Thank you please.

Now Dr. Gardner will tell his story.

The story reveals some appreciation of my message imparted in the previous week's session that one of the drawbacks of lying is that if one is discovered, one suffers social rejection.

In response, I told this story:

Once upon a time there was a girl named Susie and Susie when she was younger — hey cut down on the candy fellah. You won't be able to eat your supper. Take one more and that's it. All right. Before you go you can have one more.

Anyway, this Susie went with her parents for a — are you listening to this story?

Patient: Yeah.

Therapist: One day she went with her parents to a horse show and there she saw some very fancy — Look, I don't like you when you're sneaky. No, no. I told you no more and you've been gorging yourself. That's enough. Leave some for some of the other kids. That's enough. Don't try to do it behind my back. I don't like that. That's all. No more candy. (*Jar is removed.*)

Patient: Do you want this on your tape or not?

Therapist: Yeah. It's all right. Everything goes on the tape. When you don't steal behind my back it won't be said on the tape. All right? When you try to do it behind my back, then I'll put it on the tape. Okay? All right, back to my story.

This girl Susie went to a horse show with her family once and she enjoyed it very much and while she was watching it she really dreamed of someday riding like that herself and she walked home and she said, "I'm going to get a horse and next week I'm going to get into the show." The mother said, "Well, you have to work very hard." She said, "Naw, I can do it very easily."

Anyway, they went to the stables the next day and the girl got on the horse and she very cockily thought, "Oh, boy, here I go. I'm going to ride." Well, she fell

572

right off. Then she tried some more and she realized that it was going to take a lot of hard work. First she got discouraged and thought it really wasn't worth it, but after a while, when she started doing better, she realized that the hard work really paid off and it was a good idea anyway. So she worked very very hard and over many many months — in fact, it was a whole year before they had another horse show — and as a result of her hard work she was able to enter the show and won a prize.

Patient (in amazement): Won a prize?

Therapist: Right.

Patient: How about that. She's great!

Therapist: Yes, and she only got that way because of work. And the moral of that story is —

Patient: What?

Therapist: It's easy to dream of anything, but the way to really accomplish anything is to really work hard at it. There's no other way really. The end.

Patient: The end.

The interchange over the candy demonstrates one way in which I discourage psychopathic behavior in the context of the therapeutic situation. I not only do not permit the patient to indulge himself in anti-social behavior but, in addition, I express to him my reactions to his unacceptable activities. He is provided honest confrontation and feedback in a living situation — an experience he may not be having elsewhere. Parents of such children often condone the delinquent behavior, either overtly or covertly. Here, when Nick surreptitiously took candy after I had told him not to take any more, I not only insisted that he stop, but I also told him my reaction to his act — "I don't like that." I also conveyed my feelings about him for performing it — "I don't like you when you're sneaky." I do not tell the child that my dislike is total and permanent; it is directed only to the *sneaky part* of him *when* he steals. When he is not stealing he is once again in my favor.

When reprimanding a child for anti-social behavior, many child psychologists and psychiatrists advise confining oneself to criticizing the act and not the child. One should say to the child: "When milk is spilled, the table gets messy," rather than, "You spilled the milk. Look at the mess you've made." They claim that the latter approach will give the child the idea that clumsiness is a deep-seated part of his personality, thereby contributing to generalized feelings of low self-worth. I do not believe that one can separate the doer from his act, that one can criticize a child's act, while at the same time omitting negative implications about his personality. It is like blaming the hand only of the child who steals. A child who steals and is old enough to appreciate that he is stealing is, *at that moment*, a thief. His hand did not steal independently of any other part of him. His mind thought it, his conscience permitted it, and his total body was involved in performing the act. The fact that the child steals at a given time does not, of course, mean that he is a doomed recidivist. It means only that *at that time he is thieving*. When this aspect of his personality commands the attention of those about him, he is at that moment disliked, and he should be told so.

What should be communicated to the child is that he is a complex person with many different forms of behavior, that within him lies the potential for both acceptable and unacceptable activities. He is liked *as a person* when he behaves in a way that is acceptable to those about him; he is disliked as a person when his behavior elicits their disapprobation. When he spills his milk, he may very well have been needlessly clumsy *at that time*, and it is desirable to communicate this to him *at the moment when it happens*. If one says, "When you're clumsy, it's no fun eating with you. If you do that again you'll have to leave the table," one imparts the notion not only that clumsiness *is* in the child's repertoire of behavior and *is* something he occasionally exhibits, but also that it is believed that it *does not have to be so*.

Saying, "You're being very rude now, and people don't like you when you're that way," is a valid way of confronting a child with the social consequences of his behavior without implying that he is an inveterate and incorrigible boor.[4]

The therapist's active intervention in, or refusal to comply with, unacceptable behavior when it occurs in the office setting can be most therapeutic. In this example, I removed the jar of candy to prevent further pilfering. When a child cheats in a game such as checkers, I usually say: "Look, this game is no fun for me if you cheat. If you can't stop, we'll just have to do something else. I'm sure others feel the same way. No one likes a cheat." The child has the living experience that his unacceptable behavior may bring about the alienation of someone who is meaningful to him. In addition, it threatens disruption of a game which may be a source of pleasure to him.[5]

My comments and actions in response to Nick's candy stealing apparently reached him: he was definitely embarrassed that they were recorded and that I would not erase them — "Everything goes on the tape."

In my story, the work ethos is introduced. Through hard work and the acquisition of true expertise, one is less likely to utilize fantasied accomplishments to gain the esteem of both oneself and others. When one is truly competent, one need not resort to deceitful maneuvers to gain acceptance and respect. My hope was that the emphasis on the attractions of honest endeavor would play some role in helping this boy give up his psychopathic tendencies.

A week later, Nick told this story:

Patient: Now as we are beginning reel number two we are about to — we are still going to do our routines. Now if you forgot, if you're that stupid, you'll remember that first I tell a story and have my own moral and then the dear doctor will tell his story with his own moral.

Therapist: What a wise guy you are. "Dear doctor." Everybody is stupid except you. Huh?

Patient (laughing): And as soon as I think of my nutty story for today, we shall proceed.

Now today's story is like another chapter of the story about John Smith. You remember that story — John Smith and all that. Johann Schmidt, Jean Smithe and all that jazz.

John went to Europe with his father and he went to

France and John went to Jean's house and ended up sleeping over. That night something dreadful happened. The jewels were stolen.

Therapist: That night the jewels in Jean's house were stolen?

Patient: Yeah. They didn't know what happened and the day after the robbery John and Jean went out to play ball. John didn't feel well and Jean asked, "Why don't you feel well?" He said, "I don't know. I just don't feel well."

Therapist: Who didn't feel well?

Patient: John, and he felt just awful. And Jean thought that maybe he felt awful because he might have stolen the jewels. And he went over to John and said, "John, did you steal those jewels?" He said, "Yeah." Jean said, "How come?" "Because I need the money." "Oh," said Jean. He gave Jean the diamonds or the jewels and they gave it to Jean's parents. Jean's parents gave John fifteen dollars, I mean one hundred dollars.

The moral to my story is: if you need the money don't steal, ask.

Thank you, thank you, thank you.

Now, Dr. Gardner, the great, shall tell —

Therapist: What was that comment? You said Dr. Gardner what ——

Patient: Dr. Gardner, the great —

Therapist (sarcastically): Oh, I'm the great.

Patient: — shall tell his magnificent story.

Therapist: Okay.

Patient: We shall now proceed.

Therapist: Thank you very much for your kind permission for me to tell my story.

Patient: You're very welcome.

In his introductory comments, Nick, in his typical wise guy manner, refers to the audience as "stupid" and sarcastically calls me "the dear doctor." The therapist would be remiss, in my opinion, if he were to allow the child to go on with his story-telling without focusing in some way on this hostility. I might have suggested analytic inquiry, but for Nick, at this time in his treatment, such an approach would have been futile and would have only been met with further attempts at disparagement. I decided to respond in kind. There are some who consider sarcasm by the therapist to be totally antithetical to the therapeutic process. I do not agree. There are times, I believe, when the judicious use of sarcasm can be a very effective therapeutic tool. It can enable the therapist to impart messages with pertinent emotional impact.

In this case, I first confronted the patient with his behavior: "What a wise guy you are." Then I imitated the patient's sarcastic comment "dear doctor" with the same derogatory intonations he used. I let him know, in case he didn't, that I am fully aware of his condescension and reflect it back to him in identical form so that he can see how he appears to others. I, of course, was aware that Nick's patronizing attitude was mere facade, a pathetic compensation for his deep-seated feelings of rejection and inadequacy. He was not, however, even close to admitting to such feelings, and I felt the best way to approach the problem was via its most superficial manifestations. My hope was that getting him to appreciate how alienating his wise guy attitude was would motivate him to change. Whether imitation and sarcasm are therapeutic is determined by the therapist's intent. The patient will sense whether or not they are being used malevolently. The transcript cannot communicate the tone communicated to this boy when I said: "Everybody is stupid except you. Huh?" There was no derision or bitterness in my voice, but rather warmhearted ridicule. Nick sensed the underlying benevolence in my comments and laughed in response. His ego was strong enough for him to be able, on occasion, to laugh at himself. In the schizophrenic child, or one with a fragile ego, sarcasm and imitation are definitely contraindicated.

In Nick's story, the alter ego theme appears again. This time, however, there is some improvement. Whereas in the previous story all three boys are accomplices in the deceptive scheme, here Jean Smithe is honest and John Smith is a thief. When confronted, the latter confesses his crime — another sign of healthier superego functioning — but there is no punishment

forthcoming. Instead, all is forgiven; his motive of poverty —
"Because I need the money" — is completely accepted; and he
is even rewarded — "Jean's parents gave John fifteen dollars, I
mean one hundred dollars." Crime does pay after all.

I told this story in response:

This is another chapter in the John Smith tale.

Patient (interrupting): A guy —

Therapist: Now I will not tell my story if there are any
wisecracks from the sidelines.

Patient: There won't.

Therapist: No provocations. I will only tell my story if there
is undivided attention.

Patient: (Raps knuckles on table.)

Therapist: I won't talk while you're doing that. All right.
As long as you interrupt or play games I won't talk.

Patient: Yes sir.

Therapist: Now John Smith — I'm not going to tell my
story if you're going to whisper and —

Patient: All right, I won't. I won't. Don't worry.

Therapist: I'm going to give a name to that. It's called provocation. You're provocative. You bug people. You do
things that are irritating and I'm telling you that. This is
one of the reasons that I'm sure you have trouble with
friends. You're constantly irritating people.

Now John Smith went to France with his father and
there he went to live at the home of Jean Smith, a French
boy. When you're tapping, I stop. *(Patient stops tapping.)*
So he went to live at the home of this boy, Jean, and that
night the jewels in Jean's house were stolen.

Patient: That's the same thing as my story.

Therapist: It starts off the same way, but listen. Take it
easy. Has my story ever been an exact duplicate of your
story?

Patient: No!

Therapist: All right. Give me a chance. It starts off the
same way. Now the following morning when they found
out that the jewels were stolen, Jean noted that John
didn't feel well and he said to himself, "I wonder if that
guy John stole the jewels?" So Jean said to John, "Say,

did you steal the jewels?" And John was kind of embarrassed and ashamed and he finally had to admit that he did. Jean asked why. John said, "Well, we're very poor." Jean said, "That's no excuse." John said, "Sure it's an excuse. When you're poor, you know, that's a special circumstance." And Jean and his parents said, "Now look John. You are our friend. We brought you into our home and we trusted you and if you can turn your back on us this way and steal our jewels, well, we're sorry to tell you that you cannot remain in this house. They called John's father and they told John's father about what had happened and they said, "We are very hurt that he should do a thing like this." Of course, John thought that they would give him money if he returned the jewels. He said, "Well, I'm sorry." They said, "We can't forget things like that. Even if we were to say we forgive you, we'd only say it. We really can't forgive. 'Cause we can't forget things like that." Leave the tape alone. Leave the wire.

So anyway poor John had to leave the house and his father kept him in Europe for a while and then they went home. He had learned a very bitter lesson. You see, he lost his friend, Jean. Jean could never really forget what a terrible thing he had done to him. But he learned his lesson and in future relationships with friends he stopped stealing which he had done a number of times before. He had learned his lesson.

The moral of that story is ——

Patient: What?

Therapist: That when you steal something from someone they usually can't forget it because they're so hurt at what you have done and the only thing you can do is to try to stop doing it with other friends. The end.

Patient: Thank you.

Therapist: You're welcome.

Just as in games like checkers and cards when I refuse to continue if the patient cheats, I interrupt the storytelling if the child's behavior appears to be defeating the game's purpose. Clearly, when a child is more interested in provoking than playing the storytelling game, he will not profit from my messages. To allow oneself to be irritated only perpetuates the child's pathology. There are some therapists who deny (even to themselves) that a child's behavior is annoying them. I believe that such therapists are depriving their patients of valuable therapeutic experiences. They let the child go on uninterrupted in his antagonizing behavior and continue with the task at hand as if the distracting irritations were not present. In such situations, the therapist gets ulcers and the child gets sicker. It behooves the therapist to set a good example to his patient, to express his anger when he is irritated, and to use it to remove the hostility engendering stimuli. Here, I was annoyed by Nick's provocative interruptions, and I let him know it. This not only enabled me to "let off steam" so that I would be mentally and emotionally free to tell my story objectively, but served to deter him from further irritating me. In addition, I hoped that the confrontation would teach him something about himself that he might ultimately put to good use: "You bug people. You do things that are irritating and I'm telling you that. This is one of the reasons that I'm sure you have trouble with friends." My "wise guy" confrontation during his story was benevolent — he was not in reality doing me any harm. This confrontation was somewhat malevolent — Nick was thwarting me from proceeding with my therapeutic efforts. I was irritated, and I let Nick know it.

In my story, Jean's parents are totally unsympathetic to John's excuse that he stole the jewels because he was poor. They are disillusioned, no longer can trust him, and ask him to leave their house. John also learns that the proverbial excuse, "I'm sorry," carries no weight in the Smithe household. To them it doesn't wipe the slate clean; it doesn't recreate a situation identical to that which existed prior to the theft. Nick's antisocial tendencies were fostered, in part, by his parents' failure to punish him for transgressions if he said he was sorry. Nick is told that people do not so easily forget the pains which are inflicted upon them as his experiences with his parents would have him believe. "Forgive and forget" is a myth.

Example 3

Nancy, the girl who first came to treatment at three-and-one-half because of severe temper tantrums, disobedience both at home and school, excessive masturbation, and withdrawal, told this story in the middle of her second course of therapy, a few weeks after her sixth birthday.

Once upon a time there were about six helicopters. There were three sisters and one sister was seven, one sister was five, one sister was six, and there was a baby and she was one. And there was a mother and she was forty-nine and there was a father and he was thirty. That's what. Then — are you writing down the list?

Therapist: Yes. Then?

Patient: Then they were going to take a walk in the park. That's what they were going to do. Then they were going to — this is fun, right?

Therapist: Right.

Patient: Then they were going to look at the animals and take a train ride and then they were going to rest a little and then go on the swings and then they were going to eat some lunch there. I ate lunch in the park with my friend.

Therapist: All right and then?

Patient: Then they were going to take another trip on the train and then they were going to go on horses that had strings. I saw that when I went to Van Saun Park. I really did. They ride horses and trains there. I saw that in Van Saun Park too.

Therapist: Okay, then what happened? Now let's hear a couple of things of interest.

Patient: Oh, why?

Therapist: Come on.

Patient: Okay. What's interest?

Therapist: Different, unusual, exciting, special.

Patient: They went to a movie and then — is that exciting?

Therapist: Go ahead. What kind of movie did they see?

Patient: Well, they went to a museum and they saw the

movie in the museum. Well, it had animals and movie shows and statutes.

Therapist: Then what happened?

Patient: Then they were going to see cartoons in the movies and I saw a movie outside.

Therapist: Then what happened after that. Now make up something very exciting.

Patient: I did!

Therapist: Okay and after that — another exciting thing.

Patient: Well, they went to a whole big parade. And then they had balloons and then they were going to have some popcorn there and everything and all sorts of food and then they were going to watch the parade. And that's the end of the story.

Therapist: And the lesson of that story?

Patient: If you want to go to an exciting thing and special thing you must ask your mommy. And if you want to take a walk in the park you must ask your mommy: And that's the end of the story.

Therapist: Okay. Thank you very much. That was a very nice story. Now it's time for my story.

Patient: Thank you for saying that.

I could not be sure whether this story was told in the service of resistance or whether it reflected freedom from significant conflict. Both interpretations were possible. Nancy had indeed improved in many ways and was enjoying her relationships with family and peers to a greater extent and the story could have reflected this. On the other hand, I was not completely sure that her symptoms had subsided to the degree that termination could be considered. This can be a difficult decision when the child's symptoms are primarily of the acting-out variety. How many fights a day with one's sibling is normal? What's the average number of conflicts per day with peers? What is the normal frequency of temper outbursts for the six-year-old child? How frequently must a little girl touch her genitals for her to be considered to be pathologically masturbating?

Because of these doubts about Nancy's story, I decided to draw her into the telling of mine in the hope that I would get further information upon which to base my story. This is the interchange that took place:

> Once upon a time there was a girl and she was very, very, very, very, very, very, very, very sad. She was very unhappy. In addition, she used to cry a lot and she was very lonely.
>
> *Patient:* Why?
>
> *Therapist:* Because she had no friends.
>
> *Patient:* And no mommy and daddy?
>
> *Therapist:* She had a mommy and daddy, yes, but she had no friends. And do you know why she didn't have any friends?
>
> *Patient:* Why?
>
> *Therapist:* Why do you think?
>
> *Patient:* Because she was spitting at them, and hitting at them, and kicking them; yelling at them and saying, "Get out of here."
>
> *Therapist:* Right. Right, right, right. And what do you think happened to her?
>
> *Patient:* They didn't want to play with her.
>
> *Therapist:* Right, right. So what did she decide to do?
>
> *Patient:* Play herself; play herself.
>
> *Therapist:* She decided to play herself.
>
> *Patient:* Yeah. She played herself with nobody playing her.
>
> *Therapist:* She decided to play all by herself.
>
> *Patient:* Yeah, all by herself.
>
> *Therapist:* And then how did she feel about that? Was she happy playing all by herself?
>
> *Patient:* No.
>
> *Therapist:* Why not?
>
> *Patient:* Because she wanted someone to play with her.
>
> *Therapist:* What happened to her after that?
>
> *Patient:* Oh, she made friends.
>
> *Therapist:* How did she do that? You told me that they wouldn't play with her because she would spit, and hit, and kick.
>
> *Patient:* Oh, then she would tell her mommy and daddy.
>
> *Therapist:* Yes, but then what happened?
>
> *Patient:* Then her mommy and daddy said, "If you hit, and

spit, and kick" — hey, that rhymes!

Therapist: "Hit and spit and kick," yes, if you do that ——

Patient: "Then they won't want to play with you."

Therapist: So? So what happened then?

Patient: Then she was going to try to say hello, but she tried to, but she still kept on spitting.

Therapist: She tried to what?

Patient: She tried to say hello but she still did that spitting and hitting.

Therapist: Oh, you mean she was trying to stop it, but she still kept doing it.

Patient: Yeah.

Therapist: So then what happened?

Patient: Then her mommy and daddy said, "You kept doing that so they don't want to play with you."

Therapist: Then what happened?

Patient: Then her mommy and daddy said, "You'll have to play all by yourself."

Therapist: So what happened after that?

Patient: The girl didn't like it. She said, "Mommy, I want to have friends." "Okay, well next time we'll go out and if you say that fresh thing you're going to go to your room and never make friends."

Therapist: So what happened then? What happened after that?

Patient: I have to think. Isn't it your story?

Therapist: Yes, but we're making it together. What happened after that?

Patient: Oh, it's not my story.

Therapist: Well, I'm interested in hearing how you would end the story and then I'll tell you how I would end the story.

Patient: Okay.

Therapist: How would you end the story?

Patient: Well, I would say if you don't want to — the lesson of the story is if you, well, the lesson is if you hurt people they won't want to play with you. That's the end of the story.

Therapist: So what finally happened to this girl? Did she still stay lonely? Hhmmm?

Patient: Yes.

Therapist: Was she lonely forever and ever?

Patient: Yes, but her mommy and daddy took her out and said and the girl was trying to stop it.

Therapist: What's that?

Patient: The girl was trying to stop it and her mommy and daddy said, "Say, 'Hello. I want to play with you. I'll be nice to you.' " And she listened and said, "Hello, I want to play with you. I'll be nice to you."

Therapist: So what happened?

Patient: Then the friend wanted to make friends with her.

Therapist: Oh, and then what happened?

Patient: Then they lived happily ever after. And the lesson of that story is : if you want to have friends and you kick, and spit, and hit, then they won't want to play with you. If you do want to have friends you must say, "Hello, I want to play with you, please," and then you will have friends. And that's the end of the story.

Therapist: That's an excellent story. That's a beautiful story. You told that very well. That's really nice. You must have been proud to tell such a good story.

Patient: Then why didn't you tell it with me?

Therapist: Well, because I thought you were doing such a good job that I thought I'd let you go on and tell more. I wouldn't know how to tell a better story that's such a good story. I can't even think of a better story than that. This girl learned her lesson that if you hit and kick and spit at people they won't want to be your friends, but if you're nice to them they will be. That is the way I was going to end that story myself. The end.

I began my story with the actual situation which existed for Nancy when she began treatment. She had no friends, and the reason was that she did indeed lash out at them, spit and kick, and was most insensitive to their needs. However there had been significant improvement in her behavior with peers; so much so that, at the time of this storytelling, Nancy was enjoying very good relationships with them. Spitting and kicking were gone and her rudeness appeared to be in the normal range. Children were seeking her out — a most sensitive indication of her improvement.

The story describes Nancy's own clinical course. She had come to appreciate, in her treatment, that her antisocial behavior was alienating to other children and was the primary reason why she was lonely. In the story she describes the point where she realized this although she was still unable to control herself: "Then she was going to try to say hello, but she still kept on spitting." Finally, after many hesitations and failures she is able to say: "Hello, I want to play with you. I'll be nice to you."

The story served to further strengthen inner superego controls which were well on their way to being firmly established. At the end of the story, my reiteration of the healthy message and my praise of her for relating it served to further reinforce its incorporation into her superego.

About two months later, Nancy told this story:

Once upon a time there was a little girl and she used to catch grasshoppers. And one grasshopper had a family and she used to catch that and the family grasshoppers didn't want her to, so she catched the baby one. And the baby one wanted to come out.

Therapist: Wait a moment. I don't understand something. She used to catch grasshoppers and what was the next thing there?

Patient: Then she catched the baby one and the baby one couldn't fly and she caught the baby grasshopper and the baby grasshopper wanted to come out.

Therapist: The baby grasshopper wanted to come out of where?

Patient: Out of a cup because you put baby grasshoppers in cups.

Therapist: Then what happened?

Patient: Then the girl got a spanking.

Therapist: Why did she get a spanking?

Patient: And the girl, and the girl's mother spanked her for putting the grasshopper in the cup. And she let out the grasshopper and the baby grasshopper hopped away. And do you know what the lesson of that story is?

Therapist: What?

586

Patient: Well, the baby grasshopper didn't know how to breathe and he don't know how to fly, um, you don't catch baby grasshoppers. That's the lesson.

Therapist: Wait a minute now. When baby grasshoppers don't know how to fly you shouldn't catch them?

Patient: Yeah!

Therapist: Why not?

Patient: Well, you see grasshoppers don't know how to breathe because, you see, the girl didn't punch holes in it and he kept —

Therapist: Wait a minute. I'm not clear of the lesson of that story. Would you say it again.

Patient: The lesson of that story is when a baby grasshopper doesn't want to go in a cup and doesn't know how to fly you shouldn't catch them.

Therapist: All right, because ——

Patient: That's all.

Therapist: Okay.

Patient: Okay.

Therapist: Thank you very much. Now it's time for my story.

Patient: The voice goes through the tape?

Therapist: Right. Right. The voice goes through the tape.

One of the signs of mature superego formation is sensitivity to the feelings of others; the ability to place oneself in another person's position; to appreciate their pains almost as if one were in the painful situation oneself. (This ability naturally requires certain ego developments as well.) In this story Nancy shows that she is well along the way to the acquisition of such sensitivity. She exhibits appreciation of the baby grasshopper's feelings of suffocation and incarceration when trapped in a cup. The deterrents to repeating such unacceptable behavior are both internal and external. She appreciates that, so entrapped, the grasshopper can't breathe and that this is heartless behavior; but she also has to be dissuaded from cruelty to grasshoppers by an external reminder: her mother's spanking. The story reflects advancement in her superego development and indicates the area in which progress still has to be made.

This story was told two months prior to termination and I do not consider it pathological. Six-year-old children are not famous for their sensitivity to others, and external deterrents are still necessary to prevent them from cruel behavior.

This is the story I told in response:

> Once upon a time there was a little girl and she was catching grasshoppers. And there was a baby grasshopper and she caught the baby grasshopper in a little cup.
>
> *Patient:* Dr. Gardner?
> *Therapist:* Yes?
> *Patient:* You aren't supposed to say the same thing.
> *Therapist:* I know. I always start with your story, but now it changes. And that grasshopper felt very bad because it didn't get away. He said, "Please little girl let me out of here. There are no holes in this cup and I can hardly breathe. Also, this is a very small place and I can't jump around. Also, I'm very lonely in here; my parents aren't here and I have no friends here to play with."
>
> Well, when the girl heard that, she felt very bad about what she had done. She realized that she had done a very cruel thing. She felt sorry for the little baby grasshopper. She could see that he was having trouble breathing and that he was very lonely. So she let him out. He jumped out of the cup and there was a big happy smile on his face. He thanked her for letting him go. She too felt good when she saw how happy he was to be out. And she never did that again because she learned how terrible it made the grasshopper feel.
>
> And the lesson of that story is that if you think how the other person feels when you do something mean to them you probably won't do the mean thing. The end.

In my story, there are no external deterrents to the antisocial behavior. Her own sensitivity to the pain she is inflicting on others and the guilt she feels when she is cruel is enough to prevent repetition of her heartless behavior. The concentration is on the patient-grasshopper dyad. The grasshopper expresses his frustration and resentment and thereby communicates to the patient his pains. She, in turn, learns from him the exact consequences of her behavior and responds with sensitivity and guilt. The guilt is assuaged when she removes the grasshopper from his misery. She feels good about her benevolence and she is thereby internally rewarded for her kindness.

Nancy's treatment was terminated when she was about six-and-half-years-old because there had been such considerable improvement that I did not consider further work necessary. Her termination story was presented in Chapter 6. Six months later in a follow-up visit, Nancy told this story:

Once upon a time there was a little girl who wanted to take piano lessons and this is her first day. One day she got dressed very slowly and she got dressed; she got dressed until about eight o'clock, and then after she got dressed she went downstairs to breakfast and she really took a long time. Then when her mother drove her there the school was all — everybody wasn't there. The school ended when she was still getting dressed, and she cried and went home. That's all.
Therapist: And the lesson of that story?
Patient: You don't dawdle when something's happening in the morning.
Therapist: The lesson is ——
Patient: Don't dawdle.
Therapist: Good. Good lesson. Okay. Now I'll tell my story.

Like most seven-year-old children, Nancy did her share of dawdling. In the story, she reminds herself of the untoward consequences of such behavior. It is an attempt to strengthen a superego deficiency — a deficit which is normal and age-appropriate. The story then is not, in my opinion, pathological. In response, I told this story:

Once upon a time there was a little girl and she wanted to take piano lessons and she knew that if she dawdled she wouldn't be there on time. And when she started to get dressed, she started to dawdle and then she stopped herself and said, "Ah, ah, I'd better not dawdle or I'll be late." So she rushed up faster so that she wouldn't dawdle and her mother took her there and she made it in time and she had her piano lesson.

And the lesson of that story is: if you find yourself dawdling stop as soon as you can so that you don't miss out on anything. The end.

Patient: Oh boy!

Therapist: What are you "Oh boying" about?

Patient: Because you said it faster than a rocket going up into space.

Therapist: Yeah. Okay.

Since Nancy's story was essentially a healthy one, there was little I could do to improve upon it. What I did was to encourage forethought. In her story, the girl's dawdling results in her missing her piano lesson; in mine, she says to herself, "I'd better not dawdle or I'll be late," and she thereby avoids missing her lesson.

Example 4

George, the boy with disinterest in his schoolwork, shyness, and general timidity, told this story in his fifth month of treatment:

Once upon a time there was this person who made things, like he made little for tourists.

Therapist: He made what?

Patient: He made things for tourists. Like —

Therapist: Things for tourists.

Patient: Yeah. Like something that told them where they went and all that. He sold a lot of stuff and it cost about five dollars. This was done —

Therapist: You'll have to speak more clearly. Speak into the microphone.

Patient: This was done in the Philippines.

Therapist: In the Philippines?

Patient: Yeah and Nassau and something like that. As soon as they bought it, they gave him American money and they never knew it but everytime they were losing two cents for every dollar they gave him. A dollar down there is only ninety-eight cents. Our teacher told us this because she went down there on vacation. She told them, "You're losing money on this — "

Therapist: Wait a minute. Who told the tourists?

Patient: The guy who was selling it. "You're losing money on this because she gave me five dollars and I just gained ten cents off you." So the guy said why. He said, "Because our dollar down here is only ninety-eight cents of your dollar and I'm gaining two cents. So he found out and he told everybody and so everybody just gave him ninety-eight cents of their money and not a whole dollar.

The moral to that story is: in a different country you should check if the money is the same or different because if the amount is different then its worth a different amount.

Therapist: I see. Okay. Are you saying that this man was not honest in the beginning but then he was honest — that he turned honest?

Patient: Yes.

Therapist: What made him decide to turn honest?

Patient: I don't know! He just told this man because he was a good friend of his, you know, and he just told him.

Therapist: Why?

Patient: I don't know!

The story indicates superego growth as the dishonest man appreciates that he has been unethical and discontinues his fraudulent business practices. However, the process by which this sudden transformation takes place is not described. My question: "What made him turn honest?" is not satisfactorily answered. Accordingly, I told this story:

Once upon a time there was a man and this man lived in Nassau and Nassau was a great tourist center. Every year thousands and thousands of people would come to Nassau to buy things.

Now the situation with money in Nassau was as follows. Every American dollar there was only worth ninety-eight cents and this man was in a business where he sold things to tourists and most of the things he sold cost five dollars. So every time they gave him five dollars he was really making an extra dime. Now at first he thought that this was a great business. Oh boy, he was making even more money than he thought and he was really happy, but then gradually he became very dissatisfied with himself. He became kind of unhappy and he had these feelings of not being good and not being worthwhile and not liking himself. He began to wonder, "What am I doing? Why should I not feel good about myself? Why do I feel so lousy about myself?" Then gradually he realized it was because he was being dishonest, because he was lying, because he was taking disadvantage of people. So he decided one day that he was no longer going to do this. His conscience bothered him too much that he was taking advantage of people.

So one day people came to him to give him five dollars and he said, "No. Give me four dollars ninety cents because that's taking two cents off every dollar because your dollar is only worth ninety-eight cents here." The people were very thankful that he was so honest and he felt much better about himself because he felt good that he was being honest, whereas he felt bad when he was dishonest. And he had more friends because people liked him better that he was being honest.

And the lesson of that story is — do you know the lesson of that story? See if you can figure it out.

Patient: It's better to be honest than dishonest.

Therapist: Because?

Patient: You get more friends that way.

Therapist: You get more friends that way and what about your feelings toward yourself?

Patient: You have better feelings toward yourself.

Therapist: You feel better about yourself because you are honest and you get more friends that way. The end.

In my story the business man suffers with guilty self-loathing over his cheating innocent tourists. It is in response to his own inner pangs of remorse that he discontinues his duplicity. He then feels better about himself and as a fringe benefit enjoys the greater esteem of others. George "heard" my story and was able to figure out its moral although he probably considered the external rewards for honesty to be more important than the internal. The first reason he gave as to why it was better to be honest was, "You get more friends that way."

Example 5

Evan, an eleven-and-one-half-year old boy, was referred because of generalized inhibition and withdrawal from peers. His personality structure was schizoid, but he was not schizophrenic. He had trouble asserting himself, and showed little enthusiasm in school. His grades were quite poor although his intelligence was above average. This was the first story Evan told in treatment:

One day I went up with a group of people and a guide to go mountain climbing in Colorado. It was a big mountain and we were all very tired, but the view was fine. At about 1000 feet I picked up a rock and threw it down. It bounced off the stones and went all the way down. It was a dangerous climb, but we had ropes and a guide and waist chains. He would go up ahead of us on to a ledge. It was a very steep mountain. There were very few grips for our hands and feet. Then we got to the top of one of the ledges, but the guide fell off and he got killed. Then we built a fire and had grilled cheese sandwiches.

After that it was easier to climb because the mountain wasn't so steep. However, we couldn't get to the top, so we went all the way down and went around to the other side of the mountain. We found a spot that looked good. We got another guide, but he got killed also on the way up. We got to the top and there was a pretty view. It was 5000 feet high and it took us six hours to climb it. We could see a hundred miles in every direction. We stayed up there awhile, enjoyed the view, and then we went down. It was much easier to get down.

Therapist: What's the moral of that story?
Patient: I can't think of any moral.

The most striking thing in this story was Evan's total lack of feeling for the guides who fell and were killed. He spoke of their falls with the same emotionless tone used when he described the rock that he had thrown down the mountain. The sentence describing the death of the first one is immediately followed by: "Then we built a fire and had grilled cheese sandwiches." And the death of the second causes not a moment's hesitation or interference in the journey's progress. The story reveals severe superego deficiencies: an utter lack of sensitivity to the pains of others and an inability to place oneself in the position of someone who suffers.

This is the story I told in response:

One day a group of friends of mine and I decided to go mountain climbing. We were in Colorado and we were in the Rockies. We had a guide who was a very fine person and we all liked him very much. He had many years of experience and we felt very secure with him. He went ahead of us and we all had ropes and waist chains for protection. When we were about half-way up the mountain, he was on a ledge ahead of us and suddenly the rocks slipped from under him and, although he tried to catch on to the ledge, he slipped off and his body plummeted at least 1000 feet to the bottom of the mountain. It was a horrifying experience and we all felt completely helpless. We knew that it was sure death for him.

We were so upset that there was no question in our minds that we could not continue the trip. We were grief-stricken over this man's death, especially since he had died in the process of trying to be helpful to us in climbing this mountain. Well, we all slowly went down the mountain along the path that we had originally taken and when we got to the bottom, there we saw what we all feared and knew to be the case. There was his mangled body on the ground and it was a horrible sight. It was clear that he had probably died in the fall or died at the moment he struck the ground. Most of us cried bitterly. We then went back to the main cabin and notified the authorities. His wife was brought over and it was most painful when we had to tell her the very tragic news. The man had three children who were now left without a father as well. It was, without question, one of the most terrible experiences I have ever had.

In my story I included every ramification of the guide's death that might elicit emotional reactions. The written transscript can only convey a suggestion of the emotionalism which I tried to convey while telling my story. My hope here was to impart to Evan some sensitivity to the agony and torment which others might suffer. It would have been unreasonable to expect that this self-involved boy would, in his first session, respond significantly to an emotion-engendering story, and his overt reaction was minimal. My hope was that Evan might ultimately be reached, and this story was a step in that direction.

12. SITUATIONAL REACTIONS

The term situational reaction refers to psychogenic disturbances which arise in response to environmental experiences which have a deleterious effect upon the patient and play a significant role in the etiology of his emotional disorder. The external event is one which the patient had little or no involvement in bringing about and can do little if anything to change. He must consider it, for the most part, to be an unalterable entity to which he must adjust. The goal in treating situational reactions is to eliminate, as much as possible, inappropriate adaptations to the trauma and help the patient bear, in the least painful fashion, the uncomfortable emotional reactions which inevitably result from the detrimental experience.

The Mutual Storytelling Technique has proven particularly useful in the treatment of three common types of situational reactions in children: divorce of parents, death of a parent, and traumatic surgery.

REACTIONS TO DIVORCE

Divorce may be one of the most traumatic experiences of a child's life. Although the child is often better off living with one parent who has been healthy and strong enough to sever the troubled relationship than with two who are miserably locked together, he still usually suffers significant deprivation. I will discuss first those acute reactions which the child may exhibit around the time of the divorce, and then describe those which occur later as the child adjusts to his new way of life.

In the phase of acute reaction the child may become withdrawn, apathetic, insomnious, and anorexic. He may exhibit, that is, all the manifestations of the depressive syndrome. Or he may totally deny that his life is any different. Some become obsessed with effecting a reconciliation, and they may persist in this futile endeavor for years.

Anger is a common reaction. Sometimes it is directly expressed in an appropriate fashion. More commonly the child feels guilt over his hostility, and he may then utilize a variety of techniques to handle it. Some direct their anger toward the parent with whom they live; the absent parent not being so readily available. Others have temper tantrums. Some may utilize compulsive rituals for its symbolic discharge of hostility; others project their anger and then see themselves as innocently suffering at the hands of malevolent figures. Nightmares are another common manifestation of the repressed hostility. Some handle their anger through reaction formation: they become excessively concerned for the welfare of one or both parents and fear that they will become sick, injured, or killed. Some harbor the notion that their angry thoughts may harm the parent, and this produces guilt and fear. Separation anxiety may also develop; the child must stay with the parent to reassure himself that his hostile feelings (and even death wishes) have not been realized.

Having lost one parent, the child becomes less secure that his remaining parent will remain. He thereby becomes more generally insecure and more sensitive to rejection. Fears of total abandonment and fantasies of being sent off to hostile environments are common. No matter how much the parents may explain otherwise, the child tends to perceive the departing parent as someone who has abandoned him.

The child may feel guilty and consider the divorce to have been his fault. This reaction is often related to his desire to control this uncontrollable event in his life. Control is implied in the notion, "It's my fault."[1] A related response is the preoccupation with who is to blame.

The child of divorced parents may consider the absent parent to be unloving and himself, therefore, unlovable. He may become confused over contradictions between what his parents say about their affection for him and how they act toward him.

Father, he is told, still loves him although he never visits or sends support money. Mother is said to love him, yet she spends many nights and weekends away with strange men. His parents may adhere to the dictum that they should not speak unfavorably of one another to the child lest his respect for the criticized parent be compromised. Here again confusion is engendered: the child can only ask, "If he was so perfect, why did you divorce him?" Such parental dishonesty (no matter how well-intentioned) can only create in the child distrust of his parents.

In addition to these acute reactions to the divorce, there are a variety of problems which may then arise as the child attempts to adapt to his new way of life. He may try to take over the role of the absent parent (especially when the child is the same sex as the departed parent). Or he may regress in an attempt to get more attention as compensation for that which has been lost. He may come to view his visiting father as the "good guy" whose main purpose is to provide entertainment and his mother as "mean" because she always seems to be the one imposing restrictions on him. If the mother works, angry and depressive reactions are common — especially if she had never worked before. If his parents begin to date, the child may respond with a variety of reactions such as confusion, anger, jealousy, or denial.

The parents may attempt to use the child as a weapon against one another. The mother may refuse to let the husband see the children in retaliation for unpaid support or alimony. The father may refuse to fulfill his financial obligations unless the mother submits to certain of his demands. They may attempt to use the child to spy on one another. The child may take advantage of his parents in their discord and try to play one against the other for his own gain.

In some communities the child of divorced parents may be stigmatized. But even when this does not occur, he invariably feels different. Others live with two parents while he lives with only one. He may become ashamed to bring other children home and may even try to conceal the divorce from his friends.

The extra jobs and responsibilities which the child must take on after the divorce may become a source of deep resentment, especially if they take him away from recreational activities which his peers have the time to enjoy.

Lastly, when a divorced parent remarries, new problems may arise in the child's relationship with his stepparent. A common one is the child's displacement of hostility from the natural parent on to the stepparent.

The child's reactions to divorce are multiple. I have described them in greater detail elsewhere.[2] In addition, in *The Boys and Girls Book About Divorce*,[3] which is specifically written to be read by children, I describe many of these difficulties and suggest to the child various ways he can attempt to handle them more effectively.

Example 1

Julie, the ten-year-old girl who reacted to her parents' divorce with rage outbursts toward her mother, chronic surly attitude, and generalized antagonism toward authority figures, told this story during her second session:

Patient: Hello, everybody.
Therapist: Hi.
Patient: This story is the story of a ghost and a maniac. Well, once upon a time there was a girl ghost and a boy maniac. So the maniac was really in love with the girl ghost but he had never told anybody that. One day he asked to marry the girl ghost. The girl ghost was very pretty and beautiful but she also had another lover. So one day she and her other lover were out on a date and they got annoyed at each other. So the girl ghost said, "I don't love you anymore." So she quickly ran, uh, stomped away angrily. Of course, the lover was very disappointed to lose his beautiful girl, but that's the way it goes.

So the maniac was walking out, and the girl ghost said, "Oh, hello, is that you again?" And he said, "Yes, lovely. Will you please come on a walk with me?" "It would be my pleasure," the girl ghost said. So they each went out on a walk. Now the maniac was very ugly, but the girl ghost didn't think of his ugliness at all compared to his manners. So finally she got to like him very much and they were always going out on dates. One day the maniac bought her an engagement ring. "So," he said, "would you like to marry me?" "With pleasure," she said. So they invited some of their friends to their wedding.

Now the jealous lover had heard that she was getting married to someone else. He had to stop the wedding; so the wedding procession was now beginning when the other lover got there. "Stop the wedding," he screamed and in horror everybody turned around. He had a big witch with him. "Ha, ha, ha," the witch laughed, "I see that the girl ghost will not accept my brother. Well, I'll cast a, I'll cast a spell on everyone of you if you do not marry my brother." Well, the girl goes —

Therapist: Wait, wait a moment, I'm a little confused. The jealous lover came and he wanted who, he wanted — the witch was his sister, is that it?

Patient: Ya.

Therapist: Oh, and she said, "You've gotta marry my brother."

Patient: Well, so everybody was so unhappy, especially the girl ghost. She didn't want to marry the lover because she, she wasn't in love with him anymore; but, of course, she didn't want to be turned into anything terrible. The girl and the ugly maniac kissed each other goodbye and the girl ghost went over to the witch. "Well, have you made up your mind little twinky toes?" asked the witch meanly. "Yes," the girl ghost said sadly; so, unfortunately, they had to be married.

Well, later when they were married and living in a house the ugly maniac came, and he took the girl ghost away with him and they both ran away. Now then, by then, the girl ghost had forgotten all about the ugly maniac, so when he came she screamed in terror and when he asked her, she said, "I don't want to marry you, you are too ugly," but he was very kind, and she was having a lot of trouble with her ugly, mean old husband. So she ran away with him and they were each married. She didn't care about his ugliness anymore, and they all lived happily ever after.

The moral is it doesn't matter how ugly a person is; it's their manners and the way they feel about you.

Therapist: Okay. Thank you very much. That was an excellent story. Now it's time for me to tell my story.

Julie depicts herself as a ghost — as dead, inhuman, having no substance, and unreal. Her feelings of worthlessness are profound. She feels that only the lowest creatures could possibly be interested in her. One of her suitors is an ugly maniac and the other, the brother of a witch, is described at the end of her story as ugly and mean. In the story, she gains some ego-enhancement by getting the two men to fight over her.

Her feelings of inadequacy were in part related to her father's rejection of her. She adhered to the dicta, "If he doesn't love me, I am unlovable," and "If he has left me, there must be something terribly wrong with me." The story also reveals her feelings that all men are basically ugly, cruel, and unloving, like her father. In the story she regains her lost father; it is better to have an ugly man than no man at all. The ugly monster, however, has "good manners," in other words, he provides her with the tenderness and devotion her father deprives her of.

This is the story I told in response:

Once upon a time there was a girl ghost and there was a man whom she liked very much. He was a nice-looking man and she wanted to marry him very much and he first showed interest in her for a little while. And, then, one day they had a big fight, and he said, "You are very ugly and I never want to see you again." And he walked off and she felt very bad and she began to cry, and then a friend of hers came along and the friend said, "Why are you crying?" And she said, "Because I'm ugly." He said, "What do you mean because you're ugly?" She said, "Well, my boyfriend left me, and he said I'm ugly." The friend said, "There are two things wrong with your thinking: 1) just because somebody calls you ugly doesn't mean you're ugly and 2) just because somebody leaves you doesn't mean you're ugly." And she said, "You mean that?" And he said, "Yes," and she said, "Yeah, but you know my boyfriend is a pretty smart guy and he really knows a lot." And he said, "Yeah, he may know a lot but he's out in left field when he calls you ugly. I can tell you that you're not ugly and if you think you're ugly because he calls you ugly that means that there is something wrong with you."

Well, with that she began thinking and she realized that just because somebody leaves you, it doesn't make you ugly, and just because somebody calls you ugly, it doesn't make you ugly. So she found someone else who was very nice, she grew up, and she lived happily ever after. Do you know what the moral of that story is?

Patient: No.

Therapist: My story has two morals: if someone calls you ugly it doesn't mean you are ugly, and the other moral is if somebody leaves you, it doesn't mean you're no good. Those are the two morals of my story. What do you think of that?

Patient: I think it's a very nice story.

Therapist: What's the part you liked the most?

Patient: Um —— I liked that when the boyfriend — he told her the truth about herself.

Therapist: I see. Okay.

In my story I tried to get Julie to question two basic premises which contributed to her low self-esteem, one of the more common problems suffered by children of divorced parents. They assume that they have been abandoned because they have been bad or because they are in some way unlovable. Correction of such distortions is an important part of the treatment of these children. One must emphasize to them that the divorce is the result of the parents rejecting each other (or at least one parent rejecting the other), but that rejection of the child was in no way involved. Also, in order to help the child compensate for the loss, one must reiterate that there are many others with whom one can form gratifying relationships, both in the present and in the future.

Three weeks later, Julie told this story:

Good afternoon, ladies and gentlemen, this story is about a little girl and her talking doll. Once upon a time there was a little girl named Alice, and she had a secret because she had a talking doll who was her friend and could really walk and play. This doll was really alive. So one day the talking doll was lost. Alice burst into tears and she had to find her. Alice lived in this big spooky house so she went up to the attic where there were all different things around. She looked into all the trunks and suitcases but she couldn't find her talking doll anywhere. So, soon she saw her dog just chewing up something. Uh, she wondered if it was her talking doll or not. No, it was just the talking doll's dress. So she ran and asked the dog where was the talking doll. Now this dog could talk, too, so he said, "I think the talking doll went out to get something to eat but I don't know really 'cause that's where she usually goes."

So Alice ran out of the house to all the restaurants around the neighborhood. At one, right sitting on the table there was the talking doll, feasting and feasting. So, Alice said, "Hold on Elizabeth" — that was the talking doll's name. So, Elizabeth went back. "I'm sorry if I scared you, but I was very, very hungry and the cook is not at home now she went to do some shopping." "Oh, that's all right, Elizabeth, I'm very glad to have you back." So they all, they went —

Therapist: Hold on a second, is it that I'm sorry that I scared you by going away, but the cook wasn't there and I was hungry?

Patient: Yeah.

Therapist: Okay.

Patient: So they went back into the house and then they had even more because the talking doll had that much time to feast before Alice found her, so Alice thanked the dog very much because he's the one that had really found the talking doll.

Therapist: Did you say that the rest had more to eat? Is that it? Because the talking doll ——

Patient: Yeah, didn't have that much time to feast because Alice, um, found her.

Therapist: Oh, in other words, so that there was more food left for the rest.

Patient: Yeah.

Therapist: Okay.

Patient: And, so, they played games and danced and then the cook came back and it was dinner time and she cooked a delicious stew for everybody. Then when Alice went to bed she whispered, "Oh, Elizabeth, I'm so glad to have you back."

The moral of this story is: Don't — now let's see what's the moral of this story —— um, um —— don't look places where you know you can't find somebody. There's my moral.

Therapist: How does that apply to this story?

Patient: Well, because Alice really knew that she couldn't, um, find the doll in the attic and everything, but the dog knew where she was. The dog usually knew where Elizabeth goes, so that's why that's the moral.

Therapist: I see. Okay. Thank you. Well, that was a very good story.

Patient: Thank you.

Alice is the patient and Elizabeth, the talking doll, her alter ego. The cook, the provider of food (love), symbolizes the patient's mother. Sometimes she is home and sometimes she is not, that is, her love is not always available. When she is not there to provide affection, Julie — in the form of the doll, Elizabeth — seeks food outside the home. The restaurant, I believe, represents the father who, indeed, lived in another city. The hunt for food is her quest for affection. The moral, "Don't look places where you know you can't find somebody," refers to her quest for love. It has healthy elements in that Julie is learning from messages imparted in previous stories not to persist futilely in trying to extract love from someone who is not able to provide it. She is beginning to seek love elsewhere when it is not forthcoming. The restaurant, however, is a distorted symbol for the father in that it implies continuous availability of food. Julie sees her mother as giving affection only intermittently, and her father as continually so — a gross reversal.

With this symbolic reversal in mind, I told my story:

Now, it's time for me to tell my story. Once upon a time there was a little girl named Alice and she had a secret. She had a talking doll named Elizabeth and this talking doll was her friend and she and Elizabeth would talk about everything when they were alone. Now, in this house they had a cook and once in a while they would go out and eat in a restaurant and Elizabeth and Alice always used to argue as to who made better food, the restaurant or the cook, and they could never figure it out. Now, sometimes when the cook would make a meal Alice would say, "This meal is very good," and Elizabeth would say, "Uch, terrible. Ooh, this food is terrible. Feh!" Anyway, then sometimes the cook would make a meal and it was Elizabeth who would say, "Wow, is this food really good." And it was Alice who would say, "Ich, how could you like that? It was disgusting." And, when they had gone up to the restaurant, it was the same thing. Sometimes Alice would like the food, sometimes Elizabeth would like the food. Sometimes Alice would hate the food, sometimes Elizabeth would hate the food. So, they began to learn that no cook, be it the restaurant cook or the cook in the house, is perfect. That sometimes they make good food and sometimes they make bad food. But they decided to see who made the best food more often and they kept score and they watched carefully and they tried to see — and who do you think they finally concluded made the best food more often, not that that person made the best food all the time but had a higher percentage of times when the food was good? Who do you think it was — the cook or the restaurant?
Patient: The cook.

Therapist: Why do you say that?

Patient: Um — because, um, the cook could make their favorite foods all the time so that it would be good but the restaurant only had a menu of different things sometimes.

Therapist: Right, that's what I thought too. Besides, home cooking is usually better than restaurant cooking. You know in really home cooking, the cook can put in all the best kinds of things and tries to please the family because the family are the cook's loved ones that she often has a greater desire to make good food for. So Alice and the dog gradually realized that the cook could be counted on more often than the restaurant to make good food, although once in a while the cook would make a poor meal, but more often the restaurant would make a poor meal and you know what the morals of that, that story has a couple of morals, you know what those morals are?

Patient: Ummm ——

Therapist: Well, the morals are: nobody is perfect, everybody has their good and their bad parts like this cook. She wasn't perfect; she had times when she would cook good meals and other times when she would cook bad meals. And the second moral is: when you have a choice between two people, both of whom are not perfect, you try to spend more time with the one who will or has more to offer you and in this case it was the cook. She wasn't perfect, but she did give them more than the restaurant. But, once in a while they would go to the restaurant too. The end. What did you think of that story?

Patient: Very nice.

Therapist: What was the part about it you liked the most?

Patient: Um, when they found who was nearest perfect, who was the nearest to being perfect, not perfect, because nobody could be perfect.

Therapist: Uh-huh, right, okay.

In my story, I helped Julie gain a more accurate picture of her parents regarding their relative abilities to give her affection. This is an important goal of practically every child's therapy; but in the treatment of children whose parents are divorced, it is even more vital. Such children often have a more distorted view of their parents than those whose parents are together. There are a number of reasons for this. The divorced parents, in their antagonism, communicate to the child either overtly or covertly many criticisms of each other that are not valid. The child's fear of alienating his parents may cause him to repress his awareness of their deficiencies. An absent parent, who mainly provides recreation when visiting, is not in a situation conducive to the exposure of defects. Acquiring an accurate picture of the parents — especially regarding their abilities to give love — can help the child avoid frustration and neurotic reactions which stem from vain attempts to secure affection from an individual beyond his capacity to provide it.

During the next few weeks, I pointed out to Julie's mother that although she complained bitterly about her loneliness and frustrations, she was not actively doing those things which would increase the likelihood that she would meet a man. Her response was to make minimal and ambivalent efforts to meet men. Julie was aware of my discussions with her mother. It was during this period, three weeks after the story just presented, that she related this one:

Hello, ladies and gentlemen, this story is about two birds and a very mean one. One bird was a lady and one was a man and they were in love with each other and wanted to get married, but the bullying bird warned the lady —

Therapist: Wait a minute, does the bully make a third one?

Patient: Yeah, there are three birds.

Therapist: Well, is the bully a man or a lady?

Patient: The bully is a man, and the bully also wanted to marry the lady bird. So there were many, many fights about who would get her for the wife. Now the bully would try more and more tricks to see if he could get the girl bird but one day they were — the man bird and the girl bird were flying away and the bully flew up and bumped into the man bird and knocked him on the ground. The girl bird was very surprised and just then the bully got her and tied her up with ropes and took her to his nest. So, um, the boy bird was very hurt, was hurt very much, and tried to get up but then at the bully bird's nest the girl bird was tied and held prisoner. "I will drop you in the river if you don't marry me," the bully bird said to the girl. So the poor girl was really deeply — was deeply sad about the loss of her real boyfriend and she had no choice.

But meanwhile the boy bird was getting up now and was off to rescue the girl bird. He flew a long way, and he knew where the bully bird's nest was, and just as the bully bird was trying to fly with her in the river, he knocked the bully bird down and the girl bird flew down on the land but not in the river. So they had a terrific fight and finally the boy bird won and the bully bird was all beat up. He limped away and the girl bird and the boy bird flew off together. Soon they were married and they all lived happily ever after. And, the bully bird got another girl and married her because she was a bully too. But she never ever saw the boy bird and the girl bird again.

The moral of this story is, um, what's the moral of the story? Um, um, the moral of the story is: don't try to take somebody's else's joy away or you'll be sorry. That's the moral of my story.

Although the story could be interpreted as another example of Julie's trying to enhance her self-esteem by getting two men to fight for her affection, I believe that there is a more meaningful interpretation considering that her mother was making her first attempts to date at the time the story was told. The lady bird — first referred to as a lady, but then as a girl — represents the patient's mother, the man bird stands for her father, and the bully bird symbolizes her mother's prospective suitor. The loving relationship between the man and lady bird reveals Julie's denial of her parents' schism and her wish that they be reconciled. By making the bully bird a coercive intruder, she can deny her parents' dislike for one another as well as her mother's active interest in finding a substitute for her father.

All would be well if it weren't for some interloper who disrupts their blissful relationship. The story ends with her unrealistic wishes gratified: her parents are reconciled and suitors are removed from the picture.

Stories such as this are typical of children whose parents are divorced. In response, I told this one:

Once upon a time there was a lady bird and she felt very sad because she used to see other lady birds who would have men birds who would follow after them and want to marry them. And, she would even see some lady birds have two men fighting over them. But, this lady bird was very lonely; she not only didn't have two men fighting over her, she didn't even have one man who wanted her, so she was very lonely.

One day she was speaking to another friend and the friend said to her, "Why are you so lonely? Why are you so sad?" And she said, "I'm sad because I don't have any men fighting over me or I don't even have any men who want to be with me." So the friend said, "Well, are you doing anything about it?" She said, "What am I to do, they just don't come around?" She said, "Well, don't you go to the places where the men are, don't you go out?" And she said, "No." So she said, "Well, how do you expect to meet men if you don't go where the action is, as they say? You'll never meet a man unless you go where they are. You've got to put yourself out. You've got to be there at the same time and same place when they're there. That's the only way you're going to meet them. You can't expect them to find you if you don't put yourself in the position where they are going to meet you."

Well, the lonely lady thought about what she had been told and realized that her friend had given her good advice so she began to join clubs and organizations which men joined and gradually she began to meet men and she finally ended up marrying someone.

And, do you know what the lesson in that story is?

Patient: Um, let's see, don't, um, if you want to be with somebody, go where they are.

Therapist: Uh-huh, you just can't sit on your backside and expect it to happen. Tell me something, what about your mother, does she go out and try to be where the men are and try to meet people?

Patient: Um, yeah.

Therapist: Are you sure? Where, where does she go?

Patient: Well, she goes to dances and everything.

Therapist: When? When does she go? When was the last time?

Patient: Oh, she goes all different times.

Therapist: When? When was the last time she went out like that?

Patient: I don't know because sometimes she doesn't tell me.

Therapist: How do you know she goes to dances and everything?

Patient: Because, because sometimes she does tell me and, um —

Therapist: When was the last time she went to a dance?

Patient: The last time I know of is, um, the Jack and Jill, no, that's not the last time. I don't know, it was Friday, I don't know which Friday though.

Therapist: Was it a long time time ago or recently?

Patient: Probably, recently.

Therapist: Do you think that your mother is doing as much as she could to get married again?

Patient: No.

Therapist: Why do you say that?

Patient: Well, she could go away and try to find one. There aren't any intelligent, handsome men around here.

Therapist: Where could she go?

Patient: She could go for a trip around the world or something.

Therapist: Yes, but that costs a lot of money, doesn't it?

Patient: I suppose ——

Therapist: Well, what else do you think she could do?

Patient: I don't know. Let's do something else.

Therapist: Okay.

In my story the possibility of a reconciliation between the man and lady bird is not even discussed. To consider it — even to deny it — could have raised Julie's hopes far more than my not mentioning it at all. The divorce is a *fait accompli*. The advice regarding loneliness is really presented for both the patient and her mother. Julie handled her frustration and loneliness by outbursts of rage; the mother by depression and complaints. Both passively sat back, hoping for better days, the patient by her parents' remarriage; the mother by vague fantasies of someone pursuing her. Neither was actively seeking realistic substitutes for the lost father. In my story they are advised that passively living in a dream world isn't going to accomplish very much. It is only through active planning and realistic effort that alternative gratifications can be realized.

In my post-story discussion I attempted, through the discussion of the mother's efforts to find someone else, to encourage Julie to seek her own substitutes. However, my efforts were not too successful — Julie did not have enough interest to pursue the topic meaningfully.

Two weeks later, Julie told this story:

Um, my story is about one big bully and two little girls. Once upon a time there was a big bully named Big Bill and there were two little girls he always used to beat up. So one day the two little girls said, "We have to get away from Big Bill or else he will beat us up some more. I'm getting beat up so badly someday I might have to go to the hospital." So, there were also these two boys, also, who were the girls' friends and Big Bill got another bullying girl. So, of course, these children were much younger than Big Bill and his girlfriend.
Therapist: Wait, wait, Big Bill had one girlfriend?
Patient: Yeah, she was a bully too.
Therapist: And the two girls had two boyfriends? Right?
Patient: But they were littler. So, um, it came that they had a big fight, Big Bill and his girlfriend and the two girls and the two boys who were gonna have. And the girls were terribly afraid but the boys said, "Don't worry, we'll try to protect you." So they started to fight. At first the small children were knocked to the ground, but just then a boy sneaked up behind Big Bill and kicked him

down. His leg was hurt so bad that he never (*mumbles*). But, the girl was still there.

Therapist: Now wait. His leg was hurt so bad that he what?

Patient: His leg, but the girl was still there, and then a girl reached, went behind, and pinched her.

Therapist: This is Big Bill's girlfriend?

Patient: Yeah, and so she went home too. So the two boys and the girls had won the fight.

So the moral of my story is: four people are better than two.

This is another typical story told by children whose parents are divorced. The bully and his girlfriend are the patient's parents; the abused children are Julie and her sister (with two boys along as allies). By making her father a persecutor, Julie enjoys more involvement with him than she would were she to see him more truthfully as one who had abandoned her. In addition, Julie sees his rejection as active hostility — to which she adds her own projected anger. Her mother is once again seen as an ally of her father (again, the reconciliation theme). Her mother is seen as hostile for a number of reasons. Anger toward the father is displaced onto her mother (an available target). The mother's inability to meet the patient's insatiable demands (intensified by the absence of her father) is seen as hostility by the patient. The mother's refusal to remarry the father is seen as the mother's most hostile act. Lastly, much of Julie's own anger is projected onto her mother.

The story is one in which she simply vents the rage she feels toward her parents. She enjoys retribution for the injustices she sees herself to have suffered at their hands.

I told the following story in response:

Once upon a time there was a big bully. His name was Big Bill. And, in this neighborhood there lived these two girls. It was a funny thing about these two girls, no matter how badly Big Bill treated them, they loved him. He would humiliate them; he would laugh at them; he would ignore them; he would make appointments and not keep them; and yet, no matter what he did these two girls would say, "Oh, we love Big Bill. He's such a wonderful person and everybody should love him like we do." People said, "Look at that, look at the mark you have on your face." They said, "Oh, that's just nothing, he was just playing." No matter what he did to them these poor, foolish girls just idolized him. They loved him and, of course, people began to laugh at them and said, "Isn't it foolish how these two girls worship that Big Bill? No matter how badly he treats them, they still walk around thinking he's wonderful."

But, there were times when these two girls were very sad and upset all the time. They asked people, "Why?" "Because you let Big Bill walk all over you and you don't want to see, really, what's going on. You don't express your feelings so it comes out in other ways. You don't let your real anger come out at Big Bill. You don't let your feelings come out, and so it happens later on in a different time and a different place and then you get depressed and upset or angry at other people and other things. It's really making your life miserable in other ways." Well, what do you think the girls thought after they were told that?

Patient: That they had been silly to let Big Bill beat them up and that they still worshipped him and they didn't worship him any more.

Therapist: And they saw him as a human being after that — with both good and bad parts. When he was nice to them they enjoyed themselves with him and they respected him. But when he was not nice to them, they had nothing to do with him. They stayed away from him, and they found out that they were much less upset, angry, and depressed and things like that and the lesson of that story is what?

Patient: Look at everybody as a human being and nobody is perfect.

Therapist: Right. What did you think of that story?

Patient: I thought it was very interesting.

Julie's outward behavior toward her father revealed little, if any, of the inner rage she felt toward him. He rarely saw her, did not acknowledge her birthday, although he did send Christmas presents, was faulty in sending support money, and would cancel, at the last minute, Julie's visits to his home in another city. In spite of this, in Julie's eyes her father could do no wrong. His rationalizations became hers. His forgetting (his most common explanation) was always accepted as a reasonable excuse. To Julie, this explanation had no underlying psychodynamic meaning or implication. In my story, I tried to help Julie obtain a more accurate view of her father: a man with both assets and liabilities. In addition, I encouraged direct expression of anger toward him.

DEATH OF A PARENT

The death of a parent is, without question, even more traumatic to the child than divorce. The younger the child the greater the likelihood of psychopathological sequelae. This is especially true when there is no replacement for the deceased parent. When a parent is terminally ill, psychiatric treatment of the child may include the following: 1) preparation for the parent's death; 2) assistance at the time of the funeral; and 3) mourning and working through other post-death reactions.

Prior to the death, a parent (usually, but not necessarily, the one who will be surviving) may ask the therapist about whether to tell the child, and if so, how to go about doing it. The answer to this question cannot be separated from the issue of how the dying parent himself is handling the situation.

There is great variation in how a parent may react to a fatal illness. Some can handle the knowledge directly and make the appropriate arrangements. Others become deeply depressed and inconsolable. Others deny the obvious and pitifully clutch at every dissimulation which might support the delusion of survival. Often the person recognizes his forthcoming demise but avoids any discussion of his feelings lest he upset those who are close to him. The latter, indeed, are usually uncomfortable about communicating their knowledge and feelings to the sick person and rationalize their silence by considering such discussions deleterious to the dying one. What results is a pathetic theatrical performance in which all players make-believe that nothing serious is really happening; each avoids the unmentionable subject, ostensibly to spare the feelings of the others. The dying person is thereby deprived of salutary working-through, solace, and meaningful commiseration in his final days. At the time in his life when those close to him can be most meaningful, they become more distant than they have ever been before. In addition, added to the loved ones' burden of accepting and adjusting to the death is that of play-acting (which is made particularly difficult because they are demanding of themselves a "good show" at a time when they are least inclined to such performing). Some displace their concerns for themselves onto others: a minor illness suffered by a relatively distant friend or relative can evoke a profuse response of worry and commiseration which may preoccupy the dying person for days. Anger is another common reaction. Profound bitterness colors practically every word and action, and the dying person will seize upon every excuse to vent his rage.

The aforementioned are the more common reactions of younger and middle-aged adults. The aged seem to take death more quietly. There is far less *Sturm und Drang*. They have lived their lives through; they have loved, they have hated; they have succeeded, they have failed; they have known joy and sorrow, pleasure and heartache. For them, little is novel. They are tired, they lie down, and silently go to sleep. They appear to confirm what the poet Swinburne so eloquently tells us:

> From too much love of living,
> From hope and fear set free,
> We thank with brief thanksgiving
> Whatever gods may be
> That no life lives forever;
> That dead men rise up never;
> That even the weariest river
> Winds somewhere safe to sea.[4]

The therapist is ill-equipped to advise the child about his

parent's forthcoming death if he has not ascertained the dying parent's mode of adaptation. Ideally, the therapist should have the opportunity to interview the parent himself. In this way he can best determine what type of adjustment the sick parent is making. (When this is not possible, then a detailed inquiry of the surviving parent may have to suffice.) When interviewing the dying parent one must be respectful of his particular way of adapting. If one takes the position that it is better for everyone to know the truth, or holds that no one ever *really* wants to know, or has some other fixed idea on how to handle the dying person, considerable additional distress may be caused. A more passive approach to the interrogation is safer. If the parent will talk on his own — with primarily catalytic comments by the therapist — the mode of adjustment will often be revealed.

When the dying parent's adjustment mechanism has been determined, the therapist is better able to decide how to handle the parent's illness with the child. Another significant consideration, however, in handling the problem is the child's age. It is important for the therapist to realize that, generally, the child under the age of five is not aware of the finality of death. He may know that one is put in the ground, but he often considers the grave to be a temporary abode. From about five to nine, most children realize that death is permanent, but they do not usually consider seriously the possibility that it can happen to them. It is only after nine that the child usually appreciates, with full impact, that he too is mortal. If the parent is handling the death overtly, then the child should be directly told, by one or both of his parents, what is going to happen.

The child will usually ask questions about the hereafter. It is important for the parents to describe honestly to the child their views regarding what happens to a person after death. If they believe in some sort of existence after death, they should describe it; if they do not believe in an afterlife they should say so; and if they have no strong opinions or convictions, they should describe their inability to come to a definite conclusion. For example: "Some people believe that you do live in heaven after death and others do not. I just don't know." It is of the utmost importance that the parent be honest to the child. Dishonesty only confuses the child, brings about distrust of the parents, and adds to his burden.

After informing the child, *his* method of coping must be respected. It is important for him to have the feeling that any questions he may have will be honestly answered; it is also vital that he not be pressured into discussions when he is disinclined. Generally, the younger the child, the less he will understand of what he is being told. Even older children (pubertal and above) often exhibit what seems to the adult to be a callous disregard for the import of what they have learned.

Things are far more complicated when the dying parent utilizes denial or one of the other modes of adjustment with which he attempts to conceal from himself the full import of his condition. It is unrealistic to attempt to gain the meaningful cooperation of a child below the prepubertal period (although there are certain younger children who will show remarkable maturity in such a situation). By cooperation, I refer to the family's support and appreciation of the dying patient's adjustment mechanisms; their respect for such adaptations; and their abstaining from imposing on the sick parent what they consider to be better ways of handling death. It is unreasonable to hope that a five-year-old, whose mother is trying to deny her terminal illness, can be entrusted not to say: "Mommy, daddy says you're going to die." In some cases, it is best to withhold the information from the child in order to protect the parent. In other cases, the dying parent's defense mechanisms may be so strong that they would not be significantly affected by such a remark. Each situation must be evaluated in its own right.

A common question is whether or not the child should attend the funeral. Many parents feel that it is too traumatic a thing to expose a child to and don't even consider taking him. Such parents may be depriving the child of a most important experience. Children are concrete. Actually seeing the dead parent in a coffin and observing the burial may provide the child with a meaningful confirmation of his parent's death. Such experiences, as grueling as they may be, can make the mourning period and post-death adaptation easier. There is less question in the child's mind as to exactly what happened to the parent; there is less confusion and conjecture; and so there is less likelihood that the child will have unrealistic hopes for the parent's return or other inappropriate preoccupations. Therefore, I usually suggest that the child be invited to attend. If he refuses, I suggest that he be encouraged; but his firm refusal should be respected. Sometimes the child prefers to attend the services but not the burial; this is certainly a reasonable request. One complication arises when the child involved is so young that he might disrupt the services. In such cases, I usually suggest that the child be encouraged to go to the funeral parlor beforehand to view his parent for the last time.

Another reason why I recommend the child's involvement is that witnessing the emotional displays at the funeral often helps the child express his feelings. It is at the funeral, more than anywhere else, that he is likely to have this important experience. However, it is wise to tell the child beforehand something about what to expect regarding the family's displays of grief lest he become too frightened and overwhelmed.

Mourning involves a piecemeal desensitization to the painful loss. Vital to acceptance is free expression of the feelings of grief. The parent who is too inhibited to express his own feelings sets a poor example for his child. The parent who says to the child, "Be brave, don't cry," or "See how big a man you can be. Men don't cry," is encouraging pathological repression. He is retarding, if not entirely preventing, a salutary mourning experience.

There are some who, with the best intentions, remove or discard all of the deceased parent's belongings and personal effects. This, they claim, will help the child forget the dead parent more quickly. This is a mistake. Such memorabilia can be most helpful in the mourning period. Each child should be given some particular memento, ideally, by the dying parent himself. Having it during the mourning period serves the same purpose as the "transitional object" (the toys or blankets which children latch onto as symbols for the absent parent). It provides the child with symbolic contact with the lost parent and thereby assuages some of the pain of separation. The same object may become cherished throughout life as an important psychological tie with the lost parent. The child who reacts with apathy or who reacts as if nothing were bothering him is inhibited. Attempts should be made to encourage emotional release.

Guilt reactions may also appear in response to a parent's death. Again, I believe, that this guilt is less often related to hostility (the child believing that the parent died as the result of hostile thoughts and even death wishes which he may have harbored) and more often the result of his desire to have control over this totally uncontrollable calamity. The traditional approach to such guilt, in which the child is helped to feel more comfortable with his hostility is, in my opinion, most often misguided. The preferable approach is to help the child accept the fact that while there are certain things in life that one cannot control, this does not make one totally impotent; one can seek substitutes. Armed with the knowledge that he has *within himself* the power to gain substitutive gratifications from others (both peer and adult) and that his remaining parent has it within *his* power to remarry some day is far more effective in alleviating this type of guilt.

Some parents attempt to assuage the child's pain with comments such as, "You'll be taking daddy's place now. Now you're a big boy," or "Now you're like daddy's new wife." Whatever oedipal gratifications may be derived by the child by such statements, all things considered, they cannot but produce anxiety. Above all, the child wishes to be cared for by a parent — despite any comments he may make to the contrary. He does not really wish, nor is he in the position to assume, the awesome responsibilities of adulthood. Informing the child that every arrangement is being made to help take care of him is far more reassuring. This is not to say that some comments about his added responsibilities are not in order. However psychologically deleterious the loss of a parent may be, such new tasks may have a maturing effect. They should be presented honestly as the unfortunate result of the parent's demise and not deceptively described as a boon.

Another unfortunate practice is that of idolizing the deceased posthumously. The boy who grows up with the image of his mother as a "perfect woman," or the girl who is led to believe that no one who ever lived was as "good-natured, giving, and devoted" as her father, may have difficulty later accepting fallible human beings as mates.

During this period as well, questions about where the dead parent is should be answered in accordance with the parent's honest convictions. Statements by the child about the return of the deceased should be responded to with sympathetic denial. The same answers have to be repeated many times over before they sink in — such is the nature of the mourning period for the child.

Before going on to a case in which the Mutual Storytelling Technique was of assistance in helping a child work through his reactions to his mother's death, I would like to present the clinical experience of a child's reaction to her brother's death because it demonstrates many of the points made above.

Example 2

Ruth, a four-year-old girl, was referred because of phobic symptoms of six months' duration. When Ruth was two, her brother, Scott (then sixteen), was striken with leukemia. Scott survived one-and-a-half years, during which time the mother's involvement with the boy left her little time for Ruth. The child was not told that her brother's illness would be fatal, and at the time of his death she was told that he had gone to heaven where he was very happy. The family was South American, and the father had been temporarily assigned to his firm's New York office. The family returned to their native country for the burial. Unknown to the patient, her brother's body was in the cargo compartment of the airplane. Ruth did not attend the funeral. She was told that they had returned to South America to visit friends.

Upon returning to the United States, Ruth began exhibiting the symptoms which ultimately brought her to me. Whereas she had previously attended nursery school without hesitation, she now refused. When the doorbell rang, she became panicked and hid under the bed. She refused to visit the homes of friends. She seemed comfortable when close to both parents and would scream hysterically if they left. Upon their return to the United States, Ruth repeatedly asked questions about her brother, and she was told that he was happy in heaven with God. All of Scott's personal effects were destroyed with the exception of a few of his treasured possessions which were stored away lest the patient be upset by them. Within a week of their return, Ruth stopped asking questions.

It was quite clear that the phobic symptoms were directly related to the way the parents had handled Scott's death with Ruth. From her vantage point, people, without explanation, could suddenly disappear from the face of the earth. Every place is really dangerous because one knows nothing about the way in which such disappearances occur. It might be that people come to the door and take you away; or perhaps it happens at nursery school; or maybe neighbors do it. No place is really safe. Also, there's no point in trying to get a reasonable explanation from one's parents as to how it happens. They too cannot be trusted to be truthful. Ruth, without doubt, sensed her parents' duplicity.

I asked the parents what their genuine beliefs were concerning the dead brother's whereabouts. Both believed that there was no type of existence in the hereafter and although born Catholics, they had no particular religious convictions. They felt that divulging their true feelings about their dead son would be psychologically deleterious to their daughter. I explained to them what I considered to be the source of their child's problems. I told them that I knew that they had always done what they considered to be in the child's best interests, but that they had made some errors. I suggested that they go home and tell Ruth exactly what had happened to their son — as simply and as accurately as possible. I advised them to tell her, as best they could, what their true beliefs were regarding his present state. I suggested also that they give her one of the brother's mementos and tell her that it would always be hers. They were most reluctant at first, but they finally gained some conviction that my suggestions might be valid.

I then explained to them the psychological importance of mourning and how their child had been deprived of this important experience. I told them that it was most likely that Ruth would ask the same questions over and over again, and that it was important that they patiently continue repeating answers because this was a part of the mourning and working-through process. In addition, I suggested that they urge her to once again face the phobic situations; and each time reassure her that she, unlike Scott, would not be taken away.

The parents were seen again one week later. They reported that my suggestions had been followed, and the child had responded well. She cried bitterly when told the details of the brother's death. As I had foretold, Ruth's questions during the next few days were practically incessant. She was given a picture of her brother which she carried around at all times. She showed it to everyone she could and explained to them that it was her dead brother. She then told how he had died and said that he was in the ground in her native country.

There was a concomitant lessening of all her fears. By the time of the second visit she was again attending nursery school without difficulty; she no longer cowered at the ring of the doorbell; she was visiting friends; and she exhibited only mild anxiety when her parents went out at night. No further sessions were scheduled and the parents were advised to call me if they felt the need for such, which they did not.

Example 3

Presented here, in detail, is the case of Charles, whose thirty-eight-year-old mother died of leukemia while he was in treatment. It is an example of one of the ways the therapist can be of assistance in such a situation. Since there is great variation in the ways in which both parents and children handle death, the approaches I describe are only strictly applicable to this family. They do, however, illustrate some of the general principles I have presented.

My first contact with the mother occurred about a year before the onset of the boy's therapy. She had been referred to me by a friend who was in treatment with me. The mother called to make an appointment for Charles, then six-and-a-half. She described Charles as being minimally brain injured with normal intelligence. The primary problem was his immaturity. I was unable to take on any new patients at that time and referred her to another therapist. I heard nothing again until about a year later, when the person who had originally referred the mother told me that her friend had been diagnosed as having acute leukemia and that she was not expected to live more than a few months.

About a month later, the mother again called me for an appointment for Charles. She had not followed my recommendation to see another therapist. She described Charles as being even more immature. She felt that the organic element in his difficulties was far less significant than the emotional ones. She requested that, if possible, I see him soon but gave no reason for her sense of urgency. She told me that she had heard many good things about me and hoped that I would be able to see her son. In accord with my usual practice, I made an appointment to see the child and both parents.

Following the call, I gave some thought to the conversation. I guessed that the mother's sense of urgency related to her guilt over having let a year lapse without obtaining treatment for Charles and that now she wanted to "put him in good hands" before she died. I did not know how much conscious awareness she had of this. Her complete failure to mention her illness suggested to me that she was utilizing denial mechanisms, and I, therefore, felt that she might not be too aware of the reasons for her feelings of urgency. I also considered the possibility that she was really coming for therapy for herself while using the child as her excuse for being in my office. This is a common occurrence. Lastly,

I felt that I should also be aware of the possibility that she might be using the boy's treatment to vicariously gratify her own desires for treatment (physical and/or psychological).

In the initial interview, the parents described the child's immaturity problems. Charles played primarily with younger children; he spoke in a childish, "sing-song" manner; he cried easily; he whined when frustrated; he was the class clown; and he lied to hide transgressions and inadequacies. The organic problem was definitely improving. He had been in a class for neurologically impaired children, but he was now functioning well enough to be in a regular class. His problem there was not significantly academic but rather a lack of commitment to his studies. Again, no mention was made of the mother's illness until the end of my first interview. When I suggested appointments to see each parent separately, the mother said that she would be going into hospital in a few days and wondered whether I could see her soon because she didn't know how long she would be away. I said I would see her the next day.

Since I still did not know the mother's true motivation regarding her contact with me, I hoped that this, our first interview alone, would reveal them to me. My situation was a delicate one. On the one hand, I did not want to pressure her into talking about her illness because I already knew that she was denying it. On the other hand, I did not want to deprive her of the opportunity to discuss it with me if she only needed a little encouragement or an excuse to do so.

I began with the routine question of asking her about her reactions to the previous day's interview with her son. She said that she had had none, and that there was nothing she could add. I concluded from this that she preferred to concentrate strictly on Charles, her ostensible reason for seeing me. I explained to her that it was important for me to know about her life if I was to understand her son's problems. I then proceeded with a standard life history. (I usually begin with a more formal life history and then go on with less structured items. Providing me with the basic facts of their lives is less anxiety provoking to parents than open-ended questions. Starting with the "easier" questions makes the parent less tense during the more anxiety-provoking part of the interview.)

She related in her history a few things which provided information about the way she was handling her illness. She described a repetitious dream which had occurred intermittently since she was twenty: "I was painting a wall in the schoolyard. I was painting it white." I considered the dream to reflect a life-style of denying the unpleasant, of "whitewashing," and felt that this confirmed other observations of mine that she did not wish to talk directly about her illness. She also told me that she had had a short course of psychiatric treatment eight years previously and it had not been successful because she "couldn't open up and let go." This additional reflection of her avoidance of focusing on her inner feelings resolved me not to encourage her to talk about her illness. She also described many serious faults of her husband's which she tended to rationalize and smooth over — an additional manifestation of her utilization of the denial mechanism.

I then went into her relationship with her son. She described a number of things which suggested some deficiencies and inhibition in the expression of maternal feeling. She had never considered breast feeding; did not enjoy cuddling him; nor did she encourage him to come into her bed in the morning when he was younger. She stated, "I would have been a better mother to one than to two" — Charles had an older sister. Later, she went further, saying, "I often felt that I didn't want to have children." Such information was not only of importance in explaining the boy's regressive manifestations, but also suggested that one of her reasons for bringing Charles to me was the guilt she felt over her neglect of him. She wished to assuage this while she still could.

The mother then related a dream she had had when she had been admitted to the hospital one month previously at the onset of her illness: "I kept dreaming that I was calling out to the nurse that she had to take *her* medicine. She had a dry medicine which she had to take. Mine was wet." I felt that the dream reflected her need to focus on the treatment of others as a way of avoiding her own illness. My original supposition that one of her reasons for bringing her son to me was that it might serve both as a mechanism for her to avoid concentrating on her own illness as well as a way of vicariously receiving treatment herself, was confirmed.

I then asked her if there was anything else she wished to talk to me about; if there was anything else, not thus far discussed which she wished to mention. She replied that she assumed that I knew from her friend (who was in treatment with me) that she had chronic leukemia. She said she expected to see me after she got out of the hospital, that she didn't think that there was anything more to say about that, and so we ended the interview. As I watched her pull herself up from her chair, her emaciation and weakness led me to realize that I might never see her again. Although I hardly knew this woman, I left like crying and embracing her. Whereas there had been situations in the past when I had done exactly that, I restrained myself here because to have done so might have threatened the defensive system which she so tenaciously adhered to. She had repeatedly told me how she wanted to handle things. It would have been cruel of me to ignore her. So I played the game with her. Although I spoke to her on the phone a few times afterwards, I never saw her again. Less than two months later she was dead.

The boy's therapy can be divided into two stages. In the first, which lasted about three months, Charles brought up material which concerned his mother's death. In the second stage, which lasted about six months, what he presented suggested that my primary focus should be on the immaturity problem. In this chapter I have confined myself to the first stage. The first stage of his treatment lends itself well to further division into three phases: 1) preparation for his mother's death, 2) handling the funeral and immediate reactions to her death, and 3) treatment of post-death reactions.

During the patient's second week of treatment — about six weeks prior to his mother's death — he told this story:

Well, boys and girls, once there was a haunted house and the ghosts came over and they said, "Booo" to me; and they said, "We want everything and if you don't do it we shall kidnap you. Eeeeee."

Therapist: If you don't do what, they'll kidnap you?

Patient: If you don't listen to them.

Therapist: Okay.

Patient: So, he did not listen and uh, uh, uh, "Let me go! let me go!" they said. And, then they ran away and they never went back to the house in a million years.

Therapist: Wait a minute. Now they got hold of this boy, they got hold of you, and they tried to choke you? What did they try to do?

Patient: They tried to kidnap me and kill me and get everything of mine.

Therapist: But what happened to them?

Patient: They got all tangled up so I ran out and I never came back in a million years.

Therapist: You ran out of the house?

Patient: Uh-huh.

Therapist: Uh-huh.

Patient: Okay, and that is my story, now it is time for yours.

Therapist: What's the lesson of your story?

Patient: Never go into a house that looks too scary.

Therapist: Okay.

Charles sees his house as haunted. Frightening things are happening in it and he wishes to flee. I did not believe that it was important to analyze the exact symbolic significance of each of the dangers. They all related to horrible occurrences within the house which he did not wish to behold. At the time when Charles told this story he had been told that his mother was sick, but he had not been given any further information about the nature of her illness or its prognosis. This was consistent with the mother's pattern of denial. However, the story reveals that he was well aware that terrible things were happening. These things were made even more fearful by his ignorance of their exact nature — for ignorance only breeds further anxiety. In response, I told this story:

Once upon a time there was a boy and he was walking toward a house and a kid said, "Hey, don't go in that house" and he said, "Why?" And the second boy said, "There are ghosts, there are scary ghosts, whooo, whooo, scary ghosts," and the boy said, "Aw, I'm not scared of ghosts. There's no such thing as ghosts." Anyway, the second kid said, "There are scary ghosts" and the first boy said, "No, there aren't. If you come with me, you'll see."

So they went into the house and as soon as they came in the house they heard a noise: "Bump, boom, boom," and the boys got scared. And the second boy said, "That's a ghost, that's a ghost," and the first boy said, "No, that's not a ghost; that's just the shutter of the window flopping in the breeze against the window, bump, boom." And they went upstairs and, sure enough, they saw the flopping shutter and that's all it was.

And the second boy said, "No, you're wrong. There are still ghosts in the air." And, all of a sudden they heard: "Ooooh, oooh, oooh," and the kids were scared. "Oooh, that's a ghost," said the second boy, "Oooh, that's a ghost." And the first boy said, "No, that's not a ghost; that's just the wind blowing down the chimney, look!" And they went over to the chimney and, sure enough, they stood near the chimney and they heard: "Oooh, Oooh." It was only the wind near the chimney.

Then, all of a sudden, they heard: "Creak, creak, creak." The second boy said, "It's ghosts walking." They looked and the first boy said, "That's not ghosts walking. This house is kind of old and shaky and when the wind blows it kind of causes the wood to creak." Well, by this time, the kids began to realize that there really were no such things as ghosts and that all the sounds that they heard were really made by things that happened in the house and then they felt more comfortable and they realized that the house was not as dangerous as they first thought it was.

And the lesson in that story is what?

Patient: Never to go into a house that looks too scary.

Therapist: No, the lesson is that sometimes you may think that something is very scary, but that when you look at

it closely you find out it isn't. That's the lesson in that story.
Patient: Okay, could we hear that one over?
Therapist: Yes.

When I told my story, I knew that I would be advising the father to tell the patient the facts about his mother's condition. The purpose of my story was to communicate to Charles that there are times when things are less horrible than they may originally appear. One could argue that there can be little more horrible than a mother's death; and that he was better off in his ignorance. My belief was that the fears he harbored related more to himself — to what would happen to him if something did happen to her. I suspected that his fears in this area were exaggerated and that open discussion would lessen them. The story was told to prepare him for such confrontation and discussion.

At the time of this interchange, the mother had already entered the hospital. She was never to leave. I advised the father to tell the children that their mother had a very serious disease of the blood called leukemia, and that she might soon die of it. I suggested that they be told that the doctors were giving her various medicines to prolong her life, but that it was not too likely that they would work. (The mother had a particularly malignant form of leukemia, she had not shown any significant response to any of the known forms of treatment, and the doctors considered her early death inevitable.) The father followed my advice.

A few days after, Charles told a story in which he drowned in quicksand. I, in response, told one in which a boy stepped into quicksand but was able to pull himself out with the help of a friend. In my story, he is at first hesitant to venture forth again from his house, but he later realizes that quicksand is very rarely found and that most ground is pretty solid. In other words, the death of his mother need not mean total loss of support; there are others who are available to provide it.

A few days later, Charles told this story:

Well, I was in an office and suddenly —

Therapist: An office? In this office?

Patient: Yes. And then someone kidnaps me so they take me away and then they need ransom, four million dollars. So, we had to pay them. So then I came back home and I'm not hurt or anything but my mother was so worried, my father was so worried, Dr. Gardner was so worried, Dr. Gardner was so worried. So then I was being punished and that's the end.

Therapist: Wait a minute. Now you were being punished for what?

Patient: For just sitting, for um, for someone kidnapping me.

Therapist: Well why is it you felt if someone kidnaps you —

Patient: Well you should be more careful.

Therapist: I see, and what's the lesson of that story?

Patient: Never be sure, never be sure there is no robbers or kidnappers because there always is.

Therapist: Wait a minute. Now never be sure there are no kidnappers because there are? Now wait a minute. Now I have one question. Can you tell me the details of how, of exactly how it was that you were kidnapped?

Patient: I wasn't looking. Well, someone just pressed hard on me and they put me in a bag.

Therapist: Someone put you in a bag? Now why is that your fault?

Patient: Because I wasn't careful.

Therapist: Well, you weren't careful, in what way?

Patient: I wasn't watching.

Therapist: You weren't watching out for them?

Patient: Right.

Therapist: I see. Okay. I have a question to ask you. Now, we both know that your mother is not feeling well and that she is sick in the hospital.

Patient: Right.

Therapist: Did you ever have the feeling, at any time, that maybe it was your fault that your mother was sick?

Patient: Yes, Just a little bit.

Therapist: What was the feeling, what was the thought about that?

Patient: Well, I think we were making her get headaches but her eye, we didn't, I think we, I am sure we just couldn't make her sick because of us. Her eye couldn't get hurt.

Therapist: Now, no, no, wait a minute, now. Did you ever have the thought that maybe you were responsible for her illness?

Patient: No, not really.

Therapist: Even a little bit once?

Patient: Just a little bit.

Therapist: What was the little bit?

Patient: That I wish my Mom might get home in about a week or two weeks.

Therapist: Uh-huh. But what was the thought about being responsible for her illness. What kind of thought did you have there?

Patient: Well, I just figured that we just made her like get headaches and she would get so mad. Then she got sick and I think it's all our fault.

Therapist: You mean it's your fault?

Patient: Mine and my sister's.

Therapist: Why, because you got her mad? Because you were bad?

Patient: Uh-huh, and it upset my Dad because you should hear their fights.

Therapist: They used to fight a lot?

Patient: Yeah.

Therapist: What did they fight about?

Patient: Well, once my Dad fighted, and my Mom cried.

Therapist: I see, did that upset you very much?

Patient: And, twice it happened when my Dad pushed my Mom against the refrigerator and the whole thing, door, spilled and everything fell out.

Therapist: I see. Why did he do that?

Patient: I don't know. They probably were mad.

Therapist: Uh-huh. Do you think he made her sick? You think it's your Father's fault that she is sick?

Patient: I think it's all our fault.

Therapist: I see. So you think it's all your fault. I see, uh-huh, okay. Does it make you feel very bad when you think it's your fault?

Patient: Yes.

Therapist: Wait, hold on a second. I see. Has that been up-setting you?

Patient: Not really.

Therapist: Uh-huh.

Patient: I'm just glad she is getting out soon.

Therapist: Well, I'll tell you it's not your fault that she's sick.

Patient: It isn't?

Therapist: Nope, what about that? You're glad, it makes you feel better?

Patient: Yeah.

Therapist: Your mother's sickness could not have come from anything that you kids did. Even if you wished your mother to be sick, she wouldn't be sick. You know that. Wishing somebody sick can't make them sick. Did you know that?

Patient: No.

Therapist: It's true. Even no matter how hard you wish them sick. Even if you wish somebody sick and they got sick it wouldn't mean that the wish made them sick. You know that?

Patient: No.

Therapist: What would have made them sick?

Patient: What do you mean?

Therapist: Well, when you wish someone sick and they become sick they become sick from the illness or the accident and it has nothing to do with you. Do you understand?

Patient: Uh-huh.

Therapist: Okay.

Charles describes the kidnapping as a punishment. When asked what he was being punished for, he explained that he had not been cautious enough, so the kidnappers got him. I considered this a rationalization. I guessed that Charles in some way felt guilty about his mother's illness; he thought that it might have been his fault and was punishing himself to assuage this guilt. Accordingly, I asked him directly if he had ever had such feelings. He answered affirmatively. In response I focused on only one element of this inappropriate guilt reaction. I emphasized that angry thoughts cannot harm. As I have discussed previously, there are many factors that may contribute to such guilt; I did not know enough then to determine which ones were operative within this boy. I therefore focused on only one element — the idea that thoughts can harm — which is generally a contributory factor regardless of whatever other psychodynamic factors may be present. In addition, Charles was incapable of appreciating more than a single, simple message at a time — even then he often had trouble. This was not due to lack of intelligence but to his immaturity, lack of attention, and only intermittent involvement in the storytelling game.

In response I told this story:

Once upon a time there was a boy and this boy used to get into fights with his mother once in a while, like all kids. And sometimes when he got very mad at his mother, he would say, "I wish she were sick. I wish she were out of here. I wish she would get hit by a car. I wish she were dead. That's how angry I am at my mother."

Well, one day his mother did get sick. Now, the sickness had nothing to do with him but he started to feel very upset about it. He started to feel that it was his fault because he had even wished her to be sick and even wished her to be dead and he feared that he would be punished for such thoughts. Like he thought he might be kidnapped or taken away in a bag or something like that for thinking thoughts like that.

So this, naturally, upset him very much and one day his father noticed that he was very upset and his father said, "What's the matter?" and the boy said, "Well, I feel very bad because I think I made mommy get sick." And the father said, "What!" And he said, "Yes, I think I made mommy get sick." And the father said, "Well, how could that happen? How could you make mommy get sick?" He said, "Well, I used to wish that she were sick and sometimes

I even wished that she were dead." And the father said, "Well, practically every kid has those wishes." He said, "Yeah? Did you have wishes like that when you were a boy?" The father said, "Of course, every kid at times has thoughts like that." And the boy said, "What I'm scared about is that those wishes made her sick." The father said, "A wish cannot make anybody sick. She got sick from the illness; she caught an infection." That was the trouble in this particular woman's case. And the boy said, "You mean my wish didn't make her sick?" The father said, "No." The boy said, "Well that makes me feel better. You mean, you mean that it's normal for boys to think once in a while to wish their mother sick or dead?" And the father said, "Yes, it's normal." Well, when the boy heard that he felt much better and what do you think the lesson of that story is? See if you can figure it out.

Patient: You should, you should —— I don't know. I really don't know.

Therapist: The lesson of that story is that it's normal for kids, on occasion, to wish their parents sick or even dead. That's lesson number one. Number two: thoughts cannot harm. A thought, in itself, no matter how hard you may wish someone sick or dead, it cannot make them sick or dead. Number three: even if you wish somebody sick or dead and they become sick, they became sick from the illness, they didn't become sick because you wished them sick. And that's the end. What did you think about that story? What did you think?

Patient: I think it was very good.

Therapist: What's the part about it that you liked the most?

Patient: I think, well no, don't you learn —— I don't know. Something about a thought can't harm.

Therapist: Right! A thought can't harm.

It is clear what I attempted to do in my story. How successful I was is questionable. The story demonstrates one therapeutic approach to this type of inappropriate guilt reaction.

About three weeks later (two weeks before his mother's death), Charles told this story:

Well, I'm in the house sleeping.

Therapist: You were in the house sleeping? Yeah.

Patient: And, then a fire engine comes. I look out my window and I see that our house is on fire. So, I run out and I don't get hurt; and they got me out and I was okay. So, the lesson of that story is, never to, when you hear something, to just stay in bed it could be very, very, very dangerous.

Therapist: If you hear something, never stay in bed or do stay in bed?

Patient: Never.

Therapist: Is that the end? Okay. I want to ask you a question about your story. Tell me one thing, what about the other people, what happened to them?

Patient: Everybody was out to dinner and I was sick so I was home.

Therapist: Okay.

The house burning down represents his mother's illness which was now entering the terminal phase. Charles sees his world as collapsing, and he wishes to flee in order to survive. He sees himself as all alone; there is no one to protect him. This is the story I told in response:

Once upon a time there was a boy and he lived in a house with his older sister and his mother and his father. And one day he was in his room in bed when he thought he smelled smoke. He looked up and, sure enough, there was a little fire. Well, the first thing he did was call out to his mother and his father and his sister and he said, "Come in here, look it's all smoke. What shall we do?" And, they heard what he said and they came in and, sure enough, there was a fire. And the father said, "Okay, let's start putting it out." And he said to his mother, "You call the fire department." So, the fire department came and the fire, of course, did burn part of their house. Not too much but part of it. I would say about one quarter of it; one part, you know, one room out of four and it did burn the house but because he had caught it in time and got everybody involved in doing something about it the damage was not too great.

And the moral of that story is that if you see any danger, speak to people around you, bring it to their attention, call in help and you will, in that way, prevent terrible things from happening.

In my story I imparted two messages regarding his mother's death. I clarified that her death will not mean total destruction of his home (as is implied in his story). Only part of it — one of four family members — will be destroyed; the rest will remain intact. Secondly, in my story, he is not alone. There are others who are, and will be, available to help him and protect him from dangers.

During this period the mother called me to find out about how Charles was doing. She sounded weak and confined the conversation to the child. The father reported that the last possible drug had proven ineffective in lowering her white cell count and that there was no hope for her survival. He requested that I go to the hospital to see her. I told him that I would like to be of help if I could, but that I might do more harm than good by appearing without a specific request on her part. I suggested that he broach the subject with her and ask if she would like to see me or any other psychiatrist. She subsequently replied that she did not feel the need.

About one week later (one week before the mother's death), Charles told this story:

Well, I was writing things and I'm writing things and the page rips. So, I do the page again. The page still rips and then I told my mother and she said, "Be more careful son." So, I was more careful and I finished my homework.

The lesson of that story is to not write so hard, it makes holes. Okay.

Therapist: Now, let's take a little time out and, I want to ask you a question about that story. What were you writing when you were writing in the story?

Patient: I was doing my homework.

Therapist: I see, and what part of your homework were you doing?

Patient: I don't really remember. Okay?

Therapist: Let me ask you something now. Did you have any dreams in the last few days?

Patient: Yes, I did.

Therapist: Could I hear them? When did you have a dream?

Patient: The next day my friend Joel left to Florida, I thought he was back from Florida.

Therapist: I see, okay.

At the time of this story's telling, Charles knew that his mother's death was imminent. In the story his mother is home advising him on his homework. It reflects his wish that she return and his feeling of helplessness without her. The dream confirms this interpretation: a person, his friend, Joel, who is supposed to be away, is back home.

This is the story I told in response:

Well, once upon a time there was this boy and this boy lived at home with his mother and his father and sometimes his mother used to help him with his homework. However, one day the mother got very sick and she had to go to the hospital and he then missed her because he wanted her to help him with his homework but she wasn't there, and this made him very sad. Afterwards, his mother died, and then he felt very, very lonely and he wondered who was going to help him with his homework.

Well, after a while he found out that he could do more of it on his own than he originally did. In addition, he had an older sister who helped him out sometimes. Also, he would ask his teacher for a little extra help, and sometimes some of his friends would help him out. And, though he missed his mother very much and was very lonely, he realized that he could still get along without her. He hoped that someday his father would get married again and then he would have a stepmother. Now, how do you think it ended? Do you think he got a stepmother or not?

Patient: I think he did.

Therapist: He did and then he used to have someone to help him with his homework when he needed it. And the moral of that story is sometimes you find you can do more things on your own than you realized; so, if you don't have a mother around to help you with your homework, you may find that you can do more of it than you realize and there are always other people around who will help you if you need it. What did you think about that story?

Patient: Very good.

Therapist: What did you like about it most?

Patient: The ending.

Therapist: What was it about the ending that you liked the most?

Patient: The lesson of it, of the story.

Therapist: What was the lesson as you understood it?

Patient: Um, it was that never, you could do more when somebody doesn't help you. You can do more stuff when you try it by yourself.

Therapist: Right! Sometimes you think you need help when you don't. The end.

In my story I tried to assuage some of the patient's fears about what will happen to him after his mother dies. I reassured Charles that he will not be left alone, that there will be others who will be of help to him, and that he has the capability of handling some of life's problems himself. In addition, I gave him the hope that someday his father may remarry and provide him with a replacement for his mother. This time Charles did appreciate my message.

A few days later, while in the midst of a session with another patient, the mother called me. Quite upset, she said that she was extremely depressed and that she would like to speak to me as soon as possible. I explained that I was with a patient and that I would call her back in about fifteen minutes. When I called back she apologized for having been so distraught and told me that she was feeling better. She said that she was just having one of her "stupid hysterical outbursts" and getting to feel sorry for herself, but that she had recovered and was feeling fine now. I asked her if she would like to speak to me further, either over the phone or by visit. She thanked me for my interest; told me how much better she felt since I was seeing her son; and she did not think that she was that upset that she needed to see me. I told her that she should not hesitate to call me again if she changed her mind.

She died a few days later. Charles cried briefly when he learned of her death and was subsequently subdued and saddened. The father, with the support of relatives, thought that the funeral would be a traumatic experience for the boy. I advised him to ask his son what *he* would prefer to do. The boy emphatically stated that he wished to attend, and I strongly urged the father to respect his son's wish. He accepted my advice, but hesitatingly so because many relatives asked him to leave the boy home. Charles attended the funeral without incident. I visited the home on the evening of the funeral and spent about a half hour alone with Charles. We discussed many of the issues covered in the sessions of the previous weeks. He expressed some grief, but I felt that much was still being repressed. I reiterated hopeful messages regarding substitutive gratifications from others.

Three days after his mother's death, Charles told this story:

Well, I'm in this house and it was a party. So, my mother dies, and the next day when all the company is there, I fell asleep in the middle of it. So, my mommy comes home again and we tell her that her friend, Alice S. died. So, my mommy starts to cry because they were like sisters together and the lesson of that story is sometimes people start crying because when somebody dies because they are lonesome and they would feel like sisters.

Therapist: Sometimes people cry because when someone dies they are lonely and they feel like sisters. I'm not exactly sure what the lesson of that story is. Can you say it in other words?

Patient: Well, no I can't say it in other words.

Therapist: But I don't understand the lesson, what is the lesson?

Patient: Well, like when you are going to die you think to yourself that you don't know it, you don't want to have the other person die that day so the lesson is you ought to try to help the other person and not tell her.

Therapist: You should try and not tell her? I'm still not clear what that lesson is. Try again.

Patient: Like when you go to a hospital and like my father gave blood to my mother. You should give blood to somebody because maybe they could try to live. That's the lesson.

Therapist: Okay.

The story reflects his wish that his mother not be dead. When guests come to the house to pay their condolences, he falls asleep and removes himself from the painful confrontation. Then his mother returns to life, and he has her good friend die instead. His mother then mourns over her friend. In this way Charles vicariously gratifies through his mother his need to mourn. The story ends by touching on one of his futile attempts to prevent the calamity — giving blood to save the mother's life.

In response, I told this story:

Well, once upon a time there was this boy and this boy had a very, very sad thing happen in his life. He was only eight years old and his mother died. It was a very, very sad thing and after his mother died he hoped that it really didn't happen, that it was all really like a bad dream or something, but it really did happen and he used to hope that his mother's friend would have died instead. And he said, "Why did it have to happen to my mother? Why couldn't it happen to someone else like my mother's friend?" and though he used to wish that it happened to the mother's friend instead of the mother and also he wished that his mother was crying over the friend rather than the friend crying over his mother, it didn't happen that way, and he slowly began to realize that his mother really had died and that he would never see her again.

And he felt very sad and then he wondered what could he do to feel less sad. What can he do so that he can feel happier again, and he decided that one thing is that there are a lot of nice ladies around who would treat him very well and although not the same as his own mother, they still are very nice, as his mother had many friends and they had children his own age, so one thing he did was, he used to visit a lot. The friends of his mother who had kids his own age he used to visit, and sometimes he would sleep overnight and so that made him feel better because it made him feel like he was close to a lady again, just like his mother, and that made him feel better. And, then as he grew older, he became a teen-ager and he began to date girls and he found that girls could make him feel less lonely.

By the way, I forgot something. When he was younger, playing with his friends made him feel less lonely too. So, the two things made him feel less lonely then. One thing was to visit the homes where there were other ladies like his mother who had children like him and they would sometimes take care of him. The other thing was to play with friends and then when he got older and became a teen-ager he would go out with girls and that made him less lonely. And then finally he got married when he was older and when he was earning money he could support a wife and then he didn't feel lonely at all. But, of course, he always thought of his mother, once in a while, but as time went on he thought about her less and less and it was less painful that his mother had died. And, you know what the lessons of that story are?

Patient: No, I can't figure them out.

Therapist: The lessons are: number one, if your mother dies, one thing you can do is visit the homes of other ladies who were your mother's friends and play with their children and they can be like a mother to you. Number two: you can feel better by playing with friends. Number three: as you get older and become a teen-ager, it will help you feel better to go out on dates and be with girls. Number four: when you get really older, and you grow up and get married, then you'll have someone as a wife and she'll be companionship so you won't be so lonely. And number five: as time goes on it becomes less and less painful.

Patient: Doctor, I really liked that story.

Therapist: What was the thing about it that you liked the most.

Patient: Um, well, the boy found out that it wasn't his fault that his mother died.

Therapist: Did he find that out in my story? Tell me something, did he have, did you have some thoughts that it was your fault that your mother died? What kind of thoughts did you have like that?

Patient: Well, I thought that we made my mother sick because —— we talked about this when she was sick.

Therapist: We talked about this when she was sick but, apparently, you still have some ideas about that that we ought to talk about.

Patient: I haven't any ideas.

Therapist: Well, what did you have when your mother was sick? What was it then?

Patient: Well, I thought it was my fault because me and my sister always give my mother trouble. We always run around the house and it really was our fault I think, but not any more I do. Thank you.

Therapist: What made you change your mind?

Patient: When you told me that's what made me.

Therapist: It really wasn't your fault. Your mother got sick from leukemia and you couldn't get leukemia by having trouble with your kids. No matter how much trouble kids can give a mother, they still can't give her leukemia. Do you understand that?

Patient: Yes.

Therapist: If you were the worst kid in the whole world and that you kept bothering your mother and being naughty and really doing terrible things around the house; even if you did that you still couldn't give your mother leukemia. What do you think about that?

Patient: Yeah.

Therapist: That make you feel better?

Patient: Yeah.

Therapist: Even if you wished your mother to have leukemia, and you wished a wish like that all the time, you couldn't get her to have leukemia. Do you know that?

Patient: Then how come it happened?

Therapist: It comes from — it is probably an infection like a virus and you get an infection. She caught it probably.

Nobody knows how or where. That's what some people think.

Patient: Okay.

Therapist: Okay.

My story with five morals, which were designed to provide him with some hope and consolation, was apparently not registering while I was relating it. Charles was preoccupied with the question of his possibly having caused his mother's death, and so I readily followed up on that issue, even though it was a digression. Apparently he needed more reassurance on that problem and so I provided it.

One week later, Charles told this story:

Well, no mysteries today. No.

Therapist: Okay, any kind of story you want. it is entirely up to you.

Patient: Well, I was riding in this car and then Mrs. B. tried to get — it is a car wash.

Therapist: You were riding in a car wash?

Patient: So Mrs. B. gets out.

Therapist: Who is Mrs. B?

Patient: Joel's mother.

Therapist: Oh, who is Joel?

Patient: Joel is my friend.

Therapist: Okay, your friend's mother, Mrs. B. gets out of car.

Patient: Yeah.

Therapist: And then she — the car moves on the tracks. So then Joel gets out, so then I tried to get out and then the car moves. So I shut the door. The guy shuts the door on me.

Therapist: So you were in the car?

Patient: Yeah, and the car starts through and we go through water, through brushes, through the dryer. So, and that's my story. The lesson of that story is that when somebody tried to get out, don't be scared.

Therapist: I don't understand the moral of that story.

Patient: You shouldn't be scared because it's just one ride and nothing can happen to you.

Therapist: Okay.

The car being pulled on the track of the car wash machine symbolizes Charles himself on his life's course, He is not driving himself, but being pulled along. Although one doesn't expect eight-year-old children to represent themselves as completely independent, they still most often drive their own cars in their play and fantasy. Therefore, I considered this way of portraying his locomotion as a pathological dependency manifestation. Possibly, it reflected an intensification of his dependency cravings following his mother's death. In the fantasy he is locked into a situation where he is pulled along; even if he tried, he cannot escape and drive on his own power.

Mrs. B. stands for the patient's mother whose death is seen as abandonment. He is left all alone, but does manage to survive. So there is a positive element in the story as well: although entrapped in a dependency-gratifying situation, Charles does weather many storms (water, brushes, and dryer). He pushes through his anxiety and survives the ordeal. The moral epitomizes his experience: "You shouldn't be scared because it's just one ride and nothing can happen to you." The ride may also reflect his resolve to bravely face the world that lies ahead for him and to tolerate the associated anxiety.

This is the story I told in response:

Once upon a time there was a boy and he was in a car with Mrs. B. and her son, Joel, and another friend of his, a very good friend of his. Now they were going to a car wash and this boy was kind of scared. He thought that the car wash would be a frightening experience. So then before they got into the car wash, Mrs. B. and Joel got out, but the door was slammed on this boy and his best friend and at first he thought it was going to be very scary because he thought he was going to be alone, but he felt better because he had his friend there.

Then, the first thing that happened was they went through the place where they sprayed hot water on this car. And he thought, "Hot water, we are going to be boiling." But it turned out that he felt quite good because he didn't boil and the car protected him. He realized that there wasn't anything to be afraid of with the boiling water.

So the next thing that came along were the brushes — big brushes that started to wash the car. And he said, "Oh, we are going to be shaken up in this car." The brushes went "whurr," and he thought he was going to surely be shaken up and down and everything, but he wasn't and he was also glad he had his friend with him so that made it less scary too.

And then there were these big swirling things that put soap and water on the car and he thought he would get all wet with soap and water in his eyes, but that didn't happen either. And then they went through the cold water and he thought he would freeze, but he didn't freeze either. "Ooh," he thought, "I'm going to freeze." But he didn't freeze anyway and he got through the whole thing, and he was just perfectly fine and he said to himself, "I guess sometimes you think that things are scary but they turn out not to be so scary." Then he also said to himself, "I'll bet that it would have been more scary if I didn't have my friend."

And do you know the lesson in that story? There are two lessons in that story? You try to figure them out; what are the two lessons?

Patient: Um, you shouldn't be a scared of nothing, number one. And number two: you should always have somebody with you so you won't be very scared. Things aren't as scary as you might think in the beginning and —

Therapist: Secondly, if you have a friend, it makes things less scary. The end.

In my story I reinforced the positive element in his story: going through life can be anxiety provoking, but it is tolerable. Whereas in his story his friend leaves, in mine one stays behind to accompany him on his dangerous journey. In this way I hoped to encourage greater involvement with peers who might be helpful to him in facing life without his mother.

Three days later, Charles told this story:

Well, am I allowed to make up songs too?

Therapist: No, stories but after the stories you can make up a song.

Patient: Okay. I was playing the piano when the key sticks. So, I called my daddy, and he calls the piano man. The piano man fixes it. Then two keys happen this time. So, we call him again. Then, three keys happen this time. So, we call him again. Then, four keys and we call him again. Then, all the keys. So, we get a new piano and the lesson of that story is: when something is not working right, you should get one; get it to a real fixing store too, or get a new one, get a new piano. Thank you.

Therapist: Okay, thank you. Are you saying that the person who fixed the piano in the first place didn't do a good job? Is that it?

Patient: Right.

Therapist: He was a poor fixer? Is that why the piano finally broke down entirely?

Patient: It didn't break down entirely, but we got a new piano.

Therapist: Okay.

The piano stands for his mother. Repeated attempts to cure her failed and she was finally removed from the scene. Purchase of a new piano reveals his hope that his father will remarry — a positive and constructive wish. The story reflects progress in his working through his reactions to his mother's death.

In response, I told the following story:

Now once upon a time there was a boy and in his house he had a piano and this piano, one day, got broken. One of the keys broke. So they called in a piano tuner and he said, "Well, this piano is a pretty broken-up piano and I'll do what I can." So he tried to fix it, but a couple of days later he found two keys broken and he said, "Well, I told you this is a very broken up piano but I'll try to do what I can." So he tried to fix it again and the next day, three keys were broken. The next day, four keys were broken and, finally, the whole piano broke down and the piano tuner said, "Yes, I told you this is a very, very broken-up piano and I am not surprised to hear that."

Well, they were very sad in that house for a while when that piano broke down. The children were very sad because they liked that piano very much and they didn't know what to do, and one day they said, "Well, what can we do?" We can't afford to get a new piano right now," the father said, "because new pianos are expensive. However, why don't you children play the piano in the home of some of the neighbors?" The children thought that was an excellent idea. So they found out which of their friends had pianos, and they went over there and played the piano in the home of different neighbors and they had a good time. And then they didn't miss their piano so much.

Also, as time went on, they missed the piano less because when you are bothered about something as time goes on usually it bothers you less. And finally their father brought home a new piano and, then, they played on their own piano, and they lived happily ever after. And do you know what the lesson of that story is?

Patient: When something is broken you should either take it to the store to get it fixed or you should try to play with somebody else or get a new piano. The other thing is that if you feel sad about a piano being broken, you will find out that gradually it will not bother you so much as time goes on and especially if you use somebody else's piano. That'll make you feel better about it also. The end.

Therapist: Very good!

In his story, his lost mother is immediately replaced by a new one. Although this is good positive thinking, there was no evidence in reality that his father was going to remarry so quickly. In my story, I proposed compensations for his lost mother which are more practical and immediately available to him. Charles is encouraged to involve himself more with other adult females. He is also informed that the pain he now feels over the loss of his mother will gradually lessen — time is a great healer. Finally, however, they do get a new piano, his father remarries, that is, but the implication in my story is that this does not occur until after some significant lapse of time. The patient's statement of the moral was heartening.

One week later, Charles told this story:

Could we do the one we did on Friday?

Therapist: If you want to.

Patient: Yeah.

Therapist: You want to tell the exact same story again?

Patient: No, not the exact same story but a different story.

Therapist: Okay, tell a different one, go ahead.

Patient: No, you know like we did on Friday. Remember when a child doesn't know what story to tell, you help him?

Therapist: Okay. You want me to help you get one of them out? You have hundreds of stories inside of your head, you know. Okay.

Once upon a time a long, long, long, long time ago —— in a distant land —— far, far, far, away —— way beyond the desert —— way beyond the mountains —— way beyond the ocean, there lived a ——

Patient: Man.

Therapist: And this man ——

Patient: Worked for money.

Therapist: And what kind of work did he do?

Patient: Camels, he was like a taxi driver.

Therapist: For camels?

Patient: Yeah, like a camel, uh, huh, a camel.

Therapist: He was a camel taxi driver. Okay.

Patient: And one day this camel taxi driver got into an accident.

Therapist: He was in an accident?

Patient: And, he never rode his camel again.

Therapist: And then ——

Patient: And then the lesson of that story is that when you are a driver you should be careful, very careful, so you won't get into accidents.

Therapist: Now, I want to ask you a question. Now what kind of an accident did he get into?

Patient: Um.

Therapist: Can you tell me specifically what happened?

Patient: Um, an automobile hit him.

Therapist: He was hit by a car? I see. What happened to him as a result of this? What happened? Exactly.

Patient: He went to the hospital and he died.

Therapist: He went to the hospital and he died? I see. Um. So, no wonder he never rode his camel again. Okay.

The dead camel taxi driver is the patient's mother. As a taxi driver she rode people from place to place — she helped them on their life's path. Now that she is dead, Charles is without this service and source of gratification. The story then is a statement of his remorse over the death of his mother and the deprivations he thereby suffers.

Accordingly, I told this story:

Once upon a time there was a woman and she was a camel taxi driver and she had a family. She had a son, she had a husband, and one day she was in an accident with a car and they took her to the hospital and she was killed. She died. Well, her son was very, very sad after that and he thought for sure that he would lead a very sad life for the rest of his life. I mean he would never be happy again.

But then he spoke to a friend of his and this friend of his said, "There is no reason for you to feel that your life is sad and that nothing good will ever happen to you." He said, "What you have to do now is make friends. You have to go to the homes of other kids where they have their mothers. And then you have to know that as you grow older, you will get more and more friends and some day you'll be a teen-ager and you will go out with girls and you'll go on dates and same day you will get married and you will have a girl all to yourself. So, just because your mother died, although that is very sad, doesn't mean that you can't still have a good life." The lesson of that story is what?

Patient: You should be careful.

Therapist: Right, but sometimes accidents happen that you can't even control, and then what's the lesson for her son?

Patient: I don't know.

Therapist: What did I say the son's friend told him?

Patient: Um, I forgot.

Therapist: Well, he told him one thing, to find friends, right? What did he tell him to do about the fact that he had no mommy? How can he be with older ladies?

Patient: To find girlfriends.

Therapist: When he gets older, right. As a teen-ager he finds girlfriends, right. But, even as a young boy he can spend time with the mothers of his friends and then some day he will get married.

Patient: Okay.

Therapist: Okay.

The patient's story reflects some retrogression in working through his reactions to his mother's death. His response to my story further confirmed this. Charles was not listening while I was telling mine, and missed most of my main points. His answer to my question about the moral, "You should be careful," suggests that he was dwelling on the accident that killed the camel taxi driver, on the causes, that is, of his mother's death, rather than the more constructive issues being raised by me.

Two-and-a-half-weeks later (about five-and-a-half weeks after his mother's death), Charles told this story:

We are going to do one that's called, what is it called again? What could we call it? You know. Well, the doctor starts the story, and I will finish it. He will keep on pointing to me, and I keep on making words.

Therapist: Yes, I'm going to help make up a story by special method. There are millions of stories in every kid's head and by my special technique, I can help get out one of those stories. Like telling the story with the child. Okay?

Patient: Am I going to start the story for you?

Therapist: If you want to.

Patient: Okay, let's welcome doctor and star.

Therapist: Thank you, now I'll start off. When I point to you, you say whatever comes to your mind. Once upon a time a long, long, long time ago —— in a distant land —— far, far, far away —— way beyond the desert —— way beyond the oceans —— way beyond the mountains —— there lived a ——

Patient: Mouse.

650

Therapist: And this mouse ——

Patient: Um, oh no!

Therapist: And this mouse ——

Patient: We did this story already.

Therapist: Go ahead tell it as a different story then.

Patient: Well, this mouse sat down on a boat, and this mouse sat down on a boat, and the boat sailed away. And, he found some cheese and then there lived this mean old man.

Therapist: And then there lived an old man?

Patient: Yeah, and, who didn't like mouses eating all his cheese so they go back and they find out that the mouse was wrong. He shouldn't have ate all the man's cheese. That's all the man could eat. So, the man died.

Therapist: Wait a minute. The mouse shouldn't have eaten all the man's cheese because that's all he had? That's all the man had?

Patient: Yeah.

Therapist: Yeah, then what happened?

Patient: And then the man died.

Therapist: Why did the man die?

Patient: Because that's the only thing he brought on the boat.

Therapist: He had nothing else to eat?

Patient: So he was skinny because the mouse ate all his cheese and the lesson of that story is *(emphatically)* mice are very mean!

Therapist: Mice are very mean. Okay.

The mouse represents Charles and the man in the boat stands for his mother. The story reveals residual feelings that his mother died because of his exaggerated dependency needs. Had he not been so taking from her, she would not have been drained of vital nutriment, and she might, therefore, still be alive. The story relates to residual guilt Charles still harbors over his mother's death. As already described, such guilt has many contributing elements not all of which pertain to unconscious hostility. The factor of control of the uncontrollable is often present, and in this child guilt over his excessive dependency needs was also contributory.

Occasionally I feel that I will better communicate my messages in two stories instead of one. These are the two stories I told in response:

Patient ("announces" for therapist): Once upon a time a long, long time ago there lived a ——
Therapist: Mouse.
Patient: And this mouse had a ——
Therapist: He had some cheese and this mouse lived in the home of a man on a boat and the mouse was very hungry and he wanted to eat the cheese, he wanted to eat a lot of cheese. And he was a very hungry mouse and he used to eat a lot of the cheese and one day he thought: "Gee whiz, if I eat all that cheese maybe the man will have none for himself and maybe he will starve to death."

So one day the man said to the mouse, "You look very sad mouse, why?" And the mouse said, "I'm afraid." And the man said, "Afraid of what?" And the mouse said, "I'm afraid that if I eat all this cheese, you will starve to death." And the man said, "Well, listen to me: I think you have a problem there that you want to eat all the cheese. You have nothing to worry about. I have so much cheese here that you couldn't possibly eat me out of all of it. So you don't have to worry that I'll starve to death no matter how much cheese you eat. However, you had better find out why you have such a large appetite for cheese because little baby mice try to eat a lot of cheese but grown-up mice do other things other than just sit and eat all the time."

So the mouse thought about that and he felt good that he wasn't going to kill that man by eating too much, and he also began to realize that there are better things to do in life besides just sitting around and eating all day. He found friends and did interesting things with them and then didn't have to eat so much. Now that's my first story. Now I am going to tell a second story. Do you want to hear a second story?
Patient: Yes, I do.
Therapist: Oh, let me first tell you the lessons of the first story. The lessons of the first story are number one: that

sometimes you think that you will take so much from a person that they may die and usually that isn't the case. And the second is that if you are babyish and want to eat a lot, find friends and you will want to eat less. The end.

All right. Now for my second story.

Patient: Wait, I want to announce again this time.

Therapist: Okay, you look kind of sad. Wait. What did you think of my first story, first of all?

Patient: It was pretty good.

Therapist: What was the part you liked the best?

Patient: About the mouse, when the cat said, I mean when the man said, "You won't starve me." I liked that part the best.

Therapist: I see, no matter how much you eat you won't starve me. Okay, now for my second story.

Once upon a time there was a boy and this boy was kind of childish. He used to act like a baby and he was always clinging and whining and taking, and he never acted his own age. He was kind of lazy and sat around all day and wouldn't assume responsibility and wouldn't do anything that was unpleasant; and he was always trying to take things from people and always trying to get what he could and never really participated or gave or did his share of things. And he was a taker, he was always taking, taking, taking, and never giving and he began to worry. So then one day his mother, from whom he would take a lot, one day she died and he thought that she died —

Patient: Is that me you're talking about?

Therapist: It's something like you, something like you.

Patient (angrily): I gave you that thing. Don't say I never gave you anything!

Therapist: What do you mean?

Patient: Remember that thing I gave you.

Therapist: What?

Patient: Remember that game thing.

Therapist: Right. Right. Listen I'm not talking about you. This is another boy who has some things similar to you.

Patient: Because my mother died on me, I take —

Therapist: What's that?

Patient: I take, so I thought it was me! Because my mother died.

Therapist: Well, do you think your mother died because you took a lot?

Patient: No.

Therapist: Anyway, this boy thought his mother had died because he had taken too much from her; because he was always asking and acting like a baby, whining and crying and trying to get things from her and being lazy and not trying to do and share. He thought that he had kind of drained his mother dry or gotten everything from her and he thought that he was the death of her, so to speak. Anyway, he spoke to a friend about this and the friend said, "You know, your mother died of a disease that had nothing to do with your taking so much from her and being a baby. Even though sometimes it would get her angry and drain her and make her tired that you would be so demanding and everything. This isn't the reason why she died." He said, "However, that still doesn't mean that you should stay a baby. It would be a better idea for you to try to be more adult and grow up."

So the boy thought about that, and it made him feel good to think and realize that his being a baby did not cause his mother's death. However, he felt bad that he was so much a baby and he tried very hard to do things with other kids and to join in games and things and he knew it was uncomfortable at times but after a while he found it a lot of fun to be with friends and he missed his mother less. You know the lessons of that story?

Patient: No.

Therapist: Try to figure them out.

Patient: (rather disgustedly): I don't know.

Therapist: Well, one lesson of that story is: no matter how much of a baby you are that can't cause a mother to die. Right?

Patient: Uh-huh.

Therapist: And the second lesson is that if you are a baby, try to grow up, try to do things with other kids, and you'll find it's not as bad as you might have thought. Those are the two lessons of that story. Now do you want to — wait a minute, I want to ask you if you want to say anything about those stories. Don't turn it off yet.

Patient: Let's go.

Therapist: Now, let me ask you something, you said that you thought that this boy was like you. What do you think, do you think he's like you?

Patient: No.

Therapist: Why not?

Patient: Yes, he was like me.

Therapist: Why was he like you?

Patient: Because my mother died.

Therapist: And what else?

Patient: I'm a cry baby and I steal.

Therapist: Have you stolen anything recently?

Patient: No.

Therapist: Tell me something, do you, um, did you ever think that maybe your mother died because you were so much of a baby?

Patient: No.

Therapist: Never even once?

Patient: Maybe once I did.

Therapist: You thought that she died because of your being babyish? How would being a baby make her die?

Patient: Because of all the screaming I made.

Therapist: No that didn't cause her to die. You know that. Even though you were screaming a lot, that doesn't cause her to die. She died of a disease called leukemia, and your screaming didn't make her die. What do you think of that?

Patient: Yippee! Yippee!

Therapist: Okay, let's stop there.

In my first story, I approached the guilt problem at the most visible level. I was not sure of the deeper levels and, in addition, Charles was not ready to touch upon the profound. I reassured him that his excessively dependent demands upon his mother did not cause her to die and that taking too much love (cheese) from mother did not deplete her and starve her to death. A mother's love is too abundant to be so readily exhausted. In addition, I again imparted my advice that he seek gratifications from peers to help lessen his infantile dependency cravings. The patient's comments indicated that my main message had been received.

During the telling of my second story, my emphasis on dependent craving made Charles quite anxious. This was lessened when I assured him that my story was about another boy and not him. In the ensuing discussion, Charles made the statement: "Because my mother died on me." The implication here of anger toward his mother for having died is clear; yet he was in no way ready to touch on this issue and so I let it pass. In the second story and in the ensuing discussion I reiterated the themes of the first story and added the message that his mother's death was caused by a disease which she acquired in a way that was totally unrelated to any behavior on his part. This last message, although communicated many times previously, seemed to have sunk in this time, and his "Yippee!" response was associated with definite feelings of relief and anxiety reduction.

Two weeks later Charles told this story:

Once, long, long ago, there lived a man whose name was Dr. Gardner. He was the meanest and the sceenest, cheenest, meanest doctor in the world. He made people die. And people died no other people knew of. Well, he died.
Therapist: When other people died no one knew them?
Patient: Yeah.
So, they made Dr. Gardner —— all the people who he killed metal, that worked for him.
Therapist: I don't understand — he made people die, when people died no one knew what?
Patient: No one knew —
Therapist: When people died — what about those people who died? No one knew what?
Patient: Nobody knew where they were.

656

Therapist: Nobody knew where they were — then what happened?

Patient: So then they worked for Dr. Gardner.

Therapist: They worked for what?

Patient: They worked for Dr. Gardner.

Therapist: Who worked for Dr. Gardner?

Patient: All those people.

Therapist: Who died?

Patient: Yes.

Therapist: Oh, go ahead.

Patient: So then he died.

Therapist: Then Dr. Gardner died.

Patient: Yeah, and they made him metal. Thank you.

Therapist: Wait, wait, wait — they made him what?

Patient: They made him metal.

Therapist: What do you mean — they made him metal?

Patient: Because he made them metal, so when he died they were free. So now they made him metal, they said that. And now he works for them.

Therapist: I see. Okay. Now when you said he worked for them or they worked for him — what kind of work did they do? Listen, speak into the microphone. I want to get more information.

Patient: Slavery work.

Therapist: They did slavery work. Now hold on a second. Don't turn it off —

Patient: They did slavery work. They killed people because he made them kill people.

Therapist: They did slavery work and killed people. All right now, what's the moral of that story?

Patient: When somebody kills a person and when he dies, the person will kill them and they kill him. And thank you.

In this story Charles depicts me as a murderer. I not only kill people and turn them into metal, but the metal people, as my slaves, go on in turn to kill others. The dead metal slaves then return to life and kill me in retaliation for my heinous crimes of coercive enslavement and mass murder. The dead people represent, of course, his mother and their return to life is a manifestation of his wish, still not completely gone, that his mother become alive again. By making me her murderer, Charles places in my hands a power over life and death which neither of us has. In this way Charles gains a specious feeling of control over such calamities similar to that which he would experience were he to blame himself. Killing me also provides him with an outlet for anger — some of which is felt toward his mother for having died "on" him, some toward his father for not providing him with enough compensatory affection, and some is probably harbored toward his mother's physicians who were unsuccessful in keeping her alive.

The story reflects some regression in his working through his reactions to his mother's death. But therapy is never a straight progression, and Charles was having difficulties with his father at that time — difficulties which probably contributed to his intensified longings for his dead mother.

This is the story I told in response:

Once upon a time, a long time ago, there was a doctor and his name was Dr. Gardner. Now, this doctor, like all doctors, treated patients. And, every once in a while one of his patients would die. Which is what happens when doctors treat patients because once in a while a patient will die.

Well, the families of those dead patients sometimes would get very angry at Dr. Gardner and they would get so angry that they would wish that he was dead — wish that he were dead — and they would think, "Oh, I hate that man. He made my relative die." Whether it be a mother or a father, or a sister or a brother, and they would wish that he were dead. And some of the people would just spend all of their time wishing that Dr. Gardner were dead rather than make up for the loss by doing other things. In other words, we'll say that somebody's mother had died; so instead of going out and spending time with friends and doing things like that, making themselves feel better about the death of their mother, they would go around getting angry at Dr. Gardner and blaming him. When it wasn't his fault. The relative usually died of a disease and he couldn't cure all diseases.

Patient: Excuse me, Dr. Gardner.

Therapist: Yeah.

Patient: Do you think he was right to kill some people?

Therapist: No, in my story he didn't kill anybody.

Patient: Oh.

Therapist: In my story just some of his patients died. He didn't kill anyone.

Patient: Okay, thank you.

Therapist: Some of the people thought that he had killed. But he didn't kill. He was a doctor and he tried to help people as best as he could. And he didn't kill any of his patients, they just died. So when the relatives of these dead people began to do things with their lives and found other people to make up for their loss, and involved themselves with others, and made friends, both old and young, then they weren't so bitter with Dr. Gardner. They realized that there are things that just can't be controlled — that even doctors can't control.

Do you know what the moral of that story is?

Patient: No, I don't.

Therapist: If a relative of yours dies the best thing you can do is to make up for the loss by finding a substitute. Do you know what a substitute is?

Patient: No, I don't.

Therapist: A substitute is something instead. Like if your mother dies —

Patient: Yes, I do.

Therapist: You make friends —

Patient: And let's say, I'm only in second grade. Let's say my teacher is absent, it means she's just taking over for my teacher until she gets better.

Therapist: Right. Substitute teacher. Right. So if a relative of yours dies they can't come back, you get a permanent substitute. You get someone like another lady —

Patient: Right.

Therapist: Make friends and things like that. They can be substitutes. Counselors. Rather than to keep blaming some doctor which is what you should have done in the first place. Right? Okay, do you want to hear that?

Patient: Yes, I do.

In my story I once again communicated the notion that one must resign oneself to the painful fact that there are certain things in life over which we have no control; that there are certain diseases which physicians, in spite of their best efforts, cannot cure. Gaining control over the uncontrollable through delusional blame is a futile endeavor. One can, however, obtain compensatory gratifications with others and thereby lessen the need to utilize the maladaptive blame mechanism.

Five weeks later (less than three months after the death of his mother), Charles told this story:

Therapist: Once upon a time a long, long, long time ago —— in a distant land —— far, far, far away —— there lived a ——
Patient: Mother.
Therapist: A what?
Patient: Mother.
Therapist: There lived a mother. And this mother ——
Patient: Wasn't an ordinary mother.
Therapist: Wasn't an ordinary mother.
Patient: She always kept on getting sick and sick and sick and sicker and sicker and sick and sick and sick. Even when she got better she got sick still. And then she died.
Therapist: And she died.
Patient: And then they buried her and then the son is crying, crying, crying like this, "Ooh, ooh, ohh, ohh." And then the mother came back to life again, and then she died again, and then she came back to life again. And then finally she died. Then she never came back again.

And the lesson of that story is that when she keeps on dying and keeps coming back to life don't think she is going to stay alive. She'll die. Thank you, doctor.
Therapist: Uh-huh.
Patient: I want to say something. Soon I won't be here anymore so I would like to say now, I'll see you next time. Thank you.

The story epitomizes one facet of his working through his reactions to his mother's death. In the course of the previous months his repeated wishes for his mother's reincarnation alternated with his resignation that she would not come back to life. This was the last statement of his resignation. His subsequent stories did not reveal residual fantasies of her return. As already mentioned, it would be unreasonable to conclude that there were no such hopes; they were just of such low intensity that there was little need for their release in storytelling.

This is the story I told in response:

Once upon a time a long, long, long time ago —— in a distant land —— far, far, far away there lived a boy. And this boy had a mother and one day this boy's mother died. And he wouldn't believe it, and he said, "Oh, she'll be back to life very soon." However, that was quite foolish thinking because people really can't come back to life and he kept moping around and wishing she would come back to life and he kept hoping but nothing happened and he didn't want to accept the fact that when a person dies they really do not come back to life.

And then he wondered what could he do to make himself feel less sad. He felt very sad and he thought and he thought and then a friend came by and he spoke to him and he said, "That's an idea, I'll play with friends, that'll make me feel better." So he went out with a friend and found he had a good time and this helped him feel less sad about having lost his mother — about his mother being dead. And then he went home with his friend and he saw the friend had a mother who was a very nice person and he spoke to her a little bit, and he realized that she could answer some of the questions that his mother used to answer and that she could be like a kind of substitute mother for him sometimes. So after that happened he missed his mother less and he stopped spending all his time wishing that his mother were alive again. That's that story.

And the lesson of that story is. If your mother dies remember this: she can never come back to life again. However, that doesn't mean that you have to be sad all the the time. You can make friends and that can make you feel happy. You can spend time with the friends of your mother and some day when you are bigger and you are older, you will meet a girl whom you will marry and then you will have company again.

The end. Do you want to say anything about that story?

Patient: No.

Therapist: Okay.

As I often do in response to stories with healthy resolutions, I reiterated the child's salutary message and elaborated on it. Here I re-emphasized his resignation to the finality of his mother's death. I then again presented Charles with the grief-assuaging gratifications which are available to him if he wishes to avail himself of them.

These story sequences are representative of those Charles presented during the three months following his mother's death. They reflect various reactions, some neurotic, some healthy. Charles was not receptive to, nor probably capable of, an in-depth inquiry into the psychodynamics of his various responses. He was, therefore, approached at a most superficial level in my responding stories. It would appear then that many of his inappropriate reactions were not fully worked through. This may very well have been true, but it is possible that there was more coming-to-terms with his mother's death than his stories would suggest. Most of his subsequent stories did not touch further on his mother's death, but related more to his dependency problem and his relationship to his father. Clinically, as well, Charles did not appear to be depressed about his mother's death. However, one cannot be sure how much his mother's death was contributing to his tenacious dependency problem. One cannot be certain that his reactions to her death would have been more neurotic had he not received treatment. I would like to believe that they would have been severer, and that the Mutual Storytelling Technique was helpful to him in coping with her death in a more adaptive and less painful fashion.

TRAUMATIC SURGERY

Surgery which results in disfigurement, chronic incapacitation, or other unalterable conditions can be a cause of psychological reactions which justifiably can be considered situational. The child must learn to cope with an impairment which he cannot alter. The impairment, moreover, may be noticeable to others, and it may realistically limit him in certain areas of functioning.

Two children with such difficulties are presented here. The first is a girl with such severe temporal lobe seizures that she had to be hemispherectomized, and the second is a boy who required operative repair of a congenital harelip and cleft palate. The way in which the Mutual Storytelling Technique was utilized in their treatment will be demonstrated.

Example 4

Pam, an eighteen-and-one-half-year-old girl, contracted viral encephalitis at fourteen months of age. She was quadriplegic for one year and was left with a permanent but mild residual left hemiparesis. Whereas prior to the encephalitis there was every reason to believe that Pam was of normal intelligence, her subsequent intellectual development was retarded. Her I.Q.'s were in the 65-80 range. In addition, following the illness she developed grand mal seizures, which over the years became increasingly resistive to anticonvulsant medication. Accordingly, when she was eighteen, her right cerebral hemisphere was removed as the only alternative to her spending her life suffering intractable seizures. The operation not only left her seizure-free (with the exception of two post-operative seizures), but it also allowed her to be maintained on relatively low doses of anticonvulsant medication. Previous to the hemispherectomy, Pam had to be chronically drugged to the point of lethargy. Interestingly, the hemispherectomy in no way affected her intelligence. Prior to the operation her WAIS Full Scale I.Q. was 63 (Verbal 68 and Performance 60); afterwards it was 64 (Verbal 69 and Performance 63). The only significant untoward effect of the operation was the worsening of her pre-existing left hemiparesis. Throughout the years she had attended a school for minimally brain injured children and at the time that I saw her, Pam was functioning academically at about the fourth grade level.

She was referred about six months after her operation because of withdrawal from people, sexual problems, and dependency cravings which were considered to be exaggerated, her neurological condition notwithstanding. In my interviews with her, Pam in many respects handled herself as a nine-to-ten-year old child. She also described strong sexual urges which were occasionally gratified by masturbation. At other times she inappropriately requested sexual activities with strangers. In spite of her withdrawal, there was a strong and healthy desire for human contact, but at the most dependent level. For example, Pam fantasied marrying the interne who was involved in her care while she had been hospitalized. The life she anticipated with him was one in which she would stay at home all day and he would return home to each lunch with her, and evenings would be spent watching television and cuddling. Pam also said she was fearful of involving herself with people because she always seemed to be doing the wrong thing — a sign of good reality testing and some preservation of healthy self-awareness which served her in good stead. Lastly, Pam was preoccupied with fears for her parents' health. Although there was some reality basis for this in that her parents were elderly, her concerns were clearly exaggerated and probably were displaced worries over her own welfare.

Although most teen-agers consider the storytelling game to be beneath them, this girl did not. This was the first story she told me in treatment:

Once there were these parents who were very, very sick and they were in the house alone and they had no one for them to care for. So I heard about this and I was very concerned about the parents who were very sick because a lot of things could happen to parents when, if they don't have anyone to take care of them and to get things for them. So, I inquired about these people who were very sick, and I found out that they needed someone in the house to help them around. So, I went to this house —— *Therapist:* Uh-huh.

Patient: And, I asked, I got all of the information about what their problems were and all of that sort of thing, and they asked me if I would try to help them in some way. So, I said, "Yes, if I can." So, I told them I would come here, come to your house everyday and I'll try my best to help these two couples that are very sick. I'll do my best. I'll come in at seven o'clock. So I go to their house every day, and I stay there all night long the first night and it was really a sight because no one did anything and no one cared for them or, or really took any care of them —— so I said that I would take care of these people and see what their needs would be and I did it and was very successful.

Therapist: And the moral of that story, the lesson of that story?

Patient: Is really *(mumbles).*

Therapist: The moral, the moral is the lesson of the story, what you learn from that story.

Patient: To care for people that really needed care.

Therapist: Yes, finish the sentence.

Patient: (Pause) And, I really learned what some people could do for others.

Therapist: Uh-huh, okay, that's a very, very good story and since it was your first time on the program I think you did very well.

As mentioned, Pam displaced her concerns for herself onto her parents. The story reveals this tendency. In addition, it provides her, through fantasy, with the ego-enhancement of taking care of others. In actuality, it was she who was continually being taken care of and, at some level, this must have been quite ego-debasing. Pam compensates for such feelings of inadequacy by switching things around and making others the object of *her* ministrations. Lastly, such reversal enables her to gratify her deep-seated dependency needs. By projecting herself onto the forsaken ones she aids, she can satisfy vicariously her own desires to be cared for as a helpless infant.

This is the story I told in response:

Well, once upon a time there lived this family and there were two elderly people, an elderly couple, and they had a son and they lived in their house and their son, he was a kind of lazy guy and he wasn't very helpful when they got sick one day. He was kind of ineffective and wasn't able to care for them too well.

Fortunately, however, there was a young girl who lived in the neighborhood who heard that these people were sick, and she was concerned about them and realized that many unfortunate things could happen to people when they are very sick — especially if they didn't have someone around who could help take care of them. So, she went to the house and she asked if they needed someone, and they said, "Yes," and so they gave her the job of helping take care of them. And, when she got in there she realized that this boy was completely helpless and that he was quite scared that if his parents died he would really be alone and unable to do anything.

So this girl, as she spent her time taking care of these elderly people, she encouraged the young man to go out and learn a trade so that he could then shift for himself and support himself and be responsible for himself. So, she kept those parents alive long enough until the time came when he finished learning his trade and after that, since they were very old people, they died, but the boy was then able to take of himself because he had learned something and this girl had done two wonderful things. First of all, she had encouraged the boy to learn a trade, and secondly, she had kept the parents, these elderly people alive long enough so that the boy could learn his trade and become a useful citizen; and, do you know what the moral of my story is?

Patient: What's that?

Therapist: The lesson of my story?

Patient: Well, it ——

Therapist: The lesson of my story is that if you are lazy and shiftless and do nothing you may be frightened if your parents die, but if you learn a trade or learn something then you don't have to be so frightened because then you'll be able to stand on your own two feet even though

you may miss them when they die. The end.
Patient: That was very good.
Therapist: Good, okay.

I decided in my story to focus on a realistic element in the girl's concern for the welfare of her parents. They were elderly people compared to the parents of other teen-agers, although there was no evidence suggesting their imminent demise. However, Pam was herself almost an adult, and vocational training was being considered for her at the time of referral. My story was told in the attempt to improve her motivation for such training. Competence in some area would make her feel more secure; would lessen her dependency on her parents; and would provide her with the wherewithal for self-support when her parents would, indeed, be no longer alive.

Three weeks later, Pam related this story:

Can I think of something first?
Therapist: Yes, but say it into the microphone. Do you want to think of something first? I'll help you, and the way I do it is that I start telling a story and I stop at a certain point and point my finger at you. And, as soon as I do that, you then say the first thing that comes into your mind, and you will see that will be a story. There are millions of stories in everybody's head and all you have to do is, when I point my finger like this, you'll see. Once upon a time —— a long, long, long time ago —— in a distant land —— far, far away —— far beyond the mountains —— far beyond the desert —— there lived a ——
Patient: Girl.
Therapist: And this girl ——
Patient: Lived in a house.
Therapist: And one day ——
Patient: She went out in the desert and the mountains and she found some strange things ——
Therapist: Which were ——
Patient: Oh, bones and prehistorical creatures.
Therapist: Bones of prehistorical what?

Patient: Prehistorical creatures.
Therapist: Prehistorical creatures?
Patient: Yes.
Therapist: And when she found these she ——
Patient: She was very interested.
Therapist: She was very interested?
Patient: Yes, because she never saw bones of prehistorical creatures before.
Therapist: And so?
Patient: She was very interested and she took a bone, one of these bones, and she took it to her friend which was a scientist and she asked the scientist why these bones were there where she living ——
Therapist: Yes, and he said ——
Patient: Well, for various reasons because maybe they were buried there.
Therapist: Yes.
Patient: And someone dug them up and got frightened and just left them there to lay for a long time. And, they got very old. And, the scientist took the bones of the prehistorical creature and put it in the ——
Therapist: Put them in what? Describe it.
Patient: In a museum.
Therapist: Okay, and then?
Patient: And, they were very fascinated by this, umm, of this creature.
Therapist: All right. Is that it? What's the moral of the story?
Patient: The moral of the story is that this scientist discovered that the bone was really old.
Therapist: But, what's the moral or the lesson of the story? What's the main message?
Patient: That he discovered certain, he learned certain things from bones, dead bones that were found in the desert.
Therapist: Um, okay.

The story reflects Pam's basic attitude that she is like dead bones; that she is only of scientific interest and could very well be a museum piece. The feeling of being a scientific oddity was not without foundation. She was, indeed, presented at many medical conferences to medical students, internes, and residents. After her hemispherectomy, Pam attracted even greater medical interest from the staff of the large teaching hospital where she was operated upon. The feeling that the only thing that she was good for was to be looked upon as an interesting scientific object was intensified by the fact that she had not developed herself in other areas which might have made her attractive. Certainly, one could not expect physically and emotionally healthy young men of her age to be attracted to her. But the young men at her school — youngsters with similar difficulties — were potential social companions. Had she concerned herself more with her grooming, had she involved herself more with peers and thereby gained more of the wherewithal of socializing, had she developed skills which she was perfectly capable of performing, Pam would have been more likely to have enjoyed the attentions of youngsters her own age.

With this understanding of Pam's story, I told mine:

Well, once upon a time, a long time ago, way beyond the oceans, way beyond the desert there lived a girl. And she went out one day and she met a boy and they started just taking a walk and suddenly they saw some bones of a prehistoric creature and they were both interested in them and the boy became very interested in them and he started studying them. And, he brought a scientist to look at them and he became so fascinated and interested with the bones that he kind of forgot about the girl and he became more interested in studying those bones than in being with her.

Well, after a while she said, the heck with this. I don't have to hang around here, those bones are interesting but he seems to be more interested in the bones than in me. So she said goodbye to him and she went to a dance and she met another fellow who liked her because she was kind and pretty and worked hard at her job. And although they may have found some interesting bones too, he liked her more than the bones and she had a very good time with him, and they finally got married and lived happily ever after.

And, the moral of that story is, if someone is more interested in bones than in you, forget him, find someone else
who will be interested in you more than bones. The end.
Patient: That's good! That's an excellent story, doctor, I
can tell you that's better than mine.
Therapist: Well, it's different. What is it about it that you
liked most?
Patient: Well, there's a good ending. That's what I liked
about it.
Therapist: Uh-huh, okay, very good.

In my story Pam is told that she has the freedom to find
others whose interest in her is not confined to the scientific.
However, in order to gain the attraction of others, she has to
develop qualities which will win their attention — in this case,
"she was kind and pretty and worked hard at her job." At the
time my story was told, Pam was involved in a vocational training program where she was being evaluated for competence in
such jobs as hospital ward aide, housecleaning, factory work (of
the assembly line type), or simple clerical work. My story was
presented in the hope that it would enhance her incentive in
these pursuits and thereby improve her social attractiveness and
lessen the likelihood that she would only feel needed as a scientific oddity.
One week later, Pam told this story:

Good afternoon, I am very glad to be here and this
story that I am going to tell is going to be about some fish.
These fish are prize, I think I'll call prize-winning fish and
they do marvelous tricks and ——
Therapist: Well, go ahead, there is a prize-winning fish, and
they did marvelous tricks. For instance, one trick that
they did was ——
Patient: Jump up in the air and try to bounce, try to get
some fish to eat.
Therapist: What? They would jump up in the air and try
to get fish?
Patient: Yeah. Smaller fish.
Therapist: All right, tell me more about them —— another

thing that they could do was ——

Patient: Bounce a ball.

Therapist: And, also they could ——

Patient: Go under water and stay under water for seventy minutes.

Therapist: Water for seventy minutes?

Patient: And everyone thought that was great.

Therapist: Go ahead and these fish who could do all these tricks, now tell me, tell me something more about them. Tell me something. As a result of this ability, what happened to them?

Patient: These fish, these prize-winning fish went all around the world doing these tricks and they made people happy and they — and the people went to see them and they really did a marvelous job of doing tricks and it was just great.

The moral of the story is that ——

Therapist: Yes, go ahead.

Patient: Let me see ——

Therapist: You can't think of a moral or lesson?

Patient: No.

Therapist: All right, we'll stop and I'll tell a story.

The story is similar to the one told the previous week. Here Pam sees herself as being useful only as a kind of clown or performer of circus stunts. However, the story reflects an improvement over the previous one in that here the fish are admired because they have learned certain skills which warrant the admiration of others. The message from my other story has been heard, but she is still a long way from genuinely translating this into action. She herself had not begun to develop any particular skill of her own that would be of interest, let alone a source of admiration, to others. It was gratifying to see, however, that Pam was incorporating this value into her scheme of things.

This was the story I told in response:

Well, once upon a time there was this group of fish. And, these fish were prize-winning fish in that they could do various kinds of tricks. They could bounce a ball; they could stay under water for seventy minutes, which is not very unusual. What would be unusual for fish is that they could stay out of water for seventy minutes. I think that would be more unusual than staying under, staying under water for seventy minutes. Anyway, they went around the world doing tricks and people used to marvel at them and were amazed at what they did.

However, one of these fishes was very unhappy and he said, "I feel like a freak of some kind. I feel like my whole life, the whole purpose of my life, is just to do things for the benefit of other people, so they can watch me jump around and do fancy tricks. Sure, it's nice that they pay me to see us and they give us good food and care because we do this, and they seem to enjoy us, but I would like to get some pleasures alone." And, he was speaking to the other fish about this and they too realized that he was right — that there was something that they were missing in life. So, each one began to take up some personal hobby which he did all alone which gave him some pleasure alone, some pleasure that didn't require the fish to exhibit himself in front of others and get pleasure from being exhibited in shows. And, each one found his own hobby and interest and then they were all much happier.

And, the moral of that story is: you can get a certain amount of happiness by doing things for others, but you also have to do things for yourself if you want to be completely happy. The end. What did you think of that story?
Patient: It was very good.
Therapist: What's the part you liked the most?
Patient: I liked the ending very much.
Therapist: Uh-huh, okay.

In my story I attempted to lay down yet another goal for Pam to strive toward: the acquisition of talents and skills which could give her personal gratifications when she is alone. This girl's future, by most standards, could not be considered bright; and any activity which could provide her with genuine gratifications had to be encouraged. In the loneliness that probably lay ahead for her, a satisfying hobby could be salutary.

A psychotherapeutic approach utilizing insight and the

understanding of psychodynamics was not possible with Pam. My work with her was more along the lines of guidance and career planning. My goals, because of her intellectual deficit, had to be modest. The Mutual Storytelling Technique allowed me to supplement dramatically the advice which I provided in direct discussion.

Example 5

The full course of treatment of Chris, the boy with harelip, cleft palate, and other problems requiring surgical intervention will be described in Chapter 17. Three of his stories which demonstrated oedipal problems were presented in Chapter 8. I discuss here a situational problem which brought about his return to me for a short course of therapy fourteen months after the full course of treatment was terminated. The main reasons for his original referral were withdrawal into fantasy and such poor involvement in his school work that it was suspected that Chris might have an intellectual impairment. Chris responded well during a one year course of treatment. His reason for returning was that he was having some difficulties in his relationships with peers centered around his exaggerated reactions to the occasional teasing he was exposed to because of his harelip. He would become morose, self-deprecatory, and was reluctant to go out and play although he could usually be coaxed into it by his mother. When Chris came to his first session for the treatment of these new difficulties, he gave me this letter shown in Figure 2.

The letter is a most touching presentation of his complaint. It gives us a clue into one of the sources of his difficulty: he projects onto others (here God) his own self-loathing and considers them to hold the same deprecatory attitudes he harbors toward himself. The letter suggests that Chris utilizes the same mechanism with peers and thereby visualizes them as far more hostile than they are.

During his first return session, Chris told this story:

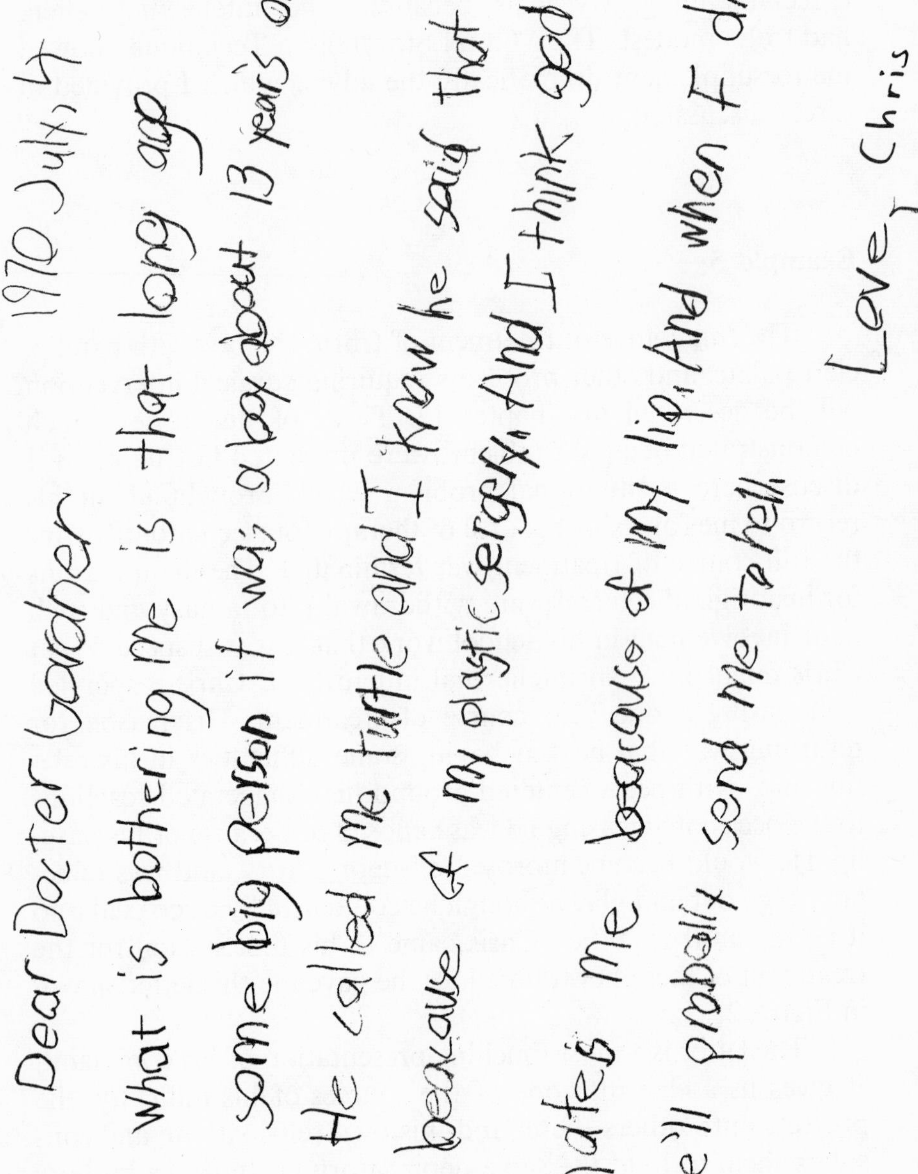

Dear Docter Gardner   1970 July, 4

What is bothering me is that long ago

some big person if was a boy about 13 years old,

He called me turtle and I know he said that

because of my plastic sergery And I think god

hates me because of my lip, And when I die

he'll probally send me to hell.

Love, Chris

Figure 2.

Well, there used to be these two boys and, um, there is this old hut and it was all wrecked up and one day they decided to fix it up and, um, they bought some things. They bought new paper and they got a man and they asked the man if he could put plugs in the wall and he did. And, it cost about ten dollars and then they got all the lights and they got all the, the mended things like, uh, the wood was broken up and they got new wood and they put in a chandelier and they made a table and they bought a television, a real little television. And, then, they well, um, the boy asked his mother, the two boys asked their mothers and fathers and invited all the other friends, if they could come and if they could have a party. Well, they did and the house looked so nice that, um, they showed it to this man and the man thought it was a very good house so they decided to put the house in the museum. That was the end.

Therapist: Uh-huh, I see, and what's the lesson of that story?

Patient: Well, it shows that it was a very good house.

Therapist: Very good. Thank you very much.

The hut requiring repair is, of course, Chris, and the man who fixes it up represents me. The story reveals his request and anticipation that I will rectify his defects so that he will no longer be exposed to the painful taunting of his peers. His hopes are that I will make him so handsome that he will be worthy of being exhibited in a museum. This last image does not have the morbid quality of the hemispherectomized girl's museum fantasy. The museum fantasy reflected Pam's feelings that she was as worthless as dead bones and was only useful as a scientific oddity. For Chris the display was of a handsomely repaired house, worthy of admiration. The element of being hopelessly rejected by everyone was not present. In spite of his withdrawal, Chris was actively involved in the world about him — a world which was basically inviting and a source of deep gratifications.

This is my story and our interchange which followed:

Once upon a time there were two boys and they saw an

old house and it was all wrecked and they decided to fix it up. Well, they got wallpaper and they bought plugs for the wall and they got new lights and they got many things. They got new wood, then they put in a chandelier and a table and a T.V. set and it really looked beautiful. One of the boys had a funny idea because there was one small part of that house that wasn't exactly perfect. It had little marks on it, uh, he wasn't happy about the house and he said, "This house is ugly. The whole house is ugly." The other boy said, "How can the whole house be ugly? What are you talking about? What do you mean the whole house is ugly? The whole house isn't ugly. Just one small part of the house is ugly. Just a little bit ugly, one small part. And, that can hardly be seen unless you are looking very hard for it." The first boy said, "Yeah, but there are some kids sometimes who make fun of us sometimes, because of that small ugly part, or that part that doesn't look as nice as the rest." The second boy said, "Ah, just ignore them — there will always be somebody to criticize you. There will always be somebody to make fun of whatever we do, even if the house was perfect, there is no such thing as a perfect house, every house has some small part that isn't perfect, there is always somebody to find fault."

Well, the first boy realized that the second boy was right that things don't have to be perfect, that one small part not being right doesn't make everything bad. And, what do you think the lesson of that story is? Can you figure it out.

Patient: What?

Therapist: What's the lesson in that story?

Patient: That every house sometimes has to have a little part of it that isn't so good.

Therapist: Right! And the second lesson is that if it has one small part that's no good then that doesn't —

Patient: Wreck it down then.

Therapist: No, that doesn't mean that the whole house is no good — only one small part is no good. Do you understand that?

Patient: Yeah.

Therapist: Say it again so that I'll be sure you understand it.

676

Patient: Well, I think, if there is one part then you just leave it there and enjoy it.

Therapist: Still enjoy the house.

Patient: Yeah.

Therapist: It doesn't mean the whole house is no good. Right. Now do you want to say that whole thing again? That's an important lesson.

Patient: Well, just because one part of it is ugly, it doesn't mean that the whole house is no good.

Therapist: Right! Excellent! Did you like that story?

Patient: Yeah.

Therapist: What part of it did you like?

Patient: When they fixed up the house.

Therapist: And, my story. Was there any part of my story that you liked?

Patient: Well, the same place.

Therapist: Remember what the lessons of my story were?

Patient: Well, just because one part is wrecked up, it doesn't mean the whole house is wrecked up.

Therapist: Right, that's the important lesson in my story. Very good.

In my story the boys repair the house themselves; I do not appear. In this way I discouraged inappropriate dependency on me. Much of the work of the therapy must be done by the patient, and I help only with those parts of the job he cannot do himself. The messages of my story are clear: no matter how hard one tries, or no matter what one is, or how one looks, there will always be someone to find fault. Secondly, everyone has at least a few defects — no one is perfect. And lastly, one small defect doesn't make one totally worthless. This last communication was most important in that Chris tended to generalize. He considered his one small imperfection — his hardly noticeable harelip — to signify that he was totally ugly and worthless. In the post-story discussion, Chris revealed his understanding of what I had imparted.

When Chris returned for his next visit, four days later, the mother reported that he was generally in better spirits and that he was playing more with his friends. This is the story he told during that session:

This person went out and saw something. It was a plant. It looked kind of strange, and he asked one of his neighbors to move it, to see what kind it was. The neighbor said, "I don't know." He called the man who looks at flowers and plants and the man said, "I'm sorry, but I don't know what it is." So this man said, "Get a scientist." The scientist said, "It can't be science fiction because it's real. It came from space." So the scientist examined the plant. He said, "This plant can spread poison."

The next morning when the neighbor woke up, he saw a man bleeding right next to the plant. The plant got bigger and bigger and soon it got to grow teeth. The man called the police, and the police called the Army. And there was a war and the monster was smashing down cities and he ate people with his mouth. A few months later they were still fighting the monster. Fifty scientists thought of a plan. They got a giant explosive plant killer. They got a high volt gun with a giant battery. They put food in the cage and the monster came into it. They shot the forty volt gun, and the monster was killed.

The lesson of the story is that there's no such thing as a plant like that.

The plant in the story symbolizes Chris. Because of his defect he abhors himself: the plant is unfamiliar to the scientist; it comes from outer space; it turns into a monster. Chris is filled with rage at the world for taunting him: the plant is poisonous, kills people, and smashes cities. Finally, to protect himself from venting his fury and to assuage the guilt he feels over his murderous impulses, Chris has himself killed. In the moral, he lessens the anxiety the story has evoked in him by making it all make-believe: "there's no such thing as a plant like that."

The reader might consider this to be the story of a very sick boy, considering all the seemingly morbid elements in it. Told by another patient, I might agree, but I knew Chris quite well, and found him to express himself in quite rich, often creative, imagery usually beyond what the clinical situation seemed to warrant. Such imagery was primarily a residuum of the fantasy pattern associated with the symptoms for which he had previously been treated. They had become his habitual pattern of depicting things, and they were related with a lightheartedness which is not present in the sicker child. And, most important, the clinical picture — which is the final determinant of the degree of pathology — was a relatively healthy one.

This is the story I told in response:

Once upon a time there was a person who went out and saw something. It was a plant and it had a little mark on it. Then the plant said to the man, "I know that everyone hates me for this mark that I have on me, for this small mark which I have. So go away and don't bother me." Then the man said, "Yes, I see the mark, but I can hardly notice it. To me you're a very beautiful plant, and I'd like to take you into my house."

The plant didn't believe it. He was very mad because he thought that he was ugly all over and he kept telling people to go away.

Then the plant met a bigger plant who had a similar line and mark on his petal. And the two began to speak. The little plant said, "Don't you think you're ugly all over?" What do you think the big plant then said?

Patient: No.

Therapist: Why?

Patient: 'Cause he didn't care about it.

Therapist: Why else?

Patient: It doesn't make the whole self ugly.

Therapist: Right! So what did the little plant think then?

Patient: He was happy.

Therapist: Was he mad anymore?

Patient: No.

Therapist: Do you know what the lesson of that story is?

Patient: One little mark doesn't make you ugly all over.

Therapist: That's right, perfectly right. A little mark in one place is hardly noticeable, but even if people notice it they just think that you have a little mark in one place. They don't think it makes you ugly all over. But if you think that one little mark makes you ugly all over you will feel bad about yourself, it may make you quite mad.

Chris readily stated the main communication of my story: "One little mark doesn't make you ugly all over." I also imparted the notion that when one feels less defective, he is less angry at the world.

Chris needed only a few more sessions for the treatment of his exaggerated reaction to teasing. He was not only generalizing far less about his defect but he was also handling those who occasionally teased him. He would either tease them back or respond with a comment like: "You must be some kind of a nut to laugh at somebody just because he has a little mark on his lip." As might have been predicted, his better handling of the teasers brought about a significant reduction in their taunts. In our last session, Chris told me that he had changed his mind and that he no longer felt that God hated him.

13. PSYCHOGENIC PROBLEMS SECONDARY TO MINIMAL BRAIN DYSFUNCTION

The term *minimal brain dysfunction* refers to a mild organic brain syndrome which manifests itself by such signs and symptoms as hyperactivity, distractability, perceptual impairments (visual and auditory being the most common), "soft neurological signs," poor memory, and figure-ground confusion. The syndrome is known by a number of other names: "brain injury," "neurological impairment," "minimal cerebral dysfunction," "hyperkinetic syndrome," and "learning disability" — to name only a few. Although their intelligence may be normal or even superior, children with this disorder often have significant difficulty in learning and in their social relationships. The exact percentage of children suffering with this syndrome is unknown. My own guess is that it is about three to five percent. However, not only is the number of such children increasing (as is to be expected in our burgeoning population), but the actual proportion of children who manifest this disorder is also on the rise. This is not the specious kind of statistical increase seen with more general awareness of the syndrome and more sensitive diagnostic techniques (although these factors are certainly contributing to the rising incidence being reported). It is rather the result of improved obstetrical and pediatric techniques. Children who, only fifteen to twenty years ago, would not have survived the perinatal period are now doing so only to suffer the effects of their premature extrauterine existence or their narrow escape from perinatal death.

Minimal brain dysfunction is seen in children whose mothers have suffered with a variety of antenatal difficulties: placenta previa and other causes of excessive bleeding; nutritional deficiencies; overexposure to radiation (including diagnostic X-rays); and infectious diseases such as rubella, toxoplasmosis, and cytomegalic inclusion disease. The syndrome is more common in primiparas (possibly related to their prolonged labors), in anomalous presentations, and when cephalopelvic disproportion is present. Eclampsia, perinatal hemorrhage, premature separation of the placenta, umbilical cord complications (such as cord prolapse and cord around the neck), and Rh and ABO incompatibility have also been implicated. Postnatally, the syndrome can result from any of the infectious disorders which can produce central nervous system involvement. It is also associated with a variety of inborn errors of metabolism such as phenylketonuria and galactosemia. Seizures, even those which are febrile in origin, are not only a manifestation of underlying organic brain dysfunction, but the seizure itself can bring about further neurological impairment — possibly as the result of the cerebral anoxemia that is produced in the apneic phase of the convulsion. The physician's traditional advice that mothers try to prevent the recurrence of febrile seizures by the rapid administration of elixir phenobarbital at the onset of the fever is without question inadequate in that children's fevers often rise so rapidly that convulsions often cannot be avoided. Most pediatric neurologists are now recommending that children with febrile seizures be placed on maintenance doses of anticonvulsant medication (either phenobarbital or diphenylhidantoin) from the first such seizure to the age of four. They advise that at age four, attempts be made to wean the child gradually from the drug regimen which is to be reinstituted, of course, should the seizures recur. I have seen a number of children whose minimal brain injury syndrome appears to have been the result of the failure to put them on such a prophylactic regimen.

There are many other diseases, agents, and predisposing factors which have been associated etiologically with minimal brain dysfunction. I have mentioned only the most common. However, in spite of the long list of entities which have been implicated, there are still many children in whom the etiology

682

is unknown; but they are so categorized because they present with the constellation of symptoms which is pathognomonic of the disorder.

THE PRIMARY SIGNS AND SYMPTOMS

Primary signs and symptoms are the direct manifestations of the basic organic impairment. The secondary signs and symptoms are psychogenic in etiology and represent the child's psychopathological reactions to his neurological deficits. The minimal brain dysfunction symptom complex is vast and complicated, and only the most obvious and well-known manifestations are outlined here.

Lag in the developmental milestones is one of the most common manifestations. The child is often late in sitting, standing, walking, talking, and bowel and bladder training. Some of the other deficits to be described may also be manifestations of developmental lag (slow maturation of the central nervous system) rather than irreversible destruction of nerve tissue. For example, the child may persist in reversing letters which are mirror images beyond the age when most children no longer exhibit such confusion. Some of the "soft neurological signs" which I shall describe are also the result of developmental lag.

Marked and continuous hyperactivity, which has an aimless quality, is often present. In many cases it may be so incessant that the child is even restless during sleep. The mother may recall that *in utero* the neurologically impaired child was more active than her other children. When hyperactivity is a manifestation of anxiety it appears primarily in association with stress, whereas the hyperactivity associated with brain injury, as already mentioned, is practically continuous. My experience has been that organic hyperactivity is reduced, in more than half of these children, by amphetamines. Similarly, the hyperactivity in such children may increase when attempts are made to reduce it with barbiturates. The amphetamines then are not only of diagnostic but also of therapeutic value in this disorder. But, it should be remembered that not all brain injured children will be sedated by them; some, like the normal child, become more hyperactive. Also, a small percentage of normal children will react paradoxically to amphetamines and barbiturates.

I usually start the child on dextroamphetamine sulphate 2.5 mgm morning and noon and then increase in 2.5 mgm increments until I reach a point when I am certain whether the child is reacting with sedation or excitation. One can go as high as 15 mgm twice daily in many of these children and derive the sedative benefits without their suffering significant side effects such as headache, dizziness, or gastric distress. When amphetamines intensify the hyperactivity I often try methylphenidate (Ritalin) in similar doses because it will often exhibit the same paradoxical effect. If neither of these work, the hyperactivity may usually be reduced with thioridazine (Mellaril) or chlorpromazine (Thorazine). With both medications I usually start on doses of 10 mgm three times a day and then increase in 10 mgm increments (that is, an increase of 30 mgm per day) until the point of lethargy is reached. I then drop the dose slightly to the sublethargic level. This is usually sufficient to control the agitation. The average child between five and twelve is usually maintained on doses of 75 to 150 mgm per day. Chlorpromazine has the advantage over thioridizine of being supplied in twelve-hour time-disintegration capsules so that one dose per day can be given. Since there is a slight, but definite, risk that chlorpromazine may produce hepatic pericanalicular inflammation (which is most often reversed on withdrawal of the drug, although chronic jaundice has been reported), one must periodically obtain a liver function test such as the alkaline phosphatase. All things considered, I prefer the chlorpromazine, not only because of its easier administration, but also because I have found it more predictably effective. Characteristically, the hyperactivity decreases spontaneously by puberty and then chemotherapy for this symptom is no longer necessary.

Because chlorpromazine and thioridizine reduce hyperactivity, they enhance the child's receptivity to learning. This is related to the fact that a child will not learn very much if he's fidgeting, jumping in his seat, or running around the classroom most of the day. The amphetamines and methylphenidate, besides reducing hyperactivity, also have an alerting effect which seems to enhance concentration. Sometimes I use a combination of one of the tranquilizers with one of the stimulants. The two must be carefully titrated to produce the maximum benefit with minimal untoward side effects.

All four of the drugs mentioned have been reported to improve various types of learning in ways which are still ill-understood. (An article by Conners, *et al.*[1] on the use of dextro-amphetamine sulphate in the treatment of children with organic learning disorders contains an excellent bibliography on the drug treatment of these children.)

Distractability, or poor attention span, is another cardinal symptom of minimal brain dysfunction. The child has difficulty differentiating between important and unimportant stimuli and thereby becomes easily diverted from the learning tasks at hand. For example, most children recognize that the teacher's words are more important to attend to than the sound made by a pencil dropped in the back of the classroom. These children do not make this differentiation. They may consider the dropped-pencil noise of equal, if not more, importance and rush to the back of the room to find out what's going on. The distractability may be visual. For example, the child may have little or no trouble reading a single word presented on a flashcard; but he will have great difficulty with the printed page where the array of words distracts him from the one he is focusing upon. Small classes and homework done in a quiet room without siblings, television and outside noises can be most useful. If a parent of such a child can be relied upon to provide supplementary home tutoring in a consistent way without significant exasperation or involvement in power struggles, the child's learning progress can be enhanced. I usually recommend that the school provide the mother with the same texts and learning materials which are used in the classroom. A few short sessions of concentrated learning are preferable to a prolonged one. Weekend and holiday tutoring is best done early in the morning when the child is most alert and unfatigued by physical activity.

The child may exhibit fine and/or gross motor coordination problems. His handwriting may be poor; he may have trouble throwing a ball, riding a bicycle, or running without tripping. His poor copying of geometric figures may be the result of motor and/or perceptual problems — the differentiation between the two may, at times, be difficult.

Perceptual problems are often seen in this syndrome and these directly interfere with learning. Visual-perceptual defects are the most common. It is not an impairment in refraction or gross perception, but rather in fine visual discrimination. For example, the child's copies of geometric figures may reveal fragmentation, angulation, rotation, and other distortions. He may have trouble differentiating between letters and words which are mirror images of one another, such as: "b" and "d," "on" and "no," or "saw" and "was." This type of letter confusion is normal to a certain extent in the first grade (We are reminded of the proverbial: "Mind your p's and q's."), but in these children the problem persists longer and in far greater severity. They may be impaired in depth perception, spatial relations, and in the differentiation of foreground from background. This is demonstrated by the child's poor performance in the hidden-picture game where he is asked to find the objects and animals which are partially concealed in a complex scene. Auditory perceptual problems may also be present. Again, this is not in the area of auditory acuity, which is usually normal, but rather in fine auditory discrimination. For example, these children may have trouble discriminating between two words of similar, but not identical sound such as: "book" and "brook." Auditory synthesis may be impaired, that is, when a word is verbally presented, but broken down into its phonic elements, the child has difficulty fusing the parts to make a word he would ordinarily recognize. For example, he does not recognize: "b — o — t" to be "boat." Also, he may not be able to accurately imitate rhythmic patterns of tapping.

Tactile perception may also be deficient. The child may exhibit astereognosis, so that he cannot recognize letters marked out on his palm or tell the denomination of a coin placed in his palm when his eyes are closed. Aphasias may also be present, as well as other problems in organizing perceptions.

Poor retention of what is learned is another common symptom of minimal brain dysfunction. This is characteristically capricious in that there are times when the child appears to have good retention, and on other occasions one gets the feeling that he has "a brain like a sieve." He may not only have difficulty remembering what he has learned in school but may also not learn from his errors — thereby repeating his mistakes, no matter how serious the consequences. Often the memory impairment is confined to a specific sensory modality. For example, auditory memory is deficient while visual and tactile memory are intact. As already mentioned, my experience has been that the amphetamines and methylphenidate can help some of these children both in concentrating upon and retaining what they have learned.

The child may have difficulty in forming concepts and abstractions at an age when others are doing so. He therefore does not appreciate age-appropriate jokes and humor, has trouble with mathematics, and cannot understand the rules of games when he plays with other children. Such deficiencies may play a role in his becoming a social outcast.

Impulsivity is another problem often exhibited by these children. The child appears as if he has trouble "putting brakes" on his thoughts, feelings, and actions. This phenomenon probably contributes to the "catastrophic reaction" observed in younger children with this disorder. In this reaction to disturbing stimuli (the exact nature of which may not be known to the observer), the child exhibits a tantrum which does not have the angry element of the traditional temper tantrum but rather a quality of frustration, helplessness, and deep pain. The older child may verbalize his frustration over not being able to control himself. His teacher finds him disruptive in the classroom: he calls out his thoughts and leaves his seat frequently. He is easy prey to bullies because he cannot refrain from responding to taunts and provocations in any but the most primitive manner. Chlorpromazine and other tranquillizers can often reduce this symptom.

Related to the impulsivity is the perseveration of speech often seen in these children. They repeat the same thing many times like a broken record. It is as if they were "hooked" on a certain word, phrase, or topic and cannot "unhook" themselves. The child may persist in asking the same question until his parents are distraught.

Cerebral dominance may not have been strongly established in some of these children which results in problems in laterality. There may be mixed dominance, right-handedness and left-footedness, for example. Ambidexterity may also be a manifestation of this problem.

So-called "soft neurological signs" are often present. These can be roughly classified in two groups. The first consists of subtle, but definite physical signs of neurological impairment: minor gross or fine motor coordination deficits, slightly hyper- or hypoactive reflexes, and minor muscle asymmetry, for example. The second group of "soft neurological signs" consists of those which represent lags in neurological development. For example, the Babinski sign is usually repressed by the growth of higher centers by the twelfth to eighteenth month of life. A child of two-and-a-half with a Babinski sign has a pathological manifestation. At three his large toe may flex on plantar stimulation — and so the sign is no longer present.

As is true of other syndromes and diseases, no child exhibits all the signs and symptoms, but each will manifest some depending on the way in which his particular brain has been affected.

The reader who is interested in further information about the primary signs and symptoms of minimal brain dysfunction is referred to two NIMH monographs[2] which contain excellent bibliographies in addition to complete basic discussions.

THE SECONDARY SIGNS AND SYMPTOMS

In the past, some children with minimal brain dysfunction were considered to be suffering from purely psychogenic difficulties. There are, in fact, still some who hold the view that the total constellation of signs and symptoms which I have described is psychogenic in etiology. The treatment of these children by traditional psychotherapeutic techniques often proved futile, and their parents were burdened with guilt and unecessary expense. In my opinion, the first step in the therapy of most of these children is educational. Everything possible must be done to enhance their learning because their psychogenic problems, more often than not, are significantly related to their learning disability. In educating such children, one must first determine the exact nature and extent of the neurological impairment (especially in perceptual areas). Attempts should be made to educate primarily through the intact or better functioning sensory systems — just as the blind man learns to read tactilely with Braille. In addition, there are special educational techniques which are designed to strengthen the defective modality(ies). The education of these children is an expanding field, and many useful devices and approaches have been developed in recent years. Chemotherapy can also be very helpful.

Most children with minimal brain dysfunction develop secondary psychogenic difficulties. These often recede as the primary neurological impairments improve through natural growth or education. Parental guidance and understanding can also be helpful in alleviating these secondary psychogenic problems. Most children do not require more than special education, chemotherapy, and parental guidance. In some, however, the secondary problems reach such severity that psychotherapy is indicated. Sometimes family psychopathology or misguidance contributes significantly to the child's psychogenic symptoms. Sometimes, in spite of the parents' deep interest, appropriate handling, and healthy involvement with the child, he still develops significant psychogenic difficulties. This should not be surprising when one realizes that the disability can be so devastating that it colors the child's whole life. Wherever he goes, his difference from others is obvious to all; he cannot escape his impairments; and he cannot run from his humiliations.

The psychogenic problems of children with minimal brain dysfunction cannot be adequately understood without detailed consideration of their parents' problems as well. For clarity of presentation, therefore, further discussion is divided into two sections: 1) the problems which primarily stem from the parents, and 2) those difficulties which, for the most part, arise in the child.

The reactions of parents are subdivided into acute and chronic adaptations. In general, the acute adaptations are transient and occur as initial reactions to learning of the child's brain dysfunction. The chronic adaptations may be prolongations of the acute or may arise afterward. The distinction is of clinical importance because the acute reactions have a good chance of resolution either without treatment or with the kind of explanatory approach I present here; whereas the chronic reactions may become deeply entrenched and may warrant psychotherapeutic intervention. In some cases, the distinction may be unclear or of little clinical significance.

The adaptational reactions of the child do not lend themselves to differentiation between the acute and the chronic. The child has no acute reaction to learning of his disability; he grows up with it. It is rather a process of gradual realization of impairment and the insidious development of neurotic and even psychotic reactions. In my discussion of the child's signs and symptoms I will include both the explanatory approaches and the specific psychotherapeutic techniques I utilize when I work with the child alone.

ACUTE PARENTAL ADAPTIVE REACTIONS

The inappropriate acute psychological reactions of the parents of the neurologically impaired child, like most neurotic reactions, are attempts at adaptation. In this case, the adaptation is to the child with brain injury. The type of reaction, however, does not arise *de novo* on learning of the child's defect, but is determined, in part, by the personality structures of the parents.

The Denial Reaction

A common reaction when the parents are first confronted

with the diagnosis is denial. It will often take the form of doubting the doctor's competence or even of castigating him. The family may then embark upon a pilgrimage that can last for years. One expert after another is consulted, and those who confirm the original diagnosis are similarly reviled. Their quest, of course, is for the physician who will say that nothing is wrong or that the child will outgrow his difficulties. They are looking for the doctor who will help them deny what they do not wish to see or hear. During this "doctor-shopping" campaign, the child is not only deprived of valuable and necessary educational and therapeutic experiences, but there usually occurs a deepening of psychogenic problems that might have been alleviated if the parents had accepted the diagnosis. Furthermore, during this search for a "good" doctor, the child receives inferentially from the parents the communication: "We don't like you the way you are. We want you to be different. We'll find a doctor who'll tell us you are the way we want you to be." The devastating effect such statements may have in lowering the child's self-esteem will be elaborated upon in the section devoted to the child's psychogenic problems.

The Overprotective Reaction

Another way of denying the child's illness in the early stages is to overprotect him. By keeping the child an infant, his parents seek not to expose his defects in maturation, and hence avoid confrontation with the painful reality. One insightful mother put it very well: "If your child can't walk, then carry him. Then no one will know what's wrong with him."

Such infantilization, of course, robs the child of the opportunity to mature in areas in which he might be capable. This not only adds to the patient's physiological and psychological pathology, but brings about even greater feelings of inadequacy than might have been appropriate or anticipated with the given defects.

The Angry Reaction

Once the parent has accepted the diagnosis, a host of further reactions are common. Anger is one of the most ubiquitous. It takes the form of preoccupation with such thoughts as: "Why me?" "Why not my neighbor or the guy at work?" or "What a curse!" Such anger, which I consider to be a normal reaction in the early stages of acceptance, stems from the feelings of helplessness and frustration one usually feels with such a child. The angry reaction becomes abnormal when it is prolonged, thereby replacing positive action. It may not ever be dissipated completely, and the physician dealing with these parents must be able to accept and handle it. Some parents direct their anger into socially useful channels. In their irritation with "neglectful and slipshod school systems" which fail to provide adequate facilities for their children, they may rise to the occasion and fight the "powers that be." Through such efforts they may be instrumental in setting up schools and other facilities for the benefit of their own and other brain injured children. Community organizations for brain injured children not only serve their overt purpose of improving the lot of these children, but are psychologically healthy and constructive outlets for many of the pent-up feelings of the parents.

The Inappropriate Guilt Reaction

The inappropriate guilt reaction is a common one in the early stages of acceptance of the brain injured child's illness. It takes the form of preoccupation with various transgressions and errors which might have brought about the illness: "It's all my fault. I didn't go to church enough." "God punished me for my sexual life before I was married." "Masturbation, that's what did it; it ruined my sperm."

Classical psychoanalytic theory postulates that such guilt is often related to unconscious hostility toward the child, and that the illness represents the magical fulfillment of these unconscious hostile wishes. It is probable that the classical formulation does apply in some cases. This guilt reaction is ubiquitous, however, and the classical position thus ascribes morbid hostility to just about all parents of organically damaged children.

In my opinion, the guilt in these parents is more often understood as a futile attempt to control an uncontrollable situation. The parent, by attributing the cause to himself, puts into his own hands the power to control what might otherwise be considered an uncontrollable disaster. By making the illness his own fault, he implies that he could prevent its recurrence in the future by not practicing those transgressions which allegedly brought it about. The guilt, then, is a defense mechanism against existential anxiety.[3] I have occasionally seen references to this type of guilt mechanism,[4] but it has not, I believe, been given the attention it deserves.

If the approach to such parents is one of uncovering unconscious hostility, they may become even more guilty and anxious. Direct denial by the physician of the parent's culpability is most often useless, because the parent must then face the existential impotency he cannot tolerate. The parents should be told that such reactions are common, that they are manifestations of their love of the child, and that it shows they care and wish they could have prevented the illness in some way. Referral to a community organization for brain injured children can be of help in relieving this guilt. Working with these associations gives such parents a feeling of some control over the child's fate and future, and mitigates the need to obtain this control through magical mechanisms such as inappropriate guilt. In addition, these activities are reparative and guilt-alleviating; that is, such action brings about the child's improvement, therefore, there is less to be guilty about.

Another form of guilt seen in the parents of these children is that which is related to the hostility which such parents must inevitably feel toward the neurologically impaired child. Many of these children are terrible burdens and may significantly disrupt their families. The frustrations and disappointments which their parents suffer cannot help but result in angry reactions toward the child — reactions which may or may not be repressed, depending on the parent's degree of comfort with his hostility. Some parents cannot accept their anger as predictable and inevitable in such a situation and feel very guilty about it.

Reassuring them that mild to moderate resentment is the norm can sometimes be helpful. Group discussions, among parents of brain injured children, may be even more effective in alleviating this form of guilt because the parent himself experiences the hostile verbalizations of others and thereby feels less unique and loathesome.

The Blame Reaction

In guilt reactions, the individual himself is blamed. In the blame reaction, someone else is considered to be at fault. Like the guilt reaction, it places responsibility in the hands of mankind and protects one against the feelings of helplessness so common in such parents.

On looking for someone to blame, the parent may select the doctor who, being fallible, has defects which now become capitalized upon. One doctor may become generalized to all doctors who are then considered bunglers, incompetents, or charlatans. The doctor "at fault" may never hear that he is to blame, but the brain injured child may never be able to forget it, so inculcated is it into him through the parents' complaints. Such an adaptation may undermine the child's faith in and respect for his physicians with resultant interference with the therapeutic benefits he might otherwise derive from the relationships.

Direct denial of culpability by the doctor or his colleagues is often of little help. But the more the parents can be helped to participate in the child's progress, the more they will feel control, with less need to utilize the blame reaction as a controlling mechanism. In addition, such an approach will lessen the anger that is also being discharged in the blame adaptation.

"What to Tell People?"

A common problem that arises in the early stages of accepting the diagnosis of minimal brain injury is that of "what to tell people?" "People" here can be broken down into three

694

groups: 1) the child, 2) the siblings, and 3) the world at large (the most important members of which are those "vicious, gossiping neighbors").

Regardless of the particular term by which the syndrome is known to the parents, the basic disorder is an organic disease of the brain, and some attempt should be made to impart this concept to the child. There is no term which is intrinsically anxiety-provoking to the child; but any term can become so if the parents consider its use to be detrimental to him. I believe that the child should be given a simple and yet meaningful explanation of his disorder — one that is commensurate with his age and ability to understand. He should be told that a small part, or parts of his brain, are not working right, and that as time goes on, as he grows and if he works at it, things should improve. Some particular reference to the child's specific impairments which result from the neurological deficit should be described to make the explanation more meaningful. For example, "The part of your brain which helps you remember is weak. You have to work harder than other children to make things stick in your brain." The explanation should be concrete because these children often have difficulties in conceptualizing. It is easier for such a child to understand that things don't stick well in his brain than to appreciate that he has a poor memory. It is important to impart the notion that the lesion is discrete (Complete neurophysiological accuracy has no place in such a discussion.) to lessen the likelihood that the child will generalize and consider his isolated impairment evidence of total worthlessness. The child is not born with an exaggerated reaction to any term; he gets it from his parents, doctors, and teachers. If they take a more matter-of-fact attitude, so will the child. To avoid disclosure or to couch explanations in euphemisms results in the child's thinking that his illness is far worse than brain damage, an illness too terrible to talk about. The anxieties thus aroused may then cause the formation of anxiety-alleviating defense mechanisms, neurotic or psychotic. In addition, such attitudes make the child distrustful of his parents, a situation which can have serious psychological consequences.

The way in which disclosure can, on occasion, dramatically alleviate such anxiety and defense mechanisms is illustrated by the following example.

Example 1

Ben was a twelve-year-old boy known to be brain damaged since age five. At age nine, he became preoccupied with dinosaurs and collected books on the subject. The topic occupied a major portion of his conversation. At the same time, he became much more withdrawn and would spend hours on the floor clapping his hands or banging blocks together. He was referred because a diagnosis of schizophrenia had been added to that of brain damage by the school psychologist, and the parents sought another professional opinion.

Clinical evaluation confirmed the psychologist's diagnosis. Ben was in a special class for children with brain injury, cerebral palsy, and other disorders associated with impaired learning. Acting on the advice of physicians and teachers, however, the parents had never told Ben what was wrong with him. His questions about this were always evaded, even though he was of normal intelligence and would have well understood reasonable explanations.

In the initial interview Ben drew a picture of a dinosaur and explained, "The dinosaur is the biggest animal that ever lived, but he was also the stupidest because he had such a very small brain. He was so big and clumsy he could destroy whole cities when he walked." Clearly, the patient considered himself big and clumsy with a small, stupid brain. The hostility expressed in the destruction of cities was found on further investigation to be related not only to the frustrations he suffered by being neurologically impaired, but also to the anger he felt toward his parents for their secretiveness about his disorder.

The parents were advised to tell Ben about his brain injury as directly and honestly as they could. They were reluctant to do this because of so many previous warnings to the contrary. They were finally convinced to follow my advice. I also told them I would continue to work with Ben, not only to discuss the diagnosis but also to help him with his reactions to the disclosure.

Two weeks and six sessions later, the child was free from the dinosaur obsession, the autistic withdrawal, and the hand-clapping and block-banging preoccupations. Although still left with a host of neurotic reactions so commonly seen in the child with minimal brain dysfunction — marked feelings of inferiority, hypersensitivity to criticism, marked difficulties in interpersonal relationships — there was no evidence of the psychotic symptomatology present for the three-year period prior to his first visit.

Although Ben's case is the most dramatic, I have seen many children in whom there has been marked alleviation of secondary neurotic and psychotic symptomatology following such open discussion.

The book I wrote for such children telling them about brain dysfunction has also been helpful.[5] It has been my experience that such direct discussion has been therapeutic in most children who are capable of appreciating the book's contents.

The general rule of openness and honesty should extend to the siblings. They, too, will become anxious and suspicious of the parents if frank discussion is avoided. The ideal attitude that the parents can transmit to the siblings is one of acceptance of the child for what he is, sympathetic tolerance for his defects, and expectation that he will contribute to the household activities in areas of competence. If parents and siblings look upon the child as a total cripple, feelings of inadequacy above and beyond what might be expected may arise in him. A statement such as, "Don't give me that excuse. Just because you're brain injured and have trouble in school doesn't mean that you can't do your share of work around the house, just like your brothers and sisters," can be salutary in many ways. It prevents the child from neurotically using the brain injury as a maneuver to avoid responsibility for acts which he can perform; it enhances the child's self-esteem by the parents' faith and expectation that he can perform well in certain areas; and it lessens the intensification of sibling rivalries which so often become exaggerated beyond their usual fierceness when the child becomes too much of a "privileged character." In regard to the latter, statements to siblings such as: "Yes, we do have to give him extra attention in certain things, but in many ways he is treated the same as you. We'd do the same for you if you were neurologically impaired," can be helpful.

The problem of what to tell the neighbors is often a difficult one. The conflict seems to revolve around two issues: if the parents are open, they may be providing an honest atmosphere, but the child may be stigmatized and rejected by the neighbors and their children. If they do not tell them openly, the child is allegedly being protected from their alienation. The latter course, however, communicates to the child that the parents are ashamed of what he is, and the previously described deleterious effects of secretiveness may result.

I favor the first course of action. All things considered, the wisest approach for the parents is one which would be similar to that recommended if the child suffered from any other chronic illness. If they are matter-of-fact, there is a greater chance that the neighbors will be. However, even with such attitudes, there may be people who will react insensitively to the child. When such a situation arises, it should be treated like any other circumstance of a neighbor reacting inappropriately to one's child. The child should be told that one occasionally meets people who have strange ideas and the neighbor should be looked upon as idiosyncratic. In addition, it has been my experience that the neighbors usually become *more* tolerant when they are told what is wrong. The "bad boy" who should be taken in hand becomes the brain injured boy who cannot be held as responsible for his antisocial behavior as can a normal boy.

Relative to the issue of "what to tell people," the therapist who does not tell the parents or who couches his explanations in platitudes or euphemisms must be mentioned briefly. It is clear that the salutary effects of all that has been said would not be possible if the therapist himself cannot or will not react to the illness with acceptance, honesty, and openness.

CHRONIC PARENTAL ADAPTIVE REACTIONS

Although the chronic adaptational reactions may be prolongations of the acute phase, they may arise insidiously months, or even years, after the diagnosis has been made. These reactions are deeper and more complex, often requiring intensive psychotherapy or psychoanalysis if there is to be any chance of their alleviation.

The Masochistic Reaction

While many theories have been proposed to explain masochistic behavior,[6] I use the term masochist primarily to refer to someone who seeks out situations which bring about personal pain. It is the masochist's idea, so well described by Thompson,[7] that the only way he can get love is to suffer. He does not consider himself worthy of attracting anyone who will treat him benevolently. He sees his choice to be between being treated malevolently and being totally ignored. He selects pain as preferable to loneliness. He is too insecure to refuse the requests and demands made upon him, no matter how inappropriate or cruel. He feels that he must submit to the will of others or be abandoned. The masochist also measures the depth of his love by the pain he will suffer for the loved one. To the latter he essentially communicates: "I must love you very much if I am willing to suffer so much on your behalf." Pertinent to this discussion is the fact that the neurologically impaired child may be utilized by the parents in the furtherance of masochistic gratification. The sicker the child is (or is kept), the greater the neurotic gratification of the masochistic parent. The therapist should recognize, then, that such parents are blocked in following through with recommendations to help the child, even though they may pay lip service to such attempts and act as if they were trying.

Masochism can be used to express hostility. Although the masochist asks for help, he may unconsciously thwart the doctor and leave him frustrated and angry. As described by Thompson,[7] additional hostility can be expressed through making the doctor feel guilty: "After all this time, you haven't helped him a bit, Doctor." The therapist may fall into the masochist's trap by reacting with hostility and retaliation, unwittingly helping the masochist add to his suffering. The child, too, can become the target of such hostility and guilt-provoking maneuvers: "Look how much I do for you, you ungrateful good-for-nothing child; you show no appreciation."

The martyr, in my opinion, is basically masochistic, and what I have said above about the masochist holds for him as well. Both believe that the only way they can get love from significant people is to suffer, but the martyr gains additional benefit by advertising his woes and misery. The martyr is saying essentially, "How noble I am to be able to endure what others cannot. People will certainly admire me when they see or hear of my courage in suffering." He attempts to enhance his self-esteem through exhibitionistic self-torture. The martyr may advertise his woes in order to elicit this sympathetic admiration, or he may suffer in silence, praising himself for his courage and strength in not crying out. Although mute, he still communicates his agony non-verbally through such mechanisms as sighs and painful facial expressions. The martyr who publicizes his agony gains the esteem of those who are impressed by such maneuvers; the martyr who mutely enjoys his pain earns *additional* veneration from those who consider suffering in silence an added virtue. By his moaning and complaining and appeals to pity, the martyr tends to evoke sympathetic comments and commiseration. Such reactions from the therapist are definitely contraindicated. They only serve to reinforce the martyristic reaction, much to the detriment of the child.

The Overprotective Reaction

The overprotective reaction often serves to help the parent

deny the child's illness by preventing him from reaching that stage of maturity which would expose his defects. In addition, such children are perfect targets for parents who have strong overprotective needs which are derived from other sources. The overprotection can be a reaction formation to unconscious hostility toward the child; it can serve to compensate for feelings of inadequacy about parenthood; and, of course, the more helpless the child is, or is made to be, the greater the opportunity to prove one's adequacy and "superadequacy" as a parent. Overprotection can also serve to gratify the parent's strong dependency needs vicariously through the child. Projection of the parent's self onto the child and excessive indulgence of the latter achieve the effect of gratifying his own great dependencies without stigma or shame. Lastly, a parent with low self-esteem and feelings of worthlessness in general may attain a feeling of being needed and wanted by deluding himself into believing he is "all the child has in the world." In all of the above, the neurotic system thrives on the child's helplessness, and unconscious mechanisms keep the parent from that which would take the child out of a dependent, helpless state.

The Withdrawal Reaction

The child might be used in the furtherance of justifying the parents' avoidance of meaningful interpersonal contacts. The mother who has "nothing else to give others," taken up as she is with ministering to the needs of the child, may also be too tired and weary for social and sexual relations with her husband. This may even extend to the avoidance of responsibility to the child's siblings. Closely related is the utilization of the child in the expression of hostility to others, for the withdrawals described above may contain not only aspects of fear of involvement but elements of hostile removal of gratification from others as well.

The "Doctor-shopping" Reaction

The doctor-shopping syndrome in the service of denial is

not always discontinued once the diagnosis is accepted. The quest now changes from one in which an attempt is made to find a physician who says nothing is wrong to one for a doctor who will provide the magical cure. Such parents often greet the newest physician with fawning flattery, praising him for his skill and deprecating the numerous doctors who have preceded him. It is the naïve physician who is taken in by all of this sycophancy and joins the parents in the delusion of his own deification. The doctor should recognize that he is being bribed with flattery and idolatrized in the service of the parents' need for a magical cure. He knows that with such a come-on, "the handwriting is on the wall," and that the parents will ultimately throw him on the ever-growing heap of fallen idols as he proves himself to be unable to bring about the miracles he was deified to perform. His successor will hear *his* name added to the list of the maligned.

As their frustration grows, the parents become prey to every quack and charlatan who offers them a miraculous cure. The quicker and more prodigious the proclaimed cures, the more enthusiastic and worshipful the parents become. Then proselytization, in the service of bolstering their hope and denying the defects of the healer, only adds more followers to the cult of the particular hero of the day.

After a succession of disillusionments, attitudes of resentment, bitterness, and distrust develop toward even the most competent and dedicated of doctors. All this, of course, has a devastating effect upon the child's ability to profit from a relationship with a therapist. Since the child's reactions to the therapist so often mirrors those of his parents, cycles of deification and subsequent iconoclasm make it extremely difficult to establish a meaningful relationship.

The therapist must try to prevent his deification at the outset. He should explain to the parents that he will do his best, but also that he has no power to grow nerve cells where they do not exist. He must try to interrupt the futile quest, confront the parents with the consequences of their behavior, assure them that he appreciates that they are trying to do the best they can for the child out of love for him, and explain that by their quest they are actually interfering with his progress. Furthermore, it must be strongly emphasized that such shifting of therapists prevents a trusting relationship from forming, not only with those treating the child for his emotional disorders, but with all other authority figures who are trying to be of help to him. Lastly, they should be told that all therapists are fallible, that none can perform miracles, but that there are many good and devoted ones who can be of help to their child. If this approach is successful, the wasteful pilgrimage may be interrupted long enough to effect some therapeutic progress.

Although the chronic adaptive reactions of the parents often require intensive psychotherapy or psychoanalysis if there is to be any progress toward their alleviation, the therapeutic value of the community organization for brain injured children cannot be overemphasized. Reference has already been made to some of the salutary aspects of these groups. A discussion of the therapy of these parents would not be complete, however, without further comment on the function and activities of these associations.

These groups are comprised primarily of parents of neurologically impaired children, but they attract professionals and interested nonparents as well. They provide a wealth of information and services for such patients and are active in forming schools, special classes, and recreational programs for these children. They are often the lobbyists who get bills passed, money allocated, funds raised, buildings built, and teachers taught. The milieu is constructive and creative. The parents' search for magical cures and bitter preoccupation with their lot in life are replaced, in part, by constructive action. Further, these groups provide the parents with hope through positive action, enhancement of self-worth, and a feeling of camaraderie. Seeing others with similar problems helps them feel less defective and depressed about their own difficulties. The groups also provide opportunities for the child to meet other brain injured children, the value of which will be discussed in the next section.

ADAPTIVE REACTIONS IN THE CHILD

The Fear Reaction

It is reasonable to expect that the brain injured child, ill-equipped as he is to cope with the world, will fear venturing forth into it. He is exposed to many frustrations and humiliations which the normal child is not. He may not run as well, get the point of a game as quickly, read as well as others in his class, or perform up to his peers in a host of other activities. He fears each new undertaking for the disappointment it may bring him. He tends to generalize and foresee failure even in areas of competence. Such fears can be reduced in a number of ways. Helping the child delineate his areas of capability so he can avoid what he is intrinsically poor in, while participating in activities of competence can be very helpful. Also, if he can improve through training, treatment, and growth, he will experience less fear of tasks in his deficient areas.

The overly permissive parent may increase the child's fears. All children need the reassurance of parental guidance and control. Deprived of this, they become fearful, anxious, and insecure. The neurologically impaired child, because of his greater degree of incapacitation, needs much more supervision and regulation than the average child. In their absence, he not only fears, but he may suffer guilt for what he does when uncontrolled. An orderly, predictable environment with appropriate restraints can be beneficial in reducing the child's fears.

If these fears have been compounded by his ignorance about his disorder, simple direct discussion, as I have shown, can help lessen them.

The Withdrawal Reaction

There are various maneuvers that the child can utilize to avoid the above-described fears, humiliations, and rejections The withdrawal reaction is one of the more common. The world of reality becomes too threatening; isolation and reversion to inner fantasy become more gratifying. In the extreme, autism and hallucinations may result. It is important to note here that in the non brain injured psychotic, the withdrawal is often on the basis of delusional ideas about the world of reality (although originally the world may really have been as malevolent as the psychotic sees it). In the brain injured child, there is often more harshness in the reality from which he is withdrawing. Because it is based on reality, this type of psychotic reaction is more amenable to change. The previously described case of Ben, the twelve-year-old boy who was psychotically obsessed with dinosaurs, is a case in point. In some brain injured children, however, as Goldfarb has demonstrated,[8] the psychotic symptoms are an intrinsic part of the brain damage syndrome, and these are most resistant to treatment.

The child's withdrawal may result in his failing to acquire skills which he might have been otherwise quite capable of learning. He becomes more inexperienced and naïve about the world than need be.

To the degree that one can make the environment less threatening and more inviting, one can also diminish the chances that the child will utilize withdrawal and autistic defenses. Placement of the child in special classes with children with similar difficulties can be of great help. In such an environment, he feels more acceptable and is less subject to exclusion and embarrassment. Social and recreational groups for brain injured children serve a similar purpose.

The Regressive Reaction

Another adaptation is that of regression to levels of behavior even more immature or infantile than might be expected from the particular degree of impairment. The most common regressive manifestations are enuresis, rocking, baby talk, whining, silliness, clinging, temper tantrums, thumbsucking, and balking at assuming age-appropriate responsibilities such as dressing, making one's bed, and doing chores. Here, too, the child is protected from the embarrassments and rejections he might encounter if he were to attempt to function at a higher level. As previously mentioned, the overprotective mother may deepen this adaptation consciously or unconsciously.

In the treatment of these regressive symptoms the therapist should strongly discourage the parental indulgence and participation which is so often present. Often this is very subtle. For example, the parent might point out all the child's homework errors so that he can get a good grade. The child is thereby deprived of the anxiety over failure which is an important impetus to learning. The child's neurological impairment may be used as the parents' rationalization for allowing a perpetuation of the regressive symptoms.

In my sessions with these children I often point out to them that these symptoms may be contributing to their alienation from peers by saying, for example, "When you get silly and use baby talk the other children don't want to play with you." I also confront the child with his regressive symptoms when he exhibits them to me, and I communicate as well my emotional reactions: "If you're going to act so silly, I'm not going to continue playing this game with you. It's no fun for me when you don't play seriously. And I know you can. I think this is one of the reasons why some of the children don't like playing with you." Most children can exert some conscious control over these symptoms, psychodynamic factors notwithstanding.

Neurotic Utilization of the Organic Symptom

Some brain injured children will use the disorder to rationalize nonaction in areas of competence. They may say, "I'm brain damaged, so I can't do anything." The answer to this, of course, should be: "Yes, you are brain damaged; and it is true that there are some things that you cannot do as well as others, but that doesn't mean you can't do anything." They may tend to generalize and interpret their isolated defects as meaning that they are totally worthless. The child might say, "I'm just no good; I can't read." A parent might reply: "There is no question that it's harder for you to learn to read; however, there are many things you do and say that make me happy to be with you and have you as a son."

706

Perseveration

Although perseveration is generally considered an organic manifestation, it also has, in my opinion, significant psychogenic elements. It can be used to gain attention. By repeating the same questions, the child prolongs a conversation and thereby avoids the dreaded isolation which is often his lot. This is not to deny that such repetitions may be related to the child's inability to understand or retain the offered answer; but often the issue is one in which the child has demonstrated understanding. I encourage parents to cease the discussion after a few rounds and to express their reactions to it: "Look, this is getting on my nerves. I've answered that question four times. That's enough. Let's talk about something else." I suggest that the parent not only provide the new topic but also start discussing it in order to divert the child. If the child still persists, I recommend that they tell the child that they will not respond to his further comments on that subject. They must then strictly carry out their warning.

Sometimes the perseverated issue is one which has important underlying psychological significance which might not be immediately apparent from the ostensible topic the child is reiterating. The next child to be presented in this chapter repetitiously complained of pain deep inside his "tushy" as well as eye pain. He also sniffed many foods before ingestion and hesitated to eat those which he considered foul. I considered these preoccupations to be a reflection of his feelings of self-loathing related to his awareness of his deficits. Obnoxious material within him (his feces) is causing him trouble (pain inside his "tushy"); he doesn't have to add to his difficulties by ingesting further objectionable material such as malodorous food. His eye pain probably symbolized his awareness of his perceptual impairment, that is, he wasn't "seeing things right." The mother was advised to state simply that there was nothing wrong with his tushy, eyes, and the food he was eating and to discuss it no further. I, too, refused to engage in similar conversations. Focus on these particular symptoms would have only served to entrench them. I believed that with enhanced competence gained through education, medication, and psycho-therapy, he would feel better about himself and these preoccupations would lessen.

Sometimes — and this is especially true of younger brain injured children — the perseveration is related to a desire for positive reinforcement of a previously rewarded response. For example, when the child is asked to count, the conversation may go like this:

Child: One.
Parent: Right, keep going.
Child: Two.
Parent: Good!
Child: Three.
Parent: Very good!
Child: Three.
Parent: Yes. Go on. What comes after three?
Child: Three.
Parent: Let's start again.
Child: One, two, three, three, three ——

The child here does not know how to count past three. Since three has been reinforced, he repeats it. He wants more compliments. He is similar to the child who tells a joke, gets a laugh, and then repeats the joke to enjoy once again the favorable response from those around him.

The Clowning Reaction

Clowning is another common adaptation. The child is referred to as a clown or freak, and he responds by playing the role to the extreme. It is as if he were saying: "They call me a freak; it's not because I am one, but it's because I *have chosen to be one.* To prove it, I'll act like one. See, I can turn on at will." The proof here, of course, is specious because, although he can turn it on at will, he cannot turn it off to the degree that he will not be labeled an "oddball." As Eisenberg puts it so well, "having been ridiculed when laughter was the very opposite of what they sought, they maintain the fiction that they are play-acting and seek the notoriety they fear they cannot escape."[9]

In my work with children who utilize this reaction I try to get them to appreciate that although they may enjoy some temporary attention by their antics, those who laugh at them are not truly their friends — they do not invite the clowner to their parties and they do not seek him out. When the child exhibits his silliness in session, I do not encourage it with laughter but rather react coldly to it and respond with comments such as: "It's behavior like that that makes children not want to play with you" or "To me, you're no fun when you act that way. Enough of that baby stuff." I then try to direct the child toward more mature activities.

Impulsivity

Although the brain injured child's impulsivity has an organic substrate there may be psychogenic contributions as well. If the child has been overprotected, the symptom may have been indulged. Anxiety increases impulsivity in most children whether or not they are neurologically impaired. The impulsive child may be singled out for bullying because the bully quickly sees that the child's inability to react with calm and restraint makes him predictably susceptible to taunts.

Most impulsive children can exert some conscious control over their outbursts — regardless of the factors, both organic and psychogenic, which may be contributing to their symptom. In the therapeutic session, one can help the organic child learn to inhibit himself. For example, the third child to be presented in this chapter often reacted with tears and effusive self-denigration when he would lose a game. During a game of checkers, as I was about to make a double jump, I said: "I'm going to make a move now which might upset you. Let me see if you can hold yourself back from screaming out and calling yourself names." When the child did exhibit self-restraint, I would compliment him. The greater the organic component in the child's impulsivity, the more one must resort to the child's utilization of conscious control as a therapeutic maneuver; but even when the psychogenic elements are significant, encouraging its use can be salutary. Helping the child appreciate the untoward consequences of his impulsivity can also help motivate him to restrain himself. I might say, for example: "Those boys pick on you because they know that you won't ignore them when they tease you. When you stop crying and screaming back, they'll stop teasing you because then it won't be any fun for them anymore."

Reactions to the Learning Impairment

Some neurologically impaired children are exquisitely sensitive to their deficits. Such insight is a mixed blessing. On the one hand, it may serve to motivate the child to improve while on the other hand, it may enhance his psychic pain. Such children have a strong tendency toward self-deprecation. They also tend to generalize and consider their isolated defects to be proof that they are totally worthless as human beings.

As mentioned, it is important to impart the notion that only one small part of the brain is affected — the part that has to do with learning. Such children must be repeatedly told that the rest of themselves works fine; that just because one small part of themselves is not working well does not mean that they are completely worthless; and that it takes them longer to learn things and they have to work harder to do so. The point that no one is perfect and that everyone makes mistakes and has defects must be repeated many times over. Often, I will comment on my own deficiencies and errors as they may be exhibited in the course of my interchanges with the child. For example, if I cannot hear the child, I might say, "Please speak a little louder. The nerves inside my ears don't work too well and I have a little trouble hearing. Just as you have to work harder to learn, I have to work harder to hear." Or, when playing checkers, I might remark: "Gee, I missed that one. I'd better pay more attention to the game."

The child's feeling of shame over his learning impairments can be lessened if he is placed in a class with children with similar problems. When a school requests my opinion regarding class placement, I give this consideration highest priority. Some schools prefer to place neurologically impaired children in normal classes and only take the child out of the classroom for special instruction. Although this plan may be all right for very *minimally* brain injured children, most are mortified by such an arrangement. With it they not only must face the painful comparison with normal peers throughout most of the day, but in addition, when they are singled out to leave the room for special instruction, they suffer further humiliation.

The Anger Reaction

There are many reasons why anger is commonly seen in these children. There is much which frustrates them — things which continue to frustrate them in spite of their strongest efforts. They are rejected by peers for reasons which they are often ill-equipped to understand. Even their parents will often prefer their normal siblings. (I have known a number of parents who consciously or unconsciously omit mentioning their brain injured children when discussing their families.) Their poor impulse control often prevents them from appropriately holding back their anger — thereby compounding their difficulties and providing them with another reason to be angry.

The anger may be directly expressed; but more often it is discharged by means of neurotic (and sometimes, psychotic) mechanisms. It can only be lessened if the basic impairments which contribute to its formation can be reduced or allievated by education, medication, and psychotherapy.

The Low Self-Esteem Reaction

The problem of low self-esteem is almost universal with brain injured children. As with most psychological symptoms, the roots are complex. In Chapter 10 I discussed factors which contribute to the self-esteem problems of children in general. Here only those factors which are of particular importance in the etiology and therapy of low self-esteem in the neurologically impaired child are discussed.

Whereas I recognize that a healthy parent will not be completely accepting of *everything* in the brain injured child, neither will the loving parent generalize and consider the child totally worthless because of certain defects. The child's self-image will, in part, mirror that of the parents and he will generalize to the extent that they do. The parents who doctor-shop, who hide the diagnosis from child, family, and neighbors, and who overprotect or deny the illness all share in common the basic attitude of not accepting the child for what he is. The parents with inordinately high academic standards who equate education and intelligence with happiness will not accept a child who might become a perfectly adequate tradesman or craftsman and, in his uncomplicated way, have a placid and rewarding life. Such parents are, in effect, saying to the child, "You are a totally worthless person because you aren't smart in school." The parents who put great emphasis on sports or physical prowess may reject the poorly coordinated child whose chances of academic gratification and competence in many other areas are good. These parents, too, may consider their child totally worthless because of their own neurotic need to mold him into some preconceived pattern of what the worthwhile child should be like. The therapist who can bring about alteration in such parental attitudes performs a vital service indeed for the child with minimal brain dysfunction.

Few of us reach the nirvana of Erikson's eighth stage wherein the individual accepts himself totally for what he is with pride and dignity.[10] However, if there is any chance of even approaching this level, it must come at the beginning from parents who accept the child with the same pride and dignity they hope some day he will have for himself.

The child whose parents do reject him significantly because of his brain syndrome must be helped to appreciate that this does not mean that he is unlovable. He must be helped to appreciate that he can get affection from others — both at present and in the future. Meaningful involvements with peers as well as with adults can provide the child with substitutive gratifications to compensate him for the deprivation he suffers at home. With peers, this is more likely to occur if they are also brain injured, and every effort should be made to place the child in situations where he is most likely to form such relationships.

The tendency to consider isolated defects as proof of total worthlessness can contribute to a child's low self-esteem problem. The therapeutic approach to such generalizing has already been described.

Another factor of significance in the formation of strong feelings of self-worth is the realization of creative and productive gratifications. Such satisfactions are necessary, I believe, if one is to feel that there is any meaning to one's existence. Traditionally, the female has derived this gratification from child rearing and the male from competence in some skill, trade, or profession. This dichotomy is not unquestionably innate, and claims by women for the opportunity for satisfactions in both the domestic and worldly realms are certainly valid.

Guiding the neurologically impaired child onto a course that might ultimately result in marriage and child rearing is certainly possible in some cases, providing, of course, he or she is capable of attracting a mate and assuming marital responsibilities. For those who do not marry, occupations which allow closely related substitutes can be relatively fulfilling. These would include activities such as childcare in nursery schools, orphanages, and hospitals or babysitting, practical nursing, and working as housekeepers in families with children. If the brain injured child's intellectual capacity is in the trainable realm, he or she should be able to realize at least some of these child rearing gratifications. In addition, there are a host of trades and occupations which can help the brain injured person achieve a sense of mastery outside the home. Early training in these, with the conviction on the parents' part that the enterprise is honorable, creative, and rewarding, helps the child achieve this goal.

Anything that either mechanically or psychologically immobilizes the child and prevents him from pursuing his capabilities must be avoided. The resultant feelings of worthlessness and inadequacy can be devastating and constitute the difference between feeling that one is a valuable person leading a useful life, and the conviction that one is useless and suffering a meaningless existence.

The causes of inappropriate low self-esteem are many and varied and pervade most neurotic and psychotic symptom complexes. Although the latter are in part created to enhance self-esteem, they almost invariably end up by lowering it. Fear and anxiety through their associated feelings of helplessness, guilt with its intrinsic component of worthlessness, and depression with its hopeless and helpless elements are only a few of the psychological mechanisms which can contribute to feelings of inferiority.

In the treatment of such patients, one must deal not only with the specific causes of lowered self-esteem which are characteristic of the brain injured child, but also help the child deal with and work through those esteem lowering mechanisms which he shares in common with other neurotic and psychotic children.

In addition to all of the aforementioned reactions, the child with minimal brain dysfunction may exhibit any other neurotic or psychotic symptom(s) known to the non brain injured child. Because of his general psychological fragility, he is probably more prone to the development of such psychogenic symptoms than the child without organic impairment. For example, in the service of expressing repressed anger without significant guilt he may utilize a variety of mechanisms: compulsions, phobias, nightmares, displacement, projection, and depression in a manner identical to that utilized by children who are free of organic injury. Therefore, the therapy of such children must be directed to these problems as well if the child is to experience alleviation of his difficulties.

The Mutual Storytelling Technique can be of great assistance in the treatment of the neurologically impaired child. With such children, the practice of home-listening to the recorded sequences can be especially valuable. I suggest that the child bring his own tape recorder to the office, and we record our stories on both tape recorders simultaneously. The patient then has the opportunity for rehearing my communications at home. For the child with memory impairment, this practice may not only be helpful but in many cases vital.

714

Example 2

Mike, a six-and-one-half-year-old boy, showed manifestations of neurological impairment as well as superimposed psychogenic symptoms. He was born at full term but there was a two-minute delay in the initial cry and oxygen was administered until twenty minutes after birth. He did not walk until seventeen months of age; he was only babbling at two years, nine months; and understandable words did not appear until age three. His IQ varied from 64 to 95 on various tests of intelligence administered during the few years prior to his first visit.

My own rough clinical estimate was that Mike was functioning in the 75-85 range with high-average verbal ability. When first seen, he could recognize a few letters of the alphabet but could not read even the simplest words. He did not know the months and seasons of the year, nor could he add the simplest numbers. His reproduction of geometric figures was impaired and he was unable to understand age-appropriate jokes. The consulting child neurologist found him to be especially distracted by an array of visual stimuli although he was quite capable of appreciating them when the visual field was restricted.

Multiple psychogenic symptoms were also present. Mike was painfully insecure and chronically anxious. He continually sought reassurance that what he was doing was acceptable. He was exquisitely sensitive to his deficits and would become acutely distressed over his failures. There was a long-standing history of compulsive smelling of objects — especially foods he was preparing to ingest. During the three months prior to his first visit (and these were the main symptoms which brought him to my attention), Mike was obsessed with concerns about his eyes and anus; he had become very withdrawn; and he would giggle inappropriately while staring into space.

Mike's father, although well-meaning, was somewhat insensitive to his son's needs and only rarely involved himself in meaningful activities with him. He was very much absorbed in his business to the further detriment of the child. His mother, on the other hand, was unusually patient with him and was deeply committed to his welfare. From the earliest years, she sought appropriate medical attention and cooperated fully in his management. She at times was overprotective — but not significantly so. All things considered, I did not think that parental psychopathology was playing a significant role in this child's psychogenic difficulties. I could not learn of any specific traumas which might have brought about the more recent intensification of psychogenic symptoms, and I considered them to be the final result of accumulated stress and anxiety related to his organic impairments.

Mike was placed on chlorpromazine and dextroamphetamine sulphate and seen once weekly in psychotherapy. In a typical session he was first seen with his mother for general discussion and advice in management. Then about fifteen minutes was spent with the Mutual Storytelling Technique, and the remainder of the session was spent with more traditional play-therapeutic modalities. During the ensuing months there was a gradual alleviation of the more recently acquired symptoms. His somatic preoccupations diminished appreciably; there was far less sniffing; and he became far less withdrawn. However, giggling and intermittent staring into space still remained a problem when Mike told this story late in his eighth month of treatment:

Therapist: Once upon a time —— a long, long time ago —— in a far off land, far, far, far away —— way beyond the deserts —— way beyond the mountains —— way beyond the ocean —— there lived a ——
Patient: A sea.
Therapist: And this sea ——
Patient: Was a make-believe sea.
Therapist: And this make-believe sea had ——
Patient: Had dancing lobsters.
Therapist: Had dancing lobsters and ——
Patient: Alice in Wonderland. This is Walt Disney's Wonderland Story.
Therapist: What's the rule of this program?
Patient: This is Walt Disney's Wonderland Story.

716

Therapist: What's the rule of this program?

Patient: No talking.

Therapist: No. What's the rule of the program about telling stories from Walt Disney? Is that against the rules or not?

Patient: No.

Therapist: It is against the rules. The rule is that it has to be your own made-up story. Right?

Patient: Yes.

Therapist: So it can't be from Walt Disney. So let's start it again. All right?

Patient: All right.

Therapist: We have the sea and dancing lobsters. That's yours. That's made-up. Okay. Now you tell me a story about the sea and the dancing lobsters.

Patient: And there were clams and swimming shrimps and big giant sharks.

Therapist: And there were clams, swimming shrimps, and big giant sharks. Okay. Then what happened?

Patient: The sharks had a little boy shark and he was seven years old and he went out to play. He wasn't hanging around the mother and he played with his friends and they haven't teased him. He played every day until he got bigger. Then he was busy working without his mother. He was busy working. He was working and doing history and science. He was working for food under the sea.

Therapist: He grew food under the sea?

Patient: No. He got some food for the people to eat at the sea from the clams and the shrimp seafood.

Therapist: Did he get the food from the sea?

Patient: The man planted bait in it and they saw the man dropping bait and the bait sunk. They were dead bait and it was chopped up and they ate it.

Therapist: I see. So a man — not the sharks — got food from the sea.

Patient: Yeah, and they ate it and they got big and strong. Then one day a bad guy came and he was strong enough to eat up a diver and it was a diver he tried to kill, but when he ate it up —

Therapist: Excuse me. You're going much too fast for me.

I don't understand that part. Tell me that part again. A man came ——

Patient: This man came and he was a bad man, and he was stronger than the shark. So he swallowed him and he swallowed him alive.

Therapist: So he swallowed who alive?

Patient: The diver.

Therapist: The bad man swallowed the diver?

Patient: No. The shark swallowed the diver.

Therapist: And where does the bad man fit in here? Is the bad man the diver?

Patient: Yes. He tried to kill the fishes to eat.

Therapist: Oh, the bad man was a diver.

Patient: Yeah, and it was a lady in it and she was a witch that couldn't melt in water or in the sea.

Therapist: Was that different from the bad man?

Patient: Yes and I made a mistake — a bad diver lady and she was a meany witch.

Therapist: Oh, the bad diver lady was a witch?

Patient: Yes. She was stronger than a witch, you know. So the shark swallowed the witch and the witch did kill the shark 'cause she was alive in the tummy and got out of the shark with a slit and the shark died. But it took very long because she was a huge huge shark, as big as a whale.

Therapist: Then what happened?

Patient: Then the shark was dead and somebody came and killed the witch with a gun, a sea gun, and then the witch died and sunk. Then all were friends and were happily ever after. That was the last witch.

Therapist: I see. Is that the end of the story?

Patient: Yes.

Therapist: And what's the lesson of that story?

Patient: And there were many other witches too.

Therapist: And the lesson of that story is? What do we learn from that story?

Patient: That when you play people don't tease, but if you don't play then people tease.

Therapist: Any other lessons?

Patient: I don't know all the others.

Therapist: Hhmmm. Okay. Thank you very much. Now it's

time for Dr. Gardner to tell his story.
Patient: Aren't I going to hear it?
Therapist: Now I'm going to tell my story.
Patient: Oh.
Therapist: We're not going to have time to hear it today, but when you go home you can hear it.
Patient: All right.

At the beginning Mike starts to tell a story from Alice in Wonderland. After more than seven months of treatment he still does not recall one of the basic rules of the game: stories must be made-up. Had I allowed him to proceed, I would have not received a more revealing original story. I also would have deprived him of an exercise in recall which is so vital to the therapy of the child with brain injury.

The story demonstrates how difficult it may be to understand the stories of neurologically impaired children. These children often do not concern themselves with using proper antecedents, and they may introduce new characters without informing the listener. On the whole, these children are quite egocentric in that they do not concern themselves with whether or not their listener understands their communications. However, their stories may be rich sources of psychodynamic data, and it therefore behooves the therapist to patiently clarify every aspect of the story by interrupting and questioning. In this story, for example, in his initial discussion of the seven-year-old shark, Mike says, "He was busy working without his mother. He was busy working. He was working and doing history and science. He was working for food under the sea." Since I had every reason to believe that the last sentence applied to the shark that he was talking about, I was confused. What could the shark actually be doing "working for food under the sea?" So I asked him: "He grew food under the sea?" His response revealed that it was a man who was fishing for food under the sea. The man appeared in the child's mind just before he verbalized the last sentence but he saw no need to inform me of the introduction of this new character. Mike's stories often required clarification. There were times, however, when parts of his stories became so complicated that it was futile to attempt to understand them. In such cases, I would ask him to start again, or I let him go on and tried to base my story on the gist of his or on those fragments which I was clear about.

The story, I believe, is about the ambivalence he feels toward his mother — his conflict over dependency on her and the anger he harbors toward her for such dependency. The first hint of these problems comes early in the story when he says: "He (the seven-year-old shark who, of course, represents the patient) was busy working without his mother." The fisher with bait (who is also a diver and who midway in the story changes into a woman) represents his mother who provides him with food. But, as he sees it, there are "strings attached." Acceptance of her food results in his being locked in a symbiotic tie which is represented by the fishing line. On a deeper level, the fishing line symbolizes the umbilical cord. Although the mother was somewhat overprotective, his own strong dependency cravings were the more significant element in the formation of the symbiotic relationship. This is poignantly demonstrated by the shark swallowing the diver — Mike literally orally incorporates his mother. Then when his mother removes herself, he dies — a clear statement of his feelings that he cannot survive without intimate involvement with her. Next, he has his mother killed, probably in revenge for her having abandoned him (cut her way out of him). His hostility toward her, however, also stems from his exaggerated dependency. The parasitic person always harbors some anger toward his host. Whatever gratifications he may derive from the relationship, his position is a dangerous one; his very survival depends on the host's benevolence. At the latter's whim, the parasite can be deprived of all sustenance — a most precarious position indeed. The host too — whose blood is being sucked — cannot help but harbor resentment toward the parasite. Killing his mother, then, probably allows some expression of this dependency-derived hostility. Seeing her as a witch probably relates to his awareness, at some level, of his mother's inevitable unconscious hostility toward him — inevitable because his care required her to assume burdens she would not have had to bear had she borne a normal child. In addition, her failure to gratify *all* his demands is seen as hostility on her part which further deepens the witch image. And lastly, Mike's own hostility projected onto her probably contributes to his viewing her as a witch.

The closing statement: "Then all were friends and were happily ever after" is a common undoing mechanism to assuage the guilt and anxiety which the story evokes in the child. All are friends again; there have been no murders; everyone is alive; and there is no subsequent hostility. They "were happily ever after."

The lesson — "That when you play, people don't tease, but if you don't play, then people tease." — has no ostensible relationship to the story. Mike had little ability to conceptualize a moral and the request for one was not made with the anticipation that he would provide an appropriate one. It was posed to elicit further information of psychodynamic significance. It was successful in providing this. The moral suggests that there is some relationship between the problems exhibited in his story and his problems with peers. I decided, therefore, to tell a story which linked these two areas of his concern:

Once upon a time there were two boys and they were twin brothers. They were seven years old and they lived with their mother. Now although they were twin brothers and they looked exactly alike, they had different kinds of personalities. One of them liked to go out and play with other kids and the other one liked to stay at home and just sit around. Now the one who liked to play with other kids had a lot of fun, and he felt very good about himself. He knew that at times when you play with other kids there are fights, there's teasing; you may fall down and hurt yourself; but that's all worth it because of the fun and the good feeling you have about yourself when you do play with them.

Now his brother, however, was very different. His brother used to like to stay at home and because he wasn't having any fun he felt very mad and angry and sad all the time and his mind was filled with all kinds of things, angry thoughts, thoughts of witches, and sharks, and lobsters, and crabs, and things like that. He was a kind of mean boy. He was very unhappy.

Now one day a friend saw these two boys and he saw that the boy who stayed at home was very sad and mean and filled with angry thoughts. He said, "What's wrong with you? Why are you so sad?" And he started to mutter and talk about the lobsters, and the sharks, and the witches. The friend said, "You know, if you went out and played like your brother, I don't think you would have so many thoughts like that." Well, the boy thought that that was kind of foolish and he didn't do it. Then he looked at his brother and he saw how happy his brother was and that his brother wasn't so angry and that his brother wasn't so sad, and his brother wasn't thinking all the time of witches and lobsters and things like that.

So he said to the brother, "Why don't you think of lobsters and witches and crabs?" And what did the brother say?

Patient: I don't know.

Therapist: He said, "Why don't you think of those?" What did the brother say? "How is it that you're not thinking of it and I am?" What did the brother say?

Patient: "'Cause you're not playing with the little children and playing outside with the friends."

Therapist: "Why should I do that?" said the sad brother. What did the happy brother say?

Patient: "Because you'll have a lot of fun."

Therapist: "What's so good about having fun?" said the sad brother.

Patient: I forgot.

Therapist: The happy brother said, "Fun is fun. Fun is a lot of fun. When you have fun you feel good and when you have fun you don't think of all kinds of things like witches and crabs."

So the sad brother decided that he would try it and he was scared at first because he hadn't done it. He didn't know how to do certain things the other kids did know how to do, but he watched carefully and he learned many of the ways of playing with other children. And it was hard and it took a long time and at times it was scary and at times he was sad and at times he would

722

make mistakes, but when he didn't make mistakes and he didn't get into trouble he had a very nice time. He realized that his brother was right — that it's much more fun to go out and play and he found that he wasn't thinking so much of crabs and witches and he was thinking more of playing with other children and having a good time.

And do you know what the lesson of that story is?

Patient: That if you will play you will have fun. If you don't then you will think of all kinds of ugly thoughts like crabs or witches or ugly thoughts like animals, like ugly animals.

Therapist: Right. And that's the lesson of that story. The end. Is there anything you want to say about that program?

Patient: No.

The mother had been advised to encourage Mike to involve himself more with peers (preferably brain injured children with whom he would be more comfortable). In my story I urged him to tolerate the anxieties that such involvements will engender in him because meaningful friendships can be salutary in many ways. Having more fun, he will be less angry. Being less dependent on his mother should also contribute to a reduction of his anger. With less anger there should be a lessening of anger-related symptomatology such as morbid preoccupations with dancing lobsters and big giant sharks; seeing his mother as a witch; and the murder fantasies revealed in his story. Conceptualization problems notwithstanding, Mike was able to provide a meaningful moral to my story.

Two weeks later, during his ninth month of treatment, Mike told this story:

Once upon a time there was a big ocean and there was a big sunny day in summer and then the children went to the beach with their parents and it was in a Hawaii beach. No natives — rightful place —

Therapist: No natives what?

Patient: And this was a Hawaii beach, the same kind of — with an ocean and they saw a big wave splashed all over the beach. And then — just like that ocean right over there. What's that? Over there?

Therapist: You mean in that picture?

Patient: Yeah.

Therapist: That's an ocean.

Patient: Well, that's what I mean. And, that's how big that wave was.

Therapist: A very big wave?

Patient: A very big wave.

Therapist: All right.

Patient: And someone got into that deep, deep ocean and it was steep all over and not one bit of shallow water. And a witch came and pushed that little boy and the baby into the ocean and they were drowning and it took a long time and finally they were going downer and downer.

Therapist: Yes.

Patient: Like this, slowly.

Therapist: Yes.

Patient: Down.

Therapist: Okay, go ahead, and then what happened?

Patient: The boy came and saved them very quickly.

Therapist: You mean there was a boy and a baby?

Patient: No, yes. And there was a big boy who saved — and there was a big boy who —

Therapist: Saved who?

Patient: There was a big boy who had no name and there was no superboy who saved them.

Therapist: Saved who? When you say them?

Patient: And then a witch pulled, um, and the boy — and the big boy saved the little boy and the baby. And they lived happily ever —

Therapist: And the big boy saved the little boy and the baby?

Patient: Yeah, and they lived happily, only they had to kill but before he pushed — a horse was looking for them and then the horse was drowning.

Therapist: Who pushed the horse in the deep water?

Patient: The witch.

Therapist: Yes.

Patient: In the big ocean and then a big, big whale; a big, big shark, ate — took one bite and got one bite of him

— of the little horsy and the shark loved the horsy and ate the little baby too which pushed the baby into the shark again and then the shark ate the witch and that was the end of it then.

That's the end of the story and the shark was so full because he was hungry. And that's the end of the story.

Therapist: Well, thank you very much. That was an excellent story.

Although parts of the story are so confusing as to be un-analyzable, there are sections which are clear and others whose meaning can be surmised. The witch again is Mike's mother. He sees her as pushing him into the ocean where he is threatened with drowning. This, I believe, symbolizes his feeling of being overwhelmed by his mother's encouraging him to enter into new situations and lessen his dependency on her. The world is a frightening place and he feels ill-equipped to cope with it. The big boy, who rescues the little boy and the baby, is an alter ego who removes the dependent parts of himself (the little boy and the baby) from life's dangers. The latter part of the story, although too chaotic to allow for complete analysis, does convey the anxiety and sense of being overwhelmed that Mike feels. The *feeling* which an otherwise confusing story may engender in the therapist can be useful data for the understanding of the child's story.

The story ends with the witch being eaten by the shark. As in the previously related story, this represents Mike's hostility toward his mother as well as his desire to orally incorporate her.

This is the story I told in response:

Once upon a time there was a big ocean and a family went to the ocean to go swimming. And this ocean was in Hawaii and there was a little boy and a baby in this family and a mother and a father and there was also a big boy in this family as well.

Now, the mother wanted the little boy and the baby to learn how to swim like big people and have a lot of fun in the water. But, these two kids, the little boy and the baby, were scared to learn how to swim and they feared that they would drown.

Now when the mother took them over to the water and said, "Now come on kids, I want you to try it," although she was being very kind and gentle, the kids thought that she was like a terrible witch. They thought that she was very cruel and that they thought she was trying to make them drown. So, they screamed out to the big brother, "She's trying to make us drown. Our mommy is like a witch."

And the big brother said, "She's not like a witch; she just wants to help you learn to swim better so that you can have a lot of fun and you can swim like the other kids. She's not a witch. Sure it's scary to go in the water for the first time and sure you're scared that you are going to drown. But, if you try it you'll see it's not so scary and then you'll see that she's not such a witch. She's not really a witch. It's just that you see her as a witch. She's just trying to help you grow up." And, he said, "She's just trying to help you grow up and learn to do grown up things."

Well, the little boy listened to that carefully and he realized that the big brother was right. The little baby was only a little kid and he still couldn't understand too well what the big brother was saying, but the little boy went into the water and he was scared but he tried and gradually he learned how to swim. It was a lot of hard work, but he gradually learned how to swim and when he did he realized that the big brother was right that his mother wasn't a witch and that many new things are scary and that sometimes you feel that terrible things will happen when they really will not.

And, that is the end of that story. Do you know what the lesson in that story is?

Patient: Um, that sometimes you think that they're a witch when you can't do it like when you swim you're afraid that your mother is a witch because they're going to drown you. But, then, when you know how to swim, then you realize that you're not scared, just a little bit scared, but you do it anyway and you realize that your mother isn't a witch anymore.

Therapist: Right. This boy's mother really wasn't a witch, right?

Patient: Right.

Therapist: He just thought she was a witch. She was really doing something to help him grow up and he found that in other situations too when his mother would try to help him study or tell him to do his homework and things. It wasn't that she was trying to be a witch, it was just that she was trying to help him learn to do things. Is that right?

Patient: Right.

Therapist: And that's the end of the story. What's the main part of it that you liked the most?

Patient: All of it.

Therapist: Do you listen to it when you go home?

Patient: Yeah.

Therapist: Okay, very good.

In my story I tried to lessen Mike's anxieties about venturing forth into the world. I let him know that new situations are anxiety-provoking, but if he is brave enough to tolerate his fears he may reap rewards which would not be his to enjoy were he to withdraw. In addition, I attempted to change one of the many elements which contributed to his viewing his mother as a witch. If he could understand that her urging him to face new situations was a manifestation of benevolence rather than hostility, he would be less prone to see her as a witch. In addition, if Mike were to derive more pleasure from friends, another element contributing to his view of his mother as a witch would be obviated.

Again, Mike's statement of the moral reflects definite insight into the meaning of my story.

At the beginning of his eleventh month of therapy, Mike related this story:

Once upon a time there was a big ghost ——

Therapist: A big ghost? Yes?

Patient: And there were tiny weensy little elves.

Therapist: Tiny elves? I see.

727

Patient: And you can't see them they are so tiny.

Therapist: You could hardly see them.

Patient: Yes, that's how small they were. This is how small they were.

Therapist: Okay.

Patient: And then there was a man coming and the man couldn't see them when he was standing up because they were so small. He didn't know they were elves so he stepped on one, and one of the elves died. So, the ghost killed the man.

Therapist: He stepped on one and the elf died and then the ghost — what?

Patient: Came and killed him.

Therapist: Who is him? The man?

Patient: Yes, and while he was killing him he was walking and he stepped on a lot of them.

Therapist: Who is them? The elves?

Patient: Yes, and after that he died.

Therapist: Who died?

Patient: The man. Because after that the ghost killed him and he died.

Therapist: Yes?

Patient: He was a big ghost but it was a spooky old man, a very, very old man.

Therapist: Okay, uh-huh, and then what happened?

Patient: And that was the end of the story.

Therapist: So let's see. Why did the ghost want to kill the man?

Patient: Because the ghost was mean. The ghost just felt like doing it. He wasn't a friendly ghost like Casper.

Therapist: He wasn't a friendly ghost. All right. What about the man, was he a friendly man?

Patient: Yes.

Therapist: Yes, I see. Now you say — Now what finally happened to the ghost?

Patient: The ghost had ate him.

Therapist: The ghost ate who?

Patient: The man, and the ghost grew bigger and bigger and was more powerful and then after that he was already very old and the ghost was very old and then the ghost died.

Therapist: All right. Anything else happen in that story?

Patient: Well, then that's the end.

Therapist: And the lesson in that story?

Patient: That there are no such things as ghosts.

Therapist: No such things as ghosts. You know that's true what you just said that there is no such thing as a ghost?

Patient: Ghosts are just make-believe.

Therapist: Yes, but your story doesn't say that. Can you tell me a lesson that comes from your story? The lesson that's in your story?

Patient: There are ghosts that just like to scare people that are make-believe for Halloween, like masks, but not real.

Therapist: I'd like you to try to think of your story and see if you can think of a lesson from your story.

Patient: No, I can't.

Therapist: Okay, that was a very good story. Thank you.

The story reveals Mike's profound feelings of impotence. He is like the miniscule elves. He is so small that he can hardly be seen and adults can capriciously crush him to death under their feet. The ghost, who kills the man who stepped on the elves (and thereby expresses the hostility the patient harbors toward those whom he sees as subjugating him), also inadvertently steps on the elves. Even his friends, who act with the best of intentions, end up his enemies — such is the lot of the impotent.

My attempts to get Mike to tell an apparently relevant moral were unsuccessful. Both of his morals refute the existence of ghosts which suggests an attempt to undo the ghost's murderous activities in the story.

This is the story I told in response:

Once upon a time there were some tiny elves. Now, they were young baby elves and naturally since they were young they were very small. In fact, they were so tiny, weeny that some of them you could hardly see at all. And, because they were so young and so small, they were scared a lot because things would happen around them like men could walk on them. Sometimes a man by mistake would step on one of them, or two men would fight and in the fight an elf might be stepped upon. They were scared about that even though it didn't happen very often. Even though it hardly happened at all, they were scared about these things.

So one day they were sitting around and talking and complaining about the fact that they were so small and that because they were small things could happen to them. And then one said, "I know what we can do. We have to speak up. We have to let them know where we are so that they will not step on us. They don't want to hurt us usually; usually it's by accident." So they said, "Let's do this. Even though we're small and our voices aren't very loud, they will hear us if we speak loud together." So, a lot of them got together when some man was passing and they said, "Hello there. Hello, mister. Hey, you up there. Hi." And the man looked down and said, "What was that? I thought I heard voices." And he looked down and then he saw these little elves and he said, "Hi. I didn't notice you fellows down there," and they said, "Yes, we've been here a long time. We want to tell you that we get scared because people step on us sometimes." He said, "I didn't know that. I'm glad you spoke up." He said, "Where do you fellows live?" And, they said, "Over there in those little houses." And they showed him the grass at the foot of the tree. He said, "You live around here, right?" They said, "Yes."

He said, "I know what I'll do. I'll build a fence and put a sign on it and then the sign will say, 'Do not step on the elves. Do not enter. No trespassing.'" So he built the fence, and he put on the sign, and then the elves felt very good and they were glad they had spoken up.

And then they began talking to this man some more. And they said, "You know we feel pretty bad that we're so small." And the man said, "Well, look, you know you're very young. It wasn't such a long time ago that you were born." He says, "You're going to grow bigger and bigger and then you won't have anything to worry about. You won't even need this fence because you will be as big as everybody else." And they didn't realize that.

Well, when they realized that they were going to grow bigger and that they were going to learn more as time went on and that they wouldn't be so scared of the world that made them feel better. And, that's exactly what happened.

Patient: I know what you mean. When they grow you can see them better so they know which way to go so they won't step on the elves. They'll see them.

Therapist: Right, and then they'll be seen and they'll be heard. They'll know more and they won't have to be so scared and that's exactly what happened. They grew up to be big people and they were no longer scared and no one stepped on them and they didn't have to worry about that anymore. And, they lived happily ever after.

Now, my story has two lessons. Can you figure them out, the lessons in my story? Try to figure them out. I think you can.

Patient: That elves will grow.

Therapist: Right. That elves and others feel small when they are little but they all grow up to be big.

Patient: And, they feel big.

Therapist: And they feel big. Well, they are big. That's the first lesson. Now the second lesson? The second lesson is in the first part of the story. When the elves are being stepped on, remember what someone said? Let's tell them what's going on. That's where the second lesson comes down from. So what's the second lesson?

Patient: The elves were scared.

Therapist: And what made them less scared?

Patient: That they were scared that someone might step on them.

Therapist: So what did they do to stop that from happening?

Patient: They had a discussion and they figured out a good idea and something happened good.

Therapist: And, what did they do after their discussion?

Patient: They built a fence.

Therapist: How did the man build a fence? What happened before he built the fence? How did he know to build the fence?

Patient: They showed the man, they were yelling.

Therapist: Right, they told the man what was bothering them.

Patient: Yes.

Therapist: And so the second lesson is: if something bothers you, speak up and tell people about it so that something can be done. If you don't say anything about it then no one will know that something is bothering you. Then, the trouble may continue; but, if you speak up and you tell people you can often stop the trouble. That's the second lesson. Okay?

Now, is there anything you want to ask me about that story?

Patient: No.

Therapist: Okay. So that's the end of our story telling.

Patient: I liked that story.

Therapist: What was the part you liked the most?

Patient: The elves.

Therapist: What part about the elves did you like?

Patient: I liked all of the parts of the elves.

Therapist: Any particular part, any special part?

Patient: No, they were all good.

Therapist: Okay. All right. Very good.

In the first part of my story, I imparted to Mike the notion that he is not as impotent as he feels. If he communicates his needs to adults, he may gain some protection from the world which he sees as overwhelming. The elves express their resentments and fears and thereby enlist the aid of a more powerful figure. Then I provided Mike with hope for the future. He will not always be a child; if he works and learns he will gain the wherewithal to handle the world more effectively.

Again, Mike was more successful in figuring out the moral of my story than he was in surmising the lesson of his.

One week later, Mike told this story:

There was a plain old wall.

Therapist: What's that? A plain old wall?

Patient: Yes, and regular people and a bat cave.

Therapist: And bats in caves?

Patient: Yeah, a bat cave. Wait, there was this magical sea

Therapist: Magical sea?

Patient: Yes, that was not so good.

Therapist: Okay, go ahead.

Patient: And there was mushrooms and an ugly monster in the sea and fishes too. And, there was a little boy.

Therapist: Yes.

Patient: He was very strong and powerful —

Therapist: He was strong and powerful. Yes?

Patient: And he could beat up all the monsters.

Therapist: He could beat up all the monsters.

Patient: And he lived happily ever after and swim to the shore and to the beach.

Therapist: I see.

Patient: So he got rid of all those monsters.

Therapist: Rid of all those monsters? Is that it?

Patient: Yes, he beat them up.

Therapist: He beat them up?

Patient: Yes.

Therapist: Okay, excellent story.

I considered the sea to represent Mike's unconscious — it is dark, deep, and much is hidden beneath its surface. The various malevolent creatures in it symbolize repressed complexes which were anxiety-provoking to him. Mike would prefer to avoid any conscious awareness of his unconscious processes. He swims to the shore (flees) and beats up (renders impotent) the monsters (fearful unconscious processes which threaten disruption into conscious awareness). He then lives "happily ever after," that is everything unpleasant is avoided.

The story is a typical resistance story. It is a common response to the anxiety that is engendered in the patient when the therapist encourages him to lift the forces of psychological repression. Accordingly, I replied with this story:

Once upon a time there was a sea. Now there was a boy who called it the magic sea because he, at that time, believed in magic. He didn't know that there is no such thing as magic. But he was a young boy and he hadn't learned a lot of things and he hadn't learned that there is no such thing as magic. So he called it the magic sea.

Now in that sea were various kinds of fishes and things. There were plants that looked like mushrooms, there were fishes and some of them were very pretty. But this boy thought that these fishes and plants were monsters and he was quite scared of them. He thought that they had magical powers and he thought that they could hurt him. So one day he was swimming at the beach and suddenly some waves came along and they carried him out — way, way, out into the sea and he was very, very scared. He thought that there were plants and fishes which were monsters and he thought that the sea was magical and he was very, very frightened.

Well he got out there and what do you think he saw but one of these sea plants, these sea mushrooms, and he was scared, but then the sea mushroom said, "What are you afraid of boy?" And then the boy said, "You're a magic monster." And the sea mushroom said, "Me a magic monster? I'm just a sea mushroom." He said, "I can't hurt you." And the boy didn't believe it and he said, "You'd better stay away from me." And the mushroom said, "Well, all right, but I'm really quite harmless. In fact, I think you're a very nice little fellow. I'm not going to hurt you."

Well the next thing that happened was that one of these fishes came along. These sea fishes. And then the boy really got scared. And he said, "Stay away from me you monster magical fish." And the fish said, "Me a magical monster?" He said, "First of all there is no such thing as magic, and, secondly, I am not going to hurt you. Where did you get that idea? I'm not so frightening." And the boy said, "I don't know, I always thought that all the plants and animals that live out in that sea are terrible. And they are frightening." And they started to laugh.

The mushrooms started to laugh and the fishes started to laugh. By this time there were a lot of them around. And you could hear the laughter all around. Even the mother and father on the shore heard them laughing. And then the boy started to laugh because he realized that they were really friendly and they didn't really want to hurt him at all. And then he realized that he had the wrong idea. He realized that those sea mushrooms were really not frightening and not monsters, not magic, and he realized that the sea fishes were not magic monsters. That there was no such thing as magic and they really weren't scary at all.

And then he started to play with some of them and he swam back to shore with their help and he brought up a couple and introduced them to his parents. And then he used to go to the beach every summer and he would meet his old friends and a couple of them he took home with him and he put them into fish pools and bowls and tanks and he had them with him all year.

And the lesson of that story is what?

Patient: There is no such thing as magic.

Therapist: Very good and the second lesson? What did the boy learn from that experience?

Patient: Not to be scared.

Therapist: Because ——

Patient: Because they're friends.

Therapist: Right.

Patient: Okay.

Therapist: That certain things that you think are scary really aren't, and then when you have a chance to be with those things or talk about those things you find out that they really aren't as scary as you once thought. Did you like listening to that story?

Patient: Yes, I liked it.

Therapist: What was the part that you liked the most?

Patient: All of it.

Therapist: Well there must have been some part that you liked more than the others.

Patient: I liked the mushrooms and the fishes.

Therapist: Okay, very good.

Patient: Well, that's thinking a little bit, but not so much about monsters.

Therapist: What?

Patient: Do you know what I mean? You say that little boy in the story he was thinking about monsters. He was scared. That's what I don't like.

Therapist: You don't like that part? Did you like the part they really weren't scary?

Patient: Yes.

Therapist: Okay. Well, thank you very much.

In my story I attempted to get Mike to reconsider his notion that his repressed complexes were significantly malevolent. I encouraged him to tolerate the anxieties which confrontation with his unconscious processes entails and to have the living experience that the terrible consequences he anticipates will not be forthcoming.

About the time Mike entered therapy, the country entered into an economic recession which deeply affected his father's business. Their financial situation was naturally a significant source of concern to the parents. Although they didn't wish to burden their children with their difficulties, Mike, at some level, was aware of some of his parents' anxieties.

At the end of his first year in treatment, when financial pressures were particularly severe, Mike told this story:

Once upon a time there was a little boy — Well this time I don't have any regular stories so I'll tell a pirate story.

Therapist: Okay. Certainly all right. Perfectly okay.

Patient: Once upon a time there was a little boy pirate and he had nothing to do, so his father was a pirate and he came and he wanted to get him a sword but his father didn't have enough money to get him a sword but had enough money to get food. So the little boy said, "I want a sword." But the father said, "You can't have a sword." So then the boy was very good and he waited, and then his father got a sword and he lived happily ever after. And he could, and he had fights and duels and he was so brave. He even got hurt and he was sick and he didn't even cry. He went to the hospital and had an operation, and he was well again and he lived happily ever after.

Therapist: How did his father get money for the sword? What did his father do?

Patient: He earned enough money from the truck.

Therapist: How is it he didn't have money at first? And how is it he then got money? How did that happen?

Patient: From his work.

Therapist: Uh-huh. Why was it that one time he couldn't, didn't have enough money, and then at another time he did have enough money? How did that happen?

Patient: Because he wasn't earning enough money for him

to get, I mean for that boy to get the sword. He didn't, I mean that man, I mean his father didn't know the boy wanted a sword. So, I mean a sword, so, I mean, so his father didn't get it.

Therapist: Yeah, but how is it that he then got it later on? How did that happen?

Patient: I don't know.

Therapist: Well, you try to figure it out. I mean it's your story. I'm asking you to explain why in the beginning —

Patient: Yeah, but it isn't a good story.

Therapist: Listen now, it's a good story. I just have one question about it. Now the question I have is: can you try to explain how it was that in the beginning of the story the father couldn't afford to buy the sword and later on in the story the father could afford to buy the sword? Now why was that?

Patient: What does that word mean, "could afford?"

Therapist: Afford means that in the beginning he didn't have enough money to buy a sword, and later on he did have enough money to buy a sword. Now how come later on he did have enough money?

Patient: 'Cause — because the boy was busy doing other things. Well, the boy was just looking for something to do. He didn't know what to do at the beginning.

Therapist: Let me ask you again. How come the father didn't have enough money in the beginning of the story, and then later on did have enough money to buy a sword? How come that happened? How did the father get more money?

Patient: From the bank?

Therapist: Does the bank just give out money like that?

Patient: No.

Therapist: Why not?

Patient: You have to earn for it.

Therapist: You have to earn for it. Right. The bank — that's very good. The bank just doesn't give out money. The bank only holds the money there for you. The money that you earn you can put in the bank, and they hold it there for you.

Patient: Yeah, is that what you wanted?

Therapist: Well, I wanted to know — I was thinking that

the father probably had to work harder to earn more money. That's what I was thinking. Is that how it happened in your story?

Patient: No.

Therapist: How did it happen? How did the father get more money?

Patient: I just don't know — I lied or something —

Therapist: Okay. We'll change the subject.

Patient: I don't have anything else.

Therapist: Okay.

Patient: Let's not — just let's not discuss about it. All right?

Therapist: Okay. We'll change the subject.

Patient: Okay. Now we'll discuss about something I can explain.

Therapist: Okay. All right. So say you don't understand it, that's all. Okay?

Patient: Yes.

Therapist: Now why are you so upset right now?

Patient: Because I don't know what you are saying.

Therapist: You don't know what I am saying? What do you mean?

Patient (calmer): I don't understand, that's all.

Therapist: Do you think you can understand now?

Patient: Yes.

Therapist: I think so too.

Patient: That's all I know. It's hard to explain.

Therapist: One way a father could earn more money would be to work harder or to get some new customers or something like that. Understand?

Patient: What are customers?

Therapist: Customers are people who buy things from the father. People who come and say, "Mister could you please sell me —" What kind of business is the father in your story in?

Patient: A workshop, a factory.

Therapist: A factory. What does he make in this factory?

Patient: Paperweights and marbles. Are marbles paperweights?

Therapist: A marble doesn't make a good paperweight because a paperweight has to have a flat bottom. Okay, he makes paperweights, yes?

Patient: Yes.

Therapist: All right. More people come and say they want to buy paperweights from him.

Patient: Yes.

Therapist: Then he got more money. That's how it works. I have another question about your story. You say that the boy pirate had some fights with the sword? Is that right?

Patient: Ummm.

Therapist: Who was he fighting with?

Patient: A mean pirate.

Therapist: A mean pirate. Yes.

Patient: That was the one that was fighting.

Therapist: Why did they fight? What happened that they started to fight?

Patient: Because the mean man was trying to kill the little boy but he was just hurt but they fixed him.

Therapist: And what happened to the mean man?

Patient: He went away because he died — Well, I didn't finish with the story. I must have made a mistake.

Therapist: Well, go ahead, do you want to finish it now?

Patient: Yes, I forgot.

Therapist: Go ahead.

Patient: Even though the boy was hurt he was still fighting, and then he got the pirate. He killed the pirate and then the pirate died and then they were going to a hospital and, well, they lived happily ever after.

Therapist: Good. Where did he get hurt when he had this fight with the pirate?

Patient: He got hurt on his hip.

Therapist: On the where?

Patient: On his hip.

Therapist: Uh-huh. He got stabbed there or something like that?

Patient: Yeah.

Therapist: Uh-huh. I see. Okay.

The interchange demonstrates the kind of difficulties one may experience when working with a child of borderline intelligence. Often the therapist, without realizing it, may use words which are not understandable to the patient. Instead of asking for clarification, the patient may provide inappropriate responses which further add to the confusion.

In the story, the boy pirate's father cannot afford to buy him a sword. This, of course, reflects Mike's awareness of the family's financial difficulties and his fear that he will suffer significant deprivations. His selection of the sword as the object he would be deprived of suggests that he anticipates that his father's business reverses will in some way jeopardize his own basic security and masculinity. Then, with no explanation provided, the father is able to provide his son with a sword. The ensuing duels, I believe, are between Mike and his father, and serve as an outlet for the anger the patient feels toward his father over the anticipated privations. Expression of such hostility can be dangerous, however, and Mike is wounded — punished for its expression. The story ends with their living happily ever after — Mike's typical anxiety- and guilt-alleviating denial and undoing of the implications in his stories.

First I attempted to get Mike to realize that no explanation was given for the father's sudden ability to provide his son a sword when he had previously been unable to afford one. The question was pursued because I believed that its clarification could provide Mike with greater appreciation of the principle that one has to work if one is to acquire something. His tendency to utilize magical solutions to solve life's problems was clearly maladaptive — especially with regard to his learning disability. When Mike became exasperated over his failure to provide the answer, I supplied it. Even then he was unable to accept it — so upset was he over his earlier failure to provide an answer to my question. My agreement to let the whole subject drop (which is the best thing one can do in such a situation) calmed him, and he was then able to understand that the father in his story might have been able to get more money by working harder.

I then inquired into the duels in the hope of gaining information to confirm my guess that they related to the hostility he felt toward his father over the latter's financial reverses. My inquiry, unfortunately, provided no clarifying information.

740

This is the story I told in response:

Once upon a time there was a boy and he was a pirate and his father was a pirate also. And his father had a factory and one day his father was very sad and he asked his father, "Why are you so sad, daddy?" And the father said, "Well my business isn't very good now. It's going down. We have enough money to buy food and clothing and things like that, it's not that bad, but we have a little problem so that I can't buy you some of the extra things that I'd like to buy you. Like I know you want to get a sword, and I know you would like to get a pirate hat. But I can't buy them for you now and that makes me sad."

Well, the boy got angry and said, "I want a sword and I want a pirate hat." And he was really mad at his father, and the father said, "I can see that you're angry and I'm glad that you're telling me that you're angry because it's no good to keep your anger in. Let's see what we can do about this to make you less angry." And the father thought and the boy thought what they could do. So the boy felt that he wanted the sword badly and he said, "Let's go to a bank they'll give us money." And the father said, "Banks just don't give out money, banks hold your money. They just save it for you and protect it and they put it in a big vault so that it will be safe and so that nothing can happen to it. But banks just don't give out money, they only give you back the money that you gave them." Well the boy realized that his father was really right and he was very sad that he didn't get his sword. And they thought again what could they do.

And then the boy came up with a good idea. He said, "Dad, do you think if I helped you in the factory that will help us get more money?" And the father said, "Yes, that's an excellent idea." He said, "You help me then I will have extra people helping and I think that would help the money situation." So the boy, he was only a boy so he couldn't do too much, but he was able to help his father in the factory and the factory earned more money and then he was able to get his sword and his pirate hat and then he wasn't angry at his father anymore.

And the lesson of that story is: number one, that

banks don't give out money that they just hold the money there for you that you earned yourself; number two, if you don't have enough money you have to work harder and earn it, and then you'll have enough money to buy the things you want. And the third lesson is that if you are angry about something, talk about it and try to figure out a solution. Try to figure out an answer to the problem. Try to figure out something to do about the problem, don't just hold it all in. The end. Now is there anything you want to say about my story?

Patient: Well, I think I rather liked it.

Therapist: What was the part you liked the most?

Patient: When the father got the sword for the little boy.

Therapist: Uh-huh. Why was the father able to get the sword then for the little boy?

Patient: Because the boy helped.

Therapist: Right, right. Excellent. So if you don't have something and you want it, you've got to do something about it and that helps you get it.

Patient: Yeah, and I liked helping my father in the shop, and I never get it for a long time and that we'll get money faster to buy the toys that I like.

Therapist: What toy are you interested in?

Patient: Umm, umm, I haven't decided. I can't think of one.

Therapist: I'm sure that if you wanted a toy that your father has enough money to buy it for you. But you know you just can't have everything you want. You know, for a special occasion, or if it is a small toy, I am sure there would be no problem.

Patient: Well how about a fish because I never took Paul's fish. How about getting fish for me? Okay? Today?

Therapist: Speak to your parents about that. I'm sure they have enough money for a fish.

In my story Mike's anger over his father's inability to buy him a sword is accepted by the father: "I can see that you're angry and I'm glad that you're telling me that you're angry because it's no good to keep your anger in." In Mike's story his anger was repressed and expressed symbolically through the slaughter of the mean pirate. In my story, the father encourages the boy to use his anger constructively to rectify the frustrations which have brought it about: "Let's see what we can do about this to make you less angry." Subsequently, through his own efforts, the boy contributes toward the family's financial improvement, and he then becomes the owner of a new sword and pirate's hat. Although Mike was clearly in no position himself to meaningfully contribute toward the betterment of his family's financial difficulties, my story was told in the hope of imparting to him the principle that one should work to contribute in accordance with one's abilities. Lastly, Mike was reassured that he need not fear that he will be deprived of the basic necessities of life.

During his thirteenth month of therapy, Mike told this story:

Once upon a time —— far, far away —— I don't know any stories.

Therapist: Well, you want me to help you?

Patient: Yeah.

Therapist: Okay. We'll play the game where I'll start telling the story and then you continue it when I point my finger at you. Okay?

Patient: All right.

Therapist: Once upon a time a long, long time ago —— in a distant land —— far, far, far away —— there lived a ——

Patient: Snake.

Therapist: A snake. Good. And that snake ——

Patient: Was a poison one.

Therapist: Was a poison snake. All right. And one day that poison snake ——

Patient: Wanted to hurt a little boy and make him poison.

Therapist: Wanted to hurt a little boy and make him what?

Patient: Make him poison.

Therapist: And make him poison and so —— what happened then?

Patient: The boy was poisoned.

Therapist: He made him into poison?

Patient: No, the boy was poisoned. See, I'm the boy and suppose I was poisoned.

Therapist: Okay, the boy was poisoned and then ——

Patient: And then the boy began to die.

Therapist: And then what happened?

Patient: The police came and took him to the hospital.

Therapist: The police came and took him to the hospital, yes?

Patient: And then they fixed him right away before he died.

Therapist: They fixed him before he died, yes?

Patient: And then he lived happily ever after.

Therapist: Okay, can you tell us what we learned from that story? Can you try to figure that out? What the lesson of that story is?

Patient: That there is such a thing as a poison snake.

Therapist: There is such a thing as a poison snake. Okay, excellent story, thank you.

Little need be said about the meaning of this story. Mike feels that he has been poisoned and that the poison may be lethal. It reveals his exquisite sensitivity to his neurological deficits, and the feeling that sometimes comes over him that he might as well be dead. There is some hope, however, in that the doctors "fixed him right away just before he died" and "then he lived happily ever after." Again, Mike employs the quick magic cure. In the moral, "There is such a thing as a poison snake," he asserts without qualification that, magic cures notwithstanding, he *is* defective.

This is the story I told in response:

Once upon a time a long, long time ago there lived a boy and this boy, like all boys, was not perfect. He had his good parts and his bad parts. He had some things that he was good at and some things that he was poor at. He had his strengths, and he had his weaknesses.

Now this boy had a very strange idea. He thought that just because he was poor in a couple of things that everything about him was no good. He thought that just because he couldn't read too well or learn as fast as the other kids at school that he was totally no good in everything, and it was as if his whole body was poisoned. He felt like every part of him was no good and that he was totally poisoned.

Well, as long as he felt that way, he felt very sad about himself. And one day he was talking to a friend and he said to the friend, "I'm no good. Everything about me is no good. My whole body is no good." And the friend said, "What are you talking about?" He said, "I can't read well in school like the other kids, and therefore I'm poisoned in my whole body." And the friend said, "That's a funny thing for you to say. Yes, I know you can't read as well as the other kids, but that doesn't mean that every part of you is no good, that you are all poisoned." He said, "That's a very silly idea." He said, "Just because one part of you is no good don't mean that your whole body is poisoned. It just means that you have one small part of you that isn't as good as the next person, that is the part of you that is poor." And the friend said, "I have parts of me that are poor." He said, "Everybody I know has good and bad parts."

Well, the boy thought about that for a while and he realized that his friend was right; that it doesn't mean that your whole body is no good or poisoned just because a part of it is no good or a part of it is poor. And after he realized that he felt much better about himself.

Do you know the lesson to that story?

Patient: Uh, no.

Therapist: The lesson to that story is: if one part of you is poor it doesn't mean that your whole body is poisoned, it just means that one part of you is poor.

Patient: I wasn't sure about it.

Therapist: You weren't sure about that, you, yourself, you mean?

Patient: I didn't know which was right, I wasn't sure.

Therapist: Did you think that if one part of a person is no good that means that everything is no good? That he's totally no good? Did you think that?

Patient: Yeah.

Therapist: Hhmmm, that's too bad.

Patient: I pictured it.

Therapist: Pardon me?

Patient: I pictured it.

Therapist: That's a wrong idea. That's a very wrong idea. It isn't that way. If a man's finger is cut that doesn't mean his whole body is cut. Right?
Patient: Yeah.
Therapist: If he has a little scar on his finger it doesn't mean his face and the rest of his body is all scarred. Right?
Patient: Yeah.
Therapist: Or, if he thought that just because he had a little scar on his finger that everybody was going to laugh at him or think he's no good.

So after that the boy was much happier. The end.

In my story I tried to help Mike feel less loathsome by pointing out to him the illogicality of his generalization that he is totally worthless because of his isolated deficiencies. I decided to reiterate this theme in my story and not introduce other elements suggested by his story. In spite of my focus on this single issue, his receptivity to my communication was questionable.

Two months later, Mike told this story:

Once upon a time there was a little boy who was sad because he didn't have any friends and so one boy then said, "Who are you?" And he said, "It's only me (*mumbles*)."
Therapist: And he said, "It's only me what?"
Patient (after a long pause): Help me get started.
Therapist: Okay. This boy ——
Patient: I don't know the name of this boy.
Therapist: You can give him any name that you want.
Patient: I don't like the name Mike because I'm Mike.
Therapist: Call him boy Number One. Okay? Then he met boy Number Two. All right?
Patient: Nope.
Therapist: You want to give him a different name?
Patient: His name was ——
Therapist: Well, you think of a name, but no one you know.
Patient: Would it be all right if I named him Mike?

Therapist: If you want to. It's okay. You can call him Mike if you want to.

Patient: You help me with this story.

Therapist: Okay. Once upon a time there was a boy, and this boy's name was Mike and he didn't have any friends. This made him very sad and one day another boy came over to him and this other boy said to him, "Who are you?" and Mike said —— you tell me —— what did Mike say?

Patient: It's a story about Charles.

Therapist: Didn't we just say that we gave the boy the name of Mike? You want to tell a different story? You want to switch to another story?

Patient: No.

Therapist: All right. What did Mike say when the boy said, "Who are you?"

Patient: No, I'd like to do "Hanzel and Gretel."

Therapist: No, you can't do "Hanzel and Gretel." You can't tell a story about something that you've read. That's against the rules.

Patient: Once upon a time there was a little boy and he had no friends and he was sad and this boy was named, um —— this boy was named Charles. This was a different Charles. And this boy Charles said, "I want some friends." And this other little friend was a bully.

Therapist: His friends were bullies?

Patient: Yes and so then he met another bully, and he said, "What are you doing here?" And he said, "I'm on my way home. Don't hurt me." And the bully said, "Come with me!"

Therapist: And the boy said what?

Patient: "Come with me. I'll push you in the fire." And the little boy said, "No please don't." And he was crying. Then the good prince was galloping along. And he came with his knight.

Therapist: Go ahead.

Patient: And the good prince —— the good prince was galloping along and came with his knight and he said, "Bullies don't have enough sense." So he killed them and that boy lived happily ever after and he got some new friends and they liked him and they used to say, "Hiya. How

are you today?" And the boy lived happily ever after. And everyone was happy that he had friends.
Therapist: Is that the end of the story?
Patient: Yes.

The initial interchange with Mike demonstrates how tolerant to frustration the therapist must be if he is to effectively work with minimally brain injured children. Continuous structuralization may be necessary if meaningful communication is to take place. After the early difficulties in getting Mike to tell a coherent story, I used his fragments to construct the beginning of a story, and I was then able to get *him* to finish it.

The story he finally presented deals with his peer problem. However, his difficulties are solved magically by others who come to his aid. A prince and knight kill the bullies, and then new friends appear on the scene without any explanation as to how they got there. Mike gives no reasons for their benevolence. Accordingly, I told this story:

Once upon a time there was a little boy. His name was Charles and they used to call him "Charles the Sissy." That's what the kids called him around the block. And they used to call him "Charles the Sissy" because they thought that Charles was very weak. Charles used to be very frightened when he'd go out into the street. He'd say, "Stay away from me, boys. I'm not big enough and strong enough and you're going to hit me." He used to cry very easily and was scared all the time. And that's why he got the name, "Charles the Sissy." He thought that he was very weak.

He said one day, "I wish there was some good prince that would come along, galloping on a horse, and beat up these boys." One day he was sitting and looking up at the sky and said, "I wish a good prince would come along." Another kid came along and said, "Did I hear you say that you wish a good prince would come along?" The boy said, "Yes." The kid said, "Listen, I have sad news for you, fellow. There's no such thing as good princes. That's in fairy tales like 'Sleeping Beauty,' 'Snow White,' and things like that. There are no good princes walking around or on horses that can change your life for you." He said, "What

748

am I going to do? All the kids pick on me." He replied, "The kids pick on you, but you don't fight back and you're scared and you think that you are not strong. You think that you can't handle yourself." The boy said, "Well, I wish the good prince would come along to give me friends." The other boy said, "The good prince isn't going to give you friends. There are no good princes around. That's a lot of fairy tale stuff. Look, there's no princes and no knights any more." He said, "Well, how can I get friends?" He replied, "Well, if you stand up for your rights and if somebody hits you, you hit him back. If somebody calls you names, call him back. If you weren't such a sissy, the kids would like you more and they wouldn't pick on you and they'd respect you and they'd want to be your friends."

So this boy Charles — "Charles the Sissy" — thought about it and the next day when a bully came along and the bully started teasing him, Charles teased him back. Well, the bully was surprised. He was really surprised! He had never seen Charles act that way before. "Is that the same Charles? Is that 'Charles the Sissy'? Are you 'Charles the Sissy'? You look like 'Charles the Sissy'?" The boy said, "My name is Charles. It's not 'Charles the Sissy.' If you call me 'Charles the Sissy,' I'm going to call you 'Herman the Scaredy Cat.'" The other boy's name was Herman. "If you call me 'Charles the Sissy,' I'll call you 'Herman the Scaredy Cat.'" So Herman said, "You're 'Charles the Sissy.'" So Charles said, "You're 'Herman the Scaredy Cat.'" Herman realized that Charles meant business and wasn't fooling around. He said, "If you don't stop calling me that, I'll hit you." Charles said, "If you hit me, I'll hit you back." So Herman hit him and Charles was scared but he made a fist and he socked that boy, Herman, right in the nose. Herman started to cry. After that Herman had a very different attitude toward Charles. He respected him. He stopped calling him names, and he said to him, "You know, I'm glad to see that you are different and I'm never going to call you 'Charles the Sissy' anymore. I'm just going to call you Charles. Can I call you Charles?" He said, "Yes. I'll call you Herman." They became friends and after that the kids liked Charles much more because he wasn't a scaredy cat and he wasn't a sissy. They stopped calling

Charles a sissy because he stopped being a sissy. He stopped being a scaredy cat and he had many more friends.

And do you know what the lesson of that story is?

Patient: Yes. Once you fight them back you'll become friends and you'll have to not be afraid and not be scared and go fight them back.

Therapist: Right! Right! What does that story tell us about good princes that gallop on horses? What does that story tell us about them?

Patient: They're only in fairy tales.

Therapist: Right. There's no such thing as good princes in real life. It's only in fairy tales. Yes, you got the moral and the lesson right, exactly right.

Patient: There's no such thing as princes?

Therapist: There are princes but they aren't the kind of princes that are in fairy tales that walk around doing good deeds for little children. That only happens in fairy tales. There are a few countries in the world that have princes, but they are like presidents and kings and things like that. They run the country. They are very busy running the country and they don't go around helping little boys get friends or beating up bullies and things like that. They don't do that. It doesn't happen that way. So that was the lesson of that story — that if you fight back and aren't a sissy, the children will like you more. But if you shake like a leaf all the time and you are quite frightened all the time and you think that you can't handle yourself, children will not like you very much. The end.

Little need be said about my story — it is self-explanatory. Generally, when telling my story I try to be sensitive to the child's involvement. If I see that he lacks interest, I will make it short; if he appears absorbed, I may extend it and "play it for all it's worth." While telling this story, I found that Mike was deeply interested and so I elaborated on my themes. His responses at the end confirmed my impression that what I was saying was registering. This interest was in marked contrast to the lack of concentration he exhibited when he began to tell his own story. This phenomenon is commonly seen in neurologically impaired children.

One week later, Mike told this story:

Once upon a time there was a Greek boy and his first name was Georgy. And he lived in an old, old house in a Greek town, in a Greek place, and then he moved to America. And he saw some kind of bully and the bully said, "What are you doing?" He started to cry and said, "No. Please don't do that." Then that bully said, "Come with me! I'll get you!" Then that boy felt like grabbing *him*! Then the Greek boy smacked him and punched him. So the other boy said, "Why did you do that to me?" This time he tried to be brave this time. He didn't cry. He fight back when it was turn to fight back, and he said, "Listen, kid. If you want to fight, go into the fire," and he pushed that boy into the fire and then got a knife and stuck it right into the boy's tummy and he died. Then this boy lived happily ever after and his friends were all happy with him.

Therapist: He stuck a knife in the bully's tummy?

Patient: Yeah. It wasn't his friend. But the friends lived happily ever after.

Therapist: You mean the Greek boy lived happily ever after?

Patient: He didn't come home to anyone else's house to help him. He just had a little argument with his friend and said, "If you want to play, you can't always do what you want to do. I got to take turns." Then they yelled a little bit and then they learned their lesson how to do it, and then they lived happily ever after. The story's name is "Georgy and His Friends."

Therapist: Very Good. Can you figure out a lesson?

Patient: Yeah. If one should have a bully fighting or if he's mean and you have arguments, you argue him back and you fight back.

Therapist: Excellent! Perfect! Excellent story!

Patient: And the title too.

Therapist: And the title too. An excellent story. And now I'll tell my story.

In this story Mike clearly reveals his recollection of the message from my previous week's story: he does not permit himself to be victimized, but rather fights back. I admit pushing a bully into a fire and sticking a knife in his belly is a little

751

excessive, but nevertheless, he fights back. In addition, Mike refers to an earlier story (not presented here) in which I emphasized the point that one has to await one's turn if one is to play successfully with peers.

This is the story I told in response:

Once upon a time there was a boy and he was a Greek boy. He lived in Greece and his name was Georgy. In Greece he lived in the capital which is called Athens. In Greece there were some kids on his block who were bullies, and they would beat him up.

One day his father said, "I have good news. We're moving to America." This boy Georgy was particularly happy because he said, "Oh boy. I'm glad we are moving to America because now the boys won't pick on me." The father said, "You know, I've been telling you a long time that there are bullies in every city in the world and I'm sure wherever we live in America there's going to be bullies there too. What you have to do is fight those bullies." Georgy said, "But I'm scared of them." The father replied, "Yes, you're scared, but you've got to fight them anyhow — even if you are scared." Georgy didn't believe his father and thought, "When I get to America, there won't be any bullies there."

So he moved away and they came to America and his first day in the United States, he was walking down the street and who do you think he meets?

Patient: A bully.

Therapist: Right! Right! He meets a bully and this bully goes over and says, "What! Are you one of those foreigners?" And the bully starts teasing him and laughing at him and all. Suddenly this boy Georgy realized that his father was right — that wherever he goes there will always be a bully. You can't run from bullies. Well, his knees started to knock. He was so scared and he started to sweat and his throat got tight. He was so scared. He was shaking a little bit, and he finally said, "If you don't cut that out" — he sounded tough but he was really scared inside — "if you don't cut that out I'm going to sock you right in the nose." So the bully said,

752

"What are you one of those wise guys?" He said, "You're the wise guy. If you don't cut that teasing out, I'll sock you right in the nose." Well, the bully didn't believe him and he said, "Yeah, yeah. You're a foreigner," and called him funny names like "You're just a stupid Greek," and things like that. This boy — he was scared — his knees were knocking — but he took his fist and he smacked that boy right in the face. Well, the boy was astounded. He was so surprised. He couldn't believe what was happening. But from that moment on that bully left him alone. He began to respect Georgy and stopped picking on him.

And the lesson of that story is what?

Patient: That once you see bad bullies, you've got to fight them back, and hit harder, and punch them in the nose and punch them all over and then they'll respect you.

Therapist: Right. And each time he met a bully who picked on him he was less and less scared because he got used to doing it. And the other lesson of that story is: there are bullies everywhere you go. Of course, most people are nice, but every once in a while you're going to meet a bully no matter where you are and if you run away from him — if you are scared of him — you are just going to be a very fearful, frightened, timid person, but if you go over to him and you don't let him tease you and you hit him back; sure you may get hit back a little bit too; sure you may get hurt, but that's the way it is. You'll feel much better about yourself and he will respect you. The end.

Anything you want to say?

Patient: That was a very nice story.

Therapist: What is the part about it that you like the most?

Patient: About when they were fighting and he learned that the bully stayed away from him when he hit the bully. That's why I liked the fighting.

Therapist: Hhmmm. Good.

Patient: I liked all of it, not when he was frightened or hating him.

Therapist: Okay. Before we stop I want to congratulate you on one thing. Your stories are much better stories now. You don't have a lot of this garbage stuff, all these strange, weird things happening. They're much nicer stories. They have a beginning, a middle, and an end, and they are about things which happen to normal people in everyday situations. They aren't about creeping, crawling monsters and slimy things. I think they are much nicer.

Patient: Yes.

Therapist: Okay, then. Anything else you want to say?

Patient: The one thing that I want to say is that I like this story and now it makes me want to try whenever they call me names, I'll call them back.

Therapist: Right. Excellent. That's one of the things I wanted you to learn from these stories. Goodbye everybody.

Patient: Goodbye.

In my story I reiterated the principle that fighting back is the best protection one has against bullies. I added that there are bullies everywhere — one cannot flee from them. I emphasized that fighting them is usually a very scary proposition, but that if one can tolerate the fears the rewards can be considerable. I was quite dramatic when imparting this last message: "he started to sweat and his throat got tight," "he was shaking," and so on. Such dramatization generally enhances the child's interest and receptivity.

The post-story discussion confirmed my impression during the story that my messages were being received. Translating all this into action was another thing. Mike still had a long way to go. The stories, however, helped him learn some principles which I hoped he would ultimately apply.

The reader may express surprise at my seemingly naïve approach to Mike's tendency to include morbid material in his stories. Although reinforcing through praise his omission of such material may appear simplistic, it has, I believe, a place in the therapy of morbid preoccupations. Certainly, my aim is to help the child change those underlying processes which give rise to the pathological fantasies. However, habitual utilization of a symptom tends to entrench it, and conscious control can lessen it.

One week later, Mike told this story:

Once upon a time there was a wicked pirate and he had some friends, some pirate friends. There was one good pirate, and he had some pirate friends and there was only one good pirate that was selected and his name was Nirvachi.

Therapist: Nirvachi?

Patient: Yes, Nirvachi, the pirate. Nirvachi the wicked pirate.

Therapist: Okay. Uh-huh.

Patient: And Nirvachi thought that he would make children slaves and big men slaves. He thought there was no such thing as a Seder (*Jewish ceremonial dinner at Passover*) and that means Nirvachi pirate was wrong about those things.

Therapist: You mean Nirvachi said there is no such thing as a Seder?

Patient: Yes, he was wrong, and Nirvachi told the children and the slaves to carry heavy things.

Therapist: Okay.

Patient: And then the children carried so then they had (*mumbles*).

Therapist: They had what?

Patient: So then the children went to the good pirate who was stronger. And he found he was a very strong man, and he came and he beat up that one and he died. And he got a gun and he stuck it out and he killed that man and they lived happily ever after. And that means that man never bothered them again and then they didn't have to bother to have slaves.

Therapist: Uh-huh. Okay. Can you tell us the lesson of that story?

Patient: No.

Therapist: Can you figure out a lesson?

Patient (Big sigh, yawn): There is no such thing as wicked pirates. And there are such things as wicked pirates who really got the slaves. Right?

Therapist: Okay, that's pretty good.

Patient: That's not too good?

Therapist: Well, it's all right. The thing is there *is* such a

thing as a pirate in your story. You made up a story
about a pirate, and the thing is there's no such thing as
real pirates, it's all make-believe. Right?
Patient: Yeah.
Therapist: Yes, that's a good lesson. Right.

The story was told during the Jewish Passover holidays
(the festival commemorating the Exodus of the Jews from
Egypt) and the enslavement theme in Mike's tale was clearly
suggested by the biblical story.

I considered Nirvachi to represent Mike the incarnation
of evil forces in the world. He does not believe in Seders, therefore, he would deprive people of pleasurable oral gratifications.
He enslaves children and makes them carry heavy things, that
is, he overwhelms them with the burdens of life. By having the
good pirate kill Nirvachi, he magically removes the oppressive
forces which bear down on him. With this understanding of
Mike's story, I related mine:

This is a story about Jewish pirates.
Well, it was Passover time and all the Jewish pirates
were getting prepared for the big annual pirate Seder.
However, there was one bad pirate guy who wasn't Jewish.
His name was Nirvachi. And Nirvachi was a very mean
pirate and he didn't believe in Passover and he didn't like
the idea that everybody was having a good time at the big
pirate Seder.
So what he wanted to do was collect all the children
and make them into slaves and some of the kids were kind
of scared. And they said, "We're scared but we're not going
to let Nirvachi ruin our fun. No siree. Seders are fun and
we're not going to let him do that to us." And another kid
said, "Oh, let's get that big good pirate, the big good Rabbi
pirate, he'll help us." And another kid said, "We don't need
him, we can do this ourselves. Look we've got fifty kids
here, fifty kids against him. We can fight him, we don't
need any help."
So all the kids surrounded this guy Nirvachi and they
were a little scared at first. They beat him up, and then he
ran away crying and was quite scared. And then they had

a wonderful Seder. The best Seder they ever had and Nirvachi learned his lesson and he never tried to stop them from having a Seder again.

And the lesson of that story is: if anybody bothers you, try to fight them off yourself if you possibly can.

Patient: Yes, but little boys can't fight big men.

Therapist: Yes, but there were fifty little boys. Together they were able to fight him pretty well.

Patient: Oh.

Therapist: See, and they joined together to fight off that mean pirate who didn't like Seders.

Patient: Oh.

Therapist: Anything you want to ask me about that story? (*Pause*) The title of that story is "Pirate Seder," or "Passover in Pirate Land."

Patient: Yes, maybe I could tell another story about pirate land?

Therapist: Oh sure, sure, go ahead.

Patient: About what a pirate does in pirate land.

Therapist: Uh-huh.

Patient: About a little pirate in pirate land.

Therapist: Uh-huh.

Patient: A very good story.

Therapist: Come on let's hear it, I'm always interested in hearing another story.

Patient: Once upon a time there was a —— the title is "The Pirate that Lived in Pirate Land."

Therapist: Okay.

Patient: Once upon a time there was a mean —— "The Pirate that Lived in Treasure Land." There was a pirate and he was a good pirate. He said, "There are poor boys and they need clothes and they need food." And then a wicked pirate came and said, "Who are you? I'll kill you if you don't listen, and I'll come and get you. (*wickedly*) Ha, ha, try to get me. Ha, ha, you won't get me at last."

And those boys were frightened, and they said, "All right we'll get this out. And we'll kill you." And then they stuck it right into him before they did it, just in time before he was ready. And then he died, and they lived happily ever after. But they weren't all happy ever after.

And then a fairy came and said, "You are good ones, that was a good deed. I will bring you a treasure and this will take you home. Watch the wand, watch the wand, watch the wand, and took them home and disappeared. And then the boy woke up and it was only a dream and they lived happily ever after and he wasn't poor.

Therapist: Well, how did it end now?

Patient: With the dream, it was only a dream.

Therapist: Yes, but before he woke up the fairy was going to take to do what?

Patient: She was going to take me, take that boy home.

Therapist: I see, from the pirate land?

Patient: Yes.

Therapist: Uh-huh.

Patient: I mean from treasure land.

Therapist: From treasure land. Did she give him treasures and presents and awards?

Patient: Yeah.

Therapist: I see, okay. Shall I tell a story now?

Patient: What?

Therapist: Shall I tell a story now?

Patient: Yes.

Therapist: Once upon a time there was a pirate and he didn't like Purim (*A Jewish festival commemorating the deliverance of the Jews in Persia from destruction by Haman.*) And all the pirates were planning to celebrate Purim. And all the kids were very happy about Purim. But he was a meany — and he didn't want to celebrate Purim. In fact what he wanted to do was to take away from the children all the food and candy and stuff like that.

Patient: The hamantashen (*Triangular cakes prepared especially for Purim*).

Therapist: Yes, and things like that. He was really a meany.

Patient: Oh, it was a pirate that had a pirate's hat, and you put it back on and it looks like a hamantashen.

Therapist: Yes, he had one of those pirate's hats. Yes.

Patient: That's the kind. It felt like a hamantashen.

758

Therapist: Yes.

Patient: Tell that.

Therapist: Are you saying that you want him to have a hat like a pirate hat?

Patient: Yes, shaped like a ——

Therapist: Hamantashen. We can give him a pirate hat like that.

Patient: Just like a pirate hat.

Therapist: Right, but he was a meany, and he didn't want the children to celebrate Purim. Now he tried to take away their candy and food and things like that.

Anyway these kids said, "We're not going to let you do that. Even though you're bigger than us, we're going to gang up on you." And they did. Off he went, he went away very sad and unhappy. And he learned his lesson and he knew he wasn't going to do that again.

Now the children said, "We did a fine deed. We got rid of that guy and now we can enjoy our Purim." And then someone said, "Well maybe we should get a reward, maybe we should get some —— a magic fairy might come and give us treasures." And another boy said, "No, we got our reward. We're having a good time. There is no such thing as magic fairies. There's no such thing as treasures. We did a good job and we feel satisfied and we feel good that we got rid of that anti-Semitic pirate, that pirate who didn't want Purim and didn't like us to have Purim.

And so they realized that they got their reward in the fun that they had and they realized that they were never going to be bothered by him again. And they realized that there is no such thing as a magic fairy and that there are no magic rewards or presents from magic fairies.

And the lesson in that story is: when you do things that are good, your reward is the good feeling you have inside yourself.

Patient: Ummm.

The somewhat humorous quality in my stories about the Jewish pirates was introduced more for my benefit than Mike's

— he was not sophisticated enough to understand my humor nor did he appreciate how amusing his own pirate Nirvachi's irreligiosity was.

In my stories I repeated the theme, emphasized in the previous week's stories, that there are no magic cures to life's problems. One must grapple directly with life's difficulties if one is to have any hope of overcoming them. Although frightened, the boys in my stories take matters into their own hands and overcome their oppressors.

In his second story, Mike reveals his appreciation of my message about fighting one's own battles (no matter how violent the measures one may be forced to take), but he ends his story with a magic fairy who ensures his living happily ever after. In my second story, therefore, I encouraged the enjoyment of the inner rewards of accomplishment and categorically denied once again the existence of magic fairies.

During his seventeenth month of therapy, Mike told this story:

> Once upon a time in a far off land there was a little island. This island was very scary. It had snails and distant jungles and on the island there were jungles and Jungle the snake.
>
> *Therapist:* You mean Jungle and Jumbo?
>
> *Patient:* No, Jungle and there was one of them named Jungle, an island was jungle, and the snake was Jungle. And this poor little snake had no friends —— he was a sad little snake, he never had friends in a long before, never had any friends. And then came a little friend and he said, "Hi," and he was a little bit happy. And then they made up friends and they had quite a lovely time and they had a good time and then they made more, and more, and more friends and the same thing again and again and they lived happily ever after. And that's the story about Jungle the snake.
>
> *Therapist:* Uh-huh. I have a question to ask you. What was it that the snake did that got him to have so many friends after he was so lonely?

Patient: Because he was looking and looking and soon he found a boy and then more, and more, and more, and then he made friends.

Therapist: Uh-huh. Had he been doing anything which made it hard for him to have friends? Did he do anything that made it —

Patient: No. He just never had friends in a long, long time. He never had friends before.

Therapist: I see.

Patient: That he needed to know.

Therapist: Uh-huh.

Patient: And then he lived happily ever after.

Therapist: I see, very good.

Patient: And his parents told him how to get friends to like him and then he knew that he would want friends very badly.

Therapist: All right, and now it's time for me to tell my story.

Mike's selection of the snake to represent himself is a reflection of his low self-regard. The snake goes from a state of loneliness to one in which he is surrounded by affectionate friends without any particular effort on his part and without any alteration of the personality characteristics which might have contributed to his earlier alienation. My questions, which were designed to draw his attention to these implausibilities, were of no avail. Accordingly, I told this story:

Once upon a time there was a snake. And I can't really tell you what his name was, I'm not sure whether his name was Jungle, Jumbo, or Jongle. And the reason I don't know what his name is —

Patient: I told you his name. He was named Jungle (*mumbled*).

Therapist: Jumbo? Jungle? Jongo?

Patient: Jongo (*mumbled*).

Therapist: Jongo?

Patient (*unclear but loud*): JUNGO!

Therapist: Jungle?

Patient: No, Jungo (*still unclear*).

Therapist: Okay. Jungle.

Patient: JUNGO! See "go" at the end, and "jun" at the beginning.

Therapist: Jungo? Okay, Jungo. Okay, fine. The reason I didn't know his name is that the boy that told me his name didn't speak clearly and kind of mumbled in such a way that I couldn't tell whether he was saying Jungle, or Jumbo, or Jongo or what. But now I got the name clear, it's Jungo. Right?

Patient: Yeah.

Therapist: Okay.

Patient: Yeah.

Therapist: This snake's name was Jungo. And one of the reasons —— and he didn't have any friends. And one of the reasons that he was sad and lonely was that he didn't speak clearly so that when he would speak to people he would mumble under his breath or he would say things in such a way that people didn't understand what he was talking about and he wouldn't speak clearly. And people would say to him, "What did you say?" He wouldn't even try to speak clearly. He just mumbled the same thing all over again. So when he mumbled the same thing all over again people said, "Well, I'm not going to be friends with him, he doesn't try to speak clearly, and when I ask him to speak clearly he just mumbles it under his breath all over again." So he was very sad and very lonely and then one day another snake came along and he said, "Do you want to be friends?" And to this snake, Jungo said, "Well, (*garbled mumble*)."

Patient: Tee, hee.

Therapist: And the snake said, "What did you say?" Jungo said, "(*garbled mumble, mumble, mumble*)." Well, the snake said, "Sorry, because if you don't want to try and speak clearly to me, I don't want to be your friend." And the snake went away.

Now what Jungo had said was, "Yes, I would like to be your friend." But he didn't speak clearly, he didn't try hard to speak clearly and so when the other snake went away, Jungo started to cry and he felt very sad.

Well, the next time another snake came along and the snake said, "Would you like to be my friend?" And Jungo said, "(*garbled mumble*)." And the snake said, "I'm sorry, I don't understand what you are saying." Jungo said, "(*garbled mumble*)." And the snake said, "Well, I don't know what's wrong with him — he may be a foreign snake or something. He may speak a different language but he certainly doesn't seem to be trying to answer my question. I'm going to go elsewhere in the jungle and find another friend."

And then Jungo said, "Hey, wait!" Well, the snake turned around and said, "Oh, you do speak English." Jungo said, "Yes, of course." The other snake said, "Well, I didn't know that. What I heard before was, '(*garbled mumble*)'." And Jungo said, "You're right, I didn't try hard enough. I didn't try to speak clearly. I've changed. I'm going to speak clearly. I realize that I have to think about the other person. I realize that I have to think about whether they can hear me or not."

Well after that Jungo had many friends. And they knew that his name was Jungo. They knew that his name wasn't Jungle or Jumbo or something like that. And when somebody said, "What's your name?" He said, "JUNGO."

And they said, "Would you like to be friends with me?" And he said, "Yes, I would like to be your friend." And after that he had many friends.

And the lesson of that story is: if you are not going to speak clearly, people won't want to bother with you. If you speak clearly, they will then want to be with you if you are nice in other ways as well. The end. Is there anything you want to say about that story?

Patient: This was the best —— happily ever after —— I liked that most of all, the happily after part.

Therapist: Uh-huh. Was there anything about this story that's like you?

Patient: Yeah, I mumble too. Like that snake, that snake was mumbling ——

Therapist: Right. I think that's one of your problems and I think you can do something about it. You mumble. I think you need practice in speaking clearly. What do you think?

Patient: Yeah.

Therapist: And I think you can speak clearly and that you have to try to speak clearly.

Patient: But can I talk?

Therapist: Can you talk?

Patient: Yes.

Therapist: Of course you can talk.

Patient: That's a relief because I always have trouble.

Therapist: You have trouble talking? I think you have a little trouble saying what's on your mind but you also don't speak clearly when you do know exactly what you want to say. You mumble and people can't hear you. Is that right?

Patient: Ummm.

Therapist: Okay, and that's the end of the story.

Patient: I mumbled again.

Therapist: Well, I think you ought to stop playing that game. I think the sooner you stop playing that game the better off you will be.

Patient: Ummm.

Therapist: That's what I think, what do you think?

Patient: Yes.

Therapist: I think you really need some practice.

Patient: Ummm.

Therapist: Okay.

I had planned to tell a story in which the snake ascertains, through discussions with his parents, the personality characteristics which were interfering with his forming friendships. I had also intended to enlist Mike's aid in describing exactly what these traits were. The boy's persistent mumbling, however, provided me with an example of one of his alienating qualities which was more meaningful to focus upon than some other characteristic which was not being exhibited at that time. Treatment is at its best when the therapist and patient direct their attention to some event which has just occurred and which they both have observed.

At the end of his twentieth month of therapy, Mike told this story:

Once upon a time there was a boy who was very lonely, who was very happy and he wanted to go to school so he was going to school and he said, "Hi," and the teacher said, "Hi, good morning." So he sat down and did his work and had a good day in school and then came home.

And then as time came by he got into a big accident and hurt part of his brain so it wouldn't —— with amnesia and he had a little part of his brain that got damaged and he had to have help, medicine, to control it. And it was called amnesia. He had to try but he couldn't help it. So they said, they just went to test him. So then they said it was all right, you don't have to control it, they gave him medicine because we're going to help you. So they took him to a hospital and gave him tests and shots because he wasn't doing so well. There was a lot of amnesia.

Therapist: I'm going to interrupt you on this story. The boy in your story has an amnesia which can be helped by drugs and medicines. This is not you. What you have can't be helped much by medicine. What you have you have to do yourself.

Patient: Yes.

Therapist: Okay, now let's hear a new story.

Patient: I don't have any good stories.

Therapist: Now, let's try it. Now let me start you off and you'll be all right. Once upon a time a long, long time ago ——

Patient: I got it, I've got a story.

Therapist: Okay, let's hear.

Patient: Once upon a time a long time ago there was a little baby. His mother always had to feed him and say, "Now come on, nice baby, you're going to have some nice breakfast." And he was happy. But sometimes he would want to cry and then as time got older, he got to be a big boy and he went to school and then. This story's name is: "A Boy Who Went To School."

Therapist: All right, go ahead.

Patient: And he had brain damage, less than mine.

Therapist: What?

Patient: Less than mine so that it would be very easy for him to control it.

Therapist: Control what?

Patient: To control his damage. He had practically the same thing only it was much less.

Therapist: All right, fine.

Patient: So he went to school. And he was, I'll show you. He was around like this high.

Therapist: Uh-huh.

Patient: And then he came home and he was still going, (*garbled*) and giggling." So his teacher and his mother said, "Please don't do that. I don't like that. Control yourself." And he said, "All right." So every day it was very, very easy. But usually it was just a little hard too. And then in school he was going, "Whee. Whee." And then the teacher said, "Please don't do it." And he was trying to do work and he was getting upset. "I can't do it," he said. And the teacher said, "Try harder, don't get upset. Now I don't want you to do that. Now you please do your work and don't be so upset." She was just talking a little tiny bit. And so he did his work and as time goes by he got so he could do it so fast he couldn't believe it. And then when he did that work he was still in the habit of (*mumble*) —

Therapist: He was still what?

Patient: He was still in the habit of getting upset. That was just when it was all harder for him to do that. But he tried and tried. So hard you wouldn't of believed it. He tried and tried and never stopped. He even did minuses! Which was very hard. He tried even doing those. He tried doing any kind of work. Though he tried, so far he wasn't very good. But he tried, tried, tried. He tried to be the goodest boy. So he learned very fast so that when he was had gone to school he was trying the same way as he did at home. And the teacher was very happy at him. And all his friends wanted to play with him all the time very much. Just like all the other kids. And they came over to play and they played all the basketballs and games and they had a good time. And he felt good.

And then he was going work and he told his mother that he then got out of the habit of getting upset because he tries to do work. And then he had the feeling of getting upset, but he tried not to say the words. So he tried to control as best as he could, and he said, "All right." You see, he had the feeling inside he had the feeling and he didn't want to let it out. He wanted to hold it in. So he wouldn't let it out because that's how he was trying to control it. He had the feeling but he didn't say it. And he didn't let it out and say, "Oh." He tried to hold it in. He was trying to control it. He really had the feeling the same feeling. So he did that too.

Therapist: Uh-huh.

Patient: So as time had gone by he got out of that habit of getting upset in learning and he knew how to do work better and and each time he slipped he said, "Oh well." Not too good. And he tried so hard with the work. And then so hard again.

When he was out of the habit about work that was so hard that the next day in other months and years he said, "There is only one mistake." And each day he was only having one mistake and as time gone by another month he said, "No mistakes, no mistakes, no mistakes." And he lived happily ever after.

And it was time for school to be over and it was beginning to be summer now. So he got out of school and he was very happy. Very, very extremely happy, and that is the story about the boy.

Therapist: Very, very good. Excellent story. Very nice story.

The stories reveal some of the therapeutic advances which Mike had made. In the first Mike demonstrates his awareness of his "focal" lesion: "he . . . hurt part of his brain," he had a little part of his brain that got damaged." Such appreciation is an important step toward the reduction of the tendency to generalize and consider the isolated defects proof of one's total worthlessness. In his first story, however, Mike is totally helpless to control his difficulties: "He had to try but he couldn't help it," and "You don't have to control it." I interrupted his story in order to emphasize the point that whereas the boy in his story might have been cured by medicines, this was most definitely not the case with Mike. The patient, at times, would attribute certain clearly psychogenic (or primarily psychogenic) symptoms such as silliness, sniffing, perseverating, and mumbling to his brain damage and thereby absolve himself from any responsibility for controlling them. I took the position that his neurological impairment did, indeed, make it more difficult for him to learn certain things, but that it had nothing to do with his silliness and other psychogenic symptoms. The former could be helped by applying himself more diligently in school, and the latter by conscious control as well as our discussions about them. Medicines, I explained, could only make these tasks a little easier. The brunt of the burden was still on his shoulders. By interrupting his story entirely and suggesting that he start a new one altogether, I let him know that I wanted to have nothing to do whatever with a boy who was helpless to control his symptoms. Although I am not certain that some of the symptoms which I considered primarily psychogenic were indeed so, I believe that erring on the side of psychogenicity offers more therapeutic hope and lessens the likelihood that the child will resign himself to his symptomatology.

In his second story, Mike demonstrates his awareness of the two classes of problems with which he suffers: organic learning and psychogenic behavioral. He also exhibits his exquisite appreciation of the efforts he must make in both of these areas. Unlike previously described stories in which the salutary maneuvers were verbalized as future *desiderata*, here they are described as experiences which have already been translated into action — with the full impact of the painful affects associated with their implementation. Mike's efforts were being rewarded: he was showing significant improvements in both schoolwork and behavior.

This is the story I told in response:

Once upon a time there was a boy and he was a very nice boy but, unfortunately, he had a little small part of

768

his brain which didn't work too well. Just a small part of his brain. And they said that he had brain damage. And that was a very poor word because he thought that he had damage all over his brain. In fact, he thought that his whole body was bad and no good and he didn't realize that there was just a small part of his brain that didn't work. So he felt terrible about himself. He felt that he was totally no good —

Patient: Well that's the time when I feel embarrassed when you help me and try to remind me and talk stern because I get silly.

Therapist: Uh-huh.

Patient: Because that gets me a little embarrassed. I can't help it all the time. You know, what we were talking about?

Therapist: Excuse me. You know you have changed the subject. You have changed the subject. Now I am telling a story.

Patient: Well, it's not about amnesia.

Therapist: You are changing the subject again. I am telling you a story. I was stern to you before because I think you can control those silly movements like your funny faces and finger movements and you are making noise and you were making funny movements with your hands and I was telling you that, if you do that, the children will not want to play with you. And that's the end of that subject. Now I will start my story again.

Now as I was saying this is a boy who had a little trouble with part of his brain and he was called brain damaged. However, he had the funny and foolish idea that all of his brain was no good. In fact, he even had worse of an idea, he had the foolish silly idea that his total whole body was no good. Just because a very small part of his brain was sore and because of that he felt very bad about himself. He said to himself, "I'm no good. I'm nothing. I'm terrible. Everything about me is no good." And that was sad because he really was a very fine fellow, he was very good looking and he could do many things very well. However, he had a lot of trouble learning because that small part of his brain that's involved with learning had some trouble and he had to work much harder but he gradually did learn and then he felt much better.

Now another thing that this boy did once in a while was that, well, before we go on to the second thing, did you understand what I said about the first thing? What did I say about the first thing that this boy thought that was a wrong thought?

Patient: I wasn't listening because I was trying to think. Trying to practice with my eyes not to move them.

Therapist: Okay, I'll say it again once more.

Patient: Ummm.

Therapist: Now you listen very carefully because I am going to ask you what I said.

Patient: Okay.

Therapist: Now this boy had trouble with a small part of his brain and he thought that his whole brain was no good and he even thought that his whole body was no good which was a silly idea. Why was that a silly idea?

Patient: Because that's not true.

Therapist: Why is it not true?

Patient: Because that is wrong.

Therapist: Why is it wrong?

Patient: Because he can control it.

Therapist: Oh, well. You weren't listening again.

Patient: Well I don't. I was listening. I heard. I remember what you said.

Therapist: What did I say?

Patient: I remember the words.

Therapist: What did I say?

Patient: That you can control it.

Therapist: No, no, now I'll try again. He had one small part of his brain that was no good or that was sore and he thought that his whole brain was no good. What did I just say?

Patient: There was one part of his brain that was no good and that was sore.

Therapist: Yes, and what did he think?

Patient: His whole brain was no good.

Therapist: Right, and he even thought his whole body was no good.

Patient: Is my brain really sore?

Therapist: There's a small part of it that's sore, yes.

Patient: Why it doesn't hurt!

Therapist: Well, but there's a small part of it that doesn't work too well. It's when you were born something happened that made a small part of your brain not work too well. Just a small part.

Patient: Is this true? Is it sore?

Therapist: Well you can call it sore if you want.

Patient: It isn't really because it doesn't hurt.

Therapist: It's sore in a way. It doesn't hurt, but it's sore. It doesn't work too well.

Patient: It makes you be silly this soreness? Right?

Therapist: No!

Patient: What?

Therapist: No, you are silly, that part of the brain doesn't make you be silly. You, yourself, are making yourself become silly. You see, you think the little boy in my story, whatever he did that was strange or different he used to blame on that small part of his brain so, in other words, if he would move his hand around or move his eyes around he would say, "Oh I have no control over that. I'm sorry I can't stop that. That's that brain thing again. That's that sore in my brain. That's the thing that does it." And that was his excuse.

Patient: Well what does this thing make you do?

Therapist: The sore only did one thing. It made his memory poor for learning.

Patient: Oh.

Therapist: But the sore did not make him move his hands around, it did not make him move his eyes around, it did not make him be silly. That he did on his own.

Patient: Oh.

Therapist: But every time he would do something like that he would say, "Don't blame me. It's my sore. That's what does it." Do you understand that?

Patient: Yes.

Therapist: What have I just said about that boy?

Patient: I forgot.

Therapist: Try to think about what I just said. What did this boy say about that sore?

Patient: Remember what I said before? That I couldn't help it.

Therapist: Yes.

Patient: And you say yes.

Therapist: I said yes what?

Patient: That it's all right. So I could help it.

Therapist: That you could help it.

Patient: Uh-hum. No, that you could help me! So it will be easier.

Therapist: You have to help yourself. I just point it out. You have to help yourself. I say to you that you are making those motions again. That isn't caused by the sore in your brain.

Patient: Well, what motions?

Therapist: When you move your hands like that.

Patient: I don't know, I don't know, I was just —

Therapist: Before you were doing it.

Patient: Oh, I didn't even know that.

Therapist: Okay, the thing is this boy used to blame everything on the sore in his brain. And everything that he did that was funny or different he would say it was the sore in his brain. And as a result of that he had very few friends because he would do all kinds of silly things. And when somebody would say, "Hey, stop that." He would say, "I can't stop that, I can't stop it. I have a sore in my brain and that makes me do it." And his mother and father said, "It's not been caused from the sore in your brain. You're just doing that by yourself on purpose and you can stop it."

Well one day the boy realized that his mother and father were right. And so he tried very hard and he stopped doing those things and then he had more friends.

And the lesson of that story is: if you have a sore in your brain that can stop you from learning, that can make it harder for you to learn but it doesn't make you move your eyes funny and it doesn't make you move your hands funny and it doesn't make you be silly. Those are things you have to stop yourself.

Patient: But you didn't even help me. Continue the story. I couldn't help it! Don't make it — don't kill it!

Therapist: Don't kill what?

Patient (crying): You're making it worse, you're breaking the brain.

Therapist: How?

Patient (crying): Sure, I'm going to end up with a whole big brain damage. And you're going to make all those amnesias and all that. You're going to make it worse. Aren't you?

Therapist: No.

Patient: You're going to make it worse.

Therapist: How am I going to make it worse?

Patient: You're just going to make it worse.

Therapist: How?

Patient: Because I can't help it. I forgot. I can't think. What am I going to do to think? It was too hard.

Therapist: Some things you can help and some things you can't.

Patient: See that, it, that, but I couldn't. I couldn't do that.

Therapist: You couldn't do what?

Patient: I couldn't help it. I couldn't remember. I really couldn't. That's the bad part.

Therapist: The memory part you can't help, but the movement of your hands you can help. And the movement of your eyes you can help, and the silliness you can help. Right?

Patient: Yes.

Therapist: Okay. That's all I'm saying. What did I just say? What did I just say to you now?

Patient: Well you can't help the memory but the movements of hands and movements of eyes you can help.

Therapist: Right, right, and the silliness you can help. Okay?

Patient (relaxed): Yes.

Therapist: The end.

In my story I merely tried to reiterate the healthy insights present in his. In spite of the fact that his story reflected awareness of the messages I was trying to emphasize and in spite of clinical behavior which revealed incorporation of these insights, Mike's reactions during the early part of my story would lead one to doubt that he had learned anything. This was the result of his attending to other things while I was relating my story: "I wasn't listening because I was trying to think. Trying to practice with my eyes not to move them." Although I am most sensitive to the child's involvement and responsivity while telling my story, there are times when I may consider him to be absorbed in my story when he is, in fact, concentrating on something else entirely. This was the situation here and it was with some difficulty that I finally managed to communicate meaningfully with Mike again — and then only after he had become upset.

During the week following this interchange, the mother reported significant diminution in silliness, extraneous eye and finger movements, and finger smelling. Also, she was able to engage Mike in meaningful discussions in which he revealed his appreciation of the fundamental issues discussed by us during the interchange.

During Mike's twenty-first month of therapy, this interchange took place.

> Once upon a time there was a girl named Laura and she thought to herself, " Maybe I ought to go on a trip to Bali."
>
> *Therapist:* A trip to where?
> *Patient:* To Bali.
> *Therapist:* To Bali.
> *Patient:* I'm always worrying about going on trips to Bali and all different islands that we've learned, and being there when I go to sleep, pretending I'm in Bali, and I'm swimming in the ocean and catching fish and then I wake up and that's why he yells at me. I'm waking him up.
> *Therapist:* Okay. So go ahead. Tell more of the story.
> *Patient:* And Laura was thinking, "I think I'm going on a trip to Bali." And she told her father and her mother and they both said, "No! You may not go on a trip. We don't have enough money. You have to wait." "Oh, please," said Laura. " No Laura. You may not go to a trip to Bali. We do not have enough money. You have to be patient. It might take awhile, but you've got to be

774

patient." So Laura said — are you writing this story down?

Therapist: You don't worry about what I'm writing. You finish your story. Yes, I'm writing the story. Go ahead. I'm writing parts of it. Go ahead.

Patient: So Laura was very sad and then she thought of another idea: "Maybe I ought to go to someone's house or to one of my neighbors or any other house to take me to a trip to Bali." So she did. She tried to do it. And she went to the neighbors — going visiting she went. She went to her neighbors and she said, "Hey," and she asked a young lady for the mother and the little children were named Mark and Dan, which were Laura's friends. And the family had a young lady for Mark and Dan, had a young lady for the mother and a young man for the father. There were two little boys and the girl Laura came over to the mother and father of Mark and Dan and said, "Will you take me to Bali?" They said, "No! We don't have enough money. You have to be patient."

And then she went to another house called — she went to another house which had a mother and a father and two children and she asked the mother and father. And she said, "Can I go to a trip to Bali?" and they said, "No, you may not!" She tried and tried but it didn't work, so then she became very sad and cried, and cried, and cried, and then had a dream about — but dreams can't come true if you say. Dreams only come out the way they want to. Right? They can't come out if you make — they can't — you know —

Therapist: You can't make a dream come out the way you want it. Right. It comes out on its own.

Patient: Yeah, Yeah. So —

Therapist: What was the dream that she had?

Patient: So she knew that she couldn't make the dream perfect. She couldn't make it come out what she wanted it to be, but she dreamed — she fell asleep and had a dream. It was a beautiful dream. She didn't even know that she was going to have a dream about Bali. She was very sad and she fell asleep and had a dream and the dream was about Bali. Laura was at home and she said, "Mother, can I go on a trip to Bali?"

Therapist: This is the dream now?

Patient: Yes. And she said, "Yes, sure. We have enough money to go." And she was very happy and she went on a plane to Bali. And she dreamed that she was on a plane flying in the sky. She looked below. It was real fun. It felt funny. It felt funny when you land, you know. It feels funny.

Therapist: Hhmmm.

Patient: So that's how it felt to Laura. So she was flying on a plane and then it was time to land and she saw beautiful palm trees and she was so happy. She said, "Oh, goody, goody, gum drops. We're at Bali!" Her mother and father were very — they talked like this. And her mother and father were very happy too and they said, "Yeah, we're really at Bali. Maybe we can go naturing and find animals and see the beautiful villagers here and the Polynesian natives." So they went there. They went naturing. They went to the beautiful seashore and they went on a boat. They decided to go on a boat. So they went on a boat to catch fish in the deep water. She was dying to catch fish. She was eight years old. She was an eight-year-old girl. So they put a big lump of bread in case she catched any of the big fish. So she put the rod down in the water and then became a big — is a mackerel bigger than a bass?

Therapist: I don't know.

Patient: Well, she caught a big fat mackerel, and the second time she caught a big trout and then she caught a big —— and then — guess what? Her father — does everyone know how to swim in deep water? Everyone knows if you don't get tired. Right?

Therapist: Right. Most people know.

Patient: Well, all seven-year-olds know how to swim in the deep water. Right?

Therapist: Most of them, but not all of them. Some of them.

Patient: Well, Laura knew. Most of them do. Right? Right?

Therapist: Some do, not most. Some do, some don't. I don't know whether most or not.

Patient: Well, Laura knew how to swim in deep water. She could almost swim far, but not too far — far enough for a seven-year-old. She could swim all the way from the side of a pool to the end of a pool. But she can swim much much farther. She could swim for two half-hours because she practiced a lot high high speed diving because she practiced so hard you wouldn't believe it. She practiced so hard her diving and her swimming and never stopped —

Therapist: All right. So go ahead.

Patient: But way down in the deep water — they got so tired; they never stopped. She wanted to practice and she wanted to learn quick, so she could swim in the ocean in case she ever goes. So she did and she learned so well that she could swim in the ocean for one-half hour and then with this boy for one-half hour. So she did and she wanted to go underneath the water —

Therapist: Excuse me. You're going to have to come to the end of this story because I have to tell mine, so make it quick.

Patient: Okay. Yeah. So then she went underneath the water. They put a snorkel diving mask in — they had to put air in so she could breathe underneath the water. So she went down underneath the water. She knew how to swim for a half hour and she saw a big lobster so she — they gave her a net too. So she brang down the nets and she had to hold it by this so she doesn't — so the lobster doesn't come out to bite her. So she holds it by the stick of the net and as she came up she was swimming with one arm because she can't swim with both arms because then —

Therapist: You're going to have to hurry up and get to the end of the story. I'm just giving you another minute.

Patient: All right.

Therapist: Go ahead.

Patient: She came up with the lobster; she came up with one arm; and they were so happy they put sticks in it and they brang it home to the motel in Bali and saw the neighbors and went naturing.

Then they decided to go home. So they went home

and she woke up and then she found out it was only a dream. She was so happy because she didn't even know she was going to have a dream about Bali and she did! And then —

Therapist: Now how does the story end?

Patient: So her mother and father were very happy and then she said, "If you want it that way it will be all right. I changed my mind. I did learn. Even though you don't want me to go, I'll listen, even though it takes very long. It doesn't matter. But it sure will be when I'm old enough to play with friends. When I'm this age I play with nine-year-olds when I'm nine. But I'm ten. I hope when I'm nine — next year maybe — I hope — "

Therapist: Hope what?

Patient: To go on a trip. So they almost had enough money, but not enough yet. So they said. "Maybe we'll be able to go on a trip next year. We almost have enough — "

Therapist: Now you're going to have to hurry up and finish this story.

Patient: Yes.

Therapist: Hurry up.

Patient: So it became next year. They had enough money to go to Bali. So they went to Bali and she was very happy. So that's the end of the story of Laura going to Bali.

Therapist: Okay. Very good. Now that was an excellent story. It was very good. You asked me before about talking about your stories. You asked me why I ask you to tell stories and I told you that I would tell you about the story that you told today. Right?

Patient: Yes.

Therapist: And I would help you understand what it means. What this story tells me is that you are getting much better in your thinking. You're thinking more clearly.

Patient: About my silliness?

Therapist: You're thinking clearly about a lot of things, that you're not thinking all over the place and many different things at the same time. You're thinking in straight lines — that one thing follows another and that you're not jumping around in your thinking. Do you know what

I am talking about?

Patient: Yes.

Therapist: You used to jump from one thing to the next.

Patient: What does that mean?

Therapist: You wouldn't care whether the second sentence had anything to do with the first sentence. Then, the second thing you said had nothing to do with the first thing you said. Now you try to make them connected. Well, anyway, the stories are better stories. They are not as silly; they are connected together well.

Patient: Oh, they're better!

Therapist: Yes, they're better. One thing follows another; they aren't all over the place. And it's a happy story, and it shows that you're thinking about pleasant things.

Patient: Yeah, and it's more like your stories that you always tell. Right?

Therapist: Right. Right. It's more like my stories and it shows that this girl isn't a baby, like when a baby is told no, it cries and he says, "I want what I want when I want it. I want it right now." In your story the girl can wait. She knows, she appreciates, she realizes that her mother and father don't have the money then, but she's willing to wait until she's older to get money, whereas babies will want just what they want at that moment. They can't wait. They get very angry that they have to wait. So I think it's a very good story in many ways — that she learned to be patient, that she learned to wait, and that she realized that it was a dream. It wasn't real. Sometimes you would have trouble —

Patient: Well, that's what I'm doing!

Therapist: Sometimes you confuse things with things in your imagination and this shows that you aren't confusing those things that — you're clear as to what's your imagination and what's real. Right?

Patient: My imagination is going to Greece and going to Bali. Sometimes in the day I forget all about it. I listen. I do whatever my mother says. It's the same as what Laura did. That's what I do too.

Therapist: Hhmmm. Right.

Patient: Be patient. That's why instead of going to Bali I could pretend and like that.

Therapist: Right. Listen, it's fun to pretend, but it's important to know when you're pretending and when you're not, and you're learning to do that pretty well. Like when you were telling your grandfather last week or the other day, whenever it was —

Patient: Yeah, the other day.

Therapist: Right, that you were in a regular second grade class, you knew you were making believe then. Right?

Patient: Yeah.

Therapist: Now you didn't really think you were in a second grade class, did you?

Patient: No.

Therapist: You see, that's important. If you want to tell jokes like that and have fun and say things like that, it's important that you know exactly what's real and what's make-believe. And sometimes you have to think about that — what's the real thing and what's the make-believe, but I think you're getting much better at that.

Patient: Yes. Say that again.

Therapist: You want me to tell you something again. What I want to tell you is that it's important that you know the difference between what's make-believe and what's real. Sometimes you were a little confused there, but now you're clearer on what the make-believe things are and what the real things are, and what you are dreaming about and what is really happening. And I think the important thing for you, although it's fun to think about nice things and dream about them once in a while, is not to spend too much of your time dreaming about these things — just part of the time and that you have to spend a lot of time getting real pleasures, having real fun, friends, and going out and doing things like that. But it's also fun to enjoy the dreams and the nice thoughts that you have as well.

Okay. Let's stop here. I won't tell a story today. What we did instead was to discuss the story and sometimes we do that instead of my telling a story.

Patient: I think that would be better.

Therapist: Anything else you want to say before we stop.
Patient: No.
Therapist: Okay then.
Patient: But one thing. It was a very good story. I loved it.
Therapist: Good.
Patient: But I have to tell you other things too.
Therapist: Okay. Next time.

The conversation presented here is typical of the kind I conduct with brain injured children. With patient repetition, the messages sink in. Here Mike reveals acceptance of the adjustments and minor frustrations he has to make because of his father's financial difficulties. He provides himself with compensatory gratification by dreaming about travel — not a completely healthy adaptation in view of his tendency to withdraw into fantasy. He advises himself, however, to be patient which implies hope for future satisfaction. Although the dream also has a quality of narcotic desensitization to the pains and frustrations of his world of reality, it does have some important symbolism which reveals definite therapeutic advance. Whereas in Mike's earlier stories lobsters and fish (representative of unconscious complexes) were presented as chaotic and anxiety-provoking, in this story they are clearly delineated and fearlessly pursued (fished out of the water) — a clear statement of the patient's increasing comfort in being confronted with previously repressed material. The swimming in the sea also reveals his lessening anxiety over involving himself in life's endeavors.

Now in his twenty-fourth month of therapy, Mike is still being seen once weekly. He is on a much lower dose of chlorpromazine than when he started therapy, and his dextroamphetamine has also been reduced. Whereas when he began treatment he could not read, he is now reading at the early second grade level. Mathematics is now at the first to second grade level. Although educational efforts and his normal growth have certainly contributed to these academic advances, these improvements would not have been as great, I believe, had not therapy enhanced his motivation significantly. Silliness and abnormal eye and finger movements, although still present, are vastly reduced. Hypochondriacal preoccupations are practically absent and perseveration is at a minimum. His awareness of the world and his relative place in it is dramatically improved. Mike is much more sensitive to the role he plays in his difficulties. With peers, his relationships have definitely improved. He exhibits far less of his bizarre behavior and so is accepted more by them. Mike is still, however, very much the second class citizen with normal peers. He is called upon when no one else is available; and he is the last choice when teams are chosen. He is most sensitive to these slights, but nevertheless has his fun when he can. Contacts with neurologically impaired children have also improved. After being teased, he tells a good tale about how well he fought back — so he has learned the principles although he still cannot really hold his own.

Mike still has a long way to go and I will most likely be working with him for many years to come. What his future will bring is hard for anyone to predict. There is good reason to believe that he will ultimately be able to master some trade or skill and be self-supporting. More gratifying relationships with peers (especially handicapped) is also a reasonable expectation for him. It is toward these goals that his therapy is aimed.

Example 3

Steve, the boy with a disciplinary problem had a basic organic problem which contributed to the previously described psychogenic difficulties. He was born with his umbilical cord twisted around his neck, and although briefly flaccid, he quickly recovered. At age five, in association with otitis media, he had an afebrile convulsion of the focal motor type which was followed by a flaccid right hemiparesis of five hours duration. An electroencephalogram taken at that time was grossly abnormal with continuous paroxysmal discharges of the spike, and the spike and wave type. From that time — and throughout his course of treatment — Steve was maintained on anticonvulsant medication. At age five-and-one-half, he suffered a mild case of meningitis, probably due to Coxsackie B virus. At six-and-one-half, he experienced a psychomotor seizure after an attempt to wean him from anticonvulsants. His only other seizure occurred while in treatment — at a time when attempts were made to further alter his drug regimen.

The primary manifestation of his organic difficulties was his impulsivity. Although psychogenic elements were contributing to his angry outbursts, there was no question in my mind that neurophysiologic impairments in impulse control were also operative. He was acutely aware of this defect in his ability to control himself and would often castigate himself mercilessly after his outbursts. Less dramatic, was his inability to suppress critical comments — criticisms which others often shared but could restrain themselves from verbalizing. Chlorpromazine was helpful in reducing some of his impulsivity, but even at sublethargic doses, his outbursts remained a major problem.

The sequences presented here occurred during the middle and late phases of his therapy. During his eighth month of therapy, Steve told this story:

> Once upon a time there was a boy and this boy wanted a girl friend and he said, "Will you be my girl friend?" And the girl said, "No, I won't be your girl friend." And he says, "Why?" And she says, "Well you're always getting into trouble." And he was trying for about nine years and he was still getting into a lot of trouble. He even got into trouble in the major leagues playing.
>
> And he still didn't realize that since he's in the trouble he would never have a wife. One day when he was about ninety-nine, he realized his problem and so he stopped getting into trouble and he had a wife and lived happily ever after. He even got back into trouble. I think my story is no good.
>
> *Therapist:* It's good, but kind of short compared to many you've told.
> *Patient:* I just can't think of any more.
> *Therapist:* All right. Let me tell a story about yours, okay?
> *Patient:* No, let me try another. Once upon a time there was a prince and this prince went —— and this prince was a dragon killer. He used to go out every day and kill dragons. Ha, ha, ha. And he killed, and one day he met a

dragon and the dragon said, "Don't touch me." Then he ignored it and he killed the dragon and he put his hide on the shelf. And then that night a huge giant, one of the most dreadful things in the world, came rising out and with footsteps crumpled up the house and all the horrible things began to eat every part inside it.

The prince was waking up on this and he had to run away. All the court, the king, the queen, and the princess escaped and they built another castle. And the same thing happened again. He went out and he found a dragon and he said, "You better not kill me." He killed it and then it happened for ten years until he realized how cruel he was being to this world. He was killing everything. He was destroying everything.

That made him so mad that he started riots in the castle. He burned up the chairs and beds. He did all that and pretty soon his whole family, uch, said, "Leave us alone." He said, "Good." And he was very lonely for a lot of years until he realized that he apologized to the next dragon he met and then forgot about it. Now he was very unhappy for the rest of his life.

Therapist: Very unhappy?

Patient: Yes.

Therapist: Why was he unhappy?

Patient: Because his family had left him.

Therapist: Yes, and it was all because he had killed so many dragons.

Patient: Yes, and he was so mad that he had killed so many and that he had started riots in the —

Therapist: Um-hmmm.

Patient: They started riots in the castle like burning chairs and he burned the king's private papers.

Therapist: I see.

Patient: Okay, the end. Um, um, I haven't finished yet. The moral: do not get angry if you have done something wrong.

Therapist: Uh-huh.

Patient: Does that story show more imagination?

Therapist: Yes, and that was an excellent story.

In Steve's first story here he reveals his feelings of helplessness over controlling his angry outbursts. No woman would marry him because of his behavior — it is not until age ninety-nine that he is able to bring it under control — and even then only temporarily.

In his second story Steve (represented by the prince), kills a dragon without provocation. The giant's vengeance is something horrible — his whole family cannot escape from the ensuing devastation. However, he does not learn from this terrible retribution and once again wantonly murders a dragon — a clear statement of Steve's appreciation that punishment is often of little avail in deterring him from repeating his hostile outbursts. The prince's frustration over his inability to inhibit himself from acting out his anger produces even further rage which is directed against himself: "he started riots in the castle. He burned up the chairs and beds."

This behavior relates clearly to the clinical situation in which Steve deprecated himself relentlessly for his poor self-control. In the story, his self-destructiveness then alienates his family: "He did all that and pretty soon his whole family, uch, said, 'Leave us alone.' " This also was reflected in the reality of his life — his self-deprecation was at times irritating and did contribute toward his being lonely. The castle destruction melee is not symbolic of hostility directed toward himself alone. In the process "he burned the king's private papers," which suggests that anger toward his father is also being vented. The moral, "Do not get angry if you have done something wrong," reflects Steve's wish that he be less enraged at himself for his poor impulse control.

This is the story I told in response:

Once upon a time there was a prince and one time he was walking down a path in a forest and suddenly what does he see ahead of him but a dragon. And this dragon started snorting fire and started to attack this prince. So the prince said to this dragon, "If you don't stop, I'm going to have to fight you with my sword." And the dragon said,

"Okay, ha, ha, ha, ha, ha." So, anyway this dragon didn't listen to the prince and they started to fight and the dragon started to attack the prince and the prince fought him and beat him and killed him.

And the prince said, "Well I got rid of that guy." And the prince's friend said, "Don't you feel bad that you killed that dragon?" And he said, "Not particularly." And he said, "I would have felt bad if I was the kind of person who would pick on innocent dragons," he said, "but this dragon started to pick on me. This dragon started to fight with me. I was minding my own business, I wasn't bothering him and he deserves that. He was going to try to kill me so I don't feel bad about killing someone who tried to kill me."

And the friend thought. Yes, the prince is probably right. Anyway the friend came across a dragon that was bothering him and he said, "I wish that dragon were dead." And the friend was overwhelmed with guilt. He felt so terrible. He said to himself, "What a worm I am, what a worm I am. I just want to kill. I'm a killer and —"

And the prince said, "You're not a killer. When you are with a dragon who bothers you, it's reasonable. It's reasonable to want to do something terrible. Even though you want to kill him. That's one of the thoughts that human beings have."

Well, this friend had a lot of trouble accepting that fact but gradually as time went on he realized that the prince was right that when people bother you it is reasonable that you have terrible thoughts. Thoughts of killing, thoughts of harming, and things of this sort. And when he realized that, he felt better about himself.

And the lesson in that story is: it's normal to have feelings of wanting to hurt someone if they bother you. The end. Do you have any comments you want to make with that story?

Patient: Okay, yeah, it's a good story.

Therapist: Well, okay.

In my story, I directed myself to the exaggerated guilt over the expression of anger which was contributing significantly to

Steve's need to flagellate himself psychologically. In the patient's story, the hostile expression was invariably unprovoked — the dragon slaying was wanton. In reality, Steve did at times initiate hostile interchanges; however, he was often victimized since he was excellent prey for bullies by predictably gratifying their need for violent response. He felt equally guilty whether his anger was provoked or unprovoked. Angry expression, no matter how justified, was cause for Steve to loathe himself and to assuage his guilt with extreme self-deprecation. This attitude derived, in part, from his parents' (especially his mother's) inhibitions in this area. My story was told in the hope of alleviating some of this guilt and of making him more comfortable with his expression of hostility. Conferences were also held with the parents and they were flexible enough to appreciate their own distortions regarding angry expression and to be more tolerant of it in their child.

My story had a relatively narrow aim: to assuage guilt over the appropriate expression of hostility. It was not my intention that Steve end up guiltless when guilt would be appropriate. It was also told as a step toward my goal of getting him to realize that his neurological impairment made it difficult for him to control himself and that greater concentration in self-control would be much more helpful to him than self-flagellation.

Five months later, Steve told this story:

> Once upon a time there was a giant sea monster. It went around wrecking ships. He couldn't control himself. When he'd wreck a ship he'd eat the sailors. His other problem was that he wrecked too many ships.
>
> One day a huge whale was seen over the horizon. They thought it was a whale, but it really was the sea monster. After he wrecked the ship and ate the sailors, he was in big trouble because the Royal Navy was after him. A destroyer shot a bomb. It landed very close to him and blew off half his body. He didn't grow a new half body. He was very unhappy. That really gave him a pain. Then he stopped wrecking ships. He found other food like fish, huge salmons, and octopuses.

The lesson of that story is: if you get out of control and you sock too many people you're in big trouble. Something bad may happen to you and you may regret it.

The story reflects some of the inner turmoil and repressed hostility this boy harbored. Whereas in the previous sequence, Steve is helpless to control the expression of his hostility — regardless of the consequences — here he suppresses it out of his appreciation of the consequences of its unbridled release: "He was very unhappy. That really gave him a pain. Then he stopped wrecking ships." In addition, Steve finds substitutive gratifications: instead of eating sailors who call out the Royal Navy, "He found other food like fish, huge salmons, and octopuses." Such a diet is far more appropriate nutriment, even for a sea monster. The lesson epitomizes his resolve to control himself: "If you get out of control and you sock too many people you're in big trouble. Something bad may happen to you and you may regret it."

This is the story I told in response:

Once upon a time there was a giant sea animal. This animal used to think a lot about how much fun it would be to go around sinking ships and eating sailors instead of eating the fish and the salmon and the octopuses which he always used to eat. He spoke about this to a friend of his who told him that he didn't think that doing that would be all that great. They discussed it for a long time and the sea monster gradually realized that if he were to do that, all the ships and sailors in the oceans would be very frightened of him and he realized that it would be much better to be liked by them than to be feared by them. In addition, they both decided that if he did that he would lead a very sad and lonely life because all the ships and sailors would run away from him and that he would have no friends, whereas if he was friendly with the ships and sailors he could have good times with them. Lastly, he realized that it would be a terrible thing to eat the sailors. They were human beings and to take their lives would be cruel because he knew that he would not want anyone to take his life. So when he thought about all these things, he knew it was better to control himself and not sink the ships and eat the sailors.

The moral of this story is that there are three good reasons to control yourself from doing harmful things to others. The first is that if everyone is afraid of you they will not like you. The second is that if you do things like that you will be sad and lonely and you won't have any friends. The third and last is that it's a terrible thing to do to others. Harming someone or hurting someone is cruel.

In my story I appealed further to his reason to assist in the suppressive process. Fuller appreciation of the untoward consequences of one's behavior (psychodynamic pressures notwithstanding) can help one inhibit himself from acting out impulses.

I am well aware that many factors contributed to Steve's hostility, and that encouraging suppression alone would not have been of much help to him. The elements which engendered his anger were also focused upon in treatment. The sequences presented in earlier chapters demonstrate some of the approaches used to elucidate and treat these underlying psychologic problems. Here I have focused only on Steve's impulsivity problem and the appeal to conscious control which is an intrinsic part of the treatment of children with minimal brain dysfunction.

Section III

Clinical Examples of
Full Courses of
Treatment

14. A GIRL WITH A PSYCHOGENIC LEARNING DISORDER

Difficulty in learning is probably the most common reason for referral to the child therapist. Many children's psychological problems are either denied or unrecognized by parents, but when they enter school and are observed more objectively their problems are detected. The more rigid demands of the school situation may also cause problems to manifest themselves for the first time. The difficulties which cause the learning disorder are most often in the home and so a detailed evaluation of the child's family is necessary if the therapist is to adequately appreciate the factors which are bringing it about.

Extreme learning disability results in total separation from school. When older, such children will often be referred to as "college or high school dropouts." There are children, however, who have "dropped out" at lower levels, but the law does not permit them to leave the school situation. Such "grade school dropouts" — and even "kindergarten dropouts" — remain physically in the classroom but learn little.

Although a parent may complain that his child isn't learning in school, this does not mean that the parent himself is fully involved in the child's learning process. Often the parent's interest is minimal or he is ambivalent — the noncommitted elements may even be unconscious. Children reflect and comply with their parents real, even though unexpressed, attitudes. The parent with a basically healthy investment in the educational process will transmit this to the child, either overtly or covertly. One child comes home from school, proudly displays his work, and is given enthusiastic support and praise; another is ignored or receives only a perfunctory reply. Some parents are solely concerned with performance in sports and inquire only how the child did in physical education. Others consider the educational process a necessary evil, an experience which must be patiently tolerated until one is old enough to go out into the world and begin living. There are parents who see the total purpose of education to be the diploma whose only value is that it is a ticket to a higher paying job. In other homes there is a total lack of intellectual curiosity or enthusiasm for learning. It is in atmospheres such as these that the child's basic, and probably inborn, desire to learn, to discover, and to master the unknown becomes atrophied.

The healthy child wants to learn, in part, out of the desire to identify with, emulate, and grow up to be like an admired adult figure. If a father is inadequate or a failure in life, whether it be the result of his own personal problems or of external factors such as discrimination, poverty, and war, he is less likely to provide his son with a model which engenders productive emulation. If a parent's attitudes are that "It's not what you know but who you know;" that the good student is a "sissy;" or that intellectuals, teachers, and "highbrows" are communists and are, therefore, to be distrusted, the child's desire to learn will be undermined.

Emotional deprivation is another cause of disinterest in learning. In the extreme, the child with severe emotional deprivation in the first few months of life may lose his appetite, become marasmic, and even die. Lesser degrees of deprivation can result in psychosis — with its associated withdrawal from life and preoccupation with inner fantasy. In such a state the child is little inclined toward meaningful involvement in the educational process. Psychotic children may, however, exhibit an uncanny ability to learn such things as species of dinosaurs, railroad schedules, and baseball statistics. They may have such a vast storehouse of knowledge in their areas of interest that they may give the impression that they are, at the very least, brilliant. But their knowledge is quite restricted and totally unrelated to the human scene. Although their memory for baseball minutiae may be prodigious, they cannot, and may never have, played the game. Although a walking railroad information booth, they have little interest in using a train to visit any person or place of interest. In other psychotic children, the failure to learn may give one the impression that they are retarded. In reality, they are pseudoretardates, that is, they are perfectly capable of learning but their severe emotional problems prevent them from doing so.

Children whose emotional deprivation has not been severe enough to produce psychosis may still react in such a way that learning is interfered with. They may exhibit antisocial personality disorders in which they live for the moment, want immediate satisfaction, and cannot wait for the more remote gratifications that education offers. Others, who are deprived, may react with the attitude: "The world offers me little warmth or pleasure. There's nothing to work for. There's nothing to learn for."

The overprotective parent may interfere in many ways with a child's learning. By doing homework for him and assuming many other educational responsibilities the child becomes an educational cripple — incapacitated in learning on his own, unable to figure things out for himself, and ill-equipped to undertake his scholastic obligations. The child is also deprived of the gratifications associated with mastering tasks, doing things on his own, and solving problems for himself — experiences which make school work more pleasurable and interesting and which serve to enhance his incentive to learn. Such parents may need the child to remain in the home; for the child's growth, development, and ultimate independence may deprive them of their only meaningful feelings of usefulness. Although they may profess interest in the child's educational advancement, their behavior will often reveal their unconscious tendencies to maintain him in the infantile state. The child may try to comply with these diametrically opposed demands. A part of him attempts to succeed in accordance with his parents' overt statements which encourage academic success; other forces within him drive him to failure, in compliance with their unconscious desires that he do so.

A related phenomenon is what I call the "Rich Man's Son

Syndrome." The child who grows up knowing that no matter how poorly he may do in school he will ultimately take over his father's lucrative business may have little incentive to learn. A small amount of anxiety about the future outcome of an endeavor enhances our efficiency; too much may paralyze us; but none at all may result in a total lack of incentive. Such fathers are in a difficult position. It is reasonable that they may want to hand down to their progeny the products of their labors and make their children's lives easier than theirs may have been. However, by so doing they are depriving their children of incentive-engendering anxiety and the opportunity to enjoy the ego-enhancing sense of mastery that comes from building something by oneself. Children who grow up in this manner bring to mind James Thurber's comment: "And then he was as happy as a king. And everybody knows how happy kings are." Of course, to take father's business and expand it creatively can provide gratifications. On the whole, however, real satisfactions are more likely to be achieved when one "starts from scratch." What are such fathers to do then? Are they to inform their children that they will never be allowed to enter the business; that upon the father's retirement or death it will be sold to strangers? It is indeed a dilemma. The therapist can only present the problem to the parents; he must be most cautious not to impose any decisions on anyone.

Some parents are extremely distrustful of the world, or they may exhibit phobic attitudes toward many aspects of the environment. They are constantly communicating to the child that terrible things can happen outside the home. The neighborhood is too rough; streets are too dangerous for bike riding; the child will get lost, and so on. When the child does venture forth into the world — which he has come to see as perilous — he knows that he can flee back home at the first sign of danger. But in school he is captive; running home is not possible — so he either refuses to go or is panicked when sent.

Parental overcommitment to the educational process is also a common problem. Such a parent may have been unsuccessful in obtaining the education he wanted and may hope to satisfy vicariously through the child his frustrated desire for academic success. To an extent this phenomenon is normal. When, however, the parent's need for such compensation is so great that he places undue pressure on the child, then the foundation for a psychogenic learning problem is laid. The child usually senses that his parents' deep involvement in his school performance has little to do with their genuine interest in him and is more related to their own inappropriate needs. Such a child may respond by doing poorly; and his parents may respond with: "How can you do this to us?" Although these children are "cutting off their noses to spite their faces," for many of them the personal loss is worth the vengeful gratification. Other children whose parents do not have excessive involvement in education may have other reasons to be angry at their parents and this hostility may be expressed through school failure. Russell, the boy described in Chapter 9 whose severe learning disability related in part to the hostility he harbored toward his rejecting parents, told this story:

> This took place in the Civil War. Me and another lieutenant commander had to fly in a balloon above the clouds. We are supposed to plot out the enemy troops. It was a deep fog and we got very low. We were looking for the enemy stockade or their fortress. They were using trees in a circle. It was a good defense because who would suspect trees. But someone made a bad mistake. We thought they were three miles away and really they were eleven-and-a-half miles away. Finally we found their fortress and when we went in, there was no one there.
>
> So we went back to our fortress and there we found that they had taken over our fortress while we were away. So we attacked the place and blew it up. We blew up our own fortress in order to overcome our enemy.
>
> The moral of that story is: seek and you shall find.

Russell is represented by his own side's fortress. So walled in, he can protect himself from the traumas he anticipates will be inflicted upon him by a hostile world. It is common for the child to view his parents' rejection as hostility and to enhance such hostility with his own projected anger. Russell's attempt to vent his own rage on his parents (the enemy fortress) proves futile at first — his foe eludes him. He finally finds the hated parents within himself (the parts of them which have been incorporated), and he destroys his own fortress for the satisfaction of killing them. In a sense he is saying: "My hatred of my parents is so great, and my frustration over not being able to enjoy vengeance so profound, that I am willing to kill myself if, in the process, I can destroy the part of them that exists within me." In addition, the suicidal gesture represents a compliance with the hostile parental introjects which would have him destroy himself. The hostile element in the parents' ambivalence was strong and each harbored deep-seated wishes for this boy's removal. Such parental impulses were incorporated and are being acted out in this fantasy. Although this boy was not overtly suicidal, his severe school problem was a form of slow suicide. It not only served to hurt himself and his parents in accordance with the aforementioned psychodynamic formulation but, on a more superficial and perhaps more conscious level, it was a source of frustration and humiliation to them and so provided the patient with retaliatory gratifications. This story has been presented here because it clearly demonstrates some of the common psychodynamic patterns present when the learning disability relates to hostility toward the parents.

In response, I told this story:

Well, this took place in the Civil War and I and my military colleague, a lieutenant commander, were involved in plotting out the position of our enemy and we were in a balloon and we were able to get pretty accurate information because they were not too far away and it was a foggy day and we were able to descend fairly low. Now, however, somebody must have goofed because when the day finally came to attack, we found that they weren't there and we figured that they could not have gone far because we certainly would have heard them. So we decided to return to our own fortress.

Well, you can't imagine how amazed we were to find

that when we returned to our fortress there they were. They had occupied our fortress. Now someone made the suggestion that the best way to get rid of them would be to destroy our own fortress, to blow it up, and then we would be blowing them up. But then someone else said, "You know. That's kind of foolish. We don't have to destroy our own fortress, the fortress that we have worked so hard in building and making. It's an excellent fortress and there must be a better way than that." So then someone else thought that there must be some other way to get them out of there. Now he decided that a good way would be to spread gas over the place. They went to a nearby town and they managed to get a large amount of gas from a chemical factory — a gas that was quite irritating, but not lethal. In other words, it wouldn't kill these men.

Well, what they did then was that they got these tanks of gas through pipes and they pumped it. It was a primitive apparatus. It was in the days of the Civil War and they pumped this gas into the fortress and what they did was they let one gate open and they pumped the gas into the back. Well, the men came tearing out right into our hands, and we took them all and made them prisoners of war. We did this in such a way that there wasn't one life lost and we won the day.

And the lesson of that story is — do you know the lesson of that story?

Patient: No, I think you better go ahead and tell it.

Therapist: Well, one lesson is: you don't have to necessarily destroy your own property in the attempt to conquer an enemy. The second lesson is: it isn't necessary to kill an enemy or blast him to smithereens in order to win a battle. You can often take him prisoner and then protect yourself from him or put yourself in such a position that you are no longer bothered by him. That's the end of my story.

Do you have any comments about that?

Patient: Yeah. This is the days of the Civil War, right?

Therapist: Right.

Patient: He got the gas from a chemical factory?

Therapist: Right. There were chemical factories in the days of the Civil War.

In my story I communicated the message that one need not destroy oneself to rid oneself of hostile introjects. Russell can preserve his own integrity and still exorcise malevolent influences within himself. The destruction of his own fortress, in his story, is in part a compliance with parental introjects which direct him to destroy himself. In mine, failure to comply with this parental dictate does not cause the dire consequences Russell might imagine, but instead the results are quite beneficial to him. In addition, he can defy his parents and remove them from the position where they can traumatize him without necessarily destroying them in the process.

Some children find that when they do well they get little response from their parents. But when they do poorly they suddenly find themselves the center of attraction. The attention may be punitive, but for such children, as it is for most, it is better to be punished than to be totally ignored.

In some homes there is an atmosphere of repressed emotions — an attitude derived from deep within our culture. The unemotional person is considered to be somehow higher and finer than someone who is more expressive of his feelings. Hardly a single television announcer failed to admire Jacqueline Kennedy's forbearance at her husband's funeral. Crying in school is one of the worst humiliations known to many children. Even in the labor room many consider it crude to cry out. And the ideal adolescent is the one who "plays it cool." When such attitudes go too far, the child becomes timid and repressed. He lacks spontaneity and the kind of self-assertiveness necessary to successful learning. He may do well in subjects like mathematics and science, where the answers are precise and reveal little of the inner self, but in liberal arts subjects like creative writing, where imagination and self-expression are required, he may fail abysmally out of the fear of exposing himself.

Some children are highly perfectionistic and are too insecure to tolerate doing average or even good work. Either they must be the best or they will do nothing. When they choose the latter course, they justify their withdrawal with the specious argument: "I'd do extremely well if I wanted to try. I've just decided not to." The flaw in their reasoning, of course, is that they probably wouldn't do as well as they would like to think. By not trying they avoid confrontation with their inadequacies and their grandiose expectations of themselves. Some children in this category have very accomplished parents and they have dropped out of the educational race because they feel that they can never reach their parents' success. My experience has been that when this occurs the parental success is not the sole cause. The parent, for example, may have been so involved in his own career that he has neglected the child; or his standards for the child may have been too high; or he may have been unconsciously in competition with the child.

In some families which have not reached their vocational, economic, or social aspirations, there is a constant condemnation of the successful which, of course, stems from jealousy. The child may fear, either consciously or unconsciously, that were he to be successful, he too would be the object of similar scorn and ridicule.

Some parents deny that their children could be anything but perfect, and consider the child's school difficulty to be the result of teacher inadequacy or school system deficiency. They further cripple the child by fostering in him delusions of competence and encouraging his tendency to blame others for his own deficits, thus depriving him of the opportunity and incentive to rectify his deficiencies.

There are many other psychological factors and situations which may interfere with learning. The child who is chronically anxious, depressed, hypochondriacal, laden with guilt, obsessed with neurotic preoccupations, or other psychopathological symptoms cannot attend properly to his school work. The child suffering severe economic deprivation is more concerned with providing himself with life's necessities than indulging himself in the luxury of learning. Therapists have recently become more sensitive to the fact that educational methods themselves have not been what they could be. Many *are* stultifying and interfere with learning. Children have had to learn in spite of these drawbacks of the system. There is no question that such antiquated methods contribute to the learning difficulty of some children. At the same time that such improved educational techniques as programmed instruction, educational television, and ingenious audio-visual aids are being introduced, parents and educators are coming to realize that the direct personal involvement of the teacher with her pupil is a vital element in the learning process. Again, many children learn in spite of their teachers' inability to form meaningful human involvements with them, but for many, such inadequacies contribute significantly to learning difficulties.

The factors which may contribute to psychogenic learning problems are multiple, and in no child is only one element the cause. Although I have outlined a few of the more common situations which bring about such learning disorders, I have by no means exhausted the possibilities.

The Mutual Storytelling Technique can be useful in the treatment of children with psychogenic learning disabilities. In this chapter I demonstrate its use in the therapy of Linda, a nine-and-one-half-year-old girl. She was referred because of negativism and chronic surly attitude. She did poorly in school in spite of high intelligence and this was primarily due to her recalcitrant attitude toward doing homework and classroom assignments. She often "split hairs" in conversations and was passive-aggressive in cooperating in household chores. Linda was generally inhibited in overtly expressing her feelings.

Linda's mother was an extremely good-looking woman whose character structure was basically hysterical. Owing to her rigid Catholic upbringing, she was sexually inhibited; however, after a few years of marriage she became orgastic. She freely walked around naked in the house; a practice consistent with other exhibitionistic tendencies. At the time of Linda's birth the mother felt too anxious to breast feed, and most of the child's care was given over to a housekeeper who was not too warm a person herself. The mother described herself as not being too interested in cuddling Linda or having her climb into her bed when she was a toddler. On projective tests the mother revealed repression of sexuality and hostility toward men. Also, the theme of symbolically castrating men was recurrent in her dreams.

Linda's father, a businessman, exhibited no definite evidence of psychopathology either in clinical interview or on projective testing. In fact, he was one of the healthiest men I can recall having seen in a clinical situation. The only area of suspected psychopathology was his marriage to an hysterical, sexually inhibited woman. However, at the time of Linda's therapy, the parents' sexual relationship was fairly satisfactory.

When Linda was two years old, a brother was prematurely born. For many months there was some question as to whether he would survive; and until Linda was four, the mother's physical and emotional involvement in his care resulted in further deprivations for Linda.

Linda was seen twice weekly. During the first five to ten minutes of each session the mother joined us to provide ancillary information about Linda's behavior. Advice and recommendations were also given to the mother at this time.

During Linda's first session, she told this story:

Once upon a time there was a boy who lived with his mother and father and sisters. He went on a picnic with his friend. He learned how to sail and went on a sailboat. Then, he saw a hurt dolphin on the edge of the beach. The dolphin had a spear in it. There was a vet's house near the beach and he took it to the vet. The vet took out the spear and the vet helped the boy put the dolphin in the water. Then, he went back to his picnic.

The moral of this story is: always help animals.

The dolphin and the boy symbolize two facets of Linda's personality. The dolphin is the part that considers itself to have been deeply wounded, perhaps sexually. The boy is the more assertive part, which seeks help from the vet who, of course, is the therapist. She anticipates that, in treatment, I will remove the source of her trauma by merely being asked to do so and that she need do no more than lie passively during the process of extraction. Then she can return to her life of fun (the picnic).

At this early phase of treatment — I had only known the girl a few minutes — I could not be sure about the exact significance of the spear (beyond the obvious hostile and sexual implications). Rather than introduce into my story elements based on my speculations about the meaning of the spear which might have been erroneous, I sidestepped this question and focused on the "safer" issue of her expectations from treatment — an issue which manifested itself with far greater certainty in her story. Accordingly, I related the following:

Once there was a boy who lived with his mother and father and two sisters. He went on a picnic with his friend. He learned how to sail and went out one day in a sailboat. While out in the sailboat he saw a dolphin rapidly swimming very close to his boat. He asked the dolphin why he was swimming so fast and the dolphin said that some people were chasing him with a spear. The boy looked up and sure enough there were people in another boat and they had a large spear which they were aiming at the dolphin. He told the dolphin to stay close behind his boat for protection. He also told him that there was a vet who lived on the beach who could help take care of him if he were to get hurt, but he hoped that that would not be necessary.

He then signaled the boat with the people with the spear, and learned that the dolphin and the people had been arguing and fighting for a long time. He suggested that they all get together at a rock near the shore and try to talk about their troubles. As they sailed toward the rock, the boy worked the sails and the dolphin helped push and steer. When they got to the rock, they all talked together about the troubles between the dolphin and the people. It took a lot of talking and sometimes they had to ask the vet for advice. But, they did most of it on their own, and finally the problems were settled because they worked hard.

My story has two morals. One, see if you can settle arguments first by talking before they get so bad that people are throwing spears at you. Two, try to help yourself first before turning to others for assistance.

As can be seen, the exact nature of the conflict that resulted in the dolphin's being speared remains unspecified, so that nothing is said about it other than to urge the child to work it through by talking and understanding rather than by hostile action. The hope here was that my story would stimulate analy-

804

tic inquiry and discourage acting out. It is, however, well known that at first the child expects the therapist to do all the work. In my story, therefore, Linda is encouraged to be much more on her own and to call on me only when she cannot.

Four weeks later (during three of which I was away on vacation), Linda told this story:

> Once upon a time there was a deer named Bambi. He lived in a forest. In a little hut in the forest lived a boy. His brother and his mother and his father lived in the hut with him. One day, the boy found Bambi in the woods where he was hurt. It was a long way to the vet's and they didn't have a car. Then the vet fixed up Bambi's leg. He stayed there one week and the leg healed. Then the boy took him back to the woods and let him go.
>
> The moral of this story is: be kind to animals.

Bambi, of course, stands for Linda. The story is quite similar to her first. It reflects Linda's feelings that the only way she can get attention and affection is to be traumatized. This attitude, I felt, was derived, in part, from her experiences at age two (the time of her brother's premature birth), when she observed that illness did, indeed, get mother's attention. In response, I told this story:

> Once upon a time there was a deer named Bambi. She lived in the woods with her mother and father and her brother. Her brother used to be sick a lot and her mother was always worrying about him and taking care of him. She seemed to have little time for Bambi. This made Bambi quite angry, but she never told anyone; she kept it all inside.
>
> One day, quite by accident, Bambi got hurt, and then she found that her mother gave her lots of attention. From then on she kept getting hurt a lot and sometimes she didn't even realize that she was doing it to get her mother's attention. But when she was sick or hurt she couldn't go out and play with the other deer and have fun with them. So she gradually realized that this wasn't a good way to

get her mother to spend time with her. This made her sad and lonely again.

One day, as she was sitting alone, sad because her mother was spending all her time with her brother, a good friend of hers passed by. Her friend said, "Why are you so sad?" "Because my mother spends all her time with my brother," she said. Her friend asked her if she had spoken to her mother and she answered that she hadn't; that she was scared to. So the friend suggested that she try to talk to her anyway and see what happens. She did this, and her mother was able to give her more time. Then she wasn't sad or lonely or angry. And also, she didn't have to get sick or hurt to get her mother's attention.

And the moral of this story is that if something bothers you, speak up. Don't hold your anger in. Don't get hurt in order to get attention, because if you do you'll miss out on all the fun with the other kids.

Subsequent stories confirmed my supposition that Linda felt that only by acting hurt and wounded could she attract affection (thus the chronic surly attitude which did, indeed, get her some attention). Further work clarified the meaning of the spear. If there were sexual elements in the symbol (a reflection of oedipal impulses toward her father) they were less meaningful than the hostile connotations. It represented her mother's rejection, which was seen as hostility (concretized as a spear) as well as her own hostility being turned onto herself because of her fear that its outward expression would result in even further rejection by her mother.

My chief aim in treatment was to help Linda assert herself and express her resentment, so that her neurotic channeling of hostility would be diminished. In addition, attempts were made to help her improve her relationship with her mother to enable her to get more affection from her and to avoid frustrations and resentment-engendering experiences. Although some improvement in the mother's feelings toward the patient was hoped for, I knew that her capacity in this area was somewhat limited. Linda was therefore encouraged to assert herself in the acquisition of friends as well. My hope also was that with less pent-up anger she would be able to concentrate better on her school work and not exhibit the passive-aggressive attitudes toward her teacher which further impaired her scholastic functioning.

At the end of her second month of treatment, Linda told this story:

> Once upon a time there was a girl named Sue who lived in the woods. She went out to get flowers for her mother and she found a baby wolf. The wolf's mother had died in a fire. She brought up the wolf and when it was older she let it go. Later, the wolf came back and played with her.
>
> Her mother didn't know about the wolf and one day her mother found her in the woods with the wolf and her mother shot the wolf, but he didn't die. Sue was angry. The wolf was her friend. She told her mother what she had done. Her mother said it would heal. She will be all right. Then her mother also played with the wolf. The moral of this story is: how the girl got the wolf for a friend.

The wolf, of course, represents Linda, who sees herself as having been injured by her mother. The mother appears twice: first as the wolf's mother and then as Sue's mother. In this way Linda can express her hostility toward her mother — the wolf's mother burns to death — and still have her available — Sue's mother is very much present. Linda expresses her resentment over her being traumatized at the mother's hands: "Sue was angry. The wolf was her friend. She told her mother what she had done." She vents her angry feelings, however, *after* the injury has been inflicted. The story represents a step forward in terms of greater freedom in the expression of feeling, in that the patient does express her anger and point out her mother's hostility. But she does not speak out early enough. Accordingly, I told this story:

> Once upon a time there was a girl named Sue. One day, while she was out gathering flowers, she found a baby wolf. She and the wolf became friends and every day Sue would

meet him in the woods and they would play together. The wolf's mother got to like Sue as well, and she was happy that her baby had such a fine playmate.

Now Sue's mother didn't know about the wolf and one day she saw Sue playing with the wolf in the woods. She went back to her house, got a gun, and came back to shoot the wolf. When Sue saw her coming with the gun, she got very angry because she knew that her mother was going to try to kill her very good friend. So she screamed out loudly to her mother: "No, no! Don't kill this wolf. He won't harm me. He's my friend. Please don't shoot!" When her mother heard that she put down the gun. She looked closely and saw that Sue and the wolf really were playing together and that the wolf wasn't harming Sue. The mother realized that she was wrong and she let them play together as much as they wanted.

The moral of that story is that if someone is going to do something that may be harmful to you, speak up early before they have a chance to do any harm.

Whereas in her story Linda expresses her resentment after the wolf has been wounded, in mine the wolf's traumatization is prevented by her speaking up early enough. I, therefore, took the resentment-expression theme one step further. In addition, the mother of the wolf in my story is very much present — she has not been burned to death as in the patient's story. There is no need to have her killed, because the anger which provoked her murder is obviated by Linda's speaking up and preventing the mother from wounding her.

In the next session Linda told this story:

Once upon a time there was a boy. He was a prince. He went hunting with his father for a deer. When the boy was alone, he found a baby deer. It was walking to its mother. The father was going to shoot the mother deer. The father didn't know that the mother had a baby deer. Then the prince saw a second baby deer. He told the father, who had pity. When he found out that the mother deer had two babies, he didn't want to shoot her any more.

The moral of this story is: talk when it is your turn.

Here Linda demonstrates clearly that my message from the previous session has been "heard" and is now being utilized. The father is stopped *before* he shoots the deer. Of course, there are still other neurotic patterns present in the story. The patient depicts herself as a boy. I believe that this had little to do with a sexual-identity problem but more with her belief that in masculine form she would have greater strength to effectively express herself. Also, here the father threatens the mother; she uses her father to act out the hostility she feels toward her mother. With this understanding of Linda's story, I related mine:

Once upon a time there was a princess. One day she saw her father leaving the palace with a shotgun in his hand. She asked him where he was going and he told her that he was going out hunting. She asked him if she could join him and he said, "Yes." On the way he told her that he was going deer hunting. She asked him why he wanted to kill the deer and he told her that the deer were doing many things which bothered him. She then asked him if he had spoken to the deer — this is a make-believe story and in this land animals can talk — and if he had told the deer what was bothering him about them. Her father said that he hadn't and he thought that the princess's suggestion was a good one.

So they found some deer and told them that they wanted to talk. The princess and her father discussed the problems with the deer, were able to solve them, and then killing became unnecessary. And so the father stopped hunting deer.

The moral of this story is that if you have a problem with someone try to settle it by telling the other person what's on your mind rather than by just going and trying to kill him.

My story carries the theme of deliberation-before-action a little further. In Linda's story the gun is raised — the father is already aiming at the deer when the prince intervenes — in mine, the differences are resolved before guns are pointed. The prince in her story becomes the princess in mine in order to communicate the notion that females have the wherewithal to express themselves as effectively as males. Also, I specifically include the princess in the discussions with the deer (who symbolize the mother) so that the patient herself takes part in resolving the conflict with her mother, rather than leaving it all to her father (as she does in her story).

Five weeks later (during three weeks of which Linda was on vacation), she told this story:

Once upon a time there was this tramp and his wife. They had a son named William and he liked to go hunting. His father said that he should go out hunting but his mother said, "No," that he would get hurt. But the father said that they needed food and that he should go. So he went and he got food and when he came back the mother got a baby. The baby grew up to be a tramp. He — the baby — was very unhappy; he ran away from home; he went to the city and begged for food; and he came to this lady's house. He bought pants and a jacket for twenty cents. He went to the lady's house after he got some food. The lady wanted to get married to him. She asked where he came from and he said they were tramps. She invited him in for supper and he stayed overnight. She got used to him and they got married. Then they had a child. No, forget that; they didn't have a child.

They went back to the mother and father's house, and the mother and father were very sick. He showed his mother his wife and his mother said to her, "Are you a tramp or a regular person?" She said that she was a regular person. The mother clapped so hard that the exertion caused her to die. They buried the mother where they lived — near their pet dog. The father also said, "Good, good." Then the father clapped so hard that he died too. Then they had children of their own and they lived happily ever after.

The moral of that story is: before you become anything, like a tramp, find out about it so you'll avoid disappointment.

Therapist: I have a question I'd like to ask you. Exactly what is a tramp as you understand it?

Patient: It's a man who isn't rich; he begs; and he's dressed

810

in rags.The whole family was tramps because the father was lazy and he didn't like to go out shopping.
Therapist: Thank you.

Linda's family (fairly well-off, upper middle class) did not ostensibly lend itself to being symbolized as tramps. The father was industrious and dedicated to both family and occupation and could not objectively be considered lazy. The symbolism becomes meaningful in the light of the important commodity which the tramp family does not provide. The father sends the son out hunting for food; he is too lazy to go himself. In the post-story inquiry, the listener is told that the father "didn't like to go out shopping" — again a reference to his deficiencies as a provider. What Linda sees him as not providing is, of course, affection. Accordingly, she goes out symbolized as a male, the sex she considers more capable of self-assertion, and acquires a mate of her own — someone who is not a tramp, someone, that is, who works and provides. She then marries, has children, and lives happily ever after — presumably a non-tramp life. The spouse, however, is primarily a provider as well. The only things the listener is told about her are that she is not a tramp and that she offered the patient room and board when she had none. So the new-found mate is another mother figure, and depicting herself as a male allows Linda a liaison with a mother-surrogate wife. Symbolizing herself as a female would restrict her to a male spouse — a less likely indulger of her dependency needs.

The parents are both killed off as well. This, in my opinion, not only satisfies Linda's hostile wishes toward them for the deprivations she considers herself to have experienced but also symbolizes her complete resignation to their inability to provide her with the love she wants.

The story is typically oedipal in accordance with the concept of the oedipus complex described in Chapter 8. Being deprived emotionally (rather than specifically sexually), she turns to another as a substitute. She resigns herself to the fact that her parents cannot provide affection (she buries them). The relationship she forms as a "resolution," however, is immature and dependent rather than egalitarian. Accordingly, I told this story:

Once upon a time there was a family of tramps. They had a daughter named Winny. Her parents were lazy and didn't work; they used to beg for food. They used to send Winny out to beg and work. One day while she was out begging she met a teen-aged boy who asked her what she was doing. She told him that her parents were tramps and they made her go out and get food for them. He asked her if she had complained to them about this and she said that she had been afraid to. After discussing this awhile with him she got the courage to tell her parents that they were being unfair to her and that they, as parents, should be working not begging in order to get food for her. She told them that as she got older she would be willing to work and contribute more but that all the other parents were working and giving to their children

Her parents listened to what she had to say and realized that she was right. So they tried to work harder and asked her to do less. However, they couldn't give her as much food as she would have liked but there was nothing more she could do about it. She just had to accept the fact that that was all they could give her. She found, however, that when she spent more time with friends, she forgot about the fact that her parents couldn't give her too much food; and sometimes she would be given food at the homes of friends.

When she got to be a teen-ager she started to date; in fact, she dated the boy I mentioned before who had given her such good advice. Well, when she dated she became very greedy and wanted the boy to do everything for her. This was because she wanted to make up for the fact that her parents had given her so little food and attention when she was younger. This boy explained to her that it made him angry when she only wanted to take from him; when she only wanted him to give her dinners all the time; and only wanted him to buy her things. Also he told her that it feels good to give to someone who likes to give to you. He explained to her that the best kind of relationship is one in which both people give and receive with each other; not just one taking and the other receiving. The end.

In my story Linda is again encouraged to assert herself and shown that such assertion can be to her benefit. In addition, she is discouraged from forming the kind of passive-dependent relationship depicted in her story and the drawbacks of such a relationship are described.

At about this time the mother described definite improvement. Linda was more assertive; things were better between her and her parents; she was far less surly; and she was more enthusiastically applying herself to her studies.

One week later, Linda related this story:

> Once upon a time there was this rabbit. And he met up with this snake and the snake said to him, "Come a little closer, maybe I can see how fat you are for dinner." Well, the little rabbit was so young, it didn't know what to do so it came closer. Well, anyhow, the little rabbit was playful and it kind of made friends with the snake so the snake didn't want to eat it. So they made friends and every day they went out to play. The moral of this story is: try to make friends with everybody.

The story refers to another communication of mine often imparted to Linda but not mentioned in any of the stories thus far: if someone dislikes you it may be related to things which *you* may be doing which are alienating; if you can change these things, you may then gain his affection. The rabbit symbolizes Linda and the snake stands for her parents. The snake's hostility disappears when he sees that the rabbit can be playful, that is, not surly. This indeed reflected the clinical situation where one of the factors causing an improvement in Linda's relationship with her parents was her friendlier attitude.

This story is a good example of the kind one sees in the late phase of treatment.

In response, I told this story:

> Once upon a time there was a rabbit. He met a snake who said to him, "Come a little closer, maybe I can see how

fat you are for dinner." The rabbit said to the snake, "Why should you want to eat me for dinner?" Then began a discussion in which the rabbit and the snake talked all about how they had become enemies and what they could do to become friends. It ended up with their being friends most of the time but not all the time, because no two animals, or even people, can like one another all the time. When the snake was unfriendly the rabbit played with other animals, and so most of the time he had a good time.

The morals of this story are: 1) try to make friends by discussing and talking about things with someone who may look like your enemy. 2) When another person is unfriendly, and most people are, sometimes, then seek friends elsewhere.

In the late phase of treatment when the child's story reflects healthy resolution of his problems, I often introduce communications regarding other related themes which have been focused upon in treatment. Here, I reiterated the notions that quiet discussion can be helpful in resolving many problems, that hostility toward someone may be based on false assumptions about him and correcting these can obviate the anger, and that no one is friendly all the time and when a person isn't, seek affection elsewhere.

One week later, Linda told this story:

Once upon a time there was a rabbit and his name was Flower. He lived with his sister and his brother and his mother and father. His sister liked to pester him a lot. He got angry at his sister and his mother asked him why he got so angry. He said it was because his sister was always fighting with him. So his mother told his sister to stop and the boy got happy after his sister stopped picking on him.

The lesson of that story is: be kind to your brothers and sisters.

The story is essentially normal in that it depicts the usual sibling rivalry situation which, as I have said, is usually fierce. Symbolizing herself as a flower is also a healthy sign — considering its implications of beauty and femininity. Although Linda again depicts herself as a boy in this story, I saw no clinical evidence whatsoever for masculine tendencies or dissatisfaction with her feminine role. Of interest in the story is the mother's question about why the boy got angry after having been pestered by his sister. It reflects Linda's awareness of her mother's hostility-inhibition problem. She explains to the mother the obvious reasons for her anger, thereby asserting herself and enlisting her mother's aid.

At the time of the telling of this story the mother described such significant diminution of all presenting problems that a termination date was set for two weeks later. Linda was described as having made a most marked improvement in school. Her teacher described Linda as much more interested, cooperative, and outgoing. In addition, in the less than four months since therapy had begun Linda had advanced an average of one year in all her academic subjects. During the next two weeks she continued to do well in all areas. She told more sibling rivalry stories, which I considered to be in the normal range. Her treatment was discontinued after a total of twenty-one sessions over a four-month period. Two years later I, by chance, met the mother, and she told me that Linda was still continuing to do well.

In Linda's case I feel that her learning disability was related to pent-up anger which was not only interfering with her concentrating in school but was also being displaced and discharged in passive-obstructionistic maneuvers which obviated her cooperation in doing school assignments, both in the classroom and at home. By helping her express her anger more directly, and utilizing it in the service of partially altering those situations which were engendering it, Linda became less angry and thereby free to pursue her studies with significantly reduced neurotic interferences.

15. A GIRL WITH PSYCHOGENIC COUGHING

The term psychophysiologic reaction (or psychosomatic reaction) refers to that class of psychiatric disorders in which psychogenic factors bring about, or contribute to, physical pathology of organs or organ systems. Generally, the term psychophysiologic reaction is used when the organ is under autonomic nervous system innervation, and the term conversion reaction (or hysterical reaction, or conversion hysteria) is employed when the organ is under the control of the voluntary nervous system. These distinctions are at times artificial and oversimplified. For example, migraine headaches and those due to hypertension would have to be considered psychophysiologic because vascular spasm is central to their etiology; but tension headaches are the result of spasm of the external muscles of the skull and would, therefore, have to be called conversion or hysterical. Stuttering, which involves tension of skeletal articulatory musculature has to be considered an hysterical phenomenon when the aforementioned distinctions are made, whereas blobus hystericus (a feeling of a lump in the throat) involves spasm of both smooth and striated muscle. Accordingly, I prefer to use the term psychogenic when describing psychosomatic or hysterical disorders such as psychogenic paraplegia, or psychogenic contributions to the patient's ulcerative colitis.

There is still much controversy in the field of medicine as to the etiology of many of the disorders classed as psychophysiologic (there is far less dispute regarding the conversion reactions, most agreeing that the organic element is minimal, if not entirely absent). I agree with the most widely accepted concept of multidetermination. Bronchial asthma, for example, results from a combination of one or more of a number of factors. There is

816

first a predisposition toward bronchial spasm (genetic and/or acquired). Such spasm may result from tension, infection, or allergic sensitivity. The patient becomes symptomatic when the etiologic factors combine and reach the threshold of symptom expression. Patients vary considerably as to the relative significance of the contributing elements. In one patient the allergic factor is the most significant — environmental change may be the most rapid and effective method of therapy. In another, the infectious element predominates — antibiotics, therefore, are the treatment of choice. In others, the bronchial musculature and glandular secretion are particularly sensitive to stress — so methods to reduce tension (one of which is psychotherapy) are indicated. Many patients require a combination of therapeutic approaches if there is to be symptomatic alleviation.

The underlying organic element in psychophysiologic disorders can roughly be divided into two categories: the physiologically idiosyncratic and the physically pathologic.

In the first category, the tissue is essentially normal when viewed microscopically but reacts exaggeratedly to physiologic stimuli. There is an "organ inferiority," as Alfred Adler called it — a *locus minoris resisentiae*. In periods of stress, some get diarrhea, others palpitations, others nausea and vomiting, etc. The particular organ or organ system seems to react in an exaggerated fashion to the stress. If this recurs frequently enough, permanent damage may result — and this may be then seen in standard pathologic examination.

In the second category, there is a primary disease process which is independent of any psychogenic factors (whether primary, secondary, or superimposed). I consider ulcerative colitis to be in this group. I believe these patients to be suffering with a disease which is primarily physical in its etiology. Superimposed stress exacerbates their condition, and so any method which may serve to reduce such stress (such as psychotherapy) can have a salutary, but not, in itself, curative, effect.

In some patients the choice of organ is less the result of some specific weakness (be it physiologic or pathologic) and more the result of specific environmental experiences which tend to focus on the particular organ. For example, a mother who is overly involved in her child's toilet training may cause the bowel to be selected for symptomatic expression such as constipation, encopresis, and soiling. In some, the organ lends itself to symbolic utilization. Soiling or vomiting may be an expression of hostility, and pseudocyesis may compensate for sterility. The organ selection may be conscious or unconscious: the encopretic child may not be aware that his symptom serves to express his anger whereas the pubescent girl with anorexia nervosa may be quite determinedly starving herself, in part, to prevent sexual development.

While this brief discussion by no means covers the complications and ramifications of the psychophysiologic reactions, by showing my basic orientation in the area, will enable the reader to better appreciate my approach to Lucy, the child with psychogenic coughing.

Lucy, an eight-and-one-half-year-old girl was referred by her pediatrician because of severe coughing spells of four months' duration. She would cough almost continuously for periods of up to eighteen hours a day but she did not cough while she was sleeping. Complete medical evaluations during two hospitalizations were not able to reveal any physical etiology. Coughing episodes would begin a few days prior to her father's departure on business trips; they would cease on his return. One year previously her mother had suffered severe coughing spells in conjunction with an episode of pneumonia. During this period, much of the family's attention had centered around the mother. Now Lucy was able to enjoy similar engrossment of the family.

Both parents were moderately devout Catholics. They were inhibited in the expression of their feelings — especially of anger. Lucy also showed these inhibitions in her shyness and timidity. But she "kept a cheerful face" in adversity and was easily taken advantage of by her peers because of her refusal to assert herself and stand up for her rights.

The mother described herself as "a loner" when she was a child. She was quite repressed in expressing anger: "I keep quiet and seethe inside when I'm mad." However, she intermittently

818

displayed violent outbursts of rage which were quite frightening to Lucy. She was exaggeratedly concerned over her children's manners and punished them severely over the use of profanity. Although the mother professed strong feelings of love for the patient, she was quite restrained in the expression of meaningful affection.

During the first two years of Lucy's life, she saw little of her father because he was working in the day and attending school at night. Although her subsequent relationship with him was warmer than that which she had with her mother, his frequent business trips resulted in separations up to three weeks in duration. He, like the mother, had a strong aversion to profanity.

During her first session in treatment, Lucy drew a picture of a bird (Figure 3). She said it was a parrot and described the enclosed area in front of the parrot's mouth as "the place where in comic strips they put in the words." The area was colored deep yellow and when asked why she hadn't put any words in it she replied, "I don't know. I just drew it that way." In addition, she could not tell me what the parrot might be saying.

The fact that the parrot, who is known, above all, as the bird that talks, was specifically depicted as mute, suggested to me that the patient had a problem about verbalizing her thoughts. I suspected that this might be related to her coughing problem. This hypothesis was confirmed in her second session when she told her first tape recorded story:

Once upon a time there was a snake named Sandy. He lived with his mother and his father and his seven brothers and his six sisters.

One day he woke up mad because his friends called him lots of bad names — like "hissy-missy" because he hissed. His friend Stripey the Tiger came over. Stripey didn't call him names. Stripey said, "Let's play a game." Sandy said, "Go away. I know you're going to call me names. Shoo!" He sent away all the friends. He did nothing; he just sat around all day and said, "Shoo!"

His friends said they were sorry — "It's just that you hiss a lot; you should see a doctor." Sandy went to the

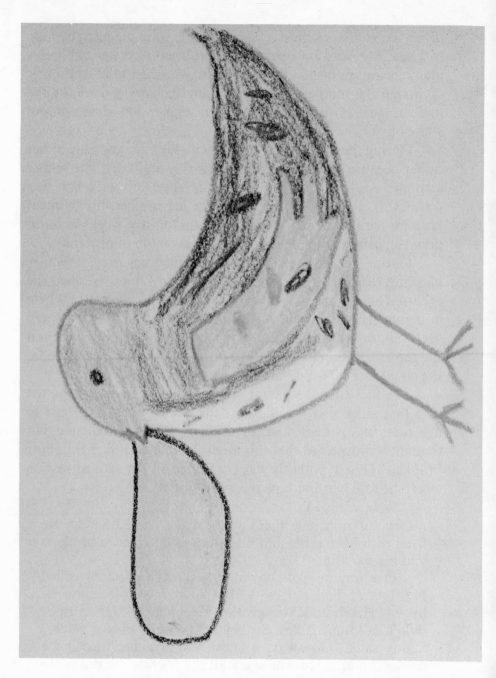

Figure 3.

doctor with his hiss. The doctor said he had choked on a piece of candy. His mother had given him the candy. The doctor got it out. That stopped the hiss and then he got friends. He said to everybody: "I'm sorry for hurting your feelings."

The moral of the story is: "Never get mad at your friends."

This story is most revealing of Lucy's main symptoms and conflicts. She portrays herself as a snake — a reflection of her low self-esteem. The hissing symbolizes the partially suppressed verbalization of hostility. Such suppression is the result of a piece of candy put into her mouth by her mother — that is, her mother's displays of affection, as symbolized by the candy, are being "shoved down her throat" and inhibiting her expression of anger. To put it differently: one cannot really get angry at someone who gives you candy. Lucy's cough is clearly the clinical representation of the hiss. She expects her animal friends (her peers) and Stripey the Tiger (the symbol of authority and parental figures) to call her names such as "hissy-missy," and to derogate her for the expression of her resentment — even though it is expressed in the disguised form of a hiss. By sending them away, she protects herself from their criticism.

She then sees a doctor (the therapist) who removes the candy — that is, the symbol of mother's love — which has served not to transmit affection but rather to suppress hostility. After this, she apologizes to the parental and peer figures for having been angry and hopes to regain their love. The moral: "Never get mad at your friends," epitomizes the core conflict around the repression of rage.

On the basis of this interpretation, I concluded that two main themes should be introduced into the child's therapy. One would attempt to lessen Lucy's guilt over the expression of hostility; the second would help her obtain gratification from her friends and thus compensate for the deficiencies of her mother. If this could be accomplished, there would be less anger on her part toward her mother. With these goals in mind, I told the following story:

Once upon a time there was a snake named Sandy. He lived with his mother and his father and his seven brothers and his six sisters.

His mother was very busy with all his brothers and sisters and spent little time with Sandy. Whenever Sandy would get mad about this, his mother would say, "It's not nice for children to be angry at their parents," or "Here's some candy; now, don't bother me." This would make him even angrier because when she gave him candy it was even harder to tell her how angry he was.

He had learned from other animals that it wasn't so bad to get angry at your mother, especially when she doesn't spend time with you. When he was angry, he would often try to get her to spend more time with him, but she would not. He decided that his mother just wasn't going to spend that much time with him, and so he made other friends and then he was much happier and wasn't so angry.

My story has two morals. The first is if your mother doesn't spend much time with you, it's okay to get angry even if she tells you it isn't. The second is if you've tried to get your mother to spend more time with you and she won't, then get more friends and you won't feel so bad or angry.

In Lucy's first story, she revealed her expectation that I would quickly and magically provide the cure by removing the candy. As I have mentioned before, it is salutary for even the youngest child to try himself to resolve his difficulties, at least to the degree that is appropriate to his age and circumstances. Therefore, I usually try to keep therapeutic intervention and manipulation out of my stories. Instead, the child is depicted as resolving his difficulties through his own efforts. In my story the doctor does not appear; the child performs the healthy maneuvers on her own — that is, she expresses her hostility; attempts to utilize it to get her mother to give her more attention and affection; and, when this fails, she seeks gratification elsewhere.

It is of interest that Lucy coughed only during the first session. During the second session, when this first taped story was told, the cough was absent. It was never seen again. Since the fundamental problems that brought it about were clearly still present, the therapy was continued in the hope that she would remain asymptomatic following future separations from her father. Furthermore, Lucy had other problems in functioning: shyness, passivity, and difficulty in maintaining meaningful friendships. It was for the treatment of these symptoms as well that therapy was continued.

Six days later, Lucy told this story:

Once there was a giraffe and he lived with his mother. One time he said to his mother, "Mother, why do you grow so tall?" And the mother said, "Because I get enough exercise and eat a lot." "That's what I will do," said the little giraffe.

So one time when his mother was eating, he decided, "I'm going to try running. I ate enough food already." So he started running away and the mother was running another way to find her child. Soon the baby giraffe became tired.

Therapist: Do I understand that he ran away from his mother?

Patient: Hhmmm.

Therapist: In other words, was he just going to get exercise? Was it by mistake or by intention?

Patient: By mistake.

Therapist: He ran away from his mother and she didn't know where he was. Is that it?

Patient: No, he was trying to get some exercise.

Therapist: And she couldn't find him?

Patient: Yeah.

Therapist: All right.

Patient: Soon he came to an elephant. "Oh, good morning, Mr. Elephant. Would you please help me find my mother?" The elephant said, "Oh, I haven't seen your mother in such a long time." "Thank you very much. I'll go play with your child until it's time for lunch," said the giraffe.

Therapist: All right. So then what happened?

Patient: So then he ran alone until he found a tiger. "Good morning, Mrs. Tiger. Have you seen my mother?" And she said, "Yes, she was just over there a minute ago. I think she went home." "Oh, Mrs. Tiger, would you please help me find my way home?" said the little giraffe. The tiger said, "I cannot help you find your mother." "Why can't you?" "Your mother has gone away some place. She won't be back until another week."

Therapist: Wait a minute. Who said that?

Patient: The tiger.

Therapist: Okay. Go ahead.

Patient: So the tiger took very good care of the giraffe and while these weeks were going he was getting enough exercise and enough food to eat, that he kept on growing taller and taller and taller.

Soon he found his mother and he said, "Goodbye, Tiger. Thank you very much." The tiger said, "You're welcome. I'd be glad to take care of any kind of baby, except for my enemies."

Therapist: All right. Then what happened?

Patient: So then when he came to his mother, his mother looked up and said, "My, how much you have grown!" And the little giraffe said, "You mean, Mother, that I had enough exercise and I had enough things to eat that I'm really taller than you are?" And she said, "Yes. Pretty soon I must teach you the ways of life." That's all.

Therapist: All right. Very, very good. What's the moral of that story — the lesson?

Patient: Always listen to your mother.

Therapist: How did this giraffe not listen to his mother?

Patient: Well, he listened to his mother but it kind of like proves to me that everybody should be listening to their mother or their parents.

Therapist: What happened to him because he didn't listen to his mother?

Patient: Well, while he was with his mother he didn't grow any taller, but when he was with the tiger he grew taller.

Therapist: Hhmmm. Was this a lady or a man tiger?

Patient: A lady.

Therapist: Okay. Very good story.

824

The story reveals Lucy's notion that she cannot get nutriment — that is, affection — from her mother, but she can get it from a surrogate, the lady tiger. It is not clear how the moral relates to the story and the post-story inquiry did not clarify this. Sometimes the child cannot figure out the moral of his story and presents me with one that sounds like it might be a good moral for *some* story. Lucy's "Always listen to your mother" seemed to be in this category of morals.

This is the story I told in response:

Okay, now it's time for me to tell my story. As you may recall on this program, I tell my stories and they contain the same characters as the child's story, except different things happen to them.

Once upon a time there was a giraffe and he lived with his mother. And once he said to his mother, "Why do you grow so tall?" And the mother said, "Because I get enough exercise and eat; I eat a lot." And the giraffe said, "You know, Mother, I would like to be as tall as you, but you don't let me exercise enough and you don't let me eat enough." The mother said, "Is that so?" The giraffe said, "Yes. When I want to go out and play and run around and play with all the other animals you don't let me and also you don't give me enough food in the house. When I want to eat something you always give me such a little bit, and sometimes I have thoughts of going away from home and going to live with the tiger who lives in the forest, in another part of the forest. That tiger gives her children a lot of food and lets them run around and get a lot of exercise and they're much bigger. They were born the same time that I was." The mother said, "You know, I didn't realize that." And the mother thought about it and realized that the little giraffe was right and then the mother started to give the giraffe more food and she started to let her go out and get more exercise. Sure enough the giraffe grew bigger and bigger.

And the moral of that story is — do you know the moral of that story?
Patient: No.

Therapist: The moral of that story is that if your mother is not giving you something that you want, tell her, speak to her, and maybe you'll get it. The end.

Patient: Sometimes my mother doesn't have enough money.

Therapist: Are you poor?

Patient: Well, we have to buy a lot of things. We need a new car, but we cannot afford it.

Therapist: I see.

Patient: Here we won't be able to afford another vacation.

Therapist: Oh, I see.

Patient: Up to Vermont.

Therapist: Hhmmm. Okay.

In my story Lucy is encouraged to assert herself with her mother and to express her resentment over not being given enough affection. I did not expect such assertion to result in significant affectionate display by the mother, but it could bring about some increase in attention.

Many of the stories Lucy told during the first few weeks of treatment centered around the theme of acquiring friends. This was one of her problem areas in that she tended to withdraw from meaningful involvement with her peers and did not properly assert herself with them. My stories were designed to encourage such participation, and she began introducing this theme into her stories. However, she often utilized inappropriate methods for acquiring friends, for example, coercion, bribery, and flattery. My subsequent stories, therefore, pointed out the futility and inappropriateness of such maneuvers. In addition, Lucy continued to tell stories in which animals suppressed or repressed their hostility. I responded with ones in which angry feelings were overtly expressed to the obvious benefit of the animals concerned. This is a typical interchange of this kind which occurred during the fifth week of treatment:

Once there was a turtle who everybody called Topsy Turtle 'cause every time he would walk or he would fall, he would land on his back and go sideways. So one day Topsy Turtle felt very bad and he was walking along until he saw his friend, Sally Turtle. Sally Turtle came over to him and said, "What's wrong?" And Topsy Turtle said, "I just feel bad about everybody calling me Topsy Turtle." And then Sally said, "Well, that was your name and they've got a good reason for it. My mother named me Sally Turtle. Well, there's nothing bad about your walking like you do, but she heard this name from humans talking about it. Here, I'll show you. I'll show you where a human lives and you'll go see all the names they call other people and then you won't feel so bad."

So Topsy Turtle went with Sally Turtle until they saw and they listened to some humans. They listened for an hour and then Topsy Turtle said, "Well, I really don't feel bad anymore because now that I see that humans call other people bad names, I guess I don't have to worry. That's all."

Therapist: And the moral of that story is?

Patient: Always don't feel bad when something bad happens to you because there's always something worse that might happen.

Therapist: Okay. Thank you very much.

Here Lucy, as Topsy Turtle, justifies repressing the anger she harbors toward those who are hostile to her (call her bad names) with the illogical rationalization that since humans commonly taunt each other, there's no reason to be angry. The turtle's awkward gait and propensity to fall and land on his back symbolizes Lucy's social ineptitude. The one positive feature in the story is the patient's beginning appreciation that verbal expression of hostility is ubiquitous — a notion which is new to her since she was raised in such a repressive atmosphere.

This is the story I told in response:

Once upon a time there was a turtle and everybody used to call him Topsy Turtle. Every time he would walk he didn't concern himself where he was walking or how he was walking and he would land on his back. And all the kids used to start calling him Topsy Turtle and he felt very bad about that and he got angry. He said, "Stop calling me Topsy Turtle." They started to laugh and they said, "You are Topsy Turtle."

Then he said to himself, "They're laughing at me because I can't walk too well. What can I do? I know. That one over there has a long nose. I'll call him Nosey Turtle. And that one over there — he's short — I'll call him Shorty Turtle. And there was one over there that was big and fat and he called him Fatty Turtle. So when they called him Topsy Turtle, he just went on and said, "You shut up, Fatty Turtle." To the other one he said, "You shut up Shorty Turtle, and you shut up Nosey Turtle." Well then they felt bad because they knew that he was right, that they were short and fat and nosey. So they stopped calling him Topsy Turtle, but they still thought he was clumsy and they wouldn't play with him.

Then he said to himself, "That settles that. I feel better about that, but I wonder. There is something true to what they say. I am a little bit clumsy. Maybe I ought to watch myself." So then he began to watch himself so that he wasn't so clumsy and he walked much better, and then they stopped calling him that name. Then he had friends and wasn't lonely anymore.

And they stopped calling him the name for two reasons: one, because he was no longer clumsy and the second, because they knew that if they did ridicule him and laugh at him that they would get it right back.

The moral of that story is: if somebody calls you —— do you know the morals of that story? There are two morals. See if you can figure them out.

Patient: If someone calls you a name call him back.

Therapist: Right. Any other moral?

Patient: Well, try to watch your stuff and try to make it better.

Therapist: Right! If what they're calling you is true then see what you can do about stopping it. The end.

In my story the turtle overtly expresses his resentment about the Topsy Turtle epithet in order to end the teasing. When this fails, he does not give up, but considers alternative courses of action. First, he responds in kind with denunciations appropriate to each of the taunting animal's obvious deficits. Although this is not the most adult kind of response, it is appropriate for children — "If he calls you a name, call him one back." This response allows release of Topsy's hostility and does make his taunters desist. However, the turtle is still exhibiting socially alienating behavior even though he is no longer being openly ridiculed for it. Once again he does not withdraw in response to disappointment but considers another constructive alternative solution: he decides to change the behavior which elicited the teasing in the first place. When this is accomplished, all taunting stops and the turtle acquires the friends he longed for so desperately.

About a month later, Lucy told this story:

Once there was a fly and he lived with his mother and father, but all his brothers and sisters went to school and he was the only one that was left at home. So all he could do was go among the flowers and find pollen for the family and he didn't like that very much. So he was, so he was all alone and he told his mother and father, "Mommy, why can't I have any friends? Why isn't there very many bumblebees that I can make friends with?"

Therapist: Did you say he was a fly or a bumblebee? You started off by saying he was a fly.

Patient: He was really a bumblebee.

Therapist: A bumblebee.

Patient: Yeah, and —

Therapist: He asked them why he didn't have friends. Is that it?

Patient: Yeah, and his mother said, "I don't know but I've tried and tried to find a hive that has bumblebees like us, but I just couldn't find any. All I can find is your grandmother's and your other grandmother's hive.

So the baby bumblebee began to think, "I wish I still anyway had some friends." And he went outside to play among the flowers. By and by, while he sat on a flower, he saw a bird coming along and the bird said, "Why are you so sad and lonely?" The bumblebee said, "Well, I don't have anybody to play with. I wish I did have someone to play with my own age." "Well, how old are you?" said the bird. "I'm only four." So the bird said, "I'm four, too. You can play with me. Anyway, I know another friend, a snake."

So they played along and the bumblebee never complained to his mother again.

Therapist: And the moral?

Patient: If you want a friend, don't just sit there and pout, you can just fly around, you can just go around and find your friend.

Therapist: Thank you very much for that story.

In the story Lucy expresses her desire to form relationships with friends. In the moral she professes the advice that one should be assertive in the acquisition of friends; but in the story there is no such self-assertion. She gains friendships by merely sitting and pouting. A passing bird takes pity on her and befriends her. Through the bird, she acquires another friend, a snake. The choice of other species suggests that she does not feel comfortable among those who are like herself; and the choice of a snake suggests that she does not consider herself worthy of the affection of anything but the lowest forms of life.

This is the story I told in response:

Once upon a time there was a bumblebee and he lived with his mother and father. His brothers and sisters went to school and every day he was home all alone with his parents. He was only four years old and he was too young to go to school. He spent all day looking for pollen in the flowers, but he didn't like doing that and he wished that he could have friends. And he looked out the window and he saw other bumblebees playing around, but they wouldn't play with him and he was very sad.

Actually he was able to make friends with a bird and a snake, which he did find for himself which was very good, but, you know, a bird and a snake are so much bigger than bumblebees that it's hard to find games that they can play — that they can all enjoy. And sometimes birds try to eat bumblebees, so that it wasn't — and sometimes snakes try to eat birds — so it was very hard to play with those two because it was kind of dangerous at times. Besides, as I said before, they were too big. So those friendships weren't very deep and they didn't last very long because there was a certain amount of distrust.

And he said, "I wish that I could play with those other bumblebees." But when he would go near them, they just wouldn't play and he was very sad.

Then one day, when the other bumblebees didn't know that he was coming through the woods, he overheard two of the bumblebees talking and they said, "I hope that kid doesn't come around again." They were referring to that bumblebee that didn't have any friends. The other one said, "Yeah, that bumblebee is a sore loser. Whenever he loses a game, he starts crying and stamping his feet." "Yeah," said the other one, "and he always wants his own way. He always wants to do it his way. He doesn't want to follow the rules of the game." And the other one said, "Yeah, and he doesn't respect the rights of others, and he doesn't care what others want. He just wants his own way and he doesn't care how we feel." The other bumblebee said, "Yeah, and he's also very quiet too. He doesn't express himself. He's just kind of shy."

Anyway, when the bumblebee heard this he was very hurt. He was very hurt and he didn't want to admit that they were talking about him, but he knew that they were and he went home crying. He went to his mother and his mother said, "What are you crying about?" He said, "I'm crying because the bumblebees there said that I am a sore loser, that I always want my own way, that I don't respect the rights of others, and that I don't express myself — that I'm quiet and shy. They're all lies, lies, lies. I don't do any of those things." And the mother said, "Are you sure they're lies?" And the little bumblebee said, "Yeah, they're all lies, lies. I don't do any of those things." And the mother said, "You know, I know you quite well, and I see you playing sometimes when they do play with you and I think it's true and the sooner you will accept that and start changing your ways, the sooner you'll have friends." Well, the bumblebee still said, "It's lies, lies, lies. I don't do any of those things." The mother said, "Well, maybe you'll change your mind."

Well, anyway, that night the bumblebee went to sleep and began thinking about it and said, "Maybe, it is true what they say. Maybe I am a sore loser. Maybe I do want my own way too much. Maybe I don't respect the rights of others. Maybe I should express myself more and speak up and not be so shy and timid."

So the next day the bumblebee went out and it seemed that he decided that he was going to try very hard to change these things and he went to where the other bumblebees were playing —— now how would you finish this story? You want to try to finish it?

Patient: Hhmmm. Well, he went to the other bumblebees, and they said, "Oh, get out of here!" He said, "Well, I'm sorry about the ways that I have been doing." So he tried to make up and tried not to be timid and not being a sore loser, being respectful of the other bumblebees and soon the bumblebees got to like him.

Therapist: Now what is the moral of that story?

Patient: I don't know. I can't think of one.

Therapist: This story has four morals. The first moral is that if you want to get friends you have to respect the rights of others and try to consider their desires too, not that you should do exactly what they want and not what you want, but you have to make a compromise. Do you know what a compromise is?

Patient: No.

Therapist: A compromise means that each person gives in some, so they want to do it one way, and you want to do it another, in a compromise you say, "Okay, I'll do it your way half the time and you do it my way half the time." You know, that's a compromise. That's the first moral. The second moral is don't be a sore loser. If you're a sore loser, kids won't want to play with you. The third moral is don't always want things your own way. If you do you won't have friends. And the fourth moral is if you want kids to like you, you have to express yourself, speak up and don't be shy and withdrawing. The end.

In my story, I first pointed out the inappropriateness and disadvantages of forming friendships with those who are markedly different from oneself — a bird and a snake are not particularly suitable friends for a bumblebee. I then confronted Lucy with the personality qualities which were interfering with her forming friendships by having the bumblebee overhear his antisocial personality characteristics enumerated by other bumblebees who are not aware that he is listening. These include being a sore loser, always wanting his own way and not respecting the rights of others, not following the rules of games, and failing to express himself. His first response is to deny these painful confrontations, but later he gains the ego strength to accept the criticisms as valid. He then utilizes his new insights constructively. He refrains from utilizing the alienating maneuvers and thereby enjoys his new-found friends. The acquisition of meaningful friendships was vital to Lucy's treatment because I considered such relationships to provide her with potential compensation for the deprivations she suffered at home (her mother's inhibition in expressing affection and her father's long absences).

One week later (at the beginning of her third month of treatment), Lucy told this story:

Once there was a hawk who was playing around. He had lots of friends and sometimes he would fight with them. So one day they were sitting on a branch and there wasn't enough room for him because he had come along kind of late. So he got up on the branch and he was just sitting sort of at the end and one of the little babies pushed him. Then he scolded, "Now don't you do that again."
Therapist: Wait a minute. He tried to get on the branch.
Patient: Yes.
Therapist: I see, and one of the little babies on the branch pushed him away.
Patient: Uh-huh. And the big hawk said, "Now don't you do that again." And he hit her and the baby began to cry.
Therapist: This was a big hawk, right? The story is about a big hawk.
Patient: Yeah. So then the brother of the baby girl hawk

came along and said, "Hi, but don't you hit my sister. You know it isn't nice." And he said, "Well, there was a little enough room for me, so I can sit on it first. She has no right to hit me. In fact, she's only a little baby." And then the brother comes out and said, "Okay, you hit my sister." Then he started to fight with the hawk and the hawk said, "Now please don't fight. You know we want to be friends." Then the other hawk said, "Oh, all right!"

So the next day they were playing and they saw a bunch of girls come by.

Therapist: Who is they? Who was playing?

Patient: The two hawks.

Therapist: Which two — you mean the big one and the brother?

Patient: Yeah. And so then they were playing around and then all of a sudden they see some girls and they said, "Those girls look thirsty. Let's go build a stand very quick so they can have something to drink." And the other one said, "Okay." So they built a stand and they quietly played and everytime they found new friends 'cause they were allowed to go up to the stand and buy their own stuff pretty soon.

Therapist: Now did they sell this — what did they have on this stand? What kind of stuff?

Patient: Juice, berry juice.

Therapist: Berry juice. Did they sell it or just give it away?

Patient: They sold it for nothing 'cause the girls were thirsty.

Therapist: They just gave it to them for nothing. And what's the moral of that story?

Patient: If you want to have friends just stay around and try not to have any fights.

Therapist: Thank you very much.

The story is one of many in which Lucy grapples with the problem of obtaining and keeping friends. The big hawk, the central figure in the story, is the patient. Her desire to join the other hawks on the branch is healthy. However, the friends (little babies) she chooses are inappropriately young for her, and she forces herself on them (by pushing herself onto the already filled branch) rather than joining them in a more considerate manner. When pushed by one of the little baby girl hawks, the big hawk reprimands her. Although the baby hawk is justified in pushing her, this is a good sign for this subdued girl — she isn't allowing herself to be pushed around. However, the patient's self-assertion gets her into trouble. The baby hawk has a big brother who threatens vengeance for his little sister. The big brother's retaliation reflects Lucy's fear that if she is to fight or assert herself, dire consequences will result. She begs the big brother not to be hard on her: "Now please don't fight." He, without reason, accedes to her request; and in this way she "cools off" the whole situation. The enemies suddenly become good friends, and the two hawks then make more friends by bribery (giving out free soft-drinks).

This is the story I told in response:

Once upon a time there was a big hawk and he one day felt very lonely because he didn't have any friends. So he saw a number of hawks sitting on a branch and that branch was filled. And he said, "Boy, I'd like to be friends with those hawks. How should I join them?" His first thought was to go up on the branch and to sit there and push away some of the other hawks. And then he thought, "No, that wouldn't be a good idea because then they won't like me. They'll accuse me of shoving them around and that's not a good way of getting friends." So he said, "I know what I'll do."

So he flew up and he said, "I'd like to sit on that branch. Is anybody going to be flying away soon?" And someone said, "Yes, I plan to be leaving in a few minutes and when I do you can have my spot." And the others thought, "My, what a courteous and considerate hawk he is. He is considerate of the feelings of other people. Another hawk might have come up here and sat right down on the branch, pushing the others away."

So he sat there when the other hawk left and he started to chat. They were talking with one another, but he didn't feel that they were as friendly as they might be. So he thought, "I know what I'll do. I will get some berries and make some berry juice and give them all some free juice. Then maybe they'll be friendlier." Then he said, "No, no, no. That might be bribing. They've got to like me for what I am, not because I give them berry juice. They've got to like me for what I am as a person." So he gave up that idea and he said, "Someday when I am friends with them, then I could give them berry juice. But that wouldn't be buying their friendship. That's really giving to a friend that you have already."

So he didn't give them any berry juice but he just stayed there and played with them and they began to like him more and more. Then later on when they were friends, then he gave them berry juice.

Now my story has two morals. Do you know what they are?

Patient: No.

Therapist: One moral is: don't push your way in with people. You have to play it slowly, show consideration, and that's a better way of making friends. The second moral is: you can't buy friendship. You can't get it by bribing people. You've got to get friends by being yourself and their finding you attractive. The end.

Patient: That was a very nice story.

Therapist: Thank you.

The meaning of my story is obvious. Whereas in Lucy's story, she tries to make friends by pushing herself forward and thereby alienating herself, in mine she is considerate of the feelings of others and in this way gains their genuine esteem. Bribery is also shown in my story to be an ineffective way of obtaining friendships. Clinically, Lucy was doing better than this story might suggest. She was involving herself more successfully with friends and asserting herself more effectively as well.

Two weeks later, she told this story:

Once there was a lonely deer and he lived in a forest. Many of the hunters lived there and, of course, there were many other animals. So one day the deer went down and he happened to notice some children and he saw little children on one end of the brook and big children on the other. And the others were trying to go to Mrs. Goose's eggs —

Therapist: Wait a minute now. He saw big and little children and which ones were going to Mrs. Goose — all of them?

Patient: No, just the big ones and they were going to steal her eggs that she had laid a few weeks ago.

Therapist: Yes.

Patient: And so the deer said, "Now that isn't very nice, just trying to steal Mrs. Goose's eggs. I will try to help Mrs. Goose and warn her." So the deer made a silent little sound that only animals can hear and told her what was wrong. And the goose came over and said, "You can help me too. You can keep guard over my family every day."

Therapist: This is what Mrs. Goose said to the deer?

Patient: Hhmmm.

Therapist: Anything else?

Patient: That's all.

Therapist: And the moral?

Patient: If you see something that is going to be danger to one of your friends, you can at least help them.

Therapist: In your story what happened to the children who were going to steal Mrs. Goose's eggs?

Patient: They got hurt real badly from the goose.

Therapist: What did she do?

Patient: Well, the goose screamed and pecked at them, and the deer charged at them and bunted them.

Therapist: Well, how was that a help to them?

Patient: To the ——

Therapist: To the children.

Patient: Well, the little children were watching this, and they felt glad that the big boys finally learned their lesson.

Therapist: I see. Okay.

I believe the deer, the central figure in the story, represents Lucy. Mrs. Goose stands for Lucy's mother; and the golden eggs represent mother's love. The children who plan to steal the eggs stand for the patient's siblings (Lucy's two sisters and one brother) who are her rivals for mother's affection. The story gratifies her fantasy that her mother will favor her over her siblings and join her in rejecting them. Accordingly, I told this story:

Once upon a time there was a lonely deer and she lived in the forest. Lots of hunters and animals lived there. One day the deer was walking along and she saw children standing near a brook. There were big children and little children, and the big children were planning to steal Mrs. Goose's eggs. Well, the deer thought that that was not nice and so by special signal warned Mrs. Goose.

Mrs. Goose said to her, "Well, I'm very pleased to know that this is going to happen since I certainly want to protect my eggs. I don't want them to be stolen. I like to give them out equally to all the people in the forest, children and animals alike, and I'm pleased that you gave me the information. However, I can tell you that the children, when they hear of this, are not going to be happy. They are going to call you a tattletale and you will have no friends." And the deer said, "Well, it is true I am lonely." And the goose said, "Well, maybe that's one of the reasons why you are lonely because you are a tattletale. Do you tattle often?" He said, "Well, I do. I thought it's being nice to big people and that they would like me more." "Well, big people may like you more if you do tattle," said the goose, "but they know that your friends won't like you and usually they advise children not to be tattletales."

Well, anyway, the little deer said, "What are you going to do?" Mrs. Goose said, "Well, I'm going to watch and wait and if those big boys do come, I'm certainly going to punish them." So the boys did come and try to steal, and she did punish them. And the deer said, "How are you going to punish them?" She said, "Well, I'm going to deprive them of eggs for a few days." The deer asked, "Would you make me the one to protect your house forever and ever from all these bad children?" Mrs. Goose said, "Absolutely not. I'm just going to punish those big boys for what they did now and I hope they learned their lesson, but from here on in I'm going to treat everyone equally. If I made you the protector of my house, the children would want to play with you even less. They would say, "Yah, ya, yah, ya, you're Mrs. Goose's pet." And they would be jealous of you and they would feel that you were different from the rest and they wouldn't want to play with you. I wouldn't be doing you any favors by making you my pet. The best thing that I can do is treat all of you children equally and punish those who do things wrong."

Mrs. Goose was very wise and the deer listened very carefully to what she said and then did begin playing more with the other children and animals in the forest because she stopped being a tattletale and she stopped trying to be Mrs. Goose's pet. When she did something wrong Mrs. Goose punished her by not giving her eggs and when the other children and animals did things wrong, she punished them.

Now do you know the morals of this story?

Patient: No.

Therapist: You want to figure them out?

Patient: Well, not very clearly.

Therapist: Well, even if not clearly.

Patient: That you should not be a tattletale.

Therapist: Right.

Patient: And not hide from other children. And that's all I can figure.

Therapist: Don't be a tattletale would be one of mine and the other is that if you try to be the favorite, let's say the teacher's pet or mother's pet or some other lady's pet, and try to take a position which is better than all the other children, they won't like you very much. That's the second moral of my story. The end.

Did you want to say something?

Patient: Yes. In my other school somebody became a teacher's pet and also the kids hardly play with her and she still is the teacher's pet.

Therapist: Do you think it's a good idea to be teacher's pet?

Patient: No. I never have been.

Therapist: A teacher who makes a child her pet is doing something which is not really a good thing for the child because all the other children don't like her and the child may think that she's better off, but she really isn't. And, of course, the kid is a tattletale and no one wants to play with a tattletale. Right?

Patient: Right.

Therapist: Do you want to hear this story over again?

Patient: No, thank you.

In my story, Mrs. Goose has no favorites; she dispenses the eggs equally to all the children and animals in the forest. I thereby communicated to Lucy that her fantasy of being shown special preference by her mother is not going to be gratified. In addition, the disadvantages of being a tattletale and mother's favorite are pointed out to the patient. She did have the tendency to be an "apple polisher" with her teacher, and this, of course, must have played a role in her peer difficulties. Lastly, I imparted the message that when one transgresses, one is deprived of mother's affection — Mrs. Goose punishes the bad children by temporarily withholding eggs. Lucy's mother was indeed somewhat deficient in the affection she could provide Lucy. Lucy was told that by alienating her mother she will get even less affection. By good behavior she can expect to receive the full allotment her mother is capable of providing.

Four days later, Lucy told this story:

Once upon a time there was a deer and he decided not to stay in his backyard anymore and to go out and make friends and have his own girlfriend. He said, "Hello," to a puppy dog who said, "Hello," and ran off because he was scared of the deer. Then he met a donkey. He said, "Hello," and the donkey ran off because he was scared of the deer; he was timid and shy. Then he saw a human being, but he stayed in the bushes. Then he moved into a family of deers and he saw a girl deer his own age. They became friends and they lived happily ever after.

The moral of this story is: find someone your own age who will like you.

The story incorporates healthy elements introduced by me in previous stories. In it Lucy leaves her backyard, that is, loosens herself from mother's apron strings. The story reveals her understanding that it is better to play with friends who are similar to herself. In the story this is represented by her playing with other deer rather than donkeys or dogs. In reality this related to her realization (now translated into action) that she does best with children her own age, rather than the younger ones she had gravitated toward in the past. The story, however, reveals her anticipation that some children will still be alienated by her: the donkey and the dog run from her in fear. This expectation, I felt, was a residuum of the past in that at the time this story was told, Lucy was no longer manifesting behavior which resulted in such reactions by peers.

With this understanding of Lucy's story, I related the following:

Once upon a time there was a deer and the deer decided that he spent enough time in his own backyard and that he would prefer to go out and make friends. He first met a puppy dog and he said to the puppy dog, "Are you afraid of me?" The puppy dog said, "No." Then he said to the puppy dog, "Let's be friends," and the puppy dog said, "You seem like a very nice deer, but we are very different. You are a deer and I am a puppy dog. I think you should get deer friends."

Then the deer met a donkey and he said to the donkey, "Are you afraid of me?" "No," said the donkey, "there is nothing to be afraid of." Then he asked the donkey to be his friend and the donkey told him the same thing the puppy dog had told him, that he should get friends who are similar to himself.

He realized that the puppy dog and the donkey were right — that he should get friends like himself and that's just what he did. He found some nice deer and made some good friends.

The lesson of this story is one, it is best to have friends who are like yourself because you have more in common with them, and two, sometimes you think that people will be afraid of you when they really aren't. The deer in my story thought that the puppy dog and the donkey would be afraid of him, but they turned out not to be. He had a wrong idea. The end.

In my story, the dog and donkey are in no way alienated by Lucy; they merely state (without fear or animosity) that she can readily find more appropriate friends. My attempt here was to reassure Lucy that she no longer possessed significantly alienating qualities. I hoped this would provide her with further self-confidence in her involvements with peers.

Four days later, Lucy told this story:

Once there was a deer and he was grazing and all of a sudden he saw some ducks fly south and he said, "Oh, I must get ready. I must tell my sisters and brothers to get ready because they are younger and I am in charge because my mother and father have went away someplace on vacation."

Therapist: What must he tell his brothers and sisters?

Patient: To get ready for the storm and find a cave near the woods so they could go out and eat the barks off the tree.

Therapist: Wait a minute — to get ready for the storm and to find a cave?

Patient: Hhmmm.

Therapist: So then they could go out and eat the barks off the tree?

Patient: Hhmmm. When the snow comes.

Therapist: You mean winter was coming?

Patient: Yeah. So the brothers and sisters —

Therapist: Where was the mother and father?

Patient: Away someplace.

Therapist: Okay.

Patient: So the sisters and brothers said, "No. You do all the work. You're in charge. Why don't you? You're old enough." The deer said, "Okay, but you should do your work. I'm going to only fix a cave for myself." They said, "Oh, we don't care. We'll find someplace for ourselves."

And so the deer did all the hard work while the little ones — well, they were sort of big — started playing. And then winter comes they were very unhappy that they did not obey the one that was in charge. And so they always came around to the deer's house and started begging, but no one would let them have anything.

Therapist: Who else was in the cave besides the first deer?

Patient: Oh, some of his cousins. He called some of his cousins because he would get lonely.

Therapist: Yeah, and they wouldn't let them in. And then what happened?

Patient: And they went begging to everybody and nobody would let them have any food.

Therapist: All right and then what happened?

Patient: That's all. And the moral of my story is: you should always listen to the older one when you believe that it is true and you do not have to obey all the times unless things are really true.

Therapist: Uh-huh. Very, very good.

Patient: Thank you.

Therapist: That was a fine story.

The story has many healthy elements. It reveals Lucy's willingness to accept the fact that there will be a time in the future when she will no longer have her parents available to provide for her. She will then have to assume many new responsibilities. It also suggests that she has come to terms with the fact that her parents have some limitations in what they can provide for her in the present; and she is willing to do more for herself, rather than neurotically pursue that which is not available. The lazy brothers and sisters, I believe, not only represent her siblings (who she would like to see starved out), but also a part of herself that would like to be provided for without putting in any effort. The story reveals her appreciation that the latter adaptation is a most unsatisfactory one — the shiftless ones end up as beggars.

With this understanding of Lucy's story, I related the following:

Once upon a time there was a deer and as he was grazing he looked up in the sky and he saw that the ducks were flying south. And he said, "Uh-oh, winter must be coming soon. I must tell my brothers and sisters so we can all prepare a warm cave and some extra food so that we'll be all right over the winter.

Well, he went over to the brothers and sisters — the

mother and father were away — and he asked them. Was your deer a girl or a boy deer?

Patient: A boy.

Therapist: Okay. He asked them to help him prepare a cave and they said, "Naw, we don't have to prepare a cave. You do it." He said, "No, I'm going to do it only for myself and if you don't help me you're going to find yourselves very cold when winter comes along."

Well, the brothers and sisters were kind of foolish deer. They were young and foolish and they didn't listen and sure enough when winter came, their brother, their big brother had a very nice warm cozy cave with a nice fire in it and they were out in the cold. And so what they had to do then was to try to find places where there wasn't too much snow to find firewood. They had to find another cave, which they finally did, and they had to work very hard to get firewood because most of it was under the snow and it was difficult to find. They had to dry it out. They had a hard time of it, but they finally did get a cave which was warm and protected themselves. And they said to themselves, "Boy, we've learned our lesson."

And the moral of that story is if you make a mistake, try to do something to correct it, even if it's late. The end.

Patient: That was a very good story. I liked it.

Therapist: I liked your story too. What was the best part of my story that you liked?

Patient: Well, that they learned their lesson.

Therapist: Hhmmm. Yes.

In Lucy's story, the fate of the lazy siblings is unclear; one doesn't know whether they survive. In mine, they learn their lesson the hard way by rising to the challenges and providing for themselves. My story is typical of the kind I tell when the patient's story is for the most part healthy. I elaborate on one element and introduce even further salutary adaptations.

During the "long haul," or working-through phase of therapy, clinical progress is often followed by transient regression related to the anxiety produced by the advances. The child's stories often reflect this sequence of progress and retrogression. This was true of Lucy during her middle and late phase of therapy. Following my suggestions, as communicated through my stories, the animals in the patient's stories would venture forth on their own and assert themselves more independently. However, her animals would expose themselves to many perils and risks when doing so; ofttimes they were traumatized in the process.

This is demonstrated by a typical story that she related at the end of her third month of treatment:

> Once there was a tadpole and he was swimming in the water. All the time people used to come there and splash through his home. One day when he was swimming along some children picked it up. And they said, "Let's keep it for a pet." "Yeah, it'll make a swell pet. We could have a frog out of it." When the tadpole heard this, he got very frightened and tried to wiggle out of the children's hands.
>
> They built a sand castle and lake around it near the shore. They put him in it. The tadpole tried to break through and it did. And the rest of the time he always stayed with his friends so he wouldn't get caught.
>
> The moral of this story is: never feel so lonely because there are always friends about.

As can be seen here, Lucy has ventured forth into the world. This is symbolized by her immersing herself in the world of the pond without her parents. But she also anticipates dangers. She sees herself as weak and impotent in the hands of the bigger children; but this is not so, however, when she stays with the weaker ones like herself.

I then related this story:

> Once upon a time there was a tadpole. He had a lot of friends. He and the other tadpoles had a good time swimming around.
>
> One day the tadpoles were talking and one of them said, "Do you think there's any danger around here? There are always lots of children walking around the edge of the

845

pond." One of the tadpoles answered, "Once in a while —
but it doesn't happen very often — a kid will come and try
to take one or two tadpoles out of the water. But most
often, most people know that it's better for us to stay in
here and they leave us alone." So that made the tadpole
feel good.

Well, one day a kid actually did come and he tried to
get a tadpole. He stuck his hand in the water and caught
this tadpole. Then the other tadpoles came around, and
they bit the kid's hand, so he dropped it back in the water
and then the tadpole was okay.

But that kid still wanted to get the tadpole. So he put
his hand in the water again very quickly and pulled him out
before the other tadpoles could get there. But this tadpole
remembered what had happened before and he gave the
boy a god hard bite. The boy screamed, "Owwww — that
hurts!" He dropped the tadpole in the water and the boy
learned his lesson. And he didn't try to pull tadpoles out of
the water anymore.

There are *three* morals to this story. The first is that
danger isn't as common as you might think; it is only rarely
that dangerous things happen to people or tadpoles. The
second is that if a dangerous thing does happen to you,
most of the time your friends can be relied upon to help
you. The third is that you should be able to rely upon yourself as well. And that's the most important moral of my
story. Learn to do things on your own, so that, if your
friends are not around, you can handle things yourself.

As can be seen, attempts *were* made to present a realistic
view of the world. There *are* some dangers, but they are less
common than Lucy imagines. In addition, she is not helpless to
cope with these hazards, for she can rely on the help of friends
and she has resources of her own. Lastly, implicit in my story
is the message that one has to express hostility if one is to
protect oneself successfully against the occasional dangers of
the world.

During the following week, Lucy's stories revealed far less
anxiety about involving herself with friends. This coincided with
her clinical improvement, as shown by the fact that there was a

definite increase on her part in successful peer involvement.

During the following week (in the middle of her fourth month of therapy), Lucy related this dream:

One day I was talking to Mr. B. and he said that I was a very good swimmer and that I could join the races. I won two of the races. There were four races and I won the first and the last. Mr. B. gave me the prize, which was some pens.

I regard this dream as having presaged the resolution of the major problems and the termination of treatment. Here Lucy has jumped into the water and is swimming — that is, she is successfully coping with living in the world.

During the next few weeks, her stories dealt with the theme of children who had no friends and then went out and got them. The following is typical of such stories:

Once there was a lonely leprechaun. He could do lots of magic, but he was very shy and timid and never wanted to get out of his home. He always sat on a log and never moved. And that's why he didn't have any friends.

One day he happened to look across the yard and he saw some children playing. He saw lots of them, too. He said to himself, "Why do those children just waste their time and play? They'll get all hot and tired out and then when their mothers and fathers call them, they'll be very, very hot, and it isn't fun to get hot."

While he was sitting down on the log, the next day, he began to complain again. He said, "Now I don't have anybody to play with. But, anyway, if I play, I'll get hot again. Anyway, I'll go over to those children and ask if I can play." So the leprechaun went over to see if he could play with them and, at first, they said no. Then he asked again and they said, "All right, yes, if you don't sit on that log all the time and if you promise to stay with us and join in." So the leprechaun always made friends and was never sad and shy from then on. He stopped saying: "It's no fun to play and run and get hot." But he was wrong and he learned his lesson.

The moral of this story is: you just can't sit there like a bump on a log and complain. You have to go out and make friends, and play with them even though you do get hurt once in a while.

It is clear here that Lucy sees involvement with others as being far less dangerous than she had previously felt it to be. She has overcome the anxiety associated with these anticipated discomforts and perils and she now steps forth. When a child presents a story with such a healthy resolution, I often just reinforce the salutary elements in it, without significantly altering the patient's story. Accordingly, I then related the following:

Once upon a time there was a lonely leprechaun. And he used to sit on a log all day and he had no friends. And he used to watch the children playing across the way. He used to say to himself, "Who wants to play with those kids? Look what happens when they play. They get overheated; they sweat a lot; they fall down; they get cut; they scrape themselves; sometimes they get hit and hurt; they get dirty; and their hair gets messed up. Who would ever want to play? Those kids are foolish. I'll sit here." But one thing he didn't realize: even though when you play things like that can happen to you, none of them are as painful as *loneliness*.

And so, once in a while the kids would pass by and say, "Aren't you lonely over there?" And he said, "I'd rather be lonely than to have cuts, bumps, scrapes, dirt, sweat, hair messed up, and be hurt." And they said, "We can't understand that. We really can't."

And gradually the leprechaun began to realize that loneliness was worse than those things and that those things only happen once in a while and that, most of all, play is a lot of fun. So he gradually began to play with kids and he was much happier. And he was no longer lonely.

The moral of this story is: when you play, painful things only happen once in a while. Most often they don't happen. It's no reason not to play just because you may get hurt or bothered once in a while.

During the next month there was progressive clinical improvement. Lucy formed many friendships, was definitely more outgoing and assertive, fought back when threatened, and tolerated separations from her father without coughing.

One month later, after five months of therapy, it was felt that treatment could be terminated because there had been significant clinical improvement in all areas of functioning.

During the last few sessions, Lucy told stories involving her relationships with her peers. They revealed some slight anxiety over the sexual feelings that were now being evoked by her closer contacts with boys. I regarded these stories as normal for a child of her age in her milieu.

Lucy was seen for a total of thirty-two sessions. Although I consider The Mutual Storytelling Technique to have played an important role in this child's improvement, other therapeutic modalities were utilized as well. In fact, only about fifteen minutes of each session were devoted to the tape-recording. Part of each session was spent with one or both parents as well, during which time information was obtained, suggestions were offered, and attempts were made to improve their relationship with Lucy. In addition, the patient brought in many dreams which were discussed with her. Near the termination of treatment, Lucy was able to analyze her own stories and to profit from a direct discussion of their meaning. Not all children reach this point. Nevertheless, that they do derive therapeutic benefits from analysis and discussion is shown by both their clinical improvement and their stories.

Three years after the termination of treatment, contact with the family revealed that there had been no recurrence of the coughing, in spite of many separations from her father because of his business trips to Europe and many parts of the U.S. which lasted from ten to eighteen days. All previously described gains were also maintained.

16. A GIRL WITH SCHOOL PHOBIA

Bonnie, a ten-year-old fourth grade girl entered therapy with a severe school phobia of three weeks' duration. The symptom started a few days after the assassination of President Kennedy, at a time when her maternal grandmother was on the verge of dying of cancer. Upon arising in the morning she would complain of headache, nausea, vomiting, and palpitations. As she approached school, she became increasingly panicky, clung to her mother ever more tenaciously, and would refuse to part from her to enter school. She claimed to be frightened of her teacher who was in reality a somewhat mild-mannered woman whom she had never feared before.

There was no past history of school fears (with the exception of fear of separating from her mother during the first two weeks of the first grade). From the age of five she had frequently reacted with exaggerated anxiety to minor physical illnesses, was preoccupied with "scary ghosts," was fearful of going to friends' homes, exhibited occasional facial tics, and was generally timid about playing rough games or exposing herself to even slightly dangerous situations such as riding her bicycle on the street.

The patient's mother was an extremely materialistic woman whose main pleasures were exhibiting her fine home and showing off her expensive clothing. She was not a particularly maternal woman and left the primary care of her two children to housekeepers. Bonnie's father was a successful lawyer. Although he complained of his wife's extravagance, he definitely enjoyed her displays of his wealth. He was severely claustrophobic in elevators, subways, and small rooms when the doors were closed. In addition, he was very involved with occult phenomena, communication with the dead, and various forms of extrasensory perception.

In treating school phobias there are two schools of thought regarding the question of whether the child should be pressured to return or not. There are some who consider it anti-therapeutic to advise the mother to force the child because this only increases his anxiety and resistance to therapy — the child knows that the therapist has suggested that the mother coerce him. Those who follow this approach may arrange for home tutors and wait for the child to reach the point where he has worked through his problems to the point that he himself makes the decision to go, even if he has to push through a little anxiety to do so. The child is treated with dignity, and ego-degrading coercion is avoided. Others feel that every attempt should be made to get the child to school at the earliest possible time, even though he may be suffering considerable anxiety. They hold that the longer he stays out, the harder it will be for him to return. Providing him with tutors only supports his phobic withdrawal and entrenches his pathology. Keeping the child home deprives him of the desensitization experience which is an important part of treatment.

I am a proponent of this second view. I advise the parents to do everything possible to get the child to school, starting the next day, or even that same day if feasible. I suggest that they do not get into discussions with the child about the various rationalizations and excuses he provides for not going to school. I recommend that they approach each morning with a matter-of-fact attitude about school — an attitude of quiet assumption that the child is going and surprise when he refuses. I advise them to pressure the child to go *up to the point of panic,* and only then allow the child to return home. However, there should not be one school morning when they do not at least bring the child to the schoolhouse. If he cannot make it inside in the morning, then another attempt is made after lunch hour. If he has to leave mid-morning, then he returns again after lunch. Waiting until the next day only prolongs the problem. When he is at home during school hours no television or play is permitted, only homework. Making things pleasant at home can intensify the problem.

I prescribe tranquillizers up to lethargic doses and then drop the dose slightly, maintaining the child on a sub-lethargic level. I speak personally to the child's teacher, guidance counselor, or school nurse and apprise them of my approach. I attempt to enlist their aid and sympathy. Interestingly, my experience has been that most often school personnel agree with this approach. Occasionally, someone who considers himself psychologically sophisticated becomes indignant and is overtly or covertly uncooperative ("Well, you're the doctor."). I explain to the mother (she, rather than the father, is the one who is most often involved in taking the child to school) that it will be rough-going, but the alternative (of letting the child stay home), although easier, is in the long run the less desirable because it will only prolong the child's illness. The child is also present when I describe my plan to the parents. To discuss this out of the child's awareness would only foster a distrust of me that would be so anti-therapeutic that a successful outcome of therapy would be unlikely.

All this may sound very cruel, especially to those who have used what they consider the more "humane" approach. I can only respond that I have tried both ways and that the main drawback of the "softer" approach is that some children never get back to school. My success with the "hard line" has been much greater. The children will often curse me terribly. "That big fat meany Dr. Gardner; you listen to every stupid thing he says," or "He's the stupidest doctor I ever saw in my whole life." In spite of their most vociferous vilification of me, however, they typically come willingly to each session. We learn about the underlying psychodynamics *while* the child is going to school, not before. Working through is not a sterile process which takes place in the therapist's office; it is only meaningfully accomplished in association with living experiences. Whatever ego-debasement the child may suffer in being so coerced is more than compensated for, I believe, by the sense of accomplishment he feels when he successfully stays. Also, there is no question that permitting the child to avoid the phobic situation is in itself ego-degrading to him. Staying home alone because he is "too scared" to go to school like the other children lowers every child's self respect.

This was the approach used from the first day with Bonnie. During the first few minutes of each session I discussed with the patient and her mother various problems which arose in the household, both the school problem and others. Like most mothers of school phobics, Bonnie's mother had difficulty following through with my suggestions. Besides the realistic discomforts the method caused her to suffer, her own ambivalence contributed to her inability to follow through completely. However, the therapist cannot wait to analyze the mother's ambivalence "away." She too must learn to exert some conscious control, push through her own anxieties just as her child is doing, and get the child to school, no matter what. In spite of all the brouhaha at home and school, Bonnie (like most school phobics) settled down to a conventional session in my office. We spent some time playing the storytelling game and the rest of the session was spent in traditional manner working both with the patient and her parents. Although the focus here is on the storytelling sequences, other relevant aspects of Bonnie's treatment are described.

Bonnie's first story in treatment was the story (see Chapter 2) about the kitten who was singled out for rejection by the mother cat and sold to another family which she subsequently left because of cruel treatment. The kitten then suffered a series of further harrowing experiences in catland and dogland before she woke from the nightmare.

During her second week of treatment, Bonnie told this story:

Once upon a time there were three boys and three girls, and the boys wanted to spy on the girls. So they put a tape recorder in the room where the girls were and a walkie-talkie in there so that they could hear them and tape what they say.

So the girls found out about this and so they decided that they should do a trick on the boys, so they said into

the walkie-talkie and the tape recorder that they were going to spy on the boys. So the boys said, "Let's tell on the girls that they are going to spy on us." So they went in and told.
Therapist: Who did they tell?
Patient: Their mother. And so they went in and told their mother.
Therapist: Were all of these children brothers and sisters?
Patient: Yes. And so then the mother called the girls into the house and asked if they were going to spy on the boys, and they said, "No." And so then the girls asked one of the boys how they knew that they were planning to spy. So then the boys had to tell that they were spying on them. So that's the end.
Therapist: What was the moral of that story?
Patient: That you shouldn't tattle on something that you did yourself.
Therapist: Don't tattle on someone if you do the same thing yourself.
Patient: Yes.
Therapist: I see. Thank you very much Bonnie.

The story is typical of the kind of early resistance story described in Chapter 3. The brothers represent the therapist and the girls symbolize the patient. The tape recorder and walkie-talkie which are used for spying are the therapist's devices for finding out things Bonnie does not wish to disclose. The girls foil the boys' plot, preventing further use of the bugging devices. In this way the patient satisfies her wish for privacy and protects herself from the dangers of revealing herself to me. Accordingly, I told this story:

Once upon a time there were three boys and three girls and one of these girls was upset about something and she was seeing a psychiatrist. And the psychiatrist once brought in the whole family and he said. "I'd like to get information about this girl that will help me treat her." And the girl said, "Uh, uh, uh. I don't want you to get information from my family. I don't want to let them know what's going on inside my mind." And the psychiatrist then said, "Well, this is the best way that I could help you. If I learn what is going on in your mind then I can help you with your problems. If I don't, then I can't." And the girl said, "Well, I'm a little hesitant to do that."

The psychiatrist said, "How about putting a walkie-talkie or a tape recorder in your room so that the things you do or say will be heard and then we can listen to the tapes and learn about your problems?"

Well, she was hesitant to do it. In fact, she said no. Then one of her sisters had similar problems, but this sister agreed that it might be helpful if she let them put the walkie-talkie and the tape recorder in her room. And much to her amazement, she found out that when she listened to it and when she discussed it with the doctor, she learned a lot about her troubles that she hadn't known before. And then the other sister seeing this said, "Well, all right. Try it on me too." And then they tried it on her and then both sisters got better.

The lesson of this story is that sometimes it may be frightening to reveal things about yourself to a psychiatrist, but when you do, you'll find out that it helps you very much with your problems. The end.

My story needs no interpretation. Bonnie listened with interest.

Three days later, she told this story:

Once upon a time there was this baby eagle and he lived on this nest high on top of a mountain with his brother, and his sisters and his mother and father.

One day he asked his mother if he could try to fly. And his mother said, "No, you're not old enough yet." But he still wanted to fly.

So then one day when his mother was out he crawled out from his nest and tried to fly. He couldn't fly and he fell, but he kept on falling and falling. Finally, his mother saw him falling and she ran to him and caught him. And then she put him back in the nest and he never tried to fly again. And that's the end.

The moral of the story is that you shouldn't try things that you are not suppose to.

The baby eagle is Bonnie whose overprotective mother tries to impede her from flying, that is, from acting like an adult and going out alone into the world. Instead she would have her remain longer in the nest — an infantile state of dependence. The metaphor is accurate. Bonnie's mother was quite fearful of the patient's exposing herself to the slightest dangers (bike-riding in the street, swimming in deep water, walking long distances, etc.).

When Bonnie does disobey her mother and attempts to assume some independence, the results are catastrophic. Mother's prophecy is fulfilled. The patient cannot get along without her, and she never flies again. She resigns herself, in other words, to a life in the womb.

The story reveals one of the important elements in Bonnie's fear of going to school. School is a place which teaches her to fly, that is, to be independent of mother. Although her mother ostensibly wanted her to go to school, there was another part of her that would keep the patient dependent and infantile. Bonnie's symptom was, in part, a compliance with her mother's unconscious wish that Bonnie never grow up. Accordingly, I told this story:

Once upon a time there was a baby eagle and it was in a nest with its brothers and sisters and mother and father. And he asked his mother if he could fly. His mother said, "No, you're too young. There are lots of dangerous things out in the world and you'd better stay in your nest."

So the next week he said, "Could I fly now, Momma?" And the mother said, "No, I'm very sorry. You are not old enough. It's dangerous out there. You listen to what I said."

Well, week in and week out he asked his mother and she said, "No, I want you to stay in the nest and stay around there."

Well, he looked over at the other trees and he saw other little eagles who were born around the same time he was and were just as old as he. They were starting to fly. And he said to the mother, "The other eagles are flying." And she said, "That's all right. Their mothers don't care for them the way that I care for you and I want you to stay around the nest, stay around the house."

Well, he listened to his mother and he watched the other eagles flying all around, getting bigger and bigger, and he started getting angrier and angrier because he was missing out on all the fun. The eagles were playing games and things in the air and flying about and going down into the water and up into the air and swinging all around. And he felt very jealous of them and he felt very angry at his mother until he finally said, "The heck with her."

One day he flew out of the nest and joined the other eagles and they said, "Oh, we're glad to see you. We were wondering when you were going to grow up and stop being a little baby and staying home. We are happy you are around."

Well, anyway, he did that and his mother got kind of angry at him, but he said, "You can't stop me. You can't stop me from growing up and being a big eagle like everyone else." Then the mother had no choice but to let him go, and although she was the kind of mother who tried to keep her children infants so that they would always be with her and she wouldn't be lonely, she realized that there was nothing she could do about it.

The lesson of my story is that if your mother is the kind of person who wants to keep you in the house, don't listen.

Patient: Right!

Therapist: Go out and have fun. If you are the kind that stays in the house all the time you're going to miss out on a lot of good things and a lot of good times. The end.

My story elaborates on the pleasures of independence as part of my approach to helping Bonnie break the umbilical cord: "The eagles were playing games and things in the air and flying about and going down into the water and up into the air and swinging all around." In addition, I confronted her with the unpleasant fact that being tied to mother's apron strings subjects one to a certain amount of criticism from one's peers: "We were wondering when you were going to grow up and stop being a little baby and staying home." I put Bonnie in touch with some of the anger she must harbor within her for allowing herself to be squelched by her mother: "he started getting angrier and angrier because he was missing out on all the fun." I communicated the message that if she is to take steps toward independence, she will invoke her mother's anger but that this is not so dangerous as she anticipates. In fact, mother is somewhat impotent to stop her in many areas: "Then the mother had no choice but to let him go . . . she realized that there was nothing she could do about it." Bonnie's single word response to my story — "Right!" — was stated with such enthusiasm that there was no question in my mind that my story had "reached" her.

Following my story, I asked the patient if her mother let her do the things other children do. She complained bitterly: "My mother and father don't let me ride my bike in the street the way other kids my age do. She won't let me swim in the deep end of the pool and I'm a good swimmer. I couldn't cross the street alone in front of my house until I was eight. I couldn't go to school alone until I was eight, and all the other kids in my class were going alone. She wouldn't let me play under the bridge over the brook where all the other kids used to play."

The mother was then brought in. She described how the maternal grandmother, who lived in the home until Bonnie was eight, was constantly concerned for the welfare of everyone in the family. If Bonnie were five minutes late, the grandmother expressed fears that she had been killed. She would wait up until Bonnie's parents came home, regardless of the hour, stating: "I can't go to sleep until they're home. I keep worrying that something will happen to them." In short, Bonnie had been programmed, from the beginning of her life, to see the world as a dangerous place. Death lurked everywhere; the only safe place was home with mother. Considering her family's continual state of fear, it was surprising that she wasn't more phobic than she was.

As already discussed in regard to changing parents' attitudes, the therapist must decide how much he can get the child to do on his own and how much he should assist the patient. Helping the child too much may foster pathological dependency; expecting the child to handle a task which is beyond his capabilities may overwhelm him and intensify his difficulties. In this case, I felt that Bonnie would need some assistance, and so I arranged for an interview with Bonnie and her parents. We focused on their irrational fears. They were able to see some of them as inappropriate and subsequently alter them; others they could not. For example, they were willing to give her greater freedom in the neighborhood and in the swimming pool. However, the mother could do nothing about her airplane phobia, and the father could not be expected to cease his life long claustrophobic reactions. Both parents agreed that their fears were irrational, but they could not help themselves. This was an important admission, and I emphasized it to Bonnie during the meeting. If a parent exhibits behavior which he recognizes as inappropriate but which he cannot control, it can be helpful to the child for such a parent to define to the child the exact area of pathology and state directly and unequivocally to the child that, although he cannot help himself, he recognizes the illogicality of his thinking and feelings. In this way there is less likelihood that the distorted notions will be transmitted to the child. If they have already been, clarification of their irrationality to the child can be helpful. Some parents are hesitant to reveal their defects because of the fear that their children will lose respect for them. The child is usually aware, at some level, of his parents' inadequacies and respects them less when they hide them than when they are mature enough to openly admit them. As stated many times before, one of the therapist's goals in treatment is to help the child gain a clearer view of his parents; their assets and their liabilities; their strengths and their weaknesses. Such clarification can only be salutary. In Bonnie's case it helped her remove some of the irrational dictates which she had learned from her parents and which were contributing to her fears.

A number of such family interviews were held during the first few months of treatment in order to ensure that Bonnie view her parents more accurately. In addition, the parents were advised to reiterate the new insights at home.

During her fourth week in treatment, Bonnie told this story:

Once upon a time there were these three cats and they lived alone all by themselves. There was this new cat who moved near them. They sort of liked her but she didn't act like she liked them or anything. They wanted to make friends with her but they were afraid to ask her because they thought she might not like them or anything.

So one day they were building this house — the first three cats were building this clubhouse. And so they were almost done when they saw this other cat toss this ball — roll it with its feet, you know. And so it ruined their clubhouse and then they knew that that cat really didn't like them and they thought she did it on purpose.

Therapist: Wait a minute. That fourth cat threw a ball towards the others?

Patient: Yes. He threw a ball towards the clubhouse and it fell down. And so one day she came over —

Therapist: What did they think about her throwing the ball? How did they interpret that?

Patient: Then they really knew that she didn't like them, and they didn't think that they wanted to play with her. And so they just forgot about her and, you know, and stayed away from her for all the wrong purpose and all.

And so then the next day the other cat — the one they didn't want to play with — came over and she said that she would like to play with them. No, that she was sorry about ruining the clubhouse and that it was an accident. So then they knew that she really did like them. And so then they were sort of glad that she wrecked the clubhouse because then they wouldn't have found out that she really liked them. And then they all played together.

The lesson of the story is sometimes you find out that you like somebody when you think you don't.

Therapist: Was this fourth cat a male or a female cat?

Patient: A female cat. They were all girls.

In one part of the story, the fourth cat is referred to as male: "He threw a ball towards the clubhouse and it fell down." Elsewhere, the fourth cat is referred to as "she" and is identified as female when I specifically ask its sex at the end. Considering the fourth cat male provides, in my opinion, the most meaningful interpretation. I am the fourth cat and the other three represent Bonnie. I'm the new "cat" who moves into the neighborhood. The three cats are hesitant about the newcomer: "They thought she might not like them." The clubhouse is the wall the patient builds to protect herself from my intrusions into her privacy. I penetrate her defenses — I ruin their clubhouse by rolling a ball against it. Their first response to this was to stay away from the fourth cat — no good can come from Bonnie's associating herself with me. I then explain to them that I meant no harm and that I really want to be her friend, and she accepts this. In essence Bonnie is telling me that she understands that I may cause her some pain in removing her protective shell, but that she realizes that my motives are basically benevolent. The moral epitomizes her feelings: "Sometimes you find out that you like somebody when you think you don't."

The story reveals a diminution of Bonnie's resistances and reflects increasing trust of me — the two, perforce, go together. In response, I told this story:

Once upon a time there were three cats. Now these three cats lived alone and one day a fourth cat moved into the neighborhood. And this cat wanted to be friendly with the three cats but they were kind of suspicious at first and they didn't know whether the fourth cat was really to be trusted or not.

And then one day this fourth cat rolled a ball over, and the fourth cat rolled the ball over as a sign of friendship. He wanted to be friends but they didn't interpret it right. They thought it wasn't friendship, that this cat was trying to hurt them.

Well, the next day the cat came over and told them that he wanted to be friends — mine is a boy cat — they were still a little distrustful, but they said, "Okay, we'll give him a chance." Now then this cat, as part of being friends, started to ask them a lot of questions about themselves. First they thought, "This is kind of personal." And they said to him, "Those are personal questions that you are asking." He said, "Isn't that part of being friends? When you are friendly with someone you are kind of personal and tell them things about yourself." Well, they thought about that and they realized that that was right. In real close friendships, you tell a lot of personal things. So they began to realize that the fourth cat really wanted to be their friend because he spoke about a number of personal things. And so then they started to talk about personal things and they felt much closer to him and they were very happy because then they could go to him with problems and troubles and he would try to help them with their problems and troubles when they told him personal things. Sometimes he told them personal things about himself and asked their advice.

And the lesson of that story is that in a good friendship you can tell the other person personal things because then you can help one another. The end.

Whereas in her story my intrusion — breaking down the clubhouse — was initially seen as painful and traumatic, in mine a less distorted view is presented. What she sees as an encroachment upon her privacy is really my way of demonstrating my interest and affection. Mutual revelation of intimacies is the cornerstone of friendship. In my story, then, I emphasized those elements in her story which reflected increasing trust and diminishing resistance in order to further reinforce and entrench these newly formed attitudes.

Less than a month later (near the end of her second month of treatment), Bonnie told this story:

Once there were two monkeys, a boy and a girl. They were brother and sister and their father told them: "Go out in the jungle and pick some bananas." So they went out and they looked all over the place, but they couldn't find banana trees. Then they went into a nearby jungle and they saw big palm trees and so on the palm trees they looked up there wasn't bananas on the palm trees, but there were coconuts. "Let's explain to our father that we couldn't find any bananas and I'm sure he won't mind having coconuts." But they didn't know that monkeys hate coconuts because they never tried them.

So they brought the coconuts home to their father and the father got real real mad and he said, "You know, monkeys hate coconuts. How dare you come back without bringing back bananas?" They said, "We couldn't find any." He said, "Well, that's no excuse for bringing back coconuts." So the little girl said, "How come you don't like coconuts? How come monkeys don't like coconuts?" The father said "Well, they never have." And they said, "Why?" And the father said, "Well, monkeys are used to eating bananas." And so the boy said, "Well, why don't you try it and see?" The father said, "No, that's ridiculous. No monkeys have ever liked bananas — I mean coconuts." The little boy said, "Yes, but you never tried it and none of your parents did. So maybe they do like it." The father said, "Well, only to prove to you, I'll take bananas all day."

Therapist: Coconuts.

Patient: Coconuts. "Only to prove to you that monkeys hate coconuts, I'll do it and also you two will taste it." So first the children taste it and they say, "It's not bad. It's pretty good." Then the father says, "Oh, you're just lying so that will be an excuse for me liking it." So then the father tried them and then he waited a little bit and then he said, "Hey, they are good."

Then he went all over the jungle to his monkey friends and told them there aren't many bananas now, but to try coconuts. So they all did and then the monkeys all liked coconuts afterwards.

Therapist: And the moral?

Patient: You don't know whether you'll like something unless you try it.

Therapist: Okay. Very good.

The story reveals Bonnie's willingness to try new things; to incorporate ideas which are alien to her parents; and even to attempt to change those of her parents' deep-seated notions which she considers irrational. The new ideas, of course, are the altered attitudes about the world which are replacing distortions derived from her parents. At the time of the telling of this story, definite clinical improvement was noted. Bonnie was less fearful of going to school but still required a fair amount of coaxing. She was, however, remaining in the classroom throughout the day about half the time — a marked improvement.

In response, I told this story:

Once upon a time there were two monkeys, a brother and a sister and they lived on the edge of the jungle with their father. Now this father was a very funny old man. He had some strange ideas. He used to say, "Now children don't go into the jungle. It's very dangerous in the jungle. All kinds of dangerous things can happen to you. Be very careful not to eat the coconuts. Don't eat the bananas or else you might get sick. Be very careful. Stay right around the house. Stay right around our hut — our monkey hut."

Well, these kids grew up believing that all this was so. They would see other monkeys go into the jungle and the other monkeys seemed to be all right, but these kids somehow still kept on believing that these things were dangerous. They would see a monkey coming out eating bananas and they would say, "Oh, he's eating bananas. He's going to get sick." They'd see another monkey eating coconuts and they'd say, "Ooh, he's eating coconuts. He's going to get sick. Ooh, he's playing in the jungle. Terrible things are going to happen to him." But they never saw any terrible thing happen. Nobody got sick from bananas. Nobody got sick from coconuts and nobody got hurt in the jungle.

So one day some kid came over to them and said, "Why don't you come on. We'll play in the jungle." They said, "Ooh, no. It's dangerous in the jungle." He replied, "Where did you get that idea?" He said, "My father told me." The kid said, "That's absurd. There's nothing to be frightened of in the jungle. Sure once in a while something may happen that's a little dangerous, but that is very seldom." Anyway, that got the monkeys thinking and they gradually began to realize that maybe their father wasn't right.

So one day they very carefully, very hesitantly stepped into the jungle and although they were scared at first, they gradually came to realize that the jungle wasn't a frightening thing or a frightening place. One day they even got the guts to try and taste a coconut. They did it and they found out that it was really pretty good and the same thing with a banana. So it ended up with them playing in the jungle and eating coconuts and bananas. At first their father was kind of upset, but then they said, "Look, we're big enough to make these decisions on our own. If you don't want to go into the jungle that's your problem. You can do what you want, but we're going into the jungle. We're going to have a good time."

Do you know what the moral of that story is?

Patient: Uh-huh.

Therapist: Can you try to figure it out?

Patient: That sometimes things aren't really as dangerous as people say they are.

Therapist: Right! And that's the moral of that story. The end. What did you think of that story?

Patient: It was good.

My story is also on the theme of changing parental precepts. I advised Bonnie to judge the world on the basis of her own observations and not blindly accept her parents' notions. She is encouraged to consider new and different ways of doing things and to have living experiences which will better enable her to evaluate the ideas which she has indiscriminately incorporated from her parents. She is urged to push through the inevitable anxieties associated with exposure to such new experiences. Lastly, Bonnie is advised to stand up and resist her father should he interfere with her in these pursuits: "Look, we're big enough to make these decisions on our own. If you don't want to go into the jungle that's your problem. You can do what you want, but we're going into the jungle. We're going to have a good time." The patient accurately provided a moral, "Sometimes things aren't really as dangerous as people say they are," and her final comment that my story was a "good" one was said with conviction and pleasure.

Seven weeks later, during the middle of her fourth month of treatment, Bonnie told this story:

> Once upon a time there were two kids. They were girls. They decided they wanted to go into a tunnel. One of the girls was very scared. She said, "I don't want to go. We might get trapped. It might rain and water will gush in." The second girl was scared too and she said, "You're right."
>
> Then their brother said that there was nothing to worry about. He went in and they followed him and everything was okay. There was nothing to fear. Then the brother said, "They're rats in here." The girls knew he was only kidding and they laughed.
>
> The moral of that story is: sometimes if you try something it might turn out okay. Things are safer than it looks.

The story represents another attempt to desensitize herself to situations which she has come to associate with danger. Near Bonnie's home was a brook which flowed under a bridge. Although many of the neighborhood children played there, prior to therapy, Bonnie's mother had prohibited her from joining them. The tunnel in the patient's story, where water might gush in, symbolizes, I believe, the once forbidden brook under the bridge. She accustoms herself to this dangerous place which represents all perilous places and, in addition, uses counterphobic mechanisms to assuage her anxiety: the girls laugh when their brother tells them there are rats in the tunnel.

Although the story suggests further improvement, it was told during her summer vacation from school. Only the future could determine how much of the changes exhibited in therapy would carry over into the classroom.

In response, I told this story:

> Once upon a time there was an amusement park. It was a playland, but you had to crawl through a long tunnel

866

in order to get there. The amusement park was at the end of the tunnel. There were three kids, two girls and a boy, who wanted to get to the amusement park, but they were first fearful of going through the tunnel. The girls especially were scared of getting scratched and rubbed along the sides of the tunnel. The boy, although he was scared too, said that there are a lot of things in life that you have to go to trouble for if you are to enjoy them. So they started crawling through the tunnel. They got hurt a little, a few scratches and a few bruises, but they finally got to the playland and they were happy that they had gone to all the trouble.

Do you know what the moral of this story is?

Patient: Sometimes if you go through a lot of trouble it's worth it.

Therapist: Yes. That's the moral of this story. There are many times in life when you have to suffer minor inconveniences in order to get the rewards at the end.

Whereas in Bonnie's story there are no dangers, in mine there are some to correspond with the way life really is. They are, however, not so terrible as her parents would have her believe. If she wishes to pursue pleasurable goals in life (the amusement park) she will have to expose herself to certain minor traumata (the scratches and bruises in my story). I make the point that most are willing to suffer these inconveniences for the pleasures they ultimately attain.

During her fifth month of treatment Bonnie returned to school after her summer vacation. There was anxiety, nausea, and balking but far less than she had had prior to the summer.

During her sixth month of treatment, after she had been back in school about a month, she became increasingly phobic. I could not attribute the exacerbation to any specific event or experience at school or home, and considered it to be a manifestation of the common phenomenon in treatment that with advances there comes anxiety which, in turn, is reduced by regression. At this time, Bonnie told this story:

Once there were these kids and they wanted to watch

a certain TV show. So they turned on the TV set and they found out that it was too early and it wasn't time for it. So they turned the TV off and went and played and rode their bicycles and did other things. So then one kid said, "Maybe it's time to go back in and watch the show. Maybe it's on now." Nobody else listened to him. They were having fun playing and doing other things. So the other kid just stayed out too. So finally they all got tired and they went inside and said, "Maybe it's on by now." So they turned the TV set on and they found out that they had missed the show. Because they didn't pay attention or think about what they were doing, they missed what they wanted to see — the show they wanted to watch.

Therapist: And the lesson of that story?

Patient: Pay attention and watch the time on whatever it is that you're doing if there's something you want to see because you might miss it if you don't pay attention.

Therapist: Thank you very much. Now it's time for me to tell my story.

This is a typical example of a resistance story. The picture on the television screen is what Bonnie would see in treatment if she looked into herself. It is the projection of unconscious processes. She is ambivalent about such inquiry at this time and the story reflects it. Various rationalizations are utilized to justify her not looking at herself, and the story ends with successful avoidance. With this interpretation in mind, I told this story:

Once upon a time there were some children who said they wanted to watch a TV show. Now this was a show — it was one of these family shows — and it told about things that happened between parents and children and it was a kind of serious family show. These kids had kind of mixed feelings about watching this show because they knew deep down that some of the things that would be happening on this show might be a little upsetting to them. But they said, "Let's watch the show." First they turned on the television set and it was too early. So they went outside and they started to play. Then one of them said, "Shall

868

we go back and see if the show is on yet." The others didn't listen. They just wanted to play. So finally after they played a long time they decided to go in, but by that time it was too late and the show had been over. But they had a kind of sigh of relief that it was over. They were also a little sad that they had missed it, because although it would have been a little upsetting, they might have learned some things from this family show that might have been helpful to them. All things considered, they ended up sorry that they had missed it.

The moral of that story is —— what's the moral of that story?

Patient: I don't know.

Therapist: The moral of that story is that if you do look at something that may be a little upsetting that you may learn something even though it may be a little upsetting. Don't run away from things just because they're a little upsetting. If you do you may miss out on some good things.

In my story I tried to create some incentive for Bonnie to look into herself once again because she might then learn things about herself which might be helpful to her. Another tack I often take with such stories utilizing television and movies is to have the children tolerate the anxieties they have about viewing the scary show. They then find that it not only wasn't as bad as they had anticipated, but that they learned some interesting things as well.

A week after this interchange, Bonnie's grandmother died. Interestingly, there was no intensification of her symptoms. During the subsequent weeks there was further improvement.

In the middle of her seventh month of therapy, Bonnie told this story:

Once there were these deers and they lived in the forest with a lot of other little animals. They didn't have very much fun in the winter because it got cold and it was hard to find food some of the days. But they had fun playing in the snow and all. Then in the summer they had fun too, but the hunters always came hunting sometimes in the summer. So they really didn't want to go out and play around too much in the summer.

So one time there were two little deers and they were pretty afraid of the hunter, so they always stayed inside and watched TV and played games. They didn't go outside and run around much. Everyone was telling them — all the other little deers, and rabbits and birds and chipmunks and all — "The hunters don't come around too much. Why don't you come out and play a little bit?" They said, "No, if he comes we'll be in a lot of trouble." So their parents thought it was a better idea for them to stay inside too.

So one day their grandfather came over and he said to them, "Why don't you come for a walk with me in the woods?" They said, "No, the hunters will get us." He said, "Of course not. I've been going walking around in the forest for years and I haven't gotten hurt by a hunter. Anyway, we're too fast for the hunters to catch us." So at first they were kind of scared to go out, but then, you know, the grandfather kept telling them how simple it was to get away from the hunters and they went outside. They went outside and they played around and the parents knew that they had gone out with the grandfather. They were very angry and they were afraid that they might get hurt by the hunters. So then they all came in very excited and the little deer said, "Boy, we sure had a lot of fun." The mother said, "You mean no hunters came after you?" He only said, "Oh, sure a lot of hunters came after us. The most fun was running away from them and playing games so they couldn't catch us. Grandpa showed us how." So the parents weren't afraid and the little deers weren't afraid to go out in the woods anymore.

Therapist: The lesson of that story?

Patient: That things can be less dangerous sometimes if you —— you shouldn't be too afraid if things are going to be very dangerous 'cause sometimes they are not dangerous and if you try, you might not get hurt or anything.

Therapist: Excellent story. Excellent story. Okay. I have a question. How is it that the hunters came in the summertime and not in the wintertime?

Patient: 'Cause in the wintertime it was too cold and in the summertime it was easier to find the animals because they were all out.

Therapist: And in the wintertime?

Patient: In the wintertime they were usually inside because of the cold.

Therapist: I see. Thank you very much. That was an excellent story and now it's time for me to tell my story.

The story reflects the clinical improvement Bonnie had enjoyed since the last sequence presented. She once again exposes herself to the phobic situation and finds that her fears were unfounded. In addition, counterphobic phenomena are present: tempting the hunters and then eluding them is fun. Like the boy who whistles as he walks through the cemetery at night, making believe she isn't scared helps in the desensitization process. The story also reveals her appreciation of her parents' role in her symptoms and her overt refutation of their irrational dictates.

In response, I told this story:

Once upon a time there were these two deer and they lived in the forest with the other little animals. These two deer had parents who were always seeing frightening things happening in the forest and they would exaggerate every little danger and make it a big thing. For instance, when the two deer went out in the winter their mother would say, "Don't catch a cold. Be careful. You're out in the cold. Don't catch a cold." The mother would worry, "Oh, there's so little food out there in the wintertime. Maybe they'll starve." She was constantly worried that they'd sink into the snow or get hurt or suffocate — things like that. So the mother was constantly worried. In the summer she would worry about the hunters. Sure an occasional hunter would go through, but this mother was constantly worried that these little deer would be killed by hunters. Well, as a result of that, these deer hardly went out. They didn't go out in the wintertime because their mother was afraid of colds, starvation, suffocation. They didn't go out in the summertime because the mother was afraid of death by being shot.

Anyway, one day the grandfather came and he said, "Why aren't you kids out playing?" The little deer said, "Oh, there are dangerous things out there in the world." He said, "What kind of dangerous things?" The little girls — they were girl deer — said, "Well, first of all, in the wintertime it's very cold and we can catch cold." He said, "Oh, fiddlesticks. What kind of junk is that? You aren't going to get colds that way. Colds are caused by germs. Just because you feel a little bit cold outside doesn't mean you'll catch a cold. That's a disease. All the kids are out there on their sleds, throwing snowballs, having a lot of fun. There's no reason why you kids shouldn't be out there playing. Your parents don't know what they're talking about." Then they said, "Also, there's not too much food out there." He said, "So what will happen? You're not going to starve. You're just going out for a little while. Nothing is going to happen. You get plenty of food here at home where you live in this cave and nothing is going to happen to you." Then they said, "What about sinking into the snow and suffocating?" He said, "That's a lot of bunk too. The snow isn't that deep out there. I've never heard of a deer suffocating in the snow." Anyway, he just pooh-poohed all these fears that their parents had. Then they said, "Well, what about in the summertime? You know there are hunters out there in the summer." "Yeah," he said, "there's a hunter once in a while, but you know how to run pretty fast. There's no reason to be so afraid of all these things. Your parents have some strange ideas about the dangers of the world."

Anyway, they talked more to the parents and the parents kind of admitted that they knew that their fears weren't really realistic. They really didn't believe it too much, but they couldn't help being frightened.

So the little deer said, "Let's try it." So they went out with their grandfather both in the summertime and in the wintertime. Sure they occasionally met a hunter, but, number one, this hunter, first of all, wasn't going around shoot-baby deer, and number two, they were pretty sensitive and when they would smell a hunter from a distance, before the hunter would even see them, they would get out of the way. Sure there was a rare, occasional danger, but certainly nothing like the parents had described. So these two deer gradually realized that their parents' ideas of the world were not very true, that their parents had some exaggerated fears about the world, and when they went out and saw that it wasn't that way, they felt much better about things. They had much more fun, played with other kids, began to enjoy themselves much more, and then grew up to be happy, healthy deer.

The lesson of that story is —— do you know what the lesson is?

Patient: No.

Therapist: The lesson of that story is: not all the things that your parents teach you about the dangers in the world are necessarily true. You have to look for yourself and see if it is true or not. The end. What do you think about that story?

Patient: It was a good story.

Therapist: What was the part about it you liked?

Patient: I liked it all. I don't think I liked any part better than I liked the whole part.

Therapist: I think yours was an excellent story too. I think these are very good stories. Do you think these stories have anything to do with your situation in school?

Patient: No, not in school.

Therapist: Nothing at all?

Patient: No.

Therapist: Hhmmm. I think it has a little bit to do with it in this regard. You think that there are terribly dangerous things happening in school which aren't happening.

Patient: The mother deer sounds like my maid.

Therapist: The mother?

Patient: Last winter —

Therapist: Which maid? What was her name?

Patient: Hilda. And she was so afraid I didn't have five sweaters on and I had these big boots and sometimes, you know, she wanted me to wear kneesocks. I just wore summer socks because I had big furry boots. I could be just walking out the door with my sled and she'd have to check my socks to see if they were kneesocks.

Therapist: Well, what did your mother and father do about this?

Patient: My mother went along with her pretty much.

Therapist: What do you think about that?

Patient: I think that's a little stupid.

Therapist: I think so too.

Patient: I was wearing — I wore like snowpants with pants under them and a shirt, a ski windbreaker, a pullover sweater, and they still don't think I'm warm enough.

Therapist: They have these exaggerated fears that I was talking about. Some terrible thing will happen to you. You've got to protect yourself at all times from colds or terrible dangers in the world. Huh?

Patient: Hhmmm.

Therapist: That's one of your family's problems, you know.

Patient: They used to be afraid that I'd drown.

Therapist: When was that?

Patient: When we'd go to the hotel. When we went to a hotel when I was in third grade or fourth grade or second grade and I knew how to swim pretty well for a long time, but they have ropes sometimes that divide the real shallow end from the deep end. I could swim in the deeper end, but in first grade I didn't pass my deep-water test at Town and Country Day Camp, and so by the time I was in third grade I wanted to go past the ropes in any swimming pool. "Well, you didn't pass the deep water test. You can't go swimming until you pass your deep water test, and I wasn't even going to day camp then.

Therapist: Hhmmm. So your parents are always frightened that something is going to happen to you? Huh?

Patient: Yes.

Therapist: And I think that's what happens to you in school. When you're in school you're kind of locked into a place which is separate from your home, and I think you think that terrible things can happen to you there. What do you think of that?

Patient: I don't know.

Therapist: You've been exposed to so much talk that things are dangerous that you've come to believe it yourself. You've come to believe that the world is a more dangerous place than it is. What do you think of that?

Patient: I think that's right. My father was always afraid to go in elevators and he used to tell me how everytime he got stuck in elevators. So up until fourth grade I was afraid to go on elevators.

Therapist: Well, how did you decide to change?

Patient: Well, when we go to hotels, I make friends usually and we play games, like in the elevators, if there isn't any operator in it. We, well, let's take when Alice and I went down to Florida over the weekend. There's four different hotels but they have one big lobby. There's a lot of different elevators and there's this boy here who was the son of a friend of my father's, and we got into this screwy elevator that was different from our elevator. I mean it was in a different section, in a different building from ours, and something was screwy because it always kept stopping at eight. Alice ran out of the elevator when it opened at eight. She wasn't sure she wanted to get in it, and I stayed in and then I pushed the button and then I ran out. But the boy Ralph, he didn't run too, so we got the next elevator and we kept on pushing all the elevator buttons, but we couldn't find him until about a half-hour later. He was coming down in one of the elevators. It was very funny.

Therapist: That's how you stopped being afraid of elevators?

Patient: Oh, well, no. I have ridden in elevators before then, but that's what I do with my friends if we're at a hotel or something.

Therapist: Hhmmm. Well, I think your fear of going to school has something to do with all these other things you've been told about — how dangerous things are in the world. What do you think?

Patient: I don't know.

Therapist: Do you think there might be something to what I just said?

Patient: Uh-huh.

Therapist: Have you come to realize that many of the

things that your parents are afraid of are really nonsense?

Patient: Yeah.

Therapist: That your father's fear of elevators — your father's afraid sometimes in restaurants and theaters and things like that — all kinds of closed places, you know.

Patient: Yeah.

Therapist: Don't you think that's kind of foolish when you see him so frightened?

Patient: Yes, and when I went to The Roosevelt School, the school was right down the road from me, but you just had to cross the street, and all my other friends would be going alone, but I had to have my little maid take me across the street.

Therapist: Why was that?

Patient: 'Cause my parents were afraid for me to cross the street. So finally the last two weeks of second grade or something I was allowed to cross the street by myself. The maid would walk down to the school and watch me cross the street by myself and then I was very big.

Therapist: So you thought a lot of their concern was kind of silly. Huh?

Patient: Uh-huh.

Therapist: But, you know, I think you are still afraid of one big thing. From all this stuff that they've been handing you about how dangerous and terrible the world is, although you thought it was silly some of it sunk in and you believe some of it. I think you believe it with school. What do you think?

Patient: They never told me anything about it.

Therapist: No, but I think that the kind of tension and the scared feeling that you get when you're in school is very similar to what happens to your father when he's in restaurants and elevators. What do you think?

Patient: Maybe.

Therapist: Why do you think that I may be right? How might they be similar?

Patient: Because my father is afraid to go to a theater unless he sits in the back row.

Therapist: Hhmmm.

Patient: And I guess being afraid of, you know, going to a theater and all could be similar to me being afraid to go to school, but I don't know ——

Therapist: Do you think that his fear of going into a theater is kind of silly?

Patient: Yes.

Therapist: What about your fear of going to school?

Patient: I guess it's silly, but I can't help it.

Therapist: I see. I know you can't help it just like he can't help it. But you know there's one thing that's important to remember here and that is that, as I see it, one of the reasons why you are so afraid of school is that this is part of what you've been told all these years about how dangerous various things are — you know, going out without sweaters and it's dangerous to cross the streets alone and you've been told by your father that elevators can be dangerous. Although he didn't say it, he was always afraid to go into closed places so you thought for a long time that there was something to be frightened about.

Patient: Yeah.

Therapist: So I think that you have been exposed to a lot of talk and action, talk and behavior that suggests that the world is a dangerous place. Hhmmm?

Patient: Uh-huh.

Therapist: Do you think it's as dangerous as your parents see it?

Patient: No.

Therapist: Do you think that the school is as dangerous as you see it?

Patient: I don't know.

Therapist: Anything you want to say to me.

Patient: No.

Therapist: Hhmmm. Okay. Of all the things we've spoken about since your story, which do you think is the most important?

Patient: Since the story?

Therapist: Yes. Just now.

Patient: Not before? I guess about being afraid of things.

Therapist: What particular thing?

Patient: School.

Therapist: And what is the most important thing I said about that?

Patient: That it isn't as dangerous as I think I think.

Therapist: Hhmmm. What do you think about that?

Patient: I don't know.

Therapist: Do you think I'm right or not?

Patient: Uh-huh. But I'm not really worried about the school being dangerous, just nervous.

Therapist: Well, you're nervous. But what are you nervous about?

Patient: I don't know.

Therapist: Right. It's just like your father. Your father doesn't know what he's nervous about in theaters, does he?

Patient: I think he's afraid that if there's a fire or something and he won't be able to run out.

Theapist: What about elevators? Restaurants?

Patient: Oh, elevators. He's afraid that he's going to get stuck.

Therapist: But he knows that that's not likely.

Patient: Yeah.

Therapist: Okay.

In my story I reinforced the insights and therapeutic gains manifested in Bonnie's story. The parents admit that their fears are unrealistic, which makes it easier for the patient to accept their irrationality. I point out that there are some dangers in the world but not to the degree and severity her parents would have her believe. Also, she has the wherewithal to protect herself and avoid some of these dangers: "They were pretty sensitive and when they would smell a hunter from a distance, before the hunter would even see them, they would get out of his way." In the ensuing discussion, I attempted to clarify on a conscious level Bonnie's awareness of her parents' distortions.

The reader may wonder why, by the seventh month of treatment, I still hadn't gotten into the "deeper" psychodynamics with Bonnie — elements such as the unconscious anger she harbored toward her mother for the latter's rejection; her fear that such hostility would bring about her mother's death; and the determination to stay close to her to reassure herself that her mother was still alive. First, I must follow the patient's leads. Her stories, dreams, and conscious productions directed me to the material I have presented. A few attempts to "probe deeper" were met with significant resistance. Bonnie was not ready to deal with these issues, and it would have been anti-therapeutic to pursue them. Second, the conditioning elements were certainly contributing factors to her phobias and concentration on them was proving effective — there was no reason to spoil things. I could have woven these deeper problems into my stories, but to do so would have made them so remote from the issues in the patient's story that she could not have "grabbed" them. Lastly, as I have said, I do not believe that conscious understanding of one's psychodynamics is invariably necessary for clinical improvement.

Three days after the interchange just described, Bonnie related this story:

> Once upon a time there was this alligator family and they lived in the middle of the jungle and all the other animals, like the monkey and the parrots and all, were afraid of them because they thought that alligators were mean and that he was going to bite them.
> *Therapist:* The alligator family went into the middle of the jungle and all the other animals were afraid?
> *Patient:* Yes, because he was mean.
> *Therapist:* The animals were afraid of the alligator family?
> *Patient:* Yes. So the alligator family didn't have anybody who liked them. So they were very lonesome. Then one little monkey was walking along in the woods and he saw the little alligator. They started playing. They were about three or four or five years old. Then the mother was looking for her monkey and she saw him playing with that little alligator. So she grabbed him quickly and made him come and she thought that the alligators were going to hurt him. So then the little alligator said, "Why are you taking the monkey away?" She said, "Because you're going to eat him." He said, "No, I'm not." She said, "Yes, you are. All alligators eat other animals." He

said, "No, they don't." Then the mother alligator came out, and she said, "Hello." They started to talk, I guess, and the monkey lady was still scared. But then after a while she wasn't scared anymore, and they were free and that's the end.

Therapist: And after a while they weren't scared anymore. What's the moral of that story?

Patient: If you think you're afraid of someone — if you don't know someone you shouldn't say that they'll eat you or something because they might not. They might be friendly.

Therapist: Okay. Now let me ask you a question. What was it about the conversation between the mother monkey and the mother alligator that made the mother monkey less scared of the mother alligator?

Patient: Nothing. She just, while they were talking, the alligator didn't try to eat the monkey.

Therapist: She just saw that it didn't happen. Is that it?

Patient: Yeah.

Therapist: I see. So the mother monkey saw that it didn't happen. She had never had the guts to try before. Is that it? *(Bonnie nods affirmatively.)* Hhmmm. Okay. I want to ask you a question. Do you think this story has anything to do with your situation now?

Patient: No.

Therapist: Not at all? What about the fact that you are afraid of something, like going to school and that you're seeing that it isn't as scary as you thought that it might be?

Patient: I didn't think about that when I told this story.

Therapist: That's all right. Now that I've mentioned this to you, do you think there's something to what I am saying?

Patient: No.

Therapist: You don't think so. You don't think that there might be something similar between the mother monkey seeing that it's not so frightening to be with alligators and your — are you finding that things in school aren't as frightening as you thought that they might be?

Patient: No.

Therapist: You're not finding that out at all?

Patient: No.

880

Therapist: Okay. Well, thank you very much. Now it's time for me to tell my story.

The story is another attempt at fantasy desensitization — part of the working-through process. I believed Bonnie when she told me that she did not see any relationship between her story and the actual experiences of her life where she was far less phobic than she had been. A child's story will sometimes portray his life's situation with uncanny accuracy yet he will have no conscious awareness of it. I did not, therefore, think that Bonnie here was "putting me on." But I did not believe her when she denied a lessening of her school fear. There was definite improvement (although she still had a way to go) and it was typical of her to exaggerate the horrors of school to discourage those who would urge her to go. One of her maneuvers was: "How can you be so cruel and force me to suffer such horrible tortures?" This is the story I told in response:

Once upon a time there was a family who lived in the woods and they were a monkey family. There was a mother monkey, a father monkey, and a little boy monkey. He was about five years old. Now this monkey mother and father were scared of a lot of things. For instance, the mother would say to the little monkey, "Now be very careful when you're outside. I don't want you climbing tall trees. If you climb tall trees, you'll fall off and you'll hurt yourself." Or she would say, "Now you don't walk on the coconut trees 'cause those coconuts will fall off and they'll hit you. Now don't you play with those rough kids that live over there down near the path because they're rough and they'll hurt you. I don't want you to get hurt. Now don't you stay out too late. You know, its dark and you'll get lost in the woods. Be careful." She was always telling this monkey how to watch out and be careful. She was always protecting him from all kinds of dangers that she saw in the forest.

Well, anyway, this monkey went out and he was playing with some of the kids. It got to be about five-thirty and he said, "I've got to run home." They said, "Why do you have to run home?" He said, "I have to get home before it gets dark." They said, "Why?" He said, "Well, I may get

881

lost." They said, "How can you get lost? It's just a straight path from here to your house. It would be impossible to get lost." He said, "Well, isn't it dangerous at night in the jungle?" They said, "Ah, not particularly." Anyway, he began to talk to these other kids and he found out that many of the things that his mother was afraid of, they weren't. For instance, when he said, "Do you kids ever walk under coconut trees?" They said, "Sure we walk under coconut trees." "Doesn't a coconut ever fall down on you?" he asked. They said, "Look that could happen once in a hundred years, that a coconut could fall down and hit you on the head while you are standing under the tree, but that doesn't mean that you should walk around constantly frightened that a coconut is going to fall on your head." He said, "Do you kids climb trees?" They said, "Of course. It's great fun." "But you might fall down and get hurt." "Yeah," they said, "once every few years somebody might slip and fall, but that's not a reason not to have all the fun of climbing trees." They scampered up the trees; they were jumping from tree to tree and swinging from the vines. That little monkey said, "Gee, I think I'm going to try that." He very carefully — he was kind of scared — he climbed up the side of the tree and he got onto a vine and he swung and wheee! Boy did he have a good time swinging in the trees back and forth. He said, "Boy, what I've been missing all this time."

Well, he got home later on. It was after dark and his mother said, "Oh, I was so worried about you. Oh, my, I'm so glad to see my little baby boy. Come here. I want to kiss you." She hugged him and kissed him. She smothered his face and she kissed him and it got all wet. Ich! Anyway, she said, "Oh, my little baby boy. What happened to you? What were you doing out there?" "Oh," he said, "I was swinging on the trees." She said, "Swinging on the trees? Oh, my poor boy. Look at you. Look you have a little scratch on your arm." So he said, "Yeah, so what? So what? So I have a scratch on my arm. So what about that?" She said, "Oh, my little baby. Look at you. Your hair is all messed up. Oh! oh!"
Patient: (Laughs appreciatively.)

Therapist: What tree were you swinging from?" He said, "Oh, the big one down by the brook." "The big tree by the brook! Oh, my — how terrible." He said, "It's not so terrible, Ma. All the kids swing from that tree." She said, "I hope you didn't walk home under that row of — you know what kind of trees; I don't even want to say it."

Patient: Coconut trees.

Therapist: She said, "I hope you didn't walk under that row of coconut trees?" He said, "I did." "Let me look at your head. Maybe a coconut fell on your head." He laughed at his mother and said, "Look, Ma, there's no coconuts falling down. Once every hundred years maybe a coconut falls down while a kid is there, but that doesn't mean that there's any reason not to walk under coconut trees."

Well, when the father came home he was very upset too when he had heard about all the things that the boy had done. But the boy didn't listen to them anymore. He had learned his lesson from the other kids, and after that he was a much happier boy. Do you know what happened to his parents? What do you think happened to them?

Patient: I don't know.

Therapist: They got used to the idea and he used to then have a lot more fun. He would go out with the other kids. He would play with them. Sometimes they would be fighting — a little roughnecking once in a while. Sometimes he'd get scratched, but he had so much fun with them that he didn't mind doing that and he would swing through the trees. Sometimes they would even cut the coconuts down and they'd throw them at one another and they really had a wonderful time.

And you know what the lesson of that story is?

Patient: No.

Therapist: Try to figure it out.

Patient: That if your parents are really worried about you getting hurt you should ignore their crazy ideas.

Therapist: Yes, that the world has a few little dangerous things, but that doesn't mean you should deprive yourself of all the fun that you could have by doing all the things in the world. The world is less dangerous than many people think. The end.

What do you think of that story?

Patient: I don't know.

Therapist: Do you have any thoughts about it?

Patient: No.

Therapist: Did you like it?

Patient: Yes, very much.

Therapist: What was the part you liked the most?

Patient: When the monkeys were swinging through the trees.

As described in Chapter 7, humor can be quite helpful in gaining the child's interest and thus increasing his receptivity to the therapist's story. Here, Bonnie was enraptured. She laughed heartily and clearly identified, in a deeply emotional way, with the monkey who dared defy his parents.

It was during this period of therapy that another issue arose that was crucial in Bonnie's treatment. I have already mentioned that her father was most interested in the occult and communication with the dead. Because he felt that discussing these matters would be anxiety-provoking to his daughter he never discussed them directly with her. However, his experiences in these areas were often a major topic of conversation. When Bonnie was present, her parents and their friends would speak about these subjects euphemistically. The whole area was shrouded in mystery to Bonnie, and even the most peripheral references to occult matters filled her with dread and would intensify a longstanding fearful preoccupation with ghosts.

Since I did not think that Bonnie herself was up to the task of convincing her father to discuss these matters with her, I decided that I would first meet with her father alone, in the hope that I could get him to initiate such a conversation. In our discussion he told me that his interest in communicating with the dead arose after his son from a former marriage had died of leukemia. He had visited a number of spiritualistic mediums with whom he had experiences which led him to believe that he was communicating with his dead son. He described a number of other experiences involving prediction of the future which confirmed his beliefs in these areas. I in no way felt that the father was psychotic and although I, myself, was incredulous about his experiences, I felt that they were attempts to maintain a relationship with a boy whose loss was probably the greatest trauma of his life. More than anything else, his belief in the occult was a manifestation of his love for his dead son.

I tried to explain to him that shrouding these matters in secrecy was contributing to Bonnie's anxieties and recommended that he discuss them openly with her. He flatly refused, claiming that they could only upset her more. I tried to explain to him that there was nothing intrinsically upsetting in his beliefs, and that if Bonnie were upset, it would only be because he believed that the revelations would be upsetting. None of his occult experiences had been anything but benevolent. He agreed that this was so and finally, with great hesitation and reluctance, agreed to discuss these matters with Bonnie, but in a family interview so I could be right there to "pick up the pieces." I agreed to this.

At the appointed time he asked to see me alone first, to be reassured that "I knew what I was doing." I told him that to the best of my knowledge this was a proper course and that even if I were mistaken, such revelations could not produce chronic psychiatric disorder; at worst only a little more acute anxiety. Bonnie and her mother were brought in and the father nervously told them the story of his interest in the occult, from the time of the death of his son (whom Bonnie did know about). On two occasions, he interrupted himself, turned to me and asked: "Are you sure you want me to go ahead Doctor? I think this is cruel." I urged him on. Bonnie was more anxious over her father's hesitation than about the actual material he revealed. By the end of the interview the father was surprised at Bonnie's calmness. I encouraged them all to continue the discussion at home and to answer as fully as possible any of Bonnie's questions.

During the next few weeks there was a further diminution

in Bonnie's fears, and she was balking even less about going to school.

In our sessions we spoke about the family interview with particular emphasis on these points: ignorance of a subject only increases one's anxiety over it and causes one to think that it is worse than it is; when one has the courage to face that which is anxiety-provoking, he most often reduces his fears; her father's interest in communicating with the dead arose from his desire to have some contact with the son he loved so much (just like he loves his daughter); and although she, herself, doesn't believe in such things, she can respect her father's belief.

About two weeks after the family meeting, at the beginning of her eighth month of treatment, Bonnie told this story:

Once in this town there was this man and he lived in this house and everyone didn't like him because he'd never come out of the house and they'd think he was a witch or a monster or killed little kids or something. They made up all kinds of stories about him.

So some kids one day said to some other kids that they didn't believe that he was really that mean. They, of course, thought that he was, but they were just trying to start an argument. So the other kid said, "Oh, yeah, well I heard from my grandmother that he ate his nephew or his dog or something." So then they really got mad and they began to figure out that nobody could be that bad. Then they kept trying to cause an argument like if he ate his nephew he'd be dead and all. So the little kid said, "I dare you to go and ring the doorbell on Halloween or something." So they got so mad at these other kids that they said, "All right if you really want it that way. Then we will."

So him and his sister and his brother and his sister went to the house on Halloween. They rang the doorbell and they were all kind of scared and the other kids were waiting behind a tree. Then this little man opened the door or a lady or something and she said that she didn't have any candy to give them because nobody ever comes around. So they said, "Trick or treat," and they were all very scared and this person opened the door. She was very nice. She said she didn't have any candy because nobody ever came around her house, but she did give them money. She gave them about three dollars apiece and they found out that she was really a nice lady. So then one of the kids asked her, "Why don't you ever come outside?" She said, "I come outside, but only in the backyard 'cause in the front yard it's too rocky for my feet. I'll fall 'cause I have weak ankles," or something like that. So they found out that she could only go in the backyard because there was nothing but grass there. It wasn't hard and she had a big flower garden.

So she gave them a lot of money and the other kids because they thought she was so horrible didn't get half of the money. They got about two dollars all together, and they just got two dollars from her house. So the other kids who went there to see if she was nice or not found out to be the luckiest and the other kids weren't as lucky as the other kids. That's the end.

Theapist: What's the moral of that story?

Patient: That if someone tries to get into an argument with you and disagrees with you, you should put up a fight and try to prove that you're right and if you are you'll be a lot luckier; if you're not, well then it's not that bad, but if you are it's good.

Therapist: Any other morals to that story? That's one moral.

Patient: No.

Therapist: See, the moral you gave pertains to the fact that the first group put up a fight against the second group to prove their point, but is there any moral about what their point was — about the old lady?

Patient: Oh, yes — that maybe if you don't just keep making up stories in your head that someone's bad. You should ask the person who you think is bad and if she does anything to you she'll probably get arrested anyway. So you shouldn't be that scared. The person probably could be nice to you if you go and ask her. She'll be your friend or something.

Therapist: I see. Now let me ask you this question. Why

were they scared? Why did they think that there was some kind of a monster in that house or something like that? What gave them that idea?

Patient: 'Cause no one had ever seen her. They thought that she was just some lady who didn't want anyone to know that she was there.

Therapist: Why did they think that she was a monster? Because no one had ever seen her?

Patient: Well, they didn't think that she was really a monster, but they were kind of scared of her and I guess when people would ask other people what happened or why she never came out, the other people probably just made up stories about her.

Therapist: That she was a monster or what?

Patient: Oh, that she was mean to little kids or something.

Therapist: I see, just because they never saw her. I see. Okay.

Patient: That story I just made up. It kind of reminds me of "To Kill a Mockingbird."

Therapist: How so?

Patient: Have you ever read the book?

Therapist: Quite a long time ago. I don't remember much of it.

Patient: Well, there's this guy named Bradley. He lived in such an old house that they made up stories about him like he was chained to the bedpost and all. He came out and saved John's life.

Therapist: Hhmmm.

Patient: That's why it reminds me so much.

Therapist: I see. So what's the lessons to be learned about that?

Patient: I don't know. There could be a lot of different reasons why you shouldn't make up stories about people unless you really know them.

Therapist: Right. Right. Thank you very much. Now it's time for me to tell my story.

The story reiterates one of the important lessons Bonnie had learned during the previous two weeks: ignorance enhances anxiety. When you don't know something about a situa-

888

tion, you often think the worst. Her father's interest in the supernatural was secretively concealed and this, in itself, engendered in her the notion that "If it's too terrible to talk about, it must really be dreadful." In this story Bonnie describes the reputation for violence these recluses suffered because of their inaccessibility. Bonnie pushes through her fears, directly confronts the forbidden, and finds that the dangers existed in her own mind only. This is exactly what happened when she had the courage to discuss her father's involvement with the occult.

In response, I told this story:

Once upon a time a new family moved into a neighborhood and they moved next to this house. Now the parents of the child in the new family were kind of scared people. They were very suspicious of the world and they always thought the worst in every situation. They told their daughter on the very first day that they moved into town, "We don't want you visiting the next door neighbor's house." She said, "Why?" They said, "Just so. You'll never know what will happen. Who knows who the people might be and what kind of terrible things might happen to you. Stay away from them and you'll be safe." She said, "What's to be afraid of?" They said, "We don't know. Just play it safe. Don't go near there."

Well, this girl decided that she didn't know what her parents were talking about. She had seen a glimpse of the lady who lived in the house and she looked all right. So the next day when no one was around she went into the backyard of those people and it looked like a pretty nice backyard. She couldn't see anything wrong with it. Then she went out and she looked in the front yard. It looked all right. Then she went to the window and peeked in the window. She looked around and the people weren't home. She didn't see anything particularly unusual. Then suddenly behind her she heard a footstep. She turned around and it was the nice lady who owned the house. The lady said, "Hello. What are you doing here?" The little girl said, "I just moved into the neighborhood." So the lady said, "Well, I'm very happy to have you here. Why didn't you come to the front door?" She said, "I don't know. My parents kind of told me that I should stay away and that there might be dangerous things here." She said, "I don't know whether it's dangerous, but the only criticism I have of you is that you didn't come up the front door. I don't particularly like people sneaking around my property, but outside of that I think if you come around here once in a while we'll be very happy to see you. Would you like to come in and have a cookie and some milk?"

So the little girl, having been told by her parents that things are dangerous and you should never trust people and things like that, was kind of scared at first, but she finally decided that her parents probably didn't know what they were talking about. So she went in and she had cookies and milk. This woman was a very good cook and she made very nice cookies. She had three of the most excellent and sweetest cookies you could imagine and then went home.

Her mother said, "Where were you this afternoon?" She said, "Promise you won't be angry at me?" Her mother said, "I don't know. Tell me where you were." She said, "I went to visit the people next door." Her mother said, "What? The people next door?" She said, "Yes." "Oh, you never listen to me. You're going to get into trouble." She said, "There's no trouble. They happen to be very fine people and I met the lady of the house and she gave me good cookies." "She gave you cookies. How were they?" She said, "They were fine. I liked them very much." Her mother said, "I hope you don't get sick." She said, "I'm not going to get sick. They were excellent cookies." Anyway, the next day the girl wasn't sick and then the mother and father began to realize that things weren't as bad over in that new house as they had thought and they even became friends with those people.

The lesson of my story is that many things that you think may be dangerous are not so, but the only way that you are going to find out is to look carefully and observe them and see what they are really like. Then you can decide whether or not they are dangerous. For example, this girl looked in the window to see what was really going on there, to see if there was anything dangerous. Most often things are not dangerous, but you think they might be dangerous if you do not know what's going on. However, knowing about a thing often makes you less scared. The end.

Do you have any comments about this story?

Patient: No.

Therapist: Okay then. Very good.

My story merely reiterates the main themes presented in Bonnie's. The messages were important, reflected healthier thinking, and were, therefore, worthy of repetition.

Four days later, she told this story:

Once there was a frog and it was living in a little pond with just some other frogs. It was nice there and then all of a sudden, then one day snakes started coming in and lizards. The got the pond all dirty and messy and they'd fight.

So these frogs were unhappy and so they left that pond and they decided to go find another pond. So they walked around. So they looked and they came to a pond and there were a few snakes there. One of them said, "Gee, maybe this is a good pond." Then they saw a snake and they said, "Oh, I guess not." The snake said, "Why isn't this a good pond?" The frogs said, "Oh, because there's too many other snakes in it and lizards and all. We can't stay in a place like that." The snake said, "Why not?" They said, "We don't know. It just wouldn't work out. There's too many of you and there's just a few frogs. It just won't work out." The snake said to them that maybe if they lived there for a few days they might like it and decide that snakes and lizards aren't bad.

So they did and then all of a sudden the frogs started to like the snakes and lizards and all, and thought that this would be a fun place to live with all different kinds of animals. They did and they were happier than just being with just plain old frogs in one little pond.

Therapist: Hhmmm. And what's the lesson of that story?

Patient: That if you don't like other people and all, and

you don't really know them, you should know them first and then see whether you like them.

Therapist: In other words, know them first before deciding whether or not you like them.

Patient: Yeah.

Therapist: Very good. That was an excellent story. Now it's time for me to tell my story.

As I have already described, slimy little animals, obnoxious creatures, and loathsome vermin most often symbolize unacceptable unconscious complexes. In this story, the frogs represent Bonnie and the snakes and lizards symbolize unconscious thoughts and feelings. Whereas she first fled from such complexes, her experiences in therapy have made her more comfortable with them, and the story dramatically reflects this. At a more superficial, but nonetheless meaningful, level the story reveals her increasing comfort with all the elements in her life that she once feared.

This is the story I told in response:

Once upon a time there were some frogs and they lived in a pond and then some snakes and lizards started moving into the pond. The older frogs kept telling the younger frogs that this place was becoming a terrible place to live in because of these snakes and lizards. They kept saying, "Snakes and lizards are no good. They are dangerous, terrible, and they bother people. They're really no good bums and everything else." So this kind of made these young frogs kind of scared of these snakes and lizards.

Then one day a wise old frog was passing by and he said, "Why are you kids so frightened?" "Well," they said, "there are a lot of snakes and lizards moving around here." So the wise old frog said, "Well, what can they do to you?" They said, "We don't know. It's just that our parents tell us that these snakes and lizards are dangerous." He said, "Look, I'm a wise old frog and I've been living around here longer than your parents. I know the snakes and lizards quite well and there's really nothing to be afraid of with them. They're the usual things you find in any pond. I suggest you go out and play with them and you'll find that what I'm saying is true."

So, somewhat reluctantly aand hesitatingly, the frogs decided to play with the snakes and lizards. To their surprise they found out that what the old wise frog had said was true — that these snakes and lizards were not such frightening things — and they became very good playmates and had a very good time.

Do you know what the lesson of that story is?

Patient: No.

Therapist: Try to figure it out.

Patient: That the animals weren't all that dangerous and mean and they shouldn't be that scared of them.

Therapist: Yes. And also not everything your parents may tell you about the dangers of an animal are necessarily true. Sometimes your parents say something about the dangers of certain animals that will not be true. The end.

Here, I reinforced Bonnie's message and added the element of her parent's contribution to her distortions.

Clinically, Bonnie was enjoying significant improvement. Following the family interview and during the ensuing discussions, there was a progressive diminution of her school phobic symptoms. In addition, for the first time in years, Bonnie enjoyed a remission of her preoccupation with ghosts. She was now attending school every day and stayed throughout the day with only occasional morning anxiety.

In the middle of her eighth month of treatment and one week after the sequence just presented, Bonnie told this story:

Once there was this kangaroo family and they lived in Australia and they had big places to run around and all. They had a lot of fun. One day the hunters came and they were going to take them back to this place in Florida called Jungleland. The kangaroos thought things like they were going to go to a zoo and be put in cages and have people stare at them and have no place to run around and just be in a little cage. But when they got there they found out that it was really like where they used to live — a big jungle and all — and they could run around and do everything they wanted. But there was one thing they didn't like. There were a lot of other animals in there and sometimes they wanted to stay in some special place and they found out that a giraffe was staying there or a lion, and they couldn't work anything out. They'd always fight.

So then one day the zookeeper said — well, not the zookeeper, but the man — said, "You animals are always fighting. You're always fighting about things. I don't know what you're fighting about, but you're always fighting. You should stop and I assure you you'll be a lot more happier in Jungleland." So the animals thought that he was a little crazy in telling them that they could get along with each other, but one lion said, "Maybe's he right. Maybe if we work out special places for us to stay, maybe we could be friends." So the giraffe said, "Well, I always liked the section by the tree." The kangaroos and all the other animals said, "Fine. That's all right." And the kangaroos said, "We always liked the section where it's very hot." And they said, "Fine, you can stay there." Then the lions said, "We like the section by the water." They said, "Fine. You can live there." They all had their own places to live and once in a while some other animal would go to the other animals to visit or spend the night or something. They all were friends after that. That's the end.

Therapist: And what's the lesson of that story?

Patient: That if you're always arguing with other people for what you want and all, you shouldn't just fight with them. You should work out — you should try to work out something that will make everybody happy.

Therapist: I see. Very good. Okay. Thank you very much. That was a very interesting story, unusual also. And now it's time for me to tell my story.

This is the kind of healthy story one sees in the pretermination phase of therapy. It is of interest that the antipathy among the animals does not have a fear element — it is one of anger over territorial conflict. The problem is solved in a civilized manner using discussion and compromise. I believe that in addition to earlier sources of hostility Bonnie now harbored anger toward her parents for their having inculcated in her so many anxiety-provoking notions. One could say that the story reflects repression of such anger — the animals separate to protect themselves from one another. However, even if this is so, there is no question also that it is handled in a most mature way: mutual coexistence.

I told this story in response:

> Once upon a time there were some kangaroos who lived in Africa and they roamed the plains. I'm sorry, they lived in Australia and they roamed the plains and they really enjoyed themselves. There were lots of places to run around and they had lots of fun.
>
> One day they got some news that some hunters were around and that these hunters were rounding up some of the kangaroos to bring to Florida to a place called Jungleland. Well, some of the kangaroos when they heard this kind of made believe that it didn't happen. They didn't want to talk about it and they said, "Better not discuss it. Talking about it is just going to make it worse. So let's make believe it isn't happening." So they didn't discuss it and what do you think happened to them? How do you think they felt?
>
> *Patient:* I don't know.
>
> *Therapist:* Well, they got very scared because when they did think about it, not having any information at all, they just thought the worst. They thought there would be death and destruction. They thought terrible things would happen. They thought that they would be put in cages. They thought that they would be beaten mercilessly. They thought that they would be starved. They thought that they would really be treated terribly by the keepers. But since they didn't talk about it and since they didn't ask questions, they just thought the worst. That's often what happens when you don't talk about something that you're afraid of. You think that it's far worse than it usually is.
>
> But some others asked the hunters what it was really like in Jungleland, and they told them that it was a wide open place and that there are no cages and that the keepers there are especially trained to take care of animals, that there is an abundance of food, and that none of the animals are treated poorly. Any of the conflicts that the animals have are usually discussed openly

and that they are settled by calm deliberation and conversation. Well, when they heard that, many of their fears were diminished significantly. Then when they actually went there — they were still frightened a little bit because it was a new place and strange and everything. New places are always strange no matter how much information you have about them. They always produce a little bit of fear.

So they went to the new place and they found out it was just as described and that it wasn't frightening and they got used to it. Actually they were happier there than they were in their original place because it was so well taken care of.

Do you know what the lessons of that story are?

Patient: No.

Therapist: Try to figure them out. What are some of the lessons?

Patient: That you should ask to find out if you're going to like it or not.

Therapist: Because?

Patient: Because if you don't ask you just think worse things about what it will be like and you'll never know whether you'll be happy or unhappy.

Therapist: Right. When you don't know, you usually think things will be worse than they really will be. That's the first lesson. The second lesson is that another way to reduce fears is to actually have the experience and see that it's not as frightening as you thought it might be. And that's what happened to these kangaroos. The end.

Do you want to make any comments about that story or your story?

Patient: No.

Therapist: Okay. Do you want to listen to any of them?

Patient: All right if you want.

Therapist: Well, do you want to?

Patient: All right.

Therapist: Okay. Do you want to listen to both or yours or mine or what?

Patient: Mine.

Therapist: Do you want to listen to mine too?

Patient: Okay.

Sometimes, in the pretermination phase of treatment following a healthy story I will tell one which reiterates elements from previous stages of treatment because the patient's story does not lend itself to salutary modification. This is what I did here: I demonstrated again how knowledge and direct experience can be powerful weapons against anxiety, whereas denial and ignorance only enhance it. The kangaroos that chose not to discuss the impending move were filled with horrifying fears; those who gathered information remained calm, and when they saw that their new home was as it had been described by the hunters they were even more relaxed.

During the next week Bonnie was weaned from tranquilizers and she still maintained her clinical improvement. Near the end of her eighth month of treatment, she told this story:

Once there were these kids and they wanted to go to this movie. There were about six of them and they didn't have enough money. They only had enough for maybe one ticket. So they didn't think of what they could do, so they couldn't get past the door, where the man was, without a ticket. There was an exit that they could get in, but you could only get out from the inside. You couldn't get in from the outside. So they didn't know what to do. So they thought for a while and then one kid said, "Well, I'm going to get a ticket," 'cause he had enough money. Then the other kid who had enough money said, "I guess I'll get a ticket too, but if you go around to the exit I'll let you in." So they went around to the exit.

Therapist: You mean the second kid went into the theater and opened up the exit door for the kids outside?

Patient: Yeah. So they went into the exit.

Therapist: You mean the two kids who had enough money?

Patient: Yeah. They opened the door and all the kids came in. Then the man who worked in the theater saw them all coming in and went over and caught them. He said, "If you're going to do that you can't come in this movie theater for a whole week. Then after the week is up you can come in as long as you have money."

So the kids couldn't go and see the movies for a

week and they were very disappointed. They found out that they should have waited till they got money.

Therapist: And the lesson of that story is?

Patient: That if you want to go someplace, like to the movies, you shouldn't cheat about it. You should try to get money or earn it or something, but you shouldn't just cheat or go in without paying.

Therapist: Okay. Thank you very much. Now it's time for me to tell my story.

Once again, the movie-television theme — the screen upon which the patient's unconscious is projected for therapeutic observation. The story reveals late treatment ambivalence about further confrontation with her unconscious. The previous few weeks had been somewhat harrowing, what with all the talk about communication with the dead, ghosts, and extra-sensory perception. Bonnie wants a rest, and so arranges to get suspended from the movie house for a one-week period. I do not believe that the illegal maneuvers in the story had anything to do with any psychopathic trends in Bonnie, but were rather convenient mechanisms for predictably getting banned from the movie house.

This is the story I responded with:

Once upon a time there were six kids and they were talking and they said, "Gee, what are we gonna do? What are we gonna do today? We've got three days off from school, Friday, Saturday and Sunday." It was a holiday and they didn't know what to do. So someone said, "Hey, how about going to a movie?" Someone else said, "Yeah, what's playing?" Another kid said, "Oh, there's a very scary picture playing in the neighborhood." Another kid said, "Aw, that picture isn't so scary." Anyway they started to argue over whether the picture was scary or not, and most of them thought that it was scary and they said, "Oh, we'd never go to see that movie. It's pretty scary." Others said, "Oh, it isn't so scary." So they kept arguing over whether it was scary or not. Those who thought it wasn't scary said, "We're going to go this afternoon at two o'clock and all those who want to come can meet us at two o'clock in front of the movie house and we'll go in together."

Well, see, there were six kids there. Two said it wasn't scary. There were two who said it was scary, and there were two who were in the middle. They *thought* that it wasn't scary but inside they *felt* that it was. In other words, there were two parts to them. Their conscious minds thought it wasn't scary, but their unconscious mind thought that it was scary. Do you follow that?

Patient: Yes.

Therapist: Now those two kids in the middle group whose conscious minds thought that it wasn't scary said, "Okay, we'll go with you. We'll join you at two o'clock." But their unconscious minds thought that it was scary. So they found that they weren't that interested in going to the movies, even though they thought they were. At first they couldn't find the money that they were supposed to have in order to go to the movies. Then they forgot the time and had to call up their friends and see what time it was. Then they realized that because of the fact that they forgot the time and because of the fact that they forgot their money that maybe they were a little more scared than they had thought. Do you understand that?

Patient: Yes.

Therapist: Well, anyway, they decided to try it anyway. They figured that it can't be that bad and they'd try it. So anyway the four kids finally convinced the other two who really said they were scared to try going into the movie anyway and seeing what it was like. They said, "You can go out if you want, if you're really scared."

Well, all six of them went in and, of course, some of them were a little scared at times, but all of them stayed and saw the whole movie and they realized that there was far less to be scared about than they had thought. The two who weren't scared at first said to the others, "See, it wasn't as scary as you thought." The two who were very scared said, "Yes, you're right. It isn't as scary as we had thought." The two who were in the middle, who thought that they weren't scared, but really were, said, "I guess we were a little scared, but we're glad we went anyway because we found out that it wasn't so scary."

Do you know what the lesson of that story is?

Patient: No.

Therapist: Try to figure it out.

Patient: That things aren't as scary as you think?

Therapist: Yes. Things may not be as scary as you think initially and if you try it out, you often will find out that things aren't as scary as you thought in the beginning. The end.

In this story I provided Bonnie with a few lessons in elementary psychology while trying to assuage her fears of further analytic inquiry.

Clinically, the patient continued to do well. During her ninth month of treatment, Bonnie told the story (Chapter 9) about the fairy who wins wings for not having a bad word to say about anyone. Although that story certainly pertained to the unconscious anger she felt toward her parents, there had been such significant improvement in all areas of functioning (including definite, but less dramatic, improvement in expressing hostility) that I did not feel much more work with her was warranted.

Bonnie's termination story (Chapter 6) was told at her next to last session. During nine months of treatment, Bonnie had sixty-two sessions. Her story about the grandfather who helped the little dragon learn how to fly in spite of the protests of her parents epitomized her treatment. Her termination dream (also presented in Chapter 6) about the skin diver who led Bonnie and her parents through the "scary" waters to safety on the other side of the bay, confirmed my clinical decision to terminate treatment.

The reader may wonder why this girl improved without working through the basic anger toward her mother which is often central to the school phobia problem. I believe that Bonnie, like many other children with this problem, feared separation from her mother because she needed to be reassured that her unconscious death wishes toward her mother would not be realized. The anger, in such cases, relates to deprivation and this was certainly the situation with Bonnie as she revealed in her first story about the abandoned kitten. Also, as is so often the case in the families of children with school phobia, the parents have phobias as well, and these contribute to the formation of the symptom. In Bonnie's family this element was of paramount importance. Other factors as well are often operative (See Chapter 14), and each child must be evaluated separately to determine which ones contribute to his fear of school. The stories which the child tells in the storytelling game are a valuable source of information in determining the psychodynamics of any particular child's phobia. They provide the therapist with the leads to follow in the therapeutic work. Those who criticize the Mutual Storytelling Technique as being too manipulative and coercive should appreciate that it is not done haphazardly and casually. The child's lead is followed. If, like all other forms of psychotherapy, the M.S.T. is "brainwashing," at least the patient tells what part of his brain to wash and when. Bonnie's stories and other productions led me to an approach which emphasized deconditioning and correction of the phobia-engendering notions which had been inculcated by her parents and grandmother. Improvement in these areas seemed to be enough at that time. There is no point continuing treatment of a child who is relatively asymptomatic because the therapist sees evidence of further difficulties in the patient's fantasies, dreams, and stories.

With Bonnie there was some additional improvement of the basic deprivational problem as well. Bonnie did become more assertive in getting her parents to spend more time with her. She learned that the expression of her resentment in this area was not only effective in getting her more time with them, but she also learned that they did not respond punitively to her protestations. She had living experiences that angry thoughts were acceptable and did not harm anyone. These factors also, I believe, contributed to the resolution of her school phobia.

17. A BOY WITH POST-TRAUMATIC NEUROSIS

In his excellent article on post-traumatic neuroses in children Levy states:

> An operation represents an experience of pain performed by strange persons in a strange place after forcible separation from the familiar home and the protecting mother — the main source of security. . . . One- and two-year-old children, as compared with older children, have a keener response to pain, are more dependent on their mothers and have less experience in social contacts . . . and less comprehension of what is to take place. . . . For them, the operative experience is more acute in every phase. . . . The operation, then, is a raw and brutal experience, difficult to comprehend as a health-giving device.[1]

In the literature on this syndrome, hostility is one of the most common symptoms described.[2] The child's anger has many sources. It is in part the expected, adaptive affect in response to frustration and pain which one cannot flee. It is intensified when motor restraint is present.[3] Langford considers the anger to serve the purpose of covering up the child's more basic fear. In addition, the child often interprets the pain as punishment but not finding any wrongdoing, considers himself the innocent victim of those who have inflicted pain upon him. Or the anger may serve to goad adults into punitive measures to assuage the guilt associated with the notion that the operations and their associated pain are punishments.[4] It is as if the child said: "I am being punished; I must have done something wrong; punish me further to relieve my guilt." The parents, of course, get the brunt of the anger not only because they are seen as the ones originally and ultimately responsible for having exposed the child to his suffering but, in addition, because they are safe scapegoats upon which to vent the rage. The anger may be handled by projection — and hostility toward the object upon which the anger is projected. This mechanism is described by Anna Freud who attributes its original description to Melanie Klein.[5]

Levy describes three ways in which the child releases his anger: 1) *nonspecific release* via such maneuvers as destroying objects, spilling water, and so on; 2) *impersonal play* — in which there is complicated verbalization and manipulation of objects which permits symbolic and guiltless expression of the anger such as in playing soldiers, cops and robbers, and cowboys and Indians; and 3) *personalized play* — in which the child depicts and, re-enacts the actual experience in all its aspects, for instance, playing doctor, nurse, hospital, operation.[6]

Another problem seen in such children is that of low self-esteem. Many elements contribute to this symptom. Intrinsic to the guilt associated with the notion that the sickness and operation are punishments is the feeling "I am no good for having performed the misdeeds for which I am now being punished." If in addition to the guilt elements in lowering the child's esteem parents consider him loathsome for his defects, he will incorporate their concept of himself (a phenomenon which H. S. Sullivan refers to as "reflected appraisals"[7]) and this will serve to further lower his self-image.

Some of the stories of Chris, the five-and-a-half-year-old boy with harelip and cleft palate, have already been presented. Three of his oedipal stories were discussed in Chapter 8, and in Chapter 12, I described his short course of treatment for a situational problem which arose about fourteen months after his full course of therapy.

Chris was referred for treatment because he was spending many hours each day absorbed in fantasy. When engrossed in his reveries, he would either gesticulate hostilely while articulating comments such as: "Get those guys," "Blow out his brains," "Get 'em," and "Kill 'em"; or else he would giggle utterances such as: "Bare bottom," "Look at his penis," and "I see her tushy." In addition, the parents described exaggerated fear of separation from his mother, excessive rivalry with his seven-year-old brother, and abnormal modesty over genital exposure — even with members of his family. His kindergarten teacher also observed the self-involved withdrawal, considered him to be intellectually and/or emotionally behind the rest of his class, and feared that he might not be able to advance to the first grade unless there was significant change in his behavior.

The patient was the third of five children who, at the time of referral, ranged in age from six weeks to nine years. He was born with a harelip, cleft palate, and bilateral inguinal hernias. Between the ages of eighteen days and three months, he was hospitalized on three occasions (for a total of twenty-eight days) for operative correction of these birth defects. In order to prevent the infant from putting his hand in his mouth and thereby rupturing his sutures, both arms were restrained at his sides twenty-four hours a day for many weeks following these procedures. He was rehospitalized at twenty-six months and again at twenty-nine months of age for further surgical repair of his cleft palate. At the age of three a hearing deficit, considered to be related to ear and throat infections, was first noted. At four a myringotomy was performed, and at five he was hospitalized for an adenoidectomy — with resultant improvement in his hearing. All told, by the time this child was five years of age, he had undergone seven hospitalizations for operative procedures.

Chris was a winsome little fellow whose warmth and charm were infectious. A mild but definite articulatory speech defect was present, as well as a noticeable, but not particularly unsightly, scar at the site of his repaired harelip. When attention was directed away from him, he would quickly lapse into fantasy — during which time he would giggle, gesticulate, and articulate in the manner already described.

His drawings, which were copiously produced, were primarily of monsters with prominent scars (from being stabbed) and huge pointed teeth (which were used for a variety of sadistic purposes). A typical example of the kind of picture drawn at this time is shown in Figure 4. Many of his drawings revealed

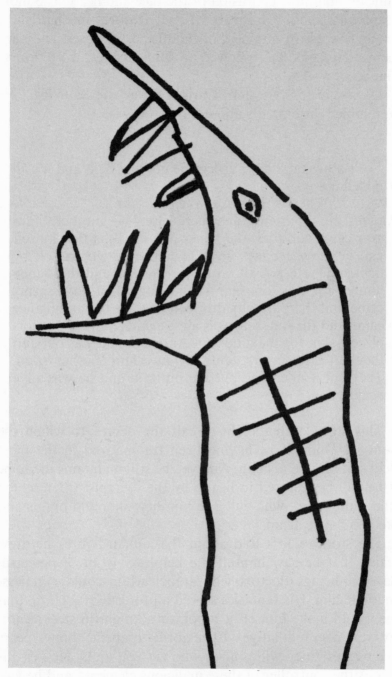

Figure 4.

significant anatomic confusion of the face and head. The monsters often exhibited misplaced facial features; unsightly defects; and excessive numbers of mouths, eyes, noses, and ears. Green and red blood also flowed profusely from various orifices of the head.

During his first session, Chris drew a "dinosaur leg." He then rambled disjointedly about his drawing:

It's a broken dinosaur leg. He got in a fight and it's all trunkled up ——
Therapist: Where's the rest of the dinosaur?
Patient: He's buried somewhere else —— another dinosaur came and took the bones out. He took the skin off and he ate the bones up — and this guy got struck by lightening. He got all on fire — this kid and these men hunted for this dinosaur — and bogeymen with spears came and the dinosaur dropped dead — the ambulance came and the dinosaur was alive again and they got lots of new skin for the dinosaur. And his brain was out and they put skins in first and they gave him another brain. They cut it open and put the brain in and he was alive again.

This story dramatically reveals the degree to which the patient sees himself as having been traumatized in the most violent and bizarre fashion. And yet, he still maintains the hope that he will be restored to health by the therapist (represented by the ambulance), who will give him new skin and brains and make him "alive again."

The stories Chris told about the human figures he drew revealed that he saw himself the helpless victim of powerful malevolent beings (doctors) who, at their whim, could mercilessly mutilate him. His fantasies served a protective function, that is, he would make himself a robot, or a knight in steel armor. They were also retaliative: "The gorilla (patient) threw spears at the pirates ('men with knives who cut you up')." He saw his father as the controller of these malicious elements, and he was therefore particularly singled out for revenge: "The mouse robot bit off the giant's leg." The obsessive preoccupation with violence also provided symbolic desensitization to his traumata. It was as if each time he exposed himself to them, even if only through substitutive imagery, they became a little more bearable. This, of course, is part of the common adaptive working through of psychic trauma.

Although oedipal problems, in accordance with classical psychoanalytic concepts, were probably operative here (for example, the penis shyness and the marked hostility to his father), I considered such difficulties to be playing a relatively minor psychodynamic role. The hostility toward the father as I saw it related not so much to the jealous rivalry with him for the mother's affection but more to his awareness that it was the father who had brought him to the doctors and had arranged for what he considered to be their mutilation of him. The penis shyness and its implied castration anxiety was, in my opinion, more significantly related to his generalized anxiety over injury and disfigurement — an almost inevitable consequence of his operative experiences.

Although his fantasies, drawings, and stories were bizarre and replete with gore and sadism, I did not consider this boy to be psychotic. He definitely preferred human involvement to his reveries and was easily distracted from them. He responded well to physical contact and involved himself with me with an enthusiasm and *joi de vivre* that made him a pleasure to be with. Even his most hostile play had none of the morbid seething rage seen in the psychotic, but rather a lightheartedness that is not seen in severely disturbed children. The parents each exhibited mild neurotic symptoms. The mother tended to be inhibited in the expression of hostile and sexual feelings, but not markedly so. Both parents exhibited somewhat excessive concern with propriety. The mother was also excessively concerned with diets, vitamins, and "health foods." I regarded the four siblings as essentially healthy psychologically. All told, there was nothing in the family environment to suggest that it was psychotogenic, or anything even conducive to the formation of severe neuroses. I concluded that Chris was suffering from a moderately severe post-traumatic neurosis related most significantly, if not completely, to his multiple operative procedures.

The psychologist who tested him at the time of referral found him to be immature, egocentric, demanding, and frequently uncooperative. His Full Scale WISC IQ was 83, with a Verbal IQ of 92 and a Performance IQ of 75. However, because of his poor cooperation, the psychologist considered her findings open to question.

Projective tests revealed "an endless amount of phobic material." The Rorschach record, with its thirteen percepts of fair quality, was filled with such responses as "explosions, giant feet, monsters, giant bats," and so on. The parents of the boy he drew in the Draw-A-Person test had died, and he on no occasion expressed to the psychologist any conscious anger or hostility toward his parents or siblings.

In describing the use of the Mutual Storytelling Technique in the treatment of Chris, it is important to bear in mind that five to six represents a borderline age for effective utilization of this method. The stories of children younger than five are most often quite fragmented, and it may be either difficult to ascertain an underlying theme or so many are suggested that it may be hard to decide which one is the most meaningful for the child at that time. Also, eliciting from the child the revealing "lesson" of the story may not be possible. Children of this patient's age usually present stories which are at best coherent but short, or at worst segmentalized, with a few dominant themes presented concurrently. However, even when the story is disjointed, the significant underlying theme can often be ascertained — a theme which lends itself to the formation of a story by the therapist. Also necessary at this age is the therapist's active participation in providing the catalytic connectives which help elicit the story.

The patient's first story in treatment is typical in form of the kind related by children his age:

Therapist: Once upon a time ——
Patient: Once upon a time ——
Therapist: Go ahead.
Patient: There was a witch — um — a ghost — and they

went out at night and — uh — they — uh — went in someone's bed and — uh — you see they made 'em have a dream ——

Therapist: Yes, and then — you're telling a good story.

Patient: And that's all.

Therapist: What did the person dream?

Patient: Oh — uh — I want to hear my story.

Therapist: You will as soon as you finish the story. What was the dream?

Patient: Uh — all the flowers got dead.

I consider this story to reflect the patient's notion that there are malevolent forces ("a witch" and "a ghost") in the world ("they went out at night") that have penetrated deep within his psyche — they have entered his bed and have caused him to dream. He sees himself a flower (with its implied beauty, fragility, and passivity) which has been destroyed ("got dead") by these malignant elements, both from within and from without. More specifically, I consider the external hostile powers to be the doctors who had subjected him to painful operative procedures and his father, whom he saw as the controller of the surgeons. The internal malicious forces consist of elements of these external figures which have been incorporated, as well as his own repressed retaliative hostility. The flower that had died is, of course, the good little boy who had been mutilated (a flower symbol appears again in the patient's termination story). This explanation lends itself well to formulation in the terminology of the Object-Relations Theory.[8] The story reflects the threat of bad objects both internal and external to destroy the good internal objects — the good boy.

Two weeks later Chris told this story:

Hello folks. Once there were a baby tree. It grows a little bit. And the baby tree was turned into a big giant — it was so big.

The ghost was in somebody's house and they went away to the ocean. He carried the cat home in a bag, like Santa Claus and he cooked it for dinner —— the cat wanted to punch the ghost and when he punched him he (*the cat*) disappeared. The ghost was behind him (*a man*). The guy (*the ghost*) put his (*the man's*) other hand behind him and he tied the man's hand. And then the ghost was —— the ghost was going to start a fire in the fireplace — to cook the man for dinner. He (*the ghost*) already ate the cat. He burned one of the man's eyes out. He had a real sharp knife and he cut his (*the man's*) hand off, and his legs, and all that. And then he (*the man*) fell down on the fire and was burned. And that's the end.

I considered the cat in this story to represent Chris from whose vantage point his operations were like being carried off suffocatingly in a bag by ghosts (the doctors). When he expresses his resentment for being so treated ("the cat wanted to punch the ghost"), he is eaten by the latter and disappears. He is, therefore, unsuccessful in effectively venting his anger, but by being eaten he has accomplished fusion with his persecutor — identification with his aggressor — and takes on the latter's powers. He then uses his new-found strength against his father (the man) and vengefully mutilates the one whom he considers to have been ultimately responsible for his own disfigurement at the hands of the surgeons. It is as if he were giving his father a taste of the latter's own medicine. The father also is an available and safe figure upon whom he can discharge his hostility: the surgeons being no longer present and not particularly trustworthy as passive scapegoats. The baby tree, in the beginning of the story, which turns into a big giant, is another manifestation of this transformation into a more potent form. With this understanding of the patient's story, I related the following:

> Once upon a time there was a cat. And this cat got hurt on his leg one day and he had a sore on his leg. The cat's father called up the doctor and he said: "Hello doctor. Can you come over and see my son, the cat? He's got a sore on his leg." So the doctor came over and he looked at it and he said: "I'm going to have to take you to the hospital and sew this up."
>
> Well, the cat was very angry because the cat thought that the doctor was going to make him worse. The cat didn't know that the doctor really wanted to make him

better. The doctor then said to the cat: "Now this is going to hurt. But when I'm through you'll be much better." The cat was scared and thought the doctor, like a ghost, wanted to scare and hurt him. Well, he had the operation and the doctor fixed him up even though it was very painful. He was much happier afterwards that he had had the operation because he didn't have the sore anymore.

When he came home he got angry at his father, and he said to his father: "You sent me to the hospital and you made that doctor, who's like a ghost, cut my leg." And the father said: "He didn't cut your leg. He didn't make the sore. You had the sore there. He just helped sew it up and make it better." The boy then changed his mind about his father and the doctor; realized that they weren't trying to hurt him but to help him; so he was then no longer angry at his father.

The lesson of this story is: sometimes you think people want to hurt you when they really want to help you. Find out first what things they're doing and why they're doing them. You may then find out that they have really wanted to help you and not hurt you. And you will then not be so angry or scared.

It is clear that in this story I attempted to correct some of this patient's distortions about his operative experiences. I considered such misconceptions to be playing a major role in his difficulties. His story reveals that he considers his father and the doctors to be basically malevolent. My story imparted the communication that, although they subjected him to pain, this was a necessary concomitant of their benevolent intentions. I worked on the assumption that with an altered concept of his situation, the emotions which followed such distortions of cognition would diminish. I worked on the principle that if Chris were to learn with conviction that his suspected enemies were really his friends, there would be considerably less anger toward, and fear of, them. It was through the Mutual Storytelling Technique, at the level of the primary process — the same level at which the patient was communicating with me — that I attempted to impart these cognitive corrections.

The parents, too, were urged, when the opportunities

arose, to discuss directly with Chris the circumstances of his illness and to impress upon him the same messages about the doctors' basic benevolence and the inevitability of the pain. Since they formerly had taken the position that such discussions might be deleterious (an attitude which certainly must have helped foster his misconceptions), this recommendation became even more vital.

Subsequent stories also revealed that the patient considered himself loathsome for harboring anger toward his father and the doctors. Such anger, as has been shown in the stories already presented, could only be expressed unconsciously and symbolically. In addition, Chris had the notion that angry thoughts, per se, could harm the objects of his hostility. When these misconceptions were presented, my stories attempted to assuage his guilt over his hostility by communicating that it was normal and expected that he would be angry even though the pain inflicted upon him was undesired by the doctors. In addition, the figures in my story found that the objects of their anger never suffered when hostile thoughts were directed against them.

Repetitious correction of his cognitive distortions concerning his operations constituted the main approach in his treatment. Over and over again my messages were related, mainly through the storytelling method, but also through traditional techniques both conscious and unconscious. He was seen twice-weekly, and not a session passed in which some opportunity was not found to impart my corrective communications. Chlorpromazine, in doses up to 30 mg per day, was given adjunctively to help alleviate his anxiety.

During his sixth week of therapy, Chris related this story:

Well, you see, this man, um, he was in the hosp and he was —
Therapist: He was in the where?
Patient: Hospital.
Therapist: Hospital. Speak into the microphone.
Patient: And he was too sick so he died. And then another man, he was old and he didn't die. He had an operation

and well, you see, his mother came and they gave him a present. And, you see, he was, um, he was sick so he died.

Therapist: Wait a minute. This was the third man? Wait a minute. Is this the second man or the third man?

Patient: It's the third man.

Therapist: The third man was sick. The second man was all right.

Patient: And he was buried in the ground where all the apples were and the grass. And you know he happened to be too —

Therapist: What is that? I didn't understand the last part. He was buried in the ground where the apples and the grass were and then what?

Patient: He was fired with spears — well, you see, she was fired with spears, and he was in the army, you know, crashed and all that and all those trees falling down, and snowing and he was cold. And he was in where all the ice was, um, and, um, she was a bad man that was in the hospital and, you know, so they fired at him cannonballs and all that. They burned him all up and lots of stuff and then they gave him sleeping ice and they gave him sleeping gas and all that in his mouth.

Therapist: They gave him sleeping gas and what else?

Patient: And oil in his mouth.

Therapist: Then what happened to him?

Patient: They tied him and exploded him with a bomb and some kids eated him and killed him.

Therapist: Some kids ate him?

Patient: And some kids eated him and killed him and bited him all up and killed him and, you know, and socked him. Suddenly a kid came and wrecked him and then he told all the big men. And he was really — and they killed him and they buried him and then they put some wake up gas on him and then all the men made him turn into a monster and then the monster hurt his thumb and then —

Therapist: And then that was the end?

Patient: He was dead.

Therapist: Is that the end of the story?

Patient: Hhmmm.

Although there is a confusing overabundance of symbolism and a plot which is anything but cohesive, I sensed the basic theme and surmised the general meaning of this story from an understanding of a few of the symbolic representations. The protagonist is subjected to multiple traumas and indignities. He is "buried in the ground . . . fired with spears . . . crashed . . . fired . . . with cannonballs," and so on. The listener also learns that Chris "had an operation," and that "they gave him sleeping gas and all in his mouth." This last information confirmed my initial supposition that the story depicts the operative experience as Chris experienced it. The sleeping gas is, of course, the anesthesia. His re-experiencing it in symbolic form is an attempt to desensitize himself to the trauma and to work it through. Self-desensitization appears to be a naturally occurring phenomenon in the post-traumatic neuroses. This process is, of course, commonly seen in the combat neuroses where the patient relives in dream, fantasy, and conscious life the military traumas.[9] It is as if each re-exposure made the experience a little less painful. Also, in mourning the preoccupation with the deceased serves a similar purpose of making the loss more bearable.[10]

With this understanding of the patient's story, I related mine:

Once upon a time there was a man who was in the hospital and he was an old man, and he didn't think too right. He didn't think straight. When the doctors came to do the operation, he thought they were trying to hurt him, when really they were trying to help him although it hurt him. He thought that the doctors were mad at him or something and he thought that the doctors wanted to kill him. The doctors didn't want to kill him; they wanted to make him better, but he thought that they wanted to kill him. He felt that they were trying to pour oil in his throat; he felt that they were trying to give him sleeping gas and that they were trying to bury him and that they were trying to put him under the ground or throw spears at him. They weren't doing these things; they were really only operating on him to make him better and because it hurt a lot, he thought that they were mad at him or something and he thought that they were trying to do terrible things to him. But when he asked his mother about it, she told him that the doctors really loved him very much and liked him and wanted to help him, and that it hurt a little bit but that didn't mean that they were mad at him or wanted to harm him.

So when he realized that and when he changed his mind and saw that these doctors really wanted to help him, but couldn't help it that it was going to hurt a little bit, he felt much better and he didn't think any longer that they were trying to kill him or do terrible things to him.

Do you understand my story? Could you tell my story the way I told it? Let's see you tell my story the way I told it?

Patient: I didn't hear some of your story.

Therapist: You want to listen to it and then try to tell it? Let's listen to my story. Okay. (*Story is replayed.*) Now Chris and I have gone over this story very carefully, and we stopped at various parts and we talked about the different parts of his story. Do you remember what the whole story was about now? Let's hear you tell the story.

Patient: Umm.

Therapist: What was the main thing in my story?

Patient: About operating.

Therapist: Yes, and what did I say about the operation that this boy had? Speak into the microphone.

Patient: They wanted to make him better.

Therapist: And what did the boy think though when the doctors were trying to make him better?

Patient: About spearing him, pouring oil down his throat, and putting him in the ground.

Therapist: Did the doctors really want to do those things?

Patient: No.

Therapist: But he thought that, right? Were they wrong thoughts that he had?

Patient: What?

Therapist: Were they wrong thoughts? Did he have the

wrong ideas, the wrong thoughts? Did he have the wrong thoughts or the right thoughts?

Patient: Wrong.

Therapist: Why were they wrong thoughts?

Patient: Because they just were.

Therapist: They were wrong thoughts. The doctors really wanted to help him, right?

Patient: Right.

Therapist: But because it hurt he thought that they were trying to kill him. Right? (*Chris nods affirmatively.*) Okay. Let's stop here.

My story is an example of how I attempted to correct his distortions in ideation — distortions which served as the basis for his fears and his anticipation of malevolent treatment. My central message, which had to be repeated many times, was that the pains Chris suffered were the inevitable concomitant of the operative procedures and were not a manifestation of the surgeon's malevolence. A child of this age cannot be expected to appreciate such a message on first hearing — such receptivity is not even expected from adult patients. Using the Mutual Storytelling Technique with a tape recorder allows for convenient re-exposure through replay and this was done here. This story demonstrates how one must patiently go over the important message(s); elicit statements of it from the patient; and have him reiterate it in many different ways to make certain that one's message has indeed been "heard." By the end of this sequence, I was satisfied that I had gotten through to Chris.

During his third month of treatment, Chris told this story:

Well, there was this plant.

Therapist: What?

Patient: Plant and it didn't have no food. It lifted into another house and garden. And then the man —

Therapist: Wait a minute. It lifted into another house?

Patient: Yeah, and then the man watered it.

Therapist: In another house a man watered it. Yes?

Patient: Then the man ran out of water. Then the plant started to another house and then they didn't run out.

Therapist: You mean the plant went to another house? Yes? And they didn't run out of water there? I see. Then what happened?

Patient: Then it started to die.

Therapist: Then the plant started to die.

Patient: It got too much water.

Therapist: It got too much water. Then what happened?

Patient: Then a man, the man, holded it up by —

Therapist: Then another man — another man?

Patient: No, the other man.

Therapist: You mean the first man? Which man was this — the one that gave it a lot of water?

Patient: Uh-huh.

Therapist: Then the man held it up by a stick. Yes. Then what happened?

Patient: Then the plant woke up and found his father and it got bigger. Then the plant was really dead and it didn't wake up and then all the people stepped on it and everything. They jumped on it and they were throwing rocks at it, stepping on him, and crunching him and ——

Therapist: And did what?

Patient: Then the father tied a child's foot up and then —

Therapist: Wait. A father tied a child's foot up? Why did a father tie up a child's foot?

Patient: Because it was stepping on the plant.

Therapist: Oh, the father tied the foot because he didn't want him to do that.

Patient: Uh-huh.

Therapist: Then what happened?

Patient: Then the father helped and they killed the child with bullets and bow and arrows and spears.

Therapist: Why did they kill the child?

Patient: Because it was stepping on the plant.

Therapist: I see.

Patient: But then another child cut the plant, it helped, but then the plant got back to its ground.

Therapist: Wait a minute. But then another child did what?

Patient: Helped him, but the child had a knife and he cut the plant up. And then he got back to his ground and he cracked both and then the giant —

Therapist: Wait a minute. I'm not clear what happened with this other child. What about this other child?

Patient: Then the giant pulled out —

Therapist: Then the giant pulled out the plant?

Patient: Then he put it into a tree.

Therapist: What did this other child do? I'm not clear. What did he do?

Patient: Then the giant put the plant into another tree.

Therapist: Why did the giant put the plant into a tree?

Patient: Because he decided he wanted to. The giant was his help and he killed all the child.

Therapist: He killed the child? Then what happened?

Patient: He was safe.

Therapist: Who was safe?

Patient: The plant.

Therapist: Then the plant was safe?

Patient: Uh-huh.

Therapist: Then what happened?

Patient: It broke down.

Therapist: The plant? Why did it break down?

Patient: Because the giant wasn't friendly anymore. It found out that uh uh, it found out that uh, that it was a little plant and he didn't like it, so he pulled it down.

Therapist: Then what happened?

Patient: And then the man killed it by spear.

Therapist: The man killed what?

Patient: The giant.

Therapist: Then what happened?

Patient: Then all the people were dead and everything, but the plant was safe.

Therapist: And how does the story end?

Patient: That if you find a plant and you don't pull it out and just look at it.

Therapist: And you shouldn't hurt it, right? And what will happen if you do that?

Patient: It will die.

Therapist: If you find a plant you shouldn't kill it? Is that it?
Patient: Hhmmm.
Therapist: Treat it nice?
Patient: Hhmmm.
Therapist: Okay. Thank you very much.

The plant represents Chris who frequently used plants to symbolize himself. Here again he is exposed to a multiplicity of traumas which, I believe, stand for his operations. However, the story differs from previous stories by introducing a new element. There is now a giant — possibly the therapist — who protects him: "The giant was his help and he killed all the child." The giant's benevolence is short-lived. The plant "breaks down" because "the giant wasn't friendly anymore." Chris does not expect his benefactor to remain benevolent for long. That would be out of keeping with his past experiences in which his curers ultimately inflicted pain upon him. All things considered, the inclusion of protective figures in his scheme of things indicated a therapeutic advance.

This is the story I told in response:

Once upon a time there was a plant and this plant was a very nice plant. It was a very handsome plant. It was a very fine plant, a very good plant, but this plant was a sick plant. It didn't feel very well. Well, because this plant was sick, the plant's daddy called in a plant doctor and this plant doctor examined this plant and said, "My, my, my. We're going to have to help this plant. We're going to have to first put a stick near it and tie a cord around the stick and a cord around the plant to help hold it up." So the plant doctor put the stick in the ground and he put the cord around the stick and he put the cord around the plant to hold it up.

But when the plant doctor tied the cord around the plant, the plant said, "Oh, this hurts, this hurts! What are you trying to do to me? What are you trying to do to me? Are you trying to kill me or something?" And the plant doctor said, "No, I'm not trying to kill you. I'm not trying to kill you. I'm just trying to make you better. I know that this hurts you and I'm sorry it hurts you. I really don't want to hurt you, but it's going to have to hurt for a little while until you get strong enough." So the plant said, "Okay, I'll take it for a while, even though it hurts."

And the plant took the pain for a while and he got better but he wasn't all better. He still had a little sickness in him. So the plant's daddy called the plant doctor again and he looked at that plant and he examined him very carefully. He said, "I think we're going to have to cut off certain parts of this plant which aren't right." And the plant doctor said to the plant, "Now look, I have this little knife here and I'm going to have to cut off parts of you that just aren't growing right." And the plant said, "Oh, that's going to hurt! What are you trying to do, kill me?" And the plant doctor said, "No, I'm not trying to kill you. I know this is going to hurt a little bit, but after I hurt you it will get better and then you will feel much better." So the plant said, "Okay, I'll do it; I'll let you hurt me, so long as it's just a little while."

So the plant doctor cut off those parts and it hurt the plant a lot, but he knew that the plant doctor wasn't trying to kill him. He was just trying to make him better. Sure enough the plant did feel better. Then the plant was almost better. When the plant doctor came again he said, "You know, I have to do one more thing. I have to stitch up certain parts of you." The plant said, "Oh, what are you trying to do? It's going to hurt. You're going to kill me!" The plant doctor said, "No, it's not to kill you; it's just to make you better." So it hurt the plant a while, but then he finally got better. And then the plant was all better.

And do you know what the lesson of that story is? What?

Patient: That you gotta protect the plant if it's going to die.

Therapist: Right. And I would say that there are a couple of other lessons — that sometimes when a doctor tries to help you it hurts a lot and you may think that he is trying to kill you, but he really isn't. He's just trying to make you better. It hurts for a while and he doesn't want to hurt you, but he may have to hurt you in order to put in the stitches or something like that. But after he does that you'll feel all better. Right?

Patient: Right.

Therapist: Okay. The end. Do you want to hear that story?

Patient: No.

Therapist: You don't want to hear it? Okay.

The story is self-explanatory. Chris, I felt, did appreciate my fundamental message and this was revealed in his proposed moral: "you gotta protect the plant if it's going to die."

At the end of his third month of treatment, Chris told this story:

Well, I've got to think —— well, okay, there was a ——

Therapist: There was a what?

Patient: There was a little tree.

Therapist: There was a little tree?

Patient: Yeah and this tree died.

Therapist: Uh-huh.

Patient: Then a man came — he was in the garden — and then a man came.

Therapist: A man came where?

Patient: A man came and watered it and it then grows up and it's alive again.

Therapist: A man waters it and it was alive again. Yes?

Patient: Then the plant got too much water and then the man gave him lots of water and she didn't grow up; she just still died.

Therapist: You mean the man gave it too much water and so it died? Is that it?

Patient: Yup! And then some people stepped on it, but then the man saved it by getting a stick and holding — and the stick holding the, the, the, the plant up.

Therapist: By holding it up, okay.

Patient: And, uh, oh, it didn't die anymore. It didn't die.

Therapist: It didn't die anymore. Then what happened?

Patient: Then it began to be winter.

Therapist: Winter came, yes.

Patient: Then it covered up and the plant couldn't breathe.

Therapist: It covered up the plant and it couldn't breathe. Then what happened?

Patient: Then the man got the snow off and it could breathe.

Therapist: The man what? I didn't understand.

Patient: The man took the snow away and then he could breathe.

Therapist: Then he could breathe. All right. Then what happened?

Patient: Um, that's the end of the story.

Therapist: What's the lesson of that story?

Patient: I'll tell you just the title.

Therapist: Just the title.

Patient: Instead.

Therapist: Okay.

Patient: Um, it's about —

Therapist: About the plant. Okay, what's the title.

Patient: That it is about the plant.

Therapist: The title is "About the Plant." That's the title?

Patient: Yep, that's the title.

Therapist: All right. Okay. Thank you for that wonderful story.

When one compares this story to previous ones, there is a definite diminution in the amount of traumatization Chris anticipates from the environment and an increase in benevolent attitudes toward him. The excessive watering represents here either his mother's tendency to be somewhat overconcerned about him (an attitude that was in part engendered by his operative experiences) or the therapeutic sessions. Chris had had more than his fill of this "good thing."

I told this story in response:

Once upon a time there was a little tree. Now this little tree when it was young had a lot of trouble. First there was no water. Then a man came and put water there so the tree grew again. Then somebody stomped and stepped on it, and then a man came and he put a stick there, so that the tree got straight again. Then it snowed and it covered up the tree, and the tree almost died because it couldn't breathe. Then a man came and he took the snow away.

But as the tree grew older it didn't need the man anymore because when it was older, it didn't need to be helped by anybody. It could do it by itself. It didn't have to be frightened, so that when it was older it sent out big long roots underground. When it was older it sent out roots under the ground to get water. When it was older it was able to push through the snow so the snow couldn't cover it. It was too big to be covered by snow. Also it was too strong to need a stick to hold it up. It was held up by itself.

And the lesson of that story it: as you grow older you get stronger and you don't need anybody else to help take care of you. You can do it yourself. The end.

Do you have anything you'd like to say about that story. No? Okay.

In my story I introduced more healthy and hopeful communications. I reassured Chris that as he gets older he will be less subject to the whims of those about him; that his water supply (source of nutriment, that is, love) will be more under his control — he will have long roots with which to acquire water. He will not be so readily overwhelmed by oppressive forces — he will be big enough to push through any snow which might cover him. And he will not be so dependent on others for physical and psychological support — he will no longer need a stick to hold him up.

Early in his fourth month of therapy, Chris told this story:

Well, um, it's a, uh, a man and the man was a bad man who was a bad guy. So the bad man set a house on fire and the house was his hide-out and someone was tied in it. So they called the police.
Therapist: It was his hide-out, yes? Who called the police?
Patient: The police was busy. He couldn't get help, but then soon it was too late. The man was dead, but he wasn't burned up. The man was real dead, but he didn't get burned. He just was poisoned by smoke. So the policeman had a secret so he gave —

Therapist: So the policeman did what?

Patient: The policeman had one of these secret pills and he gave it to him, so he woke up.

Therapist: Oh, the policeman gave him a secret pill that made him become alive again?

Patient: Yep, and then he was fighting the bad man and he was changed into superman.

Therapist: He changed into what?

Patient: Superman. And I'll tell you the title. If you see a bad guy run out of the house, just don't talk, just don't talk. The end.

Therapist: So, a good guy was tied in the house?

Patient: No, a kid was.

Therapist: Oh, a kid was tied in the house by a bad guy.

Patient: That's it.

Therapist: What was the lesson?

Patient: I told you the title.

Therapist: What was the title? What's the lesson?

Patient: Well, um, if you see a bad guy, just don't listen to him and don't talk to him or just go out of your house. That's the lesson. Goodbye everybody.

Therapist: I see. Okay.

The kid, the "good guy" — Chris — is tied up by "bad guys" — the doctors who strapped him to the operating table. He is then "poisoned by smoke" — anesthetized. A policeman — the therapist — gives him a "secret pill" which "made him become alive again." In other words, Chris now sees the therapeutic process as curative. Again positive and hopeful elements are evident in spite of the persisting anticipation that the world is a dangerous place from which one must flee if one is to survive.

In response, I told this story:

Once upon a time there was a kid and this kid had a toothache and he went to the dentist. And the dentist put him in a chair and the dentist said to him, "I'm going to have to tie your hands down before I take out this tooth. It's going to hurt a little bit, but I have to keep your hands still so that I can take out the tooth. It will hurt awhile, but then you'll be all right as soon as I take the tooth out."

Well, it hurt a lot and the boy cried, but he was happy that the dentist had told him in advance what he was going to do. And he thought at times that the dentist was really a bad guy trying to hurt him, but then he realized that the dentist wasn't a bad guy. The dentist was a good guy and he just had to hurt him because he had to take out his tooth.

And the lesson of that story is: sometimes a good guy will hurt you. He doesn't want to, but if he wants to help you, like take out your tooth, he might hurt you.

Do you understand the lesson of that story? You say the lesson of that story into the microphone.

Patient: If you'll take out a child's tooth, he'll hurt you a little bit, but he doesn't want to.

Therapist: If the dentist hurts you a little bit does that mean that he's a bad guy?

Patient: No.

Therapist: Could a dentist be a good guy and still hurt you?

Patient: No.

Therapist: What? I didn't hear you.

Patient (shouting): No, he wouldn't.

Therapist: He wouldn't be a bad guy or he would be a bad guy?

Patient: (Mumbles inaudibly.)

Therapist: I don't understand. If the dentist hurts you does that make him a bad guy?

Patient: No.

Therapist: Can a dentist be a good guy and still hurt you?

Patient: Yes.

Therapist: Does a dentist want to hurt you?

Patient: No.

Therapist: The dentist has to hurt you. Is that right?

Patient: Yes.

Therapist: Is the dentist a good guy or a bad guy?

Patient: A good guy.

Therapist: Is the dentist a good guy if he hurts you?

Patient: Yes.

Therapist: Is the dentist a bad guy if he hurts you?

Patient: No.

Therapist: Right! Good.

It is clear from my post-story discussion that my messages were sinking in and that Chris was coming to fully understand that significant figures in his world are not as harmful as he had thought. It was during this period in treatment that the mother first described a diminution in the time Chris spent in fantasy.

Another way in which attempts were made to reinforce my communications, as well as to determine whether they were being received, was to enlist the aid of Chris in telling my story and to see if he could correctly and appropriately include my messages from previous stories. A sequence from early in the fifth month of treatment demonstrates this:

> Once upon a time, there was a tree. And the tree fell on the house. And then the leaves fell off. And that's the end. And the lesson is: if you see a tree, try not to let it fall or something. Goodbye.

The story depicts the patient's traumatization. Although the "lesson" does not clearly relate to the story as told, it does incorporate messages from previous stories of mine in which trees sought help for their illness, in spite of the associated pain. I then told the patient the following story:

> Once upon a time there was a tree. And this tree began to notice that its legs were weak. So it said: "I'd better be careful. I'd better watch out, and I'd better protect myself."
>
> Well, as he was standing there a tree doctor was passing and the tree waved its leaves. Busssh — busssh — busssh went the tree. And the tree doctor heard the tree and he came over and he said: "What's wrong, tree?" And the tree said, "I feel weak in my legs." And the tree doctor then said: "So you're weak in your legs, my friend. I'm glad you called me. What you need is an operation. It's going to hurt a little bit but then you'll be all right." And the tree said, "You're a bad doctor and I hate you and you're mean." And what did the doctor say when the tree said that?
> *Patient:* He said, "No, I'm not bad."

Therapist: The tree said, "Yes, you are; you're hurting me. That must make you bad." And what did the doctor say then?

Patient: He said, "No, I ain't. No, I am not."

Therapist: So the tree said, "Why are you hurting me then?" And what did the tree doctor say then?

Patient: "I'm a good guy, but I have to hurt you."

Therapist: "Why do you have to hurt me?"

Patient: "Because then you'll feel better."

Therapist: Well the tree then thought that that doctor was a smart man. So the tree said: "Okay, go ahead. I can stand the pain."

So the doctor operated on him and then the tree felt much better. And then he was glad that he had let the tree doctor help him.

And the lesson of that story is: sometimes when a doctor helps you it may hurt a bit, but in the end you'll be much better off. The end. Do you want me to tell another story?

Patient: Hhmmm.

Therapist: What should I tell a story about? You tell me.

Patient: Well, any story.

Therapist: Any story.

Patient: Not a doctor.

Therapist: Not a what?

Patient: Not a doctor story.

Therapist: Not a doctor story?

Patient: Yes.

Therapist: How about an animal doctor story, a veterinarian?

Patient: Okay.

Therapist: Okay. Once upon a time there was a squirrel and this squirrel was living in the forest and one day he got hurt. So this squirrel hurt his foot one day and he decided that he was going to fix it himself. It was a thorn in his foot. So he said, "I know what I'm going to do. I don't need a doctor for this. I can take care of this myself." So he looked carefully at the thorn, and he got himself some tweezers and he said, "This is going to hurt, but once it's out, boy am I going to feel good."

So he got a tweezers and he took the thorn out

and he felt much better. Do you think he was a bad guy for hurting himself?

Patient: No.

Therapist: Of course not and then he felt much better. What's the lesson of that story?

Patient: I don't know.

Therapist: If something bothers you and you're sick and you can treat yourself and get better yourself, do it even though it hurts a little. The end. That's the end of my story.

Rather than "load up" a story with too many messages, if the child is interested and appears to be in a receptive mood, I sometimes will tell a second story which introduces further communications. Here, self-help and self-control over one's fate were introduced in addition to those themes which had been frequently reiterated.

Many stories during the subsequent weeks dealt with trees falling down. Repetitious stories, like repetitious dreams, are of the greatest psychologic significance in that they deal with core problems that are being worked on. It is therefore no surprise to have phases in treatment when the child's stories are similar, exhibiting only gradual change as therapy progresses. My stories were also similar to one another and reiterated major themes already described.

During the sixth month of treatment, Chris told another story which revealed that my messages were indeed being incorporated. When this occurs the therapist knows that his communications have "sunk in," and he has truly reached the child. Sometimes the child reveals his reception symbolically — indicating that the assimilation has been primarily unconscious; other times conscious understanding seems to predominate. Often there are elements of both levels of appreciation. My experience has been that each type of comprehension can be clinically helpful. The story he told on this occasion revealed that the ideas I had conveyed had been accepted more consciously:

928

Well, there was this tree, and it was sick. And this man came and said, "I'll give you this operation." He (*the tree*) said, "Will it hurt?" "Yes, it will." "That means you are a bad guy." Then he (*the tree*) said, "Okay, I see that (*you're not a bad guy*). I'll let you do the operation." So he did it. And that was the end.

The lesson is: if you see a tree sick, call the doctor.

In response, I told an identical story except mine was about a boy rather than about a tree which brought the salutary message even closer to home.

During the seventh month of treatment, the mother noted a further diminution of withdrawal into fantasy. The patient's drawings at that time were also healthier, with fewer pictures of monsters with fangs and scars. By the end of the seventh month, the chlorpromazine was discontinued without subsequent increase in anxiety.

Early in his seventh month of therapy, Chris related this story:

Well, there was this tree and fell another tree and another tree and that was the end.
Therapist: I don't understand. This tree fell on another tree?
Patient: And another tree and that's the end.
Therapist: Aw, come on. There must be more than that.
Patient: Then the doctor came and they were grown-up.
Therapist: Wait, a doctor came. Yes?
Patient: And they were grown-up, but they didn't cry.
Therapist: They were grown-up trees, but they didn't —
Patient: And they understand about doctors.
Therapist: What did they understand about doctors?
Patient: They understand that they just let them hurt you.
Therapist: They understand that what?
Patient: Because they're grown up. They're not like little
Therapist: Does it hurt the grownup when the doctor does an operation?
Patient: Yes, yes it does, but they don't care.
Therapist: Why don't they care?

Patient: Because they're grown up. They're not like little babies or something.

Therapist: What does a little baby do when a doctor does an operation?

Patient: He screams and he says, "Ahhhh, I hate you. You're not nice."

Therapist: But what does a grownup know? Speak into the microphone.

Patient: They know that it doesn't hurt you. It doesn't kill you.

Therapist: It doesn't kill you. Does it hurt?

Patient: Yes.

Therapist: Sure it hurts, but it doesn't kill. What else do the grownups know that the children don't know?

Patient: Well, a doctor is not a bad guy.

Therapist: Let me write this down. Grownups know things that children don't. They know that the doctor isn't a bad guy. What else do they know?

Patient: I don't know and that's the end.

Therapist: You said something else that grownups know — that it hurts.

Patient: This is the lesson.

Therapist: What is the lesson of this story?

Patient: I just told you about they understand —

Therapist: Just tell me again. There were two things you said that the grownups understand that the children don't. What are the two things that the grownups understand that the children don't?

Patient: That they aren't bad guys and they do not — they don't hurt.

Therapist: But they do hurt you.

Patient: Yeah, but they don't care.

Therapist: They don't care? Who doesn't care?

Patient: The grownups.

Therapist: You mean that they don't care if the doctor hurts?

Patient: Yeah!

Therapist: Why don't they care?

Patient: It doesn't hurt them! You can just ask my mother when she goes to a doctor.

Therapist: Well, it hurts her if she has to have an operation.

Patient: I know, but what if she has anesthesia?

Therapist: Then it doesn't hurt her, but afterwards, when she comes out of the anesthesia, it hurts her. Afterwards when you come out of the anesthesia where the doctor made the scar it hurts until it gets better. So it hurts a little while.

Patient: So that's the end.

Therapist: But the grownups know that the doctor isn't bad.

Patient: Yeah.

While a child is telling his story I usually take notes. As mentioned, these are helpful in the preparation of my story. Sometimes when a child, while telling his story, says something which is particularly therapeutic I will make a statement like: "Let me write that down. That's important," or "I want to get that down correctly; could you repeat that?" Having something written down is very impressive to many children and can be of help in insuring that important communications sink in. This was done here when Chris said "a doctor is not a bad guy."

The story reveals two contradictory ideas that Chris has about adults and their response to surgical pain. One is that they have pain and it doesn't bother them; the other that they do not experience it. In the discussion I attempted to clarify things for him even though I recognized that such clarification may break down his pleasant delusion that when he grows up he will not have to suffer pains.

In subsequent session we focused on the issues of the anger one may feel toward the surgeons. Through the storytelling I communicated the notions that such anger is to be expected and that it cannot harm the doctors. These themes did not appear to be important elements in this child's difficulties if significance can be determined by the frequency with which themes appear in stories and dreams.

During this period there was even further diminution in his time absorbed in fantasy. Chris was much more involved with friends and readily stayed at their homes — something he was fearful of doing when therapy began. He also told the mother that he preferred being with his friends to visiting me. Although such a comment can reflect resistance to treatment, it can also be the child's way of saying that he is ready to terminate. With Chris, I felt the latter explanation was the more reasonable.

In the middle of his eighth month of therapy, Chris told this story:

It's short. A real short. Some boys were walking to school. When they got to school the teacher taught them lots of things. The moral of the story is: if you want to learn something, then you can be healthy and strong. And that's the end.
Therapist: What are the main things these boys learned?
Patient: They learned to tie their shoes.

Since I considered this story to reflect the approaching termination of treatment, and since there had been significant clinical improvement, I decreased the frequency of his sessions from twice to once per week. The peacock shown in Figure 5 is typical of the pleasant and happy pictures Chris produced during this phase of treatment.

When asked to tell a story after eight-and-a-half months of treatment, Chris stated: "I don't want you to tell a story; I'll just tell a short one." This was agreed to, and Chris then related his:

There was this flower, in a box. Now, uh, a guy came along and found it and grew it. And then, um well, I'll tell the marble.
Therapist: Moral.
Patient: Uh-huh. It's the end.
Therapist: The moral is?
Patient: If you see a pretty flower, you can keep it but always water it. But not always — not too much, because you might drowned it. That's the end.
Therapist: And you don't want me to tell a story?
Patient: Uh-huh.

932

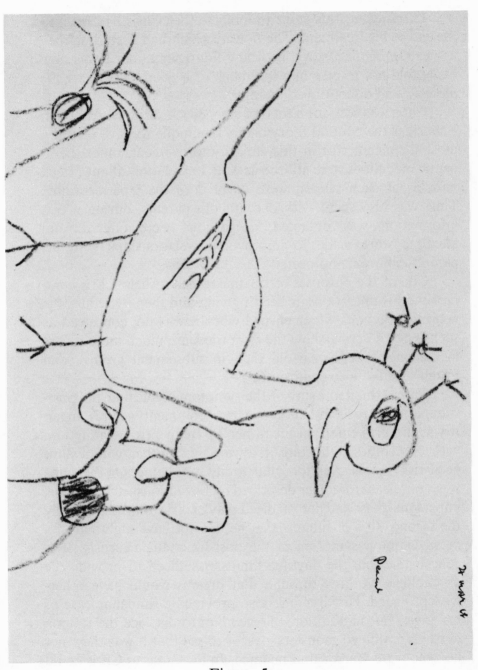

Figure 5.

Therapist: Okay, I think that's a very beautiful story.
Patient: Okay, where are the lollipops?

I considered this story to indicate that Chris had reached the end of his treatment. The flower, which had been described as dead in his first story, was now flourishing, and I was now being told not to give him too much of a good thing. *I got the message* and discontinued therapy.

Chris was seen for a total of sixty-seven sessions. Although I consider the Mutual Storytelling Technique to have played a most significant role in this child's improvement, other therapeutic modalities were utilized as well. In fact, only about fifteen minutes of each session were devoted to the tape-recording. Time was also spent with one or both parents, during which information was obtained, suggestions were offered, and attempts were made to improve his relationships with his parents, siblings, and peers.

One of the purposes of treatment was to help Chris comprehend his operations as health-giving and thereby reduce the neurotic reactions which ensued when it was not conceived as such. Levy describes how the symptoms are much more severe in the one- to two-year-old than in subsequent groups, and Prugh's study[11] also confirms this.

Chris exhibited many of the symptoms typical of the post-traumatic neurosis in children. Most prominent was his anger. It was in part vented on his father by frequently berating him with obscenities. Directing it toward his mother would have been risky — she was too vital to his well-being. Of the three types of release for anger described by Levy (nonspecific release, impersonal play, and personalized play), Chris utilized primarily the second. It is of interest that he did not have nightmares, a most common symptom in the post-traumatic neurosis. It is conceivable that the daytime fantasies sufficed to provide the psychologic working through that dreams would have otherwise provided. His drawings also provided a similar release of his anger, but in addition, allowed him to displace the trauma onto his mutilated monsters — as if to say that it was they, not he, who were scarred and maimed. In his fantasies Chris could

934

also identify with his aggressor, thereby removing himself from the vulnerable position.

It is reasonable to speculate that if this patient's mother had been freer to express her own feelings more overtly, he would have been less inhibited himself in expressing his anger and would not have resorted so much to displacement, projection, symbolization, and fantasy. One of the main emphases in treatment was to help him release his anger and feel less guilty about it — thereby reducing the necessity for expression through fantasy.

Although this child certainly withdrew in order to fantasize, he did not exhibit the severer type of withdrawal in which there are strongly autistic and/or regressive elements. The basic adequacy of the household and the pleasure in human relationships exhibited by the family served well to keep his environment an attractive one in spite of his traumas. The only manifestation of regression was his mild separation anxiety when leaving his mother to visit friends; but this problem, too, was alleviated early in treatment.

The parental contribution to the lowered self-esteem which is almost inevitably seen in child with physical defects was insignificant, if present at all. At no time did I detect any manifestation of shame on the part of either parent or any suggestion that he was less acceptable to them than their other four children. In addition, they did not exhibit the common inappropriate guilt reaction which often complicates the child's life through the overprotection and other neurotic interactions which it often engenders.[12]

In his sessions with me the retelling of the traumatic experiences even in the symbolic form of storytelling allowed a desensitization and piecemeal assimilation of experiences too overwhelming to be adjusted to in a short period of time.

Most important was my constant encouragement to the parents to discuss with the child the details of his operative procedures and to restate, when they had the opportunity, the communications which I was introducing in therapy both in my storytelling and in conscious discussion as well. Such conversations, both with me and with the parents, served not only to correct distortions but also to reduce the unnecessary anxiety that is aroused when the subject of the child's illness is considered too terrible to discuss. (I have described in Chapter 13 the salutary effects of such discussions with brain injured children.) In addition, these interchanges and confrontations helped desensitize the child to his traumas. Lastly, such discussions between the parents and the child, on a subject which was of such vital importance, helped form a tighter bond between them, and this also must have been therapeutic.

Psychologic tests were administered on the day following the termination story. This time the psychologist found him quiet, cooperative, responsive, and motivated. A comparison of his WISC scores are shown below:

Verbal	Initial Score	Termination Score
Information	9	13
Comprehension	8	12
Arithmetic	6	5
Similarities	10	13
Vocabulary	12	12
Digit Span	8	13
Performance		
Picture Completion	3	13
Picture Arrangement	7	8
Block Design	8	12
Object Assembly	8	11
Coding	6	5

	Initial Score	Termination Score	Change
Verbal IQ	92	109	+17
Performance IQ	75	99	+24
Full Scale IQ	83	104	+21

The psychologist considered the improvement too marked to be explained by practice effect alone. Whereas his previous scores suggested the possibility of borderline intelligence and visual-motor deficit, the final tests placed him well within the normal range of intelligence and suggested a bright-normal mental potential, if not a superior one. With regard to projective testing, the psychologist stated:

The human figures he drew are much more sensible and civilized than they were previously. Instead of merely covering the page in what seemed like an oral incorporative or oral aggressive mechanism, his drawings of human figures are of normal size. They earn him a rating of approximately six years (*Chris was then six years and three months old*). Moreover, his responses to the leading questions about these figures now wholly make sense. In the previous examination he seemed not even to understand some of the questions, and it was necessary to give him alternative choices so that he could respond . . . indeed, the whole tenor of his associations is within the normal range.

More instructive even is the fact that *all of the phobic, frightening percepts are gone from his Rorschach record as if a vacuum cleaner had swept them out. Not a single one of these is left.* What is left in his Rorschach is a picture of a somewhat introversive, thoughtful boy whose fantasy life is fairly active but not inappropriate. In Plate VII, interestingly, he saw a pushme-pullyou (Doctor Doolittle), without question a most creative response.

Thirteen months after termination Chris was admitted to the hospital for further operative repair of his cleft palate. In the hospital he was friendly and pleasant and tolerated the experience without any recurrence of symptoms.

Two months later he was again admitted to the hospital because of retinal changes found on routine examination. It was originally feared that he might have a brain tumor. After ten days of hospitalization (during which he did quite well, psychiatrically), a diagnosis of mild Hypervitaminosis A was made — curing the mother instantaneously of her vitamin and health food neurosis.

Two years after termination Chris was still doing well. His teacher described him as attentive, interested, and an active participant in class activities. He was getting along well with his classmates and doing quite well academically. He had developed good relationships with friends in his neighborhood and separated without anxiety from his mother in order to visit them, although he was occasionally teased about his lip deformity. I consider this an inevitable reality problem, and his upset about the teasing is quite normal.

In a recent follow-up visit the parents described inappropriate displays of hostility toward his father. I observed these myself and found them to be lighthearted rather than angry and bitter. Typical comments included: "Why don't you fill your mouth with apples and sew it up." "That car should have hit you in the tushy." For the most part I viewed his relationship with his father to be a good one and did not consider these displays pathologic, but rather age-appropriate oedipal manifestations. His story and drawings confirmed my clinical impression and did not manifest elements previously associated with the post-traumatic neurosis.

It is reasonable to assume that this patient's multiple traumas will leave him with some psychic scars that may never be completely obliterated, and it may be that at various times in his life he may again have psychologic difficulties. However, it appears that the course of treatment described here was successful in reducing his psychologic problems significantly.

CONCLUDING COMMENT

On being introduced to the Mutual Storytelling Technique many therapists have said, "It sounds like a good idea. Are you sure no one else has done it?" I had similar thoughts when I first came upon the idea. It seemed so obvious a thing to do. Children enjoy telling stories; they love hearing them; and communicating with them through stories is an ancient tradition. And yet, I was unable to find any articles in the literature describing a therapeutic procedure in which the *therapist* systematically tells stories, each of which is *specifically based on what has been elicited from the child,* and each of which is designed to introduce therapeutic messages *pertinent to the particular issue(s)* raised in the child's story. I cannot imagine, however, that others — somewhere, sometime — have not used it. What is possibly original is my systematization of it, and my detailed recording of the process.

I wish to emphasize my point that mutual storytelling is not a therapy per se, but rather one technique in the therapist's armamentarium. It is a valuable treatment modality but should be used along with other approaches if the child is to derive maximum benefit from his treatment. The method is primarily useful for verbal children with neurotic and characterological problems. It may be of value in borderline children, but would be contradicted in most psychotic children — such patients need reality confrontation more than fantasy stimulation. It can be useful in drawing out the subdued and repressed child

939

or the child with borderline intelligence. It has little place in the therapy of children below the age of four or four-and-half because such children generally do not consistently produce material which lends itself well to story formation by the therapist. The five-year-old, who represents a borderline age for the utilization of this technique, usually provides enough meaningful fragments for the therapist's story formation. He is also old enough to listen with interest to the therapist's tales. The pubertal period is the upper age limit for effective use of this method; the adolescent is usually too self-conscious to verbalize his fantasies freely and considers the game childish.

The efficacy of the Mutual Storytelling Technique is not due only to the more efficient and effective communications that it provides. Other benefits are derived by the child in a more subtle way. The telling of the stories is genuinely creative and therefore ego-enhancing. The therapist himself usually finds the procedure both enjoyable and challenging, and this affords the child the salubrious feeling that he is a person who can provide meaningful satisfactions for the therapist's needs. All too often therapists involve themselves in activities with children which they themselves find onerous or boring. When this happens, the child unerringly picks up the therapist's resentment and the activity thereby becomes psychologically deleterious, even to the point of compromising the treatment.

The Mutual Storytelling Technique, which is imaginative, constructive, and pleasure-giving, is the kind of fulfilling and rewarding experience that is salutary and meaningful in both therapeutic and non-therapeutic relationships.

It has been my purpose in this book to acquaint the child therapist with a technique which has proved valuable to me as a treatment method. My hope is that it will prove equally valuable to the readers of this book. Those of us who do utilize the method to the benefit of our child patients can enjoy a unique sense of accomplishment. When such children leave, it is as if they said to us, in the words of William Cullen Bryant:

> Deeply hath sunk the lesson thou hast given,
> And shall not soon depart.[1]

940

References

Chapter 5

1. Ames, Louise B., "Children's Stories," *Genetic Psychology Monographs*, 73 (1966), pp. 336-396.
2. Pitcher, E. G. and Prelinger, E., *Children Tell Stories*, New York: International Universities Press, Inc., 1963.

Chapter 6

1. Gardner, Richard A., "The Use of Guilt as a Defense Against Anxiety," *The Psychoanalytic Review*, 57 (1970), pp. 124-136.
   ———, "The Guilt Reaction of Parents of Children with Severe Physical Disease," *American Journal of Psychiatry*, 126 (1969), pp. 636-644.
   ———, "Guilt, Job, and J.B.," *Medical Opinion and Review*, 5, 2 (1969), pp. 146-155.
2. Kierkegaard, S., *The Concept of Dread*, trans. by Wetter Lowrie, Princeton, New Jersey: Princeton University Press, 1944.
   May, R., *The Meaning of Anxiety*, New York: Ronald Press Co., 1950.
   Chodoff, Paul, *et al.*, "Stress, Defenses, and Coping Behavior: Observations in Parents of Children with Malignant Disease," *The American Journal of Psychiatry*, 120 (1964), pp. 743-749.

Chapter 8

1. Freud, Sigmund, "The Interpretation of Dreams," in *The

Basic Writings of Sigmund Freud, trans. by A. A. Brill, New York: Modern Library, 1938.

Fenichel, Otto, *The Psychoanalytic Theory of Neurosis*, New York: W. W. Norton and Co., 1945.

2. Brenner, Charles B., *An Elementary Textbook of Psychoanalysis*, Garden City, New York: Doubleday and Co., Inc., 1957.

3. Freud, Sigmund, "Female Sexuality," trans. by Joan Riviere, in *Collected Papers*, Vol. 5, London: Hogarth Press, 1931, pp. 253-270.

———, *New Introductory Lectures on Psychoanalysis*, trans. by J. H. Sprott, New York: W. W. Norton and Co., 1933.

4. Mullahy, Patrick, *Oedipus Myth and Complex*, New York: Grove Press, 1955.

5. Freud, Sigmund, "The Passing of the Oedipus Complex," trans. by Joan Riviere, in *Collected Papers*, Vol. 2, London: Hogarth Press, 1924, pp. 269-276.

6. Jung, Carl G., "The Theory of Psychoanalysis," in *Nervous and Mental Disease Monograph Series*, No. 19, New York: Nervous and Mental Disease Publishing Co., 1915.

Campbell, J., *The Hero with a Thousand Faces*, New York: Pantheon Books, 1949.

7. Jung, Carl G., *Psychology of the Unconscious*, New York: Dodd, Mead, and Co., 1949, p. 427.

8. Adler, Alfred, *Social Interest: A Challenge to Mankind*, trans. by John Linton and Richard Vaughan, London: Faber and Faber, Ltd., 1938.

9. Rank, Otto, *The Trauma of Birth*, New York: Harcourt, Brace, and Co., 1929.

10. ———, *Will Therapy and Truth and Reality*, trans. by Jessie Taft, New York: Alfred A. Knopf, Inc., 1945.

11. ———, *Modern Education*, trans. by Mabel E. Moxon, New York: Alfred A. Knopf, Inc., 1932.

12. Forrest, Tess, "The Family Dynamics of the Oedipus Drama," *Contemporary Psychoanalysis*, 4 (1968), pp. 138-160.

13. Horney, Karen, *New Ways in Psychoanalysis*, New York: W. W. Norton and Company, 1939.
14. ———, *The Neurotic Personality of Our Time*, New York: W. W. Norton and Company, 1937.
15. Sullivan, Harry Stack, *The Interpersonal Theory of Psychiatry*, New York: W. W. Norton and Company, 1953.
16. Fromm, Erich, "The Oedipus Complex and the Oedipus Myth," in Ruth N. Anshen, ed., *The Science and Culture Series*, Vol. 5, *The Family: Its Function and Destiny*, New York: Harper and Brothers, 1948.
17. ———, *et al.,* "The Oedipus Complex: Comments on the Case of Little Hans," *Contemporary Psychoanalysis*, 4 (1968), pp. 178-188.
18. Freud, Sigmund, "Analysis of a Phobia in a Five-year-old Boy," trans. by Joan Riviere, in *Collected Papers*, Vol. 3, London: Hogarth Press, 1924, pp. 149-289.
19. Freud, Anna, *The Psychoanalytical Treatment of Children*, trans. by Nancy Proctor-Gregg, New York: Shocken Books, 1964.
    ———, *Normality and Pathology in Childhood*, New York: International Universities Press, Inc., 1965.
20. Klein, Melanie, *The Psychoanalysis of Children*, trans. by Alix Strachey, New York: Grove Press, Inc., 1960.
21. Ames, Louise B., "Children's Stories," *Genetic Psychology Monographs*, 73 (1966), pp. 336-396.
22. Pitcher, E. G. and Prelinger, E., *Children Tell Stories: An Analysis of Fantasy*, New York: International Universities Press, Inc., 1963.
23. Gardner, Richard A., "Sexual Fantasies in Childhood," *Medical Aspects of Human Sexuality*, 3, **10** (1969), pp. 121-134.
24. Schecter, David, "The Oedipus Complex: Considerations of Ego-Development and Parental Interaction," *Contemporary Psychanalysis*, 4 (1968), pp. 111-137.
25. Freud, Sigmund, *Totem and Taboo*, trans. by A. A. Brill, New York: Dodd, Mead and Company, 1918.
26. Gardner, Richard A., "A Proposed Scale for the Determination of Maternal Feeling," MSS.

27. Schecter, David, Personal communication to the author.
28. Forrest, Tess, "Paternal Roots of Female Character Development," *Contemporary Psychoanalysis*, 3 (1966), pp. 21-38.

Chapter 9

1. Gardner, Richard A., "The Use of Guilt as a Defense Against Anxiety," *The Psychoanalytic Review*, 57 (1970), pp. 124-136.
2. Ames, Louise B., "Children's Stories," *Genetic Psychology Monographs*, 73 (1966), pp. 336-396.
   Pitcher, E. G. and Prelinger, E., *Children Tell Stories: An Analysis of Fantasy*, New York: International Universities Press, Inc., 1963.
3. Woltmann, A. G., "Mud and Clay: Their Functions as Developmental Aids and as Media of Projection," in W. Wolff, ed., *Personality Symposium on Topical Issues*, No. 2, New York: Grune and Stratton, 1950, pp. 35-50.
4. Hartley, R. E., Frank, L. K., and Goldenson, R. M., "The Benefits of Water Play," in M. R. Haworth, ed., *Child Psychotherapy*, New York: Basic Books, Inc., 1964, pp. 364-371.
5. Arlow, J. A. and Kadis, A., "Fingerpainting in the Psychotherapy of Children," *American Journal of Orthopsychiatry*, 16 (1946), pp. 134-146.
6. Baruch, D. W., *New Ways in Discipline*, New York: McGraw-Hill Book Company, 1949.
7. Rogers, C. R., *Clinical Treatment of the Problem Child*, Boston: Houghton Mifflin and Company, 1939.
8. Axline, V. M., *Play Therapy*, New York: Ballantine Books, Inc., 1969.

Chapter 10

1. Mullahy, Patrick, *Psychoanalysis and Interpersonal Psychiatry*, New York: Science House, Inc., 1970.

2. Gardner, Richard A., "The Game of Checkers as a Diagnostic and Therapeutic Tool in Child Psychotherapy," *Acta Paedopsychiatrica*, 36, **5** (1969), pp. 142-152.
3. Erikson, Erik, *Childhood and Society*, rev. ed., New York: W. W. Norton and Company, 1963.
4. Sullivan, Harry Stack, *The Interpersonal Theory of Psychiatry*, New York: W. W. Norton and Company, 1953.

Chapter 11

1. Erikson, Erik, *Childhood and Society*, rev. ed., New York: W. W. Norton and Company, 1963.
2. Piers, G. and Singer, M. B., *Shame and Guilt*, Springfield, Illinois: Charles C. Thomas, 1953.
3. Freud, Sigmund, "The Economic Problem of Masochism," trans. by Joan Riviere, *Collected Papers*, Vol. 2, New York: Basic Books, 1959, pp. 255-268.
   Rado, S., "An Adaptational View of Sexual Behavior," in *Psychoanalysis of Behavior*, Vol. 1, New York: Grune and Stratton, 1956.
   Thompson, Clara, "The Interpersonal Approach to the Clinical Problems of Masochism," in J. Masserman, ed., *Individual and Family Dynamics*, New York: Grune and Stratton, 1959.
4. Gardner, Richard A., review of H. G. Ginott's *Between Parent and Child*, New York: The Macmillan Company, 1965, in *Psychology Today*, 1, **12** (1968), pp. 15-17.
5. Gardner, Richard A., "The Game of Checkers as a Diagnostic and Therapeutic Tool in Child Psychotherapy," *Acta Paedopsychiatrica*, 36, **5** (1969), pp. 142-152.

Chapter 12

1. Gardner, Richard A., "The Use of Guilt as a Defense Against Anxiety," *The Psychoanalytic Review*, 57 (1970), pp. 124-136.
   ———, "The Guilt Reaction of Parents of Children with

Severe Physical Disease," *American Journal of Psychiatry*, 126 (1969), pp. 636-644.

2. ———, review of B. Steinzor's *When Parents Divorce*, New York: Pantheon Books, 1969, in *Psychiatry and Social Science Review*, 3, **10** (1969), pp. 6-10.

———, "Psychological Aspects of Divorce," in S. Arieti, ed., *American Handbook of Psychiatry*, 3rd ed., New York: Basic Books, 1971.

3. ———, *The Boys and Girls Book About Divorce*, New York: Science House, Inc., 1970.

4. Swinburne, Algernon C., "The Garden of Proserpine." in G. B. Woods, ed., *The Literature of England*, 3rd ed., New York: Scott, Foresman, and Company, 1948, pp. 813-814.

Chapter 13

1. Conners, Keith C., *et al.,* "Dextroamphetamine Sulfate in Children with Learning Disorders: Effects on Perception, Learning, and Achievement," *Archives of General Psychiatry*, 21 (1969), pp. 182-190.

2. Clements, Sam D., "Minimal Brain Dysfunction in Children," *National Institute of Neurological Diseases and Blindness Monograph No. 3*, Washington, D.C.: U.S. Department of Health, Education, and Welfare, 1966.

"Minimal Brain Dysfunction in Children," *Neurological and Sensory Disease Control Program Monograph*, Washington, D.C.: U.S. Department of Health, Education, and Welfare, 1969.

3. Gardner, Richard A., "The Guilt Reaction of Parents of Children with Severe Physical Disease," *American Journal of Psychiatry*, 126 (1969), pp. 636-644.

———, "The Use of Guilt as a Defense Against Anxiety," *The Psychoanalytic Review*, 57 (1970), pp. 124-136.

4. Chodoff, Paul, *et al.,* "Stress, Defenses, and Coping Behavior: Observations in Parents of Children with Malignant Disease," *The American Journal of Psychiatry*, 120 (1964), pp. 743-749.

Kierkegaard, S., *The Concept of Dread*, trans. by W. Lowrie, Princeton, New Jersey: Princeton University Press, 1944.

May, R., *The Meaning of Anxiety*, New York: Ronald Press, 1950.

———, *et al., Existence,* New York: Basic Books, 1958.

5. Gardner, Richard A., *The Boys and Girls Book About Brain Dysfunction*, New York: Science House, Inc., 1972.

6. Freud, Sigmund, "The Economic Problem in Masochism," trans. by Joan Riviere, in *Collected Papers*, Vol. 2, New York: Basic Books, 1959, pp. 255-268.

   Horney, Karen, *New Ways in Psychoanalysis*, New York: W. W. Norton and Company, 1939.

   Fromm, Erich, *Escape from Freedom*, New York: Rinehart, 1941.

   Rado, S., "An Adaptational View of Sexual Behavior," in *Psychoanalysis of Behavior*, Vol. 1, New York: Grune and Stratton, 1956, pp. 186-213.

7. Thompson, Clara, "The Interpersonal Approach to the Clinical Problems of Masochism," in J. Masserman, ed., *Individual and Family Dynamics*, New York: Grune and Stratton, 1959, pp. 31-37.

8. Goldfarb, W., *Childhood Schizophrenia*, Cambridge: Harvard University Press, 1961.

9. Eisenberg, L., "Behavior Manifestations of Cerebral Damage," in H. G. Birch, ed., *Brain Damage in Children: The Biological and Social Aspects*, Baltimore: Williams and Wilkins, 1964, pp. 61-73.

10. Erikson, Erik, *Childhood and Society*, rev. ed., New York: W. W. Norton and Company, 1963, pp. 268-269.

Chapter 17

1. Levy, David M., "Psychic Trauma of Operations in Children and a Note on Combat Neurosis," *American Journal of Diseases of Children,* 69, 1945, pp. 7-25.

2. Purgh, D. G., "A Study of the Emotional Reactions of Children and Families to Hospitalization and Illness,"

American Journal of Orthopsychiatry, 23, 1953, pp. 70-106.

Bergmann, T., "Observations of Children's Reactions to Motor Restraint," *Nervous Children,* 4, 1945, pp. 318-328. (1945).

Forsyth, D., "Psychological Effects of Bodily Illness in Children," *Lancet,* 2, 1934, pp. 15-18.

Freud, Anna, "The Role of Bodily Illness in the Mental Life of Children," in *The Psychoanalytic Study of the Child,* Vol. 5, New York: International Universities Press Inc., 1952, pp. 69-81.

Langford, W. S., "The Child in the Pediatric Hospital: Adaptation to Illness and Hospitalization," *American Journal of Orthopsychiatry,* 31, 1961, pp. 667-684.

Miller, M. L., "The Traumatic Effect of Surgical Operations in Childhood on the Integrative Functions of the Ego," *Psychoanalytic Quarterly,* 20, 1951, pp. 77-92.

Pearson, G. H. J., "Effect of Operative Procedures on the Emotional Life of the Child," *American Journal of Diseases of Children,* 62, 1941, pp. 716-729.

3. Bergmann, T., *op. cit.;* and Freud, Anna, *op. cit.*

4. Langford, W. S., *op. cit.*

5. Freud, Anna, *op. cit.*

6. Levy, David M., *op. cit.*

7. Sullivan, Harry Stack, *The Interpersonal Theory of Psychiatry,* New York: W. W. Norton and Company, 1953.

8. Fairbairn, W. R. D., *Psychoanalytic Studies of the Personality,* London: Tavistock, 1952.

Guntrip, H., *Personality Structure and Human Interaction,* New York: International Universities Press, 1961.

Klein, Melanie, *Contributions to Psychoanalysis,* London: Hogarth Press, 1948.

Winnicott, D. W., *The Maturational Process and the Facilitating Environment,* New York: International Universities Press, 1965.

9. Freud, Sigmund, *Beyond the Pleasure Principle,* trans. by James Strachey, New York: Liverwright, 1950.

Kardiner, A., *The Traumatic Neuroses of War,* New York: Hoeber, 1941.

———, "The Traumatic Neuroses of War," in S. Arieti, ed., *American Handbook of Psychiatry*, New York: Basic Books, 1959.

Grinker, R. R. and Spiegel, J. P., *Men Under Stress*, New York: Blakiston, 1945.

10. Freud, Sigmund, "Mourning and Melancholia," trans. by Joan Riviere, in *Collected Papers*, Vol. 4, New York: Basic Books, 1949.

11. Purgh, D. G., *op. cit.*

12. Purgh, D. G., *op. cit.*; and Langford, W. S., *op. cit.*

Gardner, Richard A., "Psychogenic Problems of Brain Injured Children and Their Parents," *Journal of the American Academy of Child Psychiatry*, 7, pp. 471-491 (1968).

———, "The Guilt Reaction of Parents of Children with Severe Physical Disease," *American Journal of Psychiatry*, 126 (1969), pp. 636-644.

Concluding Comment

1. Bryant, W. C., "To a Waterfowl," in Kreymborg, ed., *An Anthology of American Poetry*, New.York: Tudor Publishing Company, 1941.

Patient Index*

Ben, 696-697

Bonnie, 42-45, 850-901, 483-487, 256-260

Carol, 272-279, 148-151, 506-509, 74-80, 297-303, 80-83, 253-256

Charles, 622-662, 527-529, 244-247

Chris, 903-916, 419-423, 916-921, 423-432, 921-938, 673-680

Dale, 249-253

Daniel, 352-357

David, 314-319

Donald, 539-553, 214-216, 553-556

Eric, 90-95

Evan, 593-595

Frank, 349-352

Gavin, 40-42, 366-371

George, 69-72, 495-500, 73-74, 141-145, 500-506, 145-147 590-593, 207-210

Harold, 56-58

Helen, 216-225, 243

Henry, 34-36, 561-564

Joey, 48-51, 431-434, 103-120, 287, 120-124, 434-445, 124-138, 287-291, 183-186, 458-462, 226-232, 445-451, 232-236

Julie, 599-614, 168-172, 292-296

Karen, 260-263

Larry, 61-64, 268-272

Linda, 802-815

Lucy, 818-849

Malcolm, 534-538   95-99, 487-495, 161-168

Mark, 58-61, 509-515, 264-268

Martin, 39-40, 524-527

Mike, 529-534, 714-782

Nancy, 581-586, 469-472, 586-589, 247-249, 589-590

Nick, 564-580

Pam, 663-673

Paul, 83-90, 151-161, 210-214, 236-243

Peter, 172-179, 357-366

Ronald, 51-56, 395-419, 303-310, 186-190, 310-311, 190, 279-280, 311-314, 280-281

Russell, 477-483, 796-800

Ruth, 620-622

Seymour, 344-349

Steve, 36-39, 371-386, 462-469, 66-69, 138-141, 196-206, 782-787, 386-395, 782-789

Tom, 473-477

Tony, 45-48

---

* *Indexed pages have been arranged in chronological rather than consecutive order, so that the interested reader may study each case in continuity. In addition, the stories of children whose names appear in boldface type are full-length case studies. The remaining cases do not represent a full course of therapy, or do not lend themselves to meaningful sequential reading, though they have also been listed chronologically for the convenience of the interested reader.*

Subject Index

Anger—*continued*
divorce and, 597
dreams and, 457
effective expression of, 472-473
maladaptive mechanisms and, 456
post-traumatic neurosis and, 934-935
suppressed, 181
verbal expression of, 473
See also Death wishes *and* Hostility
Anger inhibitions, 452-457
children's stories coping with, 260-262, 448-449, 458-462, 893-895
children's stories reflecting, 469-471, 478-480, 483-485, 496-498, 500-501, 506-507, 509-511, 513-514
dreams and, 457
therapist's stories coping with, 460-462, 466-469, 471-472, 480-483, 485-487, 492-495, 498-500, 501-503, 508-509, 513-514, 856-858
Anomolous presentations and minimal brain dysfunction, 682
Anorexia nervosa
divorce and, 596
psychophysiological disorders and, 818
Antenatal difficulties and minimal brain dysfunction, 682
Antibiotics and psychophysiological disorders, 817
"Anti-resistance story," 190
Anxiety
about therapy, 440
children's drawings reflecting, 86
children's stories reflecting, 69, 71, 72, 83-84, 85-88, 496-498
therapist's stories coping with, 70-71, 72-73, 84, 88-90, 498-500
basic, 328
birth, 326-327
children's stories coping with, 464-465, 866
children's stories reflecting, 173-174, 395-399, 408-414, 627, 723-725, 732-733, 845, 866-889, 891-892, 893-895
ignorance-caused, 866
incentive engendering, 796
primal, 326-327
therapist's stories coping with, 266-268, 400-408, 725-727, 846-847,

Anxiety—*continued*
864-866, 868-869, 889-891, 895-897
See also Symptoms
Anxiety-alleviation and late phase of therapy, 182
Anxiety-provoking feelings, therapist's post-story inquiry coping with, 106-117
Anxiety-provoking images
children's stories disguising, 103
therapist's stories coping with, 104-106
Apathy and divorce, 596
See also Passivity *and* Symptoms, passive
Aphasias, 687
Apneic phase of convulsion and minimal brain dysfunction, 682
Archtypal mother, 325
Arlow, J. A., 472-473
Assertive, 452
Attitude towards men, children's stories reflecting negative, 599-601
Attracting attention and learning difficulties, 800
Autonomic nervous system innervation, 816
"Autonomy vs. Shame," 557-558
Axline, V. M., 473

Babinski sign, 688
Barbituates and minimal brain dysfunction, 684
Baruch, D. W., 473
Basic
anxiety, 328
hostility, 328
Behavior problems, therapist's stories coping with, 170-172
See also Symptoms
Birth
anxiety, 326-327
trauma, 326-327
Blobus hystericus, 816
Boasting
children's stories reflecting evaluation of, 168-170
guilt due to anger causing, 48-51
Borderline intelligence, 739
children with, 529-534
Boredom
anxiety and, 568

954

Boredom—*continued*
children's stories reflecting, 207-208
Brain injury, 681
See also Minimal brain dysfunction
Bryant, William Cullen, 940

Castration
anxiety, 324-325, 336-337
children's stories reflecting, 395-399, 432-433
therapist's stories coping with, 433-434
children's stories representing, 176-177
Catharsis, 472
Cephalopelvic disproportion and minimal brain dysfunction, 682
Cerebral
anoxemia and minimal brain dysfunction, 682
dominance and minimal brain dysfunction, 688
Chemotherapy, 715, 912
minimal brain dysfunction and, 683-685, 689
See also Medication
"Children Tell Stories," 180-181
Chloropromazine, 912, 929
minimal brain dysfunction and, 684-685
Clinical
behavior, 180-183
history, children's stories relating, 765-786
improvement, children's stories following, 214-215
Clowning and self-esteem, 516
Coercion, 330
Mutual Storytelling Technique and, 208
Cognitive distortions
children's stories reflecting, 908-909, 909-910, 912-914, 923-924, 929-931
elements in child development, 341
therapist's stories coping with, 910-912, 914-916, 919-921, 924-925, 926-928
Collective unconscious and the Oedipus complex, 325-326
College dropouts, 793
Combat neurosis and self-desensitization, 914

Commercials, television
children's, 391-398, 400, 412-413
children's stories and, 279-281
Communication, non-verbal and the Mutual Storytelling Technique, 231-232
Compensation, *See* Defense mechanisms
Competence and self-esteem, 518, 523
Complacency, *See* Resignation
Complexes, children's stories reflecting unconscious, 458-460
Compliments and self-esteem, 519
Compulsive rituals and divorce, 597
Conceptualization and minimal brain dysfunction, 687
Confrontations, children's stories avoiding, 287-288
Confusion
children's stories reflecting, 90-91, 371-373
therapist's stories coping with, 92-94, 373-374
Conners, Keith, 685
Conscience, 557-560
incorporation, *See* Incorporation
Constipation and psychophysiological disorders, 818
Conversion reaction, 816
Counterphobic mechanisms, children's stories utilizing, 866, 869-871
Countertransference, 210
Criticism
children's stories reflecting fear of, 483-485
therapist's stories coping with fear of, 485-487
Crying, children's stories about, 180-181
Cytomegalic inclusion disease and minimal brain dysfunction, 682

Danger denial, *See* Defense mechanisms
Death
adjustment mechanisms to, 614-617, 622-626
children faced with, 527-529, 620-622, 622-662
children's stories about, 180-181
children's stories coping with, 527-528, 545-546, 600-661

955

956

Eclampsia and minimal brain dysfunction, 682

Education
learning difficulties and, 801-802
minimal brain dysfunction and, 689
parents and, 793-802
See also Psychogenic learning difficulties

Ego-ideal, formation of, 557, 560-561
"Ego Integrity vs. Despair," 523
"Eighth Age of Man," 523
Elixir phenobarbitol, 682
Emotional deprivation and learning, 794-795
See also Psychogenic learning disorders

Encopresis and psychophysiological disorders, 818
Engulfment, children's stories reflecting feelings of, 529-531
Environmental experiences and psychophysiological disorders, 817-818

Erikson, Erik
on "Autonomy vs. Shame," 557-558
on the "Eighth Age of Man," 523
on "Guilt vs. Initiative," 558

Escape, children's stories reflecting the desire to, 273-276
Excitation and minimal brain dysfunction, 683-685

Family, the, and therapy, 344
Fantasies
dreams and, 436
oedipal, 323
recurring, 46
young children and, 180-181

Fields, W. C., 351, 352
Figure-ground confusion and minimal brain dysfunction, 681, 686-687
Freud, Anna, 330, 903
on "identification with the aggressor," 324

Freud, Sigmund, 419
on the analysis of adults, 330
on anger expression, 472
on the incest taboo, 341
on the latency period, 339
on Little Hans, 329-330
on the Oedipus complex, 323-325, 332, 333, 335, 336, 337, 342, 343
on "secondary elaboration," 32
on Totem and Taboo, 362

Freud, Sigmund—continued
Sullivan, Harry Stack and, 329

Freudian psychoanalytic school, the, 340
Fromm, Erich, on the Oedipus complex, 332, 339
Frustration, 453-454
children's stories reflecting, 180-181
Fury, 455

Galactosemia and minimal brain dysfunction, 682
Games and self-esteem, 520-521
Gilbert and Sullivan, 281
Guilt, 455-456, 557-559, 560
adult, 258, 259
death and, 619
divorce and, 597
children's stories avoiding appropriate, 165-166
children's stories reflecting, 103, 630-633, 650-651, 783-785, 819-821
oedipal, 343-344
post-traumatic neurosis and, 902-903, 935
repression stemming from, 48-51
self-esteem and, 521, 522-523
stage, 558
therapist's stories coping with, 104-106, 106-117, 166-168, 184-186, 633-634, 640-643, 652-656, 785-787, 822

"Guilt vs. Initiative," 558

Hartley, R. E., 472-473
Helplessness, feelings of, 454
children's stories reflecting, 636-637, 643-644, 727-729, 783-785
therapist's stories coping with, 637-638, 640-645, 729-732

Hemispherectomy, 663
Hepatic pericanicular inflammation, 684
Horney, Karen on the Oedipus complex, 328
Hostility, 452-457
basic, 328
children's stories coping with, 44-45, 227-229, 310-311, 807-808, 826-827
children's stories reflecting, 48, 62, 66, 103, 120, 148-149, 173-174, 183-184, 187-189, 254, 268-271,

959

Perfectionism, 125-127
  children's stories reflecting, 125
  learning difficulties and, 800-801
  post-story inquiry reflecting children's expectations of, 107-117
  self-esteem and, 523
  therapist's stories coping with, 125, 675-677, 679-680
  See also Symptoms
Persecutory trends
  children's stories reflecting, 90-91
  therapist's stories coping with, 92-94
Perseveration and minimal brain dysfunction, 688, 707-708
Phallic phase, 323, 419
Phenlyketonuria and minimal brain dysfunction, 682
Phobias
  children's stories coping with, 862-864, 866, 869-871, 879-881, 886-889, 893-895
  children's stories reflecting, 855-856
  therapist's stories coping with, 864-866, 866-867, 871-878, 895-897, 881-884, 889-891, 898-899
  See also Parents
Pitcher, E. G., 180-181, 338-339, 340, 456
Placenta
  premature separation of and minimal brain dysfunction, 681
  previa and minimal brain dysfunction, 682
Point, Jack, 281
Post-story inquiry, the, 268-271, 873-878
  "commercials" and, 309
  therapist's stories and, 298-303
Post-traumatic neurosis, 902-903
Prelinger, I., 180-181, 338-339, 340, 456
Premature termination of therapy, *See* Therapy
Presenting complaint, *See* Symptoms
Pretermination stories, *See* Stories
"Primal Anxiety," 326-327
"Primal Wish," 327
Primiparas and minimal brain dysfunction, 682
Projection, *See* Defense mechanisms
Protective figures, children's stories utilizing, 916-919, 923-924
Provocation and therapy, 579-580

Prugh, D.G., 934
Pseudocyesis, 818
Psychodynamics of stories, *See* Interpretation of stories
Psychogenic
  children's stories reflecting awareness of problems, 765-768
  coughing, 818-820
  disorders and psychophysiological reactions, 816
  learning disorders, 793-802
  paraplegia, 816
  problems secondary to minimal brain dysfunction, 681-683, 688-714
  symptom formation and self-esteem, 516
  See also Symptoms
Psychological tests
  post-therapy, 937
  pre-therapy, 908
Psychopathic behavior and therapy, 572-575
Psychopathologic symptoms and learning difficulties, 801
Psychopaths and punishment, 559
Psychophysiological disorders
  idiosyncratic elements of, 817
  physically pathologic elements of, 816, 817
  reactions, 816-818
Psychosis
  learning and, 794-795
  minimal brain dysfunction and, 613-614
  the Mutual Storytelling Technique and, 939
Psychosomatic reactions, 816-818
Punishment and guilt, 559

"Quiet desperation," 369
  See also Resignation

Rage, 454-455
  See also Anger *and* Hostility
Rank, Otto
  on birth anxiety, 326-327
  on the Oedipus complex, 326-327
  on primal anxiety, 326-327
Reaction formations, *See* Defense mechanisms
Reactions to minimal brain dysfunction, *See* Minimal brain dysfunction

Sullivan, Harry Stack—*continued*
  on reflected appraisals, 517
  on self-esteem, 518-519
Superego, the, 557-561
  children's stories reflecting the formation of, 586-587, 590-591
  deficiencies, 557-561
    children's stories reflecting, 561-562, 564-567, 575-576, 577, 593-594
    therapist's stories coping with, 562-564, 567-571, 572-573, 575, 578-579, 580, 594-595
  development of, 100
  hypertrophied
    children's stories reflecting, 214-215
    therapist's stories coping with, 562-564, 567-571, 572-573, 575, 578-579, 580. 594-595
    therapist's stories in response to the growth of, 590-591
  therapy and, 182
Suppression, *See* Defense mechanisms
Surliness, children's stories coping with, 813
Swinburne, Algernon, 615
Symbolism analyzed with children, 265, 266-268
Symptomatology and the Oedipus complex, 334
Symptoms
  antagonistic attitude towards teachers and peers, 168-172
  authority defiance, 172-179, 186-196, 279-281, 303-314, 395-419, 599-614
  behavior problems, 247-249
  chronic anxiety, 48-51, 58-61, 103-138, 183-186, 264-268, 352-357, 509-515, 714-782
  chronic surliness, 168-172, 292-296, 599-614, 802-815
  compulsive behavior, 61-64, 268-272, 714-782
  dependency, 34-36, 58-61, 214-216, 509-515, 539-556, 663-673
  depressive moods, 74-83
  disciplinary problems, 36-39, 196-206, 581-590, 782-789
  enuresis, 48-51, 103-138, 183-186, 226-236, 281-291, 431-451, 458-462

Symptoms—*continued*
  fear of being alone, 349-352
  fear of sports and physical contact, 172-179
  feelings of inadequacy, 48-51, 103-138, 183-186, 509-515
  generalized inhibition, 593-595
  generalized tension, 74-83, 95-99, 148-151, 272-279, 297-303, 344-349, 534-538
  generalized timidity, 590-593
  guilt, excessive, over minor transgressions, 349-352
  hyperactivity, 249-253
  hypermature behavior, 216-225
  hypersensitivity to teasing, 673-680
  immaturity, 214-216, 244-247, 249-253, 527-529, 539-556, 622-662
  insecurity, 58-61, 264-268, 714-782
  insomnia, 74-83, 148-151, 272-279, 297-303, 506-509, 564-580
  irresponsibility, 244-247
  lying, 564-580
  massive tension, 349-352
  masturbation, excessive, 247-249, 469-472, 581-590
  multiple fears, 95-99, 161-168, 256-260, 487-495, 534-538
  negativism, 802-815
  negativistic behavior, 51-56, 186-196, 279-281
  nightmares, 48-51, 103-138, 183-186, 216-225, 226-236, 281-291, 431-451, 458-462
  obsession with anus and eyes, 714-782
  obsessive behavior, 216-225
  obsessive smelling of hands and objects, 529-534
  obstructionism at home, 473-477
  passivity, 39-40, 40-42, 314-318, 366-371, 524-527, 673-680, 818-849
  peer relationship problems, 34-36, 39-40, 40-42, 74-83, 148-151, 249-253, 253-256, 352-357, 473-477, 818-849
  perfectionism, 344-349
  persecutory trends, 90-95
  petty stealing, 564-580
  phobic behavior, 42-45, 256-260, 260-263, 483-487, 520-522, 850-901
  post-traumatic neurosis, 419-432, 673-680, 903-938